LINCOLN CITY F.C.
THE OFFICIAL HISTORY

By:
Ian and Donald Nannestad

Published by:
Yore Publications
12 The Furrows, Harefield,
Middx. UB9 6AT

© Ian and Donald Nannestad
....

All rights reserved
No part of this publication may be reproduced or copied in any manner
without the prior permission in writing of the copyright holders

British Library Cataloguing-in-Publication Data
A catalogue record for this book
is available from the British Library

ISBN 1 874427 47 X

YORE PUBLICATIONS specialise in football books, normally of an historic nature...
Club histories, Who's Who books, etc. plus non-league football.
Three free Newsletters are issued per year, for your first copy,
please send a S.A.E. to the address above.

Printed and bound by The Bath Press

To Mum and Dad

FOREWORD
by
Andy Graver

When I first joined the Imps I wasn't even sure where Lincoln was but like many other lads from the north I quickly settled in and have never regretted my decision to sign for the club which gave me many good times.

Although I had a trial with Coventry around 1946 my first professional club was Newcastle United where I mostly played in the Central League side. I was a little reluctant to leave St James' Park but Bill Anderson gathered a good set of players at Lincoln and in my second season we won promotion to the Second Division. The team fitted well together with players such as Tony Emery, Johnny Garvie and Doug Wright. Doug was a class above everyone, especially when going forwards, yet when Lincoln signed him he was said to be finished!

My six goals against Crewe when we overran them in the championship season are always remembered but my biggest thrill as a Lincoln player was when we beat Blackburn Rovers 8-0 in August 1953. Blackburn were a good side with two or three internationals in the team and the four goals I scored that day gave me great satisfaction.

We had a good side in the 1950s but eventually got relegated and then Bill Anderson kept the club going when the bad times came. He ran the Imps on a shoestring for so many years and they were on the point of folding in the early 1960s until Frank Eccleshare came to the rescue.

I stayed in Lincoln after my playing career was over and nowadays my sporting activities are carried out on the golf course. I enjoyed my times at Sincil Bank and hope the club soon begin to rise up the League in the near future.

Andy Graver

ACKNOWLEDGEMENTS

The authors wish to acknowledge the assistance provided by the following when compiling this book : John Reames, Claire Lait, the directors and staff of Lincoln City F.C., Billy Cobb, Tom Docherty, Roy Finch, Andy Graver, Jim Grummett jnr, Ron Harbertson, Bill Heath, Alf Jones, Jim Jones, Albert Linnecor, Bert Loxley, Bill McGlen, Trevor Meath, Fred Middleton, Dick Neal, George Nelson, Bobby Owen, Ron Smillie, Bryan Stainton, George Stillyards, Graham Taylor, Peter Wells, Willie Windle, Lincoln & District Football Supporters Club Committee, Simon Bellis, Nigel Bishop, Ian Black, Nancy Burnikell, Martin Burton, Percy Buttery, Brian Clare, Christine Clark, Frank Connell, Andrew Davies, Jack Dellar, Tom Fields, Ian Garland, Professor Charles Garton, John Gilding, Fred Green, Mabel Green, Mrs N.Hannah, Maurice Hodson, Barry Hugman, Doug Lamming, Rob Leeson, Bill Love, Harvey Lyngaas, Stuart McPhail, Deborah Manning, John Middleton, J.T.Moore, Eleanor Nannestad, Dawn Newman, Gary Parle, C.A. Pearson, Charles Raphael, Raymonds Press Agency, David Rollinson, Renee Smith, Kevin Stow, Elisabeth Sturges-Jones, Alan Thompson, Tokarskis, Les Triggs, Clive Woodhead, Syd Woodhead, H.B.Vaughan, Frank Young.

Dumfries & Galloway Family History Society, Northumberland & Durham Family History Society, Lincolnshire Archives, Liverpool Record Office, Lincoln Central Library, Northwich Library, Staffordshire Libraries, Crosby Library, Colindale Newspaper Library, Crewe Library, The Football League, and the Lincolnshire F.A.

PHOTOGRAPHIC ACKNOWLEDGEMENTS
Photographs and illustrations are courtesy of Lincoln City FC; John Middleton; the Lincolnshire Echo; the Lincoln Chronicle; Colorsport; Maurice Hodson; Alan Wilson; Charles Raphael; Martin Burton; The Local Studies Collection, Lincoln Central Library (By courtesy of Lincolnshire County Council Education and Cultural Services directorate); the Museum of Lincolnshire Life (Lincolnshire County Council); Team photographs of 1902/03; 1905/06; and 1910/11 are reproduced by permission of The British Library (ref. PIP 1859 bc). Some photographs are from the private collection of the authors and others are from collections of former players and their relatives. Every effort has been made to trace the source of these photographs but this has not been possible in all instances. Any photographer involved is cordially invited to contact the publisher in writing with proof of copyright.

CONTENTS

	Page
Introduction	6
Chapter 1: Early Days - The Period to 1919	7
Origins... The formation of Lincoln City F.C.... Early days and the rise of professionalism... The first financial crisis... The Golden Years... The re-election years... The Great War... Jack Strawson.	
Chapter 2: 1919 to 1961 - Up And Down	24
The Second Financial Crisis... Revival - and a northern section title... An expensive exercise... World War 2... After the War... Survival against the odds... Bill Anderson.	
Chapter 3: The Modern Era - 1961 to 1997	44
Hard times... Pride restored... The Taylor years... Into the Eighties... The last ten years.	
Chapter 4: The Grounds	62
Chapter 5: Supporters Organisations	65
Chapter 6: Publications	68
Chapter 7: Encyclopedia	76
Statistics Section:	
Introduction:	90
Who's Who:	91
Seasonal Statistics and Team Groups:	109
Friendly Matches, etc. :	250
Bibliography:	254
Advanced Subscribers:	255

INTRODUCTION

This book is the culmination of many years of hard work by both of us since we began serious research back in the late 1970s. At that time very little had been written on the Imps' history, one reason being the fire of 1929 which destroyed all the club's official records.

Our first task was to compile a list of results and goalscorers and this was completed by the early 1980s. Attempts to produce line-up charts from the local papers were initially successful but we encountered problems in the 1890s and early 1900s when match reports of away games were often brief with little mention of who turned out for the club. Next we visited the Football League offices in Lytham St Anne's where we were able to record all the line-ups for Football League, League Cup and war-time games from 1892 onwards. These did not prove to be without error and following this we completed the lengthy task of investigating in detail each discrepancy between our own records drawn from the press and the registers to ensure the greatest possible accuracy. There is no formal record of goalscorers and so our information is drawn from local newspapers - principally the Lincolnshire Chronicle and the Lincoln Gazette for the early years and the Lincolnshire Echo from the mid-1890s. The Football League attendance books provide our source for crowds since 1925. These official figures are often quite different to those which were shown in the newspapers of the time. Records for the F.A. Cup, Lincolnshire Cup, the non-League seasons and friendly matches have all been researched solely from newspapers. Most of this work was completed prior to the publication of our *'Who's Who of Lincoln City 1892 - 1994'* published by Yore Publications in 1994.

Well aware that the history of the club is not just the story told in newspapers we have also used two further sources which have been of great value. We are particularly grateful to John Reames and the directors for providing access to those minute books of board meetings that could be found, and to the 25 or so former players who answered our questions about events often dating back to the 1940s. Reminiscences of the period up to around 1930 appeared in the local papers and they have also proved useful. Together these have helped give a much broader balance to the book and have turned up a few stories which were new to us, and probably to most City supporters.

When we started research on this book we had very few photographs and with one or two exceptions the team groups we had were drawn from the 1980s and 1990s. It is mainly due to the help of others, particularly John Middleton, Maurice Hodson and Fred Middleton that we have been able to include over 70 team pictures. Some of these have not appeared in print for many years and it is particularly gratifying to reproduce them in the book.

It would be foolish to expect the book to be error-free and despite our careful proof-reading some typographical errors in the statistical sections will be inevitable and we apologise for these in advance. Diligent readers will also note that some of the details of pre-1939 players are slightly different to those shown in the 'Who's Who' and this is a result of further information coming to light. Views expressed in the text are our own and represent our interpretation of events drawn from the various sources available to us.

We hope that this history proves as enjoyable to read as it was for ourselves in compiling it and we wish every success to the Imps in the future.

Ian Nannestad
Donald Nannestad

September 1997

CHAPTER ONE
EARLY DAYS.... THE PERIOD TO 1919

ORIGINS

The story of Lincoln City Football Club is similar in many ways to that of several of the clubs in the lower divisions of the Football League; a tale of struggle against adversity interspersed with its own unique moments of joy and despair. High spots for the Imps have been the early years of the twentieth century when they came close to achieving First Division football, the period from 1952 to 1961 when manager Bill Anderson kept the side in Division Two against all the odds, and the 1975/76 season when Graham Taylor's team swept all before them on their way to the Fourth Division championship. Low points include the many financial crises (particularly those of 1897, 1923 and the early 1960s), and the four occasions when the club have lost their place in the Football League, each time to return after a single season's absence.

Although City were formed in 1884, it was nearly a quarter of a century before that the game of football became established in Lincoln. Football was a traditional pastime of rural England which had been taken up by the Public Schools where different rules and styles of play had evolved. The game spread to the universities and by the late 1850s the first organised clubs began to emerge in Sheffield and London, progress being hampered somewhat by the absence of a unified set of rules.

The Lincoln of early Victorian times with its stately cathedral and bustling markets was also undergoing major changes in the early 1860s. Its population of 20,999 (1861 census) would more than double over the next 40 years as the expansion of the engineering works to the south of the city led to the rapid growth of housing. In 1860 there were at least six foundries, mostly producing agricultural machinery, with the largest being the works of Messrs Clayton and Shuttleworth. The introduction of the railway line to Nottingham in 1846 had opened up the city to outside influences and acted as a catalyst to the changes that followed.

The ordinary working people, the foundrymen and the shop assistants, worked long hours but at least the former had the advantage of finishing early on a Saturday (2.30pm) when the shops remained open until 11 or 11.30pm. The principal leisure pursuits for the working men were to be found in the numerous public houses within the city. Those who sought a more respectable life looked to the Church and self improvement bodies, such as the Mechanics Institute, for guidance. Angling and bathing were popular outdoor activities and while football was not unknown it ranked alongside shinty (a form of hockey) as a game for schoolboys. Those with more spare time enjoyed rowing and cricket and by the early 1860s there were at least six local cricket clubs including Lindum which was established in 1856.

The first foundrymen's club - the Sheaf Iron Works Cricket Club - was not formed until June 1862. Spectators were attracted to the Carholme racecourse for the Spring and Autumn horse race meetings and also to regular athletics ("pedestrianism") contests, both offering the opportunity for a spot of gambling.

The first local record of the modern version of football can be found in the Lincoln Gazette of 29 November 1862 :
"Foot Ball [sic] : A match of foot ball was played on Wednesday last, between eight of the old pupils and twenty of the present pupils of Lincoln grammar school (the latter having the valuable assistance of Mr. Fowler) on their ground on the Nettleham-road, which, after a gallant struggle, resulted in a tie, each side having obtained one goal. It is in contemplation to have a match on Saturday the 6th December between fifteen of the old pupils of the grammar school and fifteen of the town. "

The return match took place on either 6 or 13 December when the school beat the town by two goals to nil, both being scored by George Apthorp. A third fixture between the two followed in January 1863, with the school winning 3-1. The school headmaster, the Rev.John Fowler, had previously taught at Marlborough College, where football was played, and he encouraged the game following his arrival in Lincoln.

The original Lincoln Football Club appears to have been formed between October 1862 (twelve months prior to the club's first annual general meeting), and 25 May 1863 when they played their first ever game against a team from the Louth club. It seems likely therefore that the games played between the school and the town in the winter of 1862/63 either provided the inspiration for the establishment of the new club or represent a series of early internal club matches. That first encounter with Louth took place on Whit Monday on a field on the Nettleham Road, almost opposite St Giles Farm. The teams played 15-a-side for just over two hours before retiring to the Queen's Inn, High Street for dinner, no goals having been scored.

The club was still in its fledgling state but by October 1863 it could count on 50 or more members, and shortly afterwards it had a set of rules, said to be based on those at Marlborough (Fowler's old school), Eton and Rugby, and a uniform of a white jersey with the Lindum arms *"worked on in the proper heraldic colours"*. A second football club, The Sons of Albion, is recorded in Lincoln at this time, although it seems to have only had a brief existence.

Meanwhile, members of the Lincoln Football Club were full of enthusiasm for their new venture and after reading about the formation of a national Football Association in the sporting press they instructed secretary Edward Chambers to make contact and enrol. The Association was only just beginning the lengthy task of producing a single set of rules and welcomed this early contact from the provinces.

A return match with Louth took place on the latter's Holmes-lane ground on 29 September with the home team winning 2-0, and a third encounter followed on the Cowpaddle in April 1864. Still playing 15-a-side, Lincoln won 2-0 with goals from J. Wiley and E. Mantle. Their opponents proved to be rather bad losers, taking exception to what they considered to be rough play: *"Apparent disregard of all rules, profuse administration of hacking, tripping-up, and what is commonly called burking, in general were the chief features of the manner of play."* (Louth & North Lincs. Advertiser, 23 Apr 1864). They also alleged Lincoln had played a professional - *"one of that craft who neither learn nor acknowledge manners."* The player concerned was Frederick Green who was indeed a professional cricketer and athlete but there is no evidence to suggest he was paid to appear in this match. The ill-feeling created was such that the two clubs never met again, although this was of little worry to Lincoln who arranged home and away fixtures with the Sheffield and Notts (Notts County) clubs in the 1864/65 season. The two Sheffield games were played with 11-a-side, Lincoln losing the first game at Newhall Cricket Ground on 25 February by one goal and three rouges to nil (a rouge was a feature of the Sheffield scoring system).

The return match at Lincoln on 8 April was played under the home side's rules and they were victorious by two goals to nil. Only one fixture with Notts took place, the clubs drawing 0-0 in a 15-a-side encounter on Nettleham Road.

The Sheffield games took place every season until 1869/70 by which time two more regular opponents, the Newark and Notts clubs, had been added to the fixture list. Matches were played to the rules of the home team and were probably closer to modern rugby than to the association game, with a limited amount of handling (although not running with the ball) being generally allowed. No copy of the Lincoln rules has survived but they were known to prohibit hacking (kicking to the shins), allow the handling or picking up of a ball which was bouncing and to include a form of offside.

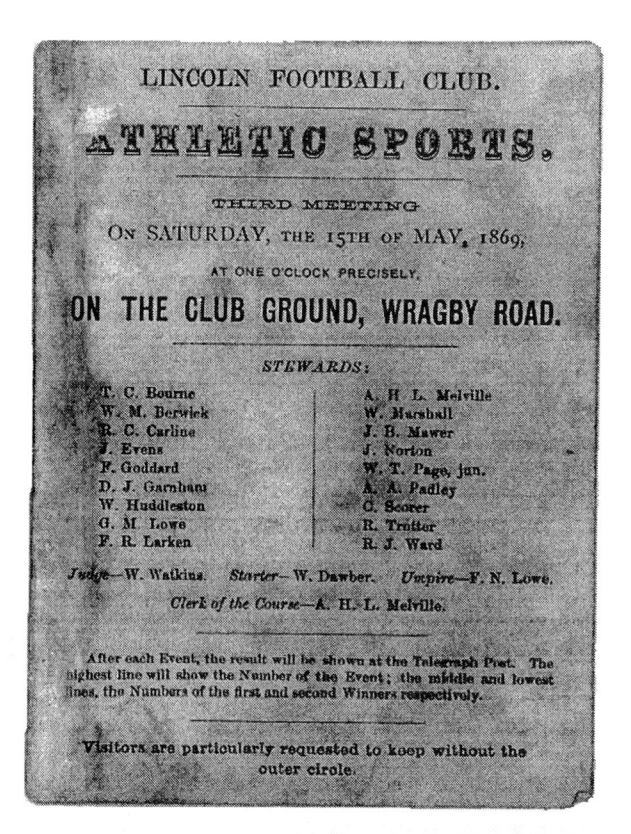

Lincoln's initial membership of the Football Association was a brief affair and the club resigned in February 1866, provoking the F.A.'s chairman, A. Pember, to suggest the club were, *"strongly opposed to anything but hacking, throttling and other violent practices"*. The Lincoln captain Devereux Garnham wrote a strong letter to the Bell's Life newspaper refuting the allegations. Lincoln had joined the F.A. because they agreed with the principle of one set of rules, they left because they could see no advantage in holding their membership.

Alterations were made to the club's own rules in October 1869 - the ball could now only be caught if it had not touched the ground, goals would be allowed even if the ball had been touched by an opponent before it passed between the posts, and a new scoring method was introduced with 'touch downs' as well as goals. The restrictions on handling brought Lincoln more in line with other clubs and in December 1869 Edward Gibney, joint secretary and a former pupil of Lincoln School, appeared for a side representing the North against the South at the Oval ground in London. In the days before international football this was the highest representative honour available to a player.

The programme for an athletic sports meeting held by the original Lincoln Football Cub at Wragby Road in May 1869.

In May 1867 an athletics sports meeting was held on the Lindum cricket ground on Nettleham Road. The event was a success attracting over 1,000 spectators who paid 6d (2.5p) each to watch. The sports were a good method of raising funds and became an annual event. Within four years the football club had merged with the Lindum Cricket Club. The two shared the football club field on Wragby Road, and they were known as the Lincoln Cricket & Football Club.

Each section retained its own committee and subscriptions were set at 7s 6d (37.5p) for football, 15s (75p) for cricket and £1 for combined membership. The original idea seems to have been to create a new county cricket team as well but this aspect of the proposals did not develop as planned. The arrangements secured the future of the Lindum C.C. but seem to have been of little direct advantage to the footballers.

The growing popularity of football allowed Lincoln to increase the number of games they played, most of their new opponents being drawn from recently established clubs within the county including Grantham, Hainton and Sleaford. The process of producing a unified set of rules continued throughout the 1870s and so the practise of playing to the home club's rules prevailed as a cause of occasional confusion. For example, when Lincoln lost 2-1 away to Derby Grammar School in March 1874 it was reported that they had been completely confused for the first half hour by the strange rules which were said to have *"an utter disregard of dribbling"*.

The number of members, many drawn from the legal profession and Public School old boys, remained fairly stable at around 60 to 80 - although it is likely that not all were active on the playing side. The 1870s were however a period of very clear decline for the club. Evidence can be found in the list of opponents which no longer included either Sheffield or (from 1874) Notts, furthermore Grantham had become the first county team to play in the F.A. Cup in 1878/79 and the initiatives to establish a Lincolnshire County F.A., in 1881, came from Brigg and not Lincoln. A clue to the reason for this may lie in a report of the club's 1879 annual general meeting which stated that they had worked their way out of debt for the first time in several years and that it was resolved to make purchases for cash only in the future and not to buy things on credit.

The Lincoln F.C. were the only club within the city until the early 1870s and it was not until the Foundrymen's Saturday half-holiday was lengthened (to 12.30 in 1872 and 12 noon in 1875) that others began to emerge. The first of these was the Recreation club formed by clerks from Clayton and Shuttleworth's Stamp End Works and from Robey's, another local engineering firm. They played on the Cowpaddle alongside Robey's foundry and in 1879 changed their name to Lincoln Rovers. The best of the working men's clubs was the Lincoln Albion, established by members of a cricket club which dated back to 1871. The players were mostly apprentices from the local foundries, however by the end of the 1870s they were competing on a level close to that of the Lincoln (now usually referred to as Lindum) and Rovers clubs.

In September 1881 H.Storm, secretary of the Brigg Town club, wrote to the leading clubs in the county suggesting they form an association and organise a cup competition. The Lincolnshire Football Association was formed later that month at a meeting held in the Queen Hotel, Lincoln, at which 12 clubs were represented: Barton, Brigg Brittania, Brigg Town, Gainsborough Recreationists, Gainsborough Town, Grantham, Grimsby Town, Horncastle, Lincoln Lindum, Lincoln Rovers, Louth and Spilsby. 16 teams entered the first Lincolnshire Cup, Rovers losing 11-0 to Spilsby in the first round while Lindum beat Horncastle and Grantham, only to fall to eventual winners Spilsby in a semi-final tie.

THE FORMATION OF LINCOLN CITY

By the autumn of 1883 the Lincolnshire Chronicle was able to report that local football was growing more and more popular day by day with hundreds now active in the game. Lindum and Rovers were still the city's premier sides with Albion, Rangers and Ramblers not far behind.

Spilsby won the Lincolnshire Cup again in 1883 leading observers to recall that Lincoln had been the top county team only a decade or so before and to consider how this situation might be rectified. The Chronicle's football writer 'Goalkeeper' raised an important question in his column : *"Is it not possible to form a Lincoln F.A. (similar to Sheffield and other towns) and to play a collective Lincoln team against all comers? A little ventilation of this subject would do no harm."* (Lincs. Chronicle 27 Oct 1883). The writer's identity has never been established but there would seem to be two main contenders - Eustace Cousans, goalkeeper for Lindum who was recovering from a recently broken arm and whose family had strong connections with the local press, and Sharpley Bainbridge who had kept goal for Lincoln back in the 1860s.

Lindum and Rovers had been bitter rivals in the recent past but their relationship was beginning to improve and perhaps in response to this appeal the Lindum included a number of Rovers players as guests for their fixtures over the Christmas and New Year period. Then on Saturday 15 March a team described as a combined Lindum and Rovers XI played Notts County second team on the Lindum's Wragby Road ground, losing 4-2. Their line-up was as follows : A.B.Porter, R.Mason, W.Heywood, F.Y.Teesdale, W.Fox, H.Simpson, C.Newsum, A.C.Newsum, E.D.Teesdale, J.Strawson, O.J.Barrett.

Nine of these men appeared for the City club on at least one occasion during the following season. If further incentive for change was needed it came from the 1883/84 Lincolnshire Cup results - Spilsby defeated Rovers (2-0) in Round 1, Lindum (3-1) in Round 2 and Albion (2-1) in the Semi-Final on their way to a hat-trick of wins in the competition.

With civic pride so severely dented a unity of purpose emerged amongst local football enthusiasts the like of which had not been seen before. Firstly Robert Dawber announced the availability of an enclosed field adjacent to the family brewery and to the rear of John O'Gaunts stables. Its High Street location close to the city centre, the foundries and the new housing developments was important for Lindum's uphill headquarters had been given as a reason why they had never developed a strong following of supporters. Shortly afterwards Sharpley Bainbridge and William Mortimer called a meeting at the Monsons Arms Hotel, then situated at the top of High Street approximately opposite where the Job Centre currently stands, and it was here on 26 June 1884 that the Lincoln City Football Club was formed.

The two founders were both active patrons of sport within the city. Bainbridge, a member of the well known local drapers family, was a City Councillor and had a variety of other sporting interests including horse racing, pigeon racing, and mountaineering. Mortimer, an architect, had been treasurer of Lincoln Rovers since the days when they were known as Recreation. He was a keen cricketer, appearing for Lincolnshire against an All-England XI in the 1860's, and like Bainbridge he was involved in the civic life of the City, serving as Sheriff in 1897.

Officers of the new club were elected as follows Vice-presidents - Sharpley Bainbridge and Robert Dawber; Secretary - Jack Strawson; Treasurer - William Mortimer; Committee - Edwin Teesdale, snr; Richard Whitton; Harry White; Ben Vickers; Will Cannon; Frank Trafford; Eustace Cousans. The presidency was left open for Mr Sibthorp the city's Member of Parliament. Club colours of red and white striped shirts were adopted, whilst season tickets and membership were available at 2s 6d (12.5p), and the admission price for matches was set at 3d (1.5p). The objectives of the new club were clearly outlined at a supper held at the Blue Anchor Public house to launch the new season. Bainbridge, speaking first, told the audience that the club had been formed *"for the benefit of football generally throughout the city, and they had got the nucleus of a very good club indeed. As they knew the Club had entered for the Lincolnshire ties and they intended to win the cup, if possible"*. Mortimer added that; *"When they strove to form that club their desire was to establish a club that should be an honour to the city and a credit to the county of which it was the capital"*. (Lincs. Chronicle 26 September 1884).

The opening match took place at the new ground on Saturday 3 October when fine weather attracted a good number of spectators to witness a one-sided affair against Sleaford. The City team lined up : H.Mantle; S.B.Barrett, W.Cannon; R.Mason, F.Y.Teesdale (capt.); G.Hallam, C.Clench; T.O.Sturges-Jones, E.D.Teesdale; H.Newsum, C.Newsum. George 'Pont' Hallam scored the first ever goal and after leading 3-1 at half-time City went on to record a 9-1 victory with goals from Hallam (3), Oliver Sturges-Jones (3), Herbert Newsum (2) and Edwin Teesdale.

The game kicked off twenty minutes late and one of the most notable incidents came in the first half when a fierce shot from Clement Newsum broke the crossbar. This match was intended as a warm up for the following week's grand opening against Nottingham Forest, unfortunately this proved to be a disappointment with Forest sending a second team and winning 4-2 into the bargain.

Where it all began - The Monson Arms Hotel, Lincoln - where the club was formed.

The early rounds of the county and national cups were negotiated with ease but they were knocked out of both at their first encounter with serious opposition. A surprise 3-0 loss to Horncastle on Boxing Day when the team appeared to be overconfident saw them exit from the Lincolnshire Cup. A week later they were out the F.A.Cup too after a 1-0 defeat at Grimsby in front of a crowd of around 3,000. City were without star forward Sturges-Jones for both games but had borrowed three Horncastle men - the Chapman brothers and Curtis - for the Grimsby match. However all three had spent the previous night at the Lincoln Cake Ball, a local society event, and perhaps because of this they were unable to inspire their new colleagues to victory. Overall City could look back on their first season with satisfaction having established themselves as the premier club in Lincoln. They had more members, more support (often up to 1,000 for home games) and a stronger fixture list than any of their local rivals. Of the 24 first team matches they had won 12, drawn three and lost nine.

Analysis of the 17 men who appeared in the F.A. Cup ties of 1884/85 reveals the majority were local born, well educated and with a professional background:

Name	Born	Club (1883/84)	Education	Career
Kenneth Bayne	Lincoln, 1858	Lincoln Albion	Lincoln School	Architect
Edmund Blyton	Lincoln, 1858	Lincoln Rovers		Solicitor
Charles Chapman	Swinstead, Lincs, 1860	Horncastle	St.Pauls, Stony Stratford / Cambridge University	Schoolmaster. (Later Clergyman)
Frank Chapman	Low Toynton, Lincs c1864	Horncastle	Oakham School / Cambridge University	Schoolmaster
David Clarke	Lincoln, 1865	Lincoln Rovers	Lincoln School	Chairman, Jackson's Laundry
Eustace Cousans	Lincoln, 1860	Lindum	Lincoln School	Printer's clerk
Harold Curtis	Cape Colony, c1866	Horncastle		Clergyman
Walter Fox	Lincoln, 1866	Lindum		Engine fitter
George Hallam	Lincoln, 1861	Lindum		Bricklayer
William Heywood	Lincoln, 1862	Lincoln Rovers		Clerk
Clement Newsum	Lincoln, 1865	Lincoln Rovers	Lincoln School	Family business
Herbert Newsum	Lincoln, 1867	Lincoln Rovers	Lincoln School	Family business
Samuel Oglesby	Canwick, Lincs, 1866			Pupil Auctioneer
Herbert Simpson	Sleaford, Lincs, 1863	Lincoln Rovers		Fitter and turner
Jack Strawson	East Firsby, Lincs 1858	Lincoln Rovers		Accountant
Oliver Sturges-Jones	Chichester, 1862	Chichester	Charterhouse School / Oxford University	Schoolmaster
Thomas Harry White	Lincoln, c1860	Lindum	Lincoln School	Dentist

[Principal Sources : 1881 Census Returns, St Catherine's House Records, Newspaper obituary notices]

The list includes two future Mayors of the city - Clement Newsum (1910) and his brother Herbert (1913) - and one Sheriff - T.H.White (1894). Charles Chapman had appeared for England at Rugby Union against Wales earlier in 1884 whilst his brother Frank was the father of A.P.F.Chapman, a future England cricket captain. Only three of the 17 were manual workers, all but two were born in Lincolnshire, and only one, Oliver Sturges-Jones, did not have strong local connections. Sturges-Jones was in fact a remarkable man and City were fortunate to have signed him up for the period when he was a master at the De Aston School, Market Rasen. After attending Charterhouse, a strong footballing school, he had a brief spell at Oxford University before he was sent down for his involvement in a series of pranks. In 1882, when just 20 years old, he had been instrumental in forming the Sussex County F.A. and served for a short period as its secretary. He became a well known player of the time appearing with Old Carthusians, Swifts and Casuals amongst other teams, before emigrating firstly to Canada and later to the United States.

As can be seen Rovers men dominated the club, providing many of the players, plus the secretary and treasurer. The Lincolnshire Chronicle, a strong supporter of the club in its infancy, condemned those it felt had been unwilling to sacrifice the interests of their own club for those of the City (clearly Lindum), but the issues were a little more complex than this. Rovers had a good team but a poor ground so it was not surprising they backed the new venture wholeheartedly, disbanding their own club in the summer of 1884 in anticipation of the City being a success. Lindum with their long history and their own enclosed ground did not have the same feelings and although they were fully in favour of a "united Lincoln Cup team" had nevertheless entered the county cup and wished to continue as an independent body.

The stage was thus set for City to replace Rovers as the traditional rivals of Lindum in a contest which was destined to be both brief and uneven.

EARLY DAYS.....
AND THE RISE OF PROFESSIONALISM

Professionalism, which had existed illegally since the late 1870s, was finally accepted by the Football Association in the summer of 1885 but strict rules were introduced to prevent men being 'imported' from other parts of the country. Players had to register annually and be qualified either by birth or two years residence within six miles of the club ground or headquarters. These regulations were not always adhered to for by Christmas 1885, City had recruited four men from Lancashire through the connections of committeeman James West and all were almost certainly professional. The most important of these was Joe Duckworth who had appeared at half-back for Blackburn Rovers in the early part of the season playing as an amateur. He was employed to coach the other players and probably because of this and his own skill and leadership the team's performances improved following his arrival. In most cases these very early professionals received a fee for their season's work and were found employment locally.

Oliver Sturges-Jones - one of the stars of the 1884-85 season

Immediately prior to the start of the 1885/86 season Lindum approached City with a proposal to enter a combined team in the Lincolnshire Cup but their plea was met with disinterest and nothing came of it. Lindum began the season with a home game versus Notts County which attracted around 1,200, and the two rivals arranged very similar fixture lists with both meeting opposition such as Attercliffe, Derby Midland and Newark from the east midlands area. However, City were able to use their greater financial resources to bring top class sides to John O'Gaunts on two occasions, arranging midweek friendlies with Blackburn Rovers in November (which they lost 1-0) and Preston North End in March (lost 4-0). In January 1886 Lindum F.C. separated from the cricket club and announced they were to hire a ground on Sincil Bank, almost exactly opposite John O'Gaunts, on the other side of the Sincil Drain. A grand opening with Notts County as the attraction was arranged for 30 January but never materialised and it was not until the visit of Gainsborough Trinity on 27 March that this ground was finally used for the first time. Both sides went out in the early stages of the F.A. Cup but reached the semi-finals of the county competition. Lindum beat Grantham Rovers 2-0 to reach the final but City drew 1-1 at Grimsby Town and then refused to play extra time, believing this had been agreed by both clubs before the tie had started. Protest and counter-protest followed with representations being made to both the Lincolnshire and Football Associations. The outcome was that Grimsby were declared winners by default, and although the protests continued into the summer they went on to win the final, which was played twice due to the various committee decisions.

For 1886/87 another professional from Lancashire was signed up. George Bone, was a Scot who had begun his career with Kilmarnock before moving south to Halliwell. Lindum, who had already begun to fall behind their local rivals, continued to decline and made early exits from both the F.A. and Lincolnshire Cups. The move downhill to Sincil Bank was not a success and they returned to their Wragby Road ground for the start of the new season. In contrast City's fortunes were improving and they reached the last 16 of the F.A. Cup for the first time. They were drawn away to Glasgow Rangers and most of the team travelled down the day before the match, although goalkeeper Kenny Bayne was forced to make the 10 hour journey overnight, arriving in Glasgow at 7am. It was a fast and exciting game, but City were hampered by an early injury to Dick Aspden and went out 3-0 in front of a 4,000 crowd. The club committee were so impressed with Gow, the Rangers full-back, that they offered him terms of £2-10s (£2.50) a week, but he turned them down. The team also progressed to the final of the Lincolnshire Cup for the first time, defeating Lindum, Humber Rovers, Gainsborough Trinity and Grantham Victoria on the way. The final took place on a neutral ground - Gainsborough's Northolme - on 2 April in front of a crowd of 7,500. Lincoln were cheered on by around 1,700 supporters, many wearing hats decorated with red and white stripes and came away with a 2-2 draw from a match which was a trial of strength and endurance. The replay took place at the same venue three weeks later when City were on top throughout a game played in hail, sleet and rain, with Duckworth dominating the Grimsby forwards. Billy Gregson shot through on 42 minutes, and a second from Jimmy Slater 10 minutes from time clinched the cup for City. When the players returned to the Great Northern Station at 10 o'clock that evening they were met by a cheering crowd and several, including captain Edwin Teesdale, were carried shoulder high to the Queen Hotel.

There were four Lincoln teams in the first round of the F.A. Cup for 1887/88, the only time this has happened. Albion (2-3 to Basford), Ramblers (0-9 to Notts County) and Lindum (0-4 to Grantham) were all defeated. City reached the third round where they fell to a Grimsby side full of Scottish imports. There was no joy in the county cup either where they were eliminated by Gainsborough Trinity.

Lindum's appearance in the Lincolnshire Cup final of 1886 proved to be the peak of their achievements. It was already clear that clubs such as City, who had greater resources and a strong commitment to the professional game, were much more likely to succeed in the long term than those who lacked these characteristics. Whilst Lindum were not completely amateur, they certainly paid some of their players in one form or another, they were unable to generate sufficient income from gate receipts to consider importing men from outside Lincoln. From around 1888 they stopped competing with City and shortly afterwards adopted a 'pure' amateur outlook, entering the F.A. Amateur Cup when it was started in 1893, and later joining the Amateur Football Association in 1908. They competed in the Midland Amateur Alliance from 1908 to 1914 and made a short visit to France in 1911. In 1901 they moved with the cricket club from Wragby Road to the present 'Lindum' ground on St Giles Avenue. They folded at the start of the Great War, reforming in 1920, and played in friendly matches until they disbanded at the end of the decade. Reconstituted in 1932, they continued to appear in friendly matches although they were now homeless as the rugby club had taken over at St Giles Avenue. They eventually hired a field on Burton Road but closed down yet again on the outbreak of war in 1939 and this time their demise was final.

The football section of the Albion club also folded around the late 1880s, although they continued as a cricket club until they were wound up in World War One. The remaining club funds were used to purchase the Albion Cup which is still competed for by local cricket clubs.

Meanwhile the wider football world underwent fundamental changes during the spring and summer of 1888. Firstly 12 of the country's leading clubs, motivated by the increasing problems of arranging a strong fixture list and by a need to generate maximum income following the spread of professionalism, split off to form the Football League. Almost immediately a group of lesser clubs led by F.A. Cup semi-finalists, Crewe Alexandra, and Bootle established a rival competition, which they called The Combination. Although not included in the original 14 members, City, Gainsborough Trinity and Grimsby Town, had all joined by the start of the season. However cup football was still the priority and as City had resigned from the county association following another dispute, their first round F.A. Cup tie with Grimsby Town took on added significance. Defeat, albeit in a second replay, and a mounting financial deficit combined to produce pressure for change. In October, the club's critics were prominent at a public meeting at the Cattle Market Hotel where they argued that membership should be open to all, particularly the foundrymen who formed the core of the club's support. The following month the committee agreed a new structure. Subscription, which included the purchase of a season ticket, would be available at three levels: 21s (£1-05), 10s-6d (52½p) and 7s-6d (37½p). The 10s-6d membership allowed free entry to all parts of the ground including the grandstands, but only those paying 21s were eligible for election to the committee. A committee of 20 was elected with a sub-committee of five running the day to day business, assisted by the secretary and treasurer. Although the critics did not achieve everything they wanted, this structure represents the most democratic in the club's history with the regular supporters able to elect the committee annually. A decision was also taken to follow the example set by Grimsby, and four Scots were quickly signed up: Quinten Neill (Queens Park), Harry Millar (Airdrieonians), Humphrey Barbour (Third Lanark) and Hugh McPhee (Hibernian). Others followed in the new year and by the end of the season the club was effectively a professional concern, drawing most of its players from outside Lincoln. The Football Association abolished its residency requirements for players in the summer of 1888. The Combination was a poorly organised competition and although most of its members played in excess of the minimum eight agreed matches, the large number of clubs and an inability to reach decisions on basic matters led to its quick demise. City played 14 fixtures, winning six and drawing two.

The club entered the newly formed Midland League for 1889/90 but there were more criticisms raised in the local press, mostly concerning the poor facilities on the John O'Gaunts ground and the fitness of the players. Shortly afterwards a trainer, Ben Smeaton, was appointed for the first time. The campaign got off to a bad start with a 2-1 defeat at Staveley, although City fielded a below strength side as a number of players were injured or suspended - either by the county association or internally by the club. The team was strengthened with several new signings in the autumn, including Mullineux and Graham from Lancashire and John Irving from Queen of the South Wanderers. These, together with the returning McPhee (he had been absent due to a bout of typhoid), inspired the team to new heights. After negotiating the early rounds of the F.A. Cup, they defeated Chester to pass into the last 16 where they were drawn away to Preston North End, winners of the League and Cup 'double' in 1888/89. City were no match for their illustrious opponents and quickly found themselves three goals down. Solid defensive work, particularly from goalkeeper Robinson, restricted the final score to 4-0 in front of a 5,000 crowd. The Midland League was a different matter however and they soon strung together a run of nine consecutive victories, suffering only one more defeat - on Easter Saturday when they went down 5-2 to Warwick County on the Edgbaston Cricket Ground. The title was won by a clear margin, and the final match, with Gainsborough Trinity, was combined with an archery tournament which helped raise the attendance to a record 6,000. The team's success on the field attracted sufficient income for the club to make a small profit, probably for the first time.

Another season of Midland League football followed, but after a good start to the campaign the team faded and defeat at Chester in the last 32 of the F.A. Cup was followed by a succession of away losses. These effectively ended their chances of retaining the title which went to Gainsborough, but there was consolation when City beat their local rivals to win the Lincolnshire Cup for only the second time.

The club took an important step upwards for the 1891/92 season, by joining the Football Alliance. Transfer activity over the summer had seen Jack Robinson move on to Derby County, where he began to establish a reputation as the country's premier goalkeeper, winning 11 England 'caps' around the turn of the century, whilst Joe Duckworth also departed. Their places were filled by two men from the Derby area, Parsons from St Lukes and Walker from Derby County. A reserve team was entered in the Midland Alliance for the first time, and admission prices were increased to 6d (2½p) although attendances held up and remained close to the break even level of 2,000. The new competition proved much harder and the team suffered several heavy defeats, notably to Newton Heath (10-1 away and 6-1 at home). Despite finishing 9th of the 12 teams, the club were accepted as founder-members of the newly formed Second Division of the Football League in May 1892.

THE FIRST FINANCIAL CRISIS

The new Second Division was slightly weaker than the Alliance for the three strongest sides - Sheffield Wednesday, Nottingham Forest and Newton Heath, had gone straight into the top division. Even so the club committee spent a sizeable sum over the close season on signing-on fees and summer wages in a bid to strengthen the side. Their first ever Football League game took place at Bramall Lane on Saturday 3rd September against Sheffield United, the kick-off being delayed until after 4 o'clock due to City's late arrival. They found themselves a goal down within three minutes, before Cameron equalised after 17 minutes play, but the Blades then dominated the match scoring three more times before Kelly netted a late consolation goal to leave the final score 4-2. The 'Cits' (as City had become known) also arrived late for their second match at Small Heath and were defeated again, this time by 4-1. It was not until their third match that a League victory was secured, Sheffield United being beaten by one goal to nil in the return fixture at John O'Gaunts. By the end of October the team were bottom of the table with three points from six games and the committee was forced to act to strengthen the side. They signed two new men - Bob Roberts the veteran Welsh international and ex-Druids, Bolton Wanderers and Preston North End half-back, and James Fleming a Scottish centre-forward who had been playing for Aston Villa. Roberts was employed as a player-coach and club captain and

The High Street entrance to the John O'Gaunts' Ground. The poster advertises a fixture between City Swifts (reserves) and Nottingham Forest on 12 September 1891

performances improved following his arrival. The team finished the season fourth from bottom which required them to apply for re-election, but all four applicants were successful as the division was expanded from 12 to 16 clubs. Despite his talents as a player and coach, Roberts was released in the summer, for as the Lincolnshire Echo noted, *"there was ONE FAILING ABOUT BOB, he gave way to drink, and just at the time when he was wanted to play in an important cup tie he was off colour."* (Lincs. Echo 15 Aug 1893). The extra costs in running a team at this level were not matched by any significant increase in gate receipts and a substantial loss was made, thus increasing accumulated debts from £110 to £309.

The financial situation necessitated a reduction in spending for the 1893/94 season as the committee and the treasurer (who was owed most of the money) acted to rectify the situation. First team players were either offered the same pay or in several cases a reduction, whilst the City Swifts (reserves) agreed to play for travel expenses and compensation for loss of time only. Isaac Moore, Frank Smallman, and James Gresham all departed but their replacements were at least as good and the team's fortunes improved. They recorded several large victories including a fine 8-2 win at Rotherham Town on 2 December which is still the club's best away win in the Football League, and went on to finish in eighth position.

Although the financial situation eased slightly there were more problems at the start of the 1894/95 season when the owner of John O'Gaunts, Robert Dawber, died and the field was put up for sale. A special meeting of club members was held at the Black Goats Hotel in January 1895 to discuss the matter and it was reported that although the debt had now fallen to £117 the treasurer, Mr F.T. Bennett, was unwilling to subsidise the move to a new ground and the possibility of establishing a limited liability company was suggested. The uncertainty created by the impending upheaval seems to have transferred to the players for only two points were gained from the first 13 games of 1895, and there were successive losses at Burslem (7-1) and Manchester City (11-3, still a club record defeat) in March. They finished in 13th position but were again successful in their re-election bid, and in the summer a new ground was obtained at Sincil Bank just a few hundred yards across the Sincil Drain from their old home. This was quite probably the same ground that the Lindum club had used briefly back in 1886.

The change of status was agreed by the membership and in October 1895 the old committee was disbanded and the Lincoln City Football Club Company Limited was incorporated, taking over the old debts by agreement. Shortly afterwards Alf Martin was engaged as secretary, the club's first paid official. The appointment was not to the liking of Jack Strawson who had been secretary of the club since its formation, and although a shareholder he temporarily ceased to play an active role in its affairs.

Martin was well known as proprietor of a series of sports papers in Grantham, as a referee, and a member of the Grantham Rovers committee. A generous and unassuming man he was considered a hard worker and a successful organiser. He faced a deepening financial crisis - the club needed to develop the Sincil Bank ground as quickly as possible yet only a small amount of the share capital had been taken up and the debts were mounting. However the enthusiasm and energy he brought with him to the club made him a popular man with the ordinary supporters and on several occasions he was cheered to the rostrum at public meetings. The team performances were of lesser importance at this time although they had some success in the F.A. Cup, registering a record 13-0 victory at Peterborough and defeating Worksop Town before being knocked out by Grimsby Town for the third year in succession. They finished fourth from bottom in the Second Division but were spared the need to seek re-election when the League changed its rules so that only the last three clubs had to enter the ballot. Meanwhile Martin set about raising money. He organised an archery tournament, a bicycle sports meeting and announced plans to obtain the £100 needed for summer wages by collecting 4,000 donations of 6d (2½p). However his lasting gift to the club was to establish the Working Men's Committee. He saw this as a way of introducing a measure of democracy by allowing the working men who formed the bulk of the club's support to become shareholders, and it survived as a valuable asset for over 30 years.

There was an air of optimism about the club as the 1896/97 season approached. There had been a number of ground improvements, including a new stand at the South Park end of the ground and several new players including Gardner Hannah (Blackburn Rovers), Jack Kirton (Oldham County), Jimmy Lynes (Leicester Fosse) and William Brown (Tottenham Hotspur) had been signed up. The pre-season practice matches attracted record attendances, but the team proved to be one of the worst ever to represent the club and in one spell suffered 18 defeats in a run of 19 League matches. The main reason for this was the growing financial crisis. In an attempt to raise money Martin had arranged a series of friendly games at the beginning of the season which resulted in the team playing six times in the first 12 days of the season, and appearing in places as far apart as New Brompton, Southampton and Manchester. The better players including Matthew Gillespie (to Newton Heath) and his brother Billy (to Manchester City for £150), were sold off as the directors tried to balance the books.

City Swifts at Sincil Bank in 1897. Back: Bayne (director), R.Strawson (director), Dickinson, Dean, R.Sharman, Shaw, Gunson, Simpson, F.Sharman (linesman). Front: Kirkham, Heywood, Scott, Ward, Ironmonger. Kenny Bayne played in the club's first season, in 1884-85.

The administration affairs were also in chaos with few of the directors taking an active interest and there was even talk of disbanding the club in mid-season. The situation came to a head early in 1897 and dramatic changes followed. Martin was forced to make a hasty departure to a post on the Grimsby Telegraph newspaper following the discovery of inaccuracies in his book keeping - the accounts showed a profit of £100 when the true position was a deficit of £400. He failed because although he was ambitious and innovative the financial situation was against him, and he never won over men such as Jack Strawson and James West who formed an 'old guard' of club officials who had worked together since the days of the Rovers club. Martin went on to a successful career in journalism, establishing the Saturday Telegraph football paper in Grimsby and the Green 'Un in Sheffield and he later served the National Union of Journalists in a number of capacities including President in 1917/18.

The company decided that they could no longer afford a paid secretary and so longstanding committeeman James West took over the position in an honorary capacity. West was very experienced in the football world and had been closely connected with the club since its formation, helping to recruit many of the early professionals as well as serving as a Football League referee. The supporters were becoming frustrated at the inept performances on the field and there were two serious incidents in early 1897. Following a rough encounter with Grimsby in January, the visiting players needed a police escort as they made way down the High Street towards the railway station amidst a hail of snowballs. A more serious incident took place during the match with Newton Heath on 1 April after the referee firstly awarded a controversial penalty to the visitors and then disallowed a seemingly legitimate City goal. At the end of the game he fled to the dressing shed through a hail of bricks and stones. He eventually escaped in a cab with the help of police and club officials although not before all the windows had been broken. As a result of this Sincil Bank was ordered to be closed for the first two weeks of the following season and boys were made to pay full price for the first two months. West meanwhile persuaded Burnley to loan two men, James Davidson and Jimmy Hartley, and the team doubled their points total over the final eight games but still finished bottom of the table. However they were successful in seeking re-election for the third time in five seasons at the Football League's annual general meeting.

The club was effectively reborn over the summer and started the 1897/98 campaign with a new playing strip of green shirts and black shorts (donated by co-founder Sharpley Bainbridge), several new faces on the board and a number of new players. The Working Men's Committee had worked hard to raise money both to pay for the new men and to help the club over the early period of the season when there would be no income from gate receipts due to the ground closure.

Playing performances improved only slightly with the team finishing in 14th position and again having to seek re-election. There was talk of the club folding if they were unsuccessful, but Jack Strawson's eloquence and popularity won the day and they topped the poll. Off the field it had been a highly successful year as a substantially reduced wage bill and increased attendances combined to produce a trading profit of £314.

Horace Fletcher - a regular in the 1897/98 forward line

The improvement in finances enabled the club to recruit better players and in March 1898 they signed the Welsh international winger Harry Pugh from Stoke. He was followed in the close season by Will Gibson, who had played in Sunderland's 'Team of all the Talents' in the early 1890s before moving to Glasgow Rangers where he appeared with the Scottish League representative side. 'Tich' Smith from Loughborough who had appeared for England in an unofficial international against Canada back in 1891 was another new face. Results improved, the team finished safely in mid-table positions in the next two seasons - 12th in 1898/99 and 9th in 1899/1900 - and for the first time ever they had a player 'capped' whilst on the books when Pugh appeared for Wales against Scotland at Aberdeen in February 1900. The threat of closure receded and there was even enough money to enter a professional reserve side in the Midland League in 1899/1900, although the extra expenses resulted in a loss of £152 and after this the second team was mostly filled by local men. The ground was also developed at this time mainly thanks to the Working Men's Committee who built a small covered stand on the Sincil Bank side and banked the standing areas with cinders to increase the capacity. In the summer of 1900 West left to become secretary-manager of Newton Heath, a post he held until the club was wound up and reformed as Manchester United at which point he retired to run a public house in the Manchester area until his death in the early 1920s.

THE GOLDEN YEARS

In September 1900 the board appointed Notts County's Scottish international centre-half David Calderhead as the new secretary-manager. He had played with City director John Irving in the Queen of the South Wanderers team of the late 1880s, had appeared in two F.A. Cup finals, and also served on the management committee of the Players Union. The club colours were changed again, reverting to red and white striped shirts with black shorts. The attack was strengthened with the signing of Tommy McInnes from Nottingham Forest, and the team performed impressively at home winning 12 of their 17 fixtures. However away results were dreadful and the total of four goals for the season (two of which came in one match) is still an all-time low in the history of the League. Even so the points gained at Sincil Bank were sufficient to enable the team to equal their highest ever position of eighth. Attendances were up to such an extent that the City Council discussed the need for an extra bridge over the Sincil Drain to cater for the volume of spectators leaving the ground on match days. A new club record was established on Boxing Day for the visit of neighbours Grimsby Town, when a crowd of around 9,000 paid receipts of £227.

The outstanding debts, which had stood at £662 at the worst point in 1897, had been reduced to just £122, and the improvement in finances meant that most of the players could be re-signed for the new season, introducing greater stability to the team. The players also benefitted in other ways - injured men were sent away for specialist treatment, long away journeys were sometimes made the day before the game and there were visits to the coast for training before important matches.

The 1901/02 season began with consecutive victories over Burnley, Burslem Port Vale and Chesterfield and only two games were lost before Christmas, but there was a disastrous 8-0 defeat at Preston on 28 December when City finished three men short due to injuries. The team remained unbeaten at home in the League all season but were only ever on the edge of the promotion race, even so

17

David 'Harry' Pugh (front row, second from right) with the Wales team that lost 6-0 to England in March 1901 - City's first International player. This was his third and final cap during his time at Sincil Bank. He later served as a gateman for City.

they finished fifth which was their highest ever position. They also had success in the F.A. Cup, easily progressing through the qualifying rounds having disposed of Worksop Town, Doncaster Rovers, Barnsley and Newton Heath. Drawn away to amateurs Oxford City in round one, City were surprised by both the strength of the opposition and the size of the crowd (around 5,000). They were content to play out a goalless draw and allow their superiority to show in the midweek replay which they won comfortably with two goals in each half. Derby's offer of £450 to switch the venue of their second round tie was rejected and grand preparations were made for the visit of their First Division opponents. Three new temporary grandstands were erected and seating provided right up to the ropes which surrounded the pitch, raising the ground capacity to around 20,000. Arrangements were made to double the width of the Sewell's Walk bridge over the Sincil Drain to cope with the large crowd which was expected.

The players were despatched to the Bacchus Hotel, Sutton-on-Sea, for a full week of special training at the coast. The game itself proved rather an anti-climax. City led 1-0 at half-time through a goal from Tommy McInnes, but were handicapped by an early injury to centre-half John Crawford which required him to leave the field for treatment at regular periods. Derby played with six forwards after the break to exploit the situation and came back strongly to finish 3-1 winners. Heavy snow on the morning of the match covered the pitch and kept the crowd down to around 10,000, although 16,435 tickets were sold to bring in record receipts of £428.

The whole of the first team squad was re-signed for the 1902/03 season and they again made a good start by winning four of the first five matches. Victory over Gainsborough Trinity on 11 October saw City at the top of the table for the first time ever but failure to win the following Saturday's game at Burton United meant they quickly dropped back to second place. A string of injuries to key players followed and by December they had fallen to sixth. In the F.A. Cup they defeated West Ham, then of the Southern League, before going out to Barnsley in the first round. Attendances dropped and Crawford was sold to Nottingham Forest to help keep the finances stable. The team finished the season in 10th position, but promotion was now seen as a distinct possibility and with this in mind the St Andrews stand was enlarged and upgraded and a cycling and athletics track laid down.

In the summer of 1903 Jimmy Hartley and Peter Proudfoot returned to Scotland and it took some time for their replacements to settle in. The team struggled in the early part of the season, suffering a 5-0 defeat at bottom of the table Glossop in October, but eventually recovered form to finish in 12th position.

The club were beginning to earn a reputation for developing new talent and in April 1904 full-back Albert Groves became the next player to move on when he was sold to Sheffield United. Secretary Calderhead travelled up to the north-east in the close season and signed up four youngsters from junior football - Dick Hood, John Martin, Magnus O'Donnell and George Buist - all of whom became first team regulars during 1904/05. There were no re-election worries and the team finished in a respectable mid-table position achieving some success in the F.A. Cup having eliminated Watford and Burnley in the qualifying rounds. Manchester City, with the great Billy Meredith, visited Sincil Bank in the first round. Despite putting up a good fight, Lincoln went two goals down, the second coming from a penalty when Meredith scored in typical style by lobbing the ball over Buist's head as the goalkeeper stayed on the six yard line (goalkeepers could position themselves anywhere in the six-yard box for a penalty at this time). Dennis O'Donnell pulled one back just before the half-time break but the forwards posed little threat in the second period and the visitors went through by 2-1. The attendance was a disappointing 8,000 with the local typhoid epidemic keeping many away.

The 1905/06 season followed a similar pattern to the two previous campaigns. Dennis O'Donnell was sold to Sunderland for a record fee of £370 and new youngsters were found, the most promising being Norrie Fairgray a brilliant but raw winger from Dumfries. The policy of selling the best players was beginning to prove unpopular with the supporters but was a useful way of making up the deficit between gate receipts and expenditure. Not only was a mid-table position achieved for the fourth year in a row but a profit of £112 was recorded, bringing the balance sheet into credit for the first time since the limited company had been formed.

Goalkeeper Buist (right with cap) and his fellow defenders keep out a Chelsea attack in their F.A.cup-tie at Stamford Bridge in January 1907.

Magnus O'Donnell and leading scorer John Martin were sold over the summer and 1906/07 began as usual with a mixture of results, although the team's fortunes were not helped by long term injuries to forwards Freddie Simpson and Peter Machin, or by the sale of centre-forward William McLeod to Leeds City for £500 in November. They met Chelsea at Sincil Bank in the first round of the F.A. Cup, and found themselves two goals behind in the closing minutes, but with the crowd streaming out Watson pulled one back with three minutes remaining. Then Fairgray won the ball straight from the kick off, raced to the goal line and crossed for Ted Dixon to equalise. An early injury to Dixon left City with only ten fit men for most of the replay. They spent much of the game on the defensive, until Fairgray struck again in extra time to clinch the tie 1-0. When the players returned to Lincoln later that evening they were met by a huge crowd and the Excelsior Band played 'See the Conquering Hero Comes' to greet them. Their reward was a trip to the Baseball Ground, but an injury to Nisbet and a nervous display by centre-forward Harry Barrick, who had been playing local football until a few weeks before, cost them dearly and they went out 1-0 to Derby. The team had been in the relative security of 15th place at the beginning of March but suffered four consecutive defeats at a crucial time, and thereby dropping into the re-election zone. Maximum points from the final two fixtures would have ensured safety but a 3-1 defeat at Nottingham Forest in the penultimate match ended these hopes and the club were forced to seek re-election. This was not the formality it had been in the 1890s for two reasons. Firstly the League was now anxious to establish itself in areas where Southern League and Northern Union (Rugby League) football were dominant, and secondly the non-League clubs were becoming increasingly professional in their applications. Oldham Athletic, for example, had produced a booklet supporting their claim for membership which they had circulated in the spring prior to the ballot. However the method of election was unchanged with a representative from each club making a short speech to try and convince League members to vote for them. Jack Strawson could rely on considerable personal support and his confident, witty, speech stressing the club's history of loyal membership was successful as City topped the poll with 28 votes.

David Calderhead was appointed secretary-manager of Chelsea in the summer of 1907. There could have been no greater contrast between life at Sincil Bank and at Stamford Bridge. Chelsea were one of the wealthiest clubs in the country, had a stadium which could hold 70 or 80,000 and regularly attracted gates ten times those at Lincoln. Calderhead had a long career at Chelsea, remaining in the post until 1933, the team reaching the 1915 F.A. Cup final and twice winning promotion to Division One under his leadership.

THE RE-ELECTION YEARS

Jack Strawson replaced Calderhead as secretary-manager, but remained on the board and was effectively managing-director for the next 12 months. After a decade of relative success the re-election application of 1906/07 proved to mark the start of a return to the days of the 1890s when such bids were required at the end of most seasons. New signings over the summer included Alston from Maxwelltown Volunteers, Law from Glasgow Rangers and Poppitt from Notts County, but the side was weakened in September when Fairgray followed his former boss to Stamford Bridge. A series of misfortunes then overtook the club with injuries to players making it impossible to field a settled team, and bad weather and poor performances produced an adverse effect on home attendances. By November the team were at the bottom of the League and the worsening financial position led to the players having their wages reduced. An early exit from the F.A. Cup at the hands of Stoke did not help and there were more problems in February when a 30 yard section of the

The damaged grandstand on the St. Andrews side caused by a freak storm during the Leeds City match.

grandstand was destroyed by a storm during the home match with Leeds City. The game resumed after a short stoppage and City went on to record a 5-0 victory which was enough to lift them off the bottom for the first time in three months. Concern over the growing financial deficit led to several local tradesman joining together to form a committee to raise funds for the club. There was no dramatic change of fortune in the team's performances and they finished bottom of the League.

Several strong clubs had applied for League membership and three of these - Bradford Park Avenue, Queens Park Rangers, and Tottenham Hotspur were expected to do well in the poll. Strawson anticipated this threat and had circulated an appeal for support well before the end of the season. There were two surprises at the Annual General Meeting. The first was the withdrawal of Q.P.R. at the last moment, the second was when Bradford, who had finished 13th in the Southern League, received two more votes than Lincoln and replaced them. Strawson's speech had placed emphasis on the loyal and conscientious nature of City's membership in the past, but the patience of other clubs had been exhausted by six re-election bids in 16 years. There was brief talk of forming a Third Division but then Stoke resigned and a Special General Meeting was called to discuss the vacancy. On the first poll Lincoln and Tottenham received 17 votes and a revived Stoke won six. A further vote then took place between Lincoln and Tottenham and on two occasions a tie resulted, 20 votes each. The Management Committee then broke the deadlock and elected Tottenham by five votes to three. City were out of the League, because the clubs had voted for the best financial option: Tottenham's gate receipts for the previous season had exceeded £8,500, whilst Lincoln's had amounted to just £1,647. The local press expressed the bitterness felt locally at the rejection: *"In practically all quarters it is held that this is the result of the most flagrant favouritism, and the prostitution of justice and established precedent to monetary considerations."* (Lincoln Leader 4 Jul 1908).

In 1908/09 the first team competed in both the Midland League and the Northern Division of the United League. The former was the more important and despite suffering a heavy defeat at the hands of Sheffield Wednesday Reserves in the opening game they went on to win 15 of the next 17 matches to head the league table. They were rarely troubled by the opposition all season, and clinched the championship with four matches remaining by beating Gainsborough Trinity Reserves 2-0 at Sincil Bank on Easter monday. They also finished runners-up to Rotherham Town in the United League. However attendances were so low that the admission price was cut from 6d (2½p) to 4d (2p) in an attempt to attract more support. Collectors were also sent round with a subscription list to raise money and help stabilise the financial position. New moves to form a Third Division again fell through, but there were high hopes of a return to League football when it became known that there were only five candidates for the two vacancies and no Southern League clubs had applied. Blackpool topped the poll with 27 votes but City were second with 24 and so resumed their place in Division Two at the expense of Chesterfield.

The club increased the number of professionals on their books for the new season and were rewarded with a mid-table position. For good measure the Lincolnshire Cup was won for only the sixth time in the club's history when Grimsby Town were defeated by four goals to nil. Attendances showed a healthy increase and the break-even figure of 5,000 per match was comfortably reached. A new ground record for a League match was set when a crowd of 10,000 turned out for the Christmas Day visit of Gainsborough, and gate receipts for the season exceeded £4,000 for the first time ever.

The team had a good start to the 1910/11 campaign and were in third place by the end of September. However when Wolves visited on 22 October, City had three men carried off through injury - Gardner, Jackson and Clarke - with both Yule and Fraser suffering cut eyes, as the visitors won 5-1. The following Saturday an understrength side went down 7-0 at Chelsea with Clem Jackson carried off for the second week in succession. The injuries affected team performances and by December they were in the bottom two and heavily involved in the fight to avoid seeking re-election. The board signed Comrie of Bradford City and Garratty, a former England international from West Bromwich, but neither proved much of a success. There was some hope of reaching safety when a four match unbeaten run in early April yielded six points, and with three games remaining City entertained leaders West Bromwich needing a victory to boost their cause. The visitors won 2-1, aided by a controversial decision by the referee who allowed a rather dubious goal to stand, and Lincoln were doomed to seek re-election. A crowd of several hundred invaded the pitch at the final whistle and chased the official to the dressing rooms. Only a police escort saved him from a ducking in the Sincil Drain on his way home. In the final analysis it was bad play and not bad refereeing which was the cause of the team's plight.

The Echo reporter despaired at the performances he had witnessed when reviewing the season *"To go to match after match and see the displays we have seen is enough to take the heart out of most people."* (Lincs. Echo 1 May 1911). Strawson again spoke of the club's loyalty to the League and of their problems through injuries at the annual general meeting, but the clubs had heard it all before and he was upstaged by Grimsby who produced the town's Member of Parliament to speak on their behalf. The leading votes were Barnsley 28, Grimsby Town 18 and Lincoln 17, so City were replaced by their county rivals, who themselves returned after a year's exile in the Midland League.

City skipper Walter Wilson receives the Lincolnshire Cup, after a victory in the competition during the Edwardian era.

In the close season the annual moves to form a Third Division failed again, but another new competition, the Central League, was successfully established. Most of the teams were drawn from reserve sides which had previously played in the Lancashire Combination but when several were forced to drop out Lincoln and Burslem Port Vale accepted invitations to replace them. There must have been a few worried faces when the first five games yielded only five points, but fortunately only one more defeat was suffered and City were crowned champions six points clear of their nearest challengers. The club also enjoyed its best F.A. Cup run for several years. In the fourth qualifying round, City met Grimsby Town a side they had been drawn against on nine previous occasions without success, but on this occasion they ran out 3-2 winners in front of a 10,000 crowd. Victories over Crook Town and Stockport County followed and they next faced Wolves away in the second round proper. The team put up a fine performance matching their opponents throughout, but fell to a last minute goal which by all accounts passed through a hole in the side netting. Attendances had held up well and a small profit was made over the year. The venture into the Central League was deemed such a success that the Working Men's Committee held a ballot of the supporters to decide whether the club should reapply for League status or not. The result was in favour of seeking readmission and the campaign was carefully planned. An appeal was issued in May outlining the club's strengths and their case for a place in Division Two. This time they were represented at the A.G.M. by John Foster Fraser the prospective Unionist (Conservative) candidate for the Lincoln parliamentary seat and the move proved a success as City finished second in the poll with 27 votes, well clear of Gainsborough Trinity whose place they took.

The side was not greatly strengthened on returning to the League, but even so the club had to pay out £900 over the summer in transfer fees. This was because the registrations of several of the existing players were held by their former clubs, and so they had to be paid for as if they were new signings. On 28 October the team went to the top of Division Two for the first time in 10 years when they won

21

2-1 away to Nottingham Forest. They stayed in the top two for three weeks but were unable to maintain a challenge for promotion and drifted away to finish in 8th position, the club's best performance since 1901/02. Attendances were at record levels, averaging around 10,000, and the grandstands were enlarged to cater for the extra interest. There was even talk of a close season tour to Denmark but this did not take place.

In December 1913 the club sold Donald Slade to Woolwich Arsenal and goalkeeper Tommy Fern to Everton. Fern had missed only two first team games since signing from Worksop in 1909 and City received a record fee of £1,500 for him. New men were brought in at some expense but by the spring they found themselves contesting the re-election positions with Glossop, Leicester Fosse and Nottingham Forest. A 5-1 defeat at home to Glossop at the beginning of April did not help the cause, although victories followed over Wolves and Stockport. The crucial match was the penultimate fixture at Leicester which was lost 2-0. Re-election could still have been avoided, but the final match at home to Bradford was also lost and they finished in 19th position on goal average and were thus doomed to face the ballot. Prior to the vote, Athletic News, the most influential football paper of the time, mounted a strong campaign for Stoke City to take the place of Lincoln. City's record was bad - eight applications in 20 years membership. Including the applications made in 1909 and 1912, when the club were seeking readmission, it was the sixth in eight years. Foster Fraser was again the spokesman and concentrated on the fact that no club had previously been cast out as a result of goal average. City had been clearly worried about their chances but the result went their way and they finished with eight more votes than Stoke. The editor of the Athletic News was furious and wrote,

"I have only one regret and that is that the reputations of 24 clubs in the Football League could do such violence to that body for commonsense as to re-elect Lincoln City to the Second Division. Never has there been a bigger and a blacker spot on the scutcheon of the League........" (Tityrus [J.H. Catton] in his Stray Leaves column, Athletic News 1 Jun 1914)

World War One broke out in August 1914 and although football continued for one more season it did so in an unreal atmosphere. When the players travelled to Leicester for the opening fixture of 1914/15, they had to fight their way through a large crowd which had gathered to meet wounded soldiers returning from the continent.

Attendances were down everywhere and the presence of khaki clad soldiers, wounded or on leave, was noted at most games. Financially City suffered more than most as the foundries started Saturday afternoon working, and on a least two occasions the club obtained handouts from the League's relief fund. Football was officially suspended in July 1915, and did not recommence until August 1919.

The captains shake hands before a pre-1914 match at Sincil Bank.

A cartoon to mark the club's opening fixture, and return to the Football League (Lincoln Leader 31 August 1912). The 'Window Blinds' refers to their nickname of the day.

THE GREAT WAR

City competed in the Midland Section of the War League during the four seasons when professional football was suspended. The season was split into two parts, a main competition which lasted for around six months followed by a subsidiary tournament usually of six games. Only three of the players signed up for war duty immediately and most of the rest took up full-time employment in the local foundries. These men were still available to play and they made an agreement with the directors that guest players would only be used when those already on the books were unavailable. The players had been concerned because several men from other Football League clubs had come to the city to work in the foundries. As a result of this agreement, Rustons Aircraftmen were often able to field a team of near Football League strength in their Lincoln League fixtures. City's team for 1915/16 differed little from that of the previous season but as the war continued the agreement reached by the players seems to have broken down as men either moved away or were prevented from travelling to away games because of work commitments. Journeys to away games were often made with an incomplete team and the numbers made up with local men on arrival. On one occasion, in April 1917, the club were required to fulfil two fixtures at the same time.

Nine players made their way to Sheffield where they made up the side with Bratley and Henry Hibbert (who had played for City back in 1909/10), and went down 7-1 to the Wednesday club. The five remaining men travelled to Birmingham filling the side with local men and came home with a 0-0 draw. In the 1917/18 season 69 different players were used in the 34 games played. Several of the winter matches finished early with the score at close of play being allowed to stand as the final result. The players trained on Saturday afternoons before the start of the season and three evenings a week when this was possible. Professional contracts had been scrapped and they appeared for expenses only. Attendances were low but this was of less importance with no wages to pay. A 1d (½p) 'War Tax' was added to admission prices from 1916/17, and the following season a permanent Entertainment Tax was introduced.

Amongst the millions who died in the hostilities were David Salkeld, whose last appearance for the club had been in December 1916, James Comrie and Tommy Strong. The war brought many new regulations into force and in August 1914 the club fell foul of one of these. A light was observed shining from the club offices in High Street during the blackout and as a result, secretary Jack Strawson was fined 10s (50p). Strawson retired in the summer of 1919 marking an end to the first period in the club's history.

JACK STRAWSON

Jack Strawson was the most influential individual in the development of the club in the period to 1919. A loyal servant for 35 years as both player and administrator he was a tireless worker and on many occasions was personally responsible for the retention of Football League status.

John Henry Strawson was born at East Firsby, near to the Lincolnshire village of Spridlington on 3 November 1858. The third of five sons of a farmer, also called John, he moved with his family to Lincoln around 1860 where they ran a cafe on the High Street known as Strawson's Dining Rooms.

His early football career was spent playing at centre forward for Lincoln Rovers. He was elected to the club committee at the age of 22 and shortly after he was appointed secretary. He had some ability as a player and appeared for the Lincs. F.A. team in the early 1880s.

He became the first secretary of the newly formed City club in July 1884 and held this honorary post until the limited company was established when a paid secretary was appointed. Unhappy at this decision he withdrew from playing an active role in the club's affairs for a short period until the departure of Alf Martin, at which point he agreed to become a director before serving as chairman from 1899 to 1908. He took on the role of secretary-manager again when David Calderhead left for Chelsea and remained in this post until the summer of 1919 when he announced his retirement from football.

Strawson was also very active in the wider world of football administration, serving on the first Midland League committee and on the Management Committee of the Football League for the 1894/95 season. His talents as an accountant were put to use when serving the League as an auditor for 24 years and he was also a well known referee in the period to 1905. In 1918 he was awarded the Football League's long service medal, given to those who had served their club for 21 years or more.

His finest hours were undoubtedly the occasions when he pleaded for the club to be re-elected at the Football League's annual general meeting - usually with success. Reports of these meetings convey something of his speeches and the sort of man he was: *"Who can stand a Strawsonian argument, composed, as it is, of sound common sense (from the point of the pleader) with an embroidery in equal proportion of soap and honey?"* (Athletic News 23 May 1898). Whilst ten years later he gave the impression that, *"... he regarded himself - not as a beggar - but as the licensed humorist of the League. There was an air of assurance about 'The Senior Auditor' as much as to say 'I know you'll vote for Strawson' ..."* (Athletic News 3 Jun 1907).

After retiring from football in 1919 he became landlord of the Red Lion Hotel in Spalding where he remained for ten years. He died in a Grimsby hospital on 4 March 1949 at the age of 90.

✣✣✣✣✣✣✣✣

CHAPTER TWO
1919 TO 1961 . . . UP AND DOWN

THE SECOND FINANCIAL CRISIS

Jack Strawson's decision to leave his post as secretary-manager after so many years at the helm came at a bad time for the club. Several of the directors had dropped out during the war years and the board were in need of an experienced figure both to reorganise the administrative affairs and to assemble a squad of players for the new season. No immediate successor was appointed and the role passed temporarily into the hands of directors Billy Pogson and Cornelius Taylor, who although enthusiastic were not as efficient as Strawson. The Lincolnshire Echo recognised the serious nature of the situation and an article was printed outlining the problems that existed, together with suggestions on how to resolve these. Shortly afterwards, long serving defender Clem Jackson was appointed player-manager with responsibility for signing up new men. With the club finances in a poor state no money was available to buy players and the team which lined up for the first post-war fixture relied heavily on the men who had appeared in 1914/15. The board were turned down by their first choice for secretary-manager, local reporter Herbert Green, and eventually appointed George Fraser at the start of the season. Fraser was well qualified for the post having appeared in a record 267 League games for City between 1901 and 1911, he also had family ties with Strawson, their wives being sisters. Since retiring from the game he had been a publican, firstly at the Turks Head on Newport, and later at the Black Bull in Welton.

The team struggled in the early fixtures, conceding 37 goals in the first ten games. Although three youngsters, Ashurst, Chipperfield and Linfoot, were obtained at the auction of players from the expelled Leeds City, fortunes did not improve and only the poor form of newcomers Coventry kept City off the bottom of the table. The fans were already worried by the team's League performances and became further alienated from the cause when the directors agreed to switch the home F.A. Cup tie with Middlesbrough to Ayresome Park for a payment of just under £1,000 - the first time in the club's history that they had resorted to this practise. By Easter they were still in trouble at the foot of the table but had to meet fellow strugglers Coventry twice, and in preparation the players were sent to Sutton-on-Sea for special training. The first meeting took place at Sincil Bank on 17 April with City winning by a comfortable 4-1 margin after the visiting 'keeper was carried off injured. It looked as if the Imps (as they were now commonly referred to) might avoid the need to seek re-election for with two matches to play the table looked thus:

	P	PTS
Lincoln City	40	27
Wolverhampton Wanderers	38	26
Coventry City	39	24
Grimsby Town	39	21

However Coventry won the return match at Highfield Road 2-0 and then picked up a point from their midweek visit to Bury leaving the Imps needing to win their final match to finish in a position of safety. They lost 4-2 at Huddersfield, Coventry beat Bury 2-1, and so Lincoln and Grimsby had to seek re-election. Voting was conducted along the same lines as before the war with City circulating an appeal for support prior to the League A.G.M. and engaging local Member of Parliament, Alfred Davies, to speak on their behalf. Unfortunately he lacked the charisma and personal following that Strawson possessed and this was reflected in the result, with City receiving just seven votes, the lowest total they had obtained in the 11 ballots they had contested since 1893. Leeds United and Cardiff topped the poll to fill the vacancies in Division Two whilst Grimsby, who had finished bottom, were invited to take part in the newly formed Division Three as they had won more votes than Lincoln.

In May 1923, an F.A. Commission ruled that the directors of Bury and Coventry had conspired to fix the result of the drawn game at Gigg Lane. Although several leading figures from both clubs were banned from the game for life, City's appeal for reinstatement to Division Two was not accepted.

The first team returned to the Midland League for 1920/21 and began the season in the second XI strip of black and white striped shirts, until permission was granted to change to the traditional red and white stripes. Five consecutive victories put City amongst the early leaders but league action soon took second place to the F.A. Cup with the team defeating Bromley and Millwall to earn a home tie with Fulham in the last 32 of the competition.

The directors decided to raise admission prices rather than switch the tie with the minimum adult charge doubled to 2s (10p) and the most expensive seats available at 10s 6d (52½p). Lincoln was in the grip of cup fever, fuelled by optimistic fans citing a vague passage in Old Moore's Almanac which suggested a midlands side would win the trophy as evidence that City were destined to win the competition. Many shops closed on the afternoon of the big match helping to boost the attendance to 12,500, paying record receipts of £1,637, but the Imps could only manage a 0-0 draw and went out 1-0 in the replay.

In March the Football League confirmed plans to form a northern section of the Third Division and City were one of 14 clubs accepted as a group, the other four places being decided by ballot. Meanwhile the team rose back to the top of the Midland League table and clinched the title for the third time in all with a 2-1 win over Rotherham County Reserves at Sincil Bank on 30 April. Attendances held up well and a profit exceeding £1,000 was made for the second year in succession thus returning the balance sheet to credit once more.

Secretary-manager Fraser left for Grimsby in April and was replaced by David Calderhead, son of the Chelsea and former City manager between 1901 and 1906.

The launch of the Northern Section coincided with the beginning of an economic slump and a growth in unemployment which combined to create severe problems for several of the member clubs in the early years of the competition. City's expenses increased dramatically as they were once again running two professional teams and so had to employ more players, whilst the widespread location of their opponents meant that travel costs rose sharply as a number of overnight stops were required. Gate receipts remained constant producing a widening gap between income and expenditure which was only reduced by selling players - George Richardson moving to Sheffield United and leading scorer Bob Chambers to Burnley. Stories began to appear in the press about the club's financial problems including one claim that City would withdraw from the League in the close season and another that the reserve side was about to be scrapped, but both proved to be incorrect. A heavy loss of £1,500 was incurred during the season with the team finishing 14th in the table, just four places off the bottom.

A number of events were organised to raise money during the summer including a gala and a carnival but they were not particularly successful. The summer wage bill was kept to a minimum as a large number of players were given free transfers and they were replaced by an equally large number of youngsters, mostly recruited from junior clubs in the north-east. Debts mounted towards the end of 1922 and further remedies were needed. There was an attempt to raise £1,000 through £10 subscriptions and an appeal to both supporters and local industry to buy shares. The situation reached crisis point in early February. The new year had seen just one home match whilst there had been long and expensive trips to Hartlepools, Barrow, Darlington, Nelson and Tranmere. Rumours circulated suggesting the club were on the point of closing down and on Thursday 8 February chairman Cornelius Taylor made a statement to the press confirming that the directors had insufficient funds to pay the players' wages. He also outlined the full extent of the club's debts which amounted to more than £3,000. The following day an agreement was reached with the players who accepted a reduction in wages, whilst those who were unhappy with this arrangement having the option of taking a free transfer and £10 in lieu of two weeks money.

Despite the turmoil off the field the following Saturday's home game with Tranmere Rovers went ahead with City winning 2-0. The drama continued to unfold in the following week as first-teamers James McGrahan and 'Yaffa' Ward were sold to Wigan Borough, and Bob Fenwick moved to Notts County, raising immediate cash for the club (most transfer deals at this time were settled by immediate payment in full), but leaving just 15 professionals on the books. The Imps met with a resounding 7-1 defeat at Durham City in their next fixture causing some supporters to stay away from the return match on 24 February as a protest. There was an even heavier defeat on 3 March when they lost 9-1 away to Wigan Borough, but the fans returned the next Saturday for the visit of the Lancashire side who included McGrahan and Ward in their line-up, and after this attendances returned to their pre-crisis level of around 5,000.

Just as major surgery was needed to reduce outgoings, so reform was needed to ensure that there was no recurrence of the symptoms. The Football League offered their assistance and on 15 March two senior members of the Management Committee, John Lewis and Charles Sutcliffe, visited the city where they addressed the Chamber of Commerce in the afternoon and a public meeting the same evening. Over 1,000 fans packed the Drill Hall to hear the message that financial stability could only be achieved if the gate money from each match was sufficient to pay three weeks wages. The revivalist atmosphere continued and a week later a supporters club was formed with the principal objective of raising money for the parent club. At the same time James Irving, son of 1890s star John, announced a scheme to raise £1,000 by 1s (5p) subscription to pay the summer wage bill. These measures proved most effective and when the accounts were produced they showed a loss of only £154, thus ensuring that League football would continue at Sincil Bank. Lincoln were not the only Northern Section club to suffer financial troubles at this time - Stalybridge Celtic, who finished 11th in the table, chose to return to the Cheshire League because of poor gate receipts, whilst Halifax also reduced wages and both Tranmere and Durham had serious problems.

There were several fund raising events that summer including open-air boxing and a revival of the bicycle sports, and together these produced sufficient income to allow most of the players to be retained for the 1923/24 campaign. The board of directors was reorganised in August with the introduction of six new members, including James Irving and his brother John, and for the first time since the war a new season was approached with a sense of optimism. The side was strengthened with new signings after the first few matches, but still struggled, and by Christmas they had fallen to 19th position where they remained until the end of the season, but with little danger of having to seek re-election. Attendances were often below 5,000 and for the third year in a row the financial deficit was rectified by selling players, with Jack Kendall departing for Everton and Archie Kean moving to Blackburn.

Calderhead resigned in May 1924 to take over the Newmarket Hotel in Sincil Street and he was replaced by Horace Henshall. The new secretary-manager was just 34 years old and had appeared in top class football with Aston Villa, Notts County and Sheffield Wednesday, although he had been playing for Chesterfield in the 1923/24 season. Signings over the summer included George Page, a full-back from Accrington, Josiah Barratt, outside-right from Birmingham, and Jimmy Heathcote, a centre-forward from Pontypridd. The team occupied a mid-table position at Christmas but improved performances in the second half of the season enabled them to finish in 8th position, their highest since joining the Northern Section. In the F.A Cup they defeated Rossington Main before falling 1-0 to Midland League side Alfreton in what was one of the worst humiliations in the club's history. Gates were up slightly and a profit of more than £800 was made.

Changes in the offside law in 1925/26 produced plenty more goals - City scored 21 in their first eight home games - but the team were unable to rise above the middle of the table and finished 15th. The established policy of selling off the best players was resorted to again with Walter Webster moving to Sheffield United and leading scorer Harry Havelock joining Portsmouth. The transactions ensured a healthy profit and brought the balance sheet back in credit for the first time since 1921.

Lincolnshire Chronicle 31 October 1925
Grimsby were beaten 4-1 at Sincil Bank one week earlier

REVIVAL - AND A NORTHERN SECTION TITLE

The club's fortunes took a turn for the better from the summer of 1926, and for the first time since the Great War, finances permitted the side to be strengthened with quality signings before the start of the season. The recruits included Billy Dinsdale, a bustling if inexperienced centre-forward from Aston Villa, 6'-5" goalkeeper Albert Iremonger, veteran of more than 500 League games with Notts County, and wingers Charlie Bosbury (Preston) and Frank Pegg (Sunderland). However the team's performances proved a disappointment and they won only three times in the first 22 League games. In the F.A. Cup, victories over Rotherham and Coventry earned them a home tie with Preston North End in the third round. The board raised admission prices but with the local economy in a poor state and bad weather on the day of the match, the attendance was only 6,656 - little more than for an ordinary League fixture. City lost 4-2, both goals coming from Dinsdale, who justified the decision to include him in the side for the second half of the season by establishing a new club record of 26 League and Cup goals. Form improved and 12 of the final 20 matches were won as they rose to finish in 11th position.

There was a most unusual incident at Wrexham on 9 April which caused the match to be abandoned after an hour's play with the home team leading 2-0. Heavy rain and hail had fallen throughout the game and early in the second half the Imps' left-half Alf Hale collapsed and was carried from the field unconscious. Shortly afterwards Bassnett, Robson and Tom Maidment all staggered off 'numbed with cold', and with City reduced to just seven men the referee called the proceedings to a halt. Rumours persisted that the 'injuries' occurred after the players had drunk from a bottle of refreshments provided by the trainer, the suggestion being that the bottle contained something considerably stronger than hot tea! The club publicly denied the players had been drinking.

Wrexham Leader 15 April 1927

Horace Henshall moved on to Notts County at the end of the season and the directors appointed Harry Parkes to replace him as secretary-manager. Parkes had played in the Southern League for Coventry before the war, later serving Newport County and Chesterfield as secretary-manager. A record loss of £2,583 was made on the previous year's business and the money for summer wages had to be raised by selling players. The deficit was later partly rectified when a Grand Bazaar was held in December, bringing in over £1,000. Meanwhile Parkes returned to Saltergate to sign up Albert Worthy, a solid and reliable full back, and the 1927/28 season began well with the team in third position at the end of October. Despite suffering heavy defeats at home to Hartlepools (5-1) and away to Darlington (9-2), they remained in the top six all season, and an unbeaten run spanning the final 13 matches enabled them to finish in the runners-up spot. Although they were well adrift of champions Bradford Park Avenue this was still the club's best performance to date in the Northern Section, and Dinsdale was again leading scorer with 27 goals in League and Cup games.

There was a belief that promotion back to Division Two was now a possibility. The players returned for the 1928/29 season a week earlier than usual and the supporters responded by buying a record number of season tickets. However the only real success achieved was in the F.A. Cup where the first two rounds were negotiated for the third year in a row to earn a home tie against First Division Leicester City. The Imps survived an early penalty scare with Len Hill making a brilliant save from the spot kick, but then went down 1-0 to a goal four minutes from time. The attendance was a record 16,849 who paid receipts of £1,391. Sadly there was a tragic aftermath when Bosbury, who had risen from his sick bed to play in the tie, fell seriously ill with tuberculosis and passed away on 15 July. Any financial problems were eased with the sale of the popular Dinsdale to Bradford Park Avenue in March for £1,500, but he was hardly missed as his replacement Harry Kitching scored in nine consecutive games as the team finished strongly in sixth place.

1929/30 began with a run of poor results and even when a win was finally obtained, at home to League leaders Port Vale on 16 September, the result was overshadowed by events off the field.

Following his release by Blackpool, Alf Freeman received a £5 signing-on fee when he joined City in July 1927, with Summer wages of £5-87 per fortnight

City's 1927-28 season squad take a break from training on the Sincil Bank pitch.

Later that evening a fire completely gutted the South Park stand. It was so fierce that only the brick foundations and sections of the corrugated iron roof remained the next morning. Some good came out of the tragedy however for it spurred the board on to make major changes to the ground for the first time since the turn of the century. The insurance company paid out compensation almost immediately, and within six weeks a new stand had been built capable of holding around twice as many fans as the original construction. Shortly afterwards a mortgage was arranged and the freehold of the Sincil Bank ground was purchased for £4,875 thus removing the main obstacle to a full redevelopment.

The fire and its aftermath dominated the early part of the season but the team put together a good run in the spring, winning nine of their last 11 fixtures. The 8-0 defeat of Tranmere Rovers on Easter Monday provided hat-tricks for both Tom Maidment and Harry Roberts and was the club's highest ever League victory. In March, goalkeeper Jack Kendall, who had rejoined City from Preston in the summer of 1928, was sold again, this time to Sheffield United.

Summer moves in the transfer market saw Evan Jenkins move to Burnley for £1,500 and Roberts sold to Port Vale for just £150. Within 12 months he had been transferred to Millwall and shortly afterwards appeared for the full England team. After losing narrowly in the season's opening match at New Brighton the team swept to the top of the Northern Section for the first time ever with a glorious run of ten consecutive victories. Included in this was a magnificent 6-1 thrashing of Stockport and a fine 3-1 win at Hull.

(Above) Prolific goalscorer Billy Dinsdale - a hero of the late 1920's. Club record F.A.Cup goalscorer with 14, plus 89 League goals.

(Below) Lincoln of Lincoln! Scored twice on his League debut in the 1931/32 season, but Andy had only two more first team games.

The run only ended on 25 October when second placed Chesterfield snatched a 1-1 draw at Sincil Bank in front of a crowd of 10,840. The team began to show occasional lapses of form and there was a surprise 6-4 defeat at Scarborough in the F.A. Cup, after City had led 4-2 at half time. However they continued to lead the table and never seemed to be beaten - even when 3-0 down to fellow promotion contenders Tranmere at the end of March - they fought back to recover a point. By mid-April it was clear the title lay between Lincoln, Chesterfield and Tranmere. On 22 April the Imps travelled to Saltergate for what was effectively the decider. In front of a record attendance of 20,092, the home side went 2-0 up before Dinsdale and Lax levelled the scores. Pynegar restored Chesterfield's lead but then City were awarded a late penalty only to have their hopes dashed when Kitching's spot kick was saved by the 'keeper, leaving the final score at 3-2 to the home side. Victory in the final two matches would still have ensured the championship but they lost 5-3 at Accrington on the following Saturday, whilst Chesterfield beat Gateshead 8-1 to take the title and promotion.

After failing by the narrowest of margins, the board decided to sell their teenage stars Ted Savage and Walter Lax, and Savage was soon bought by Liverpool for £2,500 with Blackpool paying £1,500 for Lax. Although some of this money was used to pay off old debts and pay summer wages, around £1,000 was available to strengthen the side and this was used to purchase Jim Smith (Doncaster), Harold Riley and George Whyte (Accrington), plus Frank Keetley (Bradford City). Experienced half-back Charlie Pringle arrived on a free transfer whilst other deals saw goalkeeper Jim Maidment exchanged for Portsmouth's Dan McPhail, and winger Frank Pegg swopped for Bradford City's reserve striker Allan Hall.

Despite all the personnel changes the new season began in fine style with home victories over Darlington and Hartlepools. Although defeated in the first away game at Halifax the team won the next five games to go top of the table - the most remarkable performance coming at Gateshead when they fought back to win after being reduced to 10 men through injury and trailing 2-0 at half-time. However, they were removed from their position at the top of the table by matters outside their own hands. Wigan Borough, whom City had beaten twice, resigned from the League at the end of October - crippled by debts of £20,000 - and their record, which included the four points gained by the Imps, was deleted from the table. City soon recovered from this setback, beating promotion rivals Southport 7-0 in November, and even a shock defeat at the hands of Crewe failed to dislodge them from a position in the top two.

Wins in the new year away to Darlington and home to Rochdale, when Walter Buckley suffered a broken leg, preceded a 9-1 victory over Halifax Town on 16 January, as the leadership was regained in some style. The visitors concentrated their attentions on leading scorer Hall to such an extent that Frank Keetley was able to net six times in the second half, including five in a 21 minute period. Concerns over the fitness of Hall and Keetley led to the signing of George Beel from Burnley in February. Beel had begun his career as a youngster at Sincil Bank before winning a reputation as a prolific scorer with the Turf Moor club. Defeat at Doncaster on 2 April allowed Gateshead to go top, but their stay proved only brief as victory at Carlisle three weeks later gave City the lead again. The players were sent off to Skegness for special training before the final home match with Wrexham, and the 0-0 draw they earned clinched the title for the first time. A record League crowd of 14,981 packed Sincil Bank for the historic occasion, and the game was filmed and shown at the local Exchange Kinema during the following week. City lost at Hartlepools in their final fixture and so won the championship on goal average, although they had a clear margin over second placed Gateshead. The success owed a lot to Hall's goalscoring feats, and his totals of 42 in League games and 52 in all competitive games were both club records. The Northern Section shield was presented by Billy Bassett of the Football League Management Committee at a victory ball held in the Assembly Rooms on 11 May.

AN EXPENSIVE EXERCISE

The club were optimistic about prospects on returning to Division Two after a twelve year absence. The finances were in a very healthy state and the board had invested heavily in ground improvements and new players over the Summer break. The main St Andrews stand was demolished and replaced by a new structure with increased capacity, whilst concrete terracing was laid down in front of both main stands. Around £1,500 was also spent on new signings the most expensive being Jackie Wilkinson, a clever winger from Newcastle who cost £600. Other recruits included Jack Buckley from Doncaster, Alf Horne (Preston) and 'Chick' Read (Sheffield United). The season's opening game produced a 1-1 draw at Notts County, and this was followed by a 2-0 home win over Swansea. There was a near tragedy when City travelled to South Wales for the return match on 5 September when a taxi carrying five of the players to the ground was involved in a collision with a bus. The cab driver suffered two broken legs and Walter Buckley, who was in the front seat, was showered with glass and required hospital treatment. Although badly shaken the other men were fit to play, but the match was lost 3-1.

Form improved and there were successive home victories over Grimsby (6-3) and West Ham (6-0), before they slipped back down the table. City received a free passage into the third round of the F.A. Cup, and prepared for their tie with Blackburn Rovers by spending a week by the sea at Skegness. Stand prices were increased and over 13,000 attended the match only to see the Imps beaten by five goals to one, the visitors scoring three goals in as many minutes to effectively settle the match. The team was strengthened shortly before the transfer deadline with the signings of half-backs Bill Dodgin (Huddersfield) and George Mathison (Newcastle), and safety was only ensured on 29 April in the season's penultimate fixture when Manchester United were defeated 2-0 at Sincil Bank. This limited achievement had been gained at a high price for the directors had spent over £3,000 in the transfer market - financed by a substantial overdraft from the bank and a loan of around £1,000 from director Arthur Taylor. The departure of at least one player in the summer was inevitable, and with no firm offers for Con Moulson it was agreed to sell prolific scorer Allan Hall to Tottenham Hotspur for a fee of £2,350.

1933/34 was the club's jubilee year but there was little to celebrate. Hall was badly missed and the first 14 games produced just eight goals. After trying various replacements the board paid out a record fee of £1,250 for a 23 year-old Scottish centre-forward, John Campbell from Leicester City. The team dropped to the foot of the table following the home defeat by Brentford on 16 December and although victories in the new year over Manchester United (5-1) and Fulham (5-0) provided some hope they remained bottom for the rest of the season. The inevitable relegation was confirmed after a 3-0 defeat at Oldham in early April. Symbolically the team had passed two funeral parties on their way to the match!

It had been another expensive year and the loss brought the total deficit from two years of higher grade football to almost £4,500. The financial situation was now a matter of serious concern, and in June the bank loan was increased to £6,000. Economy measures were needed and at the end of the season a number of fringe first team players were released on free transfers. Other cost-cutting moves saw several senior men listed for transfer - although only George Mathison was sold, and then for a bargain fee of £100 to Gateshead - and secretary-manager Parkes agreed to accept reduced wages of £8 a week.

City returned to the Northern Section in style, winning the first four games but a series of defeats followed, and although a comfortable mid-table position was maintained, they did not feature in the championship race. Attendances slumped dramatically, falling below 3,000 towards the end of the season, forcing the directors to sell off the talented Wilkinson (to Sunderland) and youngster Bob Iverson to Wolves. Over £2,500 was raised but this did little more than stabilise the position and for the third year in a row a loss was recorded. The team's performances seemed unaffected by the off the field problems and a fine run at the end of season saw them gain 20 points from 12 games, and rise into fourth place.

There was no money available for new signings and the summer recruits were either free transfers or men from junior clubs. The 1935/36 campaign began with a 6-0 victory over Accrington Stanley, and in September Alf Horne performed the unusual feat of scoring a hat-trick of penalties in the 3-0 home win over Stockport. Shortly afterwards the team went to the top of the table but they held the position only briefly and they were soon back in third place, trailing behind new leaders Tranmere. In January the club accepted a guarantee of 1,800 Dutch Guilders (£200) to play a game in Rotterdam, their first visit to the Continent. A party of 12 left Lincoln in the early evening of 7 January travelling by train and boat to reach Rotterdam shortly before 9.30 the next morning. The game against a Dutch National 'B' XI took place the same afternoon, and although City were 1-0 up at half-time they went down 4-2 in front of around 6,000 spectators. They departed the same evening and were back in Lincoln by Thursday lunchtime.

Meanwhile the financial position had reached a crisis point. Although a second mortgage for £2,000 had been taken out in November, the deficit continued to rise and the directors approached the Lincolnshire Echo for help. The local paper responded strongly and on 31 January ran a story telling how poor attendances threatened the club's existence beneath a banner headline *"Lincoln City Football Club Sensation, Club Will Die Unless More Support Comes."* There was little response however and gates rarely went over 4,000, with the exception of the visit of league leaders Chesterfield on Good Friday which attracted 14,668 - the best since the championship season. The team finished fourth again and in the summer centre-half Con Moulson became the first City player to be 'capped' since the early 1900s when he appeared for the Irish Free State against Hungary and Luxembourg. The low gates were the principal reason for another substantial loss (£2,442), and the immediate problem of paying summer wages was resolved by the sale of the Watson brothers to Chesterfield.

Early in May, secretary-manager Parkes was offered a three year contract by Mansfield and was allowed to resign to take up the post. Charlie Spencer, a former England international was chosen to replace him, but Wigan Athletic refused to release him from his contract and so the board returned to their original shortlist and appointed Joe McClelland who accepted the position at £6 a week - £2 less than his predecessor. The close season also saw the opening of the Lincoln Imp Social Club underneath the South Park stand - the first time in many years that alcohol had been sold on the ground. Despite inheriting only a skeleton playing staff McClelland quickly assembled a team capable of challenging for the title. The first three games of the 1936/37 season were won, and the team were soon heavily engaged in a race for the championship. Centre-forward Campbell was on top form and his five hat-tricks included all the goals in the 5-3 defeat of Rochdale in November.

City were boosted by a run of eight consecutive victories in the new year and by Easter it was clear the title would be decided between the Imps and Stockport County. Lincoln went top when they beat Barrow on 3 April and stayed there until the penultimate Saturday of the season, when they lost 3-1 at Hartlepools. They travelled to Edgeley Park for the final fixture on 1 May, knowing that a win was needed for the championship, any other result would give the title to Stockport. In front of a record crowd of 26,135, the defence held firm for an hour, but then conceded two controversial goals in quick succession. The first came when goalkeeper McPhail was bundled over the line, the second was a penalty and together they were enough to give the home side a 2-0 victory. Runners-up position was still a fine achievement for the new secretary-manager, who was rewarded with a £25 bonus and a three year contract. There was a sequel to the end of season events in November 1938 when a Football League Commission of Enquiry found one of the Stockport directors guilty of attempting to fix the results of City's two matches with Carlisle, and several Carlisle players received short suspensions. Ironically one of these was Tony Leach, who was by now the Imps' captain. Despite the disappointment of missing out on promotion there was better news on the financial front with gates close to break even point and a profit for the first time since 1932.

The usual batch of youngsters and free transfer signings arrived in the summer along with outside-left Joe Clare, a £150 buy from Norwich City. The team had another good start to the season, recording several resounding victories, including a 7-1 thrashing of Wrexham. There was a record attendance of 20,792 at Gateshead's Redheugh Park at the end of September to witness the clash of the Northern Section's top two teams which ended in a 1-1 draw. In January 1938, a group of players visited Rotterdam again to face a strong Dutch national side which included three of the men who were to represent their country in the World Cup finals later that year. The Imps were beaten 5-0 in front of a crowd of 10,000, the line-ups being :

HOLLAND : Dykstra (ZFC), Wilders (Bl.Wit), v.d. Linden (NAC), Paanwe (Feyenoord), Planter (Be-Quick), Van Heel (Feyenoord), Vondenhof (Juliana), v, Spaandonck (Neptunus), De Boer (KFC), Smit (Haarlem), Mynders (DFC).
CITY : McPhail, Hartshorne, Nevin, Forman, Meacock, Whyte, J.Callender, White, Campbell, Deacon, Clare.

The promotion race for 1937/38 was even tighter than the previous year with several teams having a good chance of the title as the second half of the season began. City still had hopes of the championship at the end of March, when just two points separated seven teams, but four defeats in the last five games saw them drop down the table to finish in 7th place. Rumours that the players were more interested in their performances at Friday night dances than in playing on Saturday afternoons led the club to threaten legal action against the accusers. However, there was substance to the allegations, and players were disciplined internally on at least two occasions after being caught out. Finances continued to remain stable although a small loss was reported on the year's business.

Letter confirming the record transfer of Bob Meacock

After narrowly failing to win the championship two years in a row it was decided to sell centre-half Bob Meacock to Birmingham for a club record fee of £3,000 and the number of players on the books was increased in the summer of 1938. Despite this the team had its worst start on record achieving just two draws from the first eight games, and following a 6-0 defeat at Crewe the club chairman Ted Simpson met McClelland and the players to discuss the poor performances. After this there was a slight improvement with a 3-3 draw at Stockport on 1 October, followed by a 3-0 victory over Accrington Stanley the next Saturday. However the team were in the bottom half of the Northern Section table for the first time in a decade and although a substantial sum was invested on Chesterfield centre-forward Walter Ponting, they struggled for the rest of the season. The final position of 17th was the lowest since 1923/24. There was at least the consolation of a run in the F.A. Cup. Barrow were knocked out in the first round, and the F.A. Amateur Cup holders Bromley were disposed of with ease in a game in which City led 7-0 at half-time before relaxing a little in the second period to finish 8-1 winners. The Imps then went down 4-0 at Portsmouth in the third round.

Towards the end of the season there was serious discussion about establishing either a nursery or a colts side for the first time. There had previously been informal links with Lincoln Corinthians for some time, but these arrangements had broken down after the Corinthians players failed to respond to a request to sign amateur forms for the club. In March it was agreed that the secretary-manager investigate the cost of running a colts team and hiring the Co-op Sports Field on Skellingthorpe Road.

In the close season several senior players were released. The list included George Whyte and Dan McPhail who had played over 600 League games for the Imps, and John Campbell whose total of 105 League goals was a club record. Recruits included 18 year-old Ron Gray, a centre-half from Sheffield United who would return to Sincil Bank some 30 years later as manager. A request to play a friendly match in Holland against the top club side Ajax was declined, a wise move as it happened for war broke out with the 1939/40 season just three matches old. The Football League reacted immediately by suspending the competition, and the football world did not return to normal for another seven years.

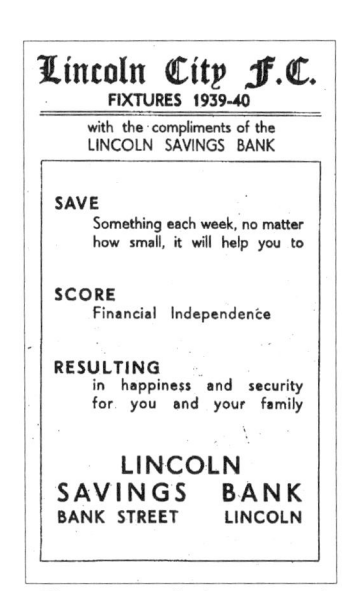

The season that never was!

WORLD WAR TWO

Immediately war broke out the Air Raids Precautions services (A.R P.) requisitioned the South Park stand and dressing room area for use as a First Aid Post and Dressing Station. The players were allowed to go home if they wished and most took advantage of this offer. The change to an emergency structure took time to organise and there was a gap of seven weeks before the regionalised competitions arranged by the League were commenced. All players' professional contracts had now been scrapped and they appeared for a standard match fee, initially £1-10s (£1.50) with no bonuses for a win or draw. Groundsman Charlie Beaumont was called up for military service, leaving assistant trainer Alf Young, who worked for Ruston's, with the task of carrying out all the maintenance work in his spare time. The team which represented City against Chesterfield in the opening fixture in the East Midlands Section of the War League was very much an experimental line-up and they were heavily defeated 8-0.

City's first game in war-time football - an 8-0 thrashing! Only five men were able to be fielded from the original first team squad that started the 1939-40 season - and they paid the penalty.

But fortunes improved and they finished in a mid-table position. There was a different structure for the following season with the clubs divided into just two groups, North and South, although matches were only played against teams within a short travelling distance.

There were two league competitions - a first championship which lasted until Christmas, and a second one which covered the period to the end of the season for which games played in the War Cup also counted.

In 1941/42 City's team of guests, former players and a few of the remaining pre-war men did remarkably well winning eight of the first nine games, and despite a 9-0 defeat at Sheffield United finished second to Blackpool in the Football League Northern Section's First Championship. The two teams were level on points but the Imps had an inferior goal average. The leading positions were :

	P	W	D	L	F - A	PTS
Blackpool	18	14	1	3	75 - 19	29
LINCOLN CITY	18	13	3	2	54 - 28	29
Preston North End	18	13	1	4	58 - 18	27
Manchester United	18	10	6	2	79 - 27	26

The A.R.P. took over most of the St Andrews stand from 1942, initially using it to store Morrison shelters. In August 1942 an increase in Entertainment Tax forced the club to raise the minimum adult admission price from 1s (5p) to 1s 6d (7½p). Full use was made of the ready supply of 'guest' players available from local R.A.F. bases during this period, and apart from 1944/45 (when they finished 51st of 54 clubs) the team generally fared well. 1945/46 was run as a transitional season with City competing in the Eastern Section of Division Three North. The F.A.Cup was also revived with ties played over two legs. 'Guest' players, although allowed for League fixtures could not take part in the Cup games, and as a result a 17 year-old centre-half named Tony Emery appeared against Yorkshire Amateurs, the beginning of a long and distinguished career at Sincil Bank.

Wartime football brought the usual quota of unusual events and high scoring feats. On Christmas Day 1940 there were two fixtures with Doncaster Rovers, the morning match at Belle Vue was drawn, and City won the return fixture at Sincil Bank by a 3-1 margin the same afternoon. In 1941/42 Mansfield were beaten 6-0 and 7-2 at home, plus 5-0 and 8-1 away in a remarkable sequence of results. Notts County were defeated 8-1 on two occasions in the following season and there was a 10-2 defeat at Sheffield United in January 1945. There were two instances of players scoring seven goals in a match - Cyril Lello achieving the feat against Notts County in December 1943, and Billy Hullett (a 'guest' from Manchester United) in the

8-1 win at Mansfield in April 1942. Another 'guest', Bert Knott, scored a total of 12 times in the three Christmas games of 1941.

The situation regarding players was very different to that in the Great War, and only three - Billy Bean, Jack Hardy and Joe Clare - turned out regularly throughout the period of emergency competition. Pre-war men who returned included Bernard Towler, Geoff Marlow, John Campbell and Allan Hall, and in 1944/45 a Polish airman named Pawlaw appeared in a few games. Amongst the many 'guests' were several who became well known players in the 1940s and '50s - Neil Franklin, Peter Doherty, George Robledo and Tommy Powell. Fortunately the loss of life incurred during the Second World War was not on the scale of that suffered in 1914-18 and there is no record of any fatalities from City's pre-war playing staff in the hostilities.

The club had entered the war with substantial loans, and came under severe pressure from the bank to repay these. Commonsense prevailed in July 1941 and it was agreed that payments of interest only would be acceptable. The board found several features of the emergency competition to their liking, particularly the playing of cup-ties on a home and away basis, the existence of a cup pool and the part-time status of the players, and these measures helped the club to record a profit in four of the seven seasons, although a small loss was made in 1945/46.

AFTER THE WAR

Although the Football League returned to a peacetime format in 1946 the game took some time to return to normal. Post-war restrictions meant that sufficient clothing coupons had to be obtained before new playing kit could be purchased whilst a delay by the League in setting a minimum admission price meant there were no season tickets available for 1946/47. Agreement on de-requisitioning the ground was reached at the end of August, ending seven years of occupation by the A.R.P. Very few of the 1939 squad had returned after the long break and only four - Billy Bean, Jack Hardy, Geoff Marlow and Alec Thompson - were re-signed. In common with other Northern Section clubs the players were part-time, receiving £5 a week when in the first team.

Training took place after work, three evenings a week during the summer, reducing to two nights during the playing season. The fixture list was exactly the same as that originally set for 1939/40 and the campaign began with a visit to Hull City's newly opened Boothferry Park stadium, with the Imps gaining a point from a goalless draw in front of a 25,000 crowd.

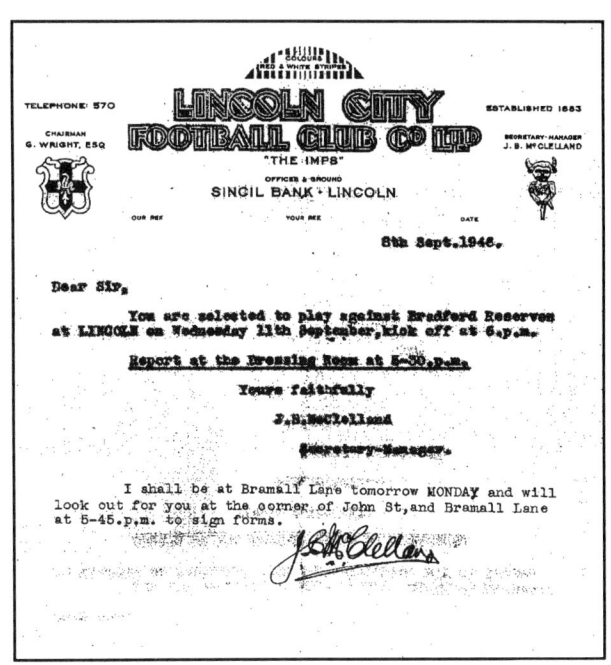

A letter from Joe McClelland making arrangements for the signing of George Nelson in September 1946.

The team was strengthened with the signing of centre-forward Jimmy Hutchinson from Bournemouth for a £750 fee, but after holding a mid-table position in December a string of poor results left them in the lower reaches throughout the second half of the season. A lengthy spell of bad weather and restrictions on midweek fixtures led to City playing their final match at Bradford City on 14 June. There was some success in the F.A. Cup and after defeating Stockton and Wrexham they were drawn at home to near neighbours Nottingham Forest in the third round. Gates were opened at 1pm for the all-ticket clash, and new records were set with an attendance of 17,092 and receipts of £2,054, but City went down 1-0.

Bill Anderson was promoted from trainer to team manager over the summer, a recognition that the task of running the club's administrative affairs was too much for one man. McClelland retained his title of secretary-manager with Anderson's role being to negotiate the signing of players and to select the team, although the final decision on who appeared in the line-up was still made by the directors. There were a number of new signings including goalkeeper George Moulson from Grimsby Town and forwards Ken Walshaw (Sunderland) and Jimmy McCormick (Fulham), but whilst other clubs in the division recruited a nucleus of full-time staff City remained part-time. This measure ensured that the wage bill was kept to a minimum, but in fact full-time status was not possible for all the players as several were in employment covered by the Essential Work Order, and permission was unlikely to be granted by the Ministry of Labour for their release.

'Keeper John Daniels is beaten at the near post, as City go down 3-1 at Oldham during the 1946-47 season.

The team started the 1947/48 season well and despite losing to non-League Workington in the F.A. Cup, they had risen to head the table by December. Two defeats by Accrington Stanley over the Christmas period allowed the Lancashire side to replace them at the top, but only temporarily, for the Imps quickly regained the leadership. They remained there until losing at Gateshead on Easter Monday and travelled to new leaders Rotherham for the season's crucial fixture with the table standing as follows:

	P	W	D	L	F - A	PTS
Rotherham United	40	24	9	7	94 - 47	57
LINCOLN CITY	40	24	8	8	74 - 40	56

A large contingent of Lincoln supporters in the all-ticket crowd of more than 20,000 who witnessed a 2-0 win for City. There was controversy over the Imps opening goal from Windle when the referee chose to over-rule a linesman's raised flag, but a second from McCormick and some fine defensive work in the second half ensured victory. Ironically both goalscorers were Rotherham men, and they were regularly reminded of this feat on future visits to their home town! On their return to Lincoln the players were met by a cheering crowd who had blocked the High Street between St Benedict's Square and the Stonebow awaiting their arrival. The scenes of jubilation were said to be reminiscent of V.E. Day, but promotion was far from assured with City requiring a win from the final match at home to Hartlepools to be certain of the title.

After conquering early nerves the team responded with a solid performance and a 5-0 victory, with leading scorer Jimmy Hutchinson hitting a hat-trick to clinch both the championship and promotion. Although assembled by McClelland, the team owed much to Anderson's ability to create a good team spirit - essential given that most of the players lived away from Lincoln and usually only met up on the Friday night or Saturday morning before a match.

Supporters with Imp symbols, in the run-in to the Championship season.

Just as important was the role played by Tom Johnson, a former colleague of Anderson's at Bramall Lane. Johnson dominated proceedings both on and off the field with little happening without his approval, although past his prime he was still a powerful no-nonsense centre half as well as a well-respected captain.

Promotion brought its rewards for all the staff. The players received 'talent money' at 12s (60p) a match with the standard first team wage up to £8 a week, and the manager was rewarded with a £100 bonus plus a five year contract at £700 a year. In May, goalkeeper George Moulson was 'capped' for the Republic of Ireland against Spain and Portugal, only the third City player to receive international honours.

During the summer break the ground capacity was increased to 25,000 with the small stand on the Sincil Bank side being demolished and the whole area terraced. The management kept faith with the existing playing staff, and a handful of men, including Hutchinson, Grummett and Bean turned full-time, but the majority remained on a part-time basis. The 1948/49 season began brightly enough with consecutive draws against West Ham, Tottenham and Bury, but it soon became evident that the team needed strengthening. In October the board paid out a record fee of £6,000 for Jock Dodds, an experienced forward from Everton, and in December former England international wing-half Doug Wright was signed from Newcastle for £600. Both were exceptional footballers and many observers still consider them to be the best two players to have appeared for the club in the post-war period.

Meanwhile the club were also hit by off the field problems, and a dispute over elections at the shareholders' annual general meeting led to the resignations of chairman George Wright and his vice-chairman Ted Simpson. Charles Applewhite was elected to replace Wright and two new members came on the board, Godfrey Holmes and Harold Allman. A group of shareholders who were unhappy with the board's policy organised themselves under the leadership of Albert Bennett, son of the club treasurer from the 1890s, and adopted the title 'The Progressives'. The team's position at the bottom of the table required urgent measures, and more than £25,000 was spent on further signings including George Eastham, Arthur Jepson, Jack Bickerstaffe, Roy Finch, Horace Green and Dick Young. Agreement was also reached with local employers to allow the players time off to train together in the mornings, but it was too late and the team never rose off the bottom of the table.

Relegation was the result of several factors: too many part-time players, failure to recognise the huge gap in standards between the Northern Section and the Second Division, a crippling injury list, and introducing too many new men at the same time. However despite the team's lowly position support was impressive and the ground record was broken on two occasions, the largest attendance being 23,146 for the visit of Grimsby on 5 March. A record loss of £7,795 was recorded, and with the prospect of Northern Section football again 17 of the 34 players were placed on the open to transfer list. At the end of May a party of 16 flew to Iceland for a short tour. Despite almost constant daylight which allowed the games to kick off at 8.30pm, freezing cold temperatures and hard pitches, City won their first three games before losing 4-1 to a strong Combined Reykjavik XI.

Chairman Charles Applewhite promised that the club would be back in Division Two as soon as was possible and Bill Anderson set out to build a team to achieve this. Winger Harry Troops arrived from Barnsley in August, and two months later Jackie Robinson was signed from Sunderland for a £3,000 fee. Robinson, like Wright and Eastham, was a pre-war England international and a skilful player. He scored on his debut at home to Darlington, but then suffered a broken leg against Wrexham on Christmas Eve, and which ended his playing career. Other new signings included inside forward Ernie Whittle from West Stanley who soon established himself as a first team regular. Considering that it was a season for rebuilding, the team's final position of fourth in the table was a worthy achievement.

Off the field the Annual General Meeting of September 1949 proved to be one of the stormiest on record. The Progressives nominated two candidates (Albert Bennett and John Holmes) who were successful in defeating board members John Irving and Edmund Fasham in a show of hands poll, only to lose to proxy votes in the ballot which followed. Uproar ensued with shouts of *"Twist!"* and *"You rigged it!"* coming from the 126 shareholders in attendance, and there was considerable animosity between the two groups with the majority present supporting The Progressives. Feelings were running high and the board agreed to investigate the possibilities of suing Bennett for slander regarding his comments about the vote. The unpleasantness continued, and on 20 September, Godfrey Holmes and Allman resigned their seats on the board, citing internal discord and the immoral use of proxy votes at the meeting as their reasons. Shortly afterwards the issue of shares was suspended by the directors.

There was a small loss of £118 on the season, but of much greater concern was the fact that the amount of loans raised by the board now exceeded £14,000. A further blow was suffered in the close season after Jock Dodds became involved in a scheme to recruit English players for the Colombian side Millionarios of Bogota and was banned from playing in the Football League. The loss of Dodds made it necessary to reshape the forward line, and in August, Preston's Johnny Garvie was signed for a fee of £750 followed by 23 year-old Andy Graver from Newcastle for £5,000. Graver, a distant relative of Harry Pringle who had served the club loyally in the 1920s, had appeared mostly in the Magpies' Central League side, understudying the likes of Roy Bentley and Jackie Milburn. He went straight in the Imps' first team and scored on his debut in a 3-1 win against Halifax Town, Echo reporter Norman Blakey noted that he *"fulfilled expectations with a steady, workmanlike display!"* (Lincs. Echo, 25 Sep 1950). The team put together a string of victories in the second half of the season, defeating Stockport 6-0 and Accrington Stanley 9-1, thus equalling the club's record League score. Although second in the table at one stage they dropped back to finish in fifth place. Graver and Garvie had already struck up a useful understanding and their partnership yielded 40 goals in its first season. The club requested a move to the Southern Section of the Third Division for 1951/52 but were turned down by the Football League Management Committee.

The board now had a policy of only signing players who were willing to live in Lincoln and to assist this a number of houses had been purchased to provide accommodation. Both Andy Graver and centre-half Tony Emery were regularly attracting interest from bigger clubs and during the summer of 1950 the board reached agreement with Norwich City to sell Graver for a fee in the region of £13,000, but the latter was unhappy with the move and it fell through. Emery however still desired higher grade football and he refused to re-sign forms for the club, leaving City to begin the season with Frank Sims at centre-half. He signed up shortly afterwards and there were some fine results in the early part of the campaign, including successive home victories over Darlington (7-2) and Crewe Alexandra (11-1). The Crewe result remains the club's record League win, with Andy Graver, who had been persuaded to play despite suffering from 'flu, hitting six goals - two with either foot and two with his head. The unfortunate visitors' goalkeeper, teenager Dennis Murray, was making his debut.

Players and officials board the aircraft at Northolt for Reykjavik and the club's Icelandic tour in May 1949. The last of the four matches was broadcast live on Icelandic radio.

The 1951 A.G.M. in September attracted yet another large turnout with almost 150 shareholders present. The Progressives were again active, ensuring the defeat of two of the three directors on a show of hands, but as usual both were re-elected in the ensuing ballot. Progressive candidate Bennett withdrew rather than submit to a ballot, and his supporters asked the board to co-opt him but this was not acted upon. Meanwhile, by early December, the team were top of the table and had reached the third round of the F.A. Cup, defeating neighbours Grimsby Town in a second round tie which attracted what may well have been the largest ever crowd to Sincil Bank. An official attendance of 21,757 was recorded, but many fans did not pass through the turnstiles and reporters estimated the actual number present at around 23,500. City went out at Portsmouth by a 4-0 margin in the next round, watched by an even larger crowd of 41,093.

The club's commitment to promotion was shown with the signing of Preston's Doug Graham for £3,500 as a replacement for the injured Varney. The 100th League goal came in a 3-1 win at Accrington towards the end of March, but although they had been top for nearly five months promotion was not clinched until the last but one game. Third placed Stockport County visited Sincil Bank on Wednesday 23 April with the Imps needing one point from their final two games to win the Northern Section championship. Two goals from Garvie had given City a 2-1 lead but in the closing minutes Graham was adjudged to have handled in the box and the visitors were awarded a penalty. Staniforth's spot kick was brilliantly saved by 'keeper Jones to win both the match and the title, thus confirming Applewhite's prediction made three years earlier. It was a season of records and to add to those already created were highest totals for points (69) and goals scored (121). A cartilage injury cost Graver a place in the England 'B' side to play Holland and also caused him to miss the final six matches, preventing him from challenging Allan Hall's record of 42 League goals in a season.

The players were rewarded with a share of 'talent money' and the offer of the maximum wage of £14 a week for first team members in the 1952/53 season. There were pay rises for all staff and Bill Anderson received a £100 bonus and a new five year contract payable at £1,000 per annum, a 25% increase on his previous salary. Attendances were up, averaging nearly 14,000, and the board gave consent for a supporters club to be formed for the first time since the war.

SURVIVAL AGAINST THE ODDS

Andy Graver prepares to shoot during the 1952-53 season public pre-season trial (matches arranged for clubs' playing staffs until the early 1960s). Bill McGlen - in white shirt - was later on the backroom staff for many years.

Promotion in 1952 paved the way for an uninterrupted period of nine seasons in Division Two, the club's second longest unbroken spell in higher grade football since entering the League. The fact that they survived for so long is testimony to the quality of players who had won the Northern Section, to Bill Anderson's ability to make the best use of limited resources, and at times to a degree of good fortune.

Although the financial position was relatively healthy only a modest sum was spent on strengthening the squad for the 1952/53 season. The new signings were Roy Killin and Bill McGlen (both from Manchester United) and Mike Ryan (Arsenal). There was tremendous support for the team - over 1,000 fans travelled to Griffin Park for the opening match at Brentford, and the first four home games each attracted gates of more than 20,000. Early results were promising, but the goal supply dried up with Johnny Garvie absent following a cartilage operation and Andy Graver unsettled due to transfer speculation.

City 'keeper Jimmy Jones safely collects a cross at Griffin Park Brentford in the opening match back in Division 2 (a 1-0 defeat).

A spell of 15 games without a win in the autumn saw the team drop to 18th place in the table, but results improved after Brian Birch was signed from Wolves for a fee of £6,000. Graver was the subject of a £25,000 bid by Portsmouth in December but this was rejected by the board. Winger Munro arrived in exchange for McGlen in the spring and the Imps finished the season in 15th position, well clear of any relegation worries.

It was during this season that the Yorkshire and England cricketer Fred Trueman signed amateur forms for the club and his presence in the Midland League side for the visit of Peterborough helped boost the attendance to 7,328 - a record for a reserve game. In May a party of 16 flew to Jersey for a short tour winning both their matches against local sides.

There was little activity in the transfer market over the close season and City began 1953/54 in disappointing fashion with a 5-0 defeat at West Ham. They managed just one goal in the first three games, but then the forwards struck form for the visit of Blackburn Rovers on 29 August, hitting eight without reply with Graver netting four of them. Five home wins in a row saw the team rise to sixth place in early October but inconsistent form meant there was to be no promotion challenge.

The season's highlight came in the F.A. Cup when victory over Walsall at the third attempt earned them a home tie with Preston North End (Division One runners-up in 1952/53). All 25,000 tickets were sold in advance and a near record attendance of 23,027 paid receipts of £3,465. The early morning snow had stopped, but a hard pitch and a strong wind contributed to many mistakes being made. Preston's England international winger Tom Finney was the visitors star man and his right-wing cross led to Baxter opening the scoring. Four minutes later City were awarded a penalty, but just as Ernie Whittle stepped up to take the kick the ball moved slightly and his mis-hit shot failed to score. Preston added a second goal on the hour to finish 2-0 winners. The Imps finished the season in a respectable mid-table position and the accounts showed another large profit of £2,725.

Manager Bill Anderson was busy over the summer break signing up an experienced goalkeeper, Mitchell Downie, and two young half-backs, Fred Middleton and Dick Neal. Amongst those leaving was Ernie Whittle who was sold to Third Division Workington. Early results saw the team occupy a comfortable position in the League table but there was a significant drop in home gates which fell below 14,000 for the first time since the promotion season. Centre-forward Andy Graver remained the subject of constant enquiries from other clubs, and in December he was sold to Leicester City for a fee of £27,000 with City also receiving Eric Littler as part of the deal. Graver was badly missed however, and the team won just two of their next 15 League games, but relegation worries were finally ended with a 3-0 win over Derby County on 23 April. The very healthy financial position enabled the board to pay off their existing debts and to purchase the St Andrews field adjacent to the Sincil Bank ground which was to be used as a training pitch. In appreciation of the successful season a bonus of £1,000 (a sum equivalent to his annual salary) was paid to the manager.

The forward line was restructured during the close season as Graver returned for a cut price fee of £14,000, Littler was offloaded to Wrexham in part-payment for Tommy Bannan, and Tommy Northcott was bought from Cardiff. The 1955/56 campaign began with consecutive victories over Blackburn, Hull and Bury. Defeat at Hull followed, but on 3 September Leicester were thrashed 7-1 at Sincil Bank, City even missing a penalty as they rose to the top of the Division Two table for the first time in 43 years.

The midweek visit of Sheffield Wednesday attracted a crowd of over 20,000, causing traffic chaos in the city, but the team could only manage a 2-2 draw and so their reign as League leaders was over just a few days after it had begun. Success on the field seems to have prompted a revival of the Progressives Group at the club's annual general meeting, but their candidate, Albert Bennett, withdrew from the election of directors rather than submit to a ballot and this was the last heard of the group. Graver was on his way again in November, this time to Stoke for £10,000 and despite suffering a surprise defeat at the hands of Third

Johnny Garvie challenges the Luton Town goalkeeper during the 1-1 draw at Sincil Bank in March 1954. Ernie Whittle looks on.

Division Southend in the F.A. Cup, the Imps remained in the top half of the table for most of the season. A 2-0 victory over Liverpool in their final match earned them eighth place - their highest League position since 1912/13.

Although there was just one summer signing, Barnsley's Ron Smillie, City's run of good form continued at the start of the 1956/57 season. They gained 17 points from the first 15 games, and at the beginning of November lay eighth in the table, however a run of defeats soon pulled them back to the more familiar territory of the lower reaches of the division. An F.A. Cup tie away to Midland League Peterborough United should have assured the team a place in the fourth round, but the match proved anything but easy and City needed a controversial last minute penalty from Harry Troops to earn a 2-2 draw. Despite the afternoon kick-off, a crowd of 18,000 attended the replay which proved to be a near repeat of the first encounter with Dick Neal's late equaliser taking the game into extra time.

Fred Middleton blasts a free-kick at the Notts County defensive wall during a mid-1950s clash at Sincil Bank.

The non-Leaguers proved to have more stamina, scoring three times in quick succession before City came back with two late goals to make the scoreline more respectable, but it was still a humiliating defeat for the club.

The dismal League form continued with only four of the remaining 17 games being won and as the supporters became disillusioned, regular attendances dipped below 10,000 for the first time since 1946/47. The fall in gate receipts led to the sale of wing-half Neal, who had gained three England Under-23 'caps' earlier in the season, with City receiving a fee of around £15,000 and Bert Linnecor from First Division Birmingham. Neal's departure provided further evidence to a section of fans that the board lacked the ambition to mount a challenge for higher grade football.

Over the close season Doug Graham, one of the few remaining players from the side that had been promoted, moved to a coaching post at St Gallen in Switzerland and Anderson signed the experienced Rotherham forward Jack Grainger. The team was further strengthened in early September with the arrival of George Hannah from Newcastle for a bargain fee of £5,000. Hannah was a very skilful player but prone to injury and on his fifth appearance for the club he suffered damaged ligaments in the 'derby' fixture against Grimsby. During his absence the team slipped towards the bottom of the table.

There was a good performance in the F.A. Cup with Wolves only winning narrowly at Sincil Bank,

'Keeper Mitchell Downie is left helpless as Peterborough score another goal. This 5-4 FA Cup defeat was one of the lowest points for the club during the 1950s.

39

but some of the League displays were pitiful and there were several heavy defeats. Throughout this period Anderson constantly juggled his resources, buying and selling players and switching the team around in an attempt to find a winning combination. There was a rare piece of fortune in early March when the home game against Cardiff was abandoned at half-time due to a heavy snowstorm, with the visitors leading 3-0, but by then the Imps were bottom of the table. There was a flurry of transfer activity just before the transfer deadline with the signing of three new men - Harold Brook (Leeds), Will Coxon (Bournemouth) and Ron Harbertson (Darlington). However defeat at home to Barnsley on Easter Monday appeared to ensure they would be relegated and in recognition of this a supporter lowered the club flag to half-mast during the game. It was now four months and 17 matches since the team had last won and although they had games in hand their fate seemed to be sealed. At this point the bottom of the table stood as follows :

City desperately defend against Wolves in the Cup the following season (1957-58) Wolves won 1-0 in front of 21,741 at Sincil Bank, and went on to reach the quarter-finals, together with winning the League championship

	P	PTS
Notts County	37	25
Swansea Town	38	24
Doncaster Rovers	39	24
LINCOLN CITY	36	19

Victory at Oakwell in the return encounter the next day made little difference to the position as both Swansea and Notts County won, but when the following three matches at Doncaster (3-1), and at home to Rotherham (2-0) and Bristol City (4-0) were also won it became clear that there was a slight chance of avoiding the drop. A cheeky back-heeled shot from close range by Harbertson was sufficient to gain a 1-0 win at Huddersfield on the final Saturday of the season, leaving the Imps requiring a draw from the re-arranged game at home to Cardiff to achieve a feat that had seemed impossible three weeks earlier. A large but noisy crowd saw a tense first-half which produced no goals, but the visitors took the lead soon after the break when Nugent lobbed goalkeeper Downie. The ground was stunned into silence save for the cheers of the five coachloads of Notts County fans and a group of their players who were hoping for a Cardiff win. City fought back and equalised when Hannah clipped the ball into the middle for Chapman to score on 69 minutes. Five minutes later, Chapman scored again, and after 79 minutes Harbertson smashed home a brilliant 25-yard shot to clinch a historic 3-1 win for the Imps and send Notts County down to the Third Division. The amount spent on transfer fees towards the end of the season helped save the club from relegation, but was the main reason for a loss of £14,000 and this prompted the directors to announce that a tight watch would be kept on finances in the coming year.

There was no money available to buy new players and before the start of the 1958/59 season the club announced they were hoping to develop talented youngsters in the future rather than resort to using the transfer market to get out of trouble. The campaign started brightly enough with a 3-1 win over Sunderland but by early September the team had sunk to the bottom of the table. George Hannah was sold to Manchester City for a fee of £10,000 with City receiving John McClelland (valued at £12,500) as part of the deal, and soon after Andy Graver returned to the club for his third spell at Sincil Bank, this time signing from Boston United. The team struggled all season and suffered a series of heavy defeats, including a 7-0 thrashing at Sheffield Wednesday on Boxing Day, and they rarely rose up out of the two relegation positions. For the second year in a row points were needed from the final match of the season to ensure safety, the table showing that any two of four teams could go down :

	P	PTS
LINCOLN CITY	41	29
Rotherham United	40	29
Grimsby Town	41	28
Barnsley	40	27

City defenders (from left) Mitchell Downie, Jeff Smith and Fred Middleton combine to fend off the challenge of Leicester's Walker, in the F.A.Cup-tie at Filbert Street in January 1959

Charlton's Summers shoots for goal as the Imps' defence, including Jeff Smith (far right) and Fred Middleton (extreme left), run back to cover. City won 5-3 at Sincil Bank, in April 1960.

City were beaten 2-1 at home by Sheffield United, but as the other three were also defeated the Imps place in Division Two was almost secure and this was confirmed on the following Wednesday when Barnsley lost at home to Leyton Orient. Although a profit of more than £4,000 was made the board continued to keep spending to a minimum and at the end of the season a total of eight men with first team experience were released including Tony Emery and Roy Finch. Emery had served the club loyally for 14 years, remaining first choice centre-half since 1959, and his aggregate of 402 Football League appearances is still a club record.

The only summer signing was Ken Barrett, a youngster from Aston Villa, and City began the 1959/60 season with a squad of just 16 full-time professionals. The team got off to a poor start losing eight of the first ten games and by the end of September were bottom of the table. Centre-half Dennis Gratton was signed from Sheffield United to strengthen the defence and a slow but steady recovery began. However, attendances rarely reached the break even level of 12-13,000, leaving no spare money to buy players and so a number of teenagers were given a run out in the first team including 17 year-olds Bob Graves, Brian Drysdale and Roger Holmes.

With such limited resources Anderson did well to steer the team into 13th place - their best League position for four seasons. In the F.A Cup, City outplayed First Division Burnley at Sincil Bank but could only draw 1-1 in front of a crowd of more than 21,000 and then went out in the midweek replay. In May the club made a short tour of the Republic of Ireland defeating Limerick, Shelbourne and Waterford in the space of five days - Andy Graver played in goal for the second-half of the Waterford game following an injury to regular 'keeper Bill Heath.

Although another small profit was made the board continued to keep a tight rein on finances and there were again only 16 full-timers on the club's books at the start of the 1960/61 campaign.

(Left) City at the Central Station, embarking for their tour of Ireland. From left: Andy Graver, Ron Allen, Bert Linnecor, C.Applewhite (director), Bill McGlen (trainer), S.Harrison (director), Roy Chapman, Fred Middleton, Mike Commons and Bill Anderson (manager). Fourteen goals were scored in the three victories.

(Below) 'Keeper Bill Heath, with Dennis Gratton (no.5) and Fred Middleton foil the Burnley attack in the FA Cup clash at Sincil Bank

Chairman Charles Applewhite tendered his resignation over the summer and new chairman Alwyne Mawer's pre-season message indicated the club would be more than happy just to retain their place in Division Two. The team had a poor start, not registering a goal until their fifth match, and attendances plummeted to their lowest level since the war. Manager Anderson was desperately in need of a goalscoring centre-forward, but then lost both his full-backs in quick succession, with Jeff Smith breaking a bone in his foot and Ron Allen suffering a double fracture of the right leg at home to Leeds on 3 December, an injury that effectively ended his career. Ian Greaves was signed from Manchester United for £2,500 as a replacement, but fortunes did not improve and the period between Christmas and Easter passed without a League win for the second time in four seasons, with the players performing as if relegation was a formality. There was a pleasant surprise in the F.A. Cup when West Bromwich Albion were beaten 3-1 - the first time in the club's history they had defeated First Division opponents in the competition. However defeat followed in the Fourth Round tie at Sheffield United. This time there was to be no miraculous escape and the team stayed bottom of the table from the end of December right through to the final match. Defeat at Brighton on 8 April confirmed the club would be appearing in the Third Division for the 1961/62 season.

Relegation came for a number of reasons. Bill Anderson struggled for several years, mainly successfully, to assemble a squad of Second Division standard but this relied to a large extent on his ability to buy good players at a cheap price and then sell them on at a profit. This in turn meant that he was rarely able to build a settled team with personnel at the club constantly changing. Every man had his price and if an acceptable offer came along he would invariably be sold. With the maximum wage rising to £20 a week from the 1958/59 season and gate receipts falling due to the supporters becoming disillusioned, the board was forced to instigate strict financial controls.

The effect was that the club began to rely heavily on a small squad of full-time players supplemented by too many part-timers, with no prospect of major signings to strengthen the side. The situation might have been different if there had been a director willing to invest a substantial amount in the team but the board were mostly elderly men and there had been no significant changes for over a decade. Several members either resigned their positions or died in the final years of Division Two status, and those remaining were either unwilling or unable to attract a wealthy investor to the club.

BILL ANDERSON

Bill Anderson ranks alongside David Calderhead Senior, and Graham Taylor, as one of the greatest managers in the club's history. Despite financial restrictions created by the relatively low attendances he twice led the Imps to promotion and kept them in Division Two from 1952 to 1961 operating on a shoe string budget.

Anderson was born at High Westwood near Newcastle on 12 January 1913. After playing for his local school team he joined Medomsley Juniors where one of his colleagues was Jock Dodds. He then had a brief spell with Nottingham Forest before joining Sheffield United where he appeared in the first team at left back. In May 1935 he was transferred to Barnsley, but then suffered a broken leg in the game against Nottingham Forest in November of the same year which effectively ended his playing career. He subsequently obtained qualifications as a masseur and chiropodist and set up a practice in Newcastle before going to work at the Vickers Armstrong factory during the Second World War.

Anderson came to Lincoln in August 1945 when he succeeded Dick Mellors as trainer, and was rapidly promoted, becoming assistant-manager in January 1947, trainer-manager in July 1947 and team manager 12 months later. On taking charge of team affairs he was just 34 years old, making him one of the youngest managers in the game. His first season as manager was a tremendous one with the club winning the Northern Section championship in style. However, some of the credit must go elsewhere for most of the team had been assembled by his predecessor Joe McClelland, and the success of the team also owed a great deal to the presence of captain Tom Johnson. Johnson was one of several former Sheffield United players recruited by Anderson in the late 1940s, others included Jimmy Hutchinson, Jock Dodds and Dick Young. The Imps were relegated after just one season in Division Two, but the side was rebuilt over the next three years and won the Division Three North title for a second time in 1951/52. That season the team netted 121 League goals and established a club record score when they beat Crewe 11-1.

Over the following years Anderson worked wonders to keep Lincoln in the Second Division earning a reputation for spotting a bargain and selling players on for a large profit. During this time he developed a special relationship with the management at Newcastle and several of his signings came from the St James' Park club. Although his transactions involving Andy Graver hit the headlines it was rare for any player to be sold at less than a substantial profit. To the tabloid press he was *"Soccer's Mr. Magic..."*, *"the game's shrewdest manager..."*, *"the No.1 Bargain Hunter"*, and even *"'Bi££' Anderson!"* However the fact that every player had a price at which he could be sold was not to the liking of all and some were glad to get away. Relegation was increasingly inevitable and after he had led the team to safety from an almost impossible position in the 1957/58 season the Imps eventually dropped to the Third Division three years later. The decline was so rapid that by the end of the 1962/63 season the club found themselves applying for re-election after finishing in the bottom four of the Fourth Division. Although the main reason for this was the financial crisis affecting the club, many supporters blamed Anderson, and there were several petitions to the board calling for his dismissal. In January 1965 all responsibility for team affairs was removed from him and he spent the last 18 months of his time at Sincil Bank working in an office with little to do. He was appointed assistant-manager at Nottingham Forest shortly after leaving Lincoln and held the post until 1975. In 1968 he was awarded the Football League's long service award for 21 years service to the game.

Anderson never married and worked tirelessly for the club travelling thousands of miles every year on scouting missions. His enthusiasm and commitment were legendary whilst his ability to bluff his opposite number in transfer negotiations helped bring many a player to Sincil Bank. One example of his tenacity when pursuing a player concerns the signing of Albert Scanlon in 1962. On hearing that the player might be for sale he called on trainer Bill McGlen at 4am and an hour later they were on their way to St James' Park. The ground was locked up when they arrived so the pair climbed over the gates and waited until the manager arrived. Needless to say Bill got his man! When Notts County made a determined bid to bring him to Meadow Lane in September 1958 he resisted the offer of a substantial increase in wages saying, *"I am happy at Lincoln, and you cannot measure that in cash. Money isn't everything... I have built my whole life round Lincoln City, and the directors are 100% behind me in anything I do."* Although he was on a lower salary at Lincoln he regularly received large bonuses when the financial situation allowed and lived rent-free in his house in Scorer Street from the mid-1950s. In the crisis of the early 1960s it was even rumoured that he paid the players wages out of his own pocket when the club ran out of money.

Known throughout as a genial warm hearted man, he smoked heavily and was accompanied everywhere by his golden labrador Sandy. He had a good sense of humour, and was well known for playing practical jokes. Outside of football he was a keen cricketer and opened the batting for the Lindum C.C. in his early years at Lincoln. He made one appearance for the Lincolnshire county team against Notts II in 1946 at Trent Bridge. In 1954 he claimed to have enjoyed the ideal summer holiday - the football World Cup, Wimbledon, the British Open golf championship and the Yorkshire - Surrey cricket match. After so many years as a loyal servant to the club his treatment in the final 18 months of his time at Sincil Bank leaves a lot to be desired. He died in February 1986 at the age of 73.

****

CHAPTER THREE:
THE MODERN ERA . . . . 1961 TO 1997

HARD TIMES

The abolition of the maximum wage in the spring of 1961 was the first in a series of changes over the next 30 years which would change the Football League from an organisation which supported each and every member to one which gave power to the rich and strong clubs and left the weak to fall by the wayside. The immediate effect on the players at Lincoln was to reduce the basic wage from £20 to £18 a week. Bonuses could be earned for results, League position, and the size of home attendances, creating potential income of £28 a week although the level set for most of these was such that they were never paid out.

City began their first season of Division Three football since 1951 with a skeleton squad of full-time players and any hopes of an easy passage were dashed in the opening game at home to Bournemouth. The Imps were well beaten and the crowd responded with a round of slow handclapping at the poverty of the performance. The squad was depleted even further when the board sold the two most effective forwards, Roy Chapman and John McClelland, for a combined fee of £20,000, and then experienced wing-half Fred Middleton went on the injury list with suspected cartilage trouble. Attendances fell to a new post-war low as the team sunk to the fringe of the relegation zone, and even the signing of Albert Broadbent and Albert Franks failed to produce any improvement. Floodlights, paid for by the supporters club, were installed by the new year and they were used for the first time in a League game on 20 January for the visit of Northampton Town. The gate was up by around 1,000 which led to several games being switched to Friday evenings in the hope that 'Pay Night football' would help bring in more money. However results did not improve and the team struggled to lift themselves out of the bottom four. Over 14,000 attended the visit of local neighbours Grimsby Town on 23 February, earning the players their first attendance bonus of the season but there was generally little for the fans to cheer. Relegation was confirmed when Queens Park Rangers sent the Imps crashing to a 5-0 home defeat, condemning them to Fourth Division football for the first time in their history.

Several of the fringe first team men were released at the end of the 1961/62 season enabling Anderson to sign up four new men - Alf Jones, Terry Kelly, Jim Campbell and Terry Carling. The campaign began in promising fashion with a 4-2 win over Tranmere and for a few months it appeared the club had finally turned the corner. When they entertained Doncaster Rovers on 19 October, City would have moved into third position had they won, but they lost 2-1 in front of a crowd of more than 10,000, and this was the beginning of a disastrous run of results. By Christmas they had fallen to 15th in the table before the dreadful winter of 1962/63 set in. They had to wait two months to play their F.A. Cup third round tie with Coventry City, the match being postponed a record 15 times, and the Sky Blues manager Jimmy Hill even suggested playing the game in Dublin.

Manager Bill Anderson (right) with trainer Bill McGlen.

When the fixture eventually took place the Imps produced a lacklustre display and were heavily defeated. The lay-off affected the team badly and by the end of April they stood 22nd in the table. A group of supporters handed a petition to chairman Edgar Gilbert calling for Bill Anderson's resignation, but the real reason for the dramatic demise was the club's chaotic financial situation. Attendances collapsed, dropping below 2,000 for the visit of Gillingham on 15 May, and they were required to seek re-election for the first time since 1919/20.

Grimsby's Cliff Portwood shoots towards the City goal in the clash at Sincil Bank in February 1962.

However the 47 votes they won at the League's A.G.M. in June were sufficient to ensure that League football could continue at Sincil Bank. Re-election was not the only worry for the club in the summer of 1963, for the administrative affairs had been steadily slipping out of control since they had been relegated from Division Two. The bad winter had left the Imps without a home game for almost ten weeks, exposing the weak financial position and bringing matters to a head. The root of the problem was the loss of income caused by falling gate receipts and an inability to create money through the transfer market to compensate for this.

Relegation in successive seasons had only served to speed up the decline and once they had fallen into this cycle it was hard to break out of it. The secretary's position had become a matter of concern too following the departure of Jack Mann and the then current incumbent, George Key, had fallen ill soon after taking up the post. The board was further depleted by death and resignation and the remaining directors were more worried about making sure that the club did not fall into the hands of a 'dictator' figure than whether it survived or not. The reality of the situation was that they were losing over £300 a week, were £10,000 in debt and had an overdraft of £7,500. The patience of creditors had run out and they faced legal action on at least two fronts concerning non-payment of rates and payments for the floodlighting. Manager Bill Anderson kept the club alive almost single handedly at times. One persistent rumour which cannot be verified is that he would pay the players out of his own pocket when there was no money available. He personally visited many of the leading local businessmen to try and persuade them to join the board. There was only firm interest from one individual, local builder Frank Eccleshare who demanded full financial control before he accepted the offer. The few remaining directors agreed to his demands and in July he was elected chairman, one of his first moves being to co-opt accountant Roy Chapman (no relation to the player of the same name) to the board. The immediate priority was to stave off the creditors demanding immediate payment of monies owed and then to work on a long term plan to reduce overheads and build up the strength of the playing staff. A retired police inspector, Thomas Aylmer, was appointed secretary and the financial position was improved through the sale of shares and donations from the supporters club - still a vibrant force despite the parent club's troubles.

The result of these dramatic off the field changes was to create an air of optimism about Sincil Bank as the 1963/64 season approached. The players' basic wage was increased to £20 a week (back to its level in 1958/59) and the bonus scheme was amended so that the targets set were more achievable. 1950s star Dick Neal returned from Middlesbrough in August for a £3,000 fee and he was to provide the leadership needed to turn the team's fortunes around. In October the attack was strengthened with the signing of Oxford's Bud Houghton and the confidence and spirit returned to the club with the team lying on the edge of the promotion race for much of the season. They defeated Hartlepools and Southport in the F.A. Cup to earn a third round tie at home to First Division Sheffield United. The game was keenly awaited in Lincoln but although City fought hard they were outclassed and went down by a 4-0 margin.

There was a near tragedy after the match when a temporary bridge over the Sincil Drain collapsed when packed with fans leaving the ground. Over 70 people fell into the mud below but fortunately only two required hospital treatment. In February there were experiments with pre-match entertainment, the usual recorded music being replaced by 'live' local pop groups, but this had no significant effect on attendances. Any remote chances of promotion were ended by three consecutive defeats over the Easter period, but the team finished the season in 11th position and for once there were no worries about relegation or re-election.

New ideas and changes continued to be implemented over the summer of 1964. Fund-raising activities included boxing, wrestling and greyhound racing while further financial measures saw the minimum adult admission price increased from 2s-6d (12½p) to 3s (15p). The junior sides were reorganised with the 'A' team withdrawn from the Lincolnshire League at a reported saving of £3,500, and youth teams entered in the Lincoln League and the Lincoln Youth League. Money was made available to strengthen the side and new signings included Joe Jacques (Preston), Brian Jackson (Peterborough) and John Hawksby (Leeds). Early results were not promising and in September the board announced that they would be selecting the team in future with Anderson and new club captain Brian Jackson to be jointly in charge of tactics. The influential Dick Neal departed to Rugby as player-manager, and without his leadership the team slipped down the table.

By Christmas they had fallen to 19th position and shortly afterwards further changes were made with Anderson now becoming general manager and former player Con Moulson entrusted with training and tactics. Moulson was rather a strange choice for although he had been helping with the youth team he was working as a machinist at Ruston's and had had no direct contact with the professional game since retiring as a player during the Second World War. His appointment was not a success and in March yet another change was announced, with Roy Chapman who had recently been brought back from Mansfield becoming player-coach with responsibility for the first team's affairs. The last victory had been recorded on Boxing Day and it was not until the defeat of Darlington on 10 April, some 17 matches later, that they managed another win. By this time City had dropped into the bottom four and for the second time in three years they were required to seek re-election. Fortunately the self-supportive nature of the League in the 1960s made it very difficult for new clubs to break through and the Imps were comfortably re-elected with the maximum 48 votes.

There were five new men in the Imps line-up for the opening game of the 1965/66 season at Doncaster, but there was still no change of fortune as they slumped to a 4-0 defeat. The defence was strengthened in October with the signing of experienced centre-half Les Moore, but the team remained in the lower reaches of the League table. The attack relied far too heavily on Barry Hutchinson for goals and by February they had slipped into the bottom four. Hutchinson was transferred to Darlington but was sorely missed as the supply of goals dried up and a dreadful run of results followed culminating in a 7-0 thrashing at Crewe, by which time the Imps had slumped to the bottom once more. The introduction of former Boston F.C. winger Harry Godbold produced some improvement in but it was too late to escape the need to apply for re-election. However City topped the poll at the League's A.G.M. to retain their position in Division Four for another season.

PRIDE RESTORED

City began the 1966/67 season in disappointing fashion and were soon bottom of the table after recording just one win from the first 14 League matches. There was the consolation of a short run in the League Cup with two fighting performances seeing off Third Division Hull City and Huddersfield Town before they met with a heavy defeat at Leicester in the third round. In September, Bill Anderson, who had spent his final years at the club in an office with little to do, finally departed after 21 years service. Shortly afterwards it was announced that player-coach Roy Chapman would step down and Ron Gray was appointed manager. Gray had played for Sheffield United and briefly for the Imps before the Second World War, later serving both Watford and Millwall as manager, although more recently he had been working as a physiotherapist and freelance scout. He brought an enthusiasm and spirit to the job which had been missing for so long. His first task was to try and lift the confidence of a team which seemed to have lost hope of winning, and considered a

New coach Con Moulson (second from right) shakes hands with club captain Roger Holmes on his introduction to the playing staff after his appointment in January 1965. During his brief period in charge, the team lost every match.

narrow defeat as a good result. Changes were made to the line-up and the second win of the season came against Tranmere in November. On 3 December Luton Town were defeated by the remarkable margin of 8-1 with new signing Billy Cobb hitting a hat-trick on his debut.

There was no sustained overall improvement in results however, and a run of 15 games without a win ensured they would finish bottom of the League for the first time since 1911. Re-election at the League's A.G.M. proved a formality again and Gray continued to restructure the side, releasing 11 men with first team experience and signing up goalkeeper John Kennedy, full back George Peden and winger Lewis Thom before the end of May.

Major changes were implemented at the club over the summer of 1967 as the club resolved to put the hard times of the last few years behind them. The team colours were changed to red shirts with white shorts, there was a new nickname - the 'Red Imps' - and the club launched their own lottery, the Imps Fighting Fund, which was run by the manager. Fans in the Sleaford area even formed their own organisation, 'The Imps Supporters Association', the first such venture in the town since the mid-1950s.

Ron Gray's arrival as manager in October 1966 began a revival. Gray (in suit) is shown shaking hands with full-back Alf Jones; other players include Roy Chapman, Tom Brooks and Geoff Heard.

John Kennedy, with Ray Harford (no.5) in attendance, gathers a high ball in the 1967/68 opening match at Sincil Bank versus Aldershot

With almost a completely new side the confidence which had been missing for so many years returned and there was a memorable run in the League Cup. Mansfield were dispatched in the first round to set up a home tie with First Division Newcastle United. City produced an inspirational performance with centre-half Ray Harford dominating his clashes with the Magpies Welsh international Wyn Davies, only to go a goal down on 70 minutes. They fought back to equalise through captain Jim Grummett then five minutes from time Jim Iley handled in the box and George Peden coolly stepped up to send the 'keeper the wrong way and gain a famous victory.

The same fighting spirit was apparent when Torquay were defeated in the third round, with the Imps racing to a 4-0 lead after just 19 minutes before eventually winning 4-2. In the last 16 of the competition they were drawn away to Derby County who had the newly appointed Brian Clough as their manager. Lincoln went a goal down but battled back and appeared to have equalised with a Jack Lewis goal on the hour, until the referee controversially disallowed it for an infringement.

Justice was done 15 minutes from time when Gregson's cross was headed home by Lewis Thom to earn a 1-1 draw. The replay took place in torrential rain in front of a record home attendance of 23,196, but with Derby leading from an early goal, City's Mick Brown was sent off in the closing stages for a head-butt and the visitors added two more goals to tie up a 3-0 victory. There was nothing in their contracts to allow a bonus for the cup run but following representations to the board a trailer loaded with potatoes was delivered to the ground and the players were given a bag each as a reward! League performances were inconsistent and the team dropped to the edge of the re-election zone, but the side was improved with new men shortly before the transfer deadline and a run of seven wins from eight games towards the end of the season enabled them to finish in 13th position.

The team was strengthened over the summer with a number of signings, including Grimsby's Graham Taylor and Dave Smith from Middlesbrough, and they began the 1968/69 season with four consecutive victories to go top of the table. A promotion challenge was maintained for much of the season until a string of poor results in the period leading up to Easter effectively ended their chances of going up. The final position of eighth was slightly disappointing but still represented the club's best performance since being relegated to the Fourth Division in 1962. The fighting qualities instilled in the team by Gray were epitomised by the display in the F.A. Cup second round replay at home to Chester. An action packed first-half saw the Imps take the lead with a goal from Peter Kearns, miss a penalty, and then lose both Kearns and goalkeeper John Kennedy through injury. Grummett took over in goal and although Chester equalised City's ten men battled on and snatched a late winner from Dave Smith to set up a third round tie at Birmingham.

The close season saw little transfer activity and in August the team made a brief visit to Northern Ireland beating both Glentoran and Ards. However, form seemed to desert them at the start of the 1969/70 campaign, and it was nine matches before a League victory was recorded, by which time they had slumped to second from bottom position. The return from injury of Gordon Hughes and the signing of Walsall's Trevor Meath led to an improvement in results but they struggled to rise up the table, eventually finishing in 8th position for the second successive year.

Board changes at the end of April saw Collingham farmer Heneage Dove replace Walter Mant as chairman, and the following month Gray was dismissed with 14 months of his contract remaining. In many ways he had become the victim of his own success having taken on a team in dire straits and transformed them into a combative outfit capable of mounting a

Trevor Meath (hands aloft) celebrates with substitute Dave Smith (no.12) after scoring in the 1-1 draw at Aldershot in October 1969.

City players and directors before flying out for the pre-season visit to Northern Ireland, August 1969. Glentoran were beaten 2-1 and City drew 2-2 with Ards.

serious challenge for Division Three football. Like Bill Anderson before him he had the ability to spot talent and persuade skilful players to join the club. His team included five men who would later manage at the highest level : Graham Taylor, Ray Harford, Jim Smith, Billy Taylor and Mick Brown. He was sacked simply because the players had failed to win promotion.

Trainer Bert Loxley was appointed to succeed Gray with the official title of 'team manager coach'. City opened the 1970/71 season with a 1-1 draw at League newcomers Cambridge United, following this up with a 2-0 home win over Brentford, a game which is remembered for the fact that the goalposts at the railway end collapsed during the closing minutes and there was a delay of three-quarters of an hour before the match could be finished. League results were inconsistent, although the new strike force of Trevis and Freeman produced several spectacular goals. However the team reached the third round in both the League and F.A. Cups, coming close to making further progress in the latter. City visited Torquay and led 3-0 at one point before the defence crumbled and they went down 4-3. By March they had slipped to the edge of the bottom four and Loxley was eased aside to be replaced by David Herd.

The new manager had enjoyed a glittering playing career, appearing with Manchester United and Arsenal, and winning five Scottish 'caps'. The initial contact had been made when he met one of the directors on holiday in the summer, and he had remained in touch with the club since, so his appointment came as no surprise. Although there were several high-scoring encounters as Herd experimented with tactics and different line-ups the results did not improve and the team finished the season in 21st position, necessitating yet another re-election bid. Fortunately, although it was the 14th occasion on which the club had been required to submit to the ballot, they had a strong case and were returned to the League without any problems.

Manager Bert Loxley, in the post for less than a year, but a loyal clubman for 20 years.

A new bonus structure was agreed with the players over the summer, allowing for payments linked to the club's position at various points in the season and to the size of home attendances. Herd brought in Frank McMahon from Irish club Waterford and several players with Central League experience, and they soon proved a match for any other side in the division. A string of home victories in the first-half of the season provided the basis for a strong promotion challenge.

Leading scorer Phil Hubbard was sold to Norwich City for a £20,000 fee shortly before Christmas and the money was used to sign up Tommy Spencer and Dixie McNeil. The new men were instrumental in leading the side to an 11 match unbeaten run and the visit of fellow promotion hopefuls Scunthorpe United on 18 March attracted an attendance of 16,498 - the best at a home League fixture since 1958. The Imps took the lead on 27 minutes when John Worsdale's cross was powerfully headed home by Alan Gilliver and they never looked liked losing a tense hard fought encounter. However the victory did not herald a renewed push for higher status and a poor run of results followed in April, and this was to cost the club promotion for they finished in 5th place, one point behind Scunthorpe who went up to Division Three along with the other Lincolnshire side Grimsby Town.

City ground-staff have to rapidly replace the goalposts after the collapse of the originals, during the Sincil Bank match versus Brentford in 1970.

THE TAYLOR YEARS

Although the public image of the club was one of a team united in their disappointment at narrowly missing out on promotion, privately the relationship between the manager and many of the playing staff was not good. After representations were made to the directors a group of three senior players were invited to express their views at a meeting of the board. The criticisms covered a wide area ranging from the manager's absences in connection with his business interests in Manchester to internal club discipline and the training methods employed. A proposal to dispense with Herd immediately was heavily defeated, but shortly afterwards a new schedule of duties for the manager was drawn up, and Graham Taylor was appointed player-coach, the role including liaison between the manager and the playing staff.

New signings for the 1972/73 season included two experienced players from the League of Ireland, in midfielder Jimmy McGeough and prolific striker Brendan Bradley. After a disappointing home defeat by Hartlepool in the opening match the team returned to form and with Bradley, McNeil and Freeman all scoring regularly they rose to third position at the start of October. Then a string of poor results left them without a win in eight games and Herd resigned at the beginning of December. The board looked to the existing staff for a replacement, interviewing Derek Trevis, Terry Branston and Graham Taylor, before appointing the latter to the position.

Taylor had won representative honours for the England Grammar Schools XI before signing up for Grimsby Town where he spent six years. He joined Lincoln in July

Graham Taylor, at 28, the youngest manager in the Football League on his appointment in December 1972, and arguably the most successful in the club's history.

1968 and shortly afterwards was appointed club captain by Ron Gray. Despite being the youngest manager in the League at the time he was certainly not naive and brought a much needed thoughtful approach to the position. One of his first tasks was to draw up a lengthy document covering almost every aspect of the club's work which he then submitted to the board for approval. He had full support from the directors who offered him a three year contract and immediately began to put his proposals into place with George Higgins arriving as trainer-coach and a junior team being entered in the Northern Intermediate League for the first time. His initial moves in the transfer market brought Dennis Leigh from Rotherham and Terry Heath from Scunthorpe with Percy Freeman leaving for Reading.

'Keeper John Kennedy under pressure from the Burnley attack in the Watney Cup match in July 1972. Other City players (from left), Percy Freeman, David Kennedy, Dave Smith, Jimmy McGeough (no.7) and Derek Trevis (no.4). Burnley won 1-0, in what was City's only experience of the sponsored tournament.

The team still struggled to find form and it took 12 matches to achieve the first victory under Taylor. A last minute header from Terry Branston gave the Imps two points against lowly Darlington to end a club run of 19 League and cup games without a win. In March Alan Harding was bought from Darlington for a substantial fee, results improved, and the team rose up the table to finish in 10th position.

The main event over the summer of 1973 was the split in the relationship between the football club and the supporters club. The dispute, which had been developing for some time, was basically over the supporters club's refusal to hand over a substantial sum of money which had been allocated for the purchase of their own premises. From now on the supporters club were known as the 'Lincoln and District Football Supporters Club', initially turning their attentions towards providing resources for the game locally. Meanwhile it was decided to change the club colours back to the traditional red and white striped shirts with black shorts. A party of players visited Billingham for pre-season training, and team building continued with the signing of defenders Ian Branfoot (Doncaster) and Sam Ellis (Mansfield). They were joined shortly after the start of the 1973/74 season by Darlington's skilful striker Peter Graham. After a moderate start the Imps put together a string of home victories and they rose to 4th in the table by the end of January, following a 2-1 win over Rotherham. The game was the first played by the club on a Sunday, the switch from Saturday being made because of restrictions on the use of floodlighting due to a strike by miners. However successive home defeats in the crucial home fixtures against Gillingham and Reading saw the team drop back down the table and they finished the season in 11th place. Chairman Dennis Bocock resigned at the end of April to be replaced by Charles Warner, and negotiations were soon held with the supporters club with the aim of making a reconciliation.

The close season was again a time for quiet rebuilding of the squad with former Welsh international winger Dick Krzywicki arriving from Huddersfield and Dennis Booth, who had previously been at the club on loan, joining from Southend. A goalkeeping crisis at the start of the 1974/75 season was resolved by signing Peter Grotier on loan from West Ham and the move was so successful that the directors agreed to buy him for a new club record fee of £16,666, with the supporters volunteering to raise part of the money. Meanwhile the club's youth policy continued to develop and in October an agreement was made to adopt Sheffield juniors Wisewood Athletic as a nursery club. The season came alive for the Imps in the autumn with a magnificent 12 match unbeaten run which included six successive victories and lifted the side into fourth position. They remained there for most of the campaign, but things began to go wrong in March with Swansea ending City's unbeaten home record with a 3-1 win, and then promotion rivals Chester inflicting a 4-1 defeat shortly afterwards. The team struggled to break down packed defences in the closing games and they travelled to Southport for the final match needing a win to go up. It was a heartbreaking performance for City however, as they went down 3-2 and so Chester took the final place in Division Three, the difference in goal average between the clubs being a margin of 0.0383.

Taylor took the view that despite their narrow failure the existing squad was good enough to win promotion and the only new signing during the summer was right-sided midfield player John Fleming. The 1975/76 campaign began with a loss at Newport but the team soon struck form and dropped just two points from the next nine games as they went to second in the table. Defeat at Northampton proved only a temporary setback as the City swept all before them, winning eleven consecutive League and cup games as they rose to lead the division. Success was not confined to League games for First Division Stoke City were beaten in the second round of the League Cup, whilst the Imps progressed to the fourth round of the F.A. Cup for the first time since 1961. Drawn to play West Bromwich Albion at the Hawthorns, they led 2-1 at half-time only to go down 3-2, the winner coming from a young Bryan Robson. Northampton, the only side who could overtake City, were beaten 3-1 at Sincil Bank, and with seven matches remaining promotion was secured against Darlington on 7 April. Dave Smith scored the 100th League goal of the campaign in a 3-0 win at Stockport, and a crowd of 14,096 packed Sincil Bank to see the title clinched in the final home game of the season against Doncaster. A draw at Bournemouth in their final fixture left City with an all-time record 74 points. They also established Fourth Division records for most wins and fewest defeats, and were the first team for a decade to score 100 League goals in a season. The side was so superior to their opponents that only two clubs came away from Sincil Bank with a point, and five of the team were selected for the P.F.A.'s representative side for the division. Success on the field was also accompanied by a profit of more than £40,000 off it.

Preparations for City's first season in Division Three for 15 years were somewhat muted with just one new recruit, Phil Hubbard, who returned to the club from Grimsby for a fee of £6,000. The Imps settled in well after an uncertain start although they tended to struggle to break down opposition defences in the higher division. Victory over Reading on 23 October put them in fourth place, but then Bury ended City's 35 match unbeaten home run and they fell back to a mid-table position. Non-League sides Morecambe and Nuneaton were defeated in the F.A. Cup, to earn a place in the third round of the competition for the third consecutive year. City battled to a 2-2 draw in an exciting game at Turf Moor, only to lose by the only goal of the match, to Burnley, in the replay on a freezing cold night. The youth policy which Taylor had started soon after being appointed manager was now beginning to bear fruit and a number of youngsters including Brendan Guest, Glenn Cockerill and Dean Crombie were introduced to first team football during the campaign.

City finished ninth in the table and there was growing speculation about the manager's future with the club. West Bromwich Albion and Watford were known to be interested and the directors signed him to a new three year contract which contained a substantial compensation clause. In June Taylor moved to Watford, who agreed to pay the Imps a £20,000 'transfer fee'. The main reasons for his departure were clear; a five-year contract said to be worth £125,000, and the almost unlimited resources of pop star Elton John to buy players. One of his final acts as manager was to tie-up the deal which brought three youngsters from the Lambton Street Boys Club to Sincil Bank - they were Mick Harford, Keith Laybourne and Mick Smith.

It was at Lincoln that Taylor began to develop many of the ideas which he used later in his career - a concentration on direct ('long ball') tactics, a belief that the football club was an integral part of the community, and a recognition that a healthy club needed a sound youth policy. Despite the 'long ball' game being associated with uninspiring monotonous football, the way it was played under Taylor was exciting to watch with plenty of attacking play and a good supply of goals. Taylor's great skills were in assembling a side in which the personalities blended so well and in getting the best out of the resources available to him. Significantly many of the 1975/76 team were 'leaders', and several - including Sam Ellis, John Ward and Ian Branfoot - later enjoyed careers in management, whilst Phil Neale became Director of Coaching at Warwickshire C.C.C. and has led England 'A' cricket teams on tour.

After leaving Lincoln, Taylor enjoyed great success at Watford taking them from the Fourth Division to runners-up position in the First Division. He later took Aston Villa to a promotion and runners-up in Division One too before spending a controversial three years as manager of the England team. He has since served Wolves as manager before returning to Watford as general manager.

INTO THE EIGHTIES

The board chose to replace Graham Taylor with an internal appointment, coach George Kerr becoming manager and Ian Branfoot stepping up to player-coach. Unlike his predecessor, Kerr was given a contract for one year only. Meanwhile, club captain Sam Ellis refused to accept the terms offered to him and followed Taylor to Watford. The new manager soon revealed his selection policies by including three teenagers in the squad for the opening game of the 1977/78 season.

The youngsters took time to settle in and the team struggled in their early fixtures, not registering a League victory until their visit to Portsmouth on 17 September. Centre-half Clive Wigginton was signed from Scunthorpe in a bid to strengthen the defence but the poor run continued. The team slumped to 22nd place in the table following defeat at Sheffield Wednesday in October and the board gave Kerr an ultimatum that results must improve or he would be sacked. The disappointing sequence continued and Kerr was dismissed in December after the home defeat by Gillingham. His successor was chosen from a short-list of four, with the two main candidates being the Bristol Rovers striker Bobby Gould and Willie Bell, a former Leeds and Scotland full back. The fact that Bristol Rovers would require a substantial fee in compensation for Gould probably went against him and Bell was appointed shortly before Christmas. With the exception of Mick Harford the youngsters were relegated to the reserves, results improved and the team finished the season in 16th position comfortably clear of relegation.

It was decided during the 1978 close season to increase the minimum admission price to £1, and a new bonus scheme was implemented for the players with payments for points won dependent on the team's position in the league table. There had been little in the way of transfer activity over the summer, but in September Ian Branfoot moved to Southampton as youth team coach and he was replaced as player-coach by Jim McCalliog.

Although the 1978/79 season began with a home win over Tranmere the Imps lost the next five games and were soon bottom of the table. The 5-0 defeat at home to Graham Taylor's Watford was particularly humiliating with some of the Lincoln fans cheering for the visitors by the end of the game. In September, Bell paid out almost £50,000 to bring in Graham Watson from Cambridge and Sheffield Wednesday's Tommy Tynan - the latter at a new club record fee of £33,000. However there was no improvement in the team's fortunes, and following a 3-0 home defeat by Swindon the manager resigned, announcing his intention to build a new career with the Campus Crusade for Christ in the United States. McCalliog served briefly as caretaker-manager

Heneage Dove - club chairman twice in the 1970s, and credited with the decision to appoint Graham Taylor as manager

before the board appointed Colin Murphy in November. Murphy had spent most of his playing career in the Southern League, and after a short period in management at Hastings United he had joined Nottingham Forest as a coach. He later followed manager Dave MacKay to Derby where he served as manager from November 1976 until January 1977. He was faced with a difficult task at Sincil Bank for the team had not won in 15 matches and were bottom of the table. The squad of players available to him comprised mostly men who were past their prime or youngsters who were a long way off achieving their full potential. One of his first moves was to restore Phil Neale to the team and another was to offload Tynan to Newport at a substantial loss to the club, just four months after he had been signed.

The team continued their dismal run of results, remaining bottom for the rest of the season and with attendances dropping below the 2,000 level the Imps were relegated back to Division Four.

Murphy signed three new men over the 1979 close season - David Carr, Tony Cunningham and Trevor Peake - and the reshaped line-up showed a new confidence in their opening matches against Third Division Barnsley in the two legs of their League Cup-tie, only to go out after a penalty shoot-out. The new strike force of Harford and Cunningham linked up well and the team quickly occupied a position on the edge of the promotion race. At the end of November the board signed Barnsley's Derek Bell for £36,000, and then sold powerful midfielder Glenn Cockerill to Swindon Town for a new club record fee of £100,000. There was a mini slump in form and Murphy returned to the transfer market in the new year, bringing in Trevor Thompson, Nolan Keeley, George Shipley and the on loan Eric McManus, with Mick Smith and Peter Grotier moving out. Results improved as the side settled down with the defence looking particularly strong - just two goals were conceded in a ten match run towards the end of the season. A 5-2 victory at Torquay in their final fixture enabled the Imps to finish seventh in the table.

By the summer of 1980 the club's financial position had become a matter of some concern. The previous two seasons had seen substantial losses made, whilst expenditure on wages was now more than double the income received from gate money. Murphy made just one new signing before the start of the 1980/81 season, with Colin Boulton the former Derby County goalkeeper filling the gap left by Peter Grotier. The team got off to a great start, despatching Third Division Hull City with ease in their League Cup-tie, and with four of the first five League games won Murphy was awarded the Manager of the Month for August.

Then, in the game at Crewe, Boulton suffered a broken leg, but although down to ten men after the dismissal of David Hughes, the Imps still won 3-0. Bolton's David Felgate was signed, initially on loan, and the team went on to record several convincing wins, including an 8-0 thrashing of Northampton Town in which Gordon Hobson scored four.

Dennis Houlston took over as chairman in December and shortly afterwards the highly promising Mick Harford was sold to Newcastle United for a new Fourth Division record fee of £160,000. The B.B.C.'s Match of the Day programme filmed the home match with Mansfield on 27 December, but only a few minutes of the game were shown, prompting the board to submit a letter of complaint. In January, Murphy was rewarded with a new contract tying him to the club until May 1984. Meanwhile City battled it out with Southend for the title. Goals began to dry up in the absence of Harford but the defence stayed firm, establishing a new record for the lowest number of goals conceded in the division, and promotion was achieved comfortably with the team finishing runners-up in the table.

In preparation for Division Three football Peterborough's David McVay and Scunthorpe striker Steve Cammack were added to the squad, whilst Glenn Cockerill returned to the club from Swindon for a cut-price fee of £40,000. The Imps made a steady start to the 1981/82 season with draws against Portsmouth and Fulham, followed by a win at Plymouth. Form then slipped and they dropped down the table, falling to 20th position after losing at home to Preston on 4 November.

The team showed some of their potential when beating First Division Notts County in both legs of their second round League Cup-tie, before going down to Watford after two brave performances. Steve Thompson returned to the line-up but it was only after a six week break due to bad weather that things improved as the team put together a 16 match unbeaten run to haul themselves into the promotion race. Comfortable wins over Chester and Exeter left the Imps needing a victory in their final match of the season against Fulham - who themselves required just a draw from the game - to go up.

The prospect of regaining their position in Division Two for the first time since 1961 ensured that over 5,000 fans travelled down to London for the vital fixture. After a tense but goalless first-half, the match turned on a crucial incident after 58 minutes. Defender Steve Thompson was dismissed for a second bookable offence, and Fulham took the lead from the free-kick that ensued. City stormed back and equalised on 71 minutes when David Carr headed home after Cockerill had flicked on Gilbert's cross. Despite pressure from Lincoln in the final minutes there were no more goals and the match finished 1-1. Any mathematical possibility of going up disappeared the following evening when Carlisle won at Chester to take the remaining promotion slot.

David Carr (no.2) celebrates with Glenn Cockerill (no.4) and Phil Turner (facing camera), after equalising for City in the promotion-decider at Fulham in May 1982. There were over 5,000 Lincoln fans in the 20,000 crowd.

A number of factors, including substantial bonus payments and a heavy loss incurred by a Country and Western Music festival, combined to produce a record loss of £259,000 on the 1981/82 season. The board responded on several fronts. The wage bill was cut with a number of players leaving on free transfers, coach Lennie Lawrence departed for Charlton, and admission prices were increased for the new campaign. The future of the club was secured by selling the ground to the City Council for £225,000 and leasing it back, initially for a period of 25 years. The 1982/83 season began with a skeleton squad of 13 men available and the players in dispute with the club over a proposal to reduce bonus payments by around 45%. Despite these off the field problems the team performed remarkably well, sweeping all before them, and by the end of September they stood at the top of the table. City also enjoyed a fine run in the Milk Cup (successor to the League Cup) disposing of York and Leicester to set up a third round tie at home to West Ham United. Their opponents were lying in third place in the First Division at the time, and after falling a goal behind, Lincoln dominated for long periods of the match, and despite Derek Bell snatching an equaliser, they were held to a 1-1 draw. The replay was delayed until 29 November, the initial date being postponed due to a waterlogged pitch, and the Imps produced another brave performance taking the match into extra time before going out of the competition.

Phil Turner goes up for a header under pressure from West Ham 'keeper Phil Parkes during the Milk Cup match.

The team peaked just before Christmas, thrashing Bournemouth 9-0 on a freezing cold afternoon. The visitors' 'keeper Kenny Allen was the star of the match pulling off a string of brilliant saves to keep the score down to single figures. The Division Three table now read:

	P	PTS
LINCOLN CITY	18	42
Bristol Rovers	20	37
Cardiff City	19	36
Newport County	19	35
Huddersfield Town	19	33

However, the dispute between the board and the playing staff, which had been the subject of widespread media attention, continued to rumble on. Matters came to a head early in the new year after the players returned from a mid-season break in Majorca as the pressures of injuries and suspensions began to tell on the small squad. Murphy publicly announced that he wished to strengthen the side with two new signings costing around £30,000 in all. Chairman Gilbert Blades refused, and the dispute blew up again with the story reaching the front page of at least one tabloid newspaper. The supporters demonstrated their backing for Murphy and the team in the home match with Plymouth, and the whole board announced their resignation on the following Monday.

Dennis Houlston took over as chairman in early March with the new board consisting of John Reames, Michael Pryor and Derek Overton. The dramatic events clearly affected the team and they slumped badly, finishing the season in sixth place. For the first time in the club's history they qualified for the final of a national competition, and met Millwall at Sincil Bank in the final of the Football League Trophy. Disappointingly this too was lost with the Imps going down 3-2 and missing a penalty in a game played in torrential rain.

Centre half Trevor Peake was sold to Coventry for £100,000 during the summer of 1983, and new faces in the team at the start of the 1983/84 season included Ross Jack and John Thomas, the two players Murphy had wanted to buy earlier in the year. The squad was strengthened in September with two new men - John Fashanu and Alan Walker - but the inspirational Steve Thompson then suffered a broken leg in the F.A. Cup tie at Port Vale. There were several dismal League performances as the team hovered in the lower reaches of the table and gates dropped below the 2,000 level by the end of the season.

There was some joy in the cup competitions however, with City drawn against Tottenham Hotspur in the second round of the Milk Cup. Despite losing the first leg 3-1, a crowd of more than 12,000 packed Sincil Bank for the return match, and although City won 2-1 on the night there was never any doubt that the London club would go through to the next round. There were fine performances in the F.A. Cup too with the Imps only going down to a very late goal at Bramall Lane after holding Sheffield United to a 0-0 draw in the first game. Meanwhile Glenn Cockerill was sold to the Blades for £140,000 and income from transfer fees contributed to a healthy profit of £88,000.

The 1984/85 season began with a goalless draw at home to Hull City, but early results were poor and the team dropped briefly to the bottom of the Third Division table. Winger John McGinley was brought in and the season's first victory was gained on 6 October when Preston were defeated 4-0 at Sincil Bank. Combative striker Fashanu was sold to Millwall in November and shortly afterwards City suffered a humiliating F.A. Cup defeat at Telford. This was the first time since 1957 that the club had been knocked out of the competition by a non-League side. The dismal League run continued and attendances rarely rose above 2,000 as the Imps struggled on the edge of the relegation zone.

On 11 May they travelled to Valley Parade to face champions Bradford City in the final game of the season. Shortly before half-time, with the game level at 0-0, a fire broke out and within minutes the main stand was engulfed in flames.

To all Lincoln City Supporters

WANT PROMOTION?

The policies of the present Chairman and Directors will mean it won't happen at Sincil Bank

These people MUST go!

A Demonstration will take place in front of the Director's Box after the final whistle

TELL THE DIRECTORS TO GO AND SHOW YOUR SUPPORT FOR COLIN AND THE PLAYERS

Printed & Distributed by Loyal Supporters

This unofficial leaflet was handed out to fans before the home clash with Plymouth. Before he resigned, chairman Gilbert Blades received death threats and his home was daubed with slogans

One of Britain's worst ever sporting disasters. The two Lincoln fans who died are remembered by the Stacey West Stand, which replaced the old railway end during the development of the ground.

A total of 56 people died and many more were injured in what was one of soccer's worst ever tragedies. Amongst the fatalities were two long-standing Lincoln supporters, Bill Stacey and Jim West.

(Left) Glenn Cockerill - City's record sale when he moved to Swindon for £100,000 in December 1979.
(Right) Gordon Hobson - one of the club's most prolific scorers with 96 League goals in two spells at Sincil Bank.

There was further drama a few weeks later when a jet carrying a party of City players on their return from holiday in Majorca overshot the runway at Leeds-Bradford airport and the passengers were forced to use the safety chutes to escape. Colin Murphy parted company with the club during the summer, and his former assistant, John Pickering, was appointed manager shortly before the 1985/86 season began. The squad had been depleted with the loss of several key men who had taken advantage of the freedom of contract to move on. Gordon Hobson, George Shipley, John Thomas, Steve Thompson and Alan Walker all left, and the new manager brought in a number of players including the former England international striker Bob Latchford. The season began brightly enough with the team playing attacking football to defeat Gillingham 1-0 at Sincil Bank, although Latchford suffered a back injury which was to rule him out of action for several weeks.

The team had risen to sixth position by early October but then fortunes changed, confidence disappeared, and the Imps began a lengthy spell without a win. The lowest point came at Derby's Baseball Ground on 9 November when they were hammered 7-0. Four members of that team never played for the club again. When City lost 4-0 at home to Cardiff on 14 December it was their 10th defeat in 11 League and cup matches, which resulted in the dismissal of Pickering as manager. The board appointed former boss George Kerr to replace him and although several experienced players were brought in to the side results did not improve Relegation to Division Four was effectively confirmed after the 2-1 defeat at Cardiff in the season's penultimate game. However, off the field there was a record profit of more than £100,000, which was mostly due to the sale of promising goalkeeper Stuart Naylor to West Bromwich Albion for a five-figure sum.

The Football League announce an end to the annual re-election procedures for the bottom four clubs, and from 1987, the team at the bottom of the League would face automatic relegation to the Vauxhall Conference.

Lincoln struggled on their return to Division Four in the 1986/87 season and slipped into the lower reaches of the table, until a series of victories inspired by Gary Lund's goalscoring raised them to a mid-table position. However a sequence of eight defeats in nine games in the new year led to the dismissal of Kerr for a second time, and he was replaced by Peter Daniel who was offered the position in a caretaker capacity. Central defender Gary Strodder was sold to West Ham for a substantial fee, and Daniel signed striker Jimmy Gilligan from Swindon and two loan players - Glenn Humphries and Derek Hood. Humphries was sent off within six minutes of his debut for the club at Hartlepool. Although there was little improvement in the team's fortunes, they appeared to be safe from relegation with one of the main candidates being Stockport County who were now managed by Colin Murphy. Victory over prospective champions Northampton Town only served to confirm this belief, but then City lost to Wolves and Scunthorpe to enter the final round of matches with the table standing as follows :

	P	Pts	Goal diff.
Rochdale	45	50	-17
LINCOLN CITY	45	48	-18
Torquay United	45	47	-16
Tranmere Rovers	45	47	-19
Burnley	45	46	-22

Tranmere played on the Friday night, winning 1-0 to reach safety but there still seemed to be little for the Imps to worry about as they faced the long journey to Swansea to play a team that had won just three times in their previous 18 games. However, City produced a lacklustre display to go down 2-0, and then had to wait for the other two games to finish to hear their fate. Burnley beat Orient 2-1 and Torquay drew two-all at home to Crewe, scoring an equaliser in injury time which had been added after a player had been bitten by a stray dog that had wandered onto the field.

Unbelievably Lincoln, who had never been bottom of the table all season, were relegated by virtue of goal difference.

City on the attack during the home victory over Northampton. City players: Willie Gamble, Gary West, John McGinley and Glenn Humphries.

THE LAST TEN YEARS

Relegation to the Vauxhall Conference was a great shock to everyone at Sincil Bank and fundamental changes were made over the summer of 1987. The healthy financial position allowed the club to remain full-time, and former manager Colin Murphy returned for a second spell in charge.

*Colin Murphy
Manager until May 1990*

He completely rebuilt the side, using money from the sale of Lee Butler (to Aston Villa for £100,000), Gary West, and others, to sign a number of players, many with either Grimsby or Stockport connections. The line-up for the opening game at Barnet included only three men from the previous season, and although City lost both this match and their next game at Weymouth, the team soon began to settle down.

The club's status as the first team to be relegated from the League ensured that each away game was played in a cup-tie atmosphere in front of a big crowd against highly motivated opponents. If this was not enough they also had to contend with a F.I.F.A. authorised offside experiment in Conference matches, which allowed players to remain on-side if receiving the ball directly from a free kick.

Paul Smith was signed for a club record fee of £48,000 in September, and a string of victories saw the team rise to a top four position. Victory over Northwich Victoria on 12 December was the start of a 15 match unbeaten run which left them challenging rivals Barnet for the championship. Attendances were boosted by the team's success, and an almost total absence of crowd violence saw an increase of over 80% on the 1986/87 figures. Three consecutive away defeats did not help City's cause and the title seemed to be slipping from their grasp, for with two matches remaining the table read:

	P	PTS
Barnet	40	77
LINCOLN CITY	40	76
Kettering Town	40	75

Stafford Rangers visited Sincil Bank on 30 April and in a tremendous atmosphere the Imps won 2-1, whilst Barnet lost by a similar score to Runcorn. The final match, at home to Wycombe, was a tense affair in front of a new Conference record crowd of 9,432. Goals from Mark Sertori and Phil Brown earned a 2-0 victory, the title, and automatic promotion back to the Football League at the expense of Newport County. 'Murphy's Mission' had been accomplished, but it been an expensive campaign and a loss of £134,000 was made on the season.

The side was strengthened with two new men over the summer - goalkeeper Mark Wallington and defender Darren Davis - but they struggled on their return to the Fourth Division, and in early September the board paid out a record £60,000 fee to bring Gordon Hobson back from Southampton. Fortunes improved slightly, and they rose to fifth position for a brief moment in November, although they had suffered the humiliation of defeat in the first round of the F.A. Cup at the hands of Conference side Altrincham. The team's form was too inconsistent to maintain a promotion challenge, and any hopes of a play-off place were dashed by successive home defeats by Burnley and Leyton Orient in early May. They finished the season in a respectable mid-table position, but for the second year in a row a substantial loss of more than £100,000 was recorded.

There were several new men in the team at the start of the 1989/90 campaign and the Imps got off to a good start by beating neighbours Scunthorpe United 1-0 with a goal from Matt Carmichael. Immediately after the game, central defender Tony James was sold to Leicester City for £150,000 with City receiving youngsters Grant Brown and Paul Groves on loan in return. Successive victories followed over Aldershot, Doncaster and Torquay, and the team went top of the table, prompting Murphy to spend £60,000 on Sheffield United winger Alan Roberts. Unfortunately Roberts suffered a serious knee injury shortly afterwards, and a series of poor results saw the team slip towards the middle of the table, although there was a fine Boxing Day win over Cambridge United when the Imps came back from 3-2 down with four minutes left to win 4-3. The board invested heavily in new players in January and the promotion challenge was briefly revived, but another poor run of results which saw just two wins from 10 games left them needing to beat champions Exeter to have a chance of qualifying for the play-offs. However the visitors won comfortably leaving City to finish in 10th position for the second year in a row, and at the end of the season Murphy left the club by mutual consent.

The former Leeds United and England striker Allan Clarke succeeded Murphy in June, and later in the summer the Stacey-West stand was opened to replace the old railway end terracing. The 1990/91 season began with great optimism, but then tragedy struck on 8 September when York's David Longhurst collapsed and died in the match at Bootham Crescent. His death seemed to affect the Lincoln players as well, for the next 18 games saw the team win only once. Following successive home defeats by Crewe Alexandra (in the F.A. Cup), and Darlington, Clarke was dismissed just 179 days after his appointment.

Steve Thompson. Manager until May 1993.

Club captain Steve Thompson replaced him, initially in a caretaker role, and although the team fell to the bottom of the table, fortunes improved from the beginning of January. The passing tactics of his predecessor were scrapped in favour of a long ball game with two big men up front, experienced players were brought in to strengthen the side, and a 6-2 thrashing of Carlisle in the last game of the season left the Imps in a creditable 14th position. It had been yet another expensive year however with the club making a record loss of £268,000.

Thompson kept faith with the same squad of players for the 1991/92 season, but after a stylish opening victory at Cardiff they crashed to a record 6-0 defeat at home to newcomers Barnet in early September. A loss of form at Sincil Bank, injuries, suspensions and an inability to score goals all contributed to the team's problems as they struggled in the lower reaches of the table. Confidence returned in the second half of the season and they finished in 10th position for the third time in four years. Victory over promotion seeking Blackpool on the final day of the season was the seventh win in a row and extended their sequence of fine results, to one defeat in 18 matches. Attendances were generally below the 3,000 level and the board sold 'keeper Matt Dickins to Blackburn Rovers for £250,000, and Shane Nicholson to Derby for £80,000, to improve the financial situation. The income from transfer fees ensured that a profit was made for the first time since 1987.

The end of season form led to hopes of automatic promotion for the 1992/93 campaign, and City began the season as joint favourites for the title with the bookmakers. Early results were disappointing, but form improved after the side achieved a creditable 1-1 draw at home to Crystal Palace in the home leg of their Coca-Cola Cup-tie, and they were soon up in fourth position. There was a shock F.A. Cup defeat at the hands of a Stafford Rangers team managed by former City player Dennis Booth, and after Christmas the team seemed to lack the confidence to finish off weaker opponents. A run of one win from eight games cost them the chance of a play-off spot, and manager Thompson departed after the board decided not to renew his contract. Youth team coach Keith Alexander was put in charge of the team for the final match of the season and with teenagers Carbon, Dixon, and Parkinson in the squad, the Imps beat Darlington 2-0 to finish eighth in the table. It was their highest position since returning to the League but attendances rose only slightly as another heavy loss of nearly £200,000 was made.

Alexander recruited the experienced Mark Smith (Notts County) and Steve Mardenborough (Darlington) over the summer break with wide man David Johnson arriving from Sheffield Wednesday for a £32,000 fee at the beginning of September. The highlight of the 1993/94 season was provided by the two Coca-Cola Cup-ties with Premiership Everton. The first leg at Sincil Bank attracted a crowd of more than 9,000, who saw City take the lead on 17 minutes when Johnson exchanged passes with David Puttnam before scoring with a clinical shot. Everton fought back to go 3-1 up, before Neil Matthews pulled a goal back. Then Grant Brown equalised with a powerful header from Puttnam's free kick, only for Paul Rideout to score again to send the Imps to a 4-3 defeat. The return leg was just as exciting, with City twice falling behind, only to equalise, before going down to two late goals, making the aggregate score 8-5 to Everton.

The long ball style had been discarded in favour of open, attacking football, and although the team looked good going forwards, the fragile nature of the defence led to a series of disappointing results and they spent the whole of the season in the lower reaches of the table. The final position of 18th was the worst since League status was regained, and it came as no surprise when manager Alexander was sacked and replaced by Sam Ellis, captain of the former Imps team under Graham Taylor, who had been assisting at the club on a casual basis since March.

Despite a return to long ball tactics, Ellis brought improvements to the team, his main achievement being to build a solid side which showed grit and determination throughout, even if the tactics employed were not always adventurous. Nevertheless the team again failed to break into the top half of the table, and the most memorable performances of the 1994/95 season came once more in the Coca-Cola Cup. Victory over Chester City earned the Imps a Second Round tie against Crystal Palace. The first leg at Sincil Bank produced a shock for the Premiership club as the hardworking Imps took the lead on 61 minutes.

David Johnson scored a simple goal after the visitors' 'keeper Martyn failed to gather a shot from winger Puttnam, and City then held on for a 1-0 win. The return leg at Selhurst Park was a dour affair with Lincoln defending in depth for most of the match. They appeared to have succeeded in blunting the Palace attack, but with the match five minutes into injury time Dean Gordon snatched a controversial goal to take the tie into extra time. Palace then scored twice to go through 3-1 on aggregate, but it had been a brave performance by the Imps.

Trevor Hebberd fires a shot towards the Palace goal during the Selhurst Park clash in 1994.

They showed similar battling qualities in the F.A. Cup, defeating Second Division Hull City and Huddersfield Town to reach the Third Round for the first time since the 1976/77 season. Drawn against Palace for a second time they were heavily defeated by a 5-1 margin. Off the field the season produced a massive loss of £464,000 - the fifth occasion in the previous seven years that a substantial deficit had been reported. But one bright spot was the completion of the Sincil Bank redevelopment, with the opening of the Linpave Stand, which had been built on the site previously occupied by uncovered terracing. The 5,700 seat structure raised the capacity of the 'new' stadium to almost 11,000.

The 1995/96 season proved to be one of the most eventful in the club's recent history. A series of uninspiring performances led to the departure of manager Ellis in September, and the appointment of the former Chelsea and Queens Park Rangers defender Steve Wicks as 'Head Coach'. Wicks possessed excellent communication skills and quickly endeared himself to the fans with a switch to a passing game with an attacking approach. Unfortunately, although sometimes exciting to watch, the new style rarely brought goals, and with the defence leaking badly at the other end just one point was gained from eight League games. The side fell to the bottom of the table and with the prospect of relegation to the Vauxhall Conference Wicks was dismissed after 42 days in office. The board then turned to John Beck who had been a controversial, but successful, proponent of the long ball game at Cambridge before moving on to Preston North End. Speedy winger Darren Huckerby was sold to Newcastle for a club record fee of £400,000, and a small amount of this was made available to Beck to restructure the team.

Sam Ellis - Manager no.1 ....Steve Wicks - Manager no.2.......... and the third manager in seven weeks - John Beck.

By Christmas only four of the side who had appeared in the opening game of the season now featured regularly in the first team. However pride was restored, results improved, and the threat of relegation receded. The Imps finished the season in 18th position - 24 points clear of bottom of the table Torquay. The sale of another talented youngster, Matt Carbon, to Derby County for £385,000 ensured that a healthy profit was made for the first time in several years.

1996/97 was Beck's first full season in charge and it proved to be a time of consolidation as he slowly reshaped the side. However the club featured regularly in national newspaper and television stories, with the debut of Newcastle's £15 million signing Alan Shearer in a pre-season friendly at Sincil Bank, a pitch invasion of home fans at Brighton in October, and Terry Fleming's mysterious 'double booking' against Wigan all making the headlines. League performances were inconsistent but a late run brought the team close to earning a place in the end-of-season play-offs, only to see their hopes dashed with a home defeat by Rochdale.

Darren Huckerby takes on a Huddersfield defender, during his brief first team career with the Imps - he developed through City's youth team.

Even so the final position of ninth was a respectable one, and a great improvement on the previous season. Once again the Coca-Cola Cup provided the main excitement. Drawn against First Division Manchester City in the second round of the competition, the Imps went a goal down in the first minute but then stormed back to dominate the game. Fleming headed home Gareth Ainsworth's cross to equalise on 30 minutes, then the visitors capitulated as headers from Steve Holmes and Gijs Bos, plus a fine shot from full-back Jon Whitney tied up a magnificent 4-1 victory. Lincoln took around 2,000 fans to Maine Road for the second leg and it was another night of celebration with a simple goal from Bos and a solid defensive performance earning them a remarkable 5-1 aggregate win. City travelled to Southampton for the third round, and again upset higher grade opposition with their direct style of play. Another fine display saw Ainsworth equalise with a goal five minutes from time to earn a 2-2 draw. The replay attracted a gate of over 10,500 to Sincil Bank, with Ainsworth giving the Imps an early lead, only for the Premiership side to draw level with a disputed penalty, and then clinch the tie with two late goals.

John Reames (City chairman since March 1983), left, presents Hall of Fame certificates to Andy Graver and Tony Emery (right) at the inaugural dinner in May 1996.

The last ten years have seen the club transform Sincil Bank from a run-down ground with poor facilities into a magnificent modern stadium. However League performances have generally been uninspiring with the team often struggling to reach a mid-table position, and yet to feature in the end-of-season play-offs. Nevertheless the club can look back with pride on its 113 years of history and look forward to the rapidly approaching millennium with a sense of optimism.

61

CHAPTER FOUR: THE GROUNDS

JOHN O'GAUNTS

Adjacent to St.Peter-at-Gowts Church, John O'Gaunts was City's home for their first eleven years. The ground takes its name from the fact that the entrance was at one time used as stables for John O'Gaunts House which stood on the opposite side of the High Street. It was chosen by the club''s founders due to its location being close to the city centre and also to the area where many of the potential supporters lived and worked. The field was owned by Robert Dawber who was a former Lincoln F.C. player and he was supportive to the club throughout their tenancy, often allowing rent to remain unpaid during times of financial difficulty.

The ground was entered through the stables which were of medieval origin, and the field was reached by a footpath through the builders yard which stood behind the entrance. The pitch lay on an east-west axis and had a noticeable slope down to the Sincil Drain end. St Peter-at-Gowts Church stood behind the other goal.

To begin with the ground was little more than an enclosed field with spectators standing on the grass to watch. Improvements were made over the summer of 1885 and by the end of the year a small, open grandstand capable of holding around 400 fans had appeared. A second uncovered stand was built for the F.A. Cup match with Middlesbrough in November 1886, although this seems to have been a temporary structure. A larger covered stand was added on the Monson Street side in September 1889, this was about 80 feet long. There is no record of any further development. The ground was rarely filled and the highest attendance was 7,000 for the visit of F.A. Cup finalists Notts County for a League match. Three early floodlit games were staged, the last of which took place on 31 January 1894 when Sheffield United were the visitors. The players seemed to have had little trouble in the dark although the generators used to power the lights were very noisy. City won 1-0 in front of around 3,000 spectators.

Robert Dawber died at the end of August 1894 and when the will was settled the ground was put up for sale by auction. It was purchased by builders, and Sibthorp, Abbot and Nelthorpe Streets currently stand on the site. The last match played there was on 30 April 1895 when City beat Gainsborough Trinity 2-0 in the Lincolnshire Charity Cup Final.

SINCIL BANK

When the club were forced to leave their home at John O'Gaunts they moved just a few hundred yards away to a site on the opposite side of the Sincil Drain. This was probably the same field that the Lindum club had hired back in the 1880s. The ground was completely undeveloped, and John Irving later recalled, *"We took an old stand from John O'Gaunts to the new ground and dressing rooms were built on practically the same site as that in use today."* (Lincs. Echo, 16 Nov 1929). The cost of the move set the club back financially and was the main reason for the change to a limited company.

The first match at the new ground was a friendly against Gainsborough Trinity, and Woolwich Arsenal provided the opposition for the first Football League game which took place on 14 September 1895. In the summer of 1896 a small uncovered stand was built at the South Park end, turnstiles were added, and the rope surrounding the pitch was replaced with wire. The ground was more fully developed between 1898 and 1902 with the help of the Working Men's Committee. Extensive banking was added around the field, and in the summer of 1899 a covered stand holding around 400 was built on the Sincil Bank side - this was known as the Working Men's Stand. In 1901 another stand was built behind the South Park goal, with the existing structure moved to the south-east corner alongside the main grandstand. In 1902 the St Andrews stand along the eastern side was enlarged and moved back to allow a permanent cycling and athletics track to be laid down in front of it.

The Working Men's Committee made small improvements every summer, adding turnstiles, extra banking, and new dressing rooms with plunge and shower baths. In February 1908 a section of the stands on the St Andrews side was destroyed by a storm which uprooted the supports, with five spectators requiring hospital treatment. By 1915 the ground consisted of three covered stands on the St Andrews, South Park, and Sincil Bank sides, with banking around the remaining areas to provide a better view for those who chose to stand up.

The ground survived the Great War intact, and when the club's finances improved in the mid-1920s further improvements were made. In 1925 a small shelter was built at the centre of the railway end, partly paid for by the supporters club which had established a fund to raise £1,200 to cover the whole of the north side of the ground, and most of the work was carried out by the Working

A panoramic view of the St.Andrews side of the ground, taken pre-1925.

Men's Committee. The area under the South Park stand was also developed at this time with new offices for the secretary, a boardroom, and a gymnasium. A wooden fence was put up around the perimeter of the pitch which had previously been roped off. By the late 1920s there was clearly a need for major improvements to the ground, particularly to the grandstands which dated from the turn of the century, but the club's position as yearly tenants made the board reluctant to act. In September 1929, the South Park stand was completely gutted by fire which also destroyed the offices and all the club records. A new structure seating 1,500 was erected within six weeks and was used for the first time for the visit of Carlisle United on 16 November.

Shortly afterwards the ground was purchased from Colonel Swann for £4,875. Ownership gave the directors the confidence to proceed with modernising the stadium and fundamental changes were made over the next few years. In the summer of 1931, the covered area at the railway end was extended by adding a second small shelter, and terracing was laid down. In the following close season the St Andrews stand was demolished to be replaced by a new structure with a capacity of 2,250, and at the same time concrete terracing was laid down in front of both this and the South Park stand. A decline in the club's finances prevented any further major developments, although in 1936 the Lincoln Imp Social Club was opened under the South Park stand to sell alcohol and refreshments, and it remained until war broke out in 1939.

Sincil Bank was requisitioned by the A. R. P. services for the duration of the Second World War, but despite the efforts of Alf Young and the volunteer work force it fell into a state of disrepair. When peace returned money was readily available for improvements but resources were scarce. Sufficient concrete blocks were obtained to replace the fencing around the pitch with a wall behind the two goals in 1945, and this was extended to the St Andrews and Sincil Bank sides twelve months later. In 1947 the A.R.P. cleansing station was converted to modern dressing rooms and the old wooden structure demolished and removed. The capacity of the ground was increased to 25,000 in 1948 when the Sincil Bank stand, which was in a poor state of repair, was demolished and the wood from it was used to create a bank of shale terracing.

From the 1950s the ground was developed further through the donations of the supporters club. Concrete terracing was laid down on the Sincil Bank side during the 1952/53 season, and by the end of the decade the 'Spion Kop' area in the north-east corner had been concreted over and covered with a shelter. Proposals by the club to build a new stand linking the St Andrews and South Park structure were discussed in detail in the mid-1950s but never came to fruition. The field at the rear of the St Andrews Stand was purchased in 1955. And this was used for training and as a venue for 'A' team fixtures.

Floodlighting was installed in 1962, again paid for by the supporters club. Two years later a social club was opened beneath the South Park stand, but the 1960s were generally a period of decline and financial crisis for the club. They began to emerge from this towards the end of the decade and the replayed League Cup-tie against Derby County in November 1967 attracted a new record attendance of 23,196. In September 1975 the wall behind the South Park goal collapsed during the League Cup match with Stoke, and this section of terracing was never used again. The original floodlights were replaced with a new and more powerful set in February 1977 with the old lights being sold to Spalding United.

Following a substantial loss in the 1981/82 season, the directors sold the ground to the City Council for £225,000 to ensure the future of League football in Lincoln. The original agreement was on a 25-year lease but this was extended to 125 years shortly after. The Safety of Sports Grounds Act of 1975 raised the profile of safety which became a top priority following the tragic fire at Bradford in May 1985. With a ground dating from the 1930s, and two stands principally of timber construction, urgent work

September 1970.
The superb view towards the railway end, as City attack the Brentford goal in the 4th Division clash at Sincil Bank.

was needed at Sincil Bank. The South Park stand was closed to spectators for the 1985/86 campaign but was then reopened in the following season after the St Andrews stand was demolished in the summer of 1986. This was the prelude to the final period of redevelopment of the ground. The first stage of this saw a new St Andrews stand seating 1,400 opened in November 1987. The South Park and railway ends were both demolished in the early months of 1990, and in August of the same year the Stacey-West stand - named after two long serving City fans who died in the Bradford fire - was opened at the north end of the ground. A new South Park stand with 17 executive boxes was operational in the summer of 1992. The E.G.T. Family stand appeared alongside the St Andrews stand in 1994, and the final stage of the redevelopment saw the completion of the 5,700 seat Linpave stand in March 1995 to replace the open terracing on the Sincil Bank side. A modern floodlighting system was also installed at this time. The total cost of rebuilding the ground amounted to around £3 million, with significant contributions coming from both the City Council and the Football Trust. Sincil Bank now has a capacity of 10,918, all under cover, and with around 9,000 seats making it one of the best stadiums in the lower divisions of the Football League.

Over the years the ground has hosted many different events including a visit from Queen Elizabeth II in June 1958, and a major pop concert in May 1966 featuring groups such as The Who, The Kinks and The Small Faces. Gainsborough Trinity used Sincil Bank on a couple of occasions around the turn of the century for Football League games when the Northolme was unavailable, whilst local cricket and football finals, boxing, wrestling, athletics, cycling, grass track motorcycling, greyhound racing, professional lawn tennis, and American football have all taken place at one time or another. However, perhaps the most unusual of all the events were the sheep dog trials held as part of the 'Holidays at Home' week in the summer of 1943.

The St.Andrews stand in the mid-1980s, shortly before it was demolished.

CHAPTER FIVE: SUPPORTERS ORGANISATIONS

THE WORKING MEN'S COMMITTEE

The Working Men's Committee was formed at the start of the 1896/97 season. The newly established limited company was having financial problems and secretary Alf Martin saw it as a way of enabling ordinary supporters to buy shares in the club. He outlined his plans at the company's half-yearly meeting in September 1896. His objective was "......to get 500 or 600 people in Lincoln to subscribe ls each and for that money to be taken up in shares, the subscribers thus being enable [sic] to send a certain number of representatives to the shareholders meeting. The subscribers to would hold a meeting every month to ventilate their opinions about the men, and the directors would thus get to know the feeling of the working classes on all matters connected with the club." (Lincs. Chronicle, 4 Sep 1896). Martin also felt that a committee could be useful in other areas such as fund raising.

The committee were very active in their early years and between 1898 and 1902 they developed the Sincil Bank ground, arranging the construction of the South Park and Sincil Bank stands and carrying out several other improvements. Once the stands were built they retained half the takings to enable them to pay off the costs. They were also involved in several schemes to raise money for the club, collecting regularly for summer wages which were always a burden for the parent club. In 1898 the committee were given the task of running the reserve team. They picked the side, accompanied the players to away games and recruited local men to supplement the professionals available to them. Amongst the talent they developed were players such as 'Corky' Blow, Wally Smith and Freddy Simpson who all became first team regulars around the turn of the century. They retained control of the reserves until around 1909 when an assistant trainer was appointed. Further recognition came to the committee at the company's 1898 annual general meeting when it was agreed to allow them three of the 12 places on the board of directors. In 1900 five of the board members had previously served the committee but only two - Fred Quincey (1900-1906) and John Burley (1900-1920) - remained for any length of time.

The committee were also active in the day-to-day activities of the club, assisting as gate men and working around the ground. In 1900 its activities were described thus: *"It is composed of working men to the number of sixteen who work, literally, in and out of season and give their service absolutely free. On match days they are on the ground an hour before the kick-off assisting in the preparation for the crowd and lending a general hand here, there and everywhere. In the 'off season' they are still of great value. Last season for several Saturdays they came along with hammer, chisel and saw and did a great deal for the improvement of the ground while they were the moving spirits in the erection of the new stand, the debt on which they are vigorously wiping out."* (Athletic News, 9 Apr 1900).

The committee continued to work for the club, although its main functions became limited to providing gatemen and undertaking minor repairs to the ground. This role continued after the First World War when they were instrumental in developing the area under the original South Park stand into a gymnasium and boardroom. In 1925 they enlarged the dressing rooms and the following summer they cleared the area behind the Sincil Bank stand and built a cycle shed. North Jubb, who had been chairman of the committee since 1899, was elected to the board in 1923, serving until his death in 1946. He had worked at Robey's at one time, but by 1901 he had a small shop on the High Street and for many years he was the local agent for the Unionist (Conservative) Party. There were a number of men who served the committee for lengthy periods. George Knott, who was one of the founder members, had acted as a volunteer cashier after the war before being appointed assistant secretary at the club in 1930, a post he held until 1939. William Gretton who was secretary of the committee from 1902 until at least 1930 worked as a gateman and then cashier at Sincil Bank for 50 years.

The last public mention of the Working Men's Committee was in 1930, although at this point it was said to be a live force. It would seem that as time went by the membership became more elderly and the formal organisation of the committee declined. There is evidence to suggest a degree of organisation even after the Second World War with the work on the perimeter wall around the pitch being completed by volunteers. Significantly when the club decided to dispense with Gretton's services in June 1953 his chosen successor refused the post and a total of eight gatemen were dismissed.

The Working Men's Committee has an important role in the wider football world as a very early example of organisation amongst a club's followers which precedes the formation of supporters clubs from the early 1900s.

It is impossible to evaluate its success against the original objectives due to an absence of factual information. There is no record of how many subscribed to the committee, how many shares they controlled or how these were allocated. However it is clear that whilst it did not herald a rush by ordinary working men to buy shares in the club it achieved great success in other areas, particularly as a fund raising body and volunteer workforce for the Imps.

The Lincoln City Football Club Supporters Club.

Statement of Accounts for the period from 17th May, 1925 to 10th August, 1926.

RECEIPTS.	£ s. d.		PAYMENTS.	£ s. d.	
To Cash at Bank, 17th May, 1925	70 0 0		By Grants to the Lincoln City Football Club, Ltd.	150 0 0	
" Subscriptions	44 12 9		" Season Tickets purchased	38 11 0	
" Advertising	4 0 0		" Shares purchased as per contra	2 0 0	
" Season Ticket Subscriptions	35 1 0		" Management Expenses:		
" Shelter Fund Subscriptions	3 7 0		Printing, Stationery, Advertising, &c.	21 8 5	
" Shares in Lincoln City Football Club, Ltd.	2 0 0		Accommodation for Meetings	2 2 0	
" Bank Interest	3 6		Mr. A. C. Walker, Honorarium 2 years	15 0 0	
" Miscellaneous	3 16 0		Mrs. Walker, Office Rent 2 years	10 0 0	
" Proceeds of Whist Drives, Draws, Band Collections, &c., viz.:			Bank Charges	1 6 0	
National Institute for the Blind	15 9 6		Miscellaneous	13 6 11	63 3 4
Alf. Jewitt	64 17 2		" Payments to the following, viz.:		
T. Anthony	12 16 7	93 3 3	National Institute for the Blind	15 9 6	
" Gross proceeds from Entertainments,			Alf. Jewitt	49 2 11	
Outing Fund	246 19 5		Expenses re Alf. Jewitt	21 9 3	
Raffles	157 9 10		T. Anthony	10 16 0	96 17 8
Concerts	105 12 11		" Expenses of Entertainments, &c., viz.:		
Boxing Match	84 10 5		Outing Fund	245 18 2	
Bands on Ground	78 11 11		Raffles	69 0 1	
Motor Cycle Sports	70 13 5		Concerts	113 11 9	
Tennis Club	70 13 4		Boxing Match	75 11 10	
Whist Drives and Dances	37 9 4		Bands on Ground	75 19 5	
Social Evening	4 2 6	856 3 1	Motor Cycle Sports	47 17 2	
			Tennis Club	62 2 2	
			Whist Drives and Dances	45 16 3	
W. A. HOWITT, *Honorary Treasurer.*			Social Evening	6 2 3	741 4 1
			" Cash at Bank, 10th August, 1926	20 10 6	
	£1112 6 7			£1112 6 7	

We have examined the foregoing Account of the Receipts and Payments with the Treasurer's Books and Vouchers and have found the same in accordance therewith.

Lincoln, 10th August, 1926.

H. BRADLEY,
A. W. BENTLEY, *Honorary Auditors.*

was handed over towards the cost of the shelter at the railway end in 1925 and they also paid for a band to entertain spectators before matches and at half-time.

In 1927 the secretary was promoted to a new job in Nottingham and transferred his allegiance to the Notts County Supporters Club. Following his departure the Lincoln club declined rapidly. Membership dropped, donations to the parent club dried up (only £38 was handed over in the 1928/29 season) and the position of secretary changed hands twice in three years. The football club's financial records show no money was received from the supporters club after September 1929, and in May of 1930 the secretary Mr H. Lill was called before the board to discuss matters. The outcome was that he announced his resignation and it seems that the club folded at this point, just seven years after it had been formed.

THE FIRST SUPPORTERS CLUB: 1923 TO 1930

The first Lincoln City Supporters Club was formed at the time of the 1923 financial crisis, the inaugural meeting taking place at the Constitutional Club. After hearing the guest speakers - football club officials, local councillors and representatives from the supporters clubs at Doncaster and Chesterfield - a small organising committee was set up. Annual subscriptions were fixed at 1s (5p) and it was decided to model the structure of the committee on the Doncaster club, with two representatives from each council ward within the city boundaries. Quarterly meetings were held for the first few years with the committee and officers elected at the annual general meeting. Their activities included regular fund-raising events (in 1926 a weekly dance and whist drive was held at the St Andrews Hall), and organising outings to an away match each season. Arrangements were also made for members to buy season tickets and shares on an instalment basis. The club worked in harmony with the Working Men's Committee who were allocated a place on the original organising group and their joint Grand Bazaar in December 1927 raised over £1,000.

The club was quite successful in its early years, mostly coinciding with the period when the secretary was a railway clerk named Walker. Three hundred members had joined in the first month and the total eventually rose to 800 at its peak, meetings were well attended, and the badge they produced sold 400 in a very short time. A substantial sum

THE SECOND SUPPORTERS CLUB: 1952 TO DATE

After their experiences in the 1920s, the board refused to allow a new supporters organisation to be formed until 1952, six years after the idea was first suggested at a shareholders' meeting. In the intervening period a number of unofficial supporters clubs had been set up including one at the Duke William public house on Bailgate.

The second Lincoln City Supporters Club was formed in April 1952, holding its first meeting in a room above Deeks hairdressers in Guildhall Street. Clarence West was elected chairman and plans were made to liaise with a similar group which existed within the local engineering works. Subscriptions were set at 2s-6d (12½p) for adults and 1s (5p) for juveniles. Membership was so popular that by June over 3,200 had joined and there were 14 rural branches as well as sections in all the engineering works. The largest and most active of the groups outside of the city was at Sleaford where there were more than 150 members under the chairmanship of Bill Stacey.

The principal objective of the club was to raise money for the football club, and their first donation was the sum of £50 for new playing kit in August 1952. Money was generally raised for specific purposes - the £1,500 handed over in the first season paid for concrete terracing on the Sincil Bank side, their next target of paying for a roof on the 'Spion Kop' section of the railway end was reached in 1957, and in August 1960 they embarked on a campaign to raise £16,000 to instal floodlights on the Sincil Bank ground. Their main source of income was a football pool competition which had over 3,000 members in August 1960, but they also organised whist drives and match day competitions such as '2d On the Ball', and a membership draw.

The Supporters Club make a presentation to chairman Frank Eccleshare (second left), in the mid-1960s. Onlookers include Ron Scott (second right) and Vic Withers (extreme right)

Apart from fund raising the club's other main activity was to arrange trips to away games and these were run by the outings committee. In 1952/53 a total of almost 7,000 adults and children were carried by rail to ten matches, but by 1961, when the team's fortunes had declined, such trips rarely took place. The club's activities were advertised on their own page of the match programme from the 1953/54 season. Membership peaked at 5,700, the numbers declining largely because many did not renew their subscriptions. Activities in the rural branches also waned and in July 1955 it was reported that the only area outside Lincoln to provide support was Sleaford. However, fund raising activities were not affected and by May 1959 more than £11,500 had been handed over to the parent club.

In 1961 former trade union official Ben Sullivan was appointed as a full-time organiser and this led to an increase in fund raising after he launched regular bingo sessions and took charge of the lottery.

The club gave full support to Frank Eccleshare when he took over control of the football club in 1963, remaining a vibrant fund-raising organisation. In September 1965, Sullivan left to take on a similar post at Newcastle United and he was replaced by Brian Baldam who still remains as one of the full-time organisers some 32 years later. Regular donations continued, but a growing disagreement came to a head in the summer of 1973 with the supporters club splitting from the parent club and renaming itself the Lincoln and District Football Supporters Club. The dispute centred around the supporters club's refusal to hand over a substantial sum of money which they had allocated towards the proposed purchase of their own building on Great Northern Terrace. The re-named club continued to raise money for local football, but the £1,000 a month they had been donating to the Imps was badly missed, until a reconciliation took place soon after Dennis Bocock resigned as chairman of the board in April 1974.

The club has since hired premises at the Drill Hall, where they now run bingo sessions twice weekly and have a small social club. Funds are also raised through the Double Chance Lottery, which has almost 7,000 members, and the Development Lottery. Total donations to the football club reached £1 million in April 1991 and currently stand in excess of £1.3 million. Annual donations peaked at £85,000 in the 1985/86 season but have since dropped off slightly - a result of the football club increasing their own fund-raising activities and of competition from the National Lottery. In addition to their much valued fund-raising, the supporters club has also organised the ballot for the football club's player of the season since it was inaugurated in the 1969/70 season.

THE RED IMPS ASSOCIATION

The Red Imps Association was formed as the club's own fund-raising body in the late 1960s. It initially ran a lottery, a re-launch of the Imps Fighting Fund Lottery, and quickly took over the organisation of providing coaches for supporters to travel to away games - a role it still plays. It acted as a volunteer workforce for many years providing staff to run the catering at home matches and looking after the club souvenir shop from when it opened in November 1971 until the early 1990s.

Apart from a period in the 1970s, the Red Imps Association was never as successful as the supporters club in raising money, and its highest annual donation was the £30,000 handed over in the 1993/94 season. Donations have dropped off since then with many of its activities being taken over by the parent club.

CHAPTER SIX .... PUBLICATIONS

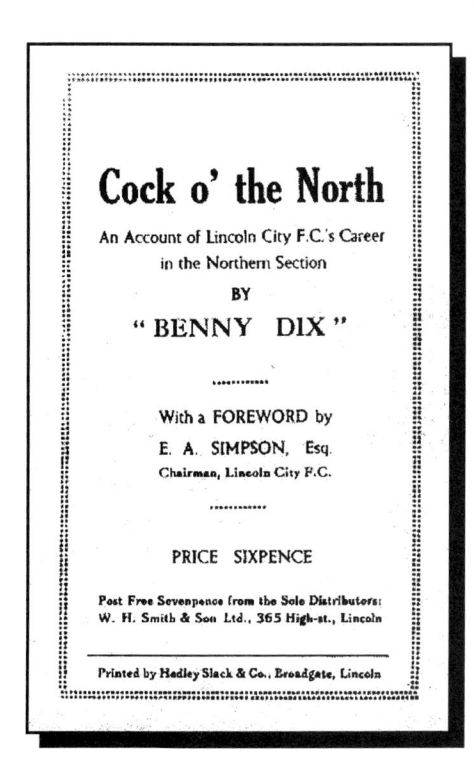

The earliest known publication about the club was a short book *'Some recollections of former players of Lincoln City F.C.'* produced by the Lincolnshire Chronicle newspaper in April 1915. The book consisted of a series of articles written about former players by Ernest Pullein which had been printed in the newspaper over the preceding four months. Pullein's book is extremely scarce with neither the British Library nor Lincoln Central Library possessing a copy.

The Chronicle went on to produce a series of annual football guides in the 1920s which included in depth coverage of City.

City's promotion to Division Two in 1932 was marked by the production of a 62-page paperback book *'Cock O' the North'* by the Lincolnshire Echo football writer Benny Dix. The book details the club's career in the Northern Section of the Third Division from 1921 to 1932. A 16-page photograph album was published at a cost of one shilling (5p) a copy to celebrate promotion in 1947/48 with the 1951/52 Division Three North title marked with a 32 page handbook.

A brief history of the club *'Down the years with Lincoln City'* was published in paperback form in 1954. The 52 page book written by John Sawyer covered the club from it's earliest days through to the end of the 1953/54 season.

A supporters' club magazine *'The Imps'* was produced from September 1967 but ran for just three issues before fading away.

Since that date a number of year books have been published along with newspaper 'specials' produced by the Lincolnshire Echo. To mark the club's centenary a 52-page paperback souvenir was produced by the Lincolnshire Standard Group.

Finally the *'Who's Who of Lincoln City 1892-1994'* was produced by Ian and Donald Nannestad and published by Yore Publications in October 1994. The 180-page paper-back book gives a brief history of the Imps together with biographical details of every player to appear for the club in the Football League along with profiles of each of the men to manage City over the years.

In 1983, the players recorded a 45 r.p.m. record with the proceeds going to the Red Imps Association, with an 'A' side of *You'll Never walk Alone'*, backed by *'The Lincolnshire Poacher'*.

69

PROGRAMMES

The earliest programme known to exist for a match involving Lincoln City is a single sheet card issued for the final of the Lincolnshire County Cup against Grimsby Town on 22 April 1887 (illustrated below). The match was played on a neutral ground at The Northolme, Gainsborough, with the match card being typical of issues of the day giving the team line-ups and space to record goals and corners gained by each team.

Many clubs began to produce programmes of a more conventional type by the late 1890s for both first team and reserve matches but Lincoln did not issue on a regular basis until well into the 20th Century. The oldest issue known is for an FA Cup first round tie against Chelsea at Sincil Bank on 12 January 1907.

Programmes were then issued for most home games, whether first team or reserves, with a redesign of the publication in 1924 producing a big increase in sales.

The eight-page issue continued until 1936/37 when City began issuing a large-sized 12-page programme. The onset of the Second World War led to a paper shortage and City ceased production until 1944/45 when a single sheet issue printed on paper so thin that it was almost transparent was sold at a penny. Normal programme production began the following season and in the ensuing seasons several changes were made before a settled format was found for the period from 1953 to 1964 with the cover dominated by a drawing of the city's famous Cathedral.

The cover appeared in colour from the 1970/71 season (having previously done so in the final two pre-war seasons) and since then the introduction of improved printing technology has seen the issue expand both in content and in quality.

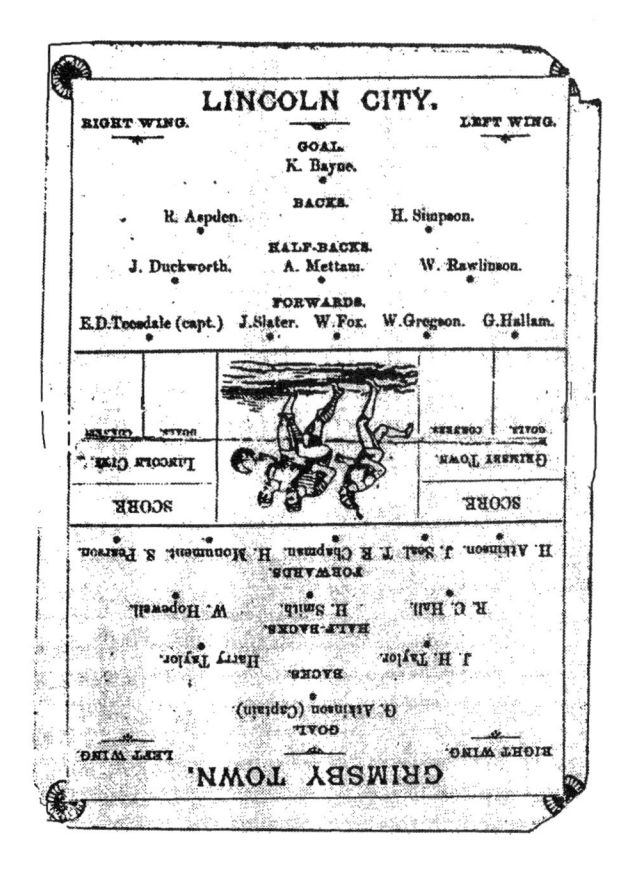

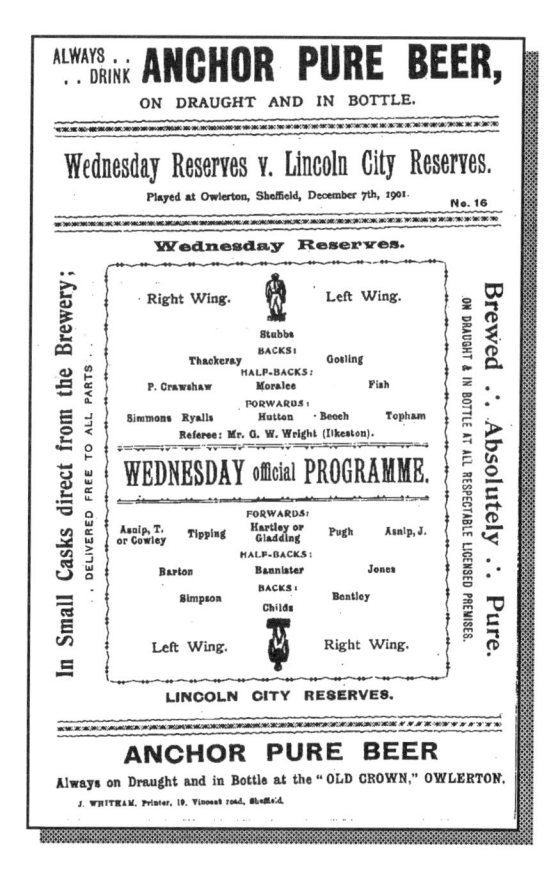

70

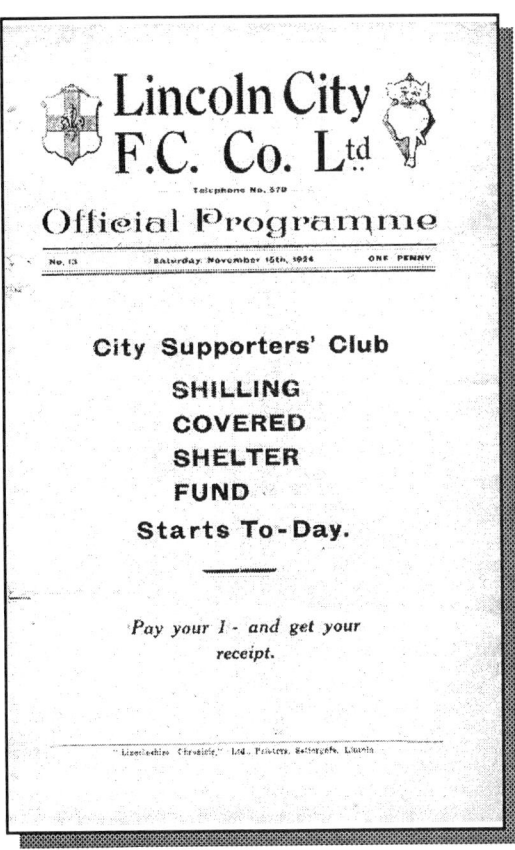

(1924/25 season)

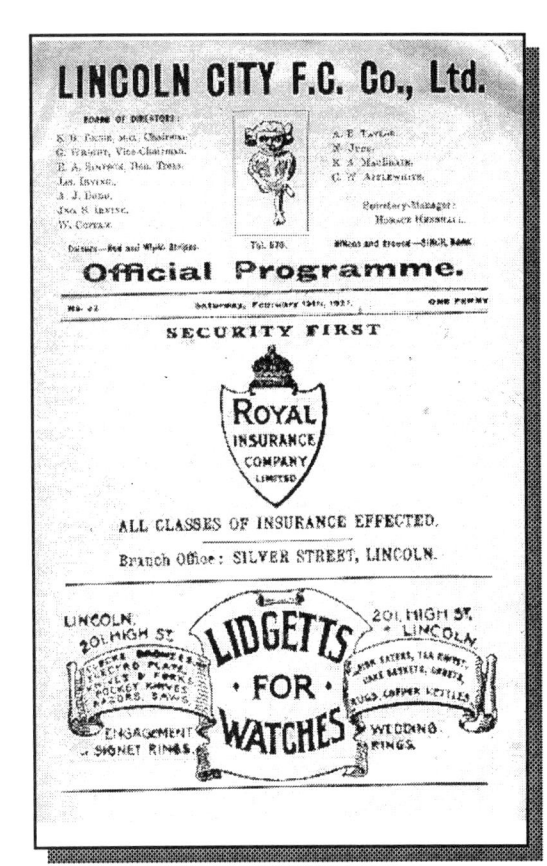

(1926/27 season)

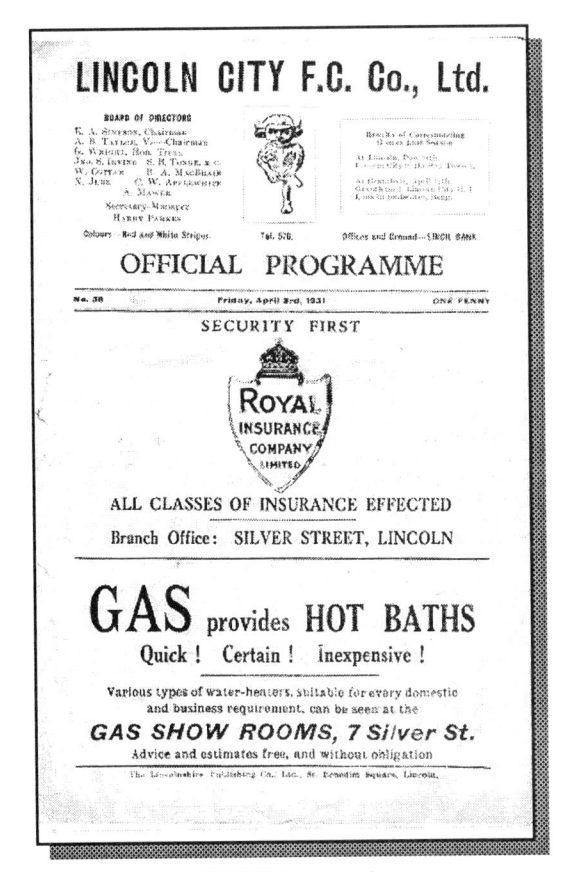

(1930/31 season)

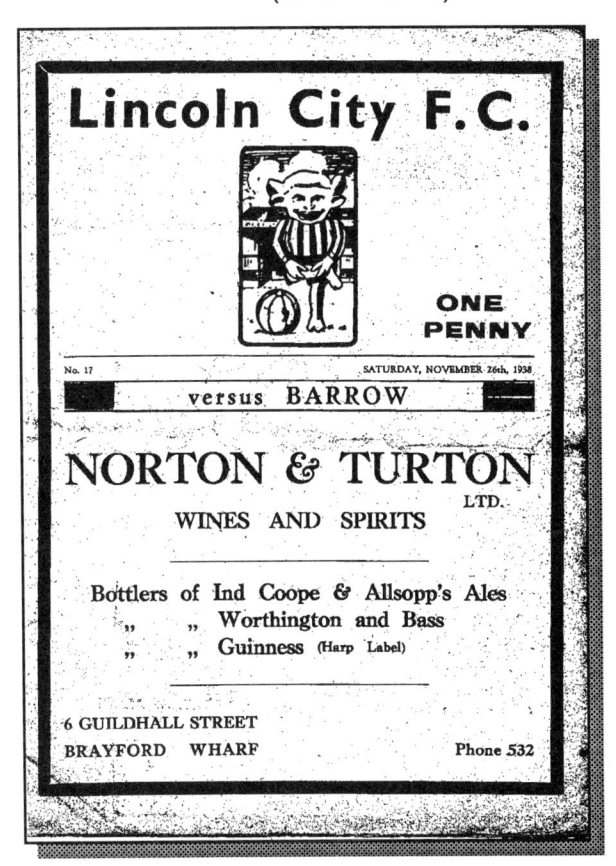

(1938/39 season)

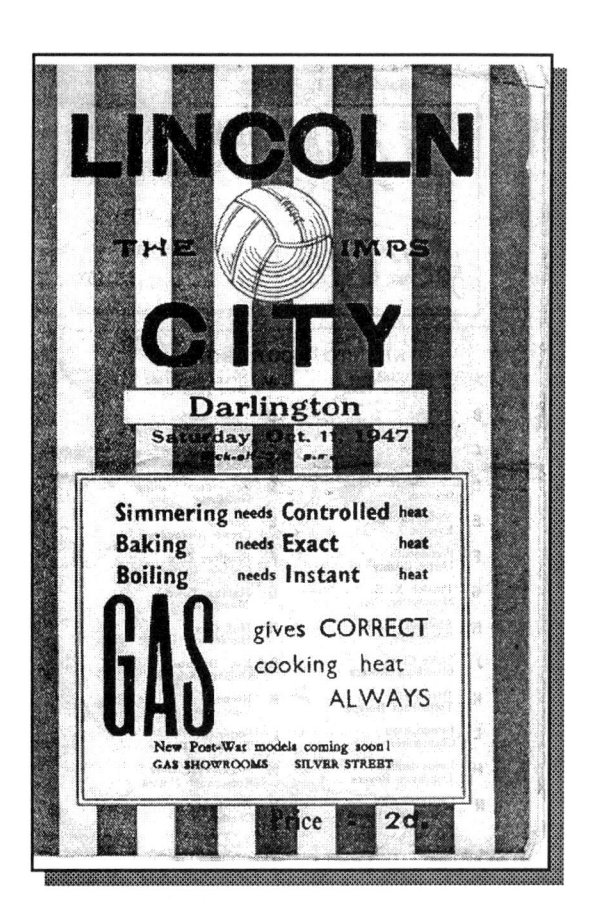

LINCOLN
THE IMPS
CITY
Darlington
Saturday, Oct. 11, 1947

Simmering needs Controlled heat
Baking needs Exact heat
Boiling needs Instant heat

GAS gives CORRECT cooking heat ALWAYS

New Post-War models coming soon!
GAS SHOWROOMS   SILVER STREET

Price — 2d.

LINCOLN CITY
versus
Tottenham Hotspur
Saturday, Aug. 28th
3 p.m. — KICK-OFF

At the top of the table:—
Blaze, Allott's Cakes

Head Office—64 Monson St., Lincoln. Tel: 376
9 Branch Shops.

Official Programme — 2d.

(1948/49 season)

LINCOLN CITY
VERSUS
TRANMERE R.
Good Friday, April 7th
Kick-off 3-0 p.m.
OFFICIAL 2d PROGRAM
No. 183

(1949/50 season)

Lincoln City
versus
Hartlepools United
SATURDAY, 1st SEPTEMBER, 1951
Kick-off 3 p.m.

OFFICIAL 3d. PROGRAMME

★ The Holder of the Winning Number of this Issue of Programme will be paid £1. Please call at Secretary's Office after the Match to receive money.

No. 2613

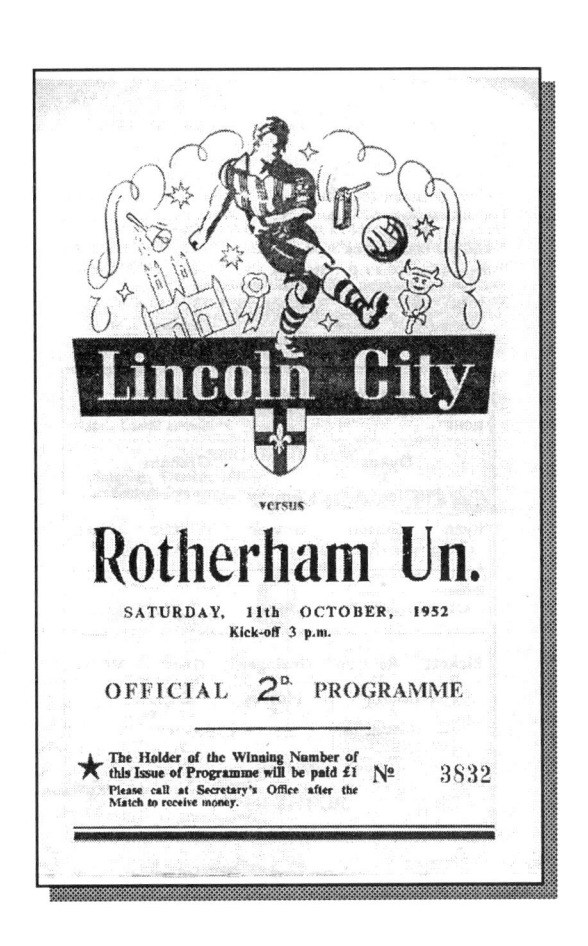

Lincoln City
versus Rotherham Un.
SATURDAY, 11th OCTOBER, 1952
Kick-off 3 p.m.

OFFICIAL 2D PROGRAMME

★ The Holder of the Winning Number of this Issue of Programme will be paid £1. Please call at Secretary's Office after the Match to receive money.

Nº 3832

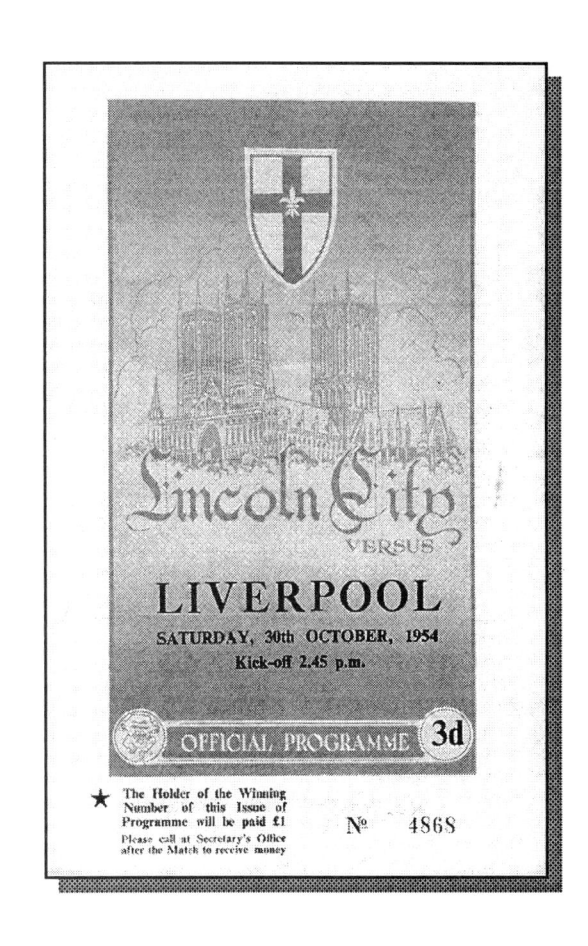

Lincoln City
versus LIVERPOOL
SATURDAY, 30th OCTOBER, 1954
Kick-off 2.45 p.m.

OFFICIAL PROGRAMME 3d

★ The Holder of the Winning Number of this Issue of Programme will be paid £1. Please call at Secretary's Office after the Match to receive money.

Nº 4868

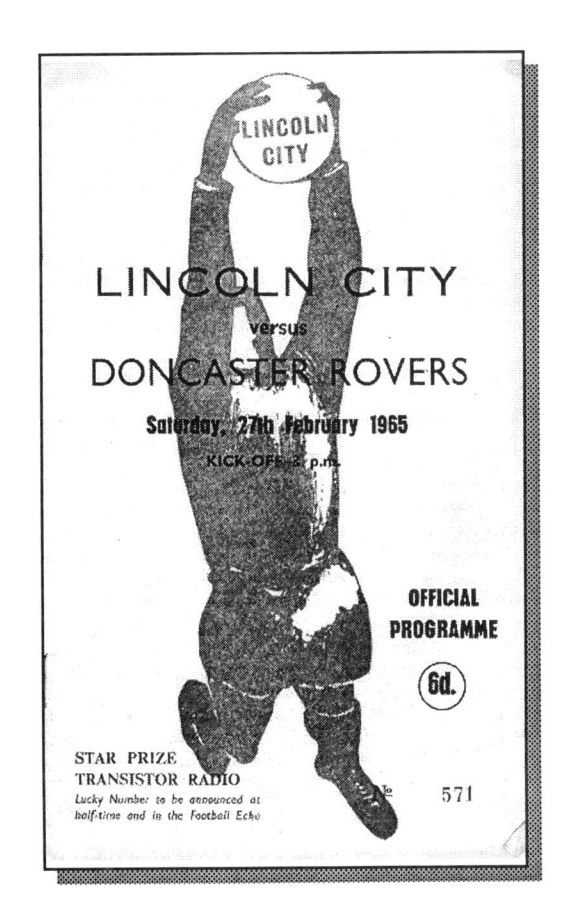

LINCOLN CITY
versus DONCASTER ROVERS
Saturday, 27th February 1965
KICK-OFF 3 p.m.

OFFICIAL PROGRAMME 6d.

STAR PRIZE TRANSISTOR RADIO
Lucky Number to be announced at half-time and in the Football Echo

Nº 571

TWO PRIZES £1/10/0 and £1/0/0
Lucky Numbers to be announced at half-time.

OFFICIAL PROGRAMME 6d.

Lincoln City
versus Colchester U.
Saturday, 12th Feb. 1966
Kick-off 3 p.m.

FOOTBALL LEAGUE DIVISION IV

Nº 646

6d
Official Programme
LINCOLN CITY
FOOTBALL CLUB
Versus
LUTON
SATURDAY 18th NOVEMBER 1967
Football League Division Four
Kick-off 3 p.m.
Next Home Game
City Res v. Halifax
WEDNESDAY 22nd NOVEMBER 1967
North Midlands League

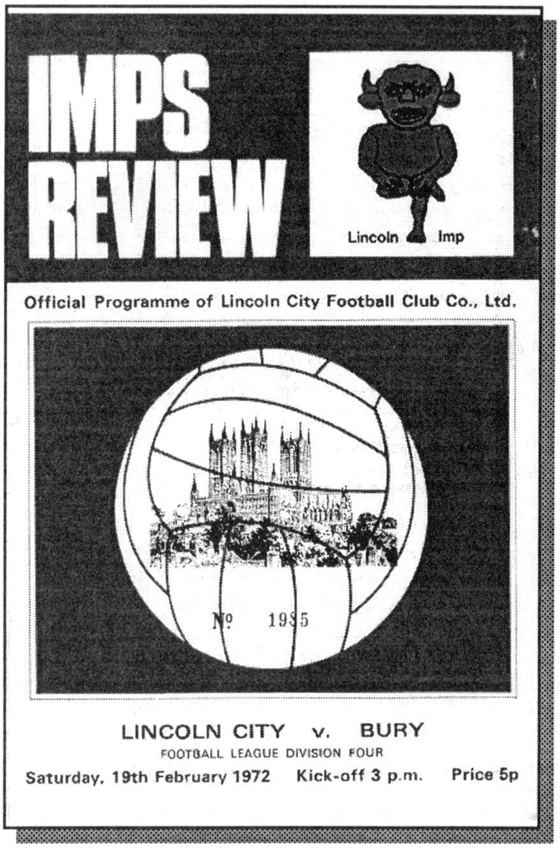
IMPS
REVIEW
Lincoln Imp
Official Programme of Lincoln City Football Club Co., Ltd.
LINCOLN CITY v. BURY
FOOTBALL LEAGUE DIVISION FOUR
Saturday, 19th February 1972
Kick-off 3 p.m.
Price 5p

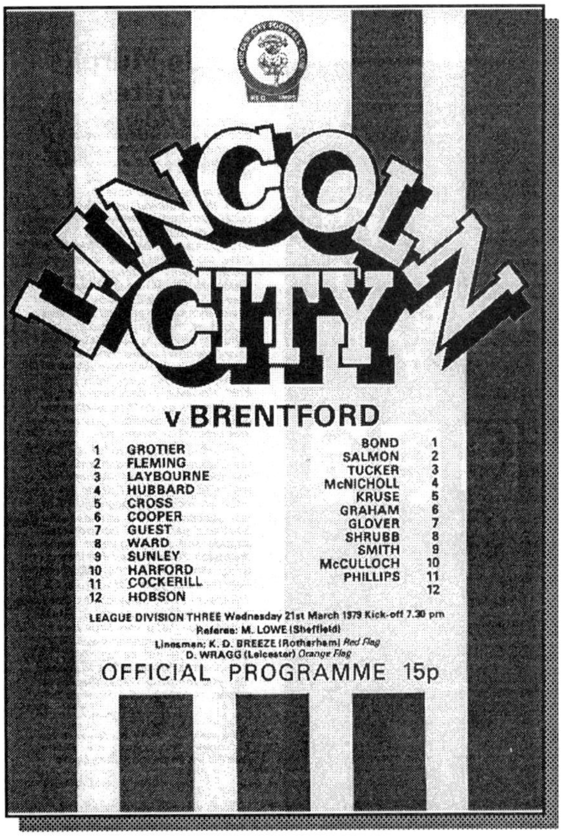
LINCOLN
CITY
v BRENTFORD
1 GROTIER
2 FLEMING
3 LAYBOURNE
4 HUBBARD
5 CROSS
6 COOPER
7 GUEST
8 WARD
9 SUNLEY
10 HARFORD
11 COCKERILL
12 HOBSON
BOND 1
SALMON 2
TUCKER 3
McNICHOLL 4
KRUSE 5
GRAHAM 6
GLOVER 7
SHRUBB 8
SMITH 9
McCULLOCH 10
PHILLIPS 11
12
LEAGUE DIVISION THREE Wednesday 21st March 1979 Kick-off 7.30 pm
Referee: M. LOWE (Sheffield)
Linesmen: K. D. BREEZE (Rotherham) Red Flag
D. WRAGG (Leicester) Orange Flag
OFFICIAL PROGRAMME 15p

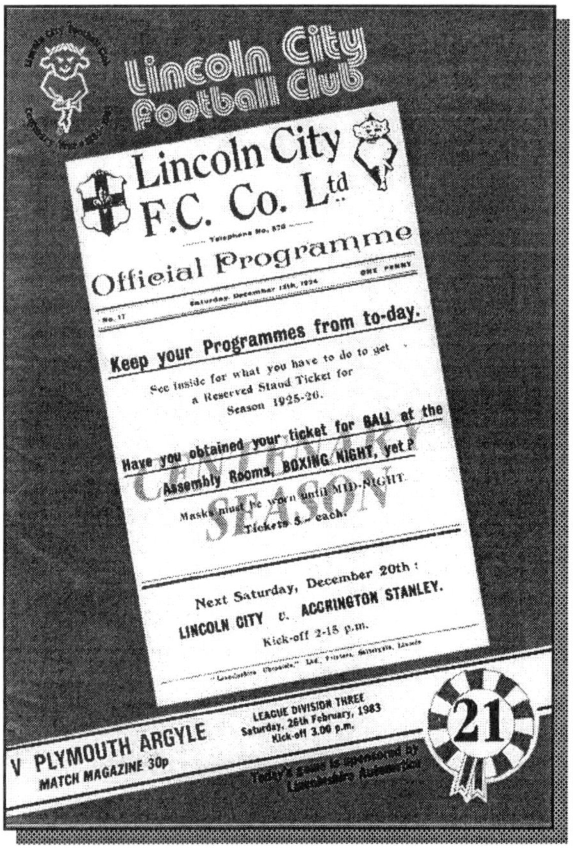
Lincoln City
Football Club
Lincoln City
F.C. Co. Ltd
Official Programme
Keep your Programmes from to-day.
See inside for what you have to do to get
a Reserved Stand Ticket for
Season 1925-26.
Have you obtained your ticket for BALL at the
Assembly Rooms, BOXING NIGHT, yet?
CENTENARY
SEASON
Next Saturday, December 20th:
LINCOLN CITY v. ACCRINGTON STANLEY.
Kick-off 2-15 p.m.
21
V PLYMOUTH ARGYLE
MATCH MAGAZINE 30p
LEAGUE DIVISION THREE
Saturday, 26th February, 1983
Kick-off 3.00 p.m.

LINCOLN CITY
Club Sponsors:
FOSSITT & THORNE
Tyre Distributors
Canon
Sunday, 16th March, 1986
SWANSEA CITY
Kick Off 3.00 p.m.
50p
DIV. III
Today's Match Sponsor is Bunny's Barge & Nightclub

Lincoln City Football Club
GMVC CHAMPIONS 1987-88
MISSION COMPLETED OVER & OUT THE IMPS 'R' BACK
BARCLAYS LEAGUE DIVISION FOUR
S.C.C.
SCARBOROUGH
Saturday, 15th October, 1988
Kick off 3.00 p.m.
60p.
Wheel Horse

season
nineteen ninety one
ninety two
£1.00
LINCOLN CITY
football club
BARCLAYS LEAGUE
DIVISION FOUR
saturday 5th october 1991
kick off 3.00 p.m.
HALIFAX TOWN
main club sponsor
FLINDALLS LTD

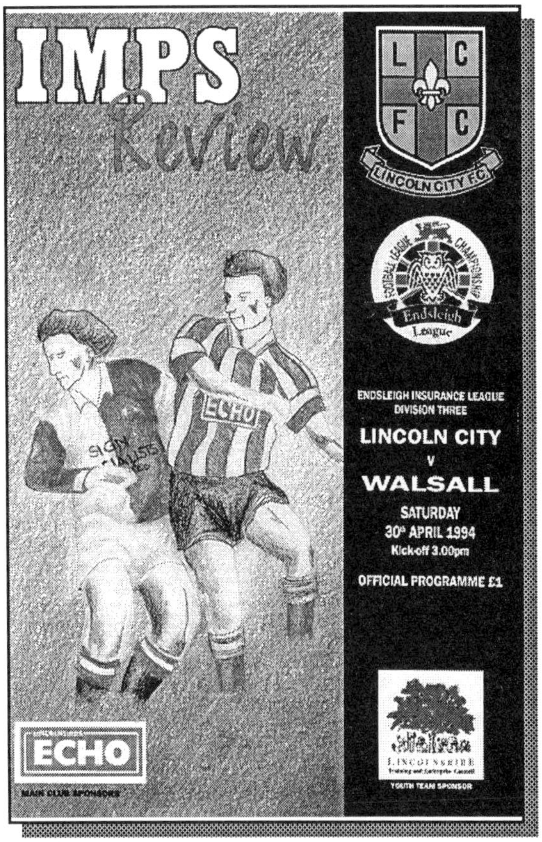
IMPS
Review
L C F C
LINCOLN CITY F.C.
Endsleigh League
ENDSLEIGH INSURANCE LEAGUE
DIVISION THREE
LINCOLN CITY
v
WALSALL
SATURDAY
30th APRIL 1994
Kick-off 3.00pm
OFFICIAL PROGRAMME £1
ECHO
MAIN CLUB SPONSORS
YOUTH TEAM SPONSOR

CHAPTER SEVEN: ENCYCLOPEDIA

ABANDONED GAMES

The Imps have been involved in the following matches abandoned before the final whistle:

Date	Year	Opponent	H/A	Score	Notes	Competition
29 Sep	1892	Grimsby Town	a	2-2	(bad weather)	Friendly
1 Dec	1894	Rotherham Town	a	1-1	(Flewitt) (65 mins - fog)	FL - Div 2
21 Mar	1896	Glossop North End	a	2-3	(80 mins - crowd trouble)	Friendly
20 Mar	1899	Gainsborough Trinity	a	0-0	(68 mins - snow)	Lincs Cup - SF
17 Mar	1900	Grimsby Town	h	0-2	(65 mins - snow)	FL - Div 2
7 Nov	1900	Gainsborough Trinity	a	1-1	(McInnes) aet (100 mins bad light)	FACup-3Qf rep
23 Nov	1907	Glossop	a	0-1	(65 mins - bad light)	FL - Div 2
27 Nov	1909	Oldham Athletic	a	2-4	(Scanlon, Langham)(81 mins bad light)	FL - Div 2
6 Jan	1912	Burnley Reserves	a	0-1	(45 mins - snow)	Central League
13 Feb	1915	Hull City	a	0-0	(54 mins - waterlogged pitch)	FL - Div 2
31 Jan	1925	Nelson	h	1-1	(Page) (70 mins - waterlogged pitch)	FL - Div 3N
9 Apr	1927	Wrexham	a	0-2	(60 mins - bad weather) att. 952	FL - Div 3N
30 Sep	1929	Stockport County	h	1-1	(own goal)(80 mins bad light) att.3,220	FL - Div 3N
28 Dec	1929	Rochdale	a	1-1	(Roberts)(45 mins mud) att 1,648	FL - Div 3N
11 Dec	1937	Mansfield Town	a	2-1	(White, Towler)(66 mins - bad light) att 11,809	FA Cup - R2
8 Mar	1958	Cardiff City	h	0-3	(45 mins - snow) att 7,101	FL - Div 2
19 Oct	1966	Crewe Alexandra	a	1-0	(Anderson)(37 mins-floodlight failure) att 3,588	FL - Div 4
21 Oct	1968	Grimsby Town	a	0-1	(21 mins - fog) att 765	Lincs Cup- R1
4 Dec	1976	Crystal Palace	h	0-1	(61 mins - frozen pitch) att 7,582	FL - Div 3
29 Dec	1976	York City	a	1-1	(Hubbard) (54 mins - frozen pitch) att 2,871	FL - Div 3
14 Dec	1979	Chesterfield	h	0-0	(52 mins - rain)	Friendly
12 Jan	1982	Luton Town	h	0-0	(51 mins - fog)	Friendly
27 Nov	1982	Oxford United	a	0-0	(64 mins - fog) att 5,540	FL - Div3
22 Dec	1982	Gainsborough Trinity	a	7-0	(70 mins - frozen pitch)	Friendly
11 May	1985	Bradford City	a	0-0	(42 mins - fire in main stand) att 11,076	FL - Div 3
8 Sep	1990	York City	a	0-0	(45 mins-death of York player D.Longhurst)att 1,900	FL-Div4
1 Feb	1992	York City	h	0-0	(45 mins - fog) att 1,749	FL - Div 4

The abandoned match against Cardiff in March 1958 led to one of the most nailbiting finishes to any season for City. The game was replayed as the last match of the season with the Imps having to draw to avoid relegation. A crowd of 18,001 packed into Sincil Bank to see Lincoln escape the drop with a 3-1 win.

The result of the Bradford fire match on 11 May 1985 was allowed to stand without being replayed. 56 people died making it one of the worst sporting tragedies in British history.

AGE

Shane Nicholson became the youngest player to appear in a competitive match for the Imps since the war when he came on as a substitute for the final five minutes of City's Littlewoods Challenge Cup second round first leg clash with Charlton on 23 September 1986. Nicholson was 16 yrs and 112 days old at the time. He made his Football League debut in the match at Burnley two months later. The only other two 16 year-olds to appear in the League for City are Carl Dawson (at 16 yrs 300 days) in 1950-51 and Craig Stones (16 yrs 309 days) in 1996-97. The oldest post-war player to appear in City's colours is goalkeeper John Burridge who was 42 yrs and 57 days when he played his final match for the Imps against Rochdale in January 1994. Veteran keeper Albert Iremonger was even older when he played for the Imps in a 3-1 win at Doncaster Rovers in April 1927 at the age of 42 yrs and 312 days.

76

APPEARANCES

The club record for appearances in Football League matches is held by centre half Tony Emery who played in 402 matches between 1946 and 1959. His only goal came against Chester in April 1951 after he was switched to play in the forward line as a result of suffering an injury.

The shortest Football League career for the Imps is that of Rick Ranshaw who spent just two minutes on the pitch after replacing the injured Bobby Cumming in the home Division Four match with Hartlepool in August 1988.

Wing-half George Whyte holds the record for consecutive Football League appearances. He did not miss a match between April 1934 and September 1938 giving him 183 consecutive appearances.

George Fraser (1901-1911) holds the FA Cup record with 27 appearances. Gordon Hobson (1977-1985 and 1988-1990) holds the Football League Cup record with 23 appearances. Dave Smith (1968-1978) made 22 starts with a further appearance as a substitute in the same competition.

ASSOCIATE MEMBERS' CUP

This competition for teams in the lower two divisions of the Football League started in 1983/84. There was little interest in the first season but the cup has since attracted sponsorship and this, together with the prospect of a Wembley final has at least meant the latter stages have attracted healthy attendances. The cup has operated under various names starting with the Freight Rover Trophy (1984-87). Subsequently it has been called the Sherpa Van Trophy (1987-89), Leyland Daf Cup (1989-91), Autoglass Trophy (1991-94) and Auto Windscreen Shield (1994 to date).

City have twice reached the last eight which is the northern section semi-final. The first occasion was in 1984/85 when they knocked out Hartlepool, Darlington and York before losing 3-1 at home to Wigan. That success was matched in 1993/94 with wins over Mansfield, Chesterfield, Darlington and Chester before going out in a 2-1 defeat at Carlisle after extra-time.

City's full record up to the end of the 1996/97 season is:

P 35   W 13   D 5   L 17   F 45   A 53

ATTENDANCES

Official attendance figures are available for F.A. Cup games from around 1900 and for Football League matches from 1925, the only figures before these dates being provided by newspaper estimates.

Attendances at John O'Gaunt's were generally quite small with the ground record being 7,000 for the visit of Notts County for a Division Two fixture on 23 March 1894. The first really big gate at Sincil Bank was for the visit of Derby County for a tie in the last 32 of the F.A. Cup on 8 February 1902. A total of 16,435 tickets were sold but bad weather on the day kept the attendance down to around 10,000. This figure was equalled on Christmas Day 1909 for the visit of Gainsborough Trinity for a Division Two game. Since then the record has increased progressively as follows:

13,000	vs Nottingham Forest	(Div 2)	1 Mar 1913
13,078	vs Grimsby Town	(Div 3 N)	24 Oct 1925
16,849	vs Leicester City	(F.A.C. -R3)	12 Jan 1929
17,092	vs Nottingham Forest	(F.A.C. - R3)	11 Jan 1947
17,657	vs Gateshead	(Div 3 N)	26 Mar 1948
20,024	vs Hartlepools United	(Div 3 N)	1 May 1948
20,662	vs Sheffield Wed.	(Div 2)	26 Feb 1949
23,146	vs Grimsby Town	(Div 2)	5 Mar 1949
23,196	vs Derby County	(Lge.Cup - R4r)	15 Nov 1967

The capacity of the "new" Sincil Bank is 10,918. The highest attendance since the ground was redeveloped is 10,523 against Southampton in the third round replayed Coca-Cola Cup tie on 12 November 1996.

HIGHEST GATES SINCE 1925 BY COMPETITION

HOME :
Football League	23,146 vs Grimsby T.	5 Mar 1949
F.A. Cup :	23,027 vs Preston N. E.	30 Jan 1954
Football League Cup :	23,196 vs Derby C.	15 Nov 1967

AWAY :
Football League :	61,231 at Everton	16 Apr 1954
F.A. Cup :	35,456 at Burnley	12 Jan 1960
Football League Cup :	25,079 at Derby County	1 Nov 1967

LOWEST GATES SINCE 1925 BY COMPETITION

HOME :
Football League:	1,186 vs Torquay U.	17 Mar 1987
F.A. Cup :	2,596 vs Blackpool	16 Nov 1985
Football League Cup:	1,737 vs Bradford P.A.	12 Oct 1960

AWAY :
Football League :	773 at Southport	2 Apr 1935
F.A. Cup:	1,450 at Witton Albion	13 Nov 1993
Football League Cup:	1,018 at Chester City	20 Aug 1991

City's highest average attendance was 16,774 for the first season back in the Second Division in 1952/53. Average attendances in Football League games since 1925 are:

1925/26	5,344	1932/33	9,758
1926/27	5,057	1933/34	7,038
1927/28	6,205	1934/35	5,227
1928/29	6,128	1935/36	5,405
1929/30	5,259	1936/37	7,138
1930/31	7,737	1937/38	7,904
1931/32	8,578	1938/39	5,090

POST-WAR

Season	Attendance	Season	Attendance
1946/47	7,614	1971/72	7,603
1947/48	13,146	1972/73	4,547
1948/49	15,890	1973/74	3,930
1949/50	12,418	1974/75	5,795
1950/51	10,440	1975/76	8,401
1951/52	13,810	1976/77	7,145
1952/53	16,774	1977/78	4,878
1953/54	14,712	1978/79	3,168
1954/55	12,067	1979/80	3,713
1955/56	13,215	1980/81	4,715
1956/57	11,179	1981/82	4,224
1957/58	10,146	1982/83	4,790
1958/59	11,334	1983/84	3,148
1959/60	10,733	1984/85	2,486
1960/61	7,429	1985/86	2,617
1961/62	5,867	1986/87	2,023
1962/63	4,629	1987/88	3,767
1963/64	5,650	1988/89	3,965
1964/65	4,475	1989/90	4,071
1965/66	3,845	1990/91	2,967
1966/67	4,087	1991/92	2,874
1967/68	6,692	1992/93	3,334
1968/69	7,912	1993/94	3,179
1969/70	6,070	1994/95	3,276
1970/71	5,499	1995/96	2,870
		1996/97	3,162

CENTRAL LEAGUE

City became founder members of the Central League and its first champions in 1911/12 after being voted out of the Football League. The league was mostly made up of reserve teams apart from City, Crewe, Burslem Port Vale and Southport Central. Lincoln lost their opening match 3-1 at Blackpool Reserves but were then defeated just once more during the season. The club used only 15 players in the 32 matches but three of those appeared in just five games between them. At the end of the season City were voted back into the Football League. The Central League later became exclusively for reserve teams with City entering in recent years (see entry on reserve team).

Record
P 32 W 18 D 12 L 2 F 81 A 30 Pts 48

CHAIRMEN

Louis Draper was the first chairman of the club being appointed in October 1895 when City were incorporated as a limited liability company. The full list of chairmen is:

Louis Draper (Oct 1895 to Feb 1897)
Thomas Bennett (Feb 1897 to Mar 1899)
Jack Strawson (Mar 1899 to Sep 1908)
Cornelius Taylor (Sep 1908 to Sep 1909)
Pearce Milner (Sep 1908 to Oct 1922).
Cornelius Taylor (Oct 1922 to Aug 1923)
Samuel Tonge (Aug 1923 to Jun 1929)
Ted Simpson (Jun 1929 to May 1939)
George Wright (May 1939 to Dec 1948);
Charles Applewhite (Dec 1948 to Aug 1960)
Alwyne Mawer (Aug 1960 to Dec 1961);
Edgar Gilbert (Dec 1961 to Jun 1963)
Frank Eccleshare (Jul 1963 to Mar 1967).
Walter Mant (Mar 1967 to Apr 1970)
Heneage Dove (Apr 1970 to Jun 1971)
Charles Warner (Jun 1971 to Jul 1972)
Dennis Bocock (Jul 1972 to Apr 1974)
Charles Warner (Apr 1974 to Aug 1975)
Heneage Dove (Aug 1975 to Dec 1980)
Dennis Houlston (Dec 1980 to May 1982)
Gilbert Blades (May 1982 to Mar 1983)
Dennis Houlston (Mar 1983 to Mar 1985)
John Reames (Mar 1985 to date).

The longest serving chairman was Pearce Milner (14 years 1 month). Current chairman John Reames is the second longest serving having reached 12 years in office in March 1997.

COLOURS

City's first shirts were red and white stripes initially playing with white shorts but very soon afterwards switching to black shorts.

The club wore green shirts with black shorts for the period from 1897 to 1900 but then went back to red and white striped shirts and continued with these until the end of the 1966/67 season. From 1967 to 1971 the team wore plain red shirts with white shorts before changing to an Arsenal-style of red shirts with white sleeves for the 1971/72 and 1972/73 seasons.

The Imps were back in red and white striped shirts from 1973 to 1983 and then had two seasons in red shirts with thin white stripes and white sleeves. The traditional red and white stripes have remained in use since 1985/86 with regular 'fashion' changes in recent years.

The shirts bore the crest of the City of Lincoln for a couple of seasons in the early 1960s before this was dropped at the end of 1963/64. An imp was put on the shirts for 1971/72 and 1972/73 but was then dropped only to be reinstated in 1975/76. The imp stayed until it was replaced by the City of Lincoln crest again in 1993/94.

DIVISION THREE NORTH CUP

The Northern Section cup was established in the 1933/34 season but attracted little interest with low attendances and clubs often fielding weakened teams.

City first entered in 1934/35 following their relegation from Division Two but they were defeated by Walsall in the first round. The Imps only success came in 1935/36 when victories over Rotherham and Chester put the club in the semi-final where they lost 3-2 at home to the eventual winners Chester. First round defeats followed in the following two seasons and City were exempt from entry in 1938/39 as they reached the FA Cup third round.

Record :
P 7 W 2 D 1 L 4 F 12 A 17

EXPUNGED MATCHES

Two games in the 1890/91 Midland League campaign were ordered to be struck from the records and replayed because of the state of the pitch. These were the matches on 3 January 1891, which City lost 1-0 at Derby Midland, and on the following Saturday when they were beaten 3-1 at Burslem Port Vale. John Irving scored the City goal.

Both matches against Wigan Borough in the 1931/32 season were declared null and void after the Lancashire club resigned from the Football League in October 1931 as a result of financial problems. Manchester Central, Prescot Cables and Merthyr Town each offered to take over Wigan's fixtures but the Football League Management Committee decided instead to delete the results of Wigan's 12 matches so depriving City of four points. The Imps still went on to take the Division Three North title that season but only on goal average from Gateshead. The two expunged games were:

9 Sep 1931 Wigan Borough 0, Lincoln City 3
                    (Hall, Cartwright, Whyte) att 4,250
14 Sep 1931 Lincoln City 3, Wigan Borough 0
                    (Riley 2, Hall) att 5,932.

The first three games of the 1939/40 season were also removed from the records after the Football League campaign was abandoned following the outbreak of war. City's matches were :

26 Aug 1939 Hull City 2, Lincoln City 2
                    (Clayton, Clare) att 6,000.
28 Aug 1939 Lincoln City 0, Darlington 2
                                            att 5,344.
2 Sep 1939 Lincoln City 4, Gateshead 3
                    (Ponting 3, Clare) att 2,856.

Finally the two fixtures against Aldershot in the 1991/92 season were also deleted from the records after City's opponents were wound up and resigned from the League. The results of these games were :

2 Nov 1991 Lincoln City 0, Aldershot 0   att 1,737.
14 Mar 1992 Aldershot 0, Lincoln City 3
                    (Kabia, Brown, Puttnam) att 1,473.

FA CUP

The club first entered the FA Cup in 1884/85 when they went to Hull Town and won 5-1 in the opening round. City received a bye in the next round before going out 1-0 at Grimsby Town.

Until 1925 City were usually required to play in the qualifying rounds which they also had to do in 1987/88 after being relegated out of the Football League.

City's biggest victory is a 13-0 success at Peterborough in a first qualifying round tie in October 1895. The goals were spread among seven players.

The heaviest defeat is 5-0 at Grimsby Town in a fourth qualifying round match in December 1892, and again at Stockport County in the first round of the 1995/96 competition.

City have three times reached the last 16. The first occasion was in 1886/87 when they went down 3-0 in Glasgow against Rangers. That was equalled in 1889/90 when Notts Olympic, Notts Rangers, Gainsborough Trinity and Chester were all defeated before City lost 4-0 to the holders Preston.

The club reached the same stage in 1901/02. Worksop Town, Doncaster Rovers, Barnsley, Newton Heath and Oxford City were all beaten before Derby County came to Sincil Bank and won 3-1.

City's full record to the end of the 1996/97 season is:

P 244 W 94 D 45 L 105 F 419 A 403
(Exludes abandoned games in 1900 and 1937, but includes replayed - after protest - match of 1892)

FANZINES

Fanzines, the word derives from a contraction of 'fan magazine', first appeared in British football in the mid-1980s providing an alternative view of the game.

There have been four fanzines covering the Imps, all unofficial publications. The first was 'The Banker', which appeared in the 1987/88 season, it later changed its name to 'The Bonker', but folded after about four issues. 'Hardaker Rides Again', was a fanzine devoted to both Chelsea and Lincoln in the late 1980s. 'The Deranged Ferret!', was launched in August 1989 with a 24 page issue for 50p. Taking its title from a phrase used by manager Colin Murphy it has appeared regularly since with issue 33 for April/May 1997 offering 56 pages for £1.

The fourth and newest Lincoln City fanzine is 'Yellowbelly' which first appeared towards the end of the 1996/97 season.

FA TROPHY

City competed in the FA Trophy in the 1987/88 season after suffering relegation to the Vauxhall Conference. The club's first match was at South Liverpool where just 350 people watched as City's almost went out to the Northern Premier Leaguers. A late goal from Bobby Cumming earned a replay but that ended at 2-2 and City needed a third game before they finally won 3-1. Both Cambridge City and Maidstone United were defeated before the Imps went down 1-0 at Enfield in the quarter-final. The North London club went on to win the trophy beating Telford 3-2 in a final replay.

FA YOUTH CUP

City first entered this competition in 1956/57 when they were defeated 6-1 at Sheffield Wednesday in a first round match. The club has entered every season since apart from 1968/69, 1970/71 and 1990/92.

The club's most successful seasons so far have been in 1978/79 and 1979/80 when they reached the third round (last 32). In 1978/79 the Imps lost 2-1 at home to Nottingham Forest and the following season they were defeated 4-2 at Manchester City with the home team going on to reach the final.

City's biggest victory is a 9-1 win over Wisbech Town in a Preliminary Round tie in 1986/87. The heaviest defeat came when the club was beaten 10-1 by Huddersfield Town in a first qualifying round match at Sincil Bank in September 1995.

FLOODLIGHTS

City's first games under floodlights were in the 1880s when they staged a couple of friendly matches on the John O'Gaunt's ground using a system known as Wells' Lights. The first of these games produced a 4-1 win over Notts County on 27 February 1889. City also played matches both home and away at Gainsborough Trinity, plus a home game with Sheffield United.

The first modern game under lights was a friendly at Grimsby Town in March 1954 which finished as a 1-1 draw.

City were one of the last teams in the Football League to install floodlights, when they finally switched on in January 1962. In the Football League, only Barrow, Chesterfield, Fulham, Gillingham and Hartlepool were later than Lincoln.

The first floodlights at Sincil Bank were financed by the Supporters Club who raised the £16,000 needed. Some of it came from individual fans who loaned money for a five year period with the reward of a free season ticket.

The lights were first switched on for a reserve match against Rotherham on 13 January 1962. They were first used in a Football League game for the latter stages of the Division Three match with Northampton on 20 January the same year. City's re-arranged match with Barnsley on 31 January 1962 was the first game entirely under lights at Sincil Bank.

A new set of lights was installed in 1977 with the original system being sold to Spalding United for £400. The current system in use was put up in 1995 following the completion of the redevelopment of the ground.

FOOTBALL ALLIANCE

City played in the Football Alliance, second only in stature to the Football League, during the 1891/92 season finishing ninth out of the 12 teams. Their biggest win came on the final match of the campaign when they defeated bottom club Birmingham St George's 5-0 at John O'Gaunt's. The heaviest defeat was 10-1 at Newton Heath. At the end of the season the top two clubs, Nottingham Forest and Newton Heath, were elected to the Football League First Division along with Sheffield Wednesday. City and seven of the remaining clubs were elected as founder-members of Division Two with Birmingham St George's disbanding due to financial problems. The Alliance was wound up in the summer of 1892.

FOOTBALL LEAGUE

Lincoln City were elected to the Football League at the 1892 annual meeting held at the Queen's Hotel, Sunderland when they became founder-members of the Second Division. The club has since lost its place on four occasions (1908, 1911, 1920 and 1987), but each time won its way back to the League after a season's absence in non-League football. Lincoln were also founder members of Division Three North when it was established in 1921.

The club's record in the League is:
Division Two   1892-1908; 1908-1911; 1912-1920
Division Three (N)   1921-1932;
Division Two   1932-1934
Division Three (N)   1934 - 1948
Division Two   1948-1949;
Division Three (N)   1949-1952
Division Two   1952-1961
Division Three   1961-1962;
Division Four   1962-1976
Division Three   1976-1979
Division Four   1979-1981;
Division Three   1981-1986
Division Four   1986-87 1988-1992
Division Three   1992 to date.

Division Four was renamed Division Three from 1992/93.

Lincoln's first match in the Football League was on 3 September 1892 when they lost 4-2 at Sheffield United. The highest final position achieved by the club was in 1901-02 when they were fifth in Division Two.

The various club records are :

Biggest win:	11-1 v Crewe Alexandra (home) 29 September 1951 (Div 3 North)
Biggest away win:	8-2 at Rotherham Town 2 December 1893 (Div 2)
Heaviest defeat:	3-11 at Manchester City 23 March 1895 (Div 2)
Heaviest home defeat:	0-6 v Barnet 4 September 1991 (Div 4)

Most wins in a season	32 in 1975/76
Least defeats in a season	4 in 1975/76
Least wins in a season	5 in 1896/97
Most defeats in a season	29 in 1964/65
Most draws in a season	18 in 1984/85
Least draws in a season	0 in 1894/95
Most goals scored in a season	121 in 1951/52
Most goals conceded in a season	101 in 1919/20
Least goals scored in a season	27 in 1896/97
Least goals conceded in a season	25 in 1980/8
Most points in a season (2 pts for a win)	74 in 1975/76
Most points in a season (3 pts for a win)	77 in 1981/82
Most players used in a season	39 in 1995/96

Record sequences
Longest unbeaten run: 18 matches
(11 March 1980 to 17 September 1980)
Longest unbeaten home run: 35 matches
(22 March 1975 to 29 October 1976)
Longest unbeaten away run: 12 matches
(11 March 1980 to 4 October 1980)
Longest winning run: 10 matches
(1 September 1930 to 18 October 1930)
Longest winning home run: 14 matches
(12 April 1982 to 18 December 1982)
Longest winning away run: 5 matches (on four occasions - most recent 3 October 1992 to 21 November 1992)
Longest run of draws: 5 matches
(21 February 1981 to 10 March 1981)
Longest run of defeats: 12 matches
(21 September 1896 to 9 January 1897)
Longest run of home defeats: 5 matches
(3 Oct 1896 - 9 Jan 1897 & 24 Jan 1961 - 18 Mar 1961)
Longest run of away defeats: 14 matches
(12 September 1896 to 4 September 1897)
Longest run without a win: 19 matches
(22 August 1978 to 23 December 1978)
Longest run without a home win: 11 matches
(2 September 1978 to 10 March 1979)

Longest run without an away win: 35 matches
(21 September 1896 to 17 December 1898)
Longest run without a draw: 36 matches
(23 March 1894 to 7 September 1895)

City's full record to the end of the 1996/97 season:
P 3,732 W 1,360 D 876 L 1,496 F 5,583 A 5,857 Pts 3,833

(Two points were awarded for a win 1892-1981. Since 1981 three points have been awarded for a win).

FOOTBALL LEAGUE CUP

City entered this competition in its inaugural season of 1960/61 when they went out in a first round replay to Bradford Park Avenue. The club's most successful run was in 1967/68 when they reached the last 16 (fourth round). Victories over Mansfield, Newcastle and Torquay set up a clash with Derby. The teams drew 1-1 at the Baseball Ground but City lost the replay 3-0 after they were reduced to 10 men with the dismissal of defender Mick Brown.

The Imps biggest victory is a 5-0 win over Hull City at Sincil Bank in a first round first leg tie in August 1980. City also won the second leg 2-0. The heaviest defeat is also 5-0 when City travelled to Leicester City for a third round tie in 1966/67.

City's full record up to the end of the 1996/97 season is:
P 111 W 38 D 28 L 45 F 160 A 174
Defeats include one game lost on penalties)

FOOTBALL LEAGUE GROUP CUP

This cup was introduced for the 1981/82 season following the withdrawal of the Scottish teams from the Anglo-Scottish Cup. 24 Football League clubs from the Second, Third and Fourth Divisions competed being split into six regional groups of four for the opening round before going into a knock-out competition. City's interest ended at the group stage where they lost to both Norwich and Peterborough and drew with Notts County.
Record :
P 3 W 0 D 1 L 2 F 2 A 5

FOOTBALL LEAGUE TROPHY

This competition replaced the Football League Group Cup for the 1982/83 season. Two First Division clubs entered (Norwich and Watford) along with 30 from the remaining three divisions. Eight regional groups of four contested the opening round with a bonus point being awarded for any team scoring three or more goals in a match.

City beat Grimsby and Sheffield United and drew with Scunthorpe in their group to progress into the quarter final.

Norwich were beaten 3-1 with Derek Bell scoring a hat-trick. and then City won 3-1 at Chester to reach the final of a national competition for the only time in their history. The Imps faced Millwall at Sincil Bank and led 1-0 at half-time but Millwall fought back and emerged 3-2 winners with City missing a crucial second half penalty.

Record :
P 6 W 4 D 1 L 1 F 14 A 8

GMAC CUP

City's only experience of this competition was in 1987/88 while in the Vauxhall Conference. Teams from the top divisions of the Vauxhall-Opel, Northern Premier and Beazer Homes Leagues competed with those from the Vauxhall Conference on a knock-out basis in the midweek tournament.

The Imps defeated Matlock Town and Bedworth United before losing 2-1 after extra-time in the third round (last 16) at Telford United.

Record :
P 3 W 2 D 0 L 1 F 7 A 5.

GOALSCORING

Two City players have scored six goals in a match in the Football League. Frank Keetley's double hat-trick against Halifax Town in a Division Three North match at Sincil Bank on 16 January 1932 included 5 goals in 21 minutes in the second half. His record was equalled by Andy Graver in the 11-1 win over Crewe Alexandra, also in a Division Three North fixture, on 29 September 1951.

Andy Graver holds the career record goals total for the club in the Football League with 143, during his three spells at Sincil Bank between 1950 and 1961.

Allan Hall holds the club record for goals in a season with 42 goals from 40 League games in the 1931/32 season. Two further goals were excluded from official records after Wigan Borough dropped out of the League in mid-season and matches against them were declared null and void.

Allan Hall scored in 12 consecutive matches between 12 December 1931 and 6 February 1932, comprising 10 League and two F.A. Cup games. Billy Dinsdale also scored in 10 consecutive League games between 29 August and 22 October 1927.

Billy Dinsdale holds the overall F.A. Cup scoring record for City with 14 goals between 1926 and 1929, and again on his return to the club for the 1930/31 season.

Two players have scored four goals in an F.A. Cup tie. Billy Gillespie managed the feat in a fourth qualifying round match at home to Worksop Town in December 1896, and that was matched the following season by Hugh Robertson against Attercliffe in the third qualifying round match in October 1897.

The overall goals record in the Football League Cup is held by Tony Cunningham (1979 to 1982) with 8. John Ward scored all four in the first round first leg tie against Chesterfield at Sincil Bank on 20 August 1975.

HALL OF FAME

The Lincoln City Hall of Fame was established in May 1996 when Tony Emery and Andy Graver were chosen as the first recipients of the honour. John Ward and Percy Freeman, who scored 47 goals between them in the 1975/76 record-breaking season, were chosen for the Hall of Fame in April 1997.

HAT-TRICKS

Frank Smallman scored City's first Football League hat-trick when he hit four goals in the 5-1 home win over Burton Swifts in a Division Two match in February 1893.

John Campbell holds the club record of five hat-tricks in a season which he achieved in 1936/37. He scored all five in the home match with Rochdale together with three in the home matches against Southport, Halifax and Darlington with his final hat-trick at Gateshead.

City's only hat-trick of penalties in a match was scored by wing-half Alf Horne against Stockport County in a Division Three North match at Sincil Bank in September 1935.

Clive Ford's hat-trick against Bradford Park Avenue in December 1967 was achieved in the first 11 minutes of the match. His final goal put City 4-0 ahead and they eventually won 5-1.

Jock Dodds' hat-trick against West Ham in December 1948 was against three different goalkeepers. His first effort beat the selected 'keeper Ernie Gregory who went off injured. George Dick replaced him until half-time, with Dodds getting one against him and another against the second-half 'keeper after Dick returned to playing outfield.

Billy Cobb is the only City player to score a hat-trick on his Football League debut for the club, scoring three goals in the 8-1 win over Luton Town in December 1966.

INTERNATIONALS

The following players have won international honours whilst on the club's books:

FULL INTERNATIONALS
David 'Harry' Pugh (Wales) 3 apps vs Scotland (Feb 1900), Scotland (March 1901), England (March 1901).
Con Moulson (Irish Free State) 2 apps vs Hungary (May 1936), Luxembourg (May 1936).
George Moulson (Eire) 3 apps vs Portugal (May 1948), Spain (May 1948), Switzerland (Dec 1948).
Arthur Fitzsimons (Eire) 1 app vs Czechoslovakia (May 1959).
David Felgate (Wales) 1 app vs Romania (Oct 1983, as sub).

UNDER-23 INTERNATIONAL
Dick Neal (England) 3 apps vs Denmark (Sept 1956), France (Oct 1956), Scotland (Feb 1957).

AMATEUR INTERNATIONAL
Harry Parr (England) 1 app vs Ireland (Feb 1947).

YOUTH INTERNATIONALS
Jim Grummett (England) 3 apps vs Wales (March 1963), Northern Ireland (May 1963), Scotland (May 1963).
Steve Adlard (England) 6 apps vs Scotland (Feb 1968), Northern Ireland, (Feb 1968), Wales (March 1968), Scotland (Feb 1969), Northern Ireland (Feb 1969), Wales (March 1969).
Brendan Guest (England) 4 apps vs Wales (9 March 1977), Wales (23 March 1977), Belgium (May 1977), Iceland (May 1977).
Stuart Naylor (England) 1 app vs Austria (Sep 1980).

OTHERS
Tony Emery toured the West Indies with an F.A. XI in the summer of 1955. Andy Graver was selected for the England 'B' team to play The Netherlands in February 1952 but had to withdraw through injury. Steve Adlard (3 apps) and Mark Wallington (2 apps) appeared for the England Schools Under-18 team whilst on the club's books. Wallington was subsequently offered full-time terms in May 1970 but turned them down as he wished to continue his studies at college. A number of players including David Wiggett, Matt Carbon and Ben Dixon have been called up to the England Youth squad without making an appearance.

JUNIOR AND YOUTH TEAMS

The club were considering forming a colts team in 1939 but war intervened and it was not until 1947 that a Lincoln City 'A' team was established. They competed in the Lincoln League (1947/48), Lincolnshire League (1948/49 to 1963/64), Lincoln League (1964/65 and 1965/66) and Lincolnshire League again (1966/67 to 1969/70 and 1972/73). A team known as Lincoln City Youths played in Division 3B of the Lincoln League in 1965/66, and Lincoln City Colts appeared in Division 2 of the Lincolnshire League in 1966/67.

A Junior team was entered in the Northern Intermediate League from 1973/74 until resigning in January 1982, and again from 1984/85 to 1987/88. The Juniors switched to the Midland Intermediate League (known as the Midland Purity Youth League and subsequently the Melville Midland Youth League), and have entered every season since 1991/92.

A Youth team also appeared in the Lincoln Sunday League from 1974/75 to 1979/80 and an 'A' team made up of schoolboys competed in the Lincoln League in 1986/87 and 1987/88. Various age group teams have represented the club from time to time in the Lincoln Youth League, Mid-Lincs. County Youth League and Yorkshire Conference.

From 1974 until the early 1980s the club had a nursery team in South Yorkshire known as Sheffield Rangers.

City 'A' played their home games on the Co-op Sports Field, Skellingthorpe Road from 1947 to around 1955, before changing to the St Andrews ground which was used until the late 1970s. In recent year the Juniors have played at a number of venues including Mulsanne Park (Nettleham), Ruston Marconi, Bishop Grosseteste College and the Lincolnshire Police ground at Nettleham.

Honours: City 'A' won the Lincolnshire League Cup in 1961/62 and the Lincs. League Charity Cup on four occasions - 1950/51, 1951/52, 1952/53 and 1961/62. The Juniors won the Lincolnshire Intermediate Cup in 1975/76 and lost to Peterborough United on penalties in the final of the Melville Midland Youth League Cup in 1995/96.

LIBEL

Cartoons were a common feature of the sports pages of local newspapers from Edwardian times through to the 1950s and beyond. The Lincolnshire Echo carried a humorous piece by 'Benny Dix' in the 1920s and 1930s whilst the Lincolnshire Chronicle had cartoon drawings in the 1920s.

In June 1930 City full-back Andy York was awarded £200 damages for libel at Lincoln Assizes, following a cartoon in the Chronicle which suggested that he was responsible for the Imps losing at York City on 22 February. York claimed that the cartoon had led to his being barracked in the following week's home game with Crewe Alexandra, thus undermining his health.

He never played for City's first team again and the Chronicle stopped carrying football cartoons after the controversy.

LIMITED COMPANY

The Lincoln City Football Club Company Limited was incorporated in 1895 with an initial share capital of £500 made up of 1,000 10s (50p) shares. In 1920 this was increased to £5,000 (10,000 shares) and there have been six further share issues. The company currently has share capital of £900,000 divided into 1.8 million 50p shares.

Most of the early directors were local businessmen from within the city but since the Second World War the board has been increasingly dominated by agricultural interests. The longest serving director was Charles Applewhite who held office from 1924 to 1960; John S. Irving (1923-1957), and Alwyne Mawer (1930-1962) also served the board for more than 30 years.

From 1898 the Working Men's Committee were allowed three places on the board although the formal arrangement ended around 1919. The last director to be associated with the committee was North Jubb who held office until his death in 1946. There has been only one woman director of the company since it was established. Mrs. E.Reames held office from October 1994 to April 1995.

A number of former City players have served on the board including Kenny Bayne, John Irving snr, and Arthur Taylor.Ted Simpson appeared for the reserves around the turn of the century. Current chairman John Reames had trials with the club in Bill Anderson's time and later played for Hykeham (Lincs. League), Lincoln Athletic, Bowham and Lincoln Rangers.

Two City directors have also held office with the Football League. Jack Strawson was on the Management Committee in the 1894/95 season and served as an auditor for 24 years. John Reames was a director of the League from 1991 to 1997 and also served on committees of the Football Association.

LINCOLN CITY 2000 +

An initiative launched by the board in February 1997 with the intention of ensuring the club's future prosperity. Its aim is to attract support and sponsorship from local businesses and to involve the fans with an individual membership scheme available at different levels.

As part of Lincoln City 2000 + a series of 'official' supporters clubs have been established in a number of areas including Spilsby, Spalding, Nottingham and London.

LINCOLN HOSPITAL CUP

The Lincoln Hospital Cup was the idea of former City defender Walter Wilson and was often referred to locally as the 'Wilson Cup'. Each year a First Division or other top club would be invited to Sincil Bank to raise money for the County Hospital. The trophy was purchased with the funds remaining when Newland Athletic F.C. was wound up, and it was first played for in May 1921 when City were defeated 2-1 by Millwall Athletic. The Imps took part until 1926/27, and after this the fixture continued to take place at Sincil Bank until the outbreak of the Second World War, usually involving a game between a Lincoln League representative XI and a local R.A.F. side. In 1938 secretary-manager Joe McClelland tried to revive the cup by inviting Leeds United to play City but he was unable to persuade the Yorkshire club to come to Sincil Bank.

Winners of the cup when it was competed for by professional clubs were:
1920/21   Millwall Athletic
1921/22   Grimsby Town
1922/23   Nottingham Forest
1923/24   CITY
1924/25   CITY and Notts County (trophy shared)
1925/26   Chesterfield
1926/27   CITY

LINCOLNSHIRE CUP

The Lincolnshire Cup, which began in 1881, was treated just as seriously as the FA Cup in the early days of the club and the need for a Lincoln team to be successful in the competition is one of the main reasons why Lincoln City were formed in 1884. The competition became much less important after entry was gained to the Football League in 1892 but it has continued in existence with the early rounds now played as pre-season matches.

City's first match produced what is still a record victory when they thrashed Boston Excelsior 11-0 in a round one game on John O'Gaunt's ground in October 1884. That scoreline was equalled in February 1928 when City travelled to Barton Town for a semi-final tie. The heaviest defeat was in 1960/61 when Grimsby Town progressed into the final by beating City 8-3 at Blundell Park. The club first won the cup in 1886/87, and in all have lifted the trophy outright on 30 occasions, sharing it another three times. City reached the final in 1973/74 but as the other semi-final was not completed the competition was left unfinished.

City's full record up to the end of the 1996/97 season is:
    P 200 W 109 D 31 L 60 F 458 A 276
Includes two games won on penalties, one won on the toss of a coin, and one lost on penalties.

MANAGERS

The men who looked after the running of team affairs in the early days of the club had various titles including secretary and secretary/manager. Alf Martin was the first paid official employed by the club when he was appointed secretary/manager in February 1896.

The committee dealt with team selection until the club became a limited company in 1895. The board of directors then took over selection with each member voting as to which player was to fill which position. In the event of a tie the chairman had a casting vote although this rarely had to be used. This situation continued until the appointment of Joe McClelland after which the secretary/manager submitted his selected team for approval by the board.

The complete list of those in charge of team affairs of the club is:

Jack Strawson (hon secretary)	July 1884 to February 1896
Alf Martin (secretary/manager)	February 1896 to March 1897
James West (hon secretary)	March 1897 to September 1900
David Calderhead (snr) (sec./man.)	September 1900 to May 1907
Jack Strawson (secretary/manager)	Summer 1907 to May 1919
Clem Jackson (player/manager)	July 1919 to September 1919
George Fraser (sec./manager)	September 1919 to April 1921
David Calderhead (jnr) (sec./man.)	April 1921 to May 1924
Horace Henshall (secretary/manager)	May 1924 to June 1927
Harry Parkes (secretary/manager)	June 1927 to May 1936
Joe McClelland (secretary/manager)	June 1936 to July 1947
Bill Anderson (manager)	July 1947 to January 1965
Con Moulson (coach)	January 1965 to March 1965
Roy Chapman (player/coach)	March 1965 to October 1966
Ron Gray (manager)	October 1966 to May 1970
Bert Loxley (manager/ coach)	July 1970 to March 1971
David Herd (manager)	March 1971 to December 1972
Graham Taylor (manager)	December 1972 to June 1977
George Kerr (manager)	June 1977 to December 1977
Willie Bell (manager)	December 1977 to October 1978
Colin Murphy (manager)	November 1978 to May 1985
John Pickering (manager)	July 1985 to December 1985
George Kerr (manager)	December 1985 to March 1987
Peter Daniel (caretaker manager)	March 1987 to May 1987
Colin Murphy (manager)	May 1987 to May 1990
Allan Clarke (manager)	June 1990 to November 1990
Steve Thompson (manager)	November 1990 to May 1993
Keith Alexander (manager)	May 1993 to May 1994
Sam Ellis (manager)	May 1994 to September 1995
Steve Wicks (head coach)	September 1995 to October 1995
John Beck (manager)	October 1995 to date.

13 of those in charge of team affairs also played for City, namely; Jack Strawson, David Calderhead (snr), Clem Jackson, George Fraser, Con Moulson, Roy Chapman, Ron Gray, Bert Loxley, Graham Taylor, Peter Daniel, Steve Thompson, Keith Alexander and Sam Ellis.

The Bell's Whisky Manager of the Year awards started in 1969 with City's only success coming in 1975/76 when Graham Taylor was the Division Four Manager of the Year. A total of 12 divisional manager of the month awards have been awarded as follows:

David Herd (1) - January 1972
Graham Taylor (5) -November 1974, September 1975, November 1975, December 1975, April 1976.
Colin Murphy (3)-August 1980, March 1982,September 1982.
Steve Thompson (2) - April 1992, October 1992.
John Beck (1) - November 1995.

Colin Murphy was the Mail on Sunday Manager of the Year for the Vauxhall Conference in 1987/88. He also won manager of the month awards in October 1987 (shared with Kettering's Alan Buckley) and January 1988.

MIDLAND LEAGUE

City entered the Midland League as founder-members in 1889 and were champions in the first season of the competition. The club finished third at the end of the following season before moving to play in the Football Alliance.

City's first team won the competition in both 1908/09 and 1920/21 after losing their place in the Football League. On each occasion they were voted back into the League after just one season's absence.

The club's reserve team competed in the league from 1899 (see reserve team entry).

Record (first team seasons only) :
P 114   W 79   D 16   L 19   F 289   A 118   Pts 174

NICKNAMES

The club's first nickname was the Citizens which was often shortened to the 'Cits'. They were also referred to as the 'Window Blinds' in their early days on account of their red and white striped shirts being similar to shop window blinds.

The first use of the name the 'Imps' comes around 1919 with the name taken from the carving inside Lincoln Cathedral which was becoming increasingly popular as a symbol of the city. From 1967 they have been known as the 'Red Imps'.

PENALTY KICKS

Penalties were first introduced by the FA in 1891 although the initial rule was different to that of today, with the goalkeeper allowed to move anywhere within his six yard box.

Sam Ellis scored 10 penalties in each of the 1974/75 and 1975/76 seasons. His best in Football League matches alone was 8 successful efforts in the former season.

Alf Horne scored a hat-trick of penalties for City in the Division Three North home match against Stockport County on 16 September 1935.

Peter Grotier is the only goalkeeper to score from the penalty spot for the Imps. He scored what proved to be the winner against both Grimsby Town and Scunthorpe United in Lincolnshire Senior Cup matches in 1976/77. The following season he scored again from the spot in a 1-1 draw with Scunthorpe in the same competition.

The first domestic match to be decided by a penalty shoot-out was the Football League Cup first round tie between City and Doncaster Rovers in 1976/77. Both legs of the tie were drawn 1-1 and the replay at the City Ground, Nottingham, on 24 August 1976 finished 2-2 after the completion of 30 minutes extra-time. The game went to penalties with Doncaster winning 3-2.

Having been the first Football League team to go out of a competition by this method it was ironic that 18 years later City should also be the first team to lose a match through the sudden death system whereby the first team to score in extra-time wins the game.

PFA AWARDS

Since 1973 the members of the Professional Footballers Association have been balloted each season to select a representative team for each division of the Football League. Lincoln players have been elected in seven seasons with the club provided five of the eleven in the 1975/76 season. City players selected are :

1973/74 (Division 4 Team) - Ian Branfoot

1974/75 (Division 4 Team) - Peter Grotier

1975/76 (Division 4 Team) - Peter Grotier, Ian Branfoot, Sam Ellis, Terry Cooper, John Ward

1980/81 (Division 4 Team) - Trevor Peake

1982/83 (Division 3 Team) - David Felgate, Trevor Peake, Glenn Cockerill.

1983/84 (Division 3 Team) - David Felgate

1996/97 (Division 3 Team) - Gareth Ainsworth

PLAYER OF THE SEASON

The annual Player of the Season award has been run by the Lincoln and District Football Supporters Club since 1969/70, apart from a break of one season in 1973/74. Votes are cast by supporters in a ballot held towards the end of each campaign. The full list of winners is:

Season	Player	Season	Player
1969/70	John Kennedy	1983/84	David Felgate
1970/71	Phil Hubbard	1984/85	Gordon Hobson
1971/72	Terry Branston	1985/86	Gary Strodder
1972/73	George Peden	1986/87	Gary West
1973/74	No Award	1987/88	Bobby Cumming
1974/75	Terry Cooper	1988/89	Tony James
1975/76	Sam Ellis	1989/90	Mark Wallington
1976/77	Sam Ellis	1990/91	Graham Bressington
1977/78	Peter Grotier	1991/92	Matt Carmichael
1978/79	Terry Cooper	1992/93	David Puttnam
1979/80	Trevor Peake	1993/94	John Schofield
1980/81	Trevor Peake	1994/95	Andy Leaning
1981/82	Steve Thompson	1995/96	Gareth Ainsworth
1982/83	Glenn Cockerill	1996/97	Gareth Ainsworth

PROMOTION

City have achieved promotion on five occasions within the Football League. They went up from Division Three North to Division Two in 1931/32, 1947/48 and 1951/52 each time as champions. Promotion was gained from Division Four to Division Three in 1975/76 (as champions again) and in 1980/81. City also won automatic promotion back to Division Four in 1987/88 after winning the Vauxhall Conference.

RE-ELECTION

The Imps have one of the worst records of any club of having to apply for re-election to the Football League. At the end of the club's first season 1892/93 they faced re-election after finishing fourth from bottom in Division Two, but City, and the other three clubs below them, were voted back in.

The situation arose again in 1894/95, 1896/97 and 1897/98 but each time the club topped the poll when votes were cast. City again came out top in the voting at the end of the 1906/07 season but their luck ran out the following season when Bradford Park Avenue replaced Lincoln with City only managing 18 votes. Lincoln received a second chance when Stoke resigned but at a special general meeting of the Football League twice tied 20-20 with Tottenham before the management committee voted 5-3 in favour of accepting Spurs.

City got back into the League for the 1909/10 season but had to apply again for re-election in 1910/11 when Grimsby Town were elected in place of Lincoln by just one vote. Again City were back after a season's absence but soon the old problem returned and at the end of the 1913/14 season again they had to rely on the votes of other clubs to stay in Division Two.

The Football League annual meeting of 1920 saw City back seeking votes and this time they were again thrown out with Leeds United (31) and Cardiff City (23) elected at the expense of Grimsby (20) and Lincoln (7). Grimsby were immediately allowed back in to the new Division Three but City were left to play in the Midland League for another season before becoming a founder-member of Division Three North in 1921.

The Imps continued until 1962/63 without having to apply for re-election but then had to survive five votes in nine seasons. They topped the voting on each occasion. On the final (and 14th) occasion City sought re-election at the 1971 annual meeting the voting was: Lincoln City 47, Barrow 38, Hartlepool 33, Newport County 33, Hereford United 22, Wigan 14, Cambridge City 2, Telford 2, Yeovil 2, Boston United and Romford one each. No votes were recorded for the other applicants - Bedford, Chelmsford, Hillingdon and Kettering.

The system of re-election was used for the last time at the 1986 annual meeting of the League. It was replaced by automatic relegation for the bottom club to be replaced by the top club in the Vauxhall Conference. City were the first team to go down under the new system.

RELEGATION

The club was relegated from Division Two to Division Three North in both the 1933/34 and 1948/49 seasons. City went down from Division Two to Division Three in 1960/61 and then from Division Three to Division Four in 1961/62, 1978/79 and 1985/86. The following season, 1986/87, saw City become the first team automatically relegated from Division Four into the Vauxhall Conference.

RESERVES

City regularly fielded two teams from their first season onwards. The first recorded game for a second team was on 4 October 1884 when local side, Albert, were defeated 5-0 on South Park. The reserve team were known as Lincoln City Swifts until around 1897. The reserves have taken part in the following competitions:

Midland Alliance	(1891/92 to 1892/93)
Lincolnshire League	(1894/95, 1896/97, 1898/99)
Midland League	(1899/1900 - 1907/08)
Lincoln League	(1908/09)
Midland League	(1909/10 - 1914/15, 1919/20)
Lincolnshire League	(1920/21)
Midland League	(1921/22-1939/40, 1945/46- 1957/58)
North Regional League	(1958/59 - 1964/65)
Midland League	(1965/66 - 1966/67)
North Midlands League	(1967/68-1974/75, 1977/78-1982/83)
Lincs. & Border Counties Floodlit League	(1983/84)
Lowfields Midland Floodlit League	(1984/85 to 1985/86)
Midland Senior League	(1988/89 to 1991/92, 1994/95)
Pontins (Central) League	(From 1995/96)

They also competed in:

Lincoln League	(1896/97)
Lincs. Midland League Clubs' League	(1933/34 - 1936/37)
Lincolnshire League Premier Division	(1961/62 - 1967/68)

City Swifts entered the Lincolnshire Cup on two occasions. In 1886/87 they were defeated 4-2 at home by Brigg Town in the first round and in 1895/96 they beat Lincoln Casuals, the 10th Lincoln Regt. and Grantham Rovers Colts, before losing to Grimsby All Saints in the final.

England cricketer Fred Trueman appeared for City reserves against Peterborough United in their Midland League fixture on 15 November 1952. The match was drawn 0-0 and attracted a record reserve game attendance of 7,328 to Sincil Bank. Reserve gates in the 1952/53 season regularly exceeded 5,000 and the visit of Boston United on Easter Monday was attended by 6,070 fans.

HONOURS : Full details are not available for the competitions in the 1890s but since then City reserves have won the Lincolnshire League (1920/21), the Midland League Subsidiary Competition (1924/25), Lincolnshire League Premier Division (1965/66, 1966/67, 1967/68), North Midlands League Cup (1967/68), and North Midlands League (1969/70). They were runners-up in the Midland League in 1932/33 (when they scored 161 goals in 44 games) and in 1996/97 won promotion from the Third Division of the Pontins League by finishing runners-up to Rochdale.

SECRETARIES

The club's administrative and team affairs were initially dealt with by one man holding the title secretary or secretary-manager. In 1948 the duties were split with Bill Anderson becoming team manager and Joe McClell-and taking charge of administration but retaining the title of secretary-manager.until he left Sincil Bank in 1949.

Jack Mann was then appointed secretary holding the position from August 1949 to June 1960. Since then the secretaries have been:

Tony Walker	(Sep 1960 to Aug 1962)
George Key	(Oct 1962 to May 1963)
Thomas Aylmer	(Aug 1963 to Feb 1964)
Roy Chapman	(Feb 1964 to Apr 1966)
Harold Pepper	(Apr 1966 to Sep 1971)
Dick Chester	(Sep 1971 to Jun 1978)
John Sorby	(Jun 1978 to Mar 1982)
Phil Hough	(Mar 1982 to Feb 1985)
Chris Rodman	(Feb 1985 to Oct 1986)
Geoff Davey	(Oct 1986 to Feb 1994)
Phil Hough	(Feb 1994 to Sep 1995)
Geoff Davey	(Sep 1995 to Oct 1996)

The post is currently split with Harold Sills as Company Secretary and Claire Lait as Football Secretary.

SHIRT SPONSORS

City's players first wore sponsored shirts for the Division Three match against Bristol Rovers on 22 January 1983 when the seed firm J Arthur Bowers' name was emblazoned across the kit. The deal lasted until the end of the season and then, following a gap, the tyre company Fossitt & Thorne took over from November 1984 through to the end of the 1987/88 season. The club wore the name Wheel Horse on their shirts for the following two seasons when they were sponsored by SCC Mowers Ltd. Deals for a season each were made with Stuart Pickford (1990/91) and Flindall's (1991/92) before the Lincolnshire Echo began their sponsorship at the start of the 1992/93 season. The Echo has kept up its sponsorship and is currently in its sixth season in partnership with the club.

SUBSTITUTES

The first substitutes were allowed in the Football League for the 1965/66 season but only to replace an injured player. The following season there was no restriction on their use and subs were also allowed in the FA Cup and the Football League Cup. In recent times clubs have been allowed two, and then three subs, in a match.

Ken Fencott was the first City player to wear the number 12 shirt in the opening game of 1965/66 but did not get on the pitch. The first sub used was Roy Chapman who replaced Bunny Larkin at Darlington on 23 August 1965.

Dean West's total of 26 appearances as a substitute is the most for the club followed by Jack Lewis with 21. Lewis was the first sub to score when he replaced Graham Parker against Grimsby on 21 September 1968 and hit the second in City's 3-0 win.

Steve Sherwood was the first substitute goalkeeper to be used when he came on for the injured Andy Leaning at Wigan on 1 April 1995.

SUDDEN DEATH

The system of deciding cup matches by sudden death if the scores were level at the end of 90 minutes was first introduced into domestic football in 1994/95 when it was used in the Auto Windscreen Shield, in place of extra-time. Teams level at the end of 90 minutes played on for a maximum of 30 minutes, but the game automatically ended if one team scored.

The first match settled in this way was City's second round tie at Huddersfield Town on 30 November 1994. The teams finished level at 2-2 at the end of normal time. Huddersfield went through as a result of a 106th minute goal from Iain Dunn which brought the game to an immediate conclusion.

SUNDAY FOOTBALL

Sunday matches were first allowed by the Football League during the power crisis early in 1974 which restricted the use of electricity. City's first Sunday game at Sincil Bank produced a gate of 6,157 to see them defeat Rotherham 2-1 on 27 January 1974. Attendances at Sunday games fell rapidly after the club dropped out of the promotion race and within a couple of months City were back to playing on a Saturday.

Experiments have since been tried with Sunday football, notably in 1986/87, but failed to produce any real increase in attendances.

TELEVISED FOOTBALL

The only occasion to date the club has appeared in a live televised match was for the meeting with Bolton Wanderers in the second round of the FA Cup on 4 December 1993. The game was shown live on Sky TV with the kick-off being switched to a Saturday night to avoid clashing with other ties. The match attracted the best crowd of the season to Sincil Bank with 6,250 watching as City went down 3-1.

Highlights of City matches were shown on a regular basis from the 1960s on Yorkshire, Anglia, and Central with occasional appearances on BBC's Match of the Day.

THE COMBINATION

The Combination was a loosely formed league made up of 20 clubs from the north and midlands who were not included in the Football League when it was formed in 1888. City were among the members for the 1888/89 season when teams were required to play a minimum of eight matches against fellow members. Most played at least 12 games with Lincoln managing 14. The Combination had problems in persuading clubs to fulfil arranged fixtures and no official league table was produced. It was disbanded after only one season with the funds going to the Derby Railway Servants Orphanage.

Record :
P 14 W 6 D 2 L 6 F 17 A 19

TOURS

A party of 16 players together with club officials toured Iceland in May and June 1949 playing four matches against local opposition. City won their first three matches before going down 4-1 to a Combined Reykjavik XI in the final match. brief tour of Jersey was made at the end of the 1952/53 season with City defeating a Jersey Saturday League XI 1-0 before easily defeating a combined Jersey-Guernsey XI 6-1.

The club travelled to Ireland in May 1960 for a short tour against League of Ireland opposition. City won all three games against Limerick, Shelbourne and Waterford.

As part of the pre-season build up to the 1969/70 season the Imps travelled to Northern Ireland where they defeated Glentoran (2-1) and then drew with Ards.

In the summer of 1976 City took part in the Gibraltar Rock Tournament on that island. The Imps played Sheffield United and Blackburn Rovers losing both games on penalties.

City have also paid one match visits to The Netherlands (1936 and 1938) and West Germany (1982).

TRAINERS

The post of trainer was first created around 1889, five years after the formation of the club. The initial holders performed the role of keeping the players fit as well as coaching. In more recent years the club has employed a coach with the physio taking over part of the work of the trainer. City trainers have been :

1889-1920 :
Ben "Yankee" Smeaton (c1889-c1895)
Cyril Crane (1897);
Tom Waterson (1897-c1908)
---- Marston (1909-1911)
Edwin Bentley (1911-1914)
Jerry Jackson (1914-c1915)
Tommy Davies (c1917 to 1920);

1920-1973 :

Billy Langham (1920-1921)	Bill Anderson (1945-1948)
Tom Anthony (1921-1925)	Jimmy Gemmell (1948-1949)
Tommy Rose (1925-1926)	Alf Young (1949-1957)
Ted Wynter (1926-1934)	Bill McGlen (1957-1965)
Steve Wright (1934-1938)	Con Moulson (1965)
Alf Young (1938-1939)	Bill McGlen (1965-1966).
Dick Mellors (1939-1945)	Bert Loxley (1966-1973).

Loxley then became physio with George Higgins taking over coaching duties alongside the manager Graham Taylor. Loxley remained with the club until the summer of 1987 as physio.

There was no physio for the Vauxhall Conference season of 1987/88, and since then the post has been held by a number of men including Adrian Davies, Gerry Brook, Neil McDiarmid, Joe Hinnigan, Mark Riley, Mark Hudson, Roger Cleary, Dave Moore and Keith Oakes.

TRANSFER FEES

Transfer fees have to be kept confidential by clubs as a result of a Football League rule introduced in 1922 but accurate estimates are given in the press and it is these figures that have been used below.

City's first big money signing was John Campbell who cost £1,250 from Leicester City in December 1933. The record continued to increase with the signing of Fred Bett from Coventry for £2,000 in September 1948 before Jock Dodds was bought the following month from Everton for £6,000. That fee was equalled when Brian Birch signed from Manchester United in December 1952.

Andy Graver smashed that record when he was brought back from Leicester for £14,000 in June 1955 and this fee was not exceeded until Peter Grotier arrived from West Ham United in September 1974 for £16,666.

Since then the tag of most expensive player has been held by Tommy Tynan (£33,000 from Sheffield Wednesday), Derek Bell (£36,000 from Barnsley), George Shipley (£45,000 from Southampton), Paul Smith (£48,000 from Port Vale) and Gordon Hobson (£60,000 from Southampton). The current record is £63,000 paid to Leicester City in January 1990 for Grant Brown.

The first big sale was that of goalkeeper Tommy Fern to Everton for £1,500 in December 1913. That was beaten when Walter Webster joined Sheffield United for £1,650 in October 1925 and again when Ted Savage went to Liverpool for £2,500 in May 1931. Bob Meacock moved to Birmingham for £3,000 in June 1938 and this record stood until February 1949 when Jimmy Hutchinson was sold to Oldham for £3,250.

In December 1954 Andy Graver was sold to Leicester City for £27,000 (the Imps also received Eric Littler in the deal), and this stood until December 1979 when Glenn Cockerill moved to Swindon Town for £100,000. Exactly 12 months later Mick Harford was sold to Newcastle United for £160,000 and then Matt Dickins went to Blackburn Rovers in March 1992 for £250,000. The current record sale is that of Darren Huckerby to Newcastle United in November 1995 for £400,000.

VAUXHALL CONFERENCE

City played in the Vauxhall Conference during the 1987/88 season after being automatically relegated from the Fourth Division. They won the title at the first attempt finishing two points clear of Barnet. City's average gate of 3,762 was a record for the competition, and the attendance of 9,432 for the home match with Wycombe when the title was clinched is still a record for a Conference game.

WATNEY CUP

This pre-season invitation tournament was competed for by the two top scoring teams from each division with the exception of clubs winning promotion or qualifying for Europe. Each club received £4,000 for qualifying with further cash incentives to reach the semi-final and final. City qualified for the 1972 competition, but were defeated 1-0 by Burnley in a first round tie at Sincil Bank.

STATISTICAL SECTION

WHO'S WHO

This section includes all players who have appeared in the Football League, FA Cup, Football League Cup, Associated Members Cups and other competitive first team matches up to the end of the 1996-97 season. The "first" and "last" seasons are the first year of each season; thus a player with the entry 1966 to 1971 appeared between the seasons 1966-67 and 1971-72. An entry in the first season column only indicates that the player only appeared in a single season. Entries on more than one line indicate a player had more than one spell at the club. Players still on the club's books at 1 August 1997 are indicated by * in the last season and next club columns. (L) in the 'Previous Club' column indicates a player who was signed on loan.

The appearances and goals column have headings for the Football League, FA Cup, Football League Cup and other games. The latter column includes matches in the Division Three North Cup, Watney Cup, Full and Associated Members' Cups. It also includes matches in the Combination (1888-89); Midland League (1889-91; 1908-09; and 1920-21); Football Alliance (1891-92); United League (1908-09); Central League (1911-12); Vauxhall Conference (1987-88); FA Trophy (1987-88) and GMAC Cup (1987-88).

Separate lists are included for players as follows:

i) Those who only appeared in the three games in 1939-40 which were later expunged from Football League records.

ii) Those whose only appearances were in games that were abandoned.

iii) Those who were unused substitutes.

iv) All players who appeared in war-time football (1915-19 and 1939-46). Where such players were guests from other teams their club is indicated.

SEASON RECORDS

The seasonal statistics pages (that follow the 'Who Who's' section) have been designed for easy reference, and are generally self-explanatory, however the following notes are given to avoid confusion.

Left hand column signifies the match number or the round number in a cup competition, e.g. 5QF = 5th qualifying round, 2R = 2nd round, 3Rr = 3rd round replay, 1R2r = 1st round second replay, 1R2L = 1st round second leg, SF = Semi-final, F = Final, NQF = Northern Quarter-final.
The second column signifies the date (month abbreviated)
The third column shows the opposition team (upper case - capital letters - a Lincoln home match, lower case - away match). Neutral, or alternative venues are indicated otherwise.
The fourth column shows the match result (Lincoln score first)
The fifth column shows the attendance - from 1925 when official records began.
The sixth column provides the Lincoln goalscorers (where known). Figure in brackets is the number of goals scored by that player, OG ('own goal') indicates a goal credited to the opposition team. Where space is limited, the goalscorers have been shown at the end of the appropriate table as indicated.

Right hand column, the players table: The numbers refer to the shirt number worn by that player in the starting line-up (or the accepted position in pre-War seasons, i.e. 1 = goalkeeper, 2 = right-back, 6 = left-half, 10 = inside-right, etc.). Unused substitutes have not been included. Used substitutes - no.12 replaced player suffixed *, no.14 replaced player suffixed #, no.15 replaced player suffixed ". No. 13 is used for substitute goalkeeper. Additional players are shown at the end of the appropriate table, the first number/letters indicating the match or round number, the second number, that player's position/shirt number (e.g. 38/6 = match 38, player number 6).

LINCOLN CITY PLAYERS WHO'S WHO

Sheet No.1 — Addinall to Bickerstaffe

Player		Date of Birth	Place of Birth	Died	First Season	Last Season	Previous Club	Next Club	League	FAC	LC	Other	Lge.	FAC	LC	Other
ADDINALL P	Percy	1888	Hull	1932	1919		West End (Lincoln)	Grantham Town	15	0	0	0	0	0	0	0
AINSWORTH G	Gareth	10/05/73	Blackburn		1995	*	Preston North End	*	77	2	6	4	34	0	2	1
AINSWORTH W	Walter	c1916			1937		Sheffield Wed	Cheltenham Town	0	0	0	1	0	0	0	0
AITKEN R	Robert	c1885			1908		Maxwelltown Vol.		0	0	0	6	0	0	0	0
ALCIDE C J	Colin	14/04/72	Huddersfield		1995	*	Emley	*	60+9	1	3+2	2	14	0	2	0
ALCOCK					1920				0	0	0	1	0	0	0	0
ALEXANDER K	Keith	14/11/56	Nottingham		1990	1992	Stockport County	Mansfield Town	26+19	1	1+4	1	4	0	0	0
ALFORD F J	Frank	14/05/01	Swindon	1982	1925		Barrow	Scunthorpe United	20	0	0	0	3	0	0	0
ALLEN P	Percy	02/07/1895	West Ham	1969	1923	1924	West Ham United	Northampton Town	59	2	0	0	4	0	0	0
ALLEN R L	Ron	22/04/35	Birmingham		1958	1960	Birmingham City	Retired	60	2	0	0	1	0	0	0
ALLISON A	Arthur				1896		Wisbech Town		1	0	0	0	0	0	0	0
ALLISON K	Ken	06/01/37	Edinburgh		1965	1966	Darlington	Rochester (USA)	41+1	1	0+1	0	13	0	0	0
ALLON J B	Joe	12/11/66	Gateshead		1995		Port Vale	Hartlepool	3+1	0	1	0	0	0	0	0
ALSTON W	Bill	19/04/1884		1971	1907		Maxwelltown Vol.	Rochdale	18	0	0	0	2	0	0	0
AMBLER E	Edward				1888		Lincoln Ramblers		0	0	0	2	0	0	0	0
ANDERSEN N J	Nicky	29/03/69	Lincoln		1989		Mansfield Town	Nuneaton Borough	1	0	0	0	0	0	0	0
ANDERSON G T	Geoff	26/11/44	Sheerness		1966		Mansfield Town	Brentford	44	1	3	0	6	0	1	0
ANDERSON R	Robert	c1902	Ardrossan		1930	1931	Newport County		27	1	0	0	0	0	0	0
ANDREWS C	Charles				1905	1907	Liberal Club (Linc)	Rotherham Town	5	0	0	0	0	0	0	0
ANDREWS H	Harold	13/08/03	Lincoln	1988	1924	1927	St. Botolph's OB	Notts County	75	7	0	0	41	2	0	0
APPLETON M A	Michael	04/12/75	Salford		1995		Manchester Utd (L)		4	0	0	1	0	0	0	0
ARMITAGE H	Harold	16/08/01	Sheffield	1973	1926		Bristol Rovers	Scarborough	9	3	0	0	0	0	0	0
ASHURST W	William	04/05/1894	Willington	1947	1919		Leeds City	Notts County	24	0	0	0	0	0	0	0
ASNIP J	John	17/07/1881	Sheffield		1901				1	0	0	0	0	0	0	0
ASNIP T	Thomas	18/02/1883	Sheffield	1918	1904		St Catherines	Adelaide	1	0	0	0	0	0	0	0
ASPDEN R	Richard				1886	1888			0	11	0	3	0	0	0	0
ATKIN A	Arthur	1893	Skegness	1952	1912	1923	Skegness FC	Boston	96	6	0	36	2	0	0	1
ATKINSON G A	Arthur	30/09/09	Goole	1983	1932		Goole Town	Hull City	9	0	0	0	5	0	0	0
ATKINSON G H	George	02/04/1869	Sleaford	1953	1890		Lincoln Amateurs		0	1	0	2	0	0	0	0
AUSTIN K L	Kevin	12/02/73	London		1996	*	Leyton Orient	*	44	0	6	1	0	0	0	0
BACON A P	Arthur	1884	Basford, Notts		1906		Sutton Junction	Sutton Town	4	0	0	0	0	0	0	0
BAGGALEY T	Thomas	c1862	Sneinton, Notts		1885	1886	Lincoln Albion		0	2	0	0	0	0	0	0
BAILEY T	Thomas				1907		Burton United	Walsall	1	0	0	0	0	0	0	0
BAINBRIDGE R	Robert				1920	1922	Jarrow	Sittingbourne	35	5	0	37	0	0	0	0
BALL A	Alf	1890	Clowne	1952	1913	1920	Clowne Rising Star	Mansfield Town	97	7	0	37	13	1	0	9
BALL S G	Gary	15/12/59	St Austell		1979		Plymouth Argyle		3	0	0	0	0	0	0	0
BANNAN T N	Tommy	13/04/36	Darngavel		1955	1956	Wrexham	Wrexham	67	2	0	0	19	3	0	0
BANNISTER C	Charlie	1879	Burton on Trent	1952	1897	1900	Oldham County	Swindon Town	106	7	0	0	10	0	0	0
BANNISTER G	Gary	22/07/60	Warrington		1994		Hong Kong Rang.	Darlington	25+4	1+1	2	1	7	1	0	0
BANNISTER N	Neville	21/07/37	Brierfield		1960	1963	Bolton Wanderers	Hartlepool	68	6	8	0	16	0	2	0
BARACLOUGH I	Ian	04/12/70	Leicester		1992	1993	Grimsby Town	Mansfield Town	68+5	4	7	7	10	0	1	0
BARBER W A J	William	20/12/08	Lincoln	1954	1933	1934	Luton Town	Crewe Alexandra	13	0	0	0	0	0	0	0
BARBOUR H	Humphrey				1888		Third Lanark		5	0	0	0	2	0	0	0
BARLOW P D	Phil	19/12/46	Shipley		1967		Bradford City		5	0	1	0	0	0	0	0
BARNARD R S	Ray	06/04/33	Middlesbrough		1960	1962	Middlesbrough	Grantham	43	2	2	0	0	0	0	0
BARNETT J V	Jason	21/04/76	Shrewsbury		1995	*	Wolves	*	60+8	1	3	4	2	0	0	0
BARRATT J	Jos	21/02/1895	Bulkington	1968	1924	1925	Pontypridd	Bristol Rovers	74	4	0	0	7	0	0	0
BARRELL G	George	07/07/1888	Lincoln	1960	1908	1914	Rustons Engineers	Rustons	141	7	0	42	26	1	0	16
BARRETT K B	Ken	05/05/38	Bromsgrove		1959	1962	Aston Villa	Stourbridge	17	0	2	0	4	0	0	0
BARRICK H	Harry	1883	Skegness		1906		Scunthorpe United	Scunthorpe United	5	1	0	0	2	0	0	0
BARTON D R	Roger	25/09/46	Jump		1964	1965	Wolves	Barnsley	28	1	1	0	1	0	0	0
BARTON W	Kenny				1898		Adelaide	Grantham	1	0	0	0	0	0	0	0
					1900		Grantham	Adelaide	1	0	0	0	0	0	0	0
BASSNETT A	Alf	10/04/1893	St Helens	1966	1926	1928	Burnley	Ballymena	89	9	0	0	6	0	0	0
BATCH N	Nigel	09/11/57	Huddersfield		1987		Grimsby Town	Darlington	0	3	38	6	0	0	0	0
BATES L					1890	1891			0	1	0	15	0	0	0	0
BATES S	Sydney	17/05/12	Wardley Colliery	1984	1934		Eighton Banks	Millwall	6	0	0	0	0	0	0	0
BATTY W	Billy	13/07/1886	Killamarsh		1911		Bristol City	Swindon Town	0	4	0	23	0	2	0	17
BAUCHOP J R	James	22/05/1886	Sauchie	1948	1923		Doncaster Rovers		28	1	0	0	11	1	0	0
BAVIN A	Arthur	05/02/1887	Nottingham	1961	1907		Liberal Club (Linc)	Worksop Town	5	1	0	0	0	0	0	0
BAYNE K	Kenny	24/01/1858	Lincoln	1924	1884	1886	Lincoln Albion		0	7	0	0	0	0	0	0
BEAN A S	Billy	25/08/1915	Lincoln	1993	1934	1948	Lincoln Corinthians	Retired	171	14	0	2	10	0	0	0
BEAUMONT S	Sydney	08/10/1889	Wrestlingworth	1939	1904		Colchester Town		5	0	0	0	0	0	0	0
BEAVON D G	David	08/12/1961	Nottingham		1981	1982	Notts County	Northampton Town	7+1	0	0	0	0	0	0	0
BEEL G W	George	26/02/1900	Lincoln	1980	1919			Merthyr Town	23	1	0	0	6	0	0	0
					1931		Burnley	Rochdale	9	0	0	0	6	0	0	0
BELL D M	Derek	30/10/56	Wyberton, Lincs		1979	1982	Barnsley	Chesterfield	69+14	2+1	10+2	3	33	0	4	3
BELL R L	Ray	06/12/30	West Seaham		1950		Seaham CW		1	0	0	0	0	0	0	0
BELL W J	William	1904	Backworth		1924		Chopwell Institute	Mansfield Town	20	2	0	0	3	1	0	0
BENNETT J C					1891		Grantham Rovers		0	0	0	5	0	0	0	0
BENNETT J W	Jack	29/11/1879	Liverpool		1900		Wellingborough	Northampton Town	4	3	0	0	0	0	0	0
BENTLEY E	Edwin				1901	1908	St Marys FC		10	0	0	9	0	0	0	0
BESTON J	James	1880	Houghton le Spring		1907	1908	Hebburn Argyle		3	0	0	6	0	0	0	0
BETT F	Fred	05/12/20	Scunthorpe		1948		Coventry City	Spalding United	14	1	0	0	2	0	0	0
BICKERSTAFFE J	Jack	08/11/1918	St Helens		1948	1950	Bury	Halifax Town	12	0	0	0	1	0	0	0

Sheet No.2   Biggins to Burnett

Player		Date of Birth	Place of Birth	Died	First Season	Last Season	Previous Club	Next Club	Appearances League	FAC	LC	Other	Goals Lge.	FAC	LC	Other
BIGGINS W	Wayne	20/11/61	Sheffield		1980		Apprentice	Kings Lynn	8	0	0	0	1	0	0	0
BIMSON S	Stuart	29/09/69	Liverpool		1996	*	Bury	*	13+2	0	0	1	1	0	0	0
BIRCH B	Brian	08/11/31	Salford		1952	1954	Wolves	Barrow	56	4	0	0	16	1	0	0
BIRCHALL R	Richard	14/10/1887	Prescot		1912		Norwich City	Worksop Town	7	0	0	0	1	0	0	0
BIRD I	Ike	14/07/1895	Kimberley	1984	1919	1920	Ilkeston United	Ilkeston United	8	4	0	33	2	2	0	14
BIRKBECK J	John	01/10/32	Lincoln		1954		Spilsby	Boston United	2	0	0	0	0	0	0	0
BISSETT J T	James	19/06/1898	Lochee		1926	1927	Middlesbrough	Dundee	32	1	0	0	6	0	0	0
BISSETT J	John				1898		Dalbeattie		18	0	0	0	0	0	0	0
BLADES W J	William				1894				3	0	0	0	1	0	0	0
BLAKEY C H S	Charles	1896	Lincoln	1962	1919			Doncaster Rovers	30	1	0	0	0	0	0	0
BLAND G P	Pat	24/02/15	Tutbury	1970	1936		Horncastle Town	Bradford PA	1	0	0	0	0	0	0	0
BLOOR M B	Micky	25/03/49	Wrexham		1971	1972	Stoke City	Darlington	71+2	3	4	0	0	0	0	0
BLOW E P	Percy	16/11/1877	North Hykeham,Lincs	1938	1900	1905	Blue Star	Horncastle United	162	18	0	0	1	0	0	0
BLYTON E V	Edmund	01/06/1858	Lincoln	1935	1884		Lincoln Rovers	Lincoln Rangers	0	1	0	0	0	0	0	0
BOAST E	Ernest	c1877		1961	1903				21	0	0	0	0	0	0	0
BODEN J G	Jackie	4/10/26	Cleethorpes		1949	1950	Skegness Town	Skegness Town	3	0	0	0	2	0	0	0
BOLAM D R	David	24/01/1898	Newcastle	1983	1924		Chester-le-Street	Exeter City	3	0	0	0	1	0	0	0
BOLTON I R	Ian	13/07/53	Leicester		1976			Notts County (L)	1	0	2	0	0	0	0	0
BONE G	George	c1863	Scotland	1936	1888	1889	Halliwell	Retired	0	1	0	2	0	0	0	0
BONHAM J W	John	11/1/1895	Wallsend	1973	1921		Wallsend Park Villa		1	0	0	0	0	0	0	0
BONSON J	Joe	19/09/36	Barnsley		1965	1966	Brentford	Hednesford Town	46+1	1	3	0	16	1	2	0
BOOTH D	Dennis	09/04/49	Stanley		1973	1977	Southend	Watford	162	13	10+1	0	9	0	1	0
BOS G	Gysbert	22/03/73	Spakenburg (Holland)		1995	1996	Ijsselmeervogels	Rotherham	28+6	1	6	1	6	1	3	0
BOSBURY C E	Charlie	05/12/1897	Newhaven	1929	1926	1928	Preston North End		85	9	0	0	30	3	0	0
BOULLEMIER L A	Leon	1874	Stoke on Trent	1954	1895	1896		Reading	49	4	0	0	0	0	0	0
BOULTON C D	Colin	12/09/45	Cheltenham		1980		Los Angeles Aztecs	Retired	4	0	3	0	0	0	0	0
BOUND M T	Matthew	09/11/72	Melksham		1995		Stockport C. (L)		3+1	0	0	1	0	0	0	0
BOWERY B N	Bert	29/10/54	St Kitts (WI)		1975		Notts Forest (L)		2+2	0	0	0	1	0	0	0
BOWLER G F	George				1893				6	0	0	0	0	0	0	0
BOWLING I	Ian	27/07/65	Sheffield		1988	1992	Gainsborough Trin.	Bradford City	59	2	3	4	0	0	0	0
BOYLEN J	John	c1898	Wishaw		1921	1922	Newmain Juniors	Wigan Borough	59	2	0	0	4	0	0	0
BRACEWELL K	Ken	05/10/36	Colne		1963	1964	Norwich City	Margate	23	0	1	0	1	0	0	0
BRADBURY J J L	John	1878	South Bank		1895		Stockport County	Ashton North End	2	0	0	0	0	0	0	0
BRADBURY					1891				0	0	0	1	0	0	0	0
BRADLEY B	Brendan	07/06/50	Derry		1972		Finn Harps	Finn Harps	31	2	0	0	12	1	0	0
BRADY					1890				0	1	0	0	1	0	0	0
BRAILSFORD J R	James	c1877	Lincoln		1895	1896	Newark Town	Notts County	20	2	0	0	0	0	0	0
BRAMMER G W	George				1890	1892	Lincoln Ramblers		2	1	0	5	0	0	0	0
BRANFOOT I G	Ian	26/01/47	Gateshead		1973	1977	Doncaster Rovers	Retired	166	11	12	0	11	1	0	0
BRANSTON T G	Terry	25/07/38	Rugby		1970	1972	Luton Town	Enderby Town	99+1	3	6	0	1	0	0	0
BRAZIER C J	Colin	06/06/57	Solihull		1982		AP Leamington	Walsall	9	0	0	1	0	0	0	0
BRENTNALL C O	Oscar				1920		Sheffield Wed.	Worksop Town	0	4	0	24	0	2	0	24
BRESSINGTON G	Graham	08/07/66	Slough		1981	1992	Wycombe Wands.	Southend United	136+5	6	10	6	7	0	2	0
BREWIS R	Robert	c1885			1907		QPR	Burnley	22	1	0	0	11	0	0	0
BRIGHTWELL D J	David	07/01/71	Lutterworth		1995		Manchester C. (L)		5	0	2	0	0	0	0	0
BRINDLEY H	Horrace	01/01/1885	Knutton, Staffs	1971	1911	1913		Chester	50	7	0	32	4	1	0	6
BRITTAIN W	William				1894		Grantham Rovers	Grantham Rovers	17	1	0	0	0	0	0	0
BROADBENT A H	Albert	20/08/34	Dudley		1961	1962	Doncaster Rovers	Doncaster Rovers	38	3	4	0	4	0	1	0
BROADBENT J	John				1894		Grantham Rovers		2	0	0	0	0	0	0	0
BROOK H	Harold	15/10/21	Sheffield		1957		Leeds United	Retired	4	0	0	0	1	0	0	0
BROOKS T W	Tom	02/02/48	Wallsend		1964	1970	Apprentice		103+10	4	2+1	0	1	0	0	0
BROWN E H	Edward				1903	1904			37	0	0	0	9	0	0	0
BROWN G A	Grant	19/11/69	Sunderland		1989		Leicester City (L)		14	0	2	1	1	0	0	0
					1989	*	Leicester City	*	274	11	16	16	11	0	1	2
BROWN M	McAndrew				1923				17	1	0	0	0	0	0	0
BROWN M J	Mick	11/07/39	Walsall		1967		Hull City	Cambridge United	38	0	5	0	0	0	0	0
BROWN P	Paul	10/12/64	Lincoln		1982		Apprentice	Lincoln United	0	0	0	0+1	0	0	0	0
BROWN P J	Phil	16/01/66	Sheffield		1987	1989	Stockport County	Kettering Town	32+11	4	5	50+2	3	1	1	19
BROWN S R	Steve	06/12/73	Southend		1995	*	Gillingham	*	31+10	1	0+3	3	5	0	0	1
BROWN T	Tom	07/11/33	Leven		1957		Newburgh	Boston United	3	0	0	0	0	0	0	0
BROWN W	William				1896			Tottenham Hotspur	1	0	0	0	0	0	0	0
BRYAN J J	Jack	22/08/1897	Langwith	1978	1919	1921		Mansfield Town	75	6	0	36	1	0	0	1
BUCKLEY J W	Jack	24/11/03	Prudhoe, Newcastle	1985	1932	1934	Doncaster Rovers	Grantham	92	2	0	0	0	0	0	0
BUCKLEY S	Steve	16/10/53	Brinsley, Notts		1986	1987	Derby County	Boston United	36	1	4	31	2	0	0	0
BUCKLEY W	Walter	30/04/06	Eccleshall		1930	1932	Bradford PA	Rochdale	81	6	0	0	1	0	0	0
BUICK J L	Joe	01/07/33	Broughty Ferry		1955	1961	Broughty Athletic	Cheltenham Town	31	1	1	0	3	0	0	0
BUIST A G	George	c1884			1904	1907	Willington Quay		83	7	0	0	0	0	0	0
BULGER C G	Charles	19/01/15	Manchester	1976	1935		Birmingham City	Walsall	22	1	0	1	10	0	0	0
BURDEN B	Brian	26/11/39	West Stockwith		1960		West Stockwith	Gainsborough Trin.	1	0	0	0	0	0	0	0
BURDETT T	Tom	22/10/15	West Hartlepool		1936	1938	Fulham	Bury	27	0	0	1	12	0	0	0
BURKE J	Jimmy				1894	1896	Grantham Rovers	Grantham Rovers	52	5	0	0	7	1	0	0
BURKE M	Marshall	26/03/59	Glasgow		1982	1983	Blackburn Rovers	Scarborough	49+1	1	5+1	4	6	0	0	2
BURKE M	Michael	28/06/04	Glasgow	1984	1934	1935	Dundalk	Southport	27	2	0	0	1	2	0	1
BURKE S J	Steve	29/09/60	Nottingham		1985		QPR (L)		4+1	0	2	0	0	0	1	0
BURNETT A P	Alf	23/7/22	Aberdeen	1977	1949		Barrow	Skegness Town	4	0	0	0	1	0	0	0

Sheet No.3 — Burnikell to Corner

Name		Date of Birth	Place of Birth	Died	First Season	Last Season	Previous Club	Next Club	League	FAC	LC	Other	Lge.	FAC	LC	Other
BURNIKELL W F	Billy	09/12/10	Southwick	1980	1929	1932		Bradford City	25	0	0	0	0	0	0	0
BURNS J					1888	1889			0	0	0	4	0	0	0	2
BURNS P	Peter				1893				2	1	0	0	0	0	0	0
BURNS R	Robert				1897		Abercorn		1	0	0	0	0	0	0	0
BURRIDGE J	John	03/12/51	Workington		1993		Scarborough	Enfield	4	0	0	0	0	0	0	0
BURROWS D W	David	07/04/61	Bilsthorpe		1978		Apprentice	Kings Lynn	1	0	0	0	0	0	0	0
BURTON T C	Thomas	c1870			1889	1890		Doncaster Rovers	0	6	0	12	0	5	0	3
BUTLER J	Joseph	1879	Horsehay, Shrops	1941	1914		Sunderland	Rochdale	37	2	0	0	0	0	0	0
BUTLER L S	Lee	30/05/66	Sheffield		1986		Harworth Colliery	Aston Villa	30	1	1	0	0	0	0	0
BUXTON G	George				1891	1892			0	1	0	7	0	0	0	0
BYRON G	Gordon	04/09/53	Prescot, Lancs		1974		Sheffield Wed	Clifton Town	3+3	3+1	0	0	0	0	0	0
CALDERHEAD D	David	19/08/1864	Hurlford	1938	1900		Notts County	Retired	2	0	0	0	0	0	0	0
CALLAND E	Ted	15/06/32	East Hedleyhope	1995	1961		Port Vale	Cheltenham Town	7	0	2	0	3	0	0	0
CALLENDER J	John	03/09/12	Wylam	1980	1936	1937	Chesterfield	Port Vale	75	6	0	1	26	0	0	0
CALLENDER T S	Tom	20/09/20	Wylam		1938		Crawcrook Albion	Gateshead	23	0	0	0	0	0	0	0
CAMERON R					1892				15	5	0	0	3	1	0	0
CAMMACK S R	Steve	20/03/54	Sheffield		1981		Scunthorpe United	Scunthorpe United	18	2+1	4+1	2+1	6	1	0	0
CAMPBELL A	Andrew		Dunfermline		1927		Brighton		5	0	0	0	4	0	0	0
CAMPBELL A	Archibald	1904	Crook, Co Durham		1925	1926	Aston Villa	Craghead United	54	3	0	0	4	0	0	0
CAMPBELL D A	David	02/06/65	Eglington, Derry		1993		Burnley (L)		2+2	0	0	1	1	0	0	0
CAMPBELL J C	James	11/04/37	St Pancras		1962	1963	Portsmouth	Wellington Town	63	7	8	0	16	3	2	0
CAMPBELL J	John	07/03/10	Stevenston		1933	1938	Leicester City	Scunthorpe United	184	9	0	5	104	4	0	2
CAPPER J	Jack	23/07/31	Wrexham		1955	1958	Headington United	Chester	21	2	0	0	0	0	0	0
CARBON M P	Matt	08/06/75	Nottingham		1992	1995	YTS	Derby County	66+3	3	4	4+3	10	0	1	0
CARGILL D A	David	21/07/36	Arbroath		1960		Derby County	Arbroath	9	1	0	0	0	0	0	0
CARLING T P	Terry	26/02/39	Otley		1962	1963	Leeds United	Walsall	84	7	8	0	0	0	0	0
CARMICHAEL M	Matt	13/05/64	Singapore		1989	1992	Basingstoke Town	Scunthorpe United	113+20	4+1	9+1	7+1	18	0	1	2
CARR D	David	31/01/57	Aylesham		1979	1982	Luton Town	Torquay United	165+3	7	18	9	4	0	1	0
CARSON A					1907				1	0	0	0	0	0	0	0
CARTWRIGHT G	George				1945				0	4	0	0	0	0	0	0
CARTWRIGHT P	Philip	08/02/08	Scarborough	1974	1930	1932	Hull City	Bournemouth	86	2	0	0	21	2	0	0
CASEY P	Paul	06/10/61	Rinteln (W Germany)		1987	1990	Boston United	Boston United	44+5	0	4	11	4	0	0	0
CAVANAGH J A	Jack	1891	Newcastle		1914		Ashington		2	0	0	0	0	0	0	0
CHADBURN J	John	1873	Mansfield	1924	1893		Mansfield Greenhalgh's	Notts County	25	2	0	0	8	1	0	0
CHAMBERS H					1888				0	3	0	5	0	0	0	0
CHAMBERS R C	Reuben	1908	Nottingham		1926		Beeston Ericssons		7	0	0	0	0	0	0	0
CHAMBERS R	Robert	11/12/1899	Newcastle	1972	1920	1921	Brighton West End	Burnley	23	1	0	19	12	0	0	8
CHAPMAN C E	Charles	26/08/1860	Swinstead, Lincs	1901	1884		Horncastle	Horncastle	0	1	0	0	0	0	0	0
CHAPMAN D P	Darren	15/11/74	Lincoln		1991		YTS	Lincoln United	0+1	0	0	0	0	0	0	0
CHAPMAN F E	Frank	c1864		1941	1884		Horncastle	Horncastle	0	1	0	0	0	0	0	0
CHAPMAN R C	Roy	18/03/34	Birmingham	1983	1957	1960	Aston Villa	Mansfield Town	103	3	2	0	45	0	1	0
					1964	1966	Mansfield Town	Port Vale	69+1	2	5	0	32	1	2	0
CHEETHAM T M	Tommy	11/10/10	Byker		1945	1947	Brentford	Retired	47	10	0	0	29	6	0	0
CHESSER W E	Billy	11/08/1893	Stockton on Tees	1949	1913	1919	Bradford City	Merthyr Town	76	2	0	0	18	2	0	0
CHIPPERFIELD F	Frank	02/12/1895	Newcastle	1979	1919		Leeds City	Middlesbrough	23	1	0	0	0	0	0	0
CLARE J	Joe	04/02/10	Westhoughton	1987	1937	1938	Norwich City	Ruston Bucyrus	68	4	0	0	23	2	0	0
CLARK D	Derek	10/08/31	Newcastle		1951		Medomsley Juniors	Ransome & Marles	4	0	0	0	1	0	0	0
CLARKE D	David	19/02/1865	Lincoln	1948	1884		Lincoln Rovers		0	1	0	0	0	0	0	0
CLARKE D A	David	03/12/64	Nottingham		1987	1993	Notts County	Doncaster Rovers	141+6	6+2	15+2	37+5	9	1	2	5
CLARKE W G	William	1880	Mauchline	1940	1909		Bradford City	Croydon Common	35	1	0	0	1	0	0	0
CLARKE W	William				1898	1899			35	2	0	0	6	2	0	0
CLEWS M D	Maxie	12/03/31	Tipton		1953	1954	Wolves		7	0	0	0	0	0	0	0
CLIFF E	Eddie	30/09/51	Liverpool		1974		Notts County (L)		3	0	0	0	0	0	0	0
CLINT T	Thomas	1892	Gateshead	1965	1921		Felling CW		1	0	0	0	0	0	0	0
CLOTWORTHY H	Hugh	08/03/14	Kilwinning	1984	1938		Kilwinning Rangers		2	0	0	0	0	0	0	0
COBB W W	Billy	29/09/40	Newark		1966	1967	Brentford	Boston United	67	1	5	0	10	1	1	0
COCKERILL G	Glenn	25/08/59	Grimsby		1976	1979	Louth United	Swindon Town	65+6	2	2	0	10	0	0	0
					1981	1983	Swindon Town	Sheffield United	114+1	7	16	8+1	25	0	1	4
CODLING J					1890	1891	Lincoln Casuals		0	1	0	7	0	0	0	0
COKER A O	Ade	19/05/54	Lagos (Nigeria)		1974		West Ham (L)		6	1	0	0	1	0	0	0
COLLINS S M	Steve	21/03/62	Stamford		1984	1985	Southend United	Peterborough Utd.	24	1	2	3	0	0	0	0
COMMONS M	Mike	18/05/40	Doncaster		1959	1960	Wath Wanderers	Workington	2	0	1	0	1	0	0	0
COMRIE J	James	31/03/1881	Denny	1916	1910		Bradford City		12	0	0	0	1	0	0	0
CONNOR J E	Edward	1884	Liverpool	1955	1907		Eccles Borough		4	0	0	0	0	0	0	0
CONNOR J	James	c1917	Cleland, Lanarks		1938		Coltess United		7	0	0	0	0	0	0	0
COOK M R	Mark	07/08/70	Boston		1988	1989	YTS	Boston United	7	0	1	1	0	0	0	0
COOPER J	Joseph	1899	Chesterfield	1959	1932		Grimsby Town		24	1	0	0	5	0	0	0
COOPER R D	Richard	07/05/65	Brent		1985	1986	Sheffield United	Exeter City	57+4	1	5	4	2	0	0	0
COOPER T	Terry	11/03/50	Croesceiliog		1971		Notts County (L)		3	0	0	0	0	0	0	0
					1972	1978	Notts County	Bradford City	265+2	15+1	13	0	12	1	0	0
COOPER W	William		Mexborough		1911		Rochdale		0	0	0	0	0	0	0	0
COPLEY D I	Dennis	21/12/21	Misterton		1946		Norwich City	Boston United	1	0	0	0	0	0	0	0
CORBETT F W	Frederick	08/10/09	Birmingham	1974	1936	1938	Manchester City		103	9	0	1	0	0	0	0
CORK A G	Alan	04/03/59	Derby		1977		Derby County (L)		5	0	0	0	0	0	0	0
CORNER J N	Norman	16/02/43	Horden		1967	1968	Hull City	Bradford City	44+1	4	3	0	12	1	1	0

Sheet No.4   Cornforth to Dunne

		Date of Birth	Place of Birth	Died	First Season	Last Season	Previous Club	Next Club	Appearances League	FAC	LC	Other	Goals Lge.	FAC	LC	Other
CORNFORTH J M	John	07/10/67	Whitley Bay		1989		Sunderland (L)		9	0	0	0	1	0	0	0
CORT C E R	Carl	01/11/77	London		1996		Wimbledon (L)		5+1	0	0	0	1	0	0	0
COSTELLO P	Peter	31/10/69	Halifax		1991		Peterborough (L)		3	0	0	0	0	0	0	0
					1992	1993	Peterborough	Kettering Town	28+10	2	2+2	4	7	1	0	1
COSTIGAN T	Thomas				1910		Seaham Harbour		2	0	0	0	1	0	0	0
COTTAM J E	John	05/06/50	Worksop		1972		Notts Forest (L)		1	0	0	0	0	0	0	0
COULTON C	Charles				1892		Birmingham St Georges		12	5	0	0	0	0	0	0
COUSANS E A	Eustace	27/05/1860	Lincoln	1943	1884		Lindum	Lindum	0	2	0	0	0	0	0	0
COWLEY B J	Jack	1877	Burton on Trent	1927	1899	1901	Hinckley Town	Swindon Town	68	3	0	0	3	0	0	0
COX M L	Mark	04/10/59	Birmingham		1976	1977	Apprentice	Doncaster Rovers	3+2	0	0	0	0	0	0	0
COXON W G	William	28/04/33	Derby		1957	1958	Norwich City	Bournemouth	11	0	0	0	1	0	0	0
CRAWFORD J	John	23/02/1880	Renton		1900	1902	Renton	Notts Forest	85	14	0	0	1	0	0	0
CRAWLEY F P	Frank	22/05/1894	Paisley	1945	1923		Blackburn Rovers	Accrington Stanley	1	0	0	0	0	0	0	0
CREANE G M	Gerard	02/02/62	Lincoln		1978	1982	Apprentice	Boston United	6+1	0	2+1	0+1	0	0	0	0
CROMBIE A	Allen	16/10/61	Lincoln		1987		Lincoln United	Boston United	0	0	0	1	0	0	0	0
CROMBIE D M	Dean	09/08/57	Lincoln		1976	1977	Ruston Bucyrus	Grimsby Town	33	0	1+1	0	0	0	0	0
					1990		Bolton Wanderers	Retired	0+1	0	0	0	0	0	0	0
CROSBY G	Gary	08/05/64	Sleaford		1986		Lincoln United	Lincoln United	6+1	0	2	0	0	0	0	0
CROSS G F	Graham	05/11/43	Leicester		1978		Enderby Town	Enderby Town	19	0	0	0	0	0	0	0
CROUCH N J	Nigel	24/11/58	Ardleigh		1979		Ipswich Town (L)		7	0	0	0	0	0	0	0
CULLEN J	Joseph			1905	1899		Tottenham Hotspur		12	1	0	0	0	0	0	0
CULLEY J	James	20/07/15	Condorrat	1981	1938		Hibernian	Alloa Athletic	5	0	0	0	0	0	0	0
CUMBERLAND T W	Thomas	1882	Derby		1902		Southwell St Marys	Southwell St Marys	5	1	0	0	0	0	0	0
CUMMING R	Bobby	07/12/55	Airdrie		1987	1988	Grimsby Town	Albany Capitals (USA)	29	4	2	41	5	2	0	9
					1989		Albany Capitals (USA)	Grimsby Borough	11+1	1	0	1	0	0	0	0
CUNNINGHAM A E	Tony	12/11/57	Kingston, Jamaica		1979	1982	Stourbridge	Barnsley	111+12	5+1	13	6	32	0	8	2
CURTIS A V	Albert	1899	Bradford	1967	1922		Robeys (Lincoln)	Gainsborough Trin.	1	0	0	0	0	0	0	0
CURTIS H E	Harold	c1866	Cape Colony	1941	1884		Horncastle	Horncastle	0	1	0	0	0	0	0	0
DAGG H C	Harry	04/03/24	Sunderland		1946		Boston United	Boston United	1	0	0	0	1	0	0	0
DAILLY J	John				1897		Hibernian		1	0	0	0	0	0	0	0
DALEY P	Phil	12/04/67	Liverpool		1994	1995	Wigan Athletic		25+7	1+1	2+1	2+2	5	0	0	1
DANIEL P W	Peter	12/12/55	Hull		1985	1986	Sunderland	Burnley	55	1	2	3	2	0	0	0
DANIELS J F	John	08/01/25	St Helens		1946		Bristol Cidac	New Brighton	17	3	0	0	0	0	0	0
D'ARCEY H C H	Harry	1874	Lincoln	1930	1894	1896			3	0	0	0	0	0	0	0
DAVIDSON J	James	1876	Edinburgh		1896		Burnley (L)		9	0	0	0	1	0	0	0
DAVIDSON R	Roger	27/10/48	Islington		1971		Fulham	Aldershot	6	1	0	0	0	0	0	0
DAVIES A M	Alec	21/05/20	Dundonald		1945	1948	Kiveton Park	Frickley Colliery	37	6	0	0	9	1	0	0
DAVIS D J	Darren	05/02/67	Sutton in Ashfield		1988	1990	Notts County	Maidstone	97+5	4	8	6	4	1	1	1
					1995		Grantham Town	Grantham Town	3	0	0	1	0	0	0	0
DAWS A	Tony	10/09/66	Sheffield		1993	1995	Grimsby Town	Scarborough	42+9	1+1	0	1	13	0	0	0
DAWSON C M	Carl	24/06/34	Harwich		1950				1	0	0	0	0	0	0	0
DAWSON					1890				0	0	0	8	0	0	0	1
DEACON R	Dickie	26/06/11	Glasgow	1986	1936	1938	Northampton Town	Retired	110	9	0	1	22	3	0	0
DENNIS J A	Tony	01/12/63	Maidenhead		1996		Colchester United	Gainsborough	23+5	0	1+2	1	2	0	0	0
DICKINS M J	Matt	03/09/70	Sheffield		1990	1991	Sheffield United	Blackburn Rovers	27	1	1	2	0	0	0	0
					1993		Blackburn Rovers (L)		0	0	0	1	0	0	0	0
DICKINSON S	Sydney	17/08/06	Nottingham	1984	1934		Port Vale	Grantham Town	14	1	0	0	3	0	0	0
DICKSON C	Charles		Dundee		1890			Bootle	0	0	0	9	0	0	0	2
DILSWORTH E	Eddie	16/04/46	Freetown, Sierra Leone		1966		Wealdstone	Wealdstone	2	0	0	0	0	0	0	0
DINSDALE W A	Billy	12/07/03	Darlington	1984	1926	1928	Aston Villa	Bradford PA	92	8	0	0	69	9	0	0
					1930		Bradford PA	Darlington	34	2	0	0	20	5	0	0
DIXON A	Andrew	19/04/68	Louth		1990		Southend United		0	0	0+1	0	0	0	0	0
DIXON B	Ben	16/09/74	Lincoln		1991	1995	YTS	Blackpool	33+10	0+1	2	3+1	0	0	0	0
DIXON E	Ted	1884	Easington		1905	1906	Sunderland	Hull City	35	2	0	0	3	1	0	0
DIXON F	Fred	c1917	Lincoln		1936		Lincoln Corinthians	Newark Town	1	0	0	0	0	0	0	0
DIXON J	Jack	c1882		1942	1901		St Mary's (Lincoln)	Gainsborough Trin	17	5	0	0	4	2	0	0
DIXON J	Joseph	c1902			1925		Penrhiceiber	Boston Town	1	0	0	0	0	0	0	0
DOBSON P	Paul	17/12/62	Hartlepool		1990	1991	Scarborough	Darlington	13+8	0	1+1	0	5	0	1	0
DOCHERTY E	Edward				1895		Duntocher Harp		5	0	0	0	2	0	0	0
DOCHERTY T	Tom	15/04/24	Penshaw		1947	1949	Murton Colliery	Norwich City	45	2	0	0	3	0	0	0
DODDS E	Jock	07/09/15	Grangemouth		1948	1949	Everton	Retired	60	2	0	0	38	2	0	0
DODGIN W	Bill	17/04/09	Gateshead		1932	1933	Huddersfield Town	Charlton	46	0	0	0	1	0	0	0
DOOLEY D	Derek	13/12/29	Sheffield		1946		Sheffield YMCA	Sheffield Wed.	2	0	0	0	2	0	0	0
DOUGHERTY J	Joseph	c1892	Darlington		1923				2	0	0	0	0	0	0	0
DOVEY D	Donald	13/04/1900	Lincoln	1979	1925	1926	Horncastle Town	Newark Town	14	0	0	0	3	0	0	0
DOWALL W	Bill		Thornliebank		1936		Bury		5	0	0	1	0	0	0	0
DOWLING M	Michael	1889	Jarrow		1914	1919	Jarrow	Ebbw Vale	28	0	0	0	4	0	0	0
DOWNIE M	Mitchell	09/12/23	Troon		1954	1958	Bradford PA	Goole Town	157	5	0	0	0	0	0	0
DOWNIE R	Robert				1897		Albion Rovers		6	0	0	0	0	0	0	0
DRANSFIELD G R	George				1935		High Green Athletic	Macclesfield Town	3	0	0	0	1	0	0	0
DRYSDALE B	Brian	24/02/43	West Hartlepool		1959	1964	Thornley CW Juniors	Hartlepool	21	2	1	0	0	0	0	0
DUCKWORTH J	Joseph				1885	1890	Blackburn Rovers		0	21	0	28	0	1	0	1
DUCKWORTH R W W	Robert	1872	Bury	1924	1894		Rossendale	Rossendale	24	1	0	0	5	0	0	0
DUNKLEY M	Malcolm	12/07/61	Wolverhampton		1988		Bromsgrove Rovers	Rovaniemi (Finland)	9+2	0	0	0	4	0	0	0
DUNNE J	Jack	1890	Donnybrook, Dublin	1974	1914		Shelbourne		23	2	0	0	0	0	0	0

Sheet No.5 — Dunphy to Gamble

Name		Date of Birth	Place of Birth	Died	First Season	Last Season	Previous Club	Next Club	League	FAC	LC	Other	Lge.	FAC	LC	Other
DUNPHY S	Sean	05/11/70	Maltby		1991	1993	Barnsley	Kettering Town	48+5	2	5+1	1	2	0	1	0
DUNWELL P M	Peter	22/11/38	Ecclesfield, Sheffield		1959	1960	Ecclesfield	Ramsgate	14	0	0	0	1	0	0	0
DWANE E J	Eddie	17/07/1896	Valetta, Malta	1973	1920	1923		Boston Town	46	2	0	4	3	0	0	3
DYE D C	Dean	14/03/69	Lincoln		1991		Charlton Athletic	Lincoln United	0+2	0	0	0	0	0	0	0
DYER A C	Alex	14/11/65	Forest Gate, London		1995		Oxford United	Barnet	1	0	1	0	0	0	0	0
DYKES D W	Don	08/06/30	Ashby by Partney, Lincs		1949	1958	British Crop Driers	Mansfield Town	95	6	0	0	4	0	0	0
EASTHAM G R	George	13/09/13	Blackpool		1948	1949	Rochdale	Hyde United	27	0	0	0	1	0	0	0
EDEN A	Alan	08/10/58	Sunderland		1977	1978	Lambton Street BC	Runcorn	5+2	0	0	0	0	0	0	0
EDWARDS R	Roy	26/11/20	Sheffield		1947	1948	Army Football	Denaby United	6	0	0	0	0	0	0	0
EDWARDS W J	Wilf	1904	Fenton		1931		Loughborough Corinthians		1	0	0	0	0	0	0	0
EGAN T W	William	1872	Chirk	1946	1896		Sheffield United		16	3	0	0	0	0	0	0
EGERTON W	Billy	1891	Bollington	1934	1913	1919	Chesterfield Town	Mid Rhondda	76	3	0	0	25	2	0	0
ELLIOTT A	Arthur	1870	Nottingham		1888		Gainsborough Trinity	Gainsborough Trinity	0	0	0	2	0	0	0	2
ELLIS K D	Keith	06/11/35	Sheffield		1965		Cardiff City		7	1	0	0	1	0	0	0
ELLIS S	Sam	12/09/46	Ashton Under Lyne		1973	1976	Mansfield Town	Watford	173	13	8	0	33	4	4	0
ELLIS W T	William	05/11/05	Wolverhampton	1971	1929		Birmingham City	York City	31	2	0	0	11	0	0	0
ELMORE E					1903			Liberal Club (Linc)	1	0	0	0	0	0	0	0
EMERY A J	Tony	04/11/27	Lincoln		1945	1958		Mansfield Town	402	22	0	0	1	0	0	0
ETCHES H	Harry				1902		Adelaide		2	0	0	0	0	0	0	0
EVANS A C	Clive	01/05/57	Birkenhead		1987	1988	Stockport County		42	3	4	46	2	0	0	8
EVANS W	William		Llansantffraid		1900		QPR		3	1	0	0	0	0	0	0
EYRE T	Thomas				1895	1897	Glasgow Ashfield	Hamilton Academicals	65	8	0	0	1	0	0	0
FAIRGRAY N M	Norrie	28/10/1880	Dumfries	1968	1905	1907	Maxwelltown Vol.	Chelsea	60	5	0	0	6	1	0	0
FAIRLEY P L	Peter				1907				4	0	0	0	0	0	0	0
FARMER M C	Mick	22/11/44	Leicester		1965		Birmingham City	Skegness Town	21+1	0	0	0	0	0	0	0
FARRALL A	Alec	03/03/36	West Kirby		1965		Gillingham	Watford	20	1	2	0	2	0	0	0
FASHANU J	John	18/09/62	Kensington		1983	1984	Norwich City	Millwall	31+5	2+1	2	1	10	0	0	0
FAWELL D S	Derek	22/03/44	Hartlepool		1965		Notts County	Wisbech Town	3	0	0	0	0	0	0	0
FEENEY T W	Tom	26/08/10	Grangetown, Yorks	1973	1933		Notts County	Stockport County	10	0	0	0	0	0	0	0
FELGATE D W	David	04/03/60	Blaenau Ffestiniog		1980	1984	Bolton Wanderers	Grimsby Town	198	10	16	9	0	0	0	0
FELL J I	Jimmy	04/01/36	Cleethorpes		1963	1965	Walsall	Boston United	64	5	1	0	10	0	0	0
FENCOTT K D W	Ken	27/12/43	Walsall		1964	1966	Aston Villa	Tamworth	67+6	4	5	0	13	1	0	0
FENTON R D	Richard				1888	1889			0	4	0	26	0	0	0	0
FENWICK R W	Robert	29/09/1894	Newcastle		1920	1922	Ashington	Notts County	49	6	0	38	2	0	0	3
					1924	1925	Notts County	Shirebrook	27	0	0	0	0	0	0	0
FERN G E	George	1874	Burton on Trent	1955	1898		Hinckley Town	Millwall Athletic	24	2	0	0	3	1	0	0
FERN T E	Tommy	01/04/1886	Measham, Leics	1966	1909	1913	Worksop Town	Everton	127	10	0	32	0	0	0	0
FINCH A R	Roy	07/04/22	Barry Island		1948	1958	WBA		275	16	0	0	56	2	0	0
FINNEY K	Kevin	19/10/69	Newcastle U.Lyme		1991	1992	Port Vale	Leek Town	31+6	1	4+1	3	2	0	1	0
FISHER J	Jackie	04/08/1897	Hodthorpe, Derbys	1954	1928	1929	Staveley Town	Denaby United	19	0	0	0	3	0	0	0
FITZSIMONS A G	Arthur	16/12/29	Dublin		1958		Middlesbrough	Mansfield Town	7	0	0	0	0	0	0	0
FLEMING J	James	1864	Leith	1934	1892		Aston Villa	Larkhall Saints	11	0	0	0	5	0	0	0
FLEMING J J	John	01/07/53	Nottingham		1975	1979	Oxford United	Port Vale	109+12	6+1	13	0	17	1	0	0
FLEMING N	Neil	09/01/50	Felixstowe		1973		Lincoln Claytons	Grantham Town	1	0	0	0	0	0	0	0
FLEMING T M	Terry	05/01/73	Marston Green		1995	*	Preston North End	*	54+5	1	6	1	0	0	1	0
FLETCHER H R	Horace	1876	Rotherham	1931	1899		Mexborough		28	2	0	0	6	0	0	0
FLETCHER J R	Rod	23/09/45	Preston		1967	1970	Crewe	Scunthorpe United	86+6	7	2	0	29	2	0	0
FLEWITT A W	Albert	1872	Beeston	1943	1893	1894	Mansfield Greenhalgh's	Everton	56	3	0	0	28	1	0	0
FLITCROFT D	David	14/01/74	Bolton		1993			Preston N E (L)	2	0	0+1	0	0	0	0	0
FOLEY S	Steve	04/10/62	Liverpool		1994		Stoke City	Bradford City	15+1	2	1	2	0	0	0	0
FOOTITT D	Don	24/05/29	Grantham		1946		Grantham St Johns	Crewe	24	2	0	0	3	0	0	0
FORAN M J	Mark	30/10/73	Aldershot		1996		Peterborough U (L)		1+1	0	0	0	0	0	0	0
FORBES J	James	14/03/1896	Newcastle	1939	1921	1922	Carlisle United	Leadgate Park	16	0	0	0	0	0	0	0
FORD C	Clive	10/04/45	West Bromwich		1966	1967	Walsall	Los Angeles Wolves	48+1	1	5	0	16	0	0	0
FORMAN R G	Reg	03/09/17	Louth, Lincs	1978	1937	1938		Gainsborough Trin.	2	0	0	1	0	0	0	0
FOSTER A W	Bertie	c1885		1959	1906	1910	Grantham Avenue		67	8	0	40	1	1	0	7
FOSTER S B	Samuel	12/11/1897	Southwell	1965	1919		Southwell Fed.	Mansfield Town	1	0	0	0	0	0	0	0
FOULKES C E	Charles	07/02/05	Bilston		1927	1929	Bournemouth	Boston	64	6	0	0	1	0	0	0
FOX K	Kevin	22/09/60	Sheffield		1979	1980		Kettering Town	4	0	1	0	0	0	0	0
FOX W	Walter				1884	1887			0	9	0	0	0	3	0	0
FRANKLIN N J	Neil	10/03/69	Lincoln		1986	1987	YTS	Nykoping (Sweden)	15	0	0	6+1	0	0	0	0
					1988		Nykoping (Sweden)	Gainsborough Trin.	0+1	1	0	0	0	0	0	0
FRANKS A J	Albert	13/04/36	Boldon, Co Durham		1961	1962	Rangers	Queen of the Sth.	58	4	4	0	5	0	1	0
FRANKS C R	Charles	15/10/1892	Gateshead	1978	1922		Close Works		1	0	0	0	0	0	0	0
FRASER D	David				1896		Leith Athletic		1	0	0	0	0	0	0	0
FRASER G	George	c1874	Elgin	1951	1901	1910	Sunderland		265	27	0	50	4	0	0	0
FREEMAN J A	Alf	13/07/04	Ilkeston	1986	1927		Blackpool	Mansfield Town	2	1	0	0	0	0	0	0
FREEMAN R P	Percy	04/07/45	Newark		1970	1972	WBA	Reading	76+4	7	7+1	1	30	5	4	0
					1974	1976	Reading	Boston United	62+10	7	6	0	34	3	0	0
FRETTINGHAM J H A	Jimmy	1871	Nottingham	1904	1894	1895	Long Eaton Rangers	New Brompton	56	4	0	0	20	2	0	0
FRY W					1888	1889			0	0	0	7	0	0	0	1
FULLALOVE					1891		Lincoln Amateurs		0	0	0	1	0	0	0	0
GALLACHER S	Sam	23/12/04	Annbank		1928		Crystal Palace	York City	13	1	0	0	0	0	0	0
GALLAGHER J C	Jackie	06/04/58	Wisbech		1976		March Town	Kings Lynn	1	0	0	0	0	0	0	0
GAMBLE S W	Willie	05/03/68	Cotham, Notts		1985	1988	Apprentice	Boston United	44+20	2+1	4+3	4+1	15	0	1	1

Name		Date of Birth	Place of Birth	Died	First Season	Last Season	Previous Club	Next Club	League	FAC	LC	Other	Lge.	FAC	LC	Other
GARDNER A	Andy	c1888	Airdrie	1934	1909	1919	Petershill		151	10	0	30	9	0	0	5
GARNER H A	Herbert	c1899	Mexborough		1921		Denaby United	Wombwell	6	0	0	0	0	0	0	0
GARRATY W	Billy	06/10/1878	Birmingham	1931	1910		WBA	Retired	16	0	0	0	2	0	0	0
GARVIE J	Johnny	16/10/27	Bellshill	1996	1950	1955	Preston North End	Carlisle United	184	8	0	0	78	2	0	0
GASH R	Robert				1894		Grantham Rovers	Grantham Rovers	14	0	0	0	1	0	0	0
GASTON R	Ray	22/12/46	Belfast		1969		Oxford United (L)		4	0	0	0	1	0	0	0
GEDNEY C	Chris	01/09/45	Boston		1962	1965	School	Spalding United	9	0	0	0	1	0	0	0
GERRY J	James				1910		Larkhall Thistle		2	0	0	0	0	0	0	0
GIBB J M	James	c1918	East Calder		1938		Manchester United	Hibernian	3	0	0	0	0	0	0	0
GIBSON C H	Colin	16/09/23	Normanby, N Yorks	1992	1955	1956	Aston Villa	Stourbridge	36	1	0	0	12	0	0	0
GIBSON R H	Bob	05/08/27	Ashington		1951	1954	Ashington	Peterborough Utd	43	4	0	0	20	0	0	0
GIBSON R J	Robert	1887	Newcastle		1912		Newcastle United		1	0	0	0	0	0	0	0
GIBSON W	Will	c1869		1911	1898	1902	Notts County	Retired	130	14	0	0	1	0	0	0
GILBERT D J	David	22/06/63	Lincoln		1980	1981	Apprentice	Scunthorpe United	15+15	3	5	0	1	0	0	0
GILLESPIE M	Matthew	24/12/1869			1895	1896		Newton Heath	36	3	0	0	10	5	0	0
GILLESPIE W J	William	02/10/1873	Strathclyde		1895	1896	Strathclyde	Manchester City	37	7	0	0	16	7	0	0
GILLIGAN J M	Jimmy	24/01/64	Hammersmith		1982		Watford (L)		0+3	0	0	0	0	0	0	0
					1986		Swindon Town	Cardiff City	11	0	0	0	1	0	0	0
GILLIVER A H	Alan	03/08/44	Swallownest		1970	1971	Brighton	Bradford City	33+4	1	4	0	8	1	0	1
GILLOTT E	Edward	14/12/02	Sheffield	1984	1924	1927	Sheffield Forge	Shirebrook	14	0	0	0	0	0	0	0
GLADDING C	Charles	1874	Louth, Lincs		1894			Gainsborough Trin.	2	0	0	0	0	0	0	0
GLENDINNING J	John				1889	1890	5th Kirkcudbrightshire RV		0	4	0	17	0	1	0	7
GODBOLD H	Harry	31/01/39	Springwell, Co Durham		1965	1966	Boston FC	Spalding United	22+1	0	1	0	3	0	0	0
GOLDSBOROUGH J	Jack	c1893	Sheffield		1913	1919	Industry FC	Boston Town	36	1	0	0	0	0	0	0
GORDON J S	Jimmy	03/09/55	Stretford		1975	1977	Luton Town	Reading	4	1	1	0	0	0	0	0
GORRINGE F C	Frederick	1903	Salford	1965	1928		Manchester City	Crewe	6	2	0	0	3	0	0	0
GORTON A W	Andy	23/09/66	Salford		1989		Stockport County	Glossop Town	20	0	2	2	0	0	0	0
GOULD G	Geoff	07/01/45	Blackburn		1967		Bradford PA	Bradford PA	1	0	0	0	0	0	0	0
GRAHAM D	Doug	15/07/21	Morpeth		1951	1956	Preston North End	St Gallen (Switz)	182	9	0	0	0	0	0	0
GRAHAM P	Peter	19/04/47	Worsborough		1973	1977	Darlington	Cambridge United	142+16	10	10	0	47	3	3	0
GRAHAM W	William				1892	1893	Burnley		21	1	0	0	2	0	0	0
GRAHAM W		c1870			1889		Southport Central		0	4	0	6	0	1	0	2
GRAINGER A	Arthur				1926		Wath Athletic	Wath Athletic	1	0	0	0	0	0	0	0
GRAINGER J	Jack	03/04/24	Havercroft	1983	1957	1958	Rotherham United	Burton Albion	42	3	0	0	14	0	0	0
GRATTON D	Dennis	21/04/34	Rotherham		1959	1960	Sheffield United	Boston Town	45	4	2	0	0	0	0	0
GRAVER A M	Andy	12/09/27	Craghead		1950	1954	Newcastle United	Leicester City	170	11	0	0	106	5	0	0
					1955		Leicester City	Stoke City	15	0	0	0	4	0	0	0
					1958	1960	Boston United	Skegness Town	89	4	0	0	33	2	0	0
GRAVES R C	Bob	07/11/42	Marylebone		1959	1964	Kirton	Retired	79	4	4	0	0	0	0	0
GRAY A	Alf	30/08/10	Bolton	1974	1934	1935	Liverpool	Newark Town	32	3	0	3	0	0	0	0
GRAY E	Ernest	c1875			1898		Mexborough	New Brompton	6	0	0	0	0	0	0	0
GRAY R	Bobby	18/06/27	Cambuslang		1949		Wishaw	Hamilton Academicals	2	0	0	0	0	0	0	0
GREAVES G H	George	20/06/1897	Nottingham		1920	1923		Scunthorpe United	72	3	0	10	0	0	0	0
GREAVES I D	Ian	26/05/32	Oldham		1960		Manchester Utd	Oldham Athletic	11	2	0	0	0	0	0	0
GREEN A	Albert	c1907	Hanley		1935		West Ham	Newark Town	23	1	0	3	6	0	0	1
GREEN H	Horace	23/04/18	Barnsley		1948	1954	Halifax Town		212	8	0	0	14	0	0	0
GREEN N R	Russell	13/08/33	Donington, Lincs		1957	1963	Corby Town	Gainsborough Trin.	125	5	5	0	8	0	0	0
GREENALL C A	Colin	30/12/63	Billinge, Lancs		1994	1995	Chester City	Wigan Athletic	43	3	6	2	3	0	0	0
GREGSON J	John	17/05/39	Skelmersdale		1967		Mansfield Town	Cambridge United	31+5	1	5	0	3	0	0	0
GREGSON W	William				1885	1886			0	6	0	0	0	2	0	0
GREIG A	Andrew	c1887	Inverness		1909		Inverness Clachnacuddin		2	0	0	0	0	0	0	0
GRESHAM J	James				1889				0	0	0	1	0	0	0	0
					1891	1892	Doncaster Rovers	Rossendale	22	5	0	8	5	0	0	1
					1894		Rossendale	Gainsborough Trin.	5	1	0	0	1	0	0	0
GRESHAM W	William				1892		Gainsborough Trin.		22	5	0	0	0	0	0	0
					1893				13	0	0	0	0	0	0	0
GREYGOOSE D	Dean	18/12/64	Thetford		1985		Cambridge Utd (L)		6	0	0	0	0	0	0	0
GRIFFIN R H G	Ronald	18/10/19	London	1987	1938		St Mirren	Brentford	1	0	0	0	0	0	0	0
GRIFFITHS C	Charles				1907		Preston North End		1	0	0	0	0	0	0	0
GRIFFITHS T	Thomas	c1902	Willington Quay		1922		Willington St Aidans	Jarrow	22	1	0	0	7	0	0	0
GROCOTT F	Frederick	c1900			1922	1924	Walker Celtic		60	1	0	0	0	0	0	0
GROTIER P D	Peter	18/10/50	Stratford, London		1974	1979	West Ham	Cardiff City	233	14	16	0	0	0	0	0
GROVES F	Fred	06/05/1892	Lincoln	1980	1909		South Bar	Worksop Town	7	0	0	0	1	0	0	0
GROVES J A	Albert	1883	South Bank		1903		South Bank	Sheffield United	29	1	0	0	2	0	0	0
GROVES P	Paul	28/02/66	Derby		1989		Leicester City (L)		8	0	2	0	1	0	0	0
GRUMMETT J	Jim	31/07/18	Barnsley	1996	1945	1951		Accrington Stanley	165	14	0	0	12	0	0	0
GRUMMETT J	Jim (Jnr)	11/07/45	Barnsley		1963	1970	Ruston Bucyrus	Aldershot	246+5	13	15	0	17	1	1	0
GRUNDY H	Harry		Reading		1907	1909			6	2	0	47	0	0	0	7
GUEST B J	Brendan	19/12/58	Nottingham		1976	1979	Apprentice	Swindon Town	99+5	6	4+2	0	2	0	0	0
GUNSON F					1891		St Catherines		0	0	0	1	0	0	0	0
					1896		Casuals (Lincoln)	Adelaide	1	0	0	0	0	0	0	0
HAILS W	Billy	19/02/35	Nettlesworth		1953	1954	Kimblesworth Jnrs	Peterborough Utd	9	0	0	0	0	0	0	0
HAINES K H	Keith	19/12/37	Wigston, Leics		1960	1962	Leeds United	Hinckley Athletic	11	0	1	0	0	0	0	0
HALE A	Alf	24/01/06	Kiveton Park	1972	1925	1929	Kiveton Park CW	Luton Town	156	11	0	0	4	0	0	0
HALL B A C	Alan	29/03/08	Deepcar	1983	1931	1932	Bradford City	Tottenham Hotspur	72	4	0	0	65	4	0	0

Sheet No.7   Hall E to Hood D

Name		Date of Birth	Place of Birth	Died	First Season	Last Season	Previous Club	Next Club	League	FAC	LC	Other	Lge.	FAC	LC	Other
HALL E	Edward				1897		Beeston Humber	Loughborough T.	18	2	0	0	3	0	0	0
HALL H	Harry	c1900			1920	1921	Pinxton		16	0	0	3	0	0	0	0
HALL J	John	c1905	Bolton		1923			Accrington Stanley	1	0	0	0	0	0	0	0
HALL S	Stuart	c1967	Worksop		1982		School		0	0	0	0+1	0	0	0	0
HALLAM G	George	17/02/1861	Lincoln	1939	1884	1889	Lindum		0	14	0	9	0	1	0	3
HALLAM H	Henry		Sleaford		1913		Peterborough GN Loco	Grantham Town	2	0	0	0	0	0	0	0
HALLIDAY J H	John	20/02/08	Dumfries		1930	1931	Boston Town	Doncaster Rovers	9	0	0	0	7	0	0	0
HAMILTON W	William	c1906	Belfast		1926	1927	Dundella	Notts County	15	3	0	0	3	0	0	0
HAMMOND G	George				1902		Barrow		1	0	0	0	0	0	0	0
HAMMOND J	John		Birtley, Co Durham		1934		RAF Cranwell		1	0	0	1	0	0	0	0
HANCOCK E	Ted	29/03/07	Rotherham		1938		Luton Town	Frickley Colliery	30	3	0	0	4	1	0	0
HANNAH G	Gardiner	04/02/1871	Baillieston		1896	1897	Blackburn Rovers		56	6	0	0	0	0	0	0
HANNAH G	George	11/12/28	Liverpool	1990	1957	1958	Newcastle United	Manchester City	38	1	0	0	4	0	0	0
HARBERTSON R	Ron	23/12/29	Redcar		1957	1959	Darlington	Wrexham	57	4	0	0	22	1	0	0
					1961		Darlington	Grantham Town	29	1	1	0	3	0	2	0
HARDIE G	George	1873	Stanley, Derbys		1898		Mexborough		12	0	0	0	0	0	0	0
HARDING A	Alan	14/05/48	Sunderland		1972	1978	Darlington	Hartlepool	203+6	12	12+1	0	38	4	1	0
HARDY J H	Jack	15/16/10	Chesterfield	1978	1945	1946	Hull City		18	4	0	0	0	0	0	0
HARFORD M G	Mick	12/02/59	Sunderland		1977	1980	Lambton Street BC	Newcastle United	109+6	3	9	0	41	0	5	0
HARFORD R T	Ray	01/06/45	Halifax		1967	1970	Exeter City	Mansfield Town	161	10	11	0	10	0	0	0
HARRIS					1920		Cranwell Works		0	0	0	2	0	0	0	0
HARRISON F N	Frank	19/09/63	Eston		1985				0+1	0	0	0	0	0	0	0
HARRISON J G	John	18/05/46	Worksop		1968		Sheffield United	Retired	4	1	0	0	0	0	0	0
HART H	Harry				1894				1	0	0	0	0	0	0	0
HART J T	John				1894				1	0	0	0	0	0	0	0
HARTLEY J	Jimmy	29/10/1876	Dumbarton		1896		Burnley (L)		9	0	0	0	5	0	0	0
					1899	1902	Tottenham Hotspur	Rangers	129	13	0	0	47	4	0	0
HARTSHORNE J	Jack	25/03/07	Willenhall	1971	1936	1938	Macclesfield Town	Grantham Town	91	6	0	1	0	0	0	0
HARVEY A	Allan	11/04/42	Barnsley		1960		Leeds United	Toronto City	0	0	1	0	0	0	0	0
HATSELL H S	Henry	c1896			1920		Bradford PA		0	0	0	2	0	0	0	0
HAVELOCK P H W	Harry	20/01/01	Hull	1973	1925		Hull City	Portsmouth	27	3	0	0	17	1	0	0
HAWKINGS B	Barry	07/11/31	Birmingham		1955	1956	Coventry City	Northampton Town	15	1	0	0	6	0	0	0
HAWKSBY J F	John	12/06/42	York		1964	1965	Leeds United	York City	64+1	6	3	0	4	1	0	0
HAWKSWORTH D M	Derek	16/07/27	Bradford		1959	1960	Huddersfield Town	Bradford City	36	0	2	0	14	0	0	0
HAYCOCK F	Frederick	1886	Smethwick	1955	1910		Portsmouth	Burslem Port Vale	25	3	0	0	5	1	0	0
HEATH R T	Terry	17/11/43	Leicester		1972	1973	Scunthorpe United	Retired	17	0	1	0	1	0	0	0
HEATH S M J P	Seamus	6/12/61	Belfast		1982		Luton Town (L)		6+1	0	1	0	0	0	0	0
HEATH W	William				1893	1895	Lindum		10	0	0	0	0	0	0	0
HEATH W H M	Bill	15/04/34	Bournemouth		1958	1961	Bournemouth	Cambridge City	84	2	2	0	0	0	0	0
HEATHCOTE J	Jimmy	17/01/1894	Bolton		1924		Pontypridd	Mansfield Town	33	1	0	0	13	0	0	0
HEBBERD T N	Trevor	19/06/58	Alresford		1994		Chesterfield	Grantham Town	20+5	3	3	2	0	0	0	0
HELLINGS D R	Dan	9/12/23	Lincoln	1996	1946		Ransome & Marles	Grantham Town	3	0	0	0	0	0	0	0
HELLIWELL D	David	28/03/48	Blackburn		1969		Blackburn Rovers	Workington	11+2	1	1	0	1	0	0	0
HEMPSALL E	Ernest	1901	Lincoln		1925		Lincoln Claytons	Lincoln Claytons	1	0	0	0	0	0	0	0
HENDERSON A					1891		Gedling Grove		0	0	0	1	0	0	0	0
HENDERSON J	John	1871	Dumfries	1930	1898	1900	Celtic	Leicester Fosse	76	7	0	0	9	1	0	0
HETHERINGTON J	Jos	11/04/1892	Sunderland	1971	1925		Preston North End	Durham City	3	2	0	0	1	0	0	0
HEWARD B	Brian	17/07/35	Lincoln		1961	1963	Scunthorpe United	Bankstown (Australia)	72	4	7	0	2	0	0	0
					1964	1965	Bankstown	Retired	25	5	1	0	0	0	0	0
HEWITT R	Ron	25/01/24	Chesterfield		1948		Sheffield United	Worksop Town	3	0	0	0	0	0	0	0
HEWS H B	Harold	1888	Honiton, Devon	1922	1909		Sleaford Town		2	0	0	0	0	0	0	0
HEYWOOD W	William	1862	Lincoln	1940	1884		Lincoln Rovers		0	1	0	0	0	0	0	0
HIBBERD S	Stuart	11/10/61	Sheffield		1980	1982	Apprentice	Boston United	36+6	0	3	3	2	0	0	0
HIBBERT H C	Henry	c1887			1909		Stockport County		4	0	0	0	1	0	0	0
HIGGINS T	Thomas				1903		Darlington St Augustines		6	1	0	0	0	0	0	0
HILL A	Amos	21/06/10	Wath-on-Dearne	1973	1935	1936	Hawson Street FC	Mansfield Town	14	0	0	1	5	0	0	1
HILL D M	David	06/06/66	Nottingham		1993	1994	Scunthorpe United		52+6	5	3+1	6	6	0	0	1
HILL K G	Ken	07/03/53	Canterbury		1974		Gillingham (L)		1	1	0	0	0	0	0	0
HILL L G	Len	15/02/1899	Islington	1979	1927	1928	Rochdale	Grays Thurrock	69	6	0	0	0	0	0	0
HINDSON E	Edward		Easington, Co Durham		1903		Southwick		11	0	0	0	0	0	0	0
HIRST L	Lee	26/01/69	Sheffield		1993		Coventry City (L)		7	0	0	2	0	0	0	0
HOBBS W T	William	c1904	Lurgan		1926		Lurgan	Belfast Celtic	1	0	0	0	0	0	0	0
HOBSON G	Gordon	27/11/57	Sheffield		1977	1984	Sheffield Rangers	Grimsby Town	260+12	9+1	21	15	73	0	3	5
					1988	1989	Southampton	Exeter City	61	2+1	2	2	23	0	0	1
HODDER W	William				1891		Sheffield Wed.		0	2	0	7	0	0	0	0
HODGES H J	Harry	1897	Edmonton	1966	1924		West Ham		7	2	0	0	0	0	0	0
HOOGKINSON V A	Vincent	01/11/06	Woollatton, Notts	1990	1933				1	0	0	0	0	0	0	0
HODSON S P	Simeon	05/03/66	Lincoln		1985	1986	Lincoln United	Newport County	54+2	1	4	5	0	0	0	0
HOGG G H	George	1900	Kiveton Park		1925		Anston FC	Southend United	5	0	0	0	0	0	0	0
HOLDER A M	Alan	10/12/31	Oxford		1955		Notts Forest	Tranmere Rovers	1	0	0	0	1	0	0	0
HOLMES M M	Maxey	24/12/08	Pinchbeck, Lincs		1938		Mansfield Town		20	1	0	0	1	0	0	0
HOLMES R W	Roger	09/09/42	Scunthorpe		1959	1971			276+2	13	16	0	36	1	3	0
HOLMES S P	Steve	13/01/71	Middlesbrough		1995		Preston N E (L)		12	0	0	2	1	0	0	0
					1995	*	Preston North End	*	38+1	0	4	0	5	0	2	0
HONE M J	Mark	31/03/68	Croydon		1996	*	Southend United	*	26+3	1	5+1	0	0	0	1	0
HOOD D	Derek	17/12/58	Washington, Co Durham		1986		York City (L)		9	0	0	0	0	0	0	0

		Date of Birth	Place of Birth	Died	First Season	Last Season	Previous Club	Next Club	League	FAC	LC	Other	Lge.	FAC	LC	Other
HOOD R P	Richard	1881	Seaham		1904	1908	Seaham Rovers		130	11	0	29	1	0	0	0
HOOPER C	Carl	23/10/03	Darlington	1972	1924	1925	Crook Town	Shildon	34	1	0	0	6	1	0	0
HOPEWELL W H	William				1888		Grimsby Town	Derby County	0	1	0	2	0	0	0	1
					1888		Derby County		0	0	0	8	0	0	0	0
HOPPER M	Matthew	c1900			1920		Ashington	Millwall	0	4	0	33	0	0	0	5
HORNE A	Alf	1903	Birmingham	1976	1932	1936	Preston North End	Mansfield Town	166	9	0	6	36	2	0	1
HOUGHTON H B	Bud	01/09/36	Madras (India)		1963	1964	Oxford United	Chelmsford City	54	7	0	0	22	3	0	0
HOUGHTON K	Keith	10/03/54	Backworth		1983		Carlisle United	Retired	26	3	3	0	0	0	1	0
HOULT A J	Alan	07/10/57	Burbage, Leics		1977		Leicester City (L)		2+2	0	0	0	1	0	0	0
HOULT R	Russell	22/11/72	Leicester		1991		Leicester City (L)		2	0	1	0	0	0	0	0
					1994		Leicester City (L)		15	0	0	1	0	0	0	0
HOWARD F	Fred		Hoyland		1897		Sheffield United	Barnsley	1	0	0	0	0	0	0	0
HUBBARD A	Ranji	1883	Leicester	1967	1912		Grimsby Town	Leicester Imperial	12	0	0	0	3	0	0	0
HUBBARD P J	Phil	25/01/49	Lincoln		1965	1971	Apprentice	Norwich City	150+2	11+1	9	0	41	1	5	0
					1976	1978	Grimsby Town	Boston United	100+9	5+1	7	0	12	0	1	0
HUCKERBY D C	Darren	23/04/76	Nottingham		1993	1995	YTS	Newcastle United	20+8	0	2	1	5	0	0	2
HUDSON G A	Geoff	14/10/31	Leeds		1965		Gillingham	Rotherham	33	1	2	0	0	0	0	0
HUGHES D T	David	19/03/58	Birmingham		1977	1980	Aston Villa	Scunthorpe United	61+1	0	2+1	0	1	0	1	0
HUGHES G	Gordon	19/06/36	Washington, Co Durham		1967	1970	Derby County	Boston United	117	9	5	0	9	0	0	0
HULME A	Arthur				1897			Gravesend United	29	2	0	0	12	1	0	0
HULME E M	Eric	14/01/49	Houghton le Spring		1972	1973	Notts Forest	Worksop Town	23	2	0	0	0	0	0	0
HULME J	James				1895		Strathclyde		0	1	0	0	0	2	0	0
HULME K	Kevin	02/12/67	Farnworth		1995		Bury	Macclesfield Town	4+1	1	0	1+1	0	0	0	0
HULMES S	Bob				1889		Heywood	New Brompton	2	0	0	0	0	0	0	0
HUMPHRIES G	Glenn	11/08/64	Hull		1986		Doncaster R (L)		9	0	0	0	0	0	0	0
HUNT S	Samuel		Smithies		1889		Doncaster Rovers	Barnsley St. Peters	0	0	0	2	0	0	0	1
HUNT S W	Walter	09/01/09	Doe Lea	1963	1933		Welbeck CW	Mansfield Town	3	0	0	0	0	0	0	0
HUNTER C	Cyril	1898	Pelaw, Newcastle		1929		Fall River FC (USA)		14	0	0	0	1	0	0	0
HUNTER G I	George	29/08/30	Troon	1990	1965		Burton Albion	Burton Albion	1	0	0	0	0	0	0	0
HUNTER L	Les	15/01/58	Middlesbrough		1987		Scunthorpe United	Chesterfield	0	0	0	3	0	0	0	1
HUNTER W	William	1888	Sunderland		1909	1910	Sunderland	Wingate Albion	32	3	0	0	8	0	0	0
HUTCHINSON J A	Jimmy	28/12/15	Sheffield		1946	1948	Bournemouth	Oldham Athletic	85	6	0	0	45	2	0	0
HUTCHINSON J B	Barry	27/01/36	Sheffield		1965		Weymouth	Darlington	24	1	2	0	18	0	2	0
HYLTON H	Herbert	c1867	Lincoln		1886				0	1	0	0	0	0	0	0
INSKIP J	John		Glengarnock		1912				1	0	0	0	0	0	0	0
IREMONGER A	Albert	15/06/1884	Wilford, Notts	1958	1926		Notts County		35	4	0	0	0	0	0	0
IREMONGER S	Sydney				1919				3	0	0	1	0	0	0	0
IRVING J	John	c1867		1942	1889	1894	Queen of the Sth	Newark Town	44	15	0	55	9	11	0	22
					1896		Newark Town		7	2	0	0	0	0	0	0
IVERSON R T J	Bob	17/10/10	Folkestone	1953	1933	1934	Ramsgate PW	Wolves	41	3	0	2	13	1	0	2
JACK J R	Ross	21/03/59	Avoch, Ross-shire		1983	1984	Norwich City	Dundee	52+8	5	5+1	4+1	16	1	1	1
JACKLIN A	Alfred				1903		Liberal Club (Linc)		3	0	0	0	0	0	0	0
JACKSON A					1892				2	1	0	0	1	0	0	0
JACKSON A E	Alan	14/02/38	Scunthorpe		1958	1960	Brigg Town	Brigg Town	4	0	0	0	0	0	0	0
JACKSON A C	Clem	1886	Kimberley, Notts	1960	1908	1919	Eastwood Rangers	Retired	184	12	0	42	0	0	0	0
JACKSON B H	Brian	01/04/33	Walton on Thames		1964		Peterborough Utd	Burton Albion	10	0	0	0	1	0	0	0
JACKSON R	Bob	05/06/34	Middleton, Lancs		1955	1963	Oldham Athletic	Wisbech Town	235	9	7	0	0	0	0	0
JACQUES J	Joe	12/09/44	Consett	1981	1964		Preston North End	Darlington	22	5	0	0	0	0	0	0
JAMES A C	Tony	27/06/67	Sheffield		1988	1989	Gainsborough Trin.	Leicester City	24+5	0	2	0+1	0	0	0	0
JEAVONS P	Pat	05/07/46	Deptford		1965		Gravesend	Wisbech Town	1	0	0	0	0	0	0	0
JEFFREY A J	Alick	29/01/39	Rawmarsh		1968	1969	Doncaster Rovers	Worksop Town	19+3	2	0	0	3	0	0	0
JEFFREY W W	William	1866	Dalderby, Lincs	1932	1887	1888	Horncastle	Boston	0	6	0	4	0	0	0	0
					1890			Burnley	0	1	0	11	0	0	0	0
JENKINS E T	Evan	26/06/06	Ynyshir	1990	1928	1929	Denaby United	Burnley	30	0	0	0	12	0	0	0
					1933		Burnley	York City	14	0	0	0	1	0	0	0
JENKINS R	Reg				1926		Chester	Chester	5	1	0	0	0	0	0	0
JEPSON A E	Arthur	12/07/15	Selston, Notts	1997	1948	1949	Stoke City	Northwich Victoria	58	2	0	0	0	0	0	0
JEWETT A W	Alf	15/11/1899	Bitterne, Hants	1980	1923		Arsenal	Wigan Borough	37	2	0	0	3	1	0	0
JOHNSON A K	Alan	19/02/71	Billinge, Lancs		1993	1995	Wigan Athletic	Sing Tau (HK)	57+6	3	1	3+1	0	0	0	1
JOHNSON D A	David	29/10/70	Rother Valley		1993	1995	Sheffield Wed	Altrincham	75+14	5	6+1	9	13	2	4	4
JOHNSON G J	George	06/10/32	Esh, Co Durham		1951		Langley Park Jnrs	Grantham Town	3	0	0	0	1	0	0	0
JOHNSON J R	Joe	13/09/20	Greenock		1952		Rangers	Workington	11	0	0	0	2	0	0	0
JOHNSON R S	Rob	22/02/62	Bedford		1983		Luton Town (L)		4	0	0	0	0	0	0	0
JOHNSON T	Tom	04/05/11	Ecclesfield	1983	1946	1948	Sheffield United	Retired	75	5	0	0	0	0	0	0
JOHNSON W T	William				1901		Chatham		6	1	0	0	0	0	0	0
JONES A	Alan	21/01/51	Grimethorpe		1977	1978	Chesterfield	Bradford City	24+2	1	0	0	4	0	0	0
JONES A	Alf	02/03/37	Liverpool		1962	1966	Leeds United	Wigan Athletic	179+1	10	10	0	3	0	0	0
JONES D T	David		Troed-y-Rhiw		1923		Chesterfield		3	0	0	0	0	0	0	0
JONES F W	Fred	1869	Llandudno	1910	1893		Small Heath		7	0	0	0	0	0	0	0
JONES G	Gary	06/04/69	Huddersfield		1993		Southend (L)		0+4	0	0	0+1	2	0	0	0
JONES J A	Jimmy	03/08/27	Birkenhead		1951	1953	New Brighton	Accrington Stanley	76	4	0	0	0	0	0	0
JONES J M	Merfyn	30/04/31	Bangor		1963		Chester		1	0	0	0	0	0	0	0
JONES W	Walter				1908		Manchester City		0	0	0	6	0	0	0	0
JUDGE A G	Alan	14/05/60	Kingsbury, London		1985		Oxford (L)		2	0	0	0	0	0	0	0
KABIA J T	Jason	28/05/69	Sutton in Ashfield		1991	1992	Oakham United	Valetta (Malta)	17+11	0+1	2+2	0+1	4	0	0	0

		Date of Birth	Place of Birth	Died	First Season	Last Season	Previous Club	Next Club	Appearances League	FAC	LC	Other	Goals Lge.	FAC	LC	Other
KEAN A	Archie	30/09/1894	Parkhead, Glasgow		1922	1923	Clapton Orient	Blackburn Rovers	76	2	0	0	11	0	0	0
KEARNS P V	Peter	26/03/37	Wellingborough		1967	1968	Aldershot	Weymouth	45+1	4	2	0	11	2	0	0
KEATING R E	Reg	14/05/04	Halton, Yorks	1961	1927		Newcastle United	Gainsborough Trin.	2	0	0	0	0	0	0	0
KEELEY N B	Nolan	24/05/51	East Barsham, Norfolk		1979	1980	Scunthorpe United	Corby Town	52	2	4	0	3	0	0	0
KEETLEY F	Frank	23/03/01	Derby	1968	1931	1932	Bradford City	Hull City	42	3	0	0	27	0	0	0
KEETLEY S	Sammy				1908		Netherfield Rangers		0	0	0	2	0	0	0	0
KEETLEY T	Tom	16/11/1898	Derby	1958	1933		Notts County	Gresley Rovers	10	0	0	0	5	0	0	0
KELLEHER J	Joe	c1949			1970		School	Ruston Bucyrus	0	1	0	0	0	0	0	0
KELLY E E	Errington	08/04/58	St Vincent (WI)		1982		Bristol Rovers	Bristol City	0+2	0	0	1	0	0	0	0
KELLY J	James				1892				8	5	0	0	1	2	0	0
KELLY M	Martin				1905	1906	Liberal Club (Linc)	Oldham Athletic	24	0	0	0	3	0	0	0
KELLY T J	Terry	14/05/42	Gateshead		1962		Newcastle United	Cambridge United	8	0	1	0	2	0	0	0
KENDALL J M	Jack	09/10/04	Broughton, Lincs	1961	1922	1923	Broughton Rangers	Everton	71	3	0	0	0	0	0	0
					1928	1929	Preston North End	Sheffield United	46	2	0	0	0	0	0	0
KENNEDY D	David	30/11/50	Sunderland		1971	1972	Leeds United		6+2	0	0+1	1	1	0	0	0
KENNEDY G	George	c1885	Dumfries	1917	1906	1907	Maxwelltown Vol.	Chelsea	42	3	0	0	0	0	0	0
KENNEDY J	John	04/09/39	Newtownards		1967	1973	Celtic	Lincoln United	251	10	16	1	0	0	0	0
KERR D	David	c1913			1937		Bangor Town	Newark Town	5	0	0	1	0	0	0	1
KERR J	Jimmy	03/03/32	Lemington		1952	1953	Blyth Spartans	Oldham Athletic	15	0	0	0	1	0	0	0
KERRIGAN D M	Don	07/05/41	Seamill	1990	1968		Fulham (L)		12	0	0	0	0	0	0	0
KEY L W	Lance	13/05/68	Kettering		1995		Sheffield Wed (L)		5	0	0	0	0	0	0	0
KILLIN H R	Roy	18/07/29	Toronto (Canada)		1953		Manchester United	Peterborough Utd	7	3	0	0	0	0	0	0
KILMORE K	Kevin	11/11/59	Scunthorpe		1985	1986	KFC Geel (Belgium)	Gainsborough Trin.	40+6	1	4	2	6	0	1	0
KIRK J J	James	c1882			1909	1910	Newark Town	Worksop Town	5	0	0	0	0	0	0	0
KIRKLAND W	William	c1915			1938		Third Lanark		3	0	0	0	0	0	0	0
KIRTON J W	Jack	02/11/1873	Pinxton, Derbys	1970	1896		Oldham County	Small Heath	27	4	0	0	5	2	0	0
KITCHING H	Harry	1905	Grimsby		1928	1930	Worksop Town	Tranmere Rovers	58	2	0	0	28	1	0	0
KNIGHTON T	Thomas				1919				2	0	0	0	0	0	0	0
KOERNER F A	Frederick		Eccleshill		1898	1899			3	0	0	0	1	0	0	0
KRZYWICKI R L	Dick	02/02/47	Penley, Flintshire		1974	1976	Huddersfield Town	Retired	55+13	5	5+1	0	11	1	0	0
KURILA J	John	10/04/41	Glasgow		1971		Colchester United	Dover	23+1	0	0	0	0	0	0	0
LAMMING W G	Walter	02/09/1896	Lincoln	1962	1919		Rustons Staff	Merthyr Town	2	0	0	0	0	0	0	0
					1921		Merthyr Town	Robeys	4	1	0	0	0	0	0	0
LANCASTER R	Roy	17/08/41	Rotherham		1966	1967	Grimsby Town	Boston United	24	0	1	0	0	0	0	0
LANGHAM W	Billy	1876	Nottingham		1906	1909	Doncaster Rovers		58	3	0	26	21	0	0	30
LARKIN B P	Bunny	11/1/36	Birmingham		1964	1965	Watford	Wisbech Town	25+2	0	2	0	3	0	0	0
LATCHFORD R D	Bob	18/1/51	Birmingham		1985		Coventry City	Newport County	14+1	1	0	0	2	0	0	0
LAVERICK C	Charles	1881			1904	1906	Doncaster Rovers		66	7	0	0	0	0	0	0
LAW J	John	c1887			1907		Rangers	Gainsborough Trin.	19	0	0	0	0	0	0	0
LAWRENCE G H	George	10/03/1889	Ilkeston	1959	1925		Bristol City	Ilkeston Town	5	2	0	0	1	0	0	0
LAWTON N	Nobby	25/03/40	Manchester		1970	1971	Brighton	Retired	20	0	1	0	0	0	0	0
LAX W	Walter	25/03/12	Gainsbrough		1929	1930	Albion Works	Blackpool	45	2	0	0	18	3	0	0
LAYBOURNE K E	Keith	27/01/59	Sunderland		1977	1978	Lambton Street BC	Runcorn	18	0	2	0	1	0	0	0
LEACH T	Tony	23/09/03	Sheffield	1970	1938		Carlisle United		25	3	0	0	2	0	0	0
LEANING A J	Andy	18/05/63	Howden, Yorks		1993	1995	Bristol City	Chesterfield	36	3	6	6	0	0	0	0
LEE J B	Jason	09/05/71	Forest Gate, London		1990	1992	Charlton	Southend	86+7	2+1	6	4	21	1	0	0
LEES J W D	Joseph	1892	Coalville	1933	1921		Rotherham County		33	1	0	0	9	1	0	0
LEES W D	Donald	1873	Cranberry		1893		Celtic	Celtic	28	2	0	0	17	0	0	0
					1894		Celtic	Barnsley St Peter	24	0	0	0	7	0	0	0
LEIGH D	Dennis	26/02/49	Barnsley		1972	1978	Rotherham United	Boston United	201+5	10	13	0	4	0	0	0
LEMONS C	Charlie	03/12/1887	Sheffield	1952	1921		Scunthorpe United	York City	22	0	0	0	4	0	0	0
LESTER A B	Benny	10/02/20	Sheffield		1947	1948	Hull City	Ransome & Marles	37	0	0	0	10	0	0	0
LEWIS F J	Jack	22/03/48	Long Eaton		1966	1969	Long Eaton United	Grimsby Town	49+21	1+1	3+1	0	11	0	2	0
LINCOLN A	Andy	17/05/02	Seaham Harbour	1977	1920		Glen Rose FC	Halifax Town	0	0	0	1	0	0	0	1
					1931		Stockport County	Gateshead	3	0	0	0	2	0	0	0
LINFOOT F	Frederick	12/03/01	Whitley Bay	1979	1919		Leeds City	Chelsea	29	1	0	0	3	0	0	0
LINNECOR A R	Bert	30/11/33	Birmingham		1956	1963	Birmingham City	Boston FC	264	13	10	0	52	1	2	0
LISHMAN W J	William	28/04/1899	Newcastle		1921		Close Works	Gateshead Town	4	0	0	0	0	0	0	0
LITTLEDYKE R	Robert	05/07/13	Chester le Street		1935		City of Durham	Mansfield Town	9	0	0	2	0	0	0	1
LITTLER J E	Eric	14/04/29	St Helens		1954		Leicester City	Wrexham	6	1	0	0	2	0	0	0
LIVINGSTONE J	James	12/01/1898	Wallsend	1984	1922		Walker Celtic		2	0	0	0	0	0	0	0
LONG H R	Ray	04/10/36	Stickney, Lincs		1959		Louth United	Louth United	1	0	0	0	0	0	0	0
LORD W	Walter	01/11/33	Grimsby		1956		Grimsby Town	Alford United	1	0	0	0	0	0	0	0
LORMOR A	Tony	29/10/70	Ashington		1989	1993	Newcastle	Peterborough Utd	90+10	4	1+2	6	30	2	2	0
LOUGHLAN A J	Tony	19/01/70	Croydon		1993		Kettering Town		4+8	1+1	0	3	2	0	0	2
LOWERY J	Jerry	19/10/24	Newcastle		1952	1953	Newcastle	Peterborough Utd	51	5	0	0	0	0	0	0
LOXLEY A D	Tony	14/12/59	Nottingham		1978		Apprentice	Sydney Olympic	1	0	0	0	0	0	0	0
LOXLEY H	Bert	03/02/34	Bonsall		1966		Lockheed	Retired	7	1	0	0	0	0	0	0
LUCAS R	Richard	22/09/70	Sheffield		1994		Preston N E (L)		4	0	0	2	0	0	0	0
LUDKIN D	Dan	01/05/1894	Ryton, Co Durham	1945	1922	1923	Close Works	Retired	14	0	0	0	1	0	0	0
LUND G J	Gary	13/09/64	Grimsby		1986		Grimsby Town	Notts County	41+3	1	4	0	13	1	1	0
LYNES J	Jimmy	1869	Cheltenham		1896		Leicester Fosse	Halifax	19	2	0	0	4	2	0	0
McALEER J	Joseph	08/03/10	Blythswood		1934		Northampton Town	Clapton Orient	6	0	0	2	5	0	0	0
McCAIRNS T	Thomas	22/12/1873	Dinsdale	1932	1899	1900	Notts County	Barnsley	35	0	0	0	14	0	0	0
McCALLIOG J	Jim	23/09/46	Glasgow		1978		Lyn, Oslo	Runcorn	9	0	0	0	0	0	0	0

Name		Date of Birth	Place of Birth	Died	First Season	Last Season	Previous Club	Next Club	League	FAC	LC	Other	Lge.	FAC	LC	Other
McCANN H	Henry	c1887	Stenhousemuir		1907	1908	Hibernian		17	2	0	32	6	0	0	7
McCARRICK M B	Mark	04/02/62	Liverpool		1984	1985	Birmingham City	Crewe	42+2	3	2	6	0	0	0	0
McCLAREN S	Steve	03/05/61	York		1986		Derby County (L)		8	0	0	0	0	0	0	0
McCLELLAND J B	John	05/03/35	Bradford		1958	1961	Manchester City	QPR	121	6	3	0	32	2	0	0
McCLELLAND J T	Jack	09/05/40	Lurgan	1976	1968		Fulham (L)		12	1	0	0	0	0	0	0
McCONVILLE P	Patrick	25/03/02	Gilford, Co Down		1925	1931	Glenavon	Glenavon	138	7	0	0	0	0	0	0
McCORMICK J	Jimmy	26/04/12	Rotherham	1968	1947	1948	Fulham	Crystal Palace	64	0	0	0	6	0	0	0
McCREADY T S	Tommy	28/09/23	Port Glasgow		1950		Hartlepool	Grantham Town	11	0	0	0	1	0	0	0
McCUBBIN A C	Sandy	1888	Greenock		1911	1913	Huddersfield Town	Newland Athletic	59	7	0	31	15	4	0	16
McCULLOCH A	Alexander		Edinburgh		1919		Hearts	Methyr Town	13	1	0	3	0	0	0	0
McCULLOCH G	Gordon	c1888	Hinckley		1913		Sutton Town	Bentley Colliery	11	1	0	0	0	0	0	0
McDERMID R	Robert	c1870			1892		Stockton	Renton	2	0	0	0	0	0	0	0
McDONALD G	George				1899		Newcastle United		2	0	0	0	0	0	0	0
McDOUGALL A	Angus	c1891	Glasgow		1913		Bathgate Linlithgow	Hartlepool	9	0	0	0	0	0	0	0
McDOWALL D	Dan	22/05/29	Kirkintilloch		1953		Workington	Millwall	17	1	0	0	4	0	0	0
McEVOY D W	Don	03/12/28	Golcar		1958	1959	Sheffield Wed.	Barrow	23	0	0	0	0	0	0	0
McFADDEN J	John	c1891	Glengarnock		1913	1914	Barrow	Barrow	19	0	0	0	0	0	0	0
McFARLANE A E	Archibald				1894	1895		Glossop North End	51	3	0	0	0	0	0	0
					1897		Glossop North End	Gravesend	10	0	0	0	0	0	0	0
McFARLANE D	David	c1890			1913			Kirkintilloch Harp	7	0	0	0	2	0	0	0
McGEOUGH J	Jimmy	14/07/46	Belfast		1972	1974	Waterford	Waterford	61+4	3	3+1	1	0	0	0	0
McGINLEY J	John	11/06/59	Rowlands Gill, Co Durham		1984	1986	Charleroi (Belgium)	Rotherham United	69+2	3	4	6	11	0	0	1
					1986	1988	Rotherham United	Doncaster Rovers	36+5	2	0	46	7	3	0	17
McGLEN W	Bill	27/04/21	Bedlington		1952		Manchester United	Oldham Athletic	13	1	0	0	0	0	0	0
McGRAHAN J	James	01/03/1898	Leadgate, Co Durham		1922		Leadgate Park	Wigan Borough	25	1	0	0	0	0	0	0
					1925	1926	Boston	Scarborough	26	3	0	0	1	0	0	0
MACHIN P	Peter	c1883			1905	1906	Wallsend Park Villa		54	5	0	0	21	0	0	0
McINALLY J S	John	26/09/51	Gatehouse of Fleet		1970	1971	Manchester United	Colchester United	22	2	0	0	0	0	0	0
McINNES I	Ian	22/03/67	Hamilton		1985	1986	Rotherham United	Kilmarnock	38+5	0	4	4	4	0	0	1
McINNES T	Thomas	29/08/1870	Glasgow	1937	1900	1902			79	11	0	0	20	4	0	0
McKAY R A	Bob	c1866			1888	1889			0	5	0	29	0	3	0	11
McKENZIE A	Aiden	15/07/59	Athlone		1979		Galway Rovers	Finn Harps	4+2	0	0	0	0	0	0	0
MacKENZIE R	Ronald	c1885			1909		Chelsea	Inverness Clachnacuddin	28	1	0	0	6	1	0	0
MACKEY J A	James	1898	Ryton, Co Durham		1923		Notts County	Luton Town	21	2	0	0	2	0	0	0
MACKIN J	John	18/11/43	Glasgow		1969		Northampton Town	York City	3	0	1	0	0	0	0	0
McLEOD W	William	1887	Hebburn, Co Durham		1906		Hebburn Argyle	Leeds City	13	0	0	0	8	0	0	0
McMAHON F G	Frank	04/01/50	Belfast		1971	1972	Waterford	Darlington	44+2	3	3	1	2	0	0	0
McMANUS C E	Eric	14/11/50	Limavady (NI)		1979		Stoke City (L)		21	0	0	0	0	0	0	0
McMILLAN S					1893			Millwall Athletic	3	0	0	0	0	0	0	0
McMILLAN W	William	c1876		1958	1898	1903	Lanark Athletic	Newark Town	176	17	0	0	1	0	0	0
					1905		Newark Town	Newark Town	2	0	0	0	0	0	0	0
McNEIL R	Dixie	16/01/47	Melton Mowbray		1971	1973	Northampton Town	Hereford United	96+1	3	2	1	53	0	0	0
McNEIL R M	Bobby	01/11/62	Bellshill		1985		Hull City	Preston North End	4	0	0	0	0	0	0	0
McPARLAND I J	Ian	04/10/61	Edinburgh		1992		Dunfermline Ath.	Sliema (Malta)	3+1	0	1	0	0	0	0	0
McPHAIL D	Dan	09/02/03	Campbelltown	1987	1931	1938	Portsmouth		309	17	0	6	0	0	0	0
McPHEE H	Hugh	C1864			1888	1889	Hibernian		0	4	0	23	0	0	0	3
McQUAKER T	Thomas	25/12/1867	Glasgow		1896				1	0	0	0	0	0	0	0
MACRILL F					1896		Grantham Rovers	St Marys (Lincoln)	3	0	0	0	0	0	0	0
McVAY D R	David	05/03/55	Workington		1981		Peterborough Utd	Grantham Town	13	0	4	2+1	0	0	0	0
McWHIRTER A					1889			Bolton Wanderers	0	0	0	2	0	0	0	0
MAIDMENT J H C	Jim	28/09/01	Sunderland	1977	1930		Newport County	Notts County	41	2	0	0	0	0	0	0
MAIDMENT T	Tom	04/11/07	Sunderland	1971	1925	1930	Sunderland	Portsmouth	126	4	0	0	43	4	0	0
MAIR G	Gordon	18/12/58	Coatbridge		1984	1985	Notts County	Motherwell	57	3	3	1+3	3	0	0	0
MANN J J	John				1895				8	2	0	0	0	0	0	0
MANNING J T	Jack	1886	Boston	1946	1911	1914	Rochdale	Rotherham County	90	9	0	31	9	1	0	10
MANSLEY A	Allan	31/08/46	Liverpool		1971		Notts County (L)		3	0	0	0	0	0	0	0
MANSON D G	David	20/09/1876	Glasgow		1896		Leicester Fosse	Warmley	4	2	0	0	1	0	0	0
MARCH H J	Harold	30/01/04	Gamston, Notts	1977	1930	1931	Hull City	Grantham Town	10	1	0	0	5	0	0	0
MARDENBOROUGH S A	Steve	11/09/64	Birmingham		1993		Darlington	Scarborough	14+7	0+1	2	1+1	2	0	0	0
MARKLEW H	Herbert	04/04/10	Dinnington	1987	1933	1934	Dinnington Main	Dinnington Main	7	0	0	0	3	0	0	0
MARLOW G A	Geoff	13/12/14	Worksop	1978	1937	1938	Dinnington Main	Newark Town	16	0	0	1	5	0	0	0
					1945	1947	Newark Town	Grantham Town	62	8	0	0	20	6	0	0
MARRIOTT A	Arthur				1891				0	2	0	18	0	0	0	1
MARRIOTT F	Frank	26/10/1893	Sutton in Ashfield		1924		Swansea Town	Grantham Town	3	1	0	0	0	0	0	0
MARSHALL J H	James	09/06/1890	Glenguie, Peterhead	1958	1924		Rotherham County	Queen of the Sth	3	0	0	0	1	0	0	0
MARSHALL L	Lester	04/02/02	Castleford		1924	1926	York City	Scarborough	19	0	0	0	6	0	0	0
MARTIN A O	Albert	19/03/1896	Lincoln	1975	1924		Rustons Staff	Rustons Staff	3	0	0	0	0	0	0	0
MARTIN J A	Jae	05/02/76	London		1996		Birmingham City		29+5	1	5	0+1	4	0	1	0
MARTIN J	John	1882	South Shields		1904	1905	Kingston Villa	Blackburn Rovers	65	7	0	0	30	3	0	0
MASON R	Richard	c1866		1954	1885		Lindum	Lindum	0	1	0	0	0	0	0	0
MATHISON G	George	24/11/09	Newcastle	1989	1932	1933	Newcastle United	Gateshead	37	0	0	0	0	0	0	0
MATTHEWS B J	Barry	18/01/26	Sheffield		1949		Sheffield United	Corby Town	2	0	0	0	0	0	0	0
MATTHEWS N	Neil	19/09/66	Grimsby		1992	1994	Stockport County	Dag. & Red.	69+14	4	2	4+3	20	0	1	1
MATTHEWSON T	Trevor	12/02/63	Sheffield		1987	1988	Stockport County	Birmingham City	43	4	3	49	2	0	0	7
MEACOCK W R	Bob	26/07/10	Hoole, Chester		1935	1937	Tranmere Rovers	Birmingham City	70	3	0	1	0	0	0	0

Sheet No.11 — Measham to Panther

Name	First	Date of Birth	Place of Birth	Died	First Season	Last Season	Previous Club	Next Club	League	FAC	LC	Other	Lge.	FAC	LC	Other
MEASHAM I	Ian	14/12/64	Barnsley		1985		Huddersfield T (L)		6	0	0	0	0	0	0	0
MEATH T J	Trevor	20/03/44	Wednesbury		1969	1971	Walsall		42+1	2	4	0	5	0	0	0
MEESON A W	Arthur	10/04/04	Oxford	1971	1929	1930	Fulham	Osberton Radiators	12	0	0	0	0	0	0	0
MEGSON G J	Gary	02/05/59	Manchester		1995		Norwich City	Shrewsbury Town	2	0	2	0	0	0	0	0
MERRITT R	Richard	22/07/1897	Shiney Row, Co Durham	1978	1925		Durham City	York City	22	3	0	0	3	1	0	0
METTAM A	Alf	22/09/1861	Lincoln	1945	1885	1888			0	9	0	2	0	0	0	0
METTAM E	Ned	18/08/1868	Lincoln	1943	1889	1895			85	7	0	7	0	0	0	1
MEUNIER J B	James	1885	Poynton, Stockport	1957	1912	1913	Everton	Coventry City	23	0	0	0	0	0	0	0
MIDDLEMASS E	Ernie	30/08/20	Newcastle		1948		South Shields	Corby Town	2	0	0	0	0	0	0	0
MIDDLETON F T	Fred	02/08/30	West Hartlepool		1954	1962	Newcastle United	Worksop Town	300	13	2	0	16	0	0	0
MILLAR H	Harry				1888		Airdrie		0	0	0	9	0	0	0	2
MILLER G	George		Riggend, Lanarks		1910		Larkhall United		22	3	0	0	0	0	0	0
MILLER W	Walter	1882	Newcastle		1911	1913	Blackpool	Merthyr Town	35	4	0	27	8	1	0	20
MILNER J	John	14/05/42	Huddersfield		1963	1966	Huddersfield Town	Bradford PA	109	9	3	0	6	1	0	0
MINETT J	Jason	12/08/71	Peterborough		1995	1996	Exeter City	Exeter City	41+5	1	2+4	4+1	5	0	0	0
MITCHELL A	Andrew				1923				1	0	0	0	0	0	0	0
MITCHELL R	Bobby	04/01/55	South Shields		1985	1986	Hamrun (Malta)	Louth United	41+3	1	1+3	2+2	2	0	1	0
MITCHELL T	Thomas	27/06/01	Trimdon Grange, Co.Dur.	1970	1929		Blackburn Rovers		3	0	0	0	0	0	0	0
MOODY V R	Roy	12/03/23	Worksop		1946			Worksop Town	1	0	0	0	0	0	0	0
MOORE A R	Andy	14/11/65	Cleethorpes		1987		Grimsby Town	Shamrock Rovers	0	3	0	32+1	0	0	0	1
MOORE I	Isaacc	08/04/1867	Dundee	1954	1890	1892	Our Boys (Dundee)	Burton Wanderers	22	11	0	38	3	8	0	15
MOORE J L	Les	07/07/33	Sheffield		1965	1966	Boston FC	Lockheed	59	0	1	0	0	0	0	0
MOORE J M	John	01/02/43	Carlton, Notts		1961	1964	Arnold St Marys	Arnold Town	30	0	1	0	5	0	1	0
MOORE W J	William	c1887	Ballyclare	1932	1923	1924	Falkirk	Ards	33	0	0	0	2	0	0	0
MORGAN E	Ernie	13/01/27	Barnsley		1952		Rawmarsh	Gillingham	3	0	0	0	0	0	0	0
MORRIS G R	George	1879	Manchester		1897	1899	M'chester St Augustines	Glossop North End	66	4	0	0	4	0	0	0
MORRIS W	William				1908		Stanton Hill Victoria	Liverpool	0	1	0	17	0	1	0	12
MORTON A	Alan	06/03/42	Peterborough		1963	1964	Peterborough United	Chesterfield	58	2	4	0	20	1	2	0
MORTON W H	William	16/12/1896	Ilkeston		1922		Newcastle United	Wigan Borough	21	0	0	0	4	0	0	0
MOSS E	Ernie	19/10/49	Chesterfield		1982		Port Vale	Doncaster Rovers	10+1	0	0	1	2	0	0	0
MOSSMAN D J	David	27/07/64	Sheffield		1987		Stockport County	Boston United	0	3	0	26+1	0	0	0	4
MOULSON C	Con	03/09/06	Clogheen (Ire)	1989	1932	1936	Bristol City	Notts County	88	3	0	2	0	0	0	0
MOULSON G B	George	06/08/14	Clogheen (Ire)	1994	1947	1948	Grimsby Town	Peterborough United	60	1	0	0	0	0	0	0
MOWATT A	Archibald	1870	South Shields		1899		Newcastle United	Newcastle United	8	1	0	0	1	0	0	0
MOWATT M J	Magnus	13/03/17	Glasgow		1938		Brentford	Clyde	6	0	0	0	1	0	0	0
MOYSES C R	Chris	01/11/65	Lincoln		1983		YTS	Halifax Town	2+2	0	0	0	0	0	0	0
MUDD P A	Paul	13/11/70	Hull		1995		Scunthorpe United	Halifax Town	2+2	0+1	0+1	1	0	0	0	0
MULLINEAUX J E B	James	1872	Blackburn		1889	1891		Burnley	0	11	0	52	0	1	0	1
MUNRO J F	Jimmy	25/03/26	Garmouth		1952	1957	Oldham Athletic	Bury	161	10	0	0	24	1	0	0
MURPHY A J	Aidan	17/09/67	Manchester		1986		Manchester Utd (L)		2	0	0	0	0	0	0	0
MURRAY J	John	09/03/45	Glasgow		1966		Stirling Albion		4	1	0	0	0	0	0	0
MURRAY J	Joseph	28/08/08	Hull	1988	1931		Hull City	Retired	1	0	0	0	0	0	0	0
MUSSON I S	Ian	13/12/53	Lincoln		1973		Sheffield Wednesday	Lincoln United	11	0	0	0	0	0	0	0
MUTCH A	Adam	07/03/01	Aberdeen		1925		Accrington Stanley	Forfar Athletic	8	0	0	0	2	0	0	0
NAYLOR S W	Stuart	06/12/62	Wetherby		1981	1985	Yorkshire Amateurs	WBA	49	2	4	8	0	0	0	0
NEAL R M	Dick	01/10/33	Dinnington		1954	1956	Wolves	Birmingham City	115	5	0	0	11	1	0	0
					1963	1964	Middlesbrough	Rugby Town	41	3	5	0	4	0	1	0
NEALE K I	Keith	19/01/35	Birmingham		1957	1958	Birmingham City	Kettering Town	8	1	0	0	1	0	0	0
NEALE P A	Phil	05/06/54	Scunthorpe		1974	1984	Lincoln United	Worcester City	327+8	16+2	11+1	4	22	0	0	0
NEAVE G D	George				1895			Dundee	29	3	0	0	0	2	0	0
NEILL Q D	Quentin	c1866	Glasgow	1901	1889	1894	Queens Park	Emigrated	59	20	0	51	0	1	0	2
NELSON G	George	05/02/25	Mexborough		1946		Sheffield United	Denaby United	1	0	0	0	0	0	0	0
NEVIN G W	George	16/12/07	Lintz	1973	1937	1938	Burnley	Rochdale	8	0	0	1	0	0	0	0
NEWSUM C H	Clement	13/06/1865	Lincoln	1947	1884		Lincoln Rovers	Lincoln RUFC	0	2	0	0	0	1	0	0
NEWSUM H E	Herbert	07/04/1867	Lincoln	1949	1884		Lincoln Rovers		0	1	0	0	0	1	0	0
NICHOLSON S M	Shane	03/06/70	Newark		1986	1991	YTS	Derby County	122+11	7	8+3	49+1	7	1	0	2
NIDD G F	Frederick	1869	Boston	1956	1897		Halliwell Rovers	Grimsby Town	9	2	0	0	0	0	0	0
NIGHTINGALE S	Samson	05/11/16	Rotherham	1982	1937		Woodhouse	Scunthorpe United	2	0	0	0	0	0	0	0
NISBET G	George				1906	1909		Maxwelltown Vol.	62	6	0	48	1	0	0	1
NORTH M V	Marc	25/09/66	Ware		1984		Luton Town (L)		4	0	0	1	0	0	0	0
NORTHCOTT T T	Tommy	05/12/31	Torquay		1955	1957	Cardiff City	Torquay United	94	3	0	0	34	1	0	0
O'CONNOR P K	Phil	10/10/53	Romford	1985	1974		Luton Town (L)		4	0	0	0	1	0	0	0
O'DONNELL D	Dennis	1880	Willington Quay		1901	1904	Willington Athletic	Sunderland	118	15	0	0	31	6	0	0
O'DONNELL M	Magnus	1882	Willington Quay		1904	1905	Wallsend Park Villa	Barnsley	45	5	0	0	11	3	0	0
OGLESBY S	Samuel	c1866	Canwick, Lincs		1884				0	1	0	0	0	0	0	0
ONWERE U A	Udo	09/11/71	Hammersmith		1994	1995	Fulham	Dover Athletic	40+3	1	5	4	4	0	0	1
ORMISTON A P	Andrew	01/03/1884	Peebles	1952	1907	1908	Hebburn Argyle	Chelsea	24	2	0	38	2	0	0	6
					1919				20	0	0	0	0	0	0	0
O'ROURKE P	Peter	22/09/1873	Newmilns	1956	1899		Burnley	Third Lanark	32	0	0	0	0	0	0	0
OSBORNE C	Charles	1873	Lincoln		1894		Adelaide	Sheppey United	6	0	0	0	0	0	0	0
OWEN R G	Bobby	05/05/24	Sunderland		1946	1954	Murton Colliery	South Shields	246	9	0	0	5	0	0	0
PAGE G	George	30/11/1898	Darlington		1924	1925	Ashington	Crewe	64	4	0	0	3	0	0	0
PALING T	Thomas				1889				0	1	0	3	0	0	0	0
PALLISTER W	William	1884	Gateshead		1902	1904	Sunderland		59	2	0	0	0	0	0	0
PANTHER F G	Fred	04/04/03	Manchester	1971	1922	1924	Celtic FC (Lincoln)	Newark Town	15	0	0	0	3	0	0	0

Sheet No.12 — Parker G S to Robinson J

		Date of Birth	Place of Birth	Died	First Season	Last Season	Previous Club	Next Club	League	FAC	LC	Other	Lge.	FAC	LC	Other
PARKER G S	Graham	23/05/46	Coventry		1968		Rotherham United	Exeter City	4+1	0	0	0	0	0	0	0
PARKER H	Harry				1903		Whitwick White Cross		30	1	0	0	3	0	0	0
PARKIN D	David	02/05/70			1986	1987	YTS	Grantham Town	0	0	0	0+2	0	0	0	0
PARKIN F W	Reg				1945			Scarborough	0	4	0	0	0	0	0	0
PARKINSON S	Steve	27/08/74	Lincoln		1992	1993	YTS	Grantham Town	1+4	0	1	0	0	0	0	0
PARR H	Harry	23/10/15	Newark		1946	1950			112	6	0	0	13	0	0	0
PARSONS D	David				1919		Eston Uited	Eston United	12	0	0	0	4	0	0	0
PARSONS W E					1891		Derby St Lukes		0	2	0	16	0	0	0	0
PATERSON W	William				1936		Stenhousemuir	Mansfield Town	2	0	0	0	0	0	0	0
PATTISON F	Frank	07/03/1889	South Bank	1950	1914		Clapton Orient	Rustons Aircraftmen	11	0	0	0	2	0	0	0
PAYNE F E	Frank	18/03/26	Ipswich		1949		Hull City	Kippax Legionnaires	5	0	0	0	0	0	0	0
PEAKE T	Trevor	10/02/57	Nuneaton		1979	1982	Nuneaton Borough	Coventry City	171	7	16	8	7	0	2	1
PEARMAN J	James	1877	Lincoln		1899		St Marys (Lincoln)		1	0	0	0	0	0	0	0
PEDEN G W W	George	12/04/43	Rosewell		1966	1973	Hearts	Worksop Town	224+1	15	12	1	16	0	3	0
PEGG F E	Frank	02/08/02	Beeston		1926	1930	Sunderland	Bradford City	115	5	0	0	51	0	0	0
PEGG G	George				1891				0	0	0	1	0	0	0	0
PHILLIPS H G	Henry				1899		Sandford Hills		2	0	0	0	1	0	0	0
PHIPPS W					1893				2	1	0	0	0	1	0	0
PICK W E	William	05/06/03	Clay Cross	1981	1925		Bury	Portsmouth	2	0	0	0	0	0	0	0
PILGRIM J A	Alan	20/07/47	Billingborough, Lincs		1965	1971	Billingborough	Boston United	20+3	1	0	0	1	0	0	0
PLATNAUER N R	Nicky	10/06/61	Leicester		1993	1995	Mansfield Town	Bedworth	26+1	0	4	0	0	0	0	0
PLATTS A J	Albert	1885	Worksop		1910	1913	Worksop Town	Scunthorpe United	29	0	0	0	4	0	0	0
POLLITT M	Mike	29/02/72	Bolton		1992		Bury (L)		5	0	1	0	0	0	0	0
					1992	1993	Bury	Darlington	52	2	4	4	0	0	0	0
PONTING W T	Walter	23/04/13	Grimsby	1960	1938		Chesterfield		23	3	0	0	15	4	0	0
POPPITT J	James	1879		1930	1907		Notts County		23	1	0	0	3	0	0	0
POSKETT T W	Thomas	26/12/09	Esh Winning	1972	1933		Grimsby Town	Notts County	10	0	0	0	1	0	0	0
POSNETT A	Arthur	1882	Leicester		1906		Liberal Club (Linc)	Gainsborough Trin.	3	0	0	0	1	0	0	0
POWELL G	Gary	02/04/69	Hoylake		1990		Everton (L)		11	0	0	0	0	0	0	0
POWELL W H	William				1932		Merthyr Town		4	0	0	0	0	0	0	0
POYNTON W	Bill	30/06/44	Shiremoor		1966		Oldham Athletic		0+1	0	0	0	0	0	0	0
PRICE T	Thomas				1902			Whitwick White Cross	11	0	0	0	3	0	0	0
PRINGLE C R	Charles	18/10/1894	Barrhead		1931	1932	Bradford PA	Stockport County	58	4	0	0	1	0	0	0
PRINGLE H	Harry	08/04/1900	Perkinsville, Co Durham	1965	1922	1933	Chester le Street	Grantham Town	292	23	0	0	60	2	0	0
PROUDFOOT P	Peter	1880	Wishaw	1941	1900	1902	Wishaw United	St Mirren	79	9	0	0	20	1	0	0
PUGH D H	David	1875	Wrexham	1945	1897	1900	Stoke City		91	7	0	0	11	1	0	0
PUNTER B	Brian	16/08/35	Bromsgrove		1959	1963	Leicester City	Hereford United	75	5	6	0	21	1	3	0
PUTTNAM D P	David	03/02/67	Leicester		1989	1995	Leicester City	Gillingham	160+17	4	13+1	8+1	21	0	1	0
PYLE T	Tom	1875	Lincoln	1958	1894	1899	Princess FC (Linc)		27	3	0	0	3	1	0	0
RABY W L	Walter	23/09/02	Lincoln	1973	1920		Robeys (Lincoln)	Grimsby Town	0	0	0	1	0	0	0	0
RABY W	Joey	03/07/1873	Heighington, Lincs	1954	1891	1893	St Catherines	Gainsborough Trin.	23	0	4	0	7	0	0	0
					1896		Gainsborough Trin.	Gainsborough Trin.	3	0	0	0	0	0	0	0
RAMSAY C J	Craig	19/09/62	Dunfermline		1979	1980	Apprentice	Yaro (Finland)	3+2	0	0	0	2	0	0	0
RANSHAW J W	Jack	19/12/16	Nettleham, Lincs		1946		Grantham Town	Peterborough Utd	3	0	0	0	0	0	0	0
RANSHAW R W G	Richard	17/04/70	Sleaford, Lincs		1988		YTS	Gainsborough Trin.	0+1	0	0	0	0	0	0	0
RANSON J G	Jack	01/04/09	Norwich		1935		Carlisle United	Blyth Spartans	5	1	0	2	1	0	0	0
RAW H	Henry	06/07/03	Tow Law	1965	1936	1937	WBA		66	6	0	0	7	0	0	0
RAWCLIFFE P	Peter	08/12/63	Grimsby		1990			Lincoln United	0+1	0	0	0	0	0	0	0
RAWLINSON W G	William	1868	Metheringham		1886	1890	Lincoln Ramblers	Gainsborough Trin.	0	15	0	25	0	0	0	0
RAYSEN L	Leonard	c1908			1926			Grantham Town	1	0	0	0	0	0	0	0
READ A H	Arthur	1894	Saxilby, Lincs		1924		Gillingham		8	1	0	0	0	0	0	0
REDDISH J	Jack	22/12/04	Nottingham	1989	1933	1934	Tottenham Hotspur	Notts County	53	2	0	0	0	0	0	0
REDFEARN N D	Neil	20/06/65	Dewsbury		1983	1985	Bolton Wanderers	Doncaster Rovers	96+4	3	4	7	13	1	0	0
REED C W	Chick	21/03/12	Holbeach, Lincs	1964	1932	1934	Sheffield United	Southport	55	5	0	2	24	4	0	0
REID J G	Jimmy	01/05/1890	Peebles	1938	1909	1911	Peebles Rovers	Airdrie	36	1	0	2	3	0	0	0
RICHARDS G V	Gary	02/08/63	Swansea		1985			Cambridge United	2+5	1	0	1	0	0	0	0
RICHARDS S C	Steve	24/10/61	Dundee		1985		Gainsborough Trin.	Cambridge United	21	0	2	0	0	0	1	0
RICHARDSON B	Barry	05/08/69	Wallsend		1995	*	Preston North End	*	70	2	5	1	0	0	0	0
RICHARDSON G W R	George	c1899	Gainsborough	1963	1920	1921	Gainsborough Wed.	Sheffield United	12	5	0	22	0	0	0	0
RICHARDSON J M	Mick	1874	Lincoln	1920	1892	1895	St Catherines	Gainsborough Trin.	64	7	0	0	6	0	0	0
RIDINGS D	David	27/02/70	Farnworth		1993		Halifax Town	Ashton United	10	0	0	0	0	0	0	0
RILEY H	Harold	02/11/09	Oldham	1982	1931	1932	Accrington Stanley	Notts County	57	2	0	0	25	2	0	0
RILEY J L	John	1888	Riddings, Derbys		1913		Sutton Town		6	0	0	0	0	0	0	0
RILEY					1920				0	0	0	0	0	0	0	0
RIPPON T	Thomas	04/02/1888	Beighton	1950	1920	1921	Grimsby Town	Worksop Town	33	5	0	35	10	4	0	23
RITCHIE R	Robert				1899		Victoria United		1	0	0	0	0	0	0	0
ROBERTS A	Alan	08/12/64	Newcastle		1989		Sheffield United	Retired	10	1	0	0	0	0	0	0
ROBERTS E E	Evan	1870	Bolton		1894			Rotherham Town	23	1	0	0	0	0	0	0
ROBERTS H	Henry	01/09/07	Barrow	1984	1928	1929	Chesterfield	Port Vale	33	4	0	0	23	0	0	0
ROBERTS R	Bob	1864	Penyace	1932	1892		Preston North End		16	1	0	0	2	0	0	0
ROBERTSON H	Hugh				1897	1898	Burnley	Millwall	65	4	0	0	34	5	0	0
ROBERTSON J N	John	08/01/74	Liverpool		1995	*	Wigan Athletic	*	36+2	1	1	1	1	0	0	0
ROBERTSON T H	Thomas	1889	Gateshead		1910		Wallsend Park Villa	Retired	8	0	0	0	0	0	0	0
ROBINSON E G	Ernest		Shiney Row, Co Durham	1991	1935	1938	Carlisle United		64	4	0	3	0	0	0	0
ROBINSON J	Jackie	10/08/17	Shiremoor	1979	1949		Sunderland	Retired	8	1	0	0	5	0	0	0

Sheet No.13   Robinson JW to Smedley

		Date of Birth	Place of Birth	Died	First Season	Last Season	Previous Club	Next Club	Appearances League	FAC	LC	Other	Goals Lge.	FAC	LC	Other
ROBINSON J W	Jack		Derby	1931	1888	1890	Derby St Lukes	Derby County	0	9	0	44	0	0	0	0
ROBINSON T E	Thomas	11/02/09	Coalville	1982	1934		Chesterfield	Northampton Town	33	1	0	1	14	0	0	0
ROBINSON W	William				1908		Walsall	Walsall	0	0	0	7	0	0	0	2
ROBINSON W A	William	20/12/1898	Pegswood Colliery	1975	1929		Bradford PA	Gainsborough Trin.	17	0	0	0	7	0	0	0
ROBSON J	James		Durham		1923		Blackburn Rovers		10	0	0	0	0	0	0	0
ROBSON J W	Joe	26/10/1899	Ryhope, Co Durham		1925	1927	Rochdale	Durham City	60	5	0	0	1	0	0	0
ROBSON M H	Matt	1891	Springwell		1909	1914	Wallsend Park Villa	Scunthorpe United	121	10	0	29	3	0	0	0
RODGERS D M	David	28/02/52	Bristol		1981		Torquay United	Forest Green Rvrs	3	0	0	0	0	0	0	0
ROE A	Archibald	09/02/1893	Hull	1947	1923	1924	Arsenal	Rotherham County	27	3	0	0	12	0	0	0
ROGERS W	William				1896		Abercorn		1	0	0	0	0	0	0	0
ROONEY R	Bobby	08/07/38	Cowie		1962	1963	Doncaster Rovers	Cambridge City	28	1	2	0	3	0	1	0
ROSS W	William	1874	Kiveton Park		1897		Sheffield United	Gravesend United	22	0	0	0	3	0	0	0
ROUND K A	Kenneth	13/10/17	Dudley	1988	1938		Dudley Town		3	0	0	0	0	0	0	0
ROWE D H	Douglas	09/07/09	Nottingham	1978	1933		Luton Town	Southampton	11	0	0	0	5	0	0	0
RUDKIN T W	Tommy	17/06/19	Peterborough		1938		Wolves	Peterborough Utd	2	0	0	0	1	0	0	0
RUSHTON R	Richard	18/09/02	Willenhall	1891	1924	1925	Willenhall Swifts	Sheffield Wed.	44	2	0	0	1	1	0	0
RYAN M J	Michael	14/10/30	Welwyn		1952		Arsenal	York City	7	0	0	0	0	0	0	0
SADDINGTON					1890		Lincoln Amateurs		0	0	0	1	0	0	0	0
SAMUELS R W L	Bobby	18/05/46	Aberdeen		1967		Dundee United	Stevenage Athletic	3+1	0	0	0	0	0	0	0
SAUNDERS J E	James		Birmingham		1906	1908	Manchester United	Chelsea	65	6	0	50	0	0	0	0
SAUNDERS J G	John	01/12/50	Worksop		1979		Barnsley	Doncaster Rovers	25+1	1	2	0	5	0	0	0
SAVAGE R E	Ted	1912	Louth	1964	1928	1930	Stewton	Liverpool	96	4	0	0	3	0	0	0
SAXBY M W	Mick	12/08/57	Mansfield		1983		Luton Town (L)		10	2	0	0	1	0	0	0
SAYER S C	Stanley	02/02/1895	Chatham	1982	1925	1926	Wigan Borough	Southend United	32	3	0	0	6	0	0	0
SCANLON A J	Albert	10/10/35	Manchester		1961	1962	Newcastle United	Mansfield Town	47	4	3	0	11	1	0	0
SCANLON E A	Edward	14/05/1890	Hebburn		1909	1910	North Shields Ath.	South Shields	29	3	0	0	3	0	0	0
SCHOFIELD H	Harry				1897	1899	M'chester St Augustines		17	1	0	0	0	0	0	0
SCHOFIELD J D	John	16/05/65	Barnsley		1988	1994	Gainsborough Trin.	Doncaster Rovers	221+10	6+2	15	14+1	11	0	4	0
SCOTT C	Chris	11/09/63	Wallsend		1987	1988	Northampton Town	Whitley Bay	4	0	0	1+1	0	0	0	0
SCOTT F	Frank	c1876	Lincoln	1937	1897	1900	Adelaide	New Brompton	45	3	0	0	8	1	0	0
SCOTT K	Keith	10/06/67	Westminster		1989	1990	Leicester United	Wycombe Wanderers	7+9	0	0+1	1+1	2	0	0	0
SCOTT K A	Kevin	12/11/54	Lincoln		1973				1	0	0	0	0	0	0	0
SCOTT R S A	Dick	26/10/41	Thetford		1964		Scunthorpe United	Kings Lynn	9+1	0	1	0	1	0	0	0
SELLARS P	Peter	15/03/58	Market Rasen		1975		Apprentice	Market Rasen Town	0+1	0	0	0	0	0	0	0
SELLARS W	William	07/10/07	Sheffield	1987	1935		Bradford PA	Norton Woodseats	33	1	0	1	2	0	0	1
SERTORI M A	Mark	01/09/67	Manchester		1987	1989	Stockport County	Wrexham	43+7	3+1	6	25+12	9	1	0	9
SHARMAN R	Richrd	c1874	Lincoln		1897	1898	Grainsborough Trin.		6	4	0	0	0	0	0	0
SHARP B C	Brittain	1883	Lincoln		1904	1905	St Catherines	Newark Town	11	0	0	0	0	0	0	0
		1891			1907		Newark Town	Worksop Town	3	0	0	0	1	0	0	0
SHARPE					1891				0	0	0	1	0	0	0	0
SHAW B	Bernard	04/09/29	Selby		1953	1954	Goole Town	Peterborough Utd	9	0	0	0	1	0	0	0
SHAW G	George	1865	Lincoln	1928	1887	1895	Lincoln Ramblers	Retired	13	17	0	56	0	3	0	20
SHAW R	Richardson	1876	Halifax		1894	1895	Peterborough GN Loco	Peterborough GN Loco	7	1	0	0	0	0	0	0
SHAW W	Wainwright	1870	Sheffield		1897		Grantham Rovers		8	0	0	0	0	0	0	0
SHAW W					1888				0	3	0	1	0	1	0	0
SHEARMAN F P	Fred				1895		Wainfleet		14	2	0	0	3	0	0	0
									3	0	0	0	0	0	0	0
SHELTON W	William				1896		Arnold St Marys	Netherfield Rangers	2	0	0	0	0	0	0	0
SHERWOOD S	Steve	10/12/53	Selby		1994		Grimsby Town	Stalybridge Celtic	6+1	0	0	0	0	0	0	0
SHIPLEY G M	George	07/03/59	Newcastle		1979	1984	Southampton	Charlton Athletic	229+1	9	22	13	42	1	8	1
SHORT D	David	14/04/41	St Neots		1958	1959	St Neots Town	Bedford Town	4	0	0	0	0	0	0	0
SILLITO H	Harry	10/07/01	Chester le Street	1993	1922	1923	Chelsea	Merthyr Town	48	3	0	0	2	0	0	0
SILVESTER T	Tom	c1861		1939	1885		Lincoln Ramblers		0	1	0	0	0	0	0	0
SIMMONITE G	Gordon	25/04/57	Sheffield		1982	1984	Blackpool		71+1	2	6	5	0	0	0	0
					1987			Gainsborough Trin.	0	0	0	16	0	0	0	0
SIMMONS A J	Tony	09/02/65	Stocksbridge		1986		Rotherham United	Gainsborough Trin.	14+5	0+1	0	1+1	5	0	0	1
SIMPSON C F	Freddy	c1883			1902	1907	Midland Athletic	Newark Town	124	9	0	0	37	2	0	0
SIMPSON H	Herbert	29/09/1863	Sleaford	1929	1884	1893	Lincoln Rovers	Retired	3	24	0	28	0	0	0	0
SIMPSON J L	John	05/10/33	Appleby	1993	1956		Netherfield	Gillingham	5	0	0	0	0	0	0	0
SIMPSON J W	John		Lincoln		1919		Army Football	Scunthorpe United	4	0	0	0	0	0	0	0
SIMPSON J W	Joe				1894	1895		Newark Town	21	1	0	0	0	0	0	0
					1896	1897	Kettering	St Marys	41	3	0	0	0	0	0	0
					1899	1900	St Marys		8	0	0	0	0	0	0	0
SIMPSON W	Walter				1897				2	0	0	0	0	0	0	0
SIMPSON W	William	c1878	Sunderland	1962	1902	1907	Sunderland	Retired	140	11	0	0	0	0	0	0
SIMS F	Frank	12/09/31	Lincoln		1951	1955	Ruston Bucyrus	Boston United	3	0	0	0	0	0	0	0
SIMS S F	Steve	02/07/57	Lincoln		1990		Burton Albion		5	0	0	0	0	0	0	0
SINGLETON A					1888				0	0	0	1	0	0	0	0
SISSON T	Thomas	19/10/1894	Basford	1976	1923	1925	Gillingham	Peterborough	75	5	0	0	1	0	0	0
SISSONS W S	William	01/02/01	Kiveton Park	1988	1924	1925	Kiveton Park	Retired	74	3	0	0	0	0	0	0
SIVELL L	Laurie	08/02/51	Lowestoft		1978		Ipswich Town (L)		2	0	0	0	0	0	0	0
SLADE D	Donald	26/11/1888	Southampton	1980	1912	1913	Southampton	Arsenal	23	2	0	0	9	2	0	0
SLATER J	James				1886	1889	Blackburn Olympic		0	9	0	2	0	2	0	0
SMALLMAN F J B	Frank	1869	Gainsborough Trin.		1889	1892	St Johns	Burton Wanderers	22	15	0	46	17	7	0	23
					1894	1895	Burton Wanderers		36	1	0	0	6	0	0	0
SMEDLEY L	Laurie	07/05/22	Sheffield		1945	1948		Frickley Colliery	11	1	0	0	7	0	0	0

Sheet No.14 — Smillie to Toman

Name		Date of Birth	Place of Birth	Died	First Season	Last Season	Previous Club	Next Club	League	FAC	LC	Other	Lge.	FAC	LC	Other
SMILLIE R D	Ron	27/09/33	Grimethorpe		1956	1959	Barnsley	Barnsley	91	4	0	0	15	0	0	0
SMITH A	Alec	07/11/1873	Old Kilpatrick	1908	1895	1896	St Mirren	Third Lanark	45	7	0	0	9	3	0	0
SMITH D	Dave	08/12/47	Thornaby		1968	1977	Middlesbrough	Rotherham United	358+13	25	22+1	1	52	5	2	0
SMITH H	Henry		Neston		1907				2	0	0	0	0	0	0	0
SMITH J	James	06/05/08	Thurnscoe	1956	1931	1935	Doncaster Rovers	Bradford City	116	7	0	4	3	0	0	0
SMITH J M	Jim	17/10/40	Sheffield		1967	1968	Halifax Town	Boston United	54	4	2	0	0	1	0	0
SMITH J E	Jeff	08/12/35	Warren		1957	1966	Sheffield United		315	18	18	0	2	0	0	0
SMITH L J	Lindsay	18/09/54	Enfield		1981		Cambridge Utd (L)		5	0	0	0	0	0	0	0
SMITH M C	Mark	21/03/60	Sheffield		1993		Notts County	Retired	20	1	3	2	1	0	0	0
SMITH M	Mick	28/10/58	Sunderland		1977	1978	Lambton Street BC	Wimbledon	20+5	0	2	0	0	0	0	0
SMITH N	Neil	10/02/70	Warley		1989	1991	Redditch United	Cheltenham	13+4	0	2	0	0	0	0	0
SMITH P M	Paul	09/11/64	Rotherham		1987	1994	Port Vale	Halifax Town	219+13	7+2	10+2	53	27	1	0	12
SMITH T	Thomas				1910				1	0	0	0	0	0	0	0
SMITH W A	Wally	1874	Lincoln	1958	1899	1902	Grantham Avenue	Small Heath	90	9	0	0	21	2	0	0
SMITH W	Tich	10/11/1871	Sawley	1907	1898		Loughborough		33	2	0	0	0	0	0	0
SNAREY C	Charles	1881	Oakham		1903				3	0	0	0	0	0	0	0
SOULSBY T	Thomas	24/10/1876	Mickley		1905			Mickley	3	0	0	0	1	0	0	0
SPEARS A F	Alan	27/12/38	Amble		1963		Millwall	Cambridge City	2	0	1	0	0	0	0	0
SPENCER T W	Thomas	22/03/14	Deptford		1936		Fulham	Ashford	4	0	0	0	1	0	0	0
SPENCER T H	Tom	28/11/45	Glasgow		1971	1973	Workington	Rotherham United	67+7	1	1	0	10	0	0	0
STAINTON B E	Bryan	08/01/42	Scampton, Lincs		1961	1964	Ingham	Gainsborough Trin.	25	0	1	0	0	0	0	0
STANT P R	Phil	13/10/62	Bolton		1990		Notts County (L)		4	0	0	0	0	0	0	0
					1996	*	Bury	*	22	0	0	1	15	0	0	0
STERLING W R	Worrell	08/06/65	Bethnal Green		1996		Bristol Rovers		15+6	0+1	3+1	0+1	0	0	0	0
STEVENSON G H	George	1905	Nottingham		1925	1926	Stamford Town	Shirebrook	11	0	0	0	6	0	0	0
STILLYARDS G W E	George	29/12/18	Whisby, Lincs		1945	1949	Lincoln Rovers	Skegness Town	100	9	0	0	2	0	0	0
STIMPSON R R	Reg	25/08/1900	Lincoln	1977	1920	1921	Robeys	Worksop Town	1	0	0	1	0	0	0	0
STONES C	Craig	31/05/80	Scunthorpe		1996	*	YTS	*	0+2	0	0	0	0	0	0	0
STOREY B B	Brett	07/07/77	Sheffield		1995		Sheffield United		0+2	0	0	0	1	0	0	0
STOREY L D	Luke	17/12/20	Dawdon		1947	1948	Blackhall Colliery	Grantham Town	11	2	0	0	2	0	0	0
STOTHERT J	James		Blackburn		1893		Brierfield	Notts County	18	0	0	0	0	0	0	0
STOUTT S P	Steve	05/04/64	Halifax		1989	1990	Grimsby Town	Boston United	36+10	1	1	3	1	0	0	0
STRAWSON J H	Jack	03/11/1858	East Firsby, Lincs	1949	1884		Lincoln Rovers	Retired	0	1	0	0	0	0	0	0
STRODDER G J	Gary	01/04/65	Cleckheaton		1982	1986	Apprentice	West Ham	122+10	2+1	7+1	6+2	6	0	0	0
STRONG T P	Tommy	1890	Newcastle	1917	1913	1914			8	0	0	0	0	0	0	0
STURGES-JONES T O	Oliver	06/06/1862	Chichester		1884		Chichester	Upton Park	0	1	0	0	0	0	0	0
STYLES					1888				0	0	0	1	0	0	0	0
SUNLEY D	David	06/02/52	Skelton		1978	1979	Hull City	Stockport County	36+5	0	2+1	0	6	0	0	0
SVARC R L	Bobby	08/02/46	Leicester		1968	1971	Leicester City	Boston United	40+5	4+2	2	0	16	4	0	0
SWAN A	Andrew	1878	Dalbeattie		1898		Dalbeattie	New Brompton	13	0	0	0	10	0	0	0
SWINBURNE T	Trevor	20/06/53	East Rainton		1985	1986	Leeds United	Retired	34	0	3	3	0	0	0	0
SYKES E A A	Albert	1900	Maltby	1994	1928	1930	Brighton	Peterborough	42	2	0	1	0	0	0	0
SYMM C	Colin	26/11/46	Dunstan on Tyne		1972	1974	Sunderland	Boston United	60+9	5	2	0+1	7	0	1	0
TAYLOR A	Albert	c1910	Ashington		1936		Bristol Rovers	Gillingham	4	0	0	1	0	0	0	0
TAYLOR A B	Arthur	c1879		1947	1905		Grantham Avenue		6	2	0	0	0	0	0	0
TAYLOR D					1889				0	1	0	0	0	0	0	0
TAYLOR D	Dave				1908				0	0	0	1	0	0	0	0
TAYLOR F	Frank	c1887		1928	1905	1907	Liberal Club (Linc)	Worksop Town	36	1	0	0	10	0	0	0
TAYLOR G A	Geoff	22/01/23	Henstead		1947		Reading	Boston United	1	0	0	0	0	0	0	0
TAYLOR G	Graham	15/09/44	Worksop		1968	1972	Grimsby Town	Retired	150+1	7	11	1	1	0	1	0
TAYLOR J	James				1923				1	0	0	0	0	0	0	0
TAYLOR J P	John	24/10/64	Norwich		1996		Luton Town (L)		5	0	0	0	2	0	0	0
TAYLOR W	Billy	31/07/39	Edinburgh	1981	1969	1970	Nottingham Forest	Retired	74+5	6	4	0	7	1	0	0
TAYLOR					1891				0	0	0	0	0	0	0	0
TEESDALE E D	Edwin	25/01/1861	Lincoln	1947	1885	1888	Lincoln Rovers		0	5	0	1	0	1	0	0
TENNANT D	David	13/06/45	Walsall		1966	1968	Grimsby Town	Rochdale	39	1	0	0	0	0	0	0
THACKER J	Jack	c1919			1938		Morris-Motors	Morris-Motors	1	0	0	0	0	0	0	0
THOM L M	Lewis	10/04/44	Stornoway		1966	1968	Shrewsbury Town	Bradford PA	45+2	4	5	0	5	1	1	0
THOMAS J W	John	05/08/58	Wednesbury		1983	1984	Chester City	Preston North End	56+11	0+1	3+1	4+1	18	0	2	0
THOMPSON A	Alex	08/12/17	Sheffield		1946	1947	Sheffield Wed.	Tranmere Rovers	34	4	0	0	1	0	0	0
THOMPSON C D	Chris	24/01/60	Walsall		1982		Bolton Wanderers	Blackburn Rovers	5+1	0	0	0	0	0	0	0
THOMPSON D	David	26/02/45	Middlesbrough		1964		Whitby Town	Kettering Town	3	0	1	0	1	0	0	0
THOMPSON J H	John	04/07/32	Newcastle		1957	1959	Newcastle United	Horden Colliery	42	1	0	0	0	0	0	0
THOMPSON J T	Trevor	21/05/55	North Shields		1979	1981	Newport County	Gainsborough Trin.	80	2	8	3	1	0	0	0
THOMPSON S P	Steve	28/07/55	Sheffield		1980	1984	Boston United	Charlton Athletic	153+1	9	17	6	8	1	0	2
					1989	1990	Sheffield United	Retired	27	3	1	1	0	0	0	0
THOMPSON T	Thomas				1903		Southwick	Southwick	6	0	0	0	0	0	0	0
THOMSON G	Gavin				1895				5	0	0	0	3	0	0	0
THORPE E	Edwin	c1898	Kiveton Park		1919	1920	Sheffield Wed.	Doncaster Rovers	12	0	0	14	0	0	0	0
THORPE L	Levy	18/11/1889	Seaham Harbour	1935	1922	1923	Blackburn Rovers	Rochdale	69	2	0	0	9	0	0	0
THURSBY R S	Stan	05/03/09	Lincoln		1929	1931	Burton Road	City School OB	21	2	0	0	6	1	0	0
TICE W					1893				10	2	0	0	0	0	0	0
TIERNEY H	Herbert	1888	Rochdale		1912		Darlington	Castleford Town	2	0	0	0	0	0	0	0
TIMMIS S	Samuel	c1872	Audley		1896		Audley		18	4	0	0	2	1	0	0
TOMAN J A	Andy	07/03/62	Northallerton		1985		Bishop Auckland	Bishop Auckland	21+3	0	2	0+1	4	0	0	0

Sheet No.15   Towler to Whyte

		Date of Birth	Place of Birth	Died	First Season	Last Season	Previous Club	Next Club	League	FAC	LC	Other	Lge.	FAC	LC	Other
TOWLER B E	Bernard	13/03/12	Ipswich	1992	1932	1937	Lincoln Corinthians	Notts County	68	5	0	0	32	4	0	0
TRACEY M G	Mike	14/02/35	Durham		1961		Luton Town	Worksop Town	21	1	1	0	5	0	1	0
TREHARNE C	Colin	30/07/37	Bridgend		1966		Mansfield Town	Ilkeston Town	20	0	3	0	0	0	0	0
TREVIS D A	Derek	09/09/42	Birmingham		1970	1972	Walsall	Philadelphia Atoms	100+8	7	7	1	18	1	2	0
TROOP F J					1890	1891	Lincoln Rangers	Newark	0	0	0	3	0	0	0	2
TROOPS H	Harold	10/02/26	Sheffield	1963	1949	1957	Barnsley	Carlisle United	295	15	0	0	32	3	0	0
TURNBULL R	Roy	22/10/48	Edinburgh		1969		Hearts		0+2	0	0	0	0	0	0	0
TURNELL F	Frederick	1868	Lincoln	1937	1890				0	0	0	1	0	0	0	0
TURNER B	Brian	27/08/25	Whittlesey		1947		March Town	March Town	5	0	0	0	0	0	0	0
TURNER C R	Chris	15/09/58	Sheffield		1978		Sheffield Wed. (L)		5	0	0	0	0	0	0	0
TURNER I	Ian	17/01/53	Middlesbrough		1978		Southampton (L)		7	1	0	0	0	0	0	0
TURNER J	John	c1868	Louth		1887		Horncastle		0	3	0	0	0	0	0	0
TURNER P	Phil	12/02/62	Sheffield		1979	1985	Apprentice	Grimsby Town	237+2	12	19	12+1	18	1	0	1
TURNER W L	Wayne	09/03/61	Luton		1981		Luton Town (L)		18	3	2	0	0	0	1	0
TYNAN T E	Tommy	17/11/55	Liverpool		1978		Sheffield Wed.	Newport County	9	0	0	0	1	0	0	0
URWIN J S	Joseph	25/02/12	High Spen, Co Durham		1933		Throckley Welfare	Stockport County	8	0	0	0	1	0	0	0
VARNEY J F	Frank	27/11/29	Oxford		1951	1952	Hull City	Headington United	20	1	0	0	4	0	0	0
VAUGHAN J	John	26/06/64	Isleworth		1996	*	Preston North End	*	10	0	1	0	0	0	0	0
VICKERS T H	Hedley	1877	Lincoln	1955	1895	1897	London Hospitals	Lindum	12	1	0	0	0	0	0	0
WADSLEY H	Harold				1908	1909	Netherfield Rangers	Sutton Junction	2	0	0	9	1	0	0	7
WAITES S H	Sydney	20/09/01	Gateshead		1920	1923	Technical Sch OB	Newark Town	3	0	0	1	0	0	0	0
WAITT M H	Mick	25/06/60	Hexham		1987	1989	Notts County	Boston United	7+1	2	0+1	16	1	1	0	8
WAKEHAM P F	Peter	14/03/36	Kingsbridge		1965		Charlton Athletic	Poole Town	44	1	2	0	0	0	0	0
WALKER A	Alan	17/12/59	Mossley		1983	1984	Telford United	Millwall	74+1	5	2	4	4	1	0	1
WALKER H	Harold				1934	1935	Usworth Colliery	Gateshead	18	0	0	0	2	0	0	0
WALKER J	John			1900	1899		Hearts	Retired	6	0	0	0	0	0	0	0
WALKER J					1891		Derby County		0	2	0	21	0	1	0	4
WALKER W	William	c1891	Durham		1921	1923	Fulham		36	0	0	0	5	0	0	0
WALLINGTON F M	Mark	17/09/52	Sleaford		1988	1990	Derby County	Retired	87	4	6	3	0	0	0	0
WALLS D	Dave	16/06/53	Leeds		1971	1972	Leeds United		9	0	0	0	0	0	0	0
WALSHAW K	Ken	28/08/18	Tynemouth		1947		Sunderland	Carlisle United	17	0	0	0	6	0	0	0
WANLESS P S	Paul	14/12/73	Banbury		1995		Oxford United	Cambridge United	7+1	0	0	2	0	0	0	0
WARD F	Fred	30/06/1894	Lincoln	1953	1914	1922	West End	Wigan Borough	99	7	0	27	8	0	0	2
					1925		Wigan Borough	Rochdale	7	3	0	0	2	0	0	0
					1930		Rochdale	Retired	2	0	0	0	0	0	0	0
WARD J	Tim				1896		Nondescripts		4	0	0	0	0	0	0	0
WARD J P	John	07/04/51	Lincoln		1970	1978	Adelaide Park	Watford	223+17	7+2	12+1	0+1	90	4	5	0
					1981		Grimsby Town	Retired	1	0	0	0	0	0	0	0
WARD P T	Paul	15/09/63	Sedgefield		1990	1992	Scunthorpe United	Gainsborough Trin.	38+1	1	3	2	0	0	1	0
WARD S	Stephen	27/12/60	Chapeltown, Sheffield		1979		Apprentice		2	0	0	0	0	0	0	0
WARD W R	Warren	25/05/62	Plympton		1985		York City	Boston United	15+6	0	1	1	8	0	0	0
WARD					1888				0	0	0	1	0	0	0	0
WARDLE G	Geoff	07/01/40	Trimdon		1961		Sunderland	Kings Lynn	1	0	0	0	0	0	0	0
WARREN L A	Lee	28/02/69	Manchester		1990		Hull City (L)		2+1	0	0	0	1	0	0	0
WARRINGTON A	Tony	12/02/34	Ecclesfield		1953	1955	Thorncliffe Juniors	Grantham Town	2	0	0	0	0	0	0	0
WATFORD A	Albert	12/02/17	Chesterfield		1946		Chesterfield	Scunthorpe United	14	1	0	0	0	0	0	0
WATSON A	Albert	c1904			1924		Yorkshire Amateurs		1	0	0	0	0	0	0	0
WATSON A E	Arthur	12/07/13	South Hiendley		1934	1935	Monckton Colliery	Chesterfield	37	0	0	3	0	0	0	0
WATSON D	Don	27/08/32	Barnsley		1956	1957	Sheffield Wed.	Bury	14	2	0	0	2	1	0	0
WATSON G S	Graham	03/08/49	Doncaster		1978	1979	Cambridge United	Cambridge United	43	2	2	0	2	0	0	0
WATSON W	William				1903	1906	South Bank	Newark Town	120	11	0	0	28	3	0	0
					1908		Newark Town	Castleford Town	0	2	0	43	0	1	0	25
WATSON W	William	29/05/16	South Hiendley		1934	1935	Monckton Colliery	Chesterfield	9	0	0	1	0	0	0	0
WEBB A R	Alan	01/01/63	Wrockwardine Wood		1983		WBA (L)		11	0	0	0	0	0	0	0
WEBB A	Alfred	c1878		1932	1899	1903	Mansfield Mechanics		131	14	0	0	0	0	0	0
WEBSTER W G	Walter	22/05/1895	West Bromwich	1980	1925		Walsall	Sheffield United	12	0	0	0	0	0	0	0
WELLS-COLE G C	Gervase	26/10/1860	Brigg	1917	1886		Lindum	Lindum	0	1	0	0	0	0	0	0
WEST D	Dean	15/12/72	Wakefield		1990	1995	YTS	Bury	93+26	6	11	5+2	20	1	1	1
WEST G	Gary	25/08/64	Scunthorpe		1985	1986	Sheffield United	Gillingham	83	2	5	4	4	0	0	0
					1990		Port Vale (L)		3	0	0	0	0	0	0	0
					1991		Port Vale	Boston United	14+4	1	2	2	1	0	0	1
WEST G					1896		GN Loco		1	0	0	0	0	0	0	0
WESTBROOK H A	Henry	24/05/1896	Chertsey	1977	1921				2	0	0	0	0	0	0	0
WESTLEY S L M	Shane	16/06/65	Canterbury		1995		Cambridge United	Retired	9	1	0	1	1	0	0	0
WHALLEY R	Robert	c1905	Flimby, Cumberland		1930		Peterborough	Peterborough	9	0	0	0	4	0	0	0
WHITE D W	Devon	02/03/64	Nottingham		1984	1985	Arnold Town	Boston United	21+8	0	0	2+1	4	0	0	2
WHITE F	Fred	05/12/16	Wolverhampton		1950		Sheffield United	Gainsborough Trin.	42	2	0	0	0	0	0	0
WHITE M	Malcolm	24/04/41	Sunderland		1964		Walsall	Bradford City	25	4	0	0	0	0	0	0
WHITE S J	Steve	02/01/59	Chipping Sodbury		1982		Charlton (L)		2+1	0	0	1	0	0	0	0
WHITE T H	Thomas	c1860	Lincoln	1915	1884		Lindum		0	2	0	0	0	0	0	0
WHITE W W	William	1911	Kirkcaldy		1936	1937	Bristol City	Hull City	46	3	0	1	11	0	0	1
WHITFIELD F	Frank	15/12/1900	Anston		1924		Wigan Borough	Southend United	23	1	0	0	1	0	0	0
WHITNEY J D	Jon	23/12/70	Nantwich		1995	*	Huddersfield Town	*	43+1	2	5	3	5	0	1	0
WHITTLE E	Ernie	25/11/25	Lanchester		1949	1953	West Stanley	Workington	145	6	0	0	62	2	0	0
WHYTE G	George	24/03/09	Cowdenbeath	1992	1931	1938	Accrington Stanley	Gainsborough Trin.	299	18	0	5	34	2	0	

Sheet No.16   Wield to Yule

Player		Date of Birth	Place of Birth	Died	First Season	Last Season	Previous Club	Next Club	League	FAC	LC	Other	Lge.	FAC	LC	Other
WIELD T W	Tommy	1886	Lincoln	1963	1904	1905	St Catherines	Grantham Avenue	13	0	0	0	0	0	0	0
					1909	1914	Grantham Avenue	Scunthorpe United	118	10	0	31	5	1	0	0
WIGGETT D J	David	25/05/57	Sheffield	1978	1973	1975	Apprentice	Hartlepool	4+2	0	0	0	0	0	0	0
WIGGINTON C A	Clive	18/10/50	Sheffield		1977	1978	Scunthorpe United	Grimsby Town	60	2	2	0	6	1	0	0
WILKINSON B J	Barry	19/07/42	Lincoln		1962	1963	Bracebridge CC	Ruston Bucyrus	6	1	3	0	3	1	1	0
WILKINSON H	Bert	02/08/22	Sunderland		1945	1950	Murton Colliery	Frickley Colliery	39	6	0	0	0	0	0	0
WILKINSON J	Jack	c1908	Wath on Dearne	1979	1932	1934	Newcastle United	Sunderland	93	4	0	0	19	2	0	0
WILKINSON W	William				1897		South Shore	Chatham	20	0	0	0	0	0	0	0
WILKINSON					1889				0	0	0	1	0	0	0	0
WILLIAMS D	Darren	15/12/68	Birmingham		1989		Leicester (L)		2	0+1	0	1	0	0	0	0
					1989		Leicester (L)		5+2	0	0	0	0	0	0	0
WILLIAMS I	Iorworth	c1914	Wales		1934		Merthyr Town	Crittalls Athletic	2	0	0	0	0	0	0	0
WILLIAMS P D	Paul	26/03/71	Burton on Trent		1989		Derby County (L)		3	2	0	1	0	0	0	0
WILLIAMS S R	Steve	03/11/75	Sheffield		1993	1995	YTS	Peterborough Utd	8+9	0+1	0+1	0+2	2	0	0	1
WILLIAMSON C H	Charlie	16/03/62	Sheffield		1983		Sheffield Wed. (L)		5	0	0	1	0	0	0	0
WILMOT J	James			1965	1910		Shildon Athletic		2	2	0	0	0	0	0	0
WILSON A	Archie	04/12/24	South Shields		1950	1951	South Shields	North Shields	4	0	0	0	0	0	0	0
WILSON D G	David	20/03/69	Todmorden		1990		Manchester Utd (L)		3	1	0	0	0	0	0	0
WILSON J	Jack	c1870	Ayrshire		1896	1897	New Brompton	Manchester City	35	4	0	0	0	0	0	0
WILSON J	Jimmy	c1916	Seaham Harbour		1937	1938	Seaham Colliery	Derby County	36	3	0	1	8	2	0	0
WILSON R	Richard	10/04/66	Grantham		1987		Grantham Town	Eastwood Town	0	0	0	13	0	0	0	0
WILSON T	Thomas	c1875			1895		Army Football	Oldham County	2	0	0	0	0	0	0	0
WILSON W	Walter	04/11/1879	Armadale	1926	1907	1914	Peebles Rovers	Fosdyke Watermen	171	14	0	81	6	0	0	2
WILTSHIRE H H	Herbert	1871	Worcester		1893				27	2	0	0	0	0	0	0
WINDLE W H	Willie	09/07/20	Maltby		1947	1951	Leeds United	Chester	91	2	0	0	22	1	0	0
WINDSOR R	Bobby	31/01/26	Stoke on Trent		1948	1949	Stoke City	Wellington Town	11	0	0	0	1	0	0	0
WINFIELD P	Phil	16/02/37	Denaby		1957		Denaby United	Ramsgate	1	0	0	0	0	0	0	0
WITHERS A	Alan	20/10/30	Bulwell		1954	1958	Blackpool	Notts County	97	1	0	0	18	0	0	0
WITHERS C C	Colin	21/03/40	Birmingham		1969		Aston Villa	Go Ahead (Holland)	1	1	1	0	0	0	0	0
WOLSTENHOLME A	Arthur	14/05/1889	Bolton		1914		Norwich City	Oldham Athletic	30	2	0	0	7	3	0	0
WOODCOCK A S	Tony	06/12/55	Eastwood, Notts		1975		Notts Forest (L)		2+2	0	0	0	1	0	0	0
WOODFIELD J	John				1897			Kettering Town	1	0	0	0	0	0	0	0
WOOLLEY					1888		Beeston St Johns		1	0	0	0	0	0	0	0
WORSDALE M J	John	29/10/48	Stoke on Trent		1971	1973	Stoke City	Worksop Town	55+12	0+1	2+1	1	9	0	0	0
WORTHY A	Albert	01/11/05	Pilsley, Derbys	1978	1927	1932	Chesterfield	Southend United	198	13	0	0	5	0	0	0
WRIGHT A	Albert				1946		Ollerton Colliery		1	0	0	0	0	0	0	0
WRIGHT B R	Brian	09/01/37	Leicester		1958	1960	Leicester City	Bedford Town	22	0	0	0	3	0	0	0
WRIGHT J D	Doug	29/04/17	Southend	1992	1948	1954	Newcastle United	Blyth Spartans	233	13	0	0	2	0	0	0
WRIGHT W S	Billy	26/04/59	Wordsley, Staffs		1978		Birmingham City	Runcorn	3	0	2	0	0	0	0	0
WRIGLEY B	Bernard	1894	Clitheroe	1965	1923	1924	Blackburn Rovers		9	0	0	0	0	0	0	0
WROE E	Edward	c1922			1945				0	4	0	0	0	1	0	0
YATES M J	Mark	24/01/70	Birmingham		1992		Burnley (L)		10+4	0	0	0	0	0	0	0
YORK A E	Andrew	14/06/1894	Blyth, Northumberland		1927	1929	Northampton Town	Newark Town	106	8	0	0	6	0	0	0
YOUNG A	Alf	27/11/1900	Wingate	1975	1929	1933	Workington Town	Retired	148	7	0	0	5	0	0	0
YOUNG E	Edward	c1915			1937		West Wylam Welfare		5	0	0	0	1	0	0	0
YOUNG J					1919				1	0	0	0	0	0	0	0
YOUNG R H	Dick	17/04/18	Gateshead	1989	1948	1953	Sheffield United	Retired	100	6	0	0	2	1	0	0
YOUNG					1890				0	0	0	4	0	0	0	0
YOUNGER W	William	22/03/40	Whitley Bay		1960		Notts Forest (L)		4	0	0	0	0	0	0	0
YULE T	Tommy	04/02/1888	Douglas Water		1909	1910	Portobello FC	Wolves	63	4	0	0	8	0	0	0

Players who only played in 1939/40 season

Player		Date of Birth	Place of Birth	Died	First	Last	Previous Club	Next Club
ASKEW W	William	1914	Coundon, Co Durham	1982			Walsall	Retired
CLAYTON R	Rex	1916	East Retford				Bristol City	
GORMLIE W J	Bill	1911	Blackpool	1976			Northampton Town	Retired
HOYLAND E	Ernest	17/01/14	Thurnscoe				W B A	Grantham Town
RIX J	Jack	12/07/08	Lintz, Co Durham	1979			W B A	Retired

Players who only played in abandoned matches

HAYDEN P	Percy				1907			
LINIGHAN B	Brian	17/03/36	West Hartlepool		1957			Ashington
ROTHWELL H	Herbert				1907			Chorlton

Players who were unused substitutes only

AUBREY A W	Alan	18/04/48	Leeds		1972		Gainsborough Trin.	Gainsborough Trin.
BLOOMER B M	Brian	03/05/52	Cleethorpes		1973		Lincoln United	Lincoln United
BOOK S	Steve	07/07/69			1994		Frome Town	Forest Green Rovers
DE GARIS P M	Paul	24/07/74	Guernsey		1994		Sheffield Wed.	Woking
DIXON A S	Andrew				1994	1995	YTS	
FRASER S M	Steve	21/02/78	Nottingham		1996		Grimsby Town	Grantham Town
GIBSON L P	Lee	03/01/78	Kettering		1995	1996	YTS	Barnet
LAWRENCE C M M	Carl	14/11/78	Leicester		1996		YTS	
MORGAN J	Jamie	11/09/75	Lincoln		1993		YTS	Boston Town
SIDDALL B	Barry	12/09/54	Ellesmere Port		1994		Burnley	Birmingham City
WHITTLE K	Ken	25/09/48	Sedgefield		1966		Apprentice	Rugby Town

WORLD WAR ONE PLAYERS

The following made appearances during World War One. The clubs of guest players are given where known.
Guest players are indicated by *

Player	Apps	Goals	Guest from
Adamson, A	1	0	
Addinall, P	105	5	
Anstey, B	1	0	
Armitage, L	3	0	
Ball, A	106	10	
Banton, J	2	1	
Barber, W	1	0	
Barrell, G	64	16	
Batefield, T	1	0	
Bavin, A	3	0	
Bell, W	1	0	
Bibby, RW	1	0	
Bird, W	1	0	
Blakey, CHS	15	0	
Blunt, W	5	0	
Borrill, W	1	0	
Bratley, PW	1	0	
Brooks, SE *	1	0	Wolverhampton W.
Brown	3	0	
Brown, W	3	0	
Bryan, JJ *	24	2	Mansfield Town
Cavanagh, JA	69	16	
Cheetham *	1	0	Stockport County
Chesser, WE	44	17	
Clements	1	0	
Colebrook, C *	1	0	Grimsby Town
Connor, W	3	0	
Cookson, W	1	0	
Cooper, A	1	0	
Crooks	1	0	
Crosan, F	1	0	
Deacon, J	1	0	
Dobson, J	1	0	
Doughty, H	4	1	
Dowling, M	3	0	
Dunne, J	38	0	
Eastmead, J	4	0	
Edgley, HH *	1	0	Aston Villa
Edwards EA	1	0	
Edwards, J	1	1	
Egerton, W	100	52	

Player	Apps	Goals	Guest from
Evans, V	10	0	
Ford, S *	1	0	Sheffield Wed.
Gardner, A	98	2	
Gibbons, A	3	0	
Gillitt, I	1	0	
Goldsborough, J	75	0	
Graham, E	2	0	
Groves, F	9	3	
Hall, B	1	0	
Harrison	2	1	
Hatton, C	1	0	
Hawley, G	1	0	
Hibbert, HC *	1	0	Chesterfield Town
Hill, J	1	0	
Hoult, W	1	0	
Humphries, H	1	0	
Jackson, AC	109	1	
Jephcott, AC *	1	0	West Bromwich A.
Jones, R	2	1	
Kenworthy, I	1	0	
Lamming, WG	21	2	
Lawrence, GH *	1	0	Derby County
Leach, JM *	1	0	Aston Villa
Lee, O	1	0	
Leyland, J	1	0	
Lindon, AE *	1	0	Barnsley
Little, I	3	1	
Lockwood, G	1	0	
Manning, JT	106	12	
Martin, J	4	0	
Millington, B	2	0	
Monks, H	1	1	
Moseley, W	3	1	
Musgrave, W	1	0	
Nash, HE *	1	0	Aston Villa
Newman	1	0	
Newton, A	1	0	
Ormiston, AP *	56	6	Chelsea
Osborne, F	9	2	
Osbourne	1	0	
Pace, A	1	0	
Parrish, J	77	30	

Player	Apps	Goals	Guest from
Pass, G	3	0	
Pattison, F	37	4	
Pennington, J *	1	0	West Bromwich A.
Phipps, C	2	0	
Phipps, L	5	0	
Price, F	1	0	
Pryce	1	0	
Reid, JG *	2	0	Airdrieonians
Reid, W	1	0	
Richardson	1	0	
Richardson, G	1	0	
Robson, MH	7	0	
Salkeld, D	9	0	
Saunders, JE	1	0	
Sewell, R	3	0	
Shaw, W	1	0	
Shorton, W	1	0	
Smelt, J	3	0	
Smith	1	0	
Smith, W	1	0	
Straughton, J	1	0	
Thompson, J	1	0	
Thorpe, E	11	1	
Thurston	1	0	
Tickle	1	0	
Timmins, W	10	0	
Tiplady, J	1	0	
Treasure, E	1	0	
Tremelling, J	4	2	
Tremelling, RD	31	0	
Tremelling, S	4	0	
Walsh, J	1	0	
Walsh, P	1	0	
Ward, F	82	1	
Ward, R	4	1	
Whipsall, J	1	0	
Wield, TW	86	1	
Wild	1	0	
Wilson, W	1	0	
Witham, V	1	0	
York, RE	1	1	

WORLD WAR TWO PLAYERS

(General notes as World One players)

Appearances do **not** include 1939/40 expunged matches, 1945/46 F.A.Cup or Lincs. Senior Cup games.

Player	Apps	Goals	Guest from	Player	Apps	Goals	Guest from:	Player	Apps	Goals	Guest from
Acton, H *	1	1		Gillan, K *	1	0	Kilmarnock	Osborne, Charles *	1	0	Millwall
Adkins, Eric	3	0		Gordon, Dennis *	5	2		Page, Albert*	1	0	Tottenham H.
Anderson, Reginald*1		0		Grainger, Dennis *	3	1	Southport	Parker, H	1	1	
Archer, Bill	6	0		Grant, Cyril	10	5		Parker, L *	1	0	Cardiff City
Bailey, Leslie *	2	0		Green, Horace *	1	0	Halifax Town	Parkin, Fred	16	0	
Barber, Arthur *	1	0		Green, S *	1	0	Newcastle	Parkinson, Kenneth	1	0	
Barton R	1	0		Groves, Ken *	14	0	Preston	Parr, Joe	6	0	
Barton, Harold *	3	1		Grummett, Jim	49	12		Pawlaw, Mieczyslaw*8		2	Notts County
Bean, Billy	204	1		Haines, John *	43	24	Swansea	Platts, Lawrie *	9	0	Nottm. Forest
Beaumont, Leonard*	5	1		Hall, Alec *	1	0	Grimsby Town	Ponting, Walter	2	0	
Bell, Tom	3	1		Hall, Allan	27	9		Powell, Tommy *	1	0	Derby County
Bellis, Alfred *	4	1	Port Vale	Hall, George *	49	1	Accrington Stan.	Ranshaw, Jack *	8	3	Grimsby Town.'
Bett, Fred *	91	36	Sunderland	Hann, Ralph *	2	0	Derby County	Ravenscroft, Alan	22	0	
Binns, Clifford *	1	0		Hardy, Jack	199	3		Rayner, Edward *	1	0	Halifax Town
Bly, Billy *	1	0	Hull City	Harper, Donald *	1	0	Chesterfield	Readett, H *	1	0	
Boyes, Lawrence	4	2		Hartshorne, Jack	2	0		Riley, Harold *	1	0	Exeter City
Bradley, Gordon *	5	0	Leicester City	Hatfield, B *	3	1	Bradford P.A.	Rix, Jack	1	0	
Bray, Norman	11	4		Hellings, Dennis	4	1		Robledo, George *	1	0	Barnsley
Brelsford, John	3	0		Hepple, Albert *	2	0	Consett	Rogers, Percy	1	0	
Broadhurst, John *	1	0		Hepworth, Ron *	1	0	Bradford P.A.	Ross, Lew *	13	0	Hibernian
Brown, Wilfred	2	1		Hetherington, G *	1	0		Rossington, K *	16	2	Sheffield United
Burton, J *	1	0		Hodgson, Jack *	1	0	Grimsby Town	Rowley, Arthur *	1	0	West Bromwich A.
Buttery, E *	1	0		Hollis, K *	4	0	Notts Forest	Rudkin, Tommy *	1	0	Peterborough Utd.
Callender, John	3	0		Howarth, Sidney	2	1		Ruecroft, Jacob *	1	0	Halifax Town
Callender, Tom	2	0		Hoyland, Ernest	15	1		Russell, George *	2	0	Notts County
Campbell, Johnny	13	4		Hullett, William *	6	11	Manchester Utd.	Rutherford, E *	16	4	Glasgow Rangers
Cartwright, Bernard	12	0		Hutchinson, Jimmy*27		15	Sheffield United	Rutherford, Joseph *1		0	Aston Villa
Cartwright, George	16	0		Jessop, Fred *	30	0	Sheffield United	Seagrave, John *	3	0	
Cheetham, Tommy*	52	47	Brentford	Johnson, George *	1	0	Watford	Settle, Alf	12	0	
Clare, Joe	147	42		Johnson, Tom	12	0		Shimwell, Eddie *	1	0	Sheffield United
Clawson H	1	0		Johnston, Bert*	104	1	Sunderland	Skelton, George	2	0	
Collindridge, Colin *	1	2	Sheffield United	Jones, Les *	4	2	Arsenal	Sleight, F *	1	0	Queens Park
Collins, Albert *	3	0	Chesterfield	Jones N *	1	0	Nottm. Forest	Smedley, Lawrie	9	3	
Connor, James	1	0		Keen, Ike *	5	0		Smith	1	0	
Cooper, Frederick*	2	0		Keggan, H *	2	0	Bury	Smith, Clem	4	1	
Cooper, Sedley *	17	3	Notts County	Knott, Bert*	31	28	Hull City	Smith, Edward *	4	0	Arsenal
Cooper, William	1	0		Laing, Fred	1	0	Airdrie	Smith, John *	12	0	Sheffield United
Corkhill, Billy *	3	0	Cardiff City	Lascelles, Reginald	2	0		Stillyards, George	24	5	
Curry, Robert *	1	0	Sheffield United	Lee, George *	2	1	York City	Taylor, Leslie	2	0	
Daniels, John	1	0		Lello, Cyril*	17	21	Derry City	Tench, Jack	2	0	
Darley, J *	1	0	Preston North End	Lewis, Glyn *	18	9	Crystal Palace	Theaker, Clarence *	1	0	Newcastle United
Davidson, Alexander*5		0	Hibernian	Liddell, J *	1	0	Queens Park	Thomas, Geoffrey *	1	0	Notts Forest
Davies, Alex	25	5		Lowrey, James *	5	1	Grimsby Town	Thompson, Alex	26	1	
Dawson, Edward *	1	0	Bristol City	Lowrie, George *	2	1	Coventry City	Thompson, Dennis *	8	3	
Day, Albert *	1	0	Brighton	Lumsden, John	4	0		Topping, Henry	7	0	
Deacon, Dickie	1	0		Lyon, J *	1	0	Everton	Towler, Bernard *	89	73	Notts County
Dean, Cyril *	3	0	Southampton	McCall, Robert *	1	1	Notts Forest	Turner, A	1	0	
Dickie, Percy *	24	2	Blackburn Rovers	McCormick, Jimmy*1		1	Tottenham H.	Turner, Hugh *	1	0	Darlington
Doherty, Peter *	3	7	Manchester City	McDermott, Joseph*	2	0	Gateshead	Tyson, W *	2	0	Southport
Dorsett, Richard *	1	0	Wolverhampton W.	McGinn, A *	1	0'	Bradford City	Walker, Harry	12	0	
Douglas, John *	20	1	Hartlepool	Makinson, James *	2	0	Leeds United	Warburton, Arthur *	1	1	Q.P.R.
Dryden, Jackie *	2	1	Charlton	Manning, Douglas	1	0		Wardle, George *	18	11	Exeter City
Drysdale, J *	1	0	Kilmarnock	Marlow, Geoff	69	26		Watford, Albert *	11	0	Chesterfield
Dulson, R *	1	0	Notts Forest	Marsh, Frank *	80	5	Chester	Watson, Frederick *	1	0	Stockport C.
Dunderdale, William*	40	29	Leeds United	Mason, Sidney	1	0		Wheat, John	1	0	
Edrich, Bill *	1	0	Chelmsford City	Meek, Joe *	20	10	Swansea	Wightman, John *	15	2	Blackburn R.
Eggleston, Tommy *1		0	Derby County	Mellors, Dick	2	0		Wilkinson, Bert	8	1	
Emery, Tony	8	0		Metcalfe, L *	1	0	Yorkshire Amat.	Williams, G *	1	0	Wrexham
Farrell, D *	2	0	Alloa	Millington, Mal *	2	0	Scunthorpe United	Williams, W *	1	0	Chester
Finan, Robert*	1	0	Blackpool	Mills, E	1	0		Wilson, Joseph *	1	0	Reading
Flack, William *	2	0	Norwich City	Moulson, Con *	97	1	Notts County	Winslow, George	1	0	
Forman, Reg	3	0		Moulson, George *103		0	Grimsby Town	Woodbridge, Gordon	3	0	
Fox, Frederick	1	0		Musson, Walter *	1	0	Derby County	Worthington, E *	4	0	Halifax Town
Franklin, Neil *	3	0	Stoke City	Nicholson, Sidney *19		0	Aberdeen	Wroe, Edward	14	0	
Gadsby, Stanley	7	0		Oakley, J *	2	0	Chesterfield	Yorston, Benny *	3	2	Middlesbrough
				O'Donnell, Hugh *	4	3	Blackpool				

SEASON 1884-85

F.A. CUP

No.	Date	Opposition	Res.	Att.	Goalscorers
1R	1 Nov	Hull Town	5-1		Scrimmage, C.Newsum, Fox(2), *
3R	3 Jan	Grimsby Town	0-1		

E.Cousans	T.White	S.Oglesby	K.Bayne	W.Fox	H.Simpson	C.Newsum	H.Newsum	J.Strawson	G.Hallam	W.Heywood
"	"	H.Curtis	H.Simpson	E.Blyton	F.Chapman	"	T.Sturges-Jones	C.Chapman	"	D.Clarke

Bye in 2R
* Additional scorer: H.Newsum

LINCOLNSHIRE CUP

1R	25 Oct	BOSTON EXCELSIOR	11-0		Kirkham, C.Newsum(2), E.Teesdale(4)*
2R	21 Nov	LINCOLN ALBION	4-0		C.Newsum,(2) E.Teesdale, Hallam
3R	26 Dec	Horncastle Town	0-3		

H.Mantle	T.White	S.Oglesby	R.Mason	H.Simpson	F.Teesdale	C.Newsum	H.Newsum	E.Teesdale	G.Hallam	W.Fox
E.Blyton	R.Mason	T.White	F.Teesdale	W.Fox	H.Simpson	"	"	"	" #	W.Kirkham
E.Cousans	S.Oglesby	"	H.Simpson	F.Teesdale	W.Fox	"	"	"	R.Mason	G.Hallam

* Additional scorers: Hallam, Simpson, Fox, White.
# G.Hallam played under the pseudonym 'Brown'.

SEASON 1885-86

F.A. CUP

No.	Date	Opposition	Res.	Att.	Goalscorers
1R	31 Oct	GRIMSBY TOWN	0-2		

| K.Bayne | R.Mason | H.Simpson | J.Duckworth | A.Mettam | W.Fox | T.Silvester | W.Gregson | E.Teesdale | T.Baggaley | G.Hallam |

LINCOLNSHIRE CUP

1R	14 Nov	LINCOLN ALBION	4-0		4 - untraced
2R	19 Dec	SPILSBY	4-0		Teesdale, Hallam, Silvester(2)
3R	30 Jan	BRIGG ANCHOLME	7-0		7 - untraced
SF	13 Mar	Grimsby Town *	1-1		untraced

S.Bainbridge	T.White	K.Bayne	W.Fox	F.Teesdale	A.Mettam	T.Silvester	Smith	T.Baggaley	G.Hallam	E.Teesdale
K.Bayne	"	H.Simpson	J.Duckworth	A.Mettam	W.Fox	"	W.Gregson	E.Teesdale	"	T.Baggaley
"	R.Aspden	"	"	"	"	"	"	"	T.Silvester	G.Hallam
"	H.Simpson	R.Aspden	"	"	"	J.Slater	"	"	"	"

* Eliminated after refusing to play extra time.

1885-86 Season
Back : Simpson, Alf Mettam, Bayne, Aspden, Fox.
Centre : Duckworth, West (umpire), Hallam.
Front : Slater, Gregson, Edwin Teesdale, Baggaley, Sylvester.

SEASON 1886-87

F.A. CUP

No.	Date	Opposition	Res.	Att.	Goalscorers										
2R	20 Nov	Middlesbrough	1-1		Slater	K.Bayne	H.Simpson	R.Aspden	J.Duckworth	A.Mettam	W.Rawlinson	J.Slater	E.Teesdale	W.Fox	W.Gregson	G.Hallam
2Rr	27	MIDDLESBROUGH	2-0		Scrimmage, Gregson	"	"	"	"	"	"	"	"	"	"	"
3R	11 Dec	Gainsborough Trinity	2-2		Gregson, Scrimmage	"	R.Aspden	H.Simpson	"	"	"	E.Teesdale	J.Slater	T.Baggaley	"	"
3Rr	24 Jan	Gainsborough Trinity	1-0		Hallam	"	G.Wells-Cole	"	"	"	"	R.Aspden	"	W.Fox	G.Hallam	W.Gregson
5R	29	Glasgow Rangers	0-3			"	R.Aspden	"	"	"	"	J.Slater	H.Hylton	"	"	"

Bye in Round 1 and 4
3R after extra time
3Rr played at Bramall Lane, Sheffield

LINCOLNSHIRE CUP

No.	Date	Opposition	Res.	Goalscorers										
1R	4 Dec	LINDUM	5-0	Hallam, Duckworth, 3 untraced	K.Bayne	R.Aspden	H.Simpson	W.Rawlinson	A.Mettam	J.Duckworth	E.Teesdale	J.Slater	T.White	G.Hallam	W.Gregson
2R	15 Jan	GRIMSBY HUMBER ROVERS	5-0	Fox(2),Hallam,Gregson,Duckworth	C.Chappell	"	"	J.Duckworth	"	W.Rawlinson	"	"	W.Fox	"	"
3R	19 Feb	GAINSBOROUGH TRINITY	5-2	Slater, Teesdale(2), Fox(2)	K.Bayne	"	"	"	"	"	"	"	"	W.Gregson	G.Hallam
SF	12 Mar	GRANTHAM VICTORIA	5-0	Duckworth,Teesdale,Gregson,2	"	"	A.Mettam	"	J.Slater	"	"	T.Baggaley	"	G.Hallam	W.Gregson
F	2 Apr	Grimsby Town	2-2	Teesdale, Slater	"	"	H.Simpson	"	A.Mettam	"	"	J.Slater	"	W.Gregson	G.Hallam
Fr	23	Grimsby Town	2-0	Gregson, Slater	"	"	"	"	"	"	"	"	"	G.Hallam	W.Gregson

2R played at Lindum ground.
F and Fr played at the Northolme, Gainsborough

SEASON 1887-88

F.A. CUP

No.	Date	Opposition	Res.	Att.	Goalscorers										
1QF	15 Oct	HORNCASTLE	4-1		Scrimmage,Slater,Teesdale,1 untraced	W.Jeffrey	R.Aspden	H.Simpson	W.Rawlinson	W.Fox	J.Duckworth	J.Slater	J.Turner	E.Teesdale	G.Shaw	G.Hallam
2QF	5 Nov	GAINSBOROUGH TRINITY	2-1		Shaw, Fox	"	"	"	"	A.Mettam	"	"	"	W.Fox	G.Hallam	G.Shaw
3QF	26	Grimsby Town	0-2			"	"	"	"	"	"	"	"	"	"	"

LINCOLNSHIRE CUP

No.	Date	Opposition	Res.	Goalscorers										
1R	22 Oct	Brigg Town	6-0	Slater,Shaw(2),Hallam(2),Turner	W.Jeffrey	R.Aspden	H.Simpson	W.Rawlinson	J.Parker	J.Duckworth	J.Slater	J.Turner	W.Fox	G.Shaw	G.Hallam
2R	3 Dec	LOUTH TOWN	9-1	Shaw(3),Teesdale,Slater,4 untraced	"	"	"	"	A.Mettam	"	E.Teesdale	J.Slater	"	G.Hallam	G.Shaw
3R	21 Jan	GAINSBOROUGH TRINITY	0-1		K.Bayne	"	"	J.Duckworth	"	W.Rawlinson	J.Slater	W.Gregson	"	G.Shaw	G.Hallam

1R played at John O'Gaunts by agreement.

SEASON 1888-89
THE COMBINATION

No.	Date	Opposition	Res.	Att.	Goalscorers
1	8 Sep	Notts Rangers	1-0		Hopewell
2	15	DERBY MIDLAND	1-4		untraced
3	20 Oct	Gainsborough Trinity	1-4		untraced
4	1 Dec	Burslem Port Vale	1-2		Hallam
5	22	BURSLEM PORT VALE	1-0		Millar
6	25	NORTHWICH VICTORIA	1-2		Millar
7	26 Jan	Derby Midland	1-0		Hallam
8	23 Feb	NOTTS RANGERS	1-1		G.Shaw
9	2 Mar	Derby Junction	2-1		Barbour(2)
10	9	Long Eaton Rangers	0-4		
11	23	GAINSBOROUGH TRINITY	0-0		
12	6 Apr	DERBY JUNCTION	2-0		G.Shaw, Fry
13	19	CREWE ALEXANDRA	0-1		
14	27	LONG EATON RANGERS	5-0		McKay,Hallam,Elliott(2),1 untraced

Full line-up has not been traced for match 6.

F.A. CUP

1QF	6 Oct	Grimsby Town	1-1		W.Shaw
1QFr	13	GRIMSBY TOWN *	1-1		OG
1QF2r	24	Grimsby Town #	1-3		Scrimmage

* after extra time   # at Bramall Lane, Sheffield

LINCOLNSHIRE CUP - No Entry.

SEASON 1889-90
MIDLAND LEAGUE

No.	Date	Opposition	Res.	Att.	Goalscorers
1	7 Sep	STAVELEY	1-2		Smallman
2	14	Gainsborough Trinity	2-1		Hunt, 1 untraced
3	28	DERBY MIDLAND	3-0		McKay(2), Mettam
4	19 Oct	SHEFFIELD	7-1		Neill(2), Burton(3), Graham, OG
5	5 Nov	Rotherham Town	1-0		Irving
6	9	Leek	5-0		Shaw(2),Irving,McPhee,1 untraced
7	30	WARWICK COUNTY	2-0		Graham, McKay
8	28 Dec	Notts Rangers	3-0		Smallman, Shaw, Irving
9	4 Jan	Burton Wanderers	3-1		Shaw, Irving, OG
10	25	DERBY JUNCTION	5-1		Smallman, McKay, Burns(2), Irving
11	22 Feb	Staveley	1-1		Scrimmage
12	1 Mar	ROTHERHAM TOWN	5-1		Irving, Shaw, 3 untraced
13	8	NOTTS RANGERS	5-0		McKay, Smallman(2), Shaw(2)
14	22	Sheffield	4-0		Irving, OG, McKay, McPhee
15	29	BURTON WANDERERS	4-0		Shaw(2), McKay, Scrimmage
16	5 Apr	Warwick County	2-5		McKay, Scrimmage
17	7	LEEK	10-2		Smallman(5),Shaw(3),Glendinning,McKay
18	8	Derby Midland	2-2		Glendinning, McKay
19	19	Derby Junction	6-0		Irving(2), Smallman(3), McPhee
20	26	GAINSBOROUGH TRINITY	3-2		Glendinning, Smallman, McPhee

3 own goals; 3 scrimmaged; 5 untraced.

F.A. CUP

2QF	26 Oct	NOTTS OLYMPIC	2-1		Neill, Smallman
3QF	16 Nov	Notts Rangers	7-2		Smallman(2),Shaw,Burton(2),McKay(2)
4QF	7 Dec	GAINSBOROUGH TRINITY	5-3		Burton(2),Shaw,Scrimmage,Graham
1R	18	CHESTER	2-0		McKay, Duckworth
2R	1 Feb	Preston North End	0-4		

1QF - bye

LINCOLNSHIRE CUP

1R		Grimsby Humber Rovers	scr		

withdrew from competition

1888/89: The Football Combination
(Latest known published table -
Athletic News 23 October 1888)
Note: Clubs listed alphabetically
rather than on a performance basis.

		P	W	D	L	F	A
1	Bootle	6	4	1	1	13	8
2	Burslem Port Vale	7	3	0	4	14	11
3	Blackpool South Shore	6	1	0	5	9	26
4	Birmingham St.George's	5	1	3	1	7	9
5	Blackburn Olympic	1	0	1	0	1	1
6	Crewe Alexandra	7	3	1	3	22	12
7	Darwen	5	2	1	2	14	12
8	Derby Junction	5	1	3	1	9	10
9	Derby Midland	5	2	1	2	9	10
10	Grimsby Town	1	0	0	1	1	3
11	Gainsborough Trinity	4	1	0	3	3	15
12	Halliwell	6	3	0	3	20	17
13	Leek	5	0	0	5	4	16
14	**Lincoln City**	**3**	**1**	**0**	**2**	**3**	**8**
15	Long Eaton Rangers	6	2	1	3	14	18
16	Newton Heath	5	4	1	0	17	6
17	Notts Rangers	5	4	0	1	15	7
18	Northwich Victoria	5	2	3	0	6	3
19	Small Heath	4	3	0	1	12	6
20	Walsall Town Swifts	6	3	2	1	11	9

Midland League: 1889/90 - Final Table

	P	W	D	L	F	A	Pts
Lincoln City	**20**	**16**	**2**	**2**	**74**	**19**	**34**
Derby Midland	19	11	3	5	41	30	25
Rotherham Town	20	11	3	6	44	27	25
Burton Wanderers	20	11	3	6	42	40	25
Staveley	20	9	4	7	46	28	22
Warwick County	20	9	4	7	36	28	22
Gainsborough Trinity	19	8	5	6	47	32	21
Derby Junction	15	7	2	9	32	49	16
Leek	20	3	2	15	26	64	8
Notts Rangers	15	1	4	10	11	36	6
Sheffield	19	2	2	15	19	66	6

SEASON 1890-91
MIDLAND LEAGUE

No.	Date	Opposition	Res.	Att.	Goalscorers
1	20 Sep	BURTON WANDERERS	4-0		Duckworth, Moore, Smallman, Glendinning
2	27	STAVELEY	8-1		Moore(3), Shaw, Irving, Smallman, *
3	18 Oct	SHEFFIELD UNITED	2-1		Shaw, Moore
4	1 Nov	Staveley	2-2		Irving, OG
5	22	Sheffield United	1-2		Irving
6	29	ROTHERHAM TOWN	0-0		
7	13 Dec	GAINSBOROUGH TRINITY	1-1		Moore
8	25	BURSLEM PORT VALE	5-0		Shaw(3), Irving, Glendinning
9	24 Jan	Gainsborough Trinity	0-3		
10	14 Feb	Derby Junction	4-0		Troop, 3 untraced
11	21	Burton Wanderers	1-2		untraced
12	28	LONG EATON RANGERS	2-1		Moore, Dickson
13	7 Mar	DERBY JUNCTION	0-0		
14	14	Long Eaton Rangers	0-5		
15	28	Derby Midland	0-1		
16	11 Apr	Rotherham Town	0-0		
17	20	Burslem Port Vale	1-1		untraced
18	25	DERBY MIDLAND	3-1		Dickson, Dawson, Moore

* Additional scorers - Glendinning, 1 untraced.

1 own goal; 6 untraced

F.A. CUP

1QF	4 Oct	Gainsborough Trinity	3-1		Moore(2), Scrimmage
2QF	25	BOSTON TOWN	9-0		Moore(2), Smallman(2), Irving(3) *
3QF	15 Nov	ECCLESFIELD	3-0		Glendinning, Moore(2)
4QF	6 Dec	STAVELEY	4-1		Moore(2), Irving, Burton
1R	17 Jan	Chester	0-1		

* Additional scorers - Shaw, Mullineux

LINCOLNSHIRE CUP

| SF | 7 Feb | Grantham Rovers | 1-0 | | Taylor |
| F | 21 Mar | Gainsborough Trinity | 1-0 | | Dickson |

F played at Harlaxton Road, Grantham

Final League Table

	P	W	D	L	F	A	Pts
1 Gainsborough Trin.	18	10	4	4	58	21	24
2 Long Eaton Rang.	18	10	2	6	50	33	22
3 *Lincoln City*	**18**	**7**	**6**	**5**	**34**	**21**	**20**
4 Derby Midland	18	8	4	6	28	28	20
5 Sheffield United	18	8	3	7	32	25	19
6 Burton Wanderers	18	7	4	7	25	33	15
7 Rotherham Town	18	7	4	7	20	28	15
8 Burslem Port Vale	18	7	2	9	35	43	16
9 Derby Junction	18	5	5	8	15	30	15
10 Staveley	18	2	4	12	19	57	8

Back: Smeaton (trainer), Simpson, Robinson, Mullineaux.
Centre: Duckworth, McKay, McPhee, Neill, Graham.
Front: Burton, Irving, Shaw.

Team group of 1889/90 season:

SEASON 1891-92
FOOTBALL ALLIANCE

No.	Date	Opposition	Res.	Att.	Goalscorers	Parsons W.E.	Neill Q.D.	Simpson H.	Bates L.	Mullineux J.E.B.	Marriott A.	Smallman F.J.B.	Walker J.	Irving J.	Moore I.	Hodder W.	Shaw G.	Codling J.	Henderson A.	Gresham J.	Buxton G.	Mettam E.	Troop F.J.	Bennett J.C.	Taylor	Bradbury	Raby W.	Sharpe	Gunson F.	Pegg G.	Fullalove	Brammer G.W.	Nuttall J.W.	Ward	Plowright
1	19 Sep	ARDWICK	3-0		Moore(2), Smallman	1	2	3	4	5	6		7	8	9	10	11																		
2	26	Small Heath	0-4			1	2	3		4	6		7	5	9	10	11	8																	
3	10 Oct	Birmingham St. George	4-2		Irving(2), Moore, Mullineux	1	3		4	5	6		7	9	8	10	11		2																
4	7 Nov	BOOTLE	1-3		Scrimmage	1	2			10	5	6	7	8	9		11		3	4															
5	21	Newton Heath	1-10		Irving	1	2		4	5	6		7	8	9	10	11		3																
6	28	Ardwick	3-2		Walker, Irving, Moore	1	2	3	5	6			7	8	9	10	11	4																	
7	12 Dec	GRIMSBY TOWN	3-2		J.Gresham, Walker(2)	1	2	3	5	6			7	8	9	10		4			11														
8	19	Walsall Town Swifts	0-2			1	2	3	5	6			7	8	9	10		4			11														
9	25	CREWE ALEXANDRA	1-1		Scrimmage	1	2	3	5	6			7	8	9	10		4			11														
10	28	Sheffield Wednesday	2-7		Irving(2)	1	2	3	5	6			7	8	9	10		4			11														
11	30 Jan	Bootle	2-3		Irving, Moore	1	2	3	5	6			7	8	9	10		4			11														
12	6 Feb	Nottingham Forest	0-0			1	2		5	6			7	8	9	10		4			11	3													
13	13	SMALL HEATH	1-1		Moore	1	2		5	6			7	8	9	10		4	3		11														
14	20	NOTTINGHAM FOREST	1-4		Smallman	1	2		5	6			7	8	9	10		4			11	3													
15	5 Mar	Grimsby Town	1-6		Troop	1	2	3		5	6		7	8	9	10					4	11													
16	12	SHEFFIELD WEDNESDAY	2-2		Irving, Marriott	1	2			5	6		7	8	9	10		4			3		11												
17	26	Burton Swifts	1-6		untraced		2		5	6			7	8	9	10	11	4						1	3										
18	2 Apr	NEWTON HEATH	1-6		Walker		2			6				8	9	10		4			3	5		1		7	11								
19	9	BURTON SWIFTS	4-0		Scrimmage, Walker, Smallman(2)		2						7	8	9	10		4			3	5		1			11	6							
20	13	Crewe Alexandra	0-3																															
21	15	WALSALL TOWN SWIFTS	1-1		Smallman		2						7	8	9	10		4			3	6		1			11		5						
22	16	BIRMINGHAM ST. GEORGE	5-0		Smallman(2),Moore,Irving,Shaw								7	8	9	10		6			2	5		1			11			3	4				

Line up has not been traced for match 20

F.A. CUP

1QF	3 Oct	DONCASTER ROVERS	3-1	Irving(3)	1	2	3		5	6	7	4	9	10	11	8			
2QF	24	Sheffield United	1-4	Walker	1	2		4	5	6	7	8	9	10	11		3		

LINCOLNSHIRE CUP

SF	30 Jan	MARKET RASEN	5-1	Hodder,Troop(2),Plowright,Mettam	... 10 ... 3 ... 5 11 1 2 7 ... 4 6 8 9
F	27 Apr	GAINSBOROUGH TRINITY	3-2	Moore, Smallman, Walker	2 ... 6 ... 7 8 9 10 ... 4 ... 3 5 ... 1 ... 11

Final League Table

		P	W	D	L	F	A	Pts
1	Nottingham Forest	22	14	5	3	59	22	33
2	Newton Heath	22	12	7	3	69	33	31
3	Small Heath	22	12	5	5	53	36	29
4	Sheffield Wednesday	22	12	4	6	65	35	28
5	Burton Swifts	22	12	2	8	54	53	26
6	Crewe Alexandra	22	7	4	11	44	49	18
7	Ardwick	22	6	6	10	39	51	18
8	Bootle	22	8	2	12	42	64	18
9	*Lincoln City*	22	6	5	11	37	65	17
10	Grimsby Town	22	6	6	10	40	39	16 *
11	Walsall Town Swifts	22	6	3	13	34	59	15
12	Birmingham St.George's	22	5	3	14	34	64	11 *

* Two points deducted

SEASON 1892-93
DIVISION TWO

No.	Date	Opposition	Res.	Att.	Goalscorers	Gresham W.	Neill Q.D.	Coulton C.	Shaw G.	Mettam E.	Moore I.	Smallman F.J.B.	Irving J.	Cameron R.	Kelly J.	Gresham J.	Richardson J.M.	Roberts R.	Fleming J.	Jackson A.	Raby W.	Brammer G.W.	McDermid R.	Graham W.	Buxton G.
1	3 Sep	Sheffield United	2-4		Cameron, Irving	1	2	3	4	5	6	7	8	9	10	11									
2	24	Small Heath	1-4		Kelly	1	2	3	4	5	6	7	8	9	10	11									
3	1 Oct	SHEFFIELD UNITED	1-0		Cameron	1	2	3	4		6	7	8	9	10	11	5								
4	8	Walsall Town Swifts	1-2		untraced	1	2	3	4		6	7	8	9	10	11	5								
5	22	BURSLEM PORT VALE	3-4		Smallman(2), J.Gresham	1	2	3		4	9	7	8	6	10	11	5								
6	12 Nov	DARWEN	1-1		Smallman	1	2	3		4	6	7	9	8	10	11		5							
7	3 Dec	Burslem Port Vale	2-1		J.Gresham, Cameron	1	2	3		4	6	7	8	9	10	11		5							
8	17	Burton Swifts	2-4		Fleming(2)	1	2	3		4	6	7		8	10	11		5	9						
9	24	ARDWICK	2-1		Smallman, Richardson	1	2	3		4	10	7	8			11	6	5	9						
10	26	CREWE ALEXANDRA	1-1		Fleming	1	2	3		4	10	7	8			11	6	5	9						
11	31	Northwich Victoria	1-2		Moore	1	2	3		4	10	7		8		11	6	5	9						
12	7 Jan	SMALL HEATH	3-4		J.Gresham, Smallman, Fleming	1	2	3		6	10	7	4	8		11	5		9						
13	14	Darwen	1-3		Roberts	1	2				10	7	8	4		11	6	5	9	3					
14	28	Crewe Alexandra	1-4		J.Gresham	1	2				10	7	8	4		11	6	5	9	3					
15	11 Feb	BURTON SWIFTS	5-1		Smallman(4), Irving	1	2			4	6	7	8			11	5	3	9		10				
16	18	Grimsby Town	2-2		Smallman(2)	1	2				6	7	8	4		11	5	3	9		10				
17	25	NORTHWICH VICTORIA	5-1		Smallman, Richardson, Raby, *	1	2				6	7	8	4		11	5	3	9		10				
18	4 Mar	GRIMSBY TOWN	1-3		J.Gresham	1	2				6	7	8	4		11	5	3	9		10				
19	31	WALSALL TOWN SWIFTS	3-1		Smallman(3)	1	2			4	10	7	9			11	6	5			8	3			
20	1 Apr	BOOTLE	5-1		Raby(2), Smallman(2), Roberts	1	2			4	10	7	9			11	6	5			8	3			
21	15	Bootle	1-4		Moore	1	2			4	10	7	9			11	6	5					3	8	
22	17	Ardwick	1-3		Moore	1	2			4	10	7	9			11	6	5			8		3		
					Apps.	22	22	12	4	15	22	22	20	15	8	22	17	16	11	2	7	2	2	1	
					Goals						3	17	2	3	1	5	2	2	5		3				

1 scrimmaged; 1 untraced

* Additional scorers - Fleming, Scrimmage

F.A. CUP

1QF	15 Oct	NEWARK TOWN *	3-1		Kelly, Irving(2)	1	2	3	6			7	8	4	10	11	5								
1QFr	27	Newark Town	4-3		Kelly, Irving(2), 1 untraced	1	2	3			4	7	9	8	10	11	5		6						
2QF	29	Greenhalgh's	3-0		Moore, Smallman, Cameron	1	2	3		5	4	7	9	8	10	11									6
3QF	19 Nov	ROTHERHAM TOWN	2-0		Smallman, Scrimmage	1	2	3		6	4	7	9	8	10	11	5								
4QF	10 Dec	Grimsby Town	0-5			1	2	3		6	4	7	9	8	10	11		5							

* Replay ordered by F.A.

LINCOLNSHIRE CUP

F	5 Apr	Gainsborough Trinity	0-4			1	2			4	10	7	9			11	5	6			8	3			

Final League Table

		Pl.	Home				Away					F.	A.	Pts
			W	D	L	F	A	W	D	L	F	A			
1	Small Heath	22	10	1	0	57	16	7	1	3	33	19	90	35	36
2	Sheffield United	22	10	1	0	35	8	6	2	3	27	11	62	19	35
3	Darwen	22	10	0	1	43	15	4	2	5	17	21	60	36	30
4	Grimsby Town	22	8	1	2	25	7	3	0	8	17	34	42	41	23
5	Ardwick	22	6	3	2	27	14	3	0	8	18	26	45	40	21
6	Burton Swifts	22	7	1	3	30	18	2	1	8	17	29	47	47	20
7	Northwich Victoria	22	7	0	4	25	26	2	2	7	17	32	42	58	20
8	Bootle	22	8	1	2	35	20	0	2	9	14	43	49	63	19
9	*Lincoln City*	*22*	*6*	*2*	*3*	*30*	*18*	*1*	*1*	*9*	*15*	*33*	*45*	*51*	*17*
10	Crewe Alexandra	22	6	1	4	30	24	0	2	9	12	45	42	69	15
11	Burslem Port Vale	22	4	1	6	16	23	2	2	7	14	34	30	57	15
12	Walsall Town Swfts	22	4	3	4	25	24	1	0	10	12	51	37	75	13

SEASON 1893-94
DIVISION TWO

No.	Date	Opposition	Res.	Att.	Goalscorers
1	2 Sep	ROTHERHAM TOWN	1-1		Irving
2	9	Liverpool	0-4		
3	16	NORTHWICH VICTORIA	4-1		Flewitt(2), Raby, Lees
4	23	GRIMSBY TOWN	1-2		Lees
5	7 Oct	NEWCASTLE UNITED	2-1		Lees, Flewitt
6	21	Crewe Alexandra	1-1		Flewitt
7	28	Grimsby Town	4-2		Lees(2), Flewitt, Richardson
8	11 Nov	SMALL HEATH	2-5		Chadburn, Flewitt
9	16	Notts County	2-1		Chadburn, Scrimmage
10	2 Dec	Rotherham Town	8-2		Chadburn(2),Flewitt,Lees(3),Irving,OG
11	23	BURTON SWIFTS	1-1		Lees
12	25	CREWE ALEXANDRA	6-1		Flewitt(2), Irving, Lees(3)
13	26	M/BROUGH IRONOPOLIS	2-3		Flewitt, Lees
14	30	Small Heath	0-6		
15	1 Jan	Newcastle United	1-5		Richardson
16	13	Middlesbrough Ironopolis	0-0		
17	20	Northwich Victoria	3-0		Irving, Chadburn, Flewitt
18	3 Feb	WOOLWICH ARSENAL	3-0		Raby(2), Flewitt
19	10	Burton Swifts	3-1		Lees, Chadburn, Graham
20	17	Woolwich Arsenal	0-4		
21	24	BURSLEM PORT VALE	2-2		Scrimmage, Lees
22	10 Mar	Burslem Port Vale	3-5		Chadburn, Irving, Scrimmage
23	17	LIVERPOOL	1-1		Flewitt
24	23	NOTTS COUNTY	0-2		
25	24	ARDWICK	6-0		Irving(2),Chadburn,Graham,Raby,Flewitt
26	26	Walsall Town Swifts	2-5		Lees(2)
27	31	Ardwick	1-0		Chadburn
28	7 Apr	WALSALL TOWN SWIFTS	0-2		

1 own goal; 3 scrimmaged

F.A. CUP

1QF	14 Oct	SHEFFIELD	2-0		Flewitt, Phipps
2QF	4 Nov	GRIMSBY TOWN	2-5		Scrimmage, Chadburn

LINCOLNSHIRE CUP

F	11 Apr	GAINSBOROUGH TRINITY	4-3		Irving(2), Lees(2)

Final League Table

		Pl.	Home W D L F A	Away W D L F A	F. A.	Pts
1	Liverpool	28	14 0 0 46 6	8 6 0 31 12	77 18	50
2	Small Heath	28	12 0 2 68 19	9 0 5 35 25	103 44	42
3	Notts County	28	12 1 1 55 14	6 2 6 15 17	70 31	39
4	Newcastle United	28	12 1 1 44 10	3 5 6 22 29	66 39	36
5	Grimsby Town	28	11 1 2 47 16	4 1 9 24 42	71 58	32
6	Burton Swifts	28	9 1 4 52 26	5 2 7 27 35	79 61	31
7	Burslem Port Vale	28	10 2 2 43 20	3 2 9 23 44	66 64	30
8	*Lincoln City*	*28*	*5 4 5 31 22*	*6 2 6 28 36*	*59 58*	*28*
9	Woolwich Arsenal	28	9 1 4 33 19	3 3 8 19 36	52 55	28
10	Walsall Town Swfts	28	8 1 5 36 23	2 2 10 15 38	51 61	23
11	Middlsbro Irnoplis	28	7 4 3 27 20	1 0 13 10 52	37 72	20
12	Crewe Alexandra	28	3 7 4 22 22	3 0 11 20 51	42 73	19
13	Ardwick	28	6 1 7 32 20	2 1 11 15 51	47 71	18
14	Rotherham Town	28	8 5 1 8 28 42	1 2 11 16 49	44 91	15
15	Northwich Victoria	28	3 3 8 17 34	0 0 14 13 64	30 98	9

SEASON 1894-95
DIVISION TWO

No.	Date	Opposition	Res.	Att.	Goalscorers
1	1 Sep	WOOLWICH ARSENAL	5-2		Flewitt(2), Frettingham(2), Gash
2	8	Darwen	0-6		
3	15	Rotherham Town	2-5		Flewitt, Frettingham
4	22	BURTON SWIFTS	3-2		Flewitt(2), Gresham
5	29	Notts County	0-3		
6	6 Oct	Woolwich Arsenal	2-5		Duckworth, Smallman
7	20	GRIMSBY TOWN	1-5		Flewitt
8	27	Crewe Alexandra	4-1		Frettingham, Richardson, Lees, Flewitt
9	10 Nov	Grimsby Town	0-3		
10	17	NEWCASTLE UNITED	3-1		Flewitt(2), Lees
11	8 Dec	BURSLEM PORT VALE	6-1		Smallman, Flewitt(2), Duckworth, Lees, OG
12	22	Newton Heath	0-3		
13	25	ROTHERHAM TOWN	2-0		Duckworth, Lees
14	26	BURY	1-3		Burke
15	29	NEWTON HEATH	3-0		Lees, Smallman, Flewitt
16	1 Jan	Newcastle United	2-4		Frettingham, Scrimmage
17	5	DARWEN	0-2		
18	12	Bury	1-4		Richardson
19	26	Burton Swifts	1-6		Frettingham
20	16 Feb	WALSALL TOWN SWIFTS	1-0		Smallman
21	23	Burton Wanderers	1-4		Duckworth
22	2 Mar	MANCHESTER CITY	0-2		
23	4	Leicester Fosse	1-2		Burke
24	16	Burslem Port Vale	1-7		Frettingham
25	23	Manchester City	3-11		Lees, Smallman, OG
26	30	BURTON WANDERERS	0-2		
27	6 Apr	LEICESTER FOSSE	1-2		Blades
28	12	NOTTS COUNTY	1-3		Flewitt
29	13	CREWE ALEXANDRA	5-2		Lees, Frettinghm(2), Duckwrth, Smallmn
30	20	Walsall Town Swifts	2-1		Frettingham, 1 untraced

F.A. CUP

| 1QF | 13 Oct | GRIMSBY TOWN | 0-3 | | |

LINCOLNSHIRE CUP

| F | 19 Jan | GAINSBOROUGH TRINITY | 1-1 | | Richardson |
| Fr | 17 Apr | Gainsborough Trinity | 1-2 | | Flewitt |

Final League Table

```
                   Pl.  Home              Away            F.  A.  Pts
                        W  D  L  F  A   W  D  L  F  A
 1  Bury           30  15  0  0 48 11   8  2  5 30 22  78  33  48
 2  Notts County   30  12  2  1 50 15   5  3  7 25 30  75  45  39
 3  Newton Heath   30   9  6  0 52 18   6  2  7 26 26  78  44  38
 4  Leicester Fosse 30 11  2  2 45 20   4  6  5 27 33  72  53  38
 5  Grimsby Town   30  14  0  1 51 16   4  1 10 28 36  79  52  37
 6  Darwen         30  13  1  1 53 10   3  3  9 21 33  74  43  36
 7  Burton Wanderers 30 10 3  2 49  9   4  4  7 18 30  67  39  35
 8  Woolwich Arsenal 30 11 3  1 54 20   3  3  9 21 38  75  58  34
 9  Manchester City 30  9  3  3 56 28   5  0 10 26 44  82  72  31
10  Newcastle United 30 11 1  3 51 28   1  2 12 21 56  72  84  27
11  Burton Swifts  30   9  2  4 34 20   2  1 12 18 54  52  74  25
12  Rotherham Town 30  10  0  5 37 22   1  2 12 18 40  55  62  24
13  Lincoln City   30   8  0  7 32 27   2  0 13 20 65  52  92  20
14  Walsall Town Swfts 30 8 0 7 35 25   2  0 13 12 67  47  92  20
15  Burslem Port Vale 30 6 3 6 30 23   1  1 13  9 54  39  77  18
16  Crewe Alexandra 30  3  4  8 20 34   0  0 15  6 69  26 103  10
```

SEASON 1895-96
DIVISION TWO

No.	Date	Opposition	Res.	Att.	Goalscorers	Mann J.J.	McFarlane A.G.	Simpson J.W.	Richardson J.M.	Neave G.D.	Burke J.	Mettam E.	Smith A.	Thomson G.	Wilson T.	Docherty E.	Heath W.	Frettingham J.H.A.	Gillespie M.	Shaw R.	Eyre T.	Gillespie W.J.	Shaw G.	Shearman F.P.	Boullemier L.A.	Smallman F.J.B.	Bradbury J.J.L.	Brailsford J.R.	Pyle T.	Vickers T.H.	Hulme J.
1	7 Sep	Grimsby Town	2-4		Thomson(2)	1	2	3	4	5	6	7	8	9	10	11															
2	14	WOOLWICH ARSENAL	1-1		Thomson	1	2		5	6	11	4	8	9		10	3	7													
3	21	Woolwich Arsenal	0-4			1	2	3	5	6		4	8			11	10	7	9												
4	28	GRIMSBY TOWN	2-5		Docherty(2)	1	2	3	5	7	6	4	8	9		11			10												
5	30	Burton Swifts	0-4			1	2	3	5	6	4		8			11		7	10												
6	5 Oct	BURTON SWIFTS	1-2		Frettingham		2		5	6	11	4	8	9			3	7	10	1											
7	19	Notts County	0-2				2		4	5	6		8					7	10	1	3	9	11								
8	26	Loughborough Town	0-3			1	2		5	11	6	4	8					7	10		3	9									
9	9 Nov	LOUGHBOROUGH TOWN	4-1		W.Gillespie(2),M.Gillespie,Frettingham		2		5	6	4		8					11	10		3	9		7							
10	16	Newton Heath	5-5		Smith(2), Frettingham, Burke, *	1	2		5	4	6		8					11	10		3	9		7							
11	30	BURTON WANDERERS	1-2		Shearman		2		5	6	4		8					11	10	1	3	9		7							
12	21 Dec	LIVERPOOL	0-1				2		5	6	4		8					11	10		3	9		7	1						
13	26	CREWE ALEXANDRA	6-2		M.Gillespie(2),W.Gillespie(3),Smith				5	6	4		8				2	11	10		3	9			1	7					
14	28	NEWCASTLE UNITED	4-0		M.Gillespie(3),W.Gillespie		2		5	6	4		8					11	10		3	9			1	7					
15	2 Jan	Newcastle United	0-5				2		5	6	4		8					11	10		3	9			1	7					
16	11	MANCHESTER CITY	1-2		Smith		2		5	6	4		8					11	10		3	9			1	7					
17	25	Liverpool	1-6		W.Gillespie		2		5	6	4		8					11	10		3	9		7	1						
18	1 Feb	ROTHERHAM TOWN	5-0		W.Gillespie,Smith,Frettingham,Burke(2)		2		5	6	4		8					11	10		3	9		7	1						
19	8	Crewe Alexandra	2-2		W.Gillespie, Scrimmage		2		5	6		4					3	11	10			9		7	1	8					
20	15	LEICESTER FOSSE	2-3		M.Gillespie, Shearman		2		5	6	4						3	11	10			9		7	1	8					
21	22	Burslem Port Vale	1-0		Frettingham		2		5	6	4		8					11	10		3	9		7	1						
22	29	Leicester Fosse	3-1		Eyre, M.Gillespie, Shearman		2		5	6	4		8					11	10		3	9		7	1						
23	7 Mar	DARWEN	1-0		Burke		2		5	6			8					11	10		3	9		7	1		4				
24	14	Manchester City	0-4				2		5	6			8						10		3	9		7	1		4	11			
25	16	Rotherham Town	2-2		M.Gillespie, Frettingham		2		5	6	4		8					11	10		3	9			1	7		4				
26	28	Darwen	0-5				2		5	6	4		8					11	10		3	9			1	7					
27	3 Apr	NOTTS COUNTY	2-3		W.Gillespie, Smith		2		5	6	4		8					11	10		3	9			1	7					
28	4	Burton Wanderers	1-4		Frettingham		2		5	6	4		8					11	10		3	9			1	7					
29	11	NEWTON HEATH	2-0		Smith, Frettingham		2		5	6			8					11	10		3	9		7	1					4	
30	18	BURSLEM PORT VALE	4-2		M.Gillespie, Frettingham(2), Smith		2			4	6		8					11	10		5	9		7	1			3			
				Apps.		8	29	4	9	29	29	22	29	5	2	5	5	27	28	3	22	24	1	14	19	8	2	4	1	1	
				Goals							4		8	3		2		10	10			1	11		3							

* Additional scorer - W.Gillespie

1 scrimmaged

F.A. CUP

1QF	12 Oct	Peterborough	13-0		Frettingham(2), Smith, *		2		4	5	6		8					7	10	1	3	9									11
2QF	2 Nov	Worksop Town	3-0		OG, M.Gillespie(2)	1	2			5	6	4	8					11	10		3	9		7							
3QF	23	GRIMSBY TOWN	2-4		Smith, Neave	1	2		5	4	6		8					11	10		3	9		7							

* M.Gillespie(3), W.Gillespie(2), Hulme(2), Burke(2), Neave

LINCOLNSHIRE CUP (City Swifts entered - results only given)

1R	14 Dec	CASUALS (LINCOLN)	7-0	Pyle(2), Murley, Irving(3), G.Shaw
2R	29 Feb	10TH LINCOLN REGT.	6-0	Macrill(2), Smallman, G.Shaw, *
SF	28 Mar	Grantham Rovers Colts	5-3	Darcey(2), West, Macrill, 1 untraced
F	25 Apr	GRIMSBY ALL SAINTS	2-2	Smallman, Macrill
Fr	30	Grimsby All Saints	0-2	

* Additional scorers - Pyle, Darcey

Final - after extra time

Final League Table

		Pl.	Home				Away			F.	A.	Pts
			W	D	L	F	A	W	D	L	F	A			
1	Liverpool	30	14	1	0	65	11	8	1	6	41	21	106	32	46
2	Manchester City	30	12	3	0	37	9	9	1	5	26	29	63	38	46
3	Grimsby Town	30	14	1	0	51	9	6	1	8	31	29	82	38	42
4	Burton Wanderers	30	12	1	2	43	15	7	3	5	26	25	69	40	42
5	Newcastle United	30	14	0	1	57	14	2	2	11	16	36	73	50	34
6	Newton Heath	30	12	2	1	48	15	3	1	11	18	42	66	57	33
7	Woolwich Arsenal	30	11	1	3	42	11	3	3	9	16	31	58	42	32
8	Leicester Fosse	30	10	0	5	40	16	4	4	7	17	28	57	44	32
9	Darwen	30	9	4	2	55	22	3	2	10	17	45	72	67	30
10	Notts County	30	8	1	6	41	22	4	1	10	16	32	57	54	26
11	Burton Swifts	30	7	2	6	24	26	3	2	10	15	43	39	69	24
12	Loughborough	30	7	3	5	32	25	2	2	11	8	41	40	66	23
13	*Lincoln City*	*30*	*7*	*1*	*7*	*36*	*24*	*2*	*3*	*10*	*17*	*51*	*53*	*75*	*22*
14	Burslem Port Vale	30	6	4	5	25	24	1	0	14	18	54	43	78	18
15	Rotherham Town	30	7	2	6	27	26	0	1	14	7	71	34	97	17
16	Crewe Alexandra	30	5	2	8	22	28	0	1	14	8	67	30	95	13

SEASON 1896-97
DIVISION TWO

No.	Date	Opposition	Res.	Att.	Goalscorers
1	5 Sep	BLACKPOOL	3-1		Lynes, Kirton(2)
2	12	Newton Heath	1-3		Lynes
3	19	Small Heath	2-1		W.Gillespie(2)
4	21	Manchester City	0-3		
5	26	Grimsby Town	1-3		Kirton
6	3 Oct	LOUGHBOROUGH TOWN	0-2		
7	24	NEWCASTLE UNITED	1-2		W.Gillespie
8	7 Nov	Leicester Fosse	1-4		Timmis
9	14	Blackpool	1-3		W.Gillespie
10	5 Dec	WOOLWICH ARSENAL	2-3		W.Gillespie, Burke
11	19	Darwen	1-4		Irving
12	25	Woolwich Arsenal	2-6		Timmis, OG
13	26	BURTON WANDERERS	2-3		Kirton, Smith
14	2 Jan	Newcastle United	1-2		Kirton
15	9	GRIMSBY TOWN	0-3		
16	16	DARWEN	1-0		Pyle
17	23	Notts County	0-8		
18	6 Feb	Burton Swifts	0-4		
19	13	MANCHESTER CITY	0-1		
20	20	GAINSBOROUGH TRINITY	0-2		
21	6 Mar	Loughborough Town	0-3		
22	13	SMALL HEATH	1-3		Hartley
23	20	BURTON SWIFTS	1-1		Hartley
24	27	Gainsborough Trinity	0-7		
25	31	NOTTS COUNTY	1-1		Lynes
26	1 Apr	NEWTON HEATH	1-3		Hartley
27	3	Burton Wanderers	0-2		
28	10	LEICESTER FOSSE	2-1		Hartley, Lynes
29	16	WALSALL	2-1		Hartley, Davidson
30	17	Walsall	0-5		

Additional players: W.Rogers 18/9, A.Allison 20/7

1 own goal

F.A. CUP

3QF	21 Nov	GAINSBOROUGH TRINITY	1-0		W.Gillespie
4QF	12 Dec	Worksop Town	3-3		Kirton, Manson, OG
4QFr	23	WORKSOP TOWN	8-0		Lynes(2),Smith,W.Gillespie(4),Kirton
5QF	28	BARNSLEY ST. PETERS	1-2		Timmis

LINCOLNSHIRE CUP

SF	3 Apr	GRANTHAM AVENUE	3-1		Shaw, Ward, West
F	29	Grimsby Town	2-6		Raby, Hartley

Additional players - R.Sharman SF/1, F.W.Dickinson SF & F/2, G.Dean SF/6, G.Shaw SF/10 & F/4

Final League Table

		Pl.	Home				Away			F.	A.	Pts
			W D L F A				W D L F A					
1	Notts County	30	12 1 2 60 18				7 3 5 32 25			92	43	42
2	Newton Heath	30	11 4 0 37 10				6 1 8 19 24			56	34	39
3	Grimsby Town	30	12 2 1 44 15				5 2 8 22 30			66	45	38
4	Small Heath	30	8 3 4 36 23				8 2 5 33 24			69	47	37
5	Newcastle United	30	13 1 1 42 13				4 0 11 14 39			56	52	35
6	Manchester City	30	10 3 2 39 15				2 5 8 19 35			58	50	32
7	Gainsborough Trin.	30	10 2 3 35 16				2 5 8 15 31			50	47	31
8	Blackpool	30	11 3 1 39 16				2 2 11 20 40			59	56	31
9	Leicester Fosse	30	11 2 2 44 20				2 2 11 15 37			59	57	30
10	Woolwich Arsenal	30	10 1 4 42 20				3 3 9 26 50			68	70	30
11	Darwen	30	13 0 2 54 16				1 0 14 13 45			67	61	28
12	Walsall	30	8 5 2 37 25				3 2 10 17 44			54	69	26
13	Loughborough	30	10 0 5 37 14				2 1 12 13 50			50	64	25
14	Burton Swifts	30	7 4 4 33 20				2 1 13 13 41			46	61	24
15	Burton Wanderers	30	8 1 6 22 22				1 1 13 9 45			31	67	20
16	Lincoln City	30	4 2 9 17 27				1 0 14 10 58			27	85	12

Back: Simpson, Wilson, Hannah, Boullemier, Timmis, Eyres, Smith, Martin (sec/manager).
Centre: Lynes, William Gillespie, Matthew Gillespie, Kirton.
Front: Brown.

SEASON 1897-98
DIVISION TWO

No.	Date	Opposition	Res.	Att.	Goalscorers
1	4 Sep	Newton Heath	0-5		
2	11	Woolwich Arsenal	2-2		Downie, Robertson
3	18	Darwen	2-3		Fletcher, Hulme
4	25	NEWCASTLE UNITED	2-3		Hall, Robertson
5	2 Oct	Grimsby Town	2-4		Hall, Robertson
6	9	DARWEN	2-2		Hulme, Fletcher
7	16	Gainsborough Trinity	0-4		
8	23	LOUGHBOROUGH TOWN	2-3		Fletcher, Robertson
9	6 Nov	NEWTON HEATH	1-0		Robertson
10	13	GAINSBOROUGH TRINITY	2-1		Hulme(2)
11	27	Loughborough Town	2-4		Hulme, Hall
12	4 Dec	LUTON TOWN	4-2		Morris, Ross, Hulme, Robertson
13	18	Luton Town	3-9		Fletcher, Hulme, Ross
14	25	GRIMSBY TOWN	1-1		Robertson
15	27	WOOLWICH ARSENAL	2-3		Morris, Robertson
16	1 Jan	Burnley	1-2		Robertson
17	8	Burton Swifts	1-1		Robertson
18	15	SMALL HEATH	1-2		Fletcher
19	24	Manchester City	1-3		Robertson
20	29	BURTON SWIFTS	3-0		Hulme(2), Robertson
21	5 Feb	BLACKPOOL	3-2		Scott(2), Hulme
22	12	Leicester Fosse	1-3		Robertson
23	19	Blackpool	0-5		
24	26	Newcastle United	0-3		
25	5 Mar	LEICESTER FOSSE	1-4		Fletcher
26	12	Walsall	1-3		Hulme
27	19	MANCHESTER CITY	2-1		Hulme, Pugh
28	8 Apr	BURNLEY	1-1		Ross
29	9	WALSALL	0-2		
30	16	Small Heath	0-4		

F.A. CUP

3QF	30 Oct	ATTERCLIFFE	5-0		Robertson(4), Pyle
4QF	20 Nov	Gainsborough Trinity	1-5		Hulme

LINCOLNSHIRE CUP

SF	4 Apr	GAINSBOROUGH TRINITY	0-0		
SFr	18	Gainsborough Trinity	1-2		Robertson

Final League Table

		Pl.	Home W D L F A	Away W D L F A	F. A. Pts
1	Burnley	30	14 1 0 64 13	6 7 2 16 11	80 24 48
2	Newcastle United	30	14 0 1 43 10	7 3 5 21 22	64 32 45
3	Manchester City	30	10 4 1 45 15	5 5 5 21 21	66 36 39
4	Newton Heath	30	11 2 2 42 10	5 4 6 22 25	64 35 38
5	Woolwich Arsenal	30	10 4 1 41 14	6 1 8 28 35	69 49 37
6	Small Heath	30	11 1 3 37 18	5 3 7 21 32	58 50 36
7	Leicester Fosse	30	8 5 2 26 11	5 2 8 20 24	46 35 33
8	Luton Town	30	10 2 3 50 13	3 2 10 18 37	68 50 30
9	Gainsborough Trin.	30	10 4 1 30 12	2 2 11 20 42	50 54 30
10	Walsall	30	9 3 3 42 15	3 2 10 16 43	58 58 29
11	Blackpool	30	8 4 3 32 15	2 1 12 17 46	49 61 25
12	Grimsby Town	30	9 1 5 44 24	1 3 11 8 38	52 62 24
13	Burton Swifts	30	7 3 5 25 21	1 2 12 13 48	38 69 21
14	*Lincoln City*	*30*	*6 3 6 27 27*	*0 2 13 16 55*	*43 82 17*
15	Darwen	30	4 1 10 21 32	2 1 12 10 44	31 76 14
16	Loughborough	30	5 2 8 15 26	1 0 14 9 61	24 87 14

SEASON 1898-99
DIVISION TWO

No.	Date	Opposition	Res.	Att.	Goalscorers
1	1 Sep	BARNSLEY	1-0		Robertson
2	3	Leicester Fosse	2-3		Robertson(2)
3	5	Small Heath	1-4		Robertson
4	10	DARWEN	2-0		Henderson, Robertson
5	17	Gainsborough Trinity	2-2		Fern, Robertson
6	24	MANCHESTER CITY	3-1		Robertson(3)
7	1 Oct	Glossop North End	0-2		
8	8	WALSALL	1-1		Robertson
9	22	BURSLEM PORT VALE	1-0		Robertson
10	5 Nov	LOUGHBOROUGH TOWN	6-0		Henderson(2),Robertson,Clarke,Morris,*
11	12	Blackpool	0-3		
12	26	Newton Heath	0-1		
13	17 Dec	Woolwich Arsenal	2-4		Pugh, Clarke
14	24	LUTON TOWN	2-0		Robertson, Clarke
15	26	GLOSSOP NORTH END	2-2		Robertson, Henderson
16	27	NEW BRIGHTON TOWER	1-2		Clarke
17	31	LEICESTER FOSSE	3-1		Robertson(2), Pugh
18	7 Jan	Darwen	2-1		Robertson, Morris
19	14	GAINSBOROUGH TRINITY	1-0		Henderson
20	4 Feb	Walsall	2-3		Swan, Bannister
21	11	BURTON SWIFTS	1-1		Robertson
22	18	Burslem Port Vale	1-2		Swan
23	22	Manchester City	1-3		Swan
24	4 Mar	Loughborough Town	4-2		Swan(3), Fern
25	11	BLACKPOOL	0-0		
26	18	Grimsby Town	1-1		Clarke
27	25	NEWTON HEATH	2-0		Robertson, Swan
28	31	SMALL HEATH	2-2		Pyle, Robertson
29	1 Apr	New Brighton Tower	1-4		Swan
30	3	Barnsley	0-1		
31	8	GRIMSBY TOWN	1-6		Swan
32	12	Burton Swifts	1-2		Swan
33	15	WOOLWICH ARSENAL	2-0		Clarke, Robertson
34	22	Luton Town	0-2		

* Additional scorer: Fern

F.A. CUP

3QF	29 Oct	ATTERCLIFFE	5-0		Henderson,Clarke(2),Fern,Robertson
4QF	19 Nov	Grimsby Town	1-2		Pugh

LINCOLNSHIRE CUP

2R	18 Feb	GRANTHAM OLYMPIC	7-0		Kiddle,Barton,Scott,Gray,Fern(3)
SF	17 Apr	GAINSBOROUGH TRINITY	1-1		Scott
SFr	19	GAINSBOROUGH TRINITY	2-3		Clarke(2)

Final League Table

```
                  Pl.    Home         Away          F.  A.  Pts
                         W  D  L  F  A   W  D  L  F  A
 1  Manchester City 34  15  1  1 64 10   8  5  4 28 25  92  35  52
 2  Glossop         34  12  1  4 48 13   8  5  4 28 25  76  38  46
 3  Leicester Fosse 34  12  5  0 35 12   6  4  7 29 30  64  42  45
 4  Newton Heath    34  12  4  1 51 14   7  1  9 16 29  67  43  43
 5  New Brighton T. 34  13  2  2 48 13   5  5  7 23 39  71  52  43
 6  Walsall         34  12  5  0 64 11   3  7  7 15 25  79  36  42
 7  Woolwich Arsenal 34 14  2  1 55 10   4  3 10 17 31  72  41  41
 8  Small Heath     34  14  1  2 66 17   3  6  8 19 33  85  50  41
 9  Burslem Port Vale 34 12 2  3 35 12   5  3  9 21 22  56  34  39
10  Grimsby Town    34  10  3  4 39 17   5  2 10 32 43  71  60  35
11  Barnsley        34  11  4  2 44 18   1  3 13  8 38  52  56  31
12  Lincoln City    34  10  5  2 31 16   2  2 13 20 40  51  56  31
13  Burton Swifts   34   7  5  5 35 25   3  3 11 16 45  51  70  28
14  Gainsborough Trin. 34 8 4  5 40 22   2  1 14 16 50  56  72  25
15  Luton Town      34   8  1  8 37 31   2  2 13 14 64  51  95  23
16  Blackpool       34   6  3  8 35 30   2  1 14 14 60  49  90  20
17  Loughborough    34   5  4  8 31 26   1  2 14  7 66  38  92  18
18  Darwen          34   2  4 11 16 32   0  1 16 6109 22 141   9
```

SEASON 1899-1900
DIVISION TWO

No.	Date	Opposition	Res.	Att.	Goalscorers
1	2 Sep	MIDDLESBROUGH	3-0		Mowatt, Phillips, Pyle
2	9	Chesterfield	2-2		Scrimmage, Hartley
3	16	GAINSBOROUGH TRINITY	2-1		Hartley(2)
4	23	Bolton Wanderers	0-4		
5	30	LOUGHBOROUGH TOWN	3-2		Hartley(2), Scrimmage
6	2 Oct	Small Heath	0-5		
7	7	Newton Heath	0-1		
8	14	SHEFFIELD WEDNESDAY	1-2		Hartley
9	21	Burton Swift	0-0		
10	4 Nov	NEW BRIGHTON TOWER	0-0		
11	11	Grimsby Town	2-5		Scott, Koerner
12	25	Barnsley	4-0		Henderson, Hartley(2), Pugh
13	2 Dec	LEICESTER FOSSE	2-0		Hartley(2)
14	16	BURSLEM PORT VALE	1-1		McCairns
15	23	Walsall	1-3		Clarke
16	25	WOOLWICH ARSENAL	5-0		Pugh(2), Scott, McCairns, OG
17	26	WALSALL	3-1		Pugh, Henderson, Hartley
18	30	Middlesbrough	1-1		Hartley
19	6 Jan	CHESTERFIELD	2-0		Scrimmage, Pugh
20	13	Gainsborough Trinity	1-3		McCairns
21	20	BOLTON WANDERERS	1-0		Scott
22	10 Feb	NEWTON HEATH	1-0		McCairns
23	24	BURTON SWIFTS	3-0		Scott, Hartley(2)
24	3 Mar	LUTON TOWN	2-0		Hartley, McCairns
25	10	New Brighton Tower	0-3		
26	24	Woolwich Arsenal	1-2		McCairns
27	31	BARNSLEY	1-1		Cowley
28	7 Apr	Leicester Fosse	0-2		
29	13	SMALL HEATH	0-0		
30	16	Luton Town	2-0		Hartley, McCairns
31	17	Sheffield Wednesday	0-1		
32	21	Burslem Port Vale	1-2		McCairns
33	23	Loughborough Town	1-0		McCairns
34	27	GRIMSBY TOWN	1-1		Pugh

1 own goal; 3 scrimmaged

F.A. CUP

3QF	28 Oct	BARNSLEY	0-1		

LINCOLNSHIRE CUP

3R	21 Mar	GRIMSBY ALL SAINTS	3-1		McCairns(2), Hartley
SF	12 Apr	ADELAIDE (LINCOLN)	1-5		Scrimmage

Additional players - J.Dixon SF/8, Morphett SF/9

Final League Table

		Pl.	Home W D L F A	Away W D L F A	F.	A.	Pts
1	Sheffield Wed.	34	17 0 0 61 7	8 4 5 23 15	84	22	54
2	Bolton Wanderers	34	14 2 1 47 7	8 6 3 32 18	79	25	52
3	Small Heath	34	15 1 1 58 12	5 5 7 20 26	78	38	46
4	Newton Heath	34	15 1 1 44 11	5 3 9 19 16	63	27	44
5	Leicester Fosse	34	11 5 1 34 8	6 4 7 19 28	53	36	43
6	Grimsby Town	34	10 3 4 46 24	7 3 7 21 22	67	46	40
7	Chesterfield	34	10 4 3 35 24	6 2 9 30 36	65	60	38
8	Woolwich Arsenal	34	13 1 3 47 12	3 3 11 14 31	61	43	36
9	*Lincoln City*	*34*	*11 5 1 31 9*	*3 3 11 15 34*	*46*	*43*	*36*
10	New Brighton T.	34	9 4 4 44 22	4 5 8 22 36	66	58	35
11	Burslem Port Vale	34	11 2 4 26 16	3 4 10 13 33	39	49	34
12	Walsall	34	10 5 2 35 18	2 3 12 15 37	50	55	32
13	Gainsborough Trin.	34	8 8 4 5 37 24	1 3 13 10 51	47	75	25
14	Middlesbrough	34	8 4 5 28 15	0 4 13 11 54	39	69	24
15	Burton Swifts	34	8 5 4 31 24	1 1 15 12 60	43	84	24
16	Barnsley	34	8 5 4 36 23	0 2 15 10 56	46	79	23
17	Luton Town	34	5 3 9 25 25	0 5 12 15 50	40	75	18
18	Loughborough	34	1 6 10 12 26	0 0 17 6 74	18	100	8

SEASON 1900-01
DIVISION TWO

Players: Webb A., McMillan W., Gibson W., Bannister C., Crawford J., Cowley B.J., Pugh D.H., Scott F., McCairns T., Hartley J., Henderson J.N., Evans W., Smith W.A., McInnes T., Bennett J.W., Calderhead D., Proudfoot P., Simpson J.W., Barton W., Blow E.P.

No.	Date	Opposition	Res.	Att.	Goalscorers
1	1 Sep	Middlesbrough	0-2		
2	8	BURNLEY	2-0		Hartley, Cowley
3	15	Burslem Port Vale	0-2		
4	22	LEICESTER FOSSE	1-0		OG
5	29	New Brighton Tower	0-2		
6	6 Oct	GAINSBOROUGH TRINITY	6-0		Scott(2), Cowley, McInnes, Henderson(2)
7	13	Walsall	0-3		
8	20	BURTON UNITED	2-1		Pugh, McInnes
9	27	Barnsley	0-0		
10	10 Nov	Blackpool	0-2		
11	24	Small Heath	0-2		
12	1 Dec	Grimsby Town	0-4		
13	8	STOCKPORT COUNTY	4-0		Hartley(3), McInnes
14	15	Newton Heath	1-4		Smith
15	25	GRIMSBY TOWN	0-1		
16	26	GLOSSOP	1-1		McInnes
17	29	MIDDLESBROUGH	1-2		Proudfoot
18	5 Jan	Burnley	0-1		
19	12	BURSLEM PORT VALE	2-2		Hartley, McInnes
20	19	Leicester Fosse	2-0		McCairns, Smith
21	26	WOOLWICH ARSENAL	3-3		McCairns(2), Smith
22	9 Feb	Gainsborough Trinity	1-1		McCairns
23	16	WALSALL	2-0		Pugh, McCairns
24	23	Burton United	0-0		
25	2 Mar	BARNSLEY	3-0		Proudfoot(2), McInnes
26	9	Woolwich Arsenal	0-0		
27	16	BLACKPOOL	3-0		Hartley(2), Crawford
28	23	Stockport County	0-1		
29	30	SMALL HEATH	3-1		Hartley(2), Smith
30	1 Apr	NEW BRIGHTON TOWER	2-0		Proudfoot, McInnes
31	5	NEWTON HEATH	2-0		Proudfoot, Hartley
32	8	Chesterfield	0-2		
33	13	CHESTERFIELD	2-0		Proudfoot, Scrimmage
34	27	Glossop	0-2		

Apps. 34 31 30 32 33 30 27 12 14 34 12 3 23 27 4 2 18 6 1 1
Goals 1 2 2 5 10 2 4 7 6

1 own goal; 1 scrimmaged

F.A. CUP

Round	Date	Opposition	Res.		Goalscorers
3QF	3 Nov	GAINSBOROUGH TRINITY	0-0		
3QFr	7	Gainsborough Trinity *	1-1		McInnes
3QF2r	12	Gainsborough Trinity #	3-1		Hartley, Scott, OG
4QF	17	Barnsley	0-1		

* after extra time, abandoned after 100mins due to bad light.
# at Bramall Lane, Sheffield.

LINCOLNSHIRE CUP

Round	Date	Opposition	Res.		Goalscorers
SF	18 Apr	Grimsby All Saints *	3-0		McCairns(2), Hartley
F	29	GRIMSBY TOWN	0-1		

* Played at Blundell Park, Grimsby

Final League Table

		Pl.	Home W D L F A	Away W D L F A	F. A. Pts
1	Grimsby Town	34	14 3 0 46 11	6 6 5 14 22	60 33 49
2	Small Heath	34	14 2 1 41 8	5 8 4 16 16	57 24 48
3	Burnley	34	15 2 0 39 6	5 2 10 14 23	53 29 44
4	New Brighton T.	34	12 5 0 34 8	5 3 9 23 30	57 38 42
5	Glossop	34	11 2 4 34 9	4 6 7 17 24	51 33 38
6	Middlesbrough	34	11 4 2 38 13	4 3 10 12 27	50 40 37
7	Woolwich Arsenal	34	13 3 1 30 11	2 3 12 9 24	39 35 36
8	*Lincoln City*	34	12 3 2 39 11	4 12 4 28	43 39 33
9	Burslem Port Vale	34	8 6 3 28 14	3 5 9 17 33	45 47 33
10	Newton Heath	34	11 3 3 31 9	3 1 13 11 29	42 38 32
11	Leicester Fosse	34	9 5 3 30 15	2 5 10 9 22	39 37 32
12	Blackpool	34	7 6 4 20 11	5 1 11 13 47	33 58 31
13	Gainsborough Trin.	34	8 4 5 26 18	2 6 9 19 42	45 60 30
14	Chesterfield	34	6 5 6 25 22	3 5 9 21 36	46 58 28
15	Barnsley	34	9 3 5 34 23	2 2 13 13 37	47 60 27
16	Walsall	34	7 7 3 29 23	0 6 11 11 33	40 56 27
17	Stockport County	34	9 2 6 25 21	2 1 14 13 47	38 68 25
18	Burton Swifts	34	7 3 7 16 21	1 1 15 18 45	34 66 20

SEASON 1901-02
DIVISION TWO

No.	Date	Opposition	Res.	Att.	Goalscorers
1	7 Sep	BURNLEY	1-0		Smith
2	14	Burslem Port Vale	2-1		Dixon, Proudfoot
3	21	CHESTERFIELD	4-0		Dixon, Hartley, McInnes, Smith
4	28	Gainsborough Trinity	2-2		McInnes, Proudfoot
5	5 Oct	MIDDLESBROUGH	2-1		O'Donnell(2)
6	12	Bristol City	1-1		Smith
7	19	BLACKPOOL	0-0		
8	26	Stockport County	1-2		O'Donnell
9	9 Nov	Glossop	1-1		Dixon
10	23	Burton United	6-0		Dixon, Smith(3), Hartley, McInnes
11	7 Dec	WOOLWICH ARSENAL	0-0		
12	9	West Bromwich Albion	1-4		Proudfoot
13	21	LEICESTER FOSSE	2-0		Smith, Hartley
14	25	DONCASTER ROVERS	0-0		
15	26	NEWTON HEATH	2-0		McInnes(2)
16	28	Preston North End	0-8		
17	4 Jan	Burnley	0-1		
18	11	BURSLEM PORT VALE	1-1		McInnes
19	18	Chesterfield	1-0		Smith
20	1 Feb	Middlesbrough	0-0		
21	15	Blackpool	0-3		
22	22	STOCKPORT COUNTY	5-0		McInnes(2), Smith(2), Scrimmage
23	1 Mar	Newton Heath	0-0		
24	8	GLOSSOP	1-0		Proudfoot
25	15	Doncaster Rovers	1-1		McInnes
26	22	BURTON UNITED	0-0		
27	28	BARNSLEY	1-1		Hartley
28	29	WEST BROMWICH ALBION	1-0		Hartley
29	5 Apr	Woolwich Arsenal	0-2		
30	12	Barnsley	2-2		Hartley(2)
31	16	GAINSBOROUGH TRINITY	3-0		O'Donnell, Proudfoot, McInnes
32	19	Leicester Fosse	1-3		Hartley
33	21	BRISTOL CITY	1-0		Hartley
34	26	PRESTON NORTH END	2-1		Proudfoot, Hartley

F.A. CUP

3QF	2 Nov	Worksop Town	4-0		O'Donnell, Dixon(2), Smith
4QF	16	DONCASTER ROVERS	1-0		O'Donnell
5QF	20	Barnsley	0-0		
5QFr	4 Dec	BARNSLEY	3-1 *		Scrimmage, McInnes, O'Donnell
Int QF	14	Newton Heath	2-1		Hartley(2)
1R	25 Jan	Oxford City	0-0		
1Rr	29	OXFORD CITY	4-0		McInnes(2), O'Donnell, Smith
2R	8 Feb	DERBY COUNTY	1-3		McInnes

* after extra time

LINCOLNSHIRE CUP

| SF | 7 Apr | GRIMSBY TOWN | 1-1 | | Smith |
| SFr | 17 | Grimsby Town | 0-3 | | |

Final League Table

		Pl.	Home W D L F A	Away W D L F A	F.	A.	Pts
1	West Bromwich Alb.	34	14 2 1 52 13	11 3 3 30 16	82	29	55
2	Middlesbrough	34	15 1 1 58 7	8 4 5 32 17	90	24	51
3	Preston North End	34	12 3 2 50 11	6 3 8 21 21	71	32	42
4	Woolwich Arsenal	34	13 2 2 35 9	5 4 8 15 17	50	26	42
5	*Lincoln City*	34	11 6 0 26 4	3 7 7 19 31	45	35	41
6	Bristol City	34	13 1 3 39 12	4 5 8 13 23	52	35	40
7	Doncaster Rovers	34	12 3 2 39 12	1 5 11 10 46	49	58	34
8	Glossop	34	7 6 4 22 15	3 6 8 14 25	36	40	32
9	Burnley	34	9 6 2 30 8	1 4 12 11 37	41	45	30
10	Burton United	34	8 6 3 32 23	3 2 12 14 31	46	54	30
11	Barnsley	34	8 6 3 25 14	3 3 11 15 30	51	63	30
12	Burslem Port Vale	34	9 7 1 36 17	2 2 12 17 42	43	59	29
13	Blackpool	34	9 3 5 27 21	2 4 11 13 35	40	56	29
14	Leicester Fosse	34	11 2 4 26 14	1 3 13 12 42	38	56	29
15	Newton Heath	34	10 2 5 27 12	1 4 12 11 41	38	53	28
16	Chesterfield	34	10 3 4 35 18	1 3 13 12 50	47	68	28
17	Stockport County	34	8 3 6 25 20	0 4 13 11 52	36	72	23
18	Gainsborough Trin.	34	4 9 4 26 25	0 2 15 4 55	30	80	19

Back : Taylor (director), McMillan, Webb, Gibson, Dick Strawson (director), Coley.
Centre : Waterson (trainer), Fraser, Crawford, Blow, Calderhead (secretary/manager).
Front : Dixon, Proudfoot, Dennis O'Donnell, Smith, McInnes.

SEASON 1902-03
DIVISION TWO

No.	Date	Opposition	Res.	Att.	Goalscorers
1	6 Sep	Manchester City	1-3		Proudfoot
2	13	BURNLEY	4-1		O'Donnell, Smith(2), Fraser
3	15	STOCKPORT COUNTY	3-1		McInnes, Hartley, C.F.Simpson
4	20	Preston North End	1-0		O'Donnell
5	27	BURSLEM PORT VALE	4-1		Hartley(2), Proudfoot, McInnes
6	4 Oct	Barnsley	0-0		
7	11	GAINSBOROUGH TRINITY	1-0		OG
8	18	Burton United	2-2		Proudfoot, O'Donnell
9	25	BRISTOL CITY	1-1		Hartley
10	8 Nov	MANCHESTER UNITED	1-3		McMillan
11	22	BLACKPOOL	0-2		
12	29	Arsenal	1-2		Proudfoot
13	6 Dec	DONCASTER ROVERS	4-2		Proudfoot(3), Hartley
14	20	Small Heath	1-3		Smith
15	25	CHESTERFIELD	0-0		
16	26	Glossop	1-0		Smith
17	27	LEICESTER FOSSE	1-2		Proudfoot
18	3 Jan	MANCHESTER CITY	1-0		McInnes
19	10	Burnley	0-1		
20	17	PRESTON NORTH END	2-3		Hartley(2)
21	24	Burslem Port Vale	1-5		C.F.Simpson
22	31	BARNSLEY	1-3		Gibson
23	14 Feb	BURTON UNITED	4-0		O'Donnell, Scrimmage, Price, Hartley
24	28	Glossop	0-2		
25	7 Mar	Manchester United	2-1		C.F.Simpson(2)
26	14	Stockport County	1-3		Smith
27	21	Blackpool	3-2		Hartley, Price, Smith
28	28	ARSENAL	2-2		C.F.Simpson, Hartley
29	30	Bristol City	2-0		Price, Smith
30	4 Apr	Doncaster Rovers	1-2		Hartley
31	10	SMALL HEATH	0-1		
32	11	Chesterfield	0-1		
33	14	Leicester Fosse	0-0		
34	15	Gainsborough Trinity	0-4		

1 own goal; 1 scrimmaged.

F.A. CUP

Int QF	13 Dec	WEST HAM UNITED	2-0		Proudfoot, Hartley
1R	7 Feb	Barnsley	0-2		

LINCOLNSHIRE CUP

SF	19 Mar	Grantham Avenue	1-1		Fraser
SFr	18 Apr	GRANTHAM AVENUE	6-0		W.Simpson, Hartley(2), Smith(2), *
F	29	GRIMSBY TOWN	1-1		OG
Fr	30	Grimsby Town	2-3		Hartley, McInnes

* Additional scorer - C.F.Simpson

Final League Table

		Pl.	Home W D L F A	Away W D L F A	F. A. Pts
1	Manchester City	34	15 1 1 64 15	10 3 4 31 14	95 29 54
2	Small Heath	34	17 0 0 57 11	7 3 7 17 25	74 36 51
3	Woolwich Arsenal	34	14 2 1 46 9	6 6 5 20 21	66 30 48
4	Bristol City	34	12 3 2 43 18	5 5 7 16 20	59 38 42
5	Manchester United	34	9 4 4 32 15	6 4 7 21 23	53 38 38
6	Chesterfield	34	11 4 2 43 10	3 5 9 24 30	67 40 37
7	Preston North End	34	10 5 2 39 12	3 5 9 17 28	56 40 36
8	Barnsley	34	9 4 4 32 13	4 4 9 23 38	55 51 34
9	Burslem Port Vale	34	11 5 1 36 16	2 3 12 21 46	57 62 34
10	Lincoln City	34	8 3 6 30 22	4 3 10 16 31	46 53 30
11	Glossop	34	9 1 7 26 19	2 6 9 17 38	43 57 29
12	Gainsborough Trin.	34	9 4 4 28 14	2 3 12 13 45	41 59 29
13	Burton United	34	9 4 4 26 20	2 3 12 13 39	39 59 29
14	Blackpool	34	7 5 5 32 24	2 5 10 12 35	44 59 28
15	Leicester Fosse	34	5 5 7 20 23	5 3 9 21 42	41 65 28
16	Doncaster Rovers	34	8 5 4 27 17	1 2 14 8 55	35 72 25
17	Stockport County	34	6 4 7 26 24	1 2 14 12 50	38 74 20
18	Burnley	34	6 7 4 25 25	0 1 16 5 52	30 77 20

Back: Calderhead (secretary), Pallister, Ashley (director), McMillan, Dick Strawson (director), Webb, Gibson, Jack Strawson (director), Billy Simpson, Waterson(trainer).
Centre: Fraser, Crawford, Blow.
Front: Proudfoot, Hartley, Dennis O'Donnell, Smith, McInnes.

SEASON 1903-04
DIVISION TWO

No.	Date	Opposition	Res.	Att.	Goalscorers	Webb A.	Groves J.A.	Pallister W.	Frazer G.	Simpson W.	Blow E.P.	O'Donnell D.	Watson W.	Higgins T.	Simpson C.F.	Parker H.	Thompson T.	Hindson E.	McMillan W.	Snarey C.	Brown E.H.	Boast E.	Jacklin A.	Elmore E.
1	5 Sep	GRIMSBY TOWN	2-1		O'Donnell, C.F.Simpson	1	2	3	4	5	6	7	8	9	10	11								
2	12	Leicester Fosse	2-2		C.F.Simpson, Groves	1	2	3	4	5	6	7	8		10	11	9							
3	19	BLACKPOOL	0-0			1	2	3	4	5	6	7	8		10	11	9							
4	26	Gainsborough Trinity	0-0			1	2	3	4	5	6	11		9	10		8	7						
5	3 Oct	BURTON UNITED	1-0		Blow	1	2	3	4	5	6	11		9	10		8	7						
6	10	Bristol City	1-3		O'Donnell	1	2		4	5	6	10	8	9		11		7	3					
7	17	MANCHESTER UNITED	0-0			1	2	3	4	5	6		8	9	10	11		7						
8	24	Glossop	0-5			1	2	3	4	5	6		8	9	10	11		7						
9	7 Nov	Arsenal	0-4			1		3	4	9	6	10				11	8	7	5	2				
10	21	Burslem Port Vale	2-2		Watson(2)	1		3	4		6	9	7		10	11	8		5	2				
11	28	Stockport County	0-4			1		3	4		6	8	7		10	11			5	2	9			
12	5 Dec	CHESTERFIELD	0-2				2	3	4		6	8	7		10	11			5		9	1		
13	12	Bolton Wanderers	2-1		C.F.Simpson, Parker		2	3	4		6	8	7		10	11			5		9	1		
14	19	BURNLEY	3-1		Brown, C.F.Simpson, Parker		2		4	3	6	8	7		10	11			5		9	1		
15	25	STOCKPORT COUNTY	3-1		Brown, C.F.Simpson(2)		2	3	4		6	8	7		10	11			5		9	1		
16	26	Preston North End	1-2		Brown		2	3	4		6		7		10	11	8		5		9	1		
17	28	BARNSLEY	0-0				2	3	4		6		7		10	11	8		5		9	1		
18	2 Jan	Grimsby Town	1-1		O'Donnell		2	3	4		6	8	7		10	11			5		9	1		
19	9	LEICESTER FOSSE	6-1		O'Donnell(3), C.F.Simpson, Brown(2)		2	3	4		6	8	7		10	11			5		9	1		
20	16	Blackpool	1-2		C.F.Simpson		2	3			6	8	7		10	11			5		9	1	4	
21	23	GAINSBOROUGH TRINITY	0-1			1	2	3	4		6	8	7		10	11			5		9	1		
22	30	Burton United	2-5		Brown, Parker		2	3	4		6	8	7		10	11			5		9	1		
23	13 Feb	Manchester United	0-2				2	3	4		6	8	7		10	11			5		9	1		
24	20	GLOSSOP	3-1		Brown(2), Groves		2	3	4		6	8	7		10	11			5		9	1		
25	27	Bradford City	1-2		O'Donnell		2	3	4		6	8	7		10	11			5		9	1		
26	5 Mar	ARSENAL	0-2				2	3	4		6	8	7		10	11			5		9	1		
27	7	BRISTOL CITY	2-6		C.F.Simpson(2)	1	2	3		4	6	8				11		7	5		9			10
28	12	Barnsley	1-2		Watson		2	3	4		6	8	10			11		7	5		9	1		
29	19	Burslem Port Vale	3-2		Watson, C.F.Simpson, O'Donnell		2	3	4		6	8	7		10	11			5		9	1		
30	1 Apr	BRADFORD CITY	1-0		Brown		2	3	4		6	8	7		10	11			5		9	1		
31	2	Chesterfield	1-0		O'Donnell		2	3	4	6		8	7		10	11			5		9	1		
32	9	BOLTON WANDERERS	1-0		O'Donnell		2	3	4	6		8	7		10	11			5		9	1		
33	16	Burnley	1-3		Watson			3	4	2		8	7		10	11			5		9	1	6	
34	23	PRESTON NORTH END	0-0					3	4	2		9	7		10	11		8	5			1	6	
				Apps.		13	29	32	32	15	30	30	30	6	32	30	6	11	27	3	23	21	3	1
				Goals			2			1		10	5		11	3					9			

F.A. CUP

| 4QF | 31 Oct | CHESTERFIELD | 0-2 | | | 1 | 2 | 3 | 4 | 5 | 6 | 7 | 8 | 9 | 10 | 11 | | | | | | | | |

LINCOLNSHIRE CUP

| SF | 16 Mar | GRIMSBY TOWN | 2-1 | | Groves, Blow | | 2 | 3 | 4 | | 6 | 8 | 10 | | 11 | | | 7 | 5 | | 9 | 1 | | |
| F | 26 Apr | Gainsborough Trinity * | 1-2 | | O'Donnell | | | 3 | 4 | 2 | | 8 | 7 | | 10 | 11 | | | 5 | | 9 | 1 | 6 | |

* played at Blundell Park, Grimsby

Final League Table

		Pl.	Home				Away				F.	A.	Pts
			W	D	L	F	A	W	D	L	F	A			
1	Preston North End	34	13	4	0	38	10	7	6	4	24	14	62	24	50
2	Woolwich Arsenal	34	15	2	0	67	5	6	5	6	24	17	91	22	49
3	Manchester United	34	14	2	1	42	14	6	6	5	23	19	65	33	48
4	Bristol City	34	14	2	1	53	12	4	4	9	20	29	73	41	42
5	Burnley	34	12	2	3	31	20	3	7	7	19	35	50	55	39
6	Grimsby Town	34	12	5	0	39	12	2	3	12	11	37	50	49	36
7	Bolton Wanderers	34	10	3	4	38	11	2	7	8	21	30	59	41	34
8	Barnsley	34	10	5	2	25	12	1	5	11	13	45	38	57	32
9	Gainsborough Trin.	34	10	2	5	34	17	4	1	12	19	43	53	60	31
10	Bradford City	34	8	5	4	30	25	4	2	11	15	34	45	59	31
11	Chesterfield	34	8	5	4	22	12	3	3	11	15	33	37	45	30
12	*Lincoln City*	34	9	4	4	25	18	2	4	11	16	40	41	58	30
13	Burslem Port Vale	34	10	3	4	44	20	0	6	11	10	32	54	52	29
14	Burton United	34	8	6	3	33	16	3	1	13	12	45	45	61	29
15	Blackpool	34	8	2	7	25	27	3	3	11	15	40	40	67	27
16	Stockport County	34	7	7	3	28	23	1	4	12	12	49	40	72	27
17	Glossop	34	7	4	6	42	25	3	2	12	15	39	57	64	26
18	Leicester Fosse	34	5	8	4	26	21	1	2	14	16	61	42	82	22

Back : Jackson (director), Hindson, Higgins, Groves, Webb, Snarey, Pallister, Waterson (trainer), Bentley (groundsman).
Centre : Dennis O'Donnell, Fraser, Billy Simpson, Blow, Calderhead (secretary/ manager), Parker.
Front : Watson, Brown, Freddy Simpson, Elmore.

SEASON 1904-05
DIVISION TWO

No.	Date	Opposition	Res.	Att.	Goalscorers	Buist A.G.	Laverick C.	Pallister W.	Fraser G.	Simpson W.	Blow E.P.	Brown E.H.	O'Donnell D.	Martin J.	O'Donnell M.	Watson W.	Simpson C.F.	Wield T.W.	Hood R.P.	Sharp B.C.	Asnip T.	Beaumont S.
1	3 Sep	Doncaster Rovers	2-0		D.O'Donnell, Watson	1	2	3	4	5	6	7	8	9	10	11						
2	10	GAINSBOROUGH TRINITY	4-1		D.O'Donnell(3), M.O'Donnell	1	2	3	4	5	6	7	8	9	10	11						
3	17	Burton United	1-2		Martin	1	2	3	4	5	6		8	9	10	11						
4	24	LIVERPOOL	0-2			1	2	3	4	5	6	9	8		10	7	11					
5	1 Oct	Burslem Port Vale	1-0		M.O'Donnell	1	2	3	4	5		9	8		10	7	11	6				
6	8	BRISTOL CITY	1-3		M.O'Donnell	1	2	3	4	5		9	8		10	7	11	6				
7	15	Manchester United	0-2			1	2		4	3	6	9			10	7			5	8	11	
8	22	GLOSSOP	3-0		Watson(2), Martin	1	2		4	3	6			10	9		7	11	5	8		
9	29	Chesterfield	0-0			1	2		4	3	6			11	9	10	7		5	8		
10	5 Nov	BRADFORD CITY	1-1		Martin	1	2		4	3	6	7	8	9	10	11			5			
11	12	Bolton Wanderers	1-4		Martin	1	2		4	3	6		11	8	9	10	7		5			
12	19	Leicester Fosse	1-0		M.O'Donnell	1	2		4	3	6		11	8	9	10	7		5			
13	26	BARNSLEY	2-0		M.O'Donnell, D.O'Donnell	1	2		4	3	6			8	9	10	7		5			11
14	3 Dec	West Bromwich Albion	0-2			1	2		4	3	6			8	9	10	7		5			11
15	17	Grimsby Town	0-1			1	2		4	3	6			8	9	10	7	11	5			
16	24	BLACKPOOL	1-0		M.O'Donnell	1	2		4	3	6			8	9	10	7	11	5			
17	26	BOLTON WANDERERS	0-2			1	2		4	3	6			8	9	10	7	11	5			
18	27	BURTON UNITED	3-1		M.O'Donnell, D.O'Donnell, Martin	1	2		4	3	6	7		8	9	10		11	5			
19	31	DONCASTER ROVERS	3-0		Martin(2), D.O'Donnell	1	2		4	3	6	7		8	9	10		11	5			
20	7 Jan	Gainsborough Trinity	0-2			1	2		4	3	6	7		8	9	10		11	5			
21	21	Liverpool	1-1		C.F.Simpson	1	2		4	3	6			8	9	10	7	11	5			
22	28	BURSLEM PORT VALE	3-3		Martin, Watson, D.O'Donnell	1	2		4	3	6			8	9		7	11	5			10
23	11 Feb	MANCHESTER UNITED	3-0		Martin, C.F.Simpson(2)	1	2		4	3	6			8	9	10	7	11	5			
24	18	Glossop	2-3		Martin(2)	1	2		4	3	6			8	9			11	5		7	
25	25	CHESTERFIELD	0-0			1	2		4	3	6			8	9	10		11	5		7	
26	4 Mar	Bradford City	0-0			1	2		4	3	6			8	9	10	7	11	5			
27	18	LEICESTER FOSSE	5-1		Martin, D.O'Donnell(3), C.F.Simpson	1	2		4	3	6		10	8	9		7	11	5			
28	25	Barnsley	1-2		M.O'Donnell	1	2	3	4		6			8	9	10	7	11	5			
29	1 Apr	WEST BROMWICH ALBION	0-2			1	2		4	3	6			8	9	10	7	11	5			
30	8	Burnley	1-2		D.O'Donnell	1	2		4	3	6			8	9	10	7	11	5			
31	15	GRIMSBY TOWN	0-0			1	2		4	3	6			8	9	10	7	11	5			
32	21	BURNLEY	2-0		Watson, D.O'Donnell	1	2		4	3	6			8	9	10	7	11	5			
33	22	Blackpool	0-1			1	2		4	3	6				9	10	7	11	5	8		
34	25	Bristol City	0-2			1	2		4	3	6			10	9		7	11	5	8		
					Apps.	34	34	7	34	33	32	14	32	30	30	29	24	2	28	5	1	5
					Goals								13	12	8	5	4					

F.A. CUP

6QF	10 Dec	Watford	1-1		Martin	1	2		4	3	6			8	9	10	7	11	5
6QFr	14	WATFORD	2-1		M.O'Donnell, D.O'Donnell	1	2		4	3	6			8	9	10	7	11	5
Int QF	14 Jan	Burnley	1-1		M.O'Donnell	1	2		4	3	6			8	9	10	7	11	5
Int QFr	18	BURNLEY	3-2		Watson, M.O'Donnell, C.F.Simpson	1	2		4	3	6			8	9	10	7	11	5
1R	4 Feb	MANCHESTER CITY	1-2		D.O'Donnell	1	2		4	3	6			8	9	10	7	11	5

LINCOLNSHIRE CUP

SF	5 Apr	GAINSBOROUGH TRINITY	2-3		Watson, Brown	1	2		4	3	6	10	8	9			7	11	5

Final League Table

		Pl.	Home						Away					F.	A.	Pts
			W	D	L	F	A	W	D	L	F	A				
1	Liverpool	34	14	3	0	60	12	13	1	3	33	13	93	25	58
2	Bolton Wanderers	34	15	0	2	53	16	12	2	3	34	16	87	32	56
3	Manchester United	34	16	0	1	60	10	8	5	4	21	20	81	30	53
4	Bristol City	34	12	3	2	40	12	7	1	9	26	33	66	45	42
5	Chesterfield	34	9	6	2	26	11	5	5	7	18	24	44	35	39
6	Gainsborough Trin.	34	11	4	2	32	15	3	4	10	29	43	61	58	36
7	Barnsley	34	11	4	2	29	13	3	1	13	9	43	38	56	33
8	Bradford City	34	8	5	4	31	20	4	3	10	14	29	45	49	32
9	**Lincoln City**	**34**	**9**	**4**	**4**	**31**	**16**	**3**	**3**	**11**	**11**	**24**	**42**	**40**	**31**
10	West Bromwich Alb.	34	8	2	7	28	20	5	2	10	28	28	56	48	30
11	Burnley	34	10	1	6	31	21	2	5	10	12	31	43	52	30
12	Glossop	34	7	5	5	23	14	3	5	9	14	32	37	46	30
13	Grimsby Town	34	9	3	5	23	14	2	5	10	11	32	33	46	30
14	Leicester Fosse	34	8	3	6	30	25	3	4	10	10	30	40	55	29
15	Blackpool	34	8	5	4	26	15	1	5	11	10	33	36	48	28
16	Burslem Port Vale	34	7	4	6	28	25	3	3	11	19	47	47	72	27
17	Burton United	34	7	2	8	20	19	1	2	14	10	55	30	84	20
18	Doncaster Rovers	34	3	2	12	12	32	0	0	17	11	49	23	81	8

Back : Giles (director), Calderhead (secretary/manager), Laverick, Buist, Pallister, Waterson (trainer), Quincey (director), Bentley (groundsman).
Centre : Fraser, Billy Simpson, Blow.
Front : Brown, Dennis O'Donnell, Martin, Magnus O'Donnell, Watson.

SEASON 1905-06
DIVISION TWO

No.	Date	Opposition	Res.	Att.	Goalscorers
1	2 Sep	BURSLEM PORT VALE	3-1		Soulsby, Machin, O'Donnell
2	9	Barnsley	2-4		Simpson, Martin
3	11	Leeds City	2-2		Dixon, Martin
4	16	CLAPTON ORIENT	2-3		F.Taylor, Dixon
5	23	Burnley	1-2		Martin
6	30	LEEDS CITY	1-2		F.Taylor
7	7 Oct	Burton United	0-2		
8	14	CHELSEA	1-4		Watson
9	21	Gainsborough Trinity	3-2		Martin, Watson, O'Donnell
10	28	BRISTOL CITY	0-3		
11	4 Nov	Manchester United	1-2		C.F.Simpson
12	11	GLOSSOP	4-1		Watson, C.F.Simpson(3)
13	18	Stockport County	0-3		
14	25	BLACKPOOL	1-1		Watson
15	2 Dec	Bradford City	2-2		Martin, Machin
16	9	WEST BROMWICH ALBION	1-2		O'Donnell
17	16	Leicester Fosse	1-3		Machin
18	23	HULL CITY	1-4		C.F.Simpson
19	25	GRIMSBY TOWN	3-1		C.F.Simpson(2), Machin
20	26	CHESTERFIELD	0-1		
21	30	Burslem Port Vale	1-3		Martin
22	6 Jan	BARNSLEY	4-1		Fairgray, Martin, Fraser, Machin
23	20	Clapton Orient	0-3		
24	27	BURNLEY	5-0		Martin, Machin(2), C.F.Simpson, Fairgray
25	10 Feb	BURTON UNITED	5-1		Kelly(2), Machin(2), Martin
26	17	Chelsea	2-4		Martin, Machin
27	24	GAINSBOROUGH TRINITY	3-0		Machin, Watson, Martin
28	3 Mar	Bristol City	0-1		
29	10	BRADFORD CITY	5-0		Martin(3), Fraser, Watson
30	17	Glossop	2-2		Machin(2)
31	24	STOCKPORT COUNTY	2-0		Kelly, Watson
32	31	Blackpool	0-2		
33	13 Apr	Grimsby Twn	2-2		Watson, OG
34	14	West Bromwich Albion	1-1		Fairgray
35	16	Chesterfield	2-1		Martin(2)
36	21	LEICESTER FOSSE	3-1		Machin, Martin, Hood
37	25	MANCHESTER UNITED	2-3		Machin(2)
38	28	Hull City	1-2		Martin

1 own goal

F.A. CUP

1R	13 Jan	STOCKPORT COUNTY	4-2		C.F.Simpson, Martin(2), Watson
2R	3 Feb	Brentford	0-3		

LINCOLNSHIRE CUP

SF	28 Mar	Grimsby Town	0-1		

Final League Table

		Pl.	Home W D L F A	Away W D L F A	F.	A.	Pts
1	Bristol City	38	17 1 1 43 8	13 5 1 40 20	83	28	66
2	Manchester United	38	15 3 1 55 13	13 3 3 35 15	90	28	62
3	Chelsea	38	15 2 2 58 16	9 5 5 32 21	90	37	53
4	West Bromwich Alb.	38	13 4 2 53 16	9 4 6 26 20	79	36	52
5	Hull City	38	10 5 4 38 21	9 1 9 29 33	67	54	44
6	Leeds City	38	15 1 5 38 19	6 4 9 21 28	59	47	43
7	Leicester Fosse	38	10 3 6 30 21	5 9 5 23 27	53	48	42
8	Grimsby Town	38	11 5 3 33 13	4 3 12 13 33	46	46	40
9	Burnley	38	9 4 6 26 23	6 4 9 16 30	42	53	38
10	Stockport County	38	11 6 2 36 16	2 3 14 8 40	44	56	35
11	Bradford City	38	7 4 8 21 22	6 4 9 25 38	46	60	34
12	Barnsley	38	11 4 4 45 17	1 5 13 15 45	60	62	33
13	*Lincoln City*	*38*	*10 1 8 46 29*	*2 5 12 23 43*	*69*	*72*	*30*
14	Blackpool	38	8 3 8 22 21	2 6 11 15 41	37	62	29
15	Gainsborough Trin.	38	10 2 7 35 22	2 2 15 9 35	44	57	28
16	Glossop	38	9 4 6 36 28	1 4 14 13 43	49	71	28
17	Burslem Port Vale	38	10 4 5 34 25	2 0 17 15 57	49	82	28
18	Chesterfield	38	8 4 7 26 24	2 4 13 14 48	40	72	28
19	Burton United	38	9 4 6 26 20	1 2 16 8 47	34	67	26
20	Clapton Orient	38	6 4 9 19 22	1 3 15 16 56	35	78	21

Back: Laverick, Buist, Billy Simpson, Calderhead (sec-manager)
Centre: Watson, Waterson (trainer), Fraser, Hood, Wield, Dixon
Front: Soulsby, Machin, Martin, Magnus O'Donnell, Freddy Simpson

SEASON 1906-07
DIVISION TWO

No.	Date	Opposition	Res.	Att.	Goalscorers
1	1 Sep	Burton United	4-3		McLeod(2), Machin, C.F.Simpson
2	8	GRIMSBY TOWN	2-1		Watson, McLeod
3	10	Leeds City	1-1		C.F.Simpson
4	15	Burslem Port Vale	2-4		Machin, C.F.Simpson
5	22	BURNLEY	1-2		McLeod
6	29	LEEDS CITY	1-1		McLeod
7	6 Oct	BARNSLEY	1-0		McLeod
8	13	Chelsea	0-2		
9	20	WOLVERHAMPTON WANDS.	0-4		
10	27	Clapton Orient	1-1		Taylor
11	3 Nov	GAINSBOROUGH TRINITY	4-0		Posnett, McLeod(2), Taylor
12	10	Stockport County	0-1		
13	17	HULL CITY	0-1		
14	24	Glossop	1-2		Machin
15	1 Dec	BLACKPOOL	0-1		
16	8	Bradford City	0-3		
17	15	WEST BROMWICH ALBION	2-1		Nisbet, Watson
18	22	Leicester Fosse	0-3		
19	25	CHESTERFIELD	1-0		Fairgray
20	29	BURTON UNITED	2-0		Dixon, Watson
21	5 Jan	Grimsby Town	0-4		
22	19	BURSLEM PORT VALE	4-0		Watson(2), Barrick, OG
23	26	Burnley	1-5		Barrick
24	9 Feb	Barnsley	2-6		Watson(2)
25	16	CHELSEA	0-5		
26	23	Wolverhampton Wanderers	0-3		
27	2 Mar	CLAPTON ORIENT	3-0		Machin(2), Fairgray
28	9	Gainsborough Trinity	1-2		Taylor
29	16	STOCKPORT COUNTY	3-1		C.F.Simpson, Taylor, Watson
30	23	Hull City	2-1		Taylor, C.F.Simpson
31	29	NOTTINGHAM FOREST	1-2		Watson
32	30	GLOSSOP	2-1		Taylor(2)
33	1 Apr	Chesterfield	0-1		
34	6	Blackpool	0-2		
35	13	BRADFORD CITY	0-2		
36	20	West Bromwich Albion	1-2		Fairgray
37	24	Nottingham Forest	1-3		Watson
38	27	LEICESTER CITY	2-2		Langham(2)

1 own goal

F.A. CUP

1R	12 Jan	CHELSEA	2-2		Watson, Dixon
1Rr	16	Chelsea *	1-0		Fairgray
2R	2 Feb	Derby County	0-1		

* after extra time

LINCOLNSHIRE CUP

| SF | 20 Mar | Gainsborough Trinity | 3-4 | | C.F.Simpson(2), Bacon |

Final League Table

		Pl.	W	D	L	F	A	W	D	L	F	A	F.	A.	Pts
1	Nottingham Forest	38	16	2	1	43	13	12	2	5	31	23	74	36	60
2	Chelsea	38	18	0	1	55	10	8	5	6	25	24	80	34	57
3	Leicester Fosse	38	15	3	1	44	12	5	5	9	18	27	62	39	48
4	West Bromwich Alb.	38	15	2	2	62	15	6	3	10	21	30	83	45	47
5	Bradford City	38	14	2	3	46	21	7	3	9	24	32	70	53	47
6	Wolverhampton W.	38	13	4	2	49	16	4	3	12	17	34	66	53	41
7	Burnley	38	12	3	4	45	13	5	2	12	17	34	62	47	40
8	Barnsley	38	14	2	3	56	21	1	6	12	17	34	73	55	38
9	Hull City	38	11	2	6	41	20	4	5	10	24	37	65	57	37
10	Leeds City	38	10	5	4	38	26	3	5	11	17	37	55	63	36
11	Grimsby Town	38	13	2	4	34	16	3	1	15	23	46	57	62	35
12	Stockport County	38	8	8	3	26	12	4	3	12	16	40	42	52	35
13	Blackpool	38	9	4	6	25	19	2	7	10	8	32	33	51	33
14	Gainsborough Trin.	38	12	3	4	33	20	2	2	15	12	52	45	72	33
15	Glossop	38	11	4	5	32	21	2	3	14	21	58	53	79	32
16	Burslem Port Vale	38	11	5	3	45	26	1	2	16	15	57	60	83	31
17	Clapton Orient	38	9	7	3	25	13	2	1	16	20	54	45	67	30
18	Chesterfield	38	10	3	6	36	26	1	4	14	14	40	50	66	29
19	*Lincoln City*	38	10	2	7	29	24	2	2	15	17	49	46	73	28
20	Burton United	38	7	3	9	24	23	1	4	14	10	45	34	68	23

Back : Dixon, Waterson (trainer), Laverick, Buist, Billy Simpson, Calderhead (sec./manager), Kelly.
Centre : Kennedy, Fraser, Hood, Nisbet.
Front : Watson, Fraser, McLeod, Freddy Simpson, Fairgray.

SEASON 1907-08
DIVISION TWO

No.	Date	Opposition	Res.	Att.	Goalscorers
1	2 Sep	Derby County	0-4		
2	7	GRIMSBY TOWN	1-0		C.F.Simpson
3	14	Fulham	1-6		Poppitt
4	16	Burnley	2-1		Brewis, Sharp
5	21	BARNSLEY	0-2		
6	28	Chesterfield	1-2		Brewis
7	5 Oct	BURNLEY	1-3		C.F.Simpson
8	12	Oldham Athletic	0-4		
9	16	FULHAM	2-4		Brewis(2)
10	26	Leeds City	1-2		Brewis
11	2 Nov	WOLVERHAMPTON WANDS.	3-1		Brewis(2), Langham
12	9	Gainsborough Trinity	1-5		C.F.Simpson
13	16	STOCKPORT COUNTY	1-1		Alston
14	30	LEICESTER FOSSE	0-3		
15	7 Dec	Blackpool	3-4		Brewis(2), Langham
16	14	STOKE CITY	1-2		Langham
17	21	West Bromwich Albion	2-5		Langham(2)
18	25	Hull City	3-5		Langham(2), Brewis
19	26	HULL CITY	0-1		
20	28	BRADFORD CITY	2-4		Wilson, Taylor
21	4 Jan	Grimsby Town	2-0		McCann, Brewis
22	18	Barnsley	1-2		Alston
23	25	CHESTERFIELD	4-0		McCann(3), Poppitt
24	1 Feb	Glossop	1-3		Langham
25	8	OLDHAM ATHLETIC	0-2		
26	15	CLAPTON ORIENT	2-2		Langham, Ormiston
27	22	LEEDS CITY	5-0		Langham(2), Wilson(2), McCann
28	29	Wolverhampton Wanderers	0-3		
29	7 Mar	GAINSBOROUGH TRINITY	2-0		Langham, Poppitt
30	14	Stockport County	1-1		Langham
31	21	GLOSSOP	0-1		
32	26	Clapton Orient	0-2		
33	28	Leicester Fosse	0-1		
34	4 Apr	BLACKPOOL	2-0		Wilson, Ormiston
35	11	Stoke City	0-3		
36	17	DERBY COUNTY	1-0		McCann
37	18	WEST BROMWICH ALBION	0-2		
38	25	Bradford City	0-2		

Additional player: T.Bailey 35/9

F.A. CUP

| 1R | 11 Jan | Stoke City | 0-5 | | |

LINCOLNSHIRE CUP

SF	19 Oct	ADELAIDE (LINCOLN)	5-0		Fraser, Brewis(3), Fairley
F	2 Apr	GAINSBOROUGH TRINITY	0-0		
Fr	27	Gainsborough Trinity	3-0		Law, Sharp, Langham

Additional player: R.Aitken SF/3

Final League Table

		Pl.	Home W D L F A	Away W D L F A	F.	A.	Pts
1	Bradford City	38	15 2 2 58 16	9 4 6 32 26	90	42	54
2	Leicester Fosse	38	14 2 3 41 20	7 8 4 31 27	72	47	52
3	Oldham Athletic	38	15 4 0 53 14	7 2 10 23 28	76	42	50
4	Fulham	38	12 2 5 50 14	10 3 6 32 35	82	49	49
5	West Bromwich Alb.	38	13 3 3 38 13	6 6 7 23 26	61	39	47
6	Derby County	38	15 1 3 50 13	6 3 10 27 32	77	45	46
7	Burnley	38	14 3 2 44 14	6 3 10 23 36	67	50	46
8	Hull City	38	15 1 3 50 23	6 3 10 23 39	73	62	46
9	Wolverhampton W.	38	11 4 4 34 11	4 3 12 16 34	50	45	37
10	Stoke	38	11 5 3 43 13	5 0 14 14 39	57	52	37
11	Gainsborough Trin.	38	9 4 6 31 28	5 3 11 16 43	47	71	35
12	Leeds City	38	6 2 11 33 28	6 2 14 20 47	53	65	32
13	Stockport County	38	9 4 6 35 26	3 4 12 13 41	48	67	32
14	Clapton Orient	38	10 4 5 28 13	1 5 13 12 52	40	65	32
15	Blackpool	38	11 3 5 33 19	0 6 13 18 39	51	58	31
16	Barnsley	38	8 3 8 31 4	4 2 13 23 37	54	68	30
17	Glossop	38	9 5 5 36 26	2 3 14 18 48	54	74	30
18	Grimsby Town	38	8 5 6 27 24	3 3 13 16 47	43	71	30
19	Chesterfield	38	6 6 7 33 38	0 5 14 13 54	46	92	23
20	**Lincoln City**	**38**	**7 2 10 27 28**	**2 1 16 19 55**	**46**	**83**	**21**

Back: Waterson (trainer), Hood, Saunders, Buist, Poppitt, Aitken, Law.
Centre: Langham, Brewis, Alston, Nisbet, Kennedy, Freddy Simpson.
Front: Fraser, Fairgray.

SEASON 1908-09
MIDLAND LEAGUE

No.	Date	Opposition	Res.	Att.	Goalscorers
1	1 Sep	Sheffield Wednesday Res.	1-5		Watson
2	3	Nottingham Forest Res.	1-0		Watson
3	5	Leicester Fosse Res.	2-1		McCann, Langham
4	12	NOTTINGHAM FOREST RES	5-1		McCann(2), Langham(2), Watson
5	19	Newark	2-1		Langham, Ormiston
6	26	MEXBOROUGH TOWN	5-1		McCann(2), Foster, Langham(2)
7	3 Oct	NEWARK	0-0		
8	7	ROTHERHAM TOWN	2-1		Langham, Watson
9	10	Sheffield United Res.	1-3		McCann
10	20	Grimsby Town Res.	2-0		Langham(2)
11	24	DONCASTER ROVERS	7-0		Langham(5), Watson(2)
12	31	DENABY UNITED	1-0		Langham
13	7 Nov	CHESTERFIELD RES.	3-0		Grundy, Robinson, Langham
14	19	Notts County Res.	3-0		Watson, Langham, Barrell
15	28	Worksop Town	2-0		Foster(2)
16	12 Dec	LEEDS CITY RES.	3-1		Langham(3)
17	19	LEICESTER FOSSE RES.	3-0		Barrell, Ormiston, Langham
18	25	NOTTS COUNTY RES.	3-1		Barrell, Watson, Langham
19	30	Gainsborough Trinity Res.	1-1		Barrell
20	2 Jan	Hull City Res.	1-3		Grundy
21	5	Bradford City Res.	2-2		Barrell, Morris
22	9	BARNSLEY RES.	1-1		Foster
23	21	Rotherham Town	2-1		Barrell, Watson
24	23	BRADFORD CITY RES.	2-4		Watson, Morris
25	30	SHEFFIELD UNITED RES.	1-0		Morris
26	6 Feb	Denaby United	3-2		Morris(2), Ormiston
27	20	Leeds City Res.	5-2		Barrell(3), Wilson, Watson
28	27	ROTHERHAM COUNTY	2-1		Watson, Foster
29	13 Mar	Chesterfield Res.	2-1		Grundy(2)
30	20	WORKSOP TOWN	2-1		Foster, Watson
31	27	Doncaster Rovers	0-0		
32	3 Apr	GRIMSBY TOWN RES.	3-2		Wadsley(2), Ormiston
33	10	Mexborough Town	3-0		Nisbet, Wadsley(2)
34	12	GAINSBOROUGH TRIN. RES	2-0		Barrell, Grundy
35	14	HULL CITY RES.	2-0		Morris, Watson
36	17	Barnsley Res.	1-0		Foster
37	21	SHEFFIELD WED. RES.	1-0		Watson
38	24	Rotherham County	4-2		Morris(2), Grundy, Wadsley

UNITED LEAGUE NORTHERN DIVISION

1	9 Sep	NORWICH CITY	0-1		
2	17	Norwich City	0-1		
3	28	Walsall	2-2		Robinson, McCann
4	2 Oct	Grantham Avenue	3-2		Watson(2), Grundy
5	14	GRANTHAM AVENUE	5-1		Langham(4), Watson
6	2 Nov	Rotherham Town	0-3		
7	14	Peterborough City	5-4		Langham(4), Watson
8	26 Dec	ROTHERHAM TOWN	2-1		Morris, Watson
9	10 Feb	PETERBOROUGH CITY	4-1		Morris, Watson(2), OG
10	10 Mar	WALSALL	5-0		Ormiston, Wilson, Wadsley(2), Watson
11	18	Coventry City	2-2		Watson(2)
12	9 Apr	COVENTRY CITY	4-0		Ormiston, OG, Morris(2)

2 own goals

F.A. CUP

| 5QF | 5 Dec | STOCKTON | 1-0 | | Watson |
| 1R | 16 Jan | Liverpool | 1-5 | | Morris |

LINCOLNSHIRE CUP

| SF | 23 Sep | Scunthorpe | 2-0 | | Watson, Langham |
| F | 28 Dec | GRIMSBY TOWN | 1-2 | | Langham |

Final League Table

		P	W	D	L	F	A	Pts
1	**Lincoln City**	**38**	**29**	**5**	**4**	**86**	**38**	**63**
2	Rotherham Town	38	22	6	10	78	53	50
3	Bradford City Res.	38	20	7	11	76	51	47
4	Barnsley Res.	38	16	12	10	68	53	44
5	Denaby United	38	18	8	12	59	49	44
6	The Wednesday Res.	38	17	8	13	80	45	42
7	Hull City Res.	38	17	7	14	79	66	41
8	Sheffield United Res.	38	16	8	14	76	63	40
9	Rotherham County	38	19	2	17	77	67	40
10	Grimsby Town Res.	38	17	5	16	69	66	39
11	Doncaster Rovers	38	18	3	17	50	58	39
12	Mexborough Town	38	13	8	17	57	88	34
13	Leicester Fosse Res.	38	13	7	18	87	70	33
14	Nottingham For. Res.	38	15	2	21	66	92	32
15	Newark	38	10	11	17	51	79	31
16	Notts County Res.	38	12	6	20	64	74	30
17	Gainsborough T. Res.	38	10	9	19	54	62	29
18	Leeds City Res.	38	12	4	22	56	90	28
19	Chesterfield T. Res.	38	9	10	19	55	101	28
20	Worksop Town	38	10	6	22	73	96	26

SEASON 1909-10
DIVISION TWO

No.	Date	Opposition	Res.	Att.	Goalscorers
1	1 Sep	Leeds City	0-5		
2	4	GRIMSBY TOWN	0-0		
3	11	Manchester City	2-6		Hibbert, Scanlon
4	18	LEICESTER FOSSE	3-1		Barrell, Scanlon, Wadsley
5	25	Bradford Park Avenue	0-4		
6	29	WEST BROMWICH ALBION	0-3		
7	2 Oct	Clapton Orient	2-1		Barrell, Foster
8	9	BLACKPOOL	2-2		Barrell, Wilson
9	16	Hull City	0-0		
10	23	DERBY COUNTY	2-3		McKenzie, Yule
11	30	Stockport County	1-1		Wilson
12	6 Nov	GLOSSOP	1-2		Langham
13	13	Birmingham	0-1		
14	11 Dec	Fulham	1-1		Hunter
15	18	BURNLEY	0-0		
16	25	GAINSBOROUGH TRINITY	4-0		Hunter(2), Yule, Langham
17	27	Wolverhampton Wanderers	2-4		Langham(2)
18	28	LEEDS CITY	0-0		
19	1 Jan	Gainsborough Trinity	0-0		
20	3	Oldham Athletic	1-6		Groves
21	8	Grimsby Town	2-1		Yule(2)
22	22	MANCHESTER CITY	0-2		
23	29	Leicester Fosse	1-4		Hunter
24	12 Feb	CLAPTON ORIENT	4-0		Barrell, Langham, Gardner, Hunter
25	19	Blackpool	0-3		
26	26	HULL CITY	1-3		Langham
27	2 Mar	BRADFORD PARK AVENUE	1-1		Hunter
28	5	Derby County	0-2		
29	12	STOCKPORT COUNTY	1-0		Clarke
30	19	Glossop	1-0		Yule
31	25	WOLVERHAMPTON WANDS.	1-0		McKenzie
32	26	BIRMINGHAM	3-2		McKenzie(2), Scanlon
33	28	Barnsley	1-2		Hunter
34	2 Apr	West Bromwich Albion	1-1		McKenzie
35	9	OLDHAM ATHLETIC	0-2		
36	16	BARNSLEY	2-1		Hunter, Fraser
37	23	FULHAM	2-2		McKenzie, Yule
38	30	Burnley	0-3		

F.A. CUP

| 4QF | 20 Nov | Crewe Alexandra | 1-2 | | McKenzie |

LINCOLNSHIRE CUP

SF	10 Nov	CLEETHORPES TOWN	0-0		
SFr	23	Cleethorpes Town	7-0		McKenzie(5), Gardner, Scanlon
F	5 Feb	GRIMSBY TOWN	4-0		Langham(2), Clarke, Hunter

Final League Table

		Pl.	Home W D L F A	Away W D L F A	F.	A.	Pts
1	Manchester City	38	15 2 2 51 17	8 6 5 30 23	81	40	54
2	Oldham Athletic	38	15 2 2 47 9	8 5 6 32 30	79	39	53
3	Hull City	38	13 4 2 52 19	10 3 6 28 27	80	46	53
4	Derby County	38	15 2 2 46 15	7 7 5 26 32	72	47	53
5	Leicester Fosse	38	15 2 2 60 20	5 2 12 19 38	79	58	44
6	Glossop	38	14 1 4 42 18	4 6 9 22 39	64	57	43
7	Fulham	38	9 7 3 28 13	5 6 8 23 30	51	43	41
8	Wolverhampton W.	38	14 3 2 51 22	3 3 13 13 41	64	63	40
9	Barnsley	38	15 3 1 48 15	1 4 14 14 44	62	59	39
10	Bradford Park Ave.	38	12 1 6 47 28	5 3 11 17 31	64	59	38
11	West Bromwich Alb.	38	8 5 6 30 23	8 0 11 28 33	58	56	37
12	Blackpool	38	7 5 24 18 7	1 11 26 34	50	52	36
13	Stockport County	38	9 6 4 37 20	4 2 13 13 27	50	47	34
14	Burnley	38	12 2 5 43 21	2 4 13 19 40	62	61	34
15	Lincoln City	38	7 6 6 27 24	3 5 11 15 45	42	69	31
16	Clapton Orient	38	10 4 5 26 15	2 2 15 11 45	37	60	30
17	Leeds City	38	8 4 7 30 33	2 3 14 16 47	46	80	27
18	Gainsborough Trin.	38	8 8 3 22 21	2 3 14 11 54	33	75	26
19	Grimsby Town	38	8 3 8 31 19	1 3 15 19 58	50	77	24
20	Birmingham	38	7 4 8 28 26	1 3 15 14 52	42	78	23

Back: Bentley (groundsman), Kirk, Jackson, Fern, Whelpton, Wield, Wilson, Marston (trainer).
Centre: Fraser, Bavin, Gardner, Robson, Hibbert, Nisbet.
Front: Foster, Moxon, Scanlon, Groves, Greig, Barrell, McKenzie, Grundy, Lindley.

SEASON 1910-11
DIVISION TWO

No.	Date	Opposition	Res.	Att.	Goalscorers
1	1 Sep	BRADFORD PARK AVENUE	0-0		
2	3	Burnley	1-3		Costigan
3	10	GAINSBOROUGH TRINITY	0-0		
4	14	GLOSSOP	2-2		Robertson, Gardner
5	17	Leeds City	1-0		Yule
6	24	STOCKPORT COUNTY	2-0		Reid, Platts
7	1 Oct	Derby County	0-5		
8	8	BARNSLEY	1-0		OG
9	15	Leicester Fosse	0-2		
10	22	WOLVERHAMPTON WANDS.	1-5		Haycock
11	29	Chelsea	0-7		
12	5 Nov	CLAPTON ORIENT	0-0		
13	12	Blackpool	1-5		Haycock
14	26	BOLTON WANDERERS	1-3		Haycock
15	10 Dec	BIRMINGHAM	0-1		
16	17	West Bromwich Albion	0-3		
17	24	HULL CITY	1-4		Platts
18	27	HUDDERSFIELD TOWN	2-2		Barrell, Platts
19	31	BURNLEY	1-0		Haycock
20	2 Jan	Bradford Park Avneue	0-6		
21	7	Gainsborough Trinity	0-1		
22	21	LEEDS CITY	1-1		Gardner
23	28	Stockport County	2-3		Garratty(2)
24	8 Feb	DERBY COUNTY	0-2		
25	11	Barnsley	2-2		Barrell, Yule
26	18	LEICESTER FOSSE	2-0		Robson, Gardner
27	4 Mar	CHELSEA	0-0		
28	11	Clapton Orient	0-2		
29	18	BLACKPOOL	0-1		
30	25	Glossop	0-2		
31	1 Apr	Bolton Wanderers	1-3		Barrell
32	8	Huddersfield Town	1-1		Haycock
33	14	FULHAM	1-0		Reid
34	15	Birmingham	1-0		Comrie
35	17	Fulham	0-0		
36	22	WEST BROMWICH ALBION	1-2		Reid
37	24	Wolverhampton Wanderers	1-2		OG
38	29	Hull City	1-2		Barrell

2 own goals

F.A. CUP

4QF	19 Nov	Huddersfield Town	1-1		Foster
4QFr	23	HUDDERSFIELD TOWN	1-0		Haycock
5QF	3 Dec	Stoke City	0-4		

LINCOLNSHIRE CUP

SF	7 Mar	Grimsby Town	1-2		Reid

Final League Table

		Pl.	Home W D L F A	Away W D L F A	F. A. Pts
1	West Bromwich Alb.	38	14 2 3 40 18	8 7 4 27 23	67 41 53
2	Bolton Wanderers	38	17 2 0 53 12	4 7 8 16 28	69 40 51
3	Chelsea	38	17 2 0 48 7	3 7 9 23 28	71 35 49
4	Clapton Orient	38	14 4 1 28 7	5 3 11 16 28	44 35 45
5	Hull City	38	8 10 1 38 21	6 6 7 17 18	55 39 44
6	Derby County	38	11 5 3 48 24	6 3 10 25 28	73 52 42
7	Blackpool	38	10 5 4 29 15	6 5 8 20 23	49 38 42
8	Burnley	38	9 9 1 31 18	4 6 9 14 27	45 45 41
9	Wolverhampton W.	38	10 5 4 26 16	5 3 11 25 36	51 52 38
10	Fulham	38	12 4 3 35 15	3 4 12 17 33	52 48 37
11	Leeds City	38	11 4 4 35 18	4 3 12 23 38	58 56 37
12	Bradford Park Ave.	38	12 4 3 44 18	2 5 12 9 37	53 55 37
13	Huddersfield Town	38	10 4 5 35 21	3 4 12 22 37	57 58 34
14	Glossop	38	11 4 4 36 21	2 4 13 12 41	48 62 34
15	Leicester Fosse	38	12 3 4 37 19	2 2 15 15 43	52 62 33
16	Birmingham	38	10 5 4 23 18	2 1 16 19 46	42 64 32
17	Stockport County	38	10 4 5 27 26	1 4 14 20 53	47 79 30
18	Gainsborough Trin.	38	9 5 5 26 16	0 6 13 11 39	37 55 29
19	Barnsley	38	5 7 7 36 26	2 7 10 16 36	52 62 28
20	Lincoln City	38	5 7 7 16 23	2 3 14 12 49	28 72 24

Back: Hunter, Jackson, Fem, Wilson, Marston (trainer)
Centre: Fraser, Gardner, George Miller
Front: Clarke, Reid, Robertson, Yule, Platts

SEASON 1911-12
CENTRAL LEAGUE

No.	Date	Opposition	Res.	Att.	Goalscorers
1	9 Sep	Blackpool Res.	1-3		Miller
2	16	Manchester United Res.	2-2		Manning, McCubbin
3	23	Bury Res.	1-1		Miller
4	30	BURY RES.	3-2		Barrell, McCubbin, Miller
5	14 Oct	Liverpool Res.	1-1		Miller
6	21	Manchester City Res.	4-0		Barrell(3), McCubbin
7	28	Oldham Athletic Res.	3-1		Miller, Brindley, Gardner
8	4 Nov	Glossop Res.	0-0		
9	11	BLACKPOOL RES.	6-2		Batty(2), Manning(2), Brindley(2)
10	16 Dec	BOLTON WANDERERS RES.	0-0		
11	23	SOUTHPORT CENTRAL	6-0		Gardner, McCubbin(3), Miller(2)
12	25	BURSLEM PORT VALE	1-0		Manning
13	26	Blackburn Rovers Res.	4-4		Batty, Miller(2), McCubbin
14	30	STOCKPORT COUNTY RES.	8-0		Barrell(2), Brindley(2), Batty(3), OG
15	1 Jan	Everton Res.	1-0		McCubbin
16	27	GLOSSOP RES.	4-0		Gardner, Batty, Manning, Miller
17	10 Feb	Stockport County Res.	3-1		McCubbin, Miller(2)
18	17	Crewe Alexandra	4-3		Miller(2), Batty, McCubbin
19	21	MANCHESTER CITY RES.	1-1		Batty
20	24	Preston North End Res.	0-0		
21	2 Mar	PRESTON NORTH END RES.	2-1		Batty, Gardner
22	9	EVERTON RES.	4-1		Miller, Brindley, Batty(2)
23	16	OLDHAM ATHLETIC RES.	6-0		Manning, Batty, McCubbin(4)
24	23	Bolton Wanderers Res.	0-0		
25	25	Burnley Res.	1-5		Batty
26	30	CREWE ALEXANDRA	1-1		McCubbin
27	5 Apr	Burslem Port Vale	1-0		Miller
28	8	BURNLEY RES.	0-0		
29	13	MANCHESTER UNITED RES.	5-0		Miller(2), Manning, McCubbin, Batty
30	15	Southport Central	1-1		Miller
31	20	LIVERPOOL RES.	3-0		Manning(2), Batty
32	27	BLACKBURN ROVERS RES.	4-0		Manning, Miller, Batty, Gardner

1 own goal

F.A. CUP

Round	Date	Opposition	Res.	Att.	Goalscorers
4QF	18 Nov	GRIMSBY TOWN	3-2		Miller, McCubbin(2)
5QF	2 Dec	Crook Town	3-2		Manning, Batty, McCubbin
1R	13 Jan	STOCKPORT COUNTY	2-0		McCubbin, Batty
2R	3 Feb	Wolverhampton Wanderers	1-2		Brindley

LINCOLNSHIRE CUP

Round	Date	Opposition	Res.	Att.	Goalscorers
SF	8 Nov	GAINSBOROUGH TRINITY	2-0		Gardner, Manning
F	6 Mar	Grimsby Town	3-2		Batty, Miller(2)

Final League Table

	P	W	D	L	F	A	Pts
1 Lincoln City	32	18	12	2	81	30	48
2 Port Vale	32	15	12	5	48	23	42
3 Crewe Alexandra	32	14	9	9	65	63	37
4 Everton Res.	32	14	8	10	66	61	36
5 Liverpool Res.	32	13	8	11	68	57	34
6 Bolton Wanderers Res.	32	9	15	8	46	45	33
7 Manchester City Res.	32	14	5	13	56	60	33
8 Manchester United Res.	32	13	6	13	56	60	32
9 Blackpool Res.	32	12	8	12	43	52	32
10 Burnley Res.	32	13	5	14	66	62	31
11 Preston North End Res.	32	10	11	11	50	40	31
12 Blackburn Rovers Res.	32	12	6	14	60	54	30
13 Oldham Athletic Res.	32	12	6	14	60	59	30
14 Bury	32	10	8	14	57	69	28
15 Glossop	32	7	10	15	29	58	24
16 Southport Central	32	8	6	18	48	79	22
17 Stockport County	32	6	9	17	27	61	21

Back: Bentley (trainer), Groves, Jackson, Goldsborough, Fern, Wilson, Wilmot, ------ (asst. groundsman).
Centre: Manning, Fraser, Robson, Hempstead, Gardner, Wield, Cooper, Platts.
Front: Foster, Reid, Durose, Miller, Gerry, Barrell, Batty, Brindley.

SEASON 1912-13
DIVISION TWO

No.	Date	Opposition	Res.	Att.	Goalscorers	Fern T.E.	Jackson A.C.	Wilson W.	Robson M.H.	Barrell G.	Wield T.W.	Manning J.T.	McCubbin A.C.	Miller W.	Hubbard A.	Brindley H.	Gardner A.	Birchall R.	Slade D.	Meunier J.B.	Tierney H.	Platts A.J.	Gibson R.J.	Inskip J.	Atkin A.
1	2 Sep	Wolverhampton Wanderers	0-2			1	2	3	4	5	6	7	8	9	10	11									
2	7	Stockport County	4-2		McCubbin, Miller(2), Manning	1	2	3	4		6	7	8	9	10	11	5								
3	9	LEICESTER FOSSE	3-0		Miller, Barrell(2)	1	2	3	4	10	6	7	8	9			5	11							
4	14	PRESTON NORTH END	0-0			1	2	3	4	10	6	7	8	9			5	11							
5	21	Burnley	1-3		Miller	1	2	3	4		6	7	8	9	10	11	5								
6	28	HULL CITY	1-1		Hubbard	1	2	3	4		6	7	8	9	10	11	5								
7	5 Oct	Glossop	1-0		Robson	1	2	3	4		6	7	8		10	11	5		9						
8	12	CLAPTON ORIENT	1-1		Gardner	1	2	3	4		6	7	8	9	10	11	5								
9	19	BLACKPOOL	1-0		McCubbin	1	2	3	4	10	6	7	8	9		11	5								
10	26	Nottingham Forest	2-1		Manning, McCubbin	1		3	4	10	6	7	8	9		11	5			2					
11	2 Nov	BRISTOL CITY	2-0		Miller, Barrell	1		3	4	10	6	7	8	9		11	5			2					
12	9	Birmingham	1-4		Gardner	1		3	4	10	6	7	8	9		11	5			2					
13	16	HUDDERSFIELD TOWN	3-1		Slade(2), McCubbin	1		3	4	10	6	7	8			11	5		9	2					
14	23	Leeds City	2-2		Slade(2)	1	2	3	4	10	6	7	8			11	5		9						
15	7 Dec	Bury	3-0		Barrell(3)	1	2	3	4	10	6	7	8			11	5		9						
16	21	Barnsley	0-4			1	2	3	4	10	6	7	8			11	5		9						
17	25	BRADFORD PARK AVENUE	1-1		Gardner	1	2		4	10	6	7	8	9		11	5			3					
18	26	Bradford Park Avenue	0-3			1	2		4	9	6	7	8		10	11	5			3					
19	28	STOCKPORT COUNTY	3-2		Barrell(2), Hubbard	1	2		4	6		9	8	7	10	11	5			3					
20	4 Jan	Preston North End	0-0			1	2		4	9			8	7	6	11	5	10		3					
21	18	BURNLEY	1-3		Wield	1	2	3		10	6	7	8	9	4	11	5								
22	25	Hull City	0-2			1	2	3		10	6	7	8	9			5	11			4				
23	1 Feb	GRIMSBY TOWN	3-0		Barrell, Slade, Hubbard	1	2	3		4	6		8	7	10		5	11	9						
24	8	GLOSSOP	0-0			1	2	3		5	6		8	7	10	11			9		4				
25	15	Clapton Orient	2-1		Miller, Slade	1	2	3	4		6	7	8	10		11	5		9						
26	22	Blackpool	1-1		Birchall	1	2	3	4	5	6	7		9		11		10	8						
27	1 Mar	NOTTINGHAM FOREST	2-1		Barrell, Slade	1	2	3	4	10	6	7		8		11	5		9						
28	8	Bristol City	0-2			1	2	3		4	6	7	10	8		11	5		9						
29	15	BIRMINGHAM	0-1			1	2	3	4	10	6	7		8		11	5		9						
30	21	FULHAM	3-0		Miller, Manning, Barrell	1	2	3	4	10	6	7	8	9			5					11			
31	22	Huddersfield Town	1-5		McCubbin	1	2	3	4	10	6	7	8	9			5					11			
32	24	WOLVERHAMPTON WANDS.	2-1		Manning, McCubbin	1	2	3	4	9	6	7	8				5	10				11			
33	25	Leicester Fosse	0-1			1	2	3	4	10	6	7	8	9			5					11			
34	29	LEEDS CITY	3-3		Barrell, McCubbin, Platts	1	2	3	4	10	6	7	8				5		9			11			
35	5 Apr	Grimsby Town	0-0			1	2	3	4	10	6	7	8	9			5					11			
36	12	BURY	0-1			1	2	3		4	6	7		9			5		10			11	8		
37	19	Fulham	1-3		Barrell	1	2	3	4	10	5	7	8	9								11		6	
38	26	BARNSLEY	2-0		McCubbin(2)	1	2	3	4	9	6	7	8			11						10			5
					Apps.	38	34	34	31	33	36	35	34	29	12	26	33	7	14	8	2	9	1	1	1
					Goals				1	13	1	4	9	7	3		3	1	7			1			

F.A. CUP

4QF	30 Nov	Rotherham County	3-1		Wield, Slade(2)	1	2	3	4	10	6	7	8			11	5		9						
5QF	14 Dec	South Shields	0-1			1	2	3	4	10	6	7	8			11	5		9						

LINCOLNSHIRE CUP

SF	26 Feb	GAINSBOROUGH TRINITY	2-2		Barrell, Platts	1	2	3	4	10	5	7		8					9			11	6		
SFr	5 Mar	Gainsborough Trinity *	1-1		Miller	1	2		4	10	5	7		8	11			9	3				6		
SF2r	8 Apr	Gainsborough Trinity #	3-1		McCubbin, Manning(2)	1	2	3		10	6	7	8	9			5					11	4		
F	28	GRIMSBY TOWN	2-3		Barrell, Gardner	1	2	3	4	9	6	7	8			11	5					10			

* Lincoln refused to play extra time
# Played at Blundell Park, Grimsby

Final League Table

		Pl.	Home W D L F A	Away W D L F A	F.	A.	Pts
1	Preston North End	38	13 5 1 34 12	6 10 3 22 21	56	33	53
2	Burnley	38	13 4 2 58 23	8 4 7 30 30	88	53	50
3	Birmingham	38	11 6 2 39 18	7 4 8 20 26	59	44	46
4	Barnsley	38	15 3 1 46 18	4 4 11 11 29	57	47	45
5	Huddersfield Town	38	13 5 1 49 12	4 4 11 17 28	66	40	43
6	Leeds City	38	12 3 4 45 22	3 7 9 25 42	70	64	40
7	Grimsby Town	38	10 8 1 32 11	5 2 12 19 39	51	50	40
8	*Lincoln City*	*38*	*10 6 3 31 16*	*5 4 10 19 36*	*50*	*52*	*40*
9	Fulham	38	13 5 1 47 16	4 0 15 18 39	65	55	39
10	Wolverhampton W.	38	10 6 3 34 16	4 4 11 22 38	56	54	38
11	Bury	38	10 6 3 29 14	5 2 12 24 43	53	57	38
12	Hull City	38	12 2 5 42 18	3 4 12 18 37	60	55	36
13	Bradford Park Ave.	38	12 4 3 47 18	2 4 13 13 42	60	60	36
14	Clapton Orient	38	8 6 5 25 20	2 8 9 9 27	34	47	34
15	Leicester Fosse	38	12 2 5 34 20	1 5 13 15 45	49	65	33
16	Bristol City	38	7 9 3 32 25	2 6 11 14 47	46	72	33
17	Nottingham Forest	38	9 3 7 35 25	3 5 11 23 34	58	59	32
18	Glossop	38	11 2 6 34 26	1 6 12 15 42	49	68	32
19	Stockport County	38	8 4 7 32 23	0 6 13 24 55	56	78	26
20	Blackpool	38	8 4 7 22 22	1 4 14 17 47	39	69	26

SEASON 1913-14
DIVISION TWO

No.	Date	Opposition	Res.	Att.	Goalscorers
1	1 Sep	Wolverhampton Wanderers	0-1		
2	6	BARNSLEY	2-2		Brindley, McCubbin
3	13	Bury	0-1		
4	20	HUDDERSFIELD TOWN	3-0		McCubbin, Slade, Brindley
5	27	Fulham	0-4		
6	2 Oct	Notts County	1-2		Brindley
7	4	Blackpool	1-2		Manning
8	11	NOTTINGHAM FOREST	1-0		Slade
9	13	Hull City	1-1		Barrell
10	18	Arsenal	0-3		
11	25	GRIMSBY TOWN	1-3		McCubbin
12	1 Nov	Birmingham	0-2		
13	8	BRISTOL CITY	2-1		Ball, McFarlane
14	15	Leeds City	0-1		
15	22	CLAPTON ORIENT	0-0		
16	6 Dec	STOCKPORT COUNTY	0-3		
17	13	Bradford Park Avenue	0-3		
18	20	NOTTS COUNTY	0-0		
19	26	LEICESTER FOSSE	3-0		Miller, Brindley, Barrell
20	27	Barnsley	0-1		
21	3 Jan	BURY	1-0		Gardner
22	17	Huddersfield Town	1-2		McCubbin
23	24	FULHAM	0-1		
24	7 Feb	BLACKPOOL	1-2		Egerton
25	10	Glossop	0-4		
26	14	Nottingham Forest	1-2		Egerton
27	21	ARSENAL	5-2		McCubbin, Ball, Egerton, Manning(2)
28	28	Grimsby Town	3-1		Chesser, Egerton, McCubbin
29	7 Mar	BIRMINGHAM	1-1		Egerton
30	11	Hull City	0-0		
31	14	Bristol City	1-4		Chesser
32	21	LEEDS CITY	1-0		McFarlane
33	28	Clapton Orient	1-5		Manning
34	4 Apr	GLOSSOP	1-5		Robson
35	10	WOLVERHAMPTON WANDS.	1-0		Egerton
36	11	Stockport County	3-2		Egerton, Barrell, Ball
37	13	Leicester Fosse	0-2		
38	18	BRADFORD PARK AVENUE	0-3		

F.A. CUP

| 1R | 10 Jan | Plymouth Argyle | 1-4 | | Barrell |

LINCOLNSHIRE CUP

| SF | 31 Jan | GRIMSBY TOWN | 2-1 | | Barrell, Brindley |
| F | 23 Apr | GAINSBOROUGH TRINITY | 3-0 | | Manning, Egerton, Barrell |

Final League Table

		Pl.		Home			Away			F.	A.	Pts
1	Notts County	38	16	2	1	55	13	7	5	7	22	23	77	36	53
2	Bradford Park Ave.	38	15	1	3	44	20	8	2	9	27	27	71	47	49
3	Woolwich Arsenal	38	14	3	2	34	10	6	6	7	20	28	54	38	49
4	Leeds City	38	15	2	2	54	16	5	5	9	22	30	76	46	47
5	Barnsley	38	14	1	4	33	15	5	6	8	18	30	51	45	45
6	Clapton Orient	38	14	5	0	38	11	2	6	11	9	24	47	35	43
7	Hull City	38	9	5	5	29	13	7	4	8	24	24	53	37	41
8	Bristol City	38	12	5	2	32	10	4	4	11	20	40	52	50	41
9	Wolverhampton W.	38	14	1	4	33	16	4	4	11	18	36	51	52	41
10	Bury	38	12	6	1	30	14	3	4	12	9	26	39	40	40
11	Fulham	38	10	8	1	34	20	6	3	10	15	23	46	43	38
12	Stockport County	38	9	6	4	32	18	4	4	11	23	39	55	57	36
13	Huddersfield Town	38	8	4	7	28	22	5	4	10	19	31	47	53	34
14	Birmingham	38	10	4	5	31	18	2	6	11	17	42	48	60	34
15	Grimsby Town	38	10	4	5	24	15	4	2	13	18	43	42	58	34
16	Blackpool	38	6	10	3	24	19	3	4	12	9	25	33	44	32
17	Glossop	38	8	8	3	32	24	3	1	13	19	43	51	67	28
18	Leicester Fosse	38	7	2	10	29	28	4	2	13	16	33	45	61	26
19	*Lincoln City*	*38*	*8*	*5*	*6*	*23*	*22*	*2*	*1*	*16*	*13*	*43*	*36*	*66*	*26*
20	Nottingham Forest	38	7	5	7	27	23	0	2	17	10	53	37	76	23

Back: W.Simpson(asst.trainer), Wilson, McFadden, Jackson, Strong, Bellamy, Fern, Gardner, Atkin, Wield, Meunier, Robson, Manning, Goldsborough
Centre: Inskip, Riley, Walter Miller, Hallam, McCubbin, Richardson, McCulloch, Barrell, Brindley, Bentley (trainer)
Front: Short, Slade, Platts.

SEASON 1914-15
DIVISION TWO

No.	Date	Opposition	Res.	Att.	Goalscorers
1	2 Sep	Leicester Fosse	2-2		Gardner, Egerton
2	5	Barnsley	1-3		Chesser
3	12	GLOSSOP	2-1		Ball, Egerton
4	19	Wolverhampton Wanderers	1-3		Pattison
5	26	FULHAM	3-1		Egerton, Pattison, Chesser
6	1 Oct	Nottingham Forest	2-3		Chesser, Ball
7	3	Stockport County	0-1		
8	10	HULL CITY	0-3		
9	17	Leeds City	1-3		Ball
10	24	CLAPTON ORIENT	1-0		Wolstenholme
11	31	Arsenal	1-1		Chesser
12	7 Nov	DERBY COUNTY	0-0		
13	14	BLACKPOOL	0-1		
14	21	Birmingham	0-2		
15	28	GRIMSBY TOWN	2-1		Wolstenholme, Wield
16	5 Dec	Huddersfield Town	1-0		Chesser
17	12	BRISTOL CITY	3-1		Ball, Wolstenholme(2)
18	14	Bury	1-1		Wolstenholme
19	25	PRESTON NORTH END	3-1		Egerton, Chesser, Wolstenholme
20	26	Preston North End	0-0		
21	2 Jan	BARNSLEY	3-0		Egerton(3)
22	16	Glossop	2-1		Egerton, Wolstenholme
23	23	WOLVERHAMPTON WANDS.	2-2		Ball, Egerton
24	6 Feb	STOCKPORT COUNTY	2-2		Wield, OG
25	20	LEEDS CITY	0-1		
26	27	Clapton Orient	1-3		Ball
27	6 Mar	ARSENAL	1-0		Chesser
28	11	Hull City	1-6		Egerton
29	13	Derby County	0-3		
30	20	Blackpool	0-0		
31	27	BIRMINGHAM	0-1		
32	29	Fulham	1-3		Manning
33	2 Apr	LEICESTER FOSSE	2-3		Ball, Egerton
34	3	Grimsby Town	1-5		Wield
35	5	NOTTINGHAM FOREST	2-1		Egerton, Wield
36	10	HUDDERSFIELD TOWN	1-1		Barrell
37	17	Bristol City	1-2		Dowling
38	24	BURY	2-3		Barrell, Chesser

1 own goal

F.A. CUP

6QF	19 Dec	ROTHERHAM COUNTY	6-0		Wolstenholme(3), Egerton, Chesser(2)
1R	9 Jan	Brighton & Hove Albion	1-2		Egerton

LINCOLNSHIRE CUP

SF	15 Apr	SCUNTHORPE UNITED	4-1		Chesser(2), Manning, Wolstenholme
F	1 May	Grimsby Town	3-2 *		Barrell, Dowling, Egerton

* After extra time

Final League Table

		Pl.	Home W D L F A	Away W D L F A	F. A. Pts
1	Derby County	38	14 3 2 40 11	9 4 6 31 22	71 33 53
2	Preston North End	38	14 4 1 41 16	6 7 6 20 26	61 42 50
3	Barnsley	38	16 2 1 31 10	6 1 12 20 41	51 51 47
4	Wolverhampton W.	38	12 4 3 47 13	7 3 9 30 39	77 52 45
5	Arsenal	38	15 1 3 52 13	4 4 11 17 28	69 41 43
6	Birmingham	38	13 3 3 44 13	6 9 18 26 62	39 43
7	Hull City	38	12 2 5 36 23	7 3 9 29 31	65 54 43
8	Huddersfield Town	38	12 4 3 36 13	5 4 10 25 29	61 42 42
9	Clapton Orient	38	12 5 2 36 17	4 4 11 14 31	50 48 41
10	Blackpool	38	11 3 5 40 22	6 2 11 18 35	58 57 39
11	Bury	38	11 5 3 39 19	4 3 12 22 37	61 56 38
12	Fulham	38	12 0 7 35 20	3 7 9 18 27	53 47 37
13	Bristol City	38	11 2 6 38 19	4 5 10 24 37	62 56 37
14	Stockport County	38	12 4 3 33 19	3 3 13 21 41	54 60 37
15	Leeds City	38	9 3 7 40 25	5 1 13 25 39	65 64 32
16	*Lincoln City*	38	9 4 6 29 23	2 5 12 17 42	46 65 31
17	Grimsby Town	38	10 4 5 36 24	1 5 13 12 52	48 76 31
18	Nottingham Forest	38	9 7 3 32 24	1 2 16 11 53	43 77 29
19	Leicester Fosse	38	8 6 4 31 41	4 0 15 16 47	47 88 24
20	Glossop	38	5 5 9 21 33	1 1 17 10 54	31 87 18

Back : Bentley (groundsman), Pearce, Goldsborough, McFadden, Clem Jackson, Butler, Dunne, Stansbury, Wield, Parker.
Centre : Manning, Downing, Wolstenholme, Robson, Egerton, Gardner, Chesser, Ball, Barrell, J.Jackson (trainer).
Front : McCubbin, Morton, Cavanagh, Oldham, Pattison.

SEASON 1915-16
WAR LEAGUE - MIDLAND SECTION

No.	Date	Opposition	Res.	Goalscorers										
1	4 Sep	SHEFFIELD UNITED	7-3	Cavanagh, Egerton(5), Chesser	Goldsborough	Jackson	F.Ward	Wield	Gardner	Barrell	Pattison	Cavanagh	Egerton	Chesser	Ball
2	11	Bradford Park Avenue	0-4		"	"	"	"	"	Robson	"	"	"	"	Salkeld
3	18	BRADFORD CITY	2-6	Egerton, Wield	Borrill	"	"	"	"	Dunne	Manning	"	"	Pattison	Ball
4	25	Leeds City	1-2	Egerton	Goldsborough	"	"	"	"	Barrell	"	"	"	Chesser	"
5	2 Oct	HUDDERSFIELD TOWN	3-0	Barrell, Egerton(2)	"	"	"	"	"	"	"	"	"	"	"
6	9	Hull City	1-1	Egerton	"	Dunne	"	"	"	"	"	"	"	Salkeld	"
7	16	GRIMSBY TOWN	1-0	Chesser	"	Jackson	"	Addinall	"	"	Pattison	"	"	Chesser	"
8	23	Nottingham Forest	2-3	Cavanagh, Egerton	"	"	"	Robson	"	"	"	"	"	"	"
9	30	NOTTS COUNTY	3-0	Ball, Chesser(2)	"	"	"	"	"	"	"	"	"	"	"
10	6 Nov	Barnsley	2-4	Egerton, Cavanagh	"	"	"	Dunne	Robson	"	"	"	"	"	"
11	13	Derby County	4-2	Gardner, Egerton(2), Cavanagh	"	"	"	Wield	Gardner	"	Manning	"	"	"	"
12	20	LEICESTER FOSSE	1-0	Chesser	"	"	"	"	"	"	"	"	"	"	Pattison
13	27	Sheffield Wednesday	1-4	Pattison	"	"	"	"	"	"	"	"	"	Pattison	Ball
14	4 Dec	Sheffield United	1-4	Egerton	"	"	"	"	"	"	"	Pattison	"	Salkeld	"
15	11	BRADFORD PARK AVENUE	2-1	Chesser, OG	"	"	"	"	"	"	"	Cavanagh	"	Chesser	"
16	18	Bradford City	0-3		"	"	Dunne	"	Robson	"	"	"	"	"	"
17	25	LEEDS CITY	2-0	Parrish, Ball	"	Dunne	F.Ward	Addinall	"	"	"	"	Parrish	"	"
18	1 Jan	Huddersfield Town	0-5		"	"	"	"	"	"	Pattison	"	Egerton	"	"
19	8	HULL CITY	4-1	Egerton(2), Manning, Cavanagh	"	"	"	Wield	Gardner	Addinall	Manning	"	"	Parrish	"
20	15	Grimsby Town	0-1		"	Jackson	"	Addinall	Wield	Barrell	"	"	"	Chesser	Pattison
21	22	NOTTINGHAM FOREST	1-4	Cavanagh	"	"	"	Wield	Gardner	"	"	"	"	"	Ball
22	29	Notts County	1-2	Barrell	"	"	"	Addinall	Wield	"	"	"	"	Parrish	"
23	5 Feb	BARNSLEY	4-1	Manning(2), Chesser, Cavanagh	Blakey	"	"	Wield	Gardner	"	"	"	"	Chesser	"
24	12	DERBY COUNTY	4-0	Egerton(3), Chesser	"	"	"	"	"	"	"	"	"	"	"
25	19	Leicester Fosse	1-1	Parrish	Goldsborough	"	"	"	"	"	"	Chesser	"	Parrish	"
26	21 Mar	SHEFFIELD WEDNESDAY	6-2	Chesser(2),Egerton(2),Ball,Cavanagh	"	"	"	"	"	"	"	Cavanagh	"	Chesser	"

P26 W12 D2 L12 F54 A54 Pts.26 Pos.9th (out of 14 teams)

MIDLAND SECTION: SUBSIDIARY COMPETITION - MIDLAND DIVISION

1	4 Mar	Sheffield Wednesday	2-2	Egerton, Chesser	Goldsborough	Jackson	Wield	Addinall	Gardner	Barrell	Manning	Cavanagh	Egerton	Chesser	Ball
2	11	HULL CITY	7-0	Chesser(2), Egerton(4), Cavanagh	"	"	F.Ward	"	Wield	"	"	"	"	"	"
3	18	Sheffield United	0-7		"	"	"	Wield	Gardner	"	"	"	"	"	"
4	25	ROTHERHAM COUNTY	1-1	Cavanagh	"	"	"	"	"	"	"	"	"	"	"
5	1 Apr	GRIMSBY TOWN	1-2	Barrell	Blakey	"	"	"	"	"	"	"	Salkeld	"	"
6	8	SHEFFIELD WEDNESDAY	3-0	Egerton(2), Barrell	"	"	"	"	"	"	"	"	"	Chesser	Salkeld
7	15	Hull City	1-2	Egerton	"	"	"	Addinall	Wield	"	"	"	"	"	"
8	22	SHEFFIELD UNITED	1-1	Parrish	"	"	"	Wield	Gardner	"	"	"	Parrish	"	Ball
9	24	Grimsby Town	0-3		"	Dunne	"	"	Bavin	"	Pattison	Dowling	Parrish	Cavanagh	Salkeld
10	29	Rotherham County	1-4	Barrell	"	Wield	"	Manning	"	Addinall	"	Cavanagh	Barrell	Chesser	Ball

P10 W2 D3 L5 F17 A22 Pts.7 Pos.6th (out of 6 teams)

Back : Robson, Salkeld, Jackson, Goldsborough, Ward, Dunne, Bentley (trainer).
Centre :--------, Wield, Gardner, Barrell, --------.
Front : Manning, Pattison, Egerton, Chesser, Ball.

SEASON 1916-17

WAR LEAGUE - MIDLAND SECTION

No.	Date	Opposition	Re.	Goalscorers
1	2 Sep	Bradford Park Avenue	0-1	
2	9	BIRMINGHAM	3-2	Cavanagh(2), Parrish
3	16	Hull City	1-2	Manning
4	23	NOTTINGHAM FOREST	1-2	Egerton
5	30	Barnsley	1-6	Ball
6	7 Oct	LEEDS CITY	2-5	Manning, Barrell
7	14	Sheffield United	1-5	Egerton
8	21	BRADFORD CITY	1-2	Barrell
9	28	Leicester Fosse	1-1	Barrell
10	4 Nov	GRIMSBY TOWN	1-1	Ball
11	11	Notts County	4-0	Pattison(2), Egerton, Barrell
12	18	ROTHERHAM COUNTY	2-0	Addinall, Egerton
13	25	Huddersfield Town	1-3	Addinal
14	2 Dec	CHESTERFIELD TOWN	1-3	Parrish
15	9	BRADFORD PARK AVE. *	1-1	Barrell
16	23	Hull City #	1-1	Barrell
17	26	SHEFFIELD WEDNESDAY	4-0	Parrish(4)
18	30	Nottingham Forest	0-2	
19	6 Jan	BARNSLEY	0-1	
20	13	Leeds City	1-3	Barrell
21	20	SHEFFIELD UNITED	0-2	
22	27	Bradford City	0-2	
23	3 Feb	LEICESTER FOSSE	3-1	Addinall, Egerton, Jackson
24	10	Grimsby Town	0-1	
25	17	NOTTS COUNTY	1-2	Addinall
26	24	Rotherham County	3-5	Barrell(2), Egerton
27	3 Mar	HUDDERSFIELD TOWN	0-1	
28	10	Chesterfield Town	3-3	Barrell, Manning(2)
29	28 Apr	Sheffield Wednesday +	1-7	Pattison
30	28	Birmingham +	0-0	

* Abandoned after 80 mins, score stands.   # Abandoned after 81 mins, score stands.   + Both matches took place at the same time.

P30 W5 D6 L19 F38 A65 Pts.16 Pos.16th (out of 16 teams)

MIDLAND SECTION: SUBSIDIARY COMPETITION - MIDLAND DIVISION

No.	Date	Opposition	Res.	Goalscorers
1	17 Mar	Grimsby Town	1-1	Parrish
2	31	HULL CITY	2-2	Barrell, Manning
3	6 Apr	CHESTERFIELD TOWN	6-1	Manning,Parrish(2),Ormiston,Ball,Barrell
4	7	GRIMSBY TOWN	1-3	Manning
5	9	Chesterfield Town	0-3	
6	21	Hull City	1-2	Parrish

P6 W1 D2 L3 F11 A12 Pts.4 Pos.13th (out of 16 teams)

SEASON 1917-18

WAR LEAGUE - MIDLAND SECTION

No.	Date	Opposition	Res.	Goalscorers
1	1 Sep	BARNSLEY	2-1	Egerton, Parrish
2	8	Barnsley *	0-1	
3	15	BRADFORD PARK AVENUE	0-0	
4	22	Bradford Park Avenue	0-1	
5	29	SHEFFIELD UNITED	0-1	
6	6 Oct	Sheffield United	0-6	
7	13	Leeds City	0-3	
8	20	LEEDS CITY	0-4	
9	27	Nottingham Forest	1-0	Parrish
10	3 Nov	NOTTINGHAM FOREST	3-1	Addinall, Manning, Egerton
11	10	Leicester Fosse	0-4	
12	17	LEICESTER FOSSE	1-1	Egerton
13	24	Hull City	0-2	
14	1 Dec	HULL CITY	1-3	Ormiston
15	8	Notts County	1-1	Parrish
16	15	NOTTS COUNTY	1-2	Parrish
17	29	HUDDERSFIELD TOWN	2-1	Egerton, Harrison
18	5 Jan	Sheffield Wednesday	2-7	Doughty, Thorpe
19	12	SHEFFIELD WEDNESDAY	3-0	Manning, Cavanagh, Egerton
20	19	Rotherham County	0-2	
21	26	ROTHERHAM COUNTY	1-1	Chesser
22	2 Feb	Bradford City	0-3	
23	9	BRADFORD CITY	2-1	Egerton(2)
24	16	Grimsby Town	1-4	Ball
25	23	GRIMSBY TOWN	1-0	Gardner
26	2 Mar	Birmingham	0-5	
27	9	BIRMINGHAM	3-3	Parrish, OG, Egerton
28	1 Apr	Huddersfield Town	0-4	

* 35 minutes each way played; score stands.

P28 W7 D5 L16 F25 A62 Pts.19 Pos.14th (out of 15 teams)

MIDLAND SECTION: SUBSIDIARY COMPETITION - MIDLAND DIVISION

No.	Date	Opposition	Res.	Goalscorers
1	26 Dec	Gainsborough	4-0	Yorke, Groves(2), Monks
2	16 Mar	Hull City	2-4	Edwards, Jones
3	23	HULL CITY	1-1	Ormiston
4	29	GAINSBOROUGH	3-1	Parrish(3)
5	30	GRIMSBY TOWN	1-0	Cavanagh
6	6 Apr	Grimsby Town	0-2	

P6 W3 D1 L2 F11 A8 Pts.7 Pos.6th (out of 16 teams)

SEASON 1918-19
WAR LEAGUE - MIDLAND SECTION

No.	Date	Opposition	Res.	Goalscorers										
1	7 Sep	Barnsley	6-2	Egerton(2), Banton, Parrish, *	D.Tremelling	Jackson	Wield	Connor	Ormiston	Addinall	Cavanagh	Egerton	Parrish	Banton	Lamming
2	14	BARNSLEY	4-2	Egerton(2), Parrish(2)	"	"	"	Addinall	"	Dunne	Ball	"	"	Cavanagh	"
3	21	Leicester Fosse	0-2		"	"	"	Bryan	Gardner	Addinall	Manning	Straughton	"	"	Banton
4	28	LEICESTER FOSSE	4-0	Egerton(2), Parrish, Cavanagh	"	"	"	Ormiston	"	"	"	Egerton	"	"	Lamming
5	5 Oct	Nottingham Forest	1-1	Egerton	"	"	"	"	"	"	"	"	"	"	"
6	12	NOTTINGHAM FOREST	1-3	Ball	"	"	Dunne	"	"	"	Ball	"	"	"	"
7	19	LEEDS CITY	1-0	Ormiston	"	"	Wield	"	"	"	Manning	"	"	"	"
8	26	Leeds City	0-2		"	"	"	"	"	"	"	"	"	"	"
9	2 Nov	SHEFFIELD UNITED	2-1	Egerton, Lamming	"	"	"	Brown	Ormiston	"	"	"	"	"	"
10	9	Sheffield United	1-6	Moseley	"	"	Addinall	Kenworthy	Connor	Lockwood	Ford	Deacon	"	Moseley	"
11	16	BRADFORD PARK AVENUE	1-1	Parrish	"	"	F.Ward	Connor	Gardner	Thompson	Blunt	Egerton	"	"	"
12	23	Bradford Park Avenue	1-6	Parrish	Smith	F.Ward	Wield	Hill	"	Ormiston	Wilson	"	"	Bell	"
13	30	HULL CITY	0-2		D.Tremelling	Jackson	Brown	Ormiston	"	Addinall	Blunt	"	"	Cavanagh	"
14	7 Dec	Hull City	1-5	Parrish	"	Pass	"	"	"	"	Manning	Bryan	"	Moseley	Ball
15	14	NOTTS COUNTY	0-1		"	Jackson	Wield	Bryan	"	"	"	Groves	Egerton	Lamming	"
16	21	Notts County	1-2	Bryan	"	Pass	"	"	Ormiston	"	"	Parrish	"	"	"
17	25	COVENTRY CITY	3-2	Groves, Parrish, Ball	"	F.Ward	"	"	"	"	"	Groves	"	Parrish	"
18	26	Coventry City	0-2		"	Pass	Jackson	"	Addinall	Edwards	"	"	Dowling	Bibby	"
19	28	HUDDERSFIELD TOWN	1-4	Parrish	"	F.Ward	Wield	"	Gardner	Addinall	"	"	Parrish	Dowling	"
20	11 Jan	SHEFFIELD WEDNESDAY	1-4	Ormiston	"	Jackson	"	"	Ormiston	"	"	"	Egerton	Parrish	"
21	18	Sheffield Wednesday	2-4	Ball, Ormiston	"	"	R.Ward	"	"	S.Tremelling	"	Parrish	"	Ball	Lamming
22	25	GRIMSBY TOWN	0-1		"	"	"	"	"	"	"	Newton	Parrish	"	"
23	1 Feb	Grimsby Town	2-1	F.Ward, R.Ward	Blakey	"	F.Ward	"	S.Tremelling	Addinall	"	Chesser	R.Ward	"	"
24	8	BRADFORD CITY	0-1		"	"	"	"	"	"	"	Osborne	"	"	"
25	15	Bradford City	2-1	Chesser(2)	D.Tremelling	Wild	"	"	Gardner	"	"	"	Chesser	Whipsall	Ball
26	22	ROTHERHAM COUNTY	2-0	Egerton, Osborne	"	Jackson	"	"	"	"	"	Egerton	Chesser	"	"
27	1 Mar	Rotherham County	0-0		"	"	"	"	"	"	"	"	"	"	"
28	8	BIRMINGHAM	1-0	Osborne	"	"	"	"	"	"	Osborne	Parrish	"	"	"
29	15	Birmingham	0-3		"	Thorpe	"	"	"	"	"	Gillitt	"	"	"
30	21 Apr	Huddersfield Town	0-0		Sewell	"	Reid	"	"	"	Manning	Osborne	Armitage	"	Pattison

* Additional scorers: Lamming, Cavanagh

P30 W10 D4 L16 F38 A59 Pts.24 Pos.12 (out of 16 teams)

MIDLAND SECTION: SUBSIDIARY COMPETITION - MIDLAND DIVISION

No.	Date	Opposition	Res.	Goalscorers										
1	22 Mar	HULL CITY	1-2	J.Tremelling	D.Tremelling	Jackson	F.Ward	Bryan	Gardner	Addinall	Thorpe	Osborne	J.Tremelling	Chesser	Ball
2	29	Hull City	2-1	Bryan, OG	"	Thorpe	"	"	"	"	Manning	Little	"	"	Lee
3	5 Apr	Grimsby Town	1-2	J.Tremelling	"	"	"	"	"	"	"	"	"	"	Ball
4	12	GRIMSBY TOWN	1-2	Little	"	Jackson	"	"	"	"	"	"	"	"	"
5	18	COVENTRY CITY	1-1	Chesser	Sewell	"	"	"	"	"	Thorpe	Armitage	"	"	"
6	19	Coventry City	0-1		"	Thorpe	Crosan	"	"	"	"	Osborne	"	"	Pattison

P6 W1 D1 L4 F6 A9 Pts.3 Pos.4th (out of 4 teams)

SEASON 1919-20
DIVISION TWO

No.	Date	Opposition	Res.	Att.	Goalscorers
1	30 Aug	West Ham United	1-1		Chesser
2	1 Sep	BLACKPOOL	0-3		
3	6	WEST HAM UNITED	1-4		McCulloch
4	8	Blackpool	0-6		
5	13	BRISTOL CITY	0-0		
6	20	Bristol City	0-6		
7	27	Tottenham Hotspur	1-6		Egerton
8	4 Oct	TOTTENHAM HOTSPUR	1-1		McCulloch
9	11	BARNSLEY	0-4		
10	18	Barnsley	3-5		Bird, Beel, Iremonger
11	25	CLAPTON ORIENT	2-1		Dowling(2)
12	1 Nov	Clapton Orient	0-1		
13	8	STOCKPORT COUNTY	2-0		Chesser, Dowling
14	15	Stockport County	0-3		
15	22	PORT VALE	0-0		
16	29	Port Vale	0-1		
17	6 Dec	Hull City	2-5		Beel(2)
18	13	HULL CITY	2-0		Egerton, Chesser
19	20	Bury	0-3		
20	25	NOTTINGHAM FOREST	1-4		Ball
21	26	Nottingham Forest	1-2		Bird
22	27	BURY	2-1		Linfoot, Bryan
23	31	HUDDERSFIELD TOWN	1-3		Ward
24	3 Jan	Wolverhampton Wanderers	0-4		
25	17	WOLVERHAMPTON WANDS.	4-0		Atkin, McCulloch, Egerton, Beel
26	24	Rotherham County	0-3		
27	31	ROTHERHAM COUNTY	0-0		
28	7 Feb	STOKE CITY	3-1		Beel, Atkin, Ball
29	14	Stoke City	2-1		Chesser(2)
30	21	Grimsby Town	2-2		Parsons, Beel
31	28	GRIMSBY TOWN	2-0		Parsons, Ward
32	6 Mar	BIRMINGHAM CITY	2-2		Linfoot, Chesser
33	13	Birmingham City	0-7		
34	20	LEICESTER CITY	0-3		
35	27	Leicester City	0-4		
36	2 Apr	South Shields	2-2		Egerton(2)
37	3	FULHAM	0-1		
38	5	SOUTH SHIELDS	1-1		Egerton
39	10	Fulham	0-3		
40	17	COVENTRY CITY	4-1		Linfoot, Chesser, Parsons(2)
41	24	Coventry City	0-2		
42	1 May	Huddersfield Town	2-4		Chesser, Ball

F.A. CUP

Int QF	14 Jan	MIDDLESBROUGH *	1-4		Ball

* Match played at Ayresome Park by agreement, Lincoln being guaranteed a sum of 'just under £1,000' in gate receipts

LINCOLNSHIRE CUP

SF	17 Mar	SCUNTHORPE UNITED	4-1		Foster(3), Bird
F	3 May	GRIMSBY TOWN	7-0		Chesser(2), Linfoot(2), Bird, *

* Additional scorers: Chipperfield, Ball

Final League Table

```
              Pl.  Home          Away        F.  A.  Pts
                   W  D  L  F  A W  D  L  F  A
1  Tottenham Hotspur 42 19 2 0 60 11 13 4 4 42 21 102 32 70
2  Huddersfield Town 42 16 4 1 58 13 12 4 5 39 25 97 38 64
3  Birmingham        42 14 3 4 54 16 10 5 6 31 18 85 34 56
4  Blackpool         42 13 4 4 40 18 8  6 7 25 29 65 47 52
5  Bury              42 14 4 3 35 15 6  4 11 25 29 60 44 48
6  Fulham            42 11 6 4 36 18 8  3 10 25 32 61 50 47
7  West Ham United   42 14 5 2 34 14 5  6 10 13 26 47 40 47
8  Bristol City      42 9  9 3 30 18 4  8 9 16 25 46 43 43
9  South Shields     42 13 5 3 47 18 2  7 12 11 30 58 48 42
10 Stoke             42 13 3 5 37 15 5  3 13 23 39 60 54 42
11 Hull City         42 13 4 4 53 23 5  2 14 25 49 78 72 41
12 Barnsley          42 9  5 7 41 28 6  5 10 20 27 61 55 40
13 Port Vale         42 11 7 3 35 27 5  5 11 24 35 59 62 40
14 Leicester City    42 8  6 7 26 29 7  4 10 15 32 41 61 40
15 Clapton Orient    42 14 3 4 34 17 2  3 16 17 42 51 59 38
16 Stockport County  42 11 4 6 34 24 3  5 13 18 37 52 61 37
17 Rotherham County  42 10 4 7 32 27 3  4 14 19 56 51 83 34
18 Nottingham Forest 42 9  4 8 23 22 2  5 14 20 51 43 73 31
19 Wolverhampton W.  42 8  4 9 41 32 2  6 13 14 48 55 80 30
20 Coventry City     42 7  7 7 20 26 2  4 15 15 47 35 73 29
21 Lincoln City      42 8  6 7 27 30 1  3 17 17 71 44 101 27
22 Grimsby Town      42 8  4 9 23 24 2  1 18 11 51 34 75 25
```

An unnamed team group, probably taken on City's visit to Birmingham.

SEASON 1920-21
MIDLAND LEAGUE

No.	Date	Opposition	Res.	Att.	Goalscorers
1	28 Aug	MEXBOROUGH TOWN	3-1		Brentall(2), Bird
2	11 Sep	SHEFFIELD WED. RES.	4-0		Brentall(2), Ball, Rippon
3	18	Mexborough Town	3-0		Brentall(2), Bird
4	25	CASTLEFORD TOWN	3-1		Bird, Brentnall, Ball
5	2 Oct	Denaby United	3-0		Brentall(2), Hooper
6	8	Notts County Res.	0-2		
7	9	NOTTS COUNTY RES.	2-1		Rippon, Fenwick
8	16	Gainsborough Trinity	0-0		
9	23	HULL CITY RES.	6-1		Rippon(2), Bird, Ward(2), Brentall
10	30	Sheffield Wednesday Res.	2-0		Hopper, Bird
11	6 Nov	Barnsley Res.	1-1		Brentnall
12	13	DONCASTER ROVERS	2-0		Brentnall, Bryan
13	20	Sheffield United Res.	6-1		Brentnall(3), Rippon, Ball, Bird
14	27	SHEFFIELD UNITED RES.	3-0		Brentnall(2), Rippon
15	4 Dec	Rotherham County Res.	0-3		
16	11	LEEDS UNITED RES.	2-2		Ball, Atkin
17	25	GRIMSBY TOWN RES.	2-1		Dwane(2)
18	27	DENABY UNITED	4-0		Hooper(2), Dwane, Rippon
19	1 Jan	Worksop Town	5-4		Brentnall(2), Hopper, Rippon, OG
20	15	Castleford Town	1-2		Chambers
21	22	WORKSOP TOWN	4-0		Bird, Fenwick, Ball, Brentnall
22	5 Feb	ROTHERHAM TOWN	3-0		Bird, Rippon, Brentnall
23	12	Leeds United Res.	2-3		Brentnall(2)
24	19	NOTTINGHAM FOR. RES.	4-1		Rippon(2), Bird(2)
25	26	Chesterfield	1-0		Rippon
26	5 Mar	CHESTERFIELD	5-3		Chambers(2), Rippon(2), Ball
27	12	Grimsby Town Res.	2-1		Ball, Rippon
28	19	SCUNTHORPE UNITED	2-0		Bird, Rippon
29	25	HALIFAX TOWN	5-1		Chambers(3), Rippon, Ball
30	26	Hull City Res.	4-0		Rippon(3), Ball
31	28	GAINSBOROUGH TRINITY	2-0		Fenwick, Bird
32	2 Apr	Scunthorpe United	0-1		
33	11	Nottingham Forest Res.	2-1		Rippon, Chambers
34	16	Halifax Town	0-1		
35	23	Rotherham Town	1-2		Bird
36	30	ROTHERHAM COUNTY RES.	2-1		Brentnall, Rippon
37	5 May	Doncaster Rovers	1-4		Rippon
38	7	BARNSLEY RES.	3-1		Lincoln, Bird, Chambers

1 own goal

F.A. CUP

Round	Date	Opposition	Res.	Goalscorers
6QF	18 Dec	BROMLEY	5-0	Bird(2), Rippon(2), Brentall
1R	8 Jan	Millwall	3-0	Rippon(2), Brentnall
2R	29	FULHAM	0-0	
2Rr	7 Feb	Fulham	0-1	

LINCOLNSHIRE CUP

Round	Date	Opposition	Res.	Goalscorers
SF	28 Feb	SCUNTHORPE UNITED	1-0	Fenwick
F	27 Apr	Grimsby Town	1-4	Rippon

Final League Table

	P	W	D	L	F	A	Pts
1 Lincoln City	38	27	3	8	95	40	57
2 Notts County Res.	38	22	9	7	80	45	53
3 Chesterfield	38	15	11	9	70	46	47
4 Scunthorpe United	36	15	9	11	64	43	45
5 Rotherham Town	38	15	8	12	68	48	44
6 Sheffield United Res.	38	16	10	12	73	63	42
7 Rotherham County Res.	38	16	9	13	57	37	41
8 Castleford Town	38	17	6	15	61	56	40
9 The Wednesday Res.	38	16	7	15	66	50	39
10 Worksop Town	38	16	7	15	62	55	39
11 Halifax Town	38	17	5	16	54	62	39
12 Leeds United Res.	38	15	8	15	49	51	38
13 Gainsborough Trinity	38	14	8	16	58	60	36
14 Nottingham Forest Res.	38	13	10	15	69	77	36
15 Hull City Res.	38	12	9	17	52	68	33
16 Doncaster Rovers	38	11	10	17	38	54	32
17 Mexborough	38	10	11	17	39	61	31
18 Grimsby Town Res.	38	11	6	21	45	72	28
19 Barnsley Res.	38	9	8	21	55	86	26
20 Denaby United	38	4	6	28	37	118	14

SEASON 1921-22
DIVISION THREE (NORTH)

No.	Date	Opposition	Res.	Att.	Goalscorers
1	27 Aug	WALSALL	1-0		Rippon
2	3 Sep	Walsall	0-3		
3	10	NELSON	0-2		
4	17	Nelson	0-0		
5	24	Wrexham	1-3		Chambers
6	1 Oct	WREXHAM	1-0		Chambers
7	22	Barrow	0-2		
8	29	BARROW	1-0		Chambers
9	5 Nov	ASHINGTON	4-1		Chambers, Boylen, Rippon, Lees
10	12	Ashington	2-4		Chambers, Boylen
11	19	Darlington	2-4		Rippon, Boylen
12	26	CREWE ALEXANDRA	2-3		Lees, Boylen
13	17 Dec	ACCRINGTON STANLEY	1-1		Rippon
14	24	Accrington Stanley	0-2		
15	26	DARLINGTON	0-2		
16	27	DURHAM CITY	3-0		Chambers(3)
17	31	CHESTERFIELD	2-1		Lemons, Walker
18	2 Jan	Durham City	0-2		
19	7	Crewe Alexandra	2-0		Rippon, Walker
20	14	Chesterfield	0-3		
21	21	HALIFAX TOWN	3-1		Rippon, Chambers, Lees
22	4 Feb	Rochdale	2-0		Lees, Walker
23	11	ROCHDALE	1-2		Rippon
24	16	Halifax Town	2-1		Chambers, Fenwick
25	18	TRANMERE ROVERS	4-1		Chambers(2), Rippon, Walker
26	25	Tranmere Rovers	0-4		
27	4 Mar	STALYBRIDGE CELTIC	2-1		Ward, Walker
28	11	Stalybridge Celtic	0-2		
29	18	Wigan Borough	1-3		Lemons
30	25	WIGAN BOROUGH	3-0		Lemons(2), Lees
31	1 Apr	Hartlepools United	1-1		Lees
32	8	HARTLEPOOLS UNITED	1-1		Lees
33	14	Grimsby Town	1-3		Ward
34	15	Southport Central	0-0		
35	17	GRIMSBY TOWN	0-2		
36	22	SOUTHPORT CENTRAL	3-1		Lees, Rippon(2)
37	29	Stockport County	2-2		Ward, Lees
38	6 May	STOCKPORT COUNTY	0-1		

F.A. CUP

| 5QF | 3 Dec | NORTHAMPTON TOWN | 1-2 | | Lees |

LINCOLNSHIRE CUP

SF	16 Mar	Grimsby Town	2-2		Lemons, Lees
SFr	22	GRIMSBY TOWN	1-0		Rippon
F	1 May	Boston	2-0		Lemons, Rippon

Final League Table

		Pl.	Home	Away	F.	A.	Pts
			W D L F A	W D L F A			
1	Stockport County	38	13 5 1 36 10	11 3 5 24 11	60	21	56
2	Darlington	38	15 2 2 52 7	7 4 8 29 30	81	37	50
3	Grimsby Town	38	15 4 0 54 15	6 4 9 18 32	72	47	50
4	Hartlepools United	38	10 6 3 33 11	7 2 10 19 28	52	39	42
5	Accrington Stanley	38	15 1 3 50 15	4 2 13 23 42	73	57	41
6	Crewe Alexandra	38	13 1 5 39 21	5 4 10 21 35	60	56	41
7	Stalybridge Celtic	38	14 3 2 42 15	4 2 13 20 48	62	63	41
8	Walsall	38	15 2 2 52 17	3 1 15 14 48	66	65	39
9	Southport	38	11 6 2 39 12	3 4 12 16 32	55	44	38
10	Ashington	38	13 2 4 42 22	4 2 13 17 44	59	66	38
11	Durham City	38	14 0 5 43 20	3 3 13 25 47	68	67	37
12	Wrexham	38	12 4 3 40 17	2 5 12 11 39	51	56	37
13	Chesterfield	38	12 2 5 33 15	4 1 14 15 52	48	67	35
14	*Lincoln City*	*38*	*11 2 6 32 20*	*3 4 12 16 39*	*48*	*59*	*34*
15	Barrow	38	11 2 6 29 18	3 13 13 36	42	54	33
16	Nelson	38	7 6 6 27 23	6 1 12 21 43	48	66	33
17	Wigan Borough	38	9 4 6 32 28	2 5 12 14 44	46	72	31
18	Tranmere Rovers	38	7 5 7 41 25	2 6 11 10 36	51	61	29
19	Halifax Town	38	9 4 6 37 28	1 5 13 19 48	56	76	29
20	Rochdale	38	9 2 8 34 24	2 2 15 18 53	52	77	26

1921-22
Back: Waites, Barnett, Lemons, Fenwick, Forbes, Bryan, Clint, Bainbridge, Stimpson, Atkin, Richardson, Lishman, Ward.
Centre: Langham(trainer), Bonham, Rippon, Garner, Chambers, Dwane, Marples, Herrick, Walker, Anthony(asst. trainer).
Front : Hall, Greaves, Lees, Moon, Travis.

1922-23
Back : McGrahan, Greaves, Kendall, Fenwick, Dwane, Ward.
Front : Kean, Boylen, Thorpe, Griffiths, Sillito.

SEASON 1922-23
DIVISION THREE (NORTH)

No.	Date	Opposition	Res.	Att.	Goalscorers
1	26 Aug	Halifax Town	1-3		Griffiths
2	2 SEP	HALIFAX TOWN	0-0		
3	9	ROCHDALE	0-1		
4	16	Rochdale	1-1		Pringle
5	23	STALYBRIDGE CELTIC	1-1		Fenwick
6	30	Stalybridge Celtic	1-0		Thorpe
7	7 OCT	Wrexham	2-0		Thorpe, Griffiths
8	14	WREXHAM	2-0		Sillito, Ward
9	21	Bradford Park Avenue	1-4		Kean
10	28	BRADFORD PARK AVENUE	0-0		
11	4 Nov	SOUTHPORT CENTRAL	2-0		Thorpe, Pringle
12	11	Southport Central	0-3		
13	25	DARLINGTON	1-1		Ward
14	9 Dec	Ashington	2-0		OG, Griffiths
15	23	HARTLEPOOLS UNITED	2-1		Pringle, Griffiths
16	25	Walsall	0-2		
17	26	Walsall	0-2		
18	30	BARROW	1-1		Griffiths
19	1 Jan	Hartlepools United	0-2		
20	6	Barrow	3-1		Griffiths(2), Dwane
21	13	Darlington	0-0		
22	20	NELSON	1-0		Ward
23	27	Nelson	1-2		Pringle
24	3 Feb	Tranmere Rovers	0-2		
25	10	TRANMERE ROVERS	2-0		Kean, Thorpe
26	17	Durham City	1-7		Thorpe
27	24	DURHAM CITY	3-1		Kean, Pringle(2)
28	3 Mar	Wigan Borough	1-9		Morton
29	10	WIGAN BOROUGH	2-1		Morton(2)
30	17	CHESTERFIELD	0-0		
31	30	ASHINGTON	2-0		Panther(2)
32	31	CREWE ALEXANDRA	1-0		Ludkin
33	2 Apr	Chesterfield	3-3		Kean, Panther, Morton
34	7	Crewe Alexandra	1-3		Pringle
35	14	GRIMSBY TOWN	1-2		Thorpe
36	21	Grimsby Town	0-0		
37	28	ACCRINGTON STANLEY	0-0		
38	5 May	Accrington Stanley	0-1		

1 own goal

F.A. CUP

4QF	18 Nov	Chesterfield	0-2		

LINCOLNSHIRE CUP

4R	16 Dec	GRANTHAM TOWN	4-0		Pringle, Griffiths(2), Ward
SF	31 Jan	SCUNTHORPE UNITED	1-0		Fenwick
F	30 Apr	Grimsby Town	1-2		Sillito

Bye in rounds 1, 2 & 3

Final League Table

		Pl.	Home					Away					F.	A.	Pts
			W	D	L	F	A	W	D	L	F	A			
1	Nelson	38	15	2	2	37	10	9	1	9	24	31	61	41	51
2	Bradford Park Ave.	38	14	4	1	51	15	5	5	9	16	23	67	38	47
3	Walsall	38	13	4	2	32	14	6	4	9	19	30	51	44	46
4	Chesterfield	38	13	5	1	49	18	6	2	11	19	34	68	52	45
5	Wigan Borough	38	14	3	2	45	11	4	5	10	19	28	64	39	44
6	Crewe Alexandra	38	13	3	3	32	9	4	6	9	16	29	48	38	43
7	Halifax Town	38	11	4	4	29	14	6	3	10	24	32	53	46	41
8	Accrington Stanley	38	14	2	3	40	14	3	5	11	19	44	59	65	41
9	Darlington	38	13	3	3	43	14	2	7	10	16	32	59	46	40
10	Wrexham	38	13	5	1	29	12	1	5	13	9	36	38	48	38
11	Stalybridge Celtic	38	13	2	4	32	18	2	4	13	10	29	42	47	36
12	Rochdale	38	8	5	6	29	22	5	5	9	13	31	42	53	36
13	*Lincoln City*	38	9	7	3	21	11	4	3	12	18	44	39	55	36
14	Grimsby Town	38	10	3	6	35	18	4	2	13	20	34	55	52	33
15	Hartlepools United	38	10	6	3	34	14	0	6	13	14	40	48	54	32
16	Tranmere Rovers	38	11	4	4	41	21	1	4	14	8	38	49	59	32
17	Southport	38	11	3	5	21	12	1	4	14	11	34	32	46	31
18	Barrow	38	11	2	6	31	17	2	2	15	19	43	50	60	30
19	Ashington	38	10	3	6	34	33	1	5	13	17	44	51	77	30
20	Durham City	38	7	9	3	31	19	2	1	16	12	40	43	59	28

SEASON 1923-24
DIVISION THREE (NORTH)

No.	Date	Opposition	Res.	Att.	Goalscorers
1	25 Aug	HALIFAX TOWN	1-0		Kean
2	1 Sep	Halifax Town	0-1		
3	5	HARTLEPOOLS UNITED	1-1		Bauchop
4	8	BARROW	4-1		Bauchop, Kean(2), Sillito
5	15	Barrow	1-2		Bauchop
6	22	GRIMSBY TOWN	1-3		Thorpe
7	29	Grimsby Town	2-2		Bauchop(2)
8	6 Oct	DARLINGTON	2-0		Thorpe, Pringle
9	13	Darlington	0-1		
10	20	Tranmere Rovers	3-1		Pringle(3)
11	27	TRANMERE ROVERS	1-1		Kean
12	3 Nov	Bradford Park Avenue	1-3		Mackey
13	10	BRADFORD PARK AVENUE	2-3		Roe, Pringle
14	24	Chesterfield	1-2		Bauchop
15	8 Dec	ROTHERHAM COUNTY	2-1		Roe(2)
16	22	WREXHAM	4-2		Roe(2), Kean, Pringle
17	25	ROCHDALE	0-2		
18	26	Rochdale	0-1		
19	29	Doncaster Rovers	2-3		Bauchop, Mackey
20	1 Jan	Hartlepools United	1-1		Bauchop
21	5	DONCASTER ROVERS	1-1		Kean
22	12	CHESTERFIELD	0-1		
23	19	ACCRINGTON STANLEY	0-2		
24	26	Accrington Stanley	1-3		Bauchop
25	2 Feb	CREWE ALEXANDRA	0-0		
26	9	Crewe Alexandra	2-1		Roe, Pringle
27	16	DURHAM CITY	3-1		Jewett, Roe, Bauchop
28	23	Durham City	0-1		
29	1 Mar	WIGAN BOROUGH	1-1		Roe
30	8	Wigan Borough	0-0		
31	12	Wrexham	1-2		Bauchop
32	15	Ashington	1-2		Roe
33	22	ASHINGTON	2-0		Jewett, Roe
34	29	Walsall	0-0		
35	5 Apr	WALSALL	2-0		Jewett, Roe
36	12	WOLVERHAMPTON WANDS.	0-0		
37	18	Southport Central	2-3		Kean, Dwane
38	19	Wolverhampton Wanderers	0-3		
39	21	SOUTHPORT CENTRAL	1-1		Thorpe
40	22	Rotherham County	0-2		
41	26	New Brighton	1-3		Roe
42	3 May	NEW BRIGHTON	1-0		Dwane

F.A. CUP

Round	Date	Opposition	Res.	Att.	Goalscorers
4QF	17 Nov	Denaby United	2-1		OG, Jewett
5QF	1 Dec	Northampton Town	1-5		Bauchop

LINCOLNSHIRE CUP

Round	Date	Opposition	Res.	Att.	Goalscorers
3R	16 Jan	Gainsborough Trinity	2-1		Jewett, Walker
SF	20 Mar	Grantham Town	2-0		Roe, Sillito
F	14 Apr	GRIMSBY TOWN	1-0		Kean

Bye 1R & 2R

Final League Table

	Pl.	W	Home D	L	F	A	W	Away D	L	F	A	F.	A.	Pts
1 Wolverhampton W.	42	18	3	0	51	10	6	12	3	25	17	76	27	63
2 Rochdale	42	17	4	0	40	8	8	5	8	20	18	60	26	62
3 Chesterfield	42	16	4	1	54	15	6	6	9	16	24	70	39	54
4 Rotherham County	42	16	3	2	46	13	7	3	11	24	30	70	43	52
5 Bradford Park Ave.	42	17	3	1	50	12	4	7	10	19	31	69	43	52
6 Darlington	42	16	5	0	51	19	4	3	14	19	34	70	53	48
7 Southport	42	13	7	1	30	10	3	7	11	14	32	44	42	46
8 Ashington	42	14	4	3	41	21	4	4	13	18	40	59	61	44
9 Doncaster Rovers	42	13	4	4	41	17	2	8	11	18	36	59	53	42
10 Wigan Borough	42	12	5	4	39	15	2	9	10	16	38	55	53	42
11 Grimsby Town	42	11	9	1	30	7	3	4	14	19	40	49	47	41
12 Tranmere Rovers	42	11	5	5	32	21	2	10	9	19	39	51	60	41
13 Accrington Stanley	42	14	4	3	35	21	4	3	14	13	40	48	61	40
14 Halifax Town	42	11	4	6	26	17	4	6	11	16	42	42	59	40
15 Durham City	42	12	5	4	40	23	3	4	14	19	37	59	60	39
16 Wrexham	42	8	11	2	24	12	2	7	12	13	32	37	44	38
17 Walsall	42	10	5	6	31	20	4	3	14	13	39	44	59	36
18 New Brighton	42	9	9	3	28	10	2	4	15	12	43	40	53	35
19 Lincoln City	**42**	**8**	**8**	**5**	**29**	**22**	**2**	**4**	**15**	**19**	**37**	**48**	**59**	**32**
20 Crewe Alexandra	42	6	7	8	20	24	1	6	14	12	34	32	58	27
21 Hartlepools United	42	5	7	9	22	24	2	4	15	11	46	33	70	25
22 Barrow	42	7	7	7	25	24	1	2	18	10	56	35	80	25

SEASON 1924-25
DIVISION THREE (NORTH)

No.	Date	Opposition	Res.	Att.	Goalscorers
1	1 Sep	WIGAN BOROUGH	1-0		Bolam
2	6	DONCASTER ROVERS	2-0		Heathcote, Pringle
3	8	Wigan Borough	0-4		
4	13	Southport	0-4		
5	17	Crewe Alexandra	1-1		Pringle
6	20	ASHINGTON	5-0		Heathcote(3), Pringle, Sisson
7	27	Nelson	0-1		
8	1 Oct	Wrexham	1-0		Heathcote
9	4	BARROW	2-1		Pringle(2)
10	11	New Brighton	1-4		Rushton
11	18	TRANMERE ROVERS	3-2		Allen, Pringle, Heathcote
12	25	GRIMSBY TOWN	0-0		
13	1 Nov	Hartlepools United	1-1		Pringle
14	8	ROCHDALE	1-2		Heathcote
15	22	BRADFORD PARK AVENUE	0-4		
16	6 Dec	ROTHERHAM COUNTY	3-1		Moore, Bell, Pringle
17	13	Rotherham County	1-1		Moore
18	20	ACCRINGTON STANLEY	3-0		Whitfield, Heathcote, Pringle
19	25	Halifax Town	0-1		
20	26	HALIFAX TOWN	1-1		Barratt
21	27	DURHAM CITY	3-0		J.Marshall, Bell(2)
22	1 Jan	Durham City	0-5		
23	3	Doncaster Rovers	1-2		Heathcote
24	17	SOUTHPORT CENTRAL	1-1		Pringle
25	24	Ashington	1-2		L.Marshall
26	7 Feb	Barrow	2-1		Heathcote, Pringle
27	11	Darlington	1-0		L.Marshall
28	14	NEW BRIGHTON	2-0		Allen(2)
29	21	Tranmere Rovers	0-0		
30	28	Grimsby Town	2-1		L.Marshall(2)
31	7 Mar	HARTLEPOOLS UNITED	2-1		Allen, Pringle
32	11	Chesterfield	0-2		
33	14	Rochdale	0-3		
34	18	NELSON	2-1		Hooper, Pringle
35	21	DARLINGTON	0-1		
36	28	Bradford Park Avenue	0-4		
37	4 Apr	WREXHAM	1-1		Pringle
38	10	WALSALL	0-1		
39	13	Walsall	0-2		
40	18	CHESTERFIELD	3-1		Heathcote(3)
41	25	Accrington Stanley	2-0		Andrews, Barratt
42	2 May	CREWE ALEXANDRA	4-1		Andrews, Barratt, Hooper, Pringle

F.A. CUP

4QF	15 Nov	ROSSINGTON MAIN	3-0		Rushton, Bell, Whitfield
5QF	29	Alfreton Town	0-1		

LINCOLNSHIRE CUP

4R	15 Jan	Boston	1-2		Pringle

Bye 1R, 2R & 3R

Final League Table

		Pl.	Home W D L F A	Away W D L F A	F. A. Pts
1	Darlington	42	16 4 1 50 14	8 6 7 28 19	78 33 58
2	Nelson	42	18 2 1 58 14	5 5 11 21 36	79 50 53
3	New Brighton	42	17 3 1 56 16	6 4 11 19 34	75 50 53
4	Southport	42	17 2 2 41 7	5 5 11 18 30	59 37 51
5	Bradford Park Ave.	42	15 5 1 59 13	4 7 10 25 29	84 42 50
6	Rochdale	42	17 2 2 53 16	4 5 12 22 37	75 53 49
7	Chesterfield	42	14 3 4 42 15	3 8 10 18 29	60 44 45
8	Lincoln City	42	13 4 4 39 19	5 4 12 14 39	53 58 44
9	Halifax Town	42	11 5 5 36 22	5 6 10 20 30	56 52 43
10	Ashington	42	13 4 4 41 24	3 6 12 27 52	68 76 42
11	Wigan Borough	42	10 7 4 39 16	5 4 12 23 49	62 65 41
12	Grimsby Town	42	10 6 5 38 21	5 3 13 22 39	60 60 39
13	Durham City	42	11 6 4 38 17	2 7 12 12 51	50 68 39
14	Barrow	42	14 4 3 39 22	2 3 16 12 52	51 74 39
15	Crewe Alexandra	42	11 7 3 35 24	2 6 13 18 54	53 78 39
16	Wrexham	42	11 5 5 37 21	4 3 14 16 40	53 61 38
17	Accrington Stanley	42	12 5 4 43 23	3 3 15 17 49	60 72 38
18	Doncaster Rovers	42	12 5 4 36 17	2 5 14 18 48	54 65 38
19	Walsall	42	10 6 5 27 16	3 5 13 17 37	44 53 37
20	Hartlepools United	42	9 8 4 28 21	3 3 15 17 42	45 63 35
21	Tranmere Rovers	42	11 3 7 40 29	3 1 17 19 49	59 78 32
22	Rotherham County	42	6 5 10 27 31	1 2 18 15 57	42 88 21

1924-25
Back : Allen, Rushton, Grocott, Wrigley, Sisson, Read, Anthony (trainer),
Hempsall, Gillott, Sissons, Brown, Page, Storey, Ludkin (assistant trainer).
Front : Barratt, Pringle, Roe, Heathcote, Moore, Dovey, Panther, Hodges, Bolam, Bell.

1925-26
Back: Rose(trainer), Page, Havelock, Webster, Lawrence, Sissons, Walker, Sisson, Marshall, Ludkin(asst. trainer).
Centre : Hempsall, Campbell, Kemp, Fenwick, Gillott, Rushton, Hale, Alford, Merritt.
Front : Barratt, Pringle, Dovey, Gordon, Walton, Mutch, Andrews, Hooper.

SEASON 1925-26
DIVISION THREE (NORTH)

No.	Date	Opposition	Res.	Att.	Goalscorers
1	29 Aug	Coventry City	2-3	15257	Merritt, Havelock
2	5 Sep	NELSON	1-3	7774	Pringle
3	7	SOUTHPORT CENTRAL	3-0	5143	Mutch, Barratt, Havelock
4	12	Barrow	0-3	4595	
5	15	Southport Central	2-3	5030	Mutch, Hooper
6	19	ASHINGTON	2-0	3138	Barratt, Havelock
7	21	CHESTERFIELD	2-1	5126	Havelock, Hooper
8	26	Wigan Borough	3-3	5434	Havelock(2), Page
9	3 Oct	NEW BRIGHTON	3-1	7124	Havelock, Page, Merritt
10	10	Crewe Alexandra	1-3	6037	Page
11	17	Bradford Park Avenue	1-4	7772	Havelock
12	24	GRIMSBY TOWN	4-1	13078	Havelock(2), Campbell, Merritt
13	31	Tranmere Rovers	0-2	5458	
14	7 Nov	WALSALL	5-1	2460	Campbell, Havelock(2), Barratt, Robson
15	14	Accrington Stanley	1-3	5649	Havelock
16	21	DURHAM CITY	1-0	4758	Hooper
17	5 Dec	ROCHDALE	0-2	5153	
18	19	HALIFAX TOWN	0-1	4444	
19	25	WREXHAM	3-2	7110	Ward, Hetherington, Andrews
20	26	Wrexham	1-1	8197	Alford
21	1 Jan	Chesterfield	0-2	6181	
22	2	COVENTRY CITY	0-3	4823	
23	9	Hartlepools United	2-4	4291	Stevenson, Alford
24	16	Nelson	2-5	5586	Stevenson, Marshall
25	23	BARROW	4-3	4109	Havelock(4)
26	30	Ashington	1-4	3595	Pringle
27	6 Feb	WIGAN BOROUGH	2-1	4575	Stevenson(2)
28	13	New Brighton	0-5	4793	
29	20	CREWE ALEXANDRA	2-2	4595	Pringle, Ward
30	27	BRADFORD PARK AVENUE	1-1	6905	Hooper
31	6 Mar	Grimsby Town	0-4	12575	
32	13	TRANMERE ROVERS	1-3	4428	Barratt
33	20	Walsall	0-0	4931	
34	27	ACCRINGTON STANLEY	3-1	3107	Andrews(3)
35	2 Apr	Doncaster Rovers	0-1	9418	
36	3	Durham City	2-3	2364	Andrews(2)
37	5	DONCASTER ROVERS	3-1	5866	Andrews(2), Sayer
38	10	HARTEPOOLS UNITED	2-1	3627	Barratt, Andrews
39	17	Rochdale	1-0	6797	Alford
40	19	Rotherham United	3-1	2458	Andrews(3)
41	24	ROTHERHAM UNITED	0-3	4883	
42	1 May	Halifax Town	2-0	1958	Dovey, Andrews

F.A. CUP

1R	28 Nov	Bradford Park Avenue	2-2	12459	Havelock, Merritt
1Rr	2 Dec	BRADFORD PARK AVE.	1-1 *	5857	McGrahan
1R2r	7	Bradford Park Avenue #	1-2	5500	Hooper

* After extra time
# Played at Bramall Lane, Sheffield

LINCOLNSHIRE CUP

3R	16 Dec	GAINSBOROUGH TRINITY	2-0	1000	Havelock, Merritt
SF	26 Jan	Grimsby Town	1-0		Merritt
F	26 Apr	BOSTON	1-2	4000	Andrews

Bye in 1R & 2R

Final League Table

		Pl.	Home W D L F A	Away W D L F A	F. A. Pts
1	Grimsby Town	42	20 1 0 61 8	6 8 7 30 32	91 40 61
2	Bradford Park Ave.	42	18 2 1 65 10	8 6 7 36 33	101 43 60
3	Rochdale	42	16 1 4 55 25	11 4 6 49 33	104 58 59
4	Chesterfield	42	18 2 1 70 19	7 3 11 30 35	100 54 55
5	Halifax Town	42	12 5 4 34 19	5 6 10 19 31	53 50 45
6	Hartlepools United	42	15 5 1 59 23	3 3 15 23 50	82 73 44
7	Tranmere Rovers	42	15 2 4 45 27	4 4 13 28 56	73 83 44
8	Nelson	42	13 2 6 37 24	4 3 14 22 42	69 71 43
9	Ashington	42	11 6 4 44 23	5 5 11 26 39	70 62 43
10	Doncaster Rovers	42	11 7 3 52 25	5 4 12 28 47	80 72 43
11	Crewe Alexandra	42	14 3 4 43 23	3 6 12 20 38	63 61 43
12	New Brighton	42	13 4 4 51 29	4 4 13 18 38	69 67 42
13	Durham City	42	14 5 2 45 19	4 1 16 18 51	63 70 42
14	Rotherham United	42	13 3 5 44 28	4 4 13 25 64	69 92 41
15	**Lincoln City**	**42**	**14 2 5 42 28**	**3 3 15 24 54**	**66 82 39**
16	Coventry City	42	13 6 2 47 19	3 0 18 26 63	73 82 38
17	Wigan Borough	42	12 5 4 53 22	1 6 14 15 52	68 74 37
18	Accrington Stanley	42	14 0 7 49 34	3 3 15 32 71	81 105 37
19	Wrexham	42	9 6 6 39 31	2 4 15 24 61	63 92 32
20	Southport	42	9 6 6 37 34	2 4 15 25 58	62 92 32
21	Walsall	42	8 4 9 40 34	1 2 18 18 73	58 107 26
22	Barrow	42	4 2 15 28 49	3 2 16 22 49	50 98 18

SEASON 1926-27
DIVISION THREE (NORTH)

No.	Date	Opposition	Res.	Att.	Goalscorers
1	28 Aug	SOUTHPORT	1-1	7287	Dinsdale
2	4 Sep	Stockport County	3-3	7474	Pegg, Bosbury, Sayer
3	6	TRANMERE ROVERS	1-2	5388	Bissett
4	11	HARTLEPOOLS UNITED	1-2	5475	Campbell
5	13	ACCRINGTON STANLEY	4-0	3340	Sayer, Andrews(3)
6	18	Crewe Alexandra	3-3	5978	Andrews(3)
7	20	Tranmere Rovers	1-1	6484	Bissett
8	25	BARROW	3-1	5574	Dovey, Hamilton, Maidment
9	28	Accrington Stanley	1-1	5292	Andrews
10	2 Oct	Halifax Town	1-2	7825	Andrews
11	9	NELSON	1-4	4920	Dovey
12	16	Bradford Park Avenue	1-3	11032	Hamilton
13	23	WALSALL	3-3	3906	Stevenson(2), Andrews
14	30	Chesterfield	2-4	7206	Andrews, Maidment
15	6 Nov	ASHINGTON	4-0	3733	Andrews(2), Campbell, Hale
16	13	New Brighton	1-1	5690	Hamilton
17	20	WREXHAM	2-2	3495	Pringle, Sayer
18	4 Dec	DONCASTER ROVERS	0-0	4487	
19	18	ROTHERHAM UNITED	1-2	3723	Bosbury
20	25	Rochdale	3-7	8921	Sayer(2), Dinsdale
21	27	ROCHDALE	2-3	7812	Pegg, Marshall
22	1 Jan	Stoke City	0-2	11082	
23	15	Southport	3-2	3910	Dinsdale, Pegg, Bosbury
24	22	STOCKPORT COUNTY	1-3	3144	Dinsdale
25	29	Hartlepools United	1-1	2452	Andrews
26	5 Feb	CREWE ALEXANDRA	3-3	2854	Pringle, Bosbury, Andrews
27	12	Barrow	3-0	3876	Pegg, Dinsdale, Bosbury
28	19	HALIFAX TOWN	3-1	4344	Pegg, Pringle(2)
29	26	Nelson	1-2	5784	Dinsdale
30	28	Wigan Borough	2-3	2835	Andrews, Bosbury
31	5 Mar	BRADFORD PARK AVENUE	5-1	6358	Dinsdale(2), Pegg(2), Andrews
32	12	Walsall	2-1	4370	Bosbury, Andrews
33	19	CHESTERFIELD	3-1	5521	Dinsdale, Bassnett, Pegg
34	26	Ashington	2-1	2623	Bissett, Dinsdale
35	2 Apr	NEW BRIGHTON	4-1	4874	Bosbury, Pegg(2), Dinsdale
36	15	DURHAM CITY	5-0	7321	Dinsdale(4), Bosbury
37	16	WIGAN BOROUGH	2-0	5836	Maidment, Bosbury
38	18	Durham City	2-4	2785	Dinsdale, Bissett
39	23	Doncaster Rovers	3-1	4366	Dinsdale, Andrews, Bissett
40	27	Wrexham	1-1	1838	Dinsdale
41	30	STOKE CITY	1-3	7861	Dinsdale
42	7 May	Rotherham United	4-2	2155	Andrews, Dinsdale(2), Bissett

F.A. CUP

1R	27 Nov	ROTHERHAM UNITED	2-0	7394	Pringle, Andrews
2R	11 Dec	Coventry City	1-1	14047	Andrews
2Rr	15	COVENTRY CITY	2-1	5398	Dinsdale(2)
3R	8 Jan	PRESTON NORTH END	2-4	6656	Dinsdale(2)

LINCOLNSHIRE CUP (bye in R1)

2R	1 Feb	Grimsby Town	3-1		Pegg, Sayer, Bosbury
SF	31 Mar	Stamford Town	2-1	1458	Andrews, Maidment
F	5 May	Boston	1-0	4500	Pegg

Final League Table

		Pl.	Home W D L F A	Away W D L F A	Pts
1	Stoke City	42	17 3 1 57 11	10 6 5 35 29	63
2	Rochdale	42	18 2 1 72 22	8 4 9 33 43	58
3	Bradford Park Ave.	42	18 3 0 74 21	6 4 11 27 38	55
4	Halifax Town	42	13 6 2 46 23	8 5 8 24 30	53
5	Nelson	42	16 2 3 64 20	6 5 10 40 55	51
6	Stockport County	42	13 4 4 60 31	9 3 9 33 38	49
7	Chesterfield	42	12 4 2 65 24	6 1 14 27 44	47
8	Doncaster Rovers	42	13 4 4 58 27	5 7 9 23 38	47
9	Tranmere Rovers	42	13 5 3 54 28	6 3 12 31 45	46
10	New Brighton	42	14 2 5 49 24	4 8 9 30 46	46
11	Lincoln City	42	9 5 7 50 33	6 7 8 40 45	42
12	Southport	42	15 5 54 32	4 4 13 26 53	41
13	Wrexham	42	12 5 6 41 26	4 5 12 24 47	42
14	Walsall	42	10 4 7 35 22	4 6 11 33 59	38
15	Crewe Alexandra	42	11 5 5 46 28	3 4 14 25 53	37
16	Ashington	42	9 8 4 42 30	3 4 14 18 60	36
17	Hartlepools Utd.	42	11 4 6 43 26	3 2 16 23 55	34
18	Wigan Borough	42	10 6 5 44 28	1 4 16 22 55	32
19	Rotherham Utd.	42	8 6 7 41 35	2 6 13 29 57	32
20	Durham City	42	8 4 8 35 35	3 2 16 23 70	30
21	Accrington Stan.	42	9 3 9 45 38	1 4 16 17 60	27
22	Barrow	42	5 6 10 22 40	2 1 17 12 77	22

Back : Crone, Hempsall, Goldsborough, Tom Maidment, Pegg.
Second Row : Wynter (trainer), Armitage, Bissett, Bailey, Iremonger, Sissons, McConville, Lester Marshall.
Third Row : Henshall (secretary-manager), Bosbury, McGrahan, Archibald Campbell, Blunt, Robson, Gillott, Hale, Hamilton, Ludkin (assistant trainer). Front : Dovey, Hobbs, Pringle, Dinsdale, Andrews, Sayer, Stevenson, Grainger.

SEASON 1927-28
DIVISION THREE (NORTH)

No.	Date	Opposition	Res.	Att.	Goalscorers	Hill L.G.	Bissett J.T.	York A.E.	Bassnett A.	Robson J.W.	Hale A.	Bosbury C.E.	Pringle H.	Dinsdale W.A.	Andrews H.	Pegg F.E.	Worthy A.	Foulkes C.E.	Freeman J.A.	Campbell, Andrew	McConville P.	Gillott E.	Keating R.E.	Maidment T.	Hamilton W.	Russell D.P.
1	27 Aug	Doncaster Rovers	0-3	8451		1	2	3	4	5	6	7	8	9	10	11										
2	29	WIGAN BOROUGH	4-1	5518	Dinsdale, Pegg(2), Bosbury	1		3	4		6	7	8	9	10	11	2	5								
3	3 Sep	DARLINGTON	1-0	7192	Dinsdale	1		3	4		6	7	8	9	10	11	2	5								
4	7	Wigan Borough	3-1	4260	Dinsdale, Pegg(2)	1		3	4		6	7	8	9	10	11	2	5								
5	10	Ashington	5-4	3066	Bosbury,Pegg,Dinsdale,Pringle(2)	1		3	4		6	7	8	9	10	11	2	5								
6	17	CREWE ALEXANDRA	5-2	7175	Dinsdale(2),Hale,Bosbury,Andrews	1		3	4		6	7	8	9	10	11	2	5								
7	24	Halifax Town	1-3	9615	Dinsdale	1		3	4		6	7	8	9	10	11	2	5								
8	1 Oct	BRADFORD CITY	2-2	6049	Dinsdale, Bosbury	1		3	4		6	7	8	9	10	11	2	5								
9	8	New Brighton	3-2	4667	Dinsdale, Bassnett, Pringle	1		3	4	6		7	8	9	10	11	2	5								
10	15	STOCKPORT COUNTY	2-0	7468	Andrews, Dinsdale	1		3	4	6		7	8	9	10	11	2	5								
11	22	Rochdale	3-0	5229	Bassnett, Dinsdale, Pegg	1		3	4		6	7	8	9	10	11	2	5								
12	29	NELSON	0-0	7956		1		3	4		6	7	8	9	10	11	2	5								
13	5 Nov	Barrow	3-3	5131	Dinsdale(2), Foulkes	1		3	4		6	7	8	9	10	11	2	5								
14	12	ROTHERHAM UNITED	4-1	5819	Pegg(2), Bosbury(2)	1		3	4		6	7	8	9	10	11	2	5								
15	19	Southport	1-3	3113	Dinsdale	1		3	4		6	7	8	9	10	11	2	5								
16	3 Dec	Wrexham	0-1	4400		1		3			6	7	8	9	10	11	2	5	4							
17	13	DURHAM CITY	2-1	1475	Bassnett, Campbell	1		3	4		6	7	8	9		11	2	5		10						
18	17	Bradford Park Avenue	0-3	10977		1		3	4		6	7	8	9	10	11	2	5								
19	24	TRANMERE ROVERS	1-1	5363	Campbell	1		3	4	6		7	8	9		11	2	5		10						
20	26	Hartlepools United	2-1	3941	Pringle, Pegg	1		3	4		6	7	8	9		11	2	5		10						
21	27	HARTLEPOOLS UNITED	1-5	9277	Bassnett	1		3	4		6	7	8	9		11	2	5		10						
22	31	DONCASTER ROVERS	2-0	8631	Andrews, Pegg	1			4		6	7	8		10	11	2				3	5	9			
23	2 Jan	Accrington Stanley	0-1	5682		1			4		6	7	8		10	11	2				3	5	9			
24	7	Darlington	2-9	8365	Dinsdale, Andrews	1			4		6	7	8	9	10	11	2				3	5				
25	21	ASHINGTON	3-1	5768	York, Hale, Bassnett	1		3	4		6	7	8	9	10	11	2	5								
26	28	Stockport County	0-2	7478		1		3	4		6	7	8	9	10	11	2	5								
27	4 Feb	HALIFAX TOWN	5-2	5515	Andrews(3), Bosbury(2)	1		3	4		6	7		9	10	11	2	5						8		
28	11	Bradford City	1-3	7229	Pegg	1		3	4		6	7		9	10	11	2	5						8		
29	18	NEW BRIGHTON	1-2	5375	Pegg	1		3	4			7	8	9	10	11	2	5	6							
30	3 Mar	ROCHDALE	3-1	5760	Dinsdale(2), Pringle	1		3	4		6	7	8	9	10	11	2	5								
31	10	Nelson	3-1	3422	Maidment, Pringle, Bosbury	1		3	4		6	7	10	9		11	2	5						8		
32	17	BARROW	5-0	5302	Campbell(2),Dinsdale(2),Maidment	1		3	4		6	7		9		11	2	5		10				8		
33	21	Crewe Alexandra	0-0	1856		1		3	4		6	7	10	9		11	2	5						8		
34	24	Rotherham United	4-2	4339	Maidment(2), Dinsdale, Bosbury	1		3	4		6	7	10	9		11	2	5						8		
35	31	SOUTHPORT	2-0	4427	York, Pegg	1		3	4		6	7		9		11	2	5						8		
36	6 Apr	ACCRINGTON STANLEY	3-1	8810	Bosbury(2), Pegg	1		3	4		6	7	10	9		11	2	5						8		
37	7	Chesterfield	1-0	4720	Dinsdale	1		3	4		6	7	10	9		11	2	5						8		
38	11	CHESTERFIELD	0-0	3650		1		3	4		6	7	10	9		11	2	5						8		
39	14	WREXHAM	5-0	4005	Dinsdale(2),Maidment(2),Bosbury	1		3	4		6	7	10	9		11	2	5						8		
40	21	Durham City	4-0	1305	Bosbury(2), Pringle, Dinsdale	1		3	4		6	7	10	9		11	2	5						8		
41	28	BRADFORD PARK AVENUE	2-0	9785	Dinsdale, Maidment	1		3	4		6	7	10	9		11	2	5						8		
42	5 May	Tranmere Rovers	2-2	4029	Pringle, Dinsdale	1		3	4		6	7	10	9		11	2	5						8		
					Apps.	42	1	39	41	4	38	42	39	40	27	41	41	38	2	5	3	3	2	14		
					Goals			2	5		2	15	8	26	7	14		1		4				7		

F.A. CUP

1R	26 Nov	Accrington Stanley	5-2	7245	Dinsdale(2),Pringle,Andrews,Bosbury	1		3	4		6	7	8	9	10	11	2	5								
2R	10 Dec	Gainsborough Trinity	2-0	7591	Bosbury(2)	1		3	4		6	7	8	9	10	11	2	5								
3R	14 Jan	Huddersfield Town	2-4	19229	Pringle, Dinsdale	1		3	4			7	8	9	10		2	5	6						11	

LINCOLNSHIRE CUP

3R	31 Jan	Cleethorpes Town *	7-1	1000	Dinsdale(2), Maidment(2), #		2	3	4	5	6	7		9		11					10			8		1
SF	25 Feb	Barton Town	11-0	1526	Andrews(3), York, Foulkes, +	1		3	4			7	8	9	10	11	2	5	6							
F	24 Apr	Grimsby Town	1-3	5000	Pegg	1		3	4		6	7	10	9		11	2	5						8		

Bye in 1R & 2R

* Played at Blundell Park, Grimsby   # Additional scorers: Bosbury, Pegg(2)   + Additional scorers: Pringle(2), Bosbury, Dinsdale(3)

Final League Table

		Pl.	Home					Away					F.	A.	Pts
			W	D	L	F	A	W	D	L	F	A			
1	Bradford Park Ave.	42	18	2	1	68	22	9	7	5	33	23	101	45	63
2	Lincoln City	42	15	4	2	53	20	9	3	9	38	44	91	64	55
3	Stockport County	42	16	5	0	62	14	7	3	11	27	37	89	51	54
4	Doncaster Rovers	42	15	4	2	59	18	8	3	10	21	26	80	44	53
5	Tranmere Rovers	42	14	6	1	68	28	8	3	10	37	44	105	72	53
6	Bradford City	42	15	4	2	59	19	3	8	10	26	41	85	60	48
7	Darlington	42	15	1	5	63	26	6	4	11	26	46	89	74	47
8	Southport	42	15	2	4	55	24	5	3	13	24	46	79	70	45
9	Accrington Stanley	42	14	4	3	49	22	4	4	13	27	45	76	67	44
10	New Brighton	42	10	7	4	45	22	4	7	10	27	40	72	62	42
11	Wrexham	42	15	1	5	48	19	3	5	13	16	48	64	67	42
12	Halifax Town	42	11	7	3	47	24	2	8	11	26	47	73	71	41
13	Rochdale	42	13	4	4	45	24	4	3	14	29	53	74	77	41
14	Rotherham United	42	11	6	4	39	19	3	5	13	26	50	65	69	39
15	Hartlepools United	42	10	3	8	41	35	6	3	12	28	46	69	81	38
16	Chesterfield	42	10	4	7	46	29	3	6	12	25	49	71	78	36
17	Crewe Alexandra	42	10	6	5	51	28	2	4	15	26	58	77	86	34
18	Ashington	42	10	5	6	54	36	1	6	14	23	67	77	103	33
19	Barrow	42	10	8	3	41	24	0	3	18	13	78	54	102	31
20	Wigan Borough	42	8	5	8	30	32	2	5	14	26	65	56	97	30
21	Durham City	42	10	5	6	37	30	1	2	18	16	70	53	100	29
22	Nelson	42	8	4	9	50	49	2	2	17	26	87	76	136	26

1927-28
Back : Wynter (trainer), Bissett, Worthy, Russell, Bassnett, Hill, York, McConville, Ludkin.(assistant trainer).
Centre : Bosbury, Richards, Gillott, Foulkes, Robson, Hale, Freeman, Hamilton,
Parkes (secretary/manager), Tyler (assistant groundsman).
Front : Todd, Pringle, Maidment, Dinsdale, Keating, Andrews, Edwards, Pegg.

1928-29
Back : Wynter (trainer), Clipson, Worthy, Hill, Kendall, McConville, York, Ludkin (assistant trainer).
Centre : Parkes (secretary/manager), Bosbury, Roberts, Hargreaves, Foulkes,
Beaman, Gallagher, Hale, Sykes, Campbell, Pegg, Jubb (director).
Front : Osgerby, Maidment, Harrison, Dinsdale, Kitching, Bassnett, Gorringe, Pringle, Warren.

SEASON 1928-29
DIVISION THREE (NORTH)

No.	Date	Opposition	Res.	Att.	Goalscorers
1	25 Aug	WIGAN BOROUGH	1-3	7913	Pegg
2	27	Rotherham United	2-3	3641	Pringle, Pegg
3	1 Sep	Crewe Alexandra	3-1	4411	Pegg, Bosbury, Pringle
4	3	ROTHERHAM UNITED	1-1	5943	Bosbury
5	8	TRANMERE ROVERS	3-1	6339	Pegg, Pringle, Kitching
6	15	Stockport County	3-7	10924	York, Pringle, Bosbury
7	22	HALIFAX TOWN	3-0	6322	Pegg, Dinsdale(2)
8	25	Nelson	4-3	4970	Pegg(2), Pringle, Gorringe
9	29	Doncaster Rovers	0-0	6727	
10	6 Oct	Bradford City	3-2	15584	Dinsdale(2), Maidment
11	13	ACCRINGTON STANLEY	3-1	6431	Dinsdale(2), Pegg
12	20	BARROW	5-0	6104	Dinsdale, Worthy, York(2), Maidment
13	27	Chesterfield	1-1	3990	York
14	3 Nov	WREXHAM	1-1	10625	Gorringe
15	10	New Brighton	1-6	4387	Dinsdale
16	17	ROCHDALE	2-0	5586	Pegg, Gorringe
17	1 Dec	DARLINGTON	0-0	5842	
18	15	SOUTH SHIELDS	5-0	5337	Roberts(2), Hale, Dinsdale, Pringle
19	22	Ashington	1-1	1129	Bosbury
20	25	Hartlepools United	2-3	3699	Dinsdale(2)
21	26	HARTLEPOOLS UNITED	7-1	9668	Dinsdale(3), Pegg(3), Bosbury
22	29	Wigan Borough	0-4	7517	
23	1 Jan	Carlisle United	1-3	10539	Dinsdale
24	5	CREWE ALEXANDRA	1-0	4832	Dinsdale
25	19	Tranmere Rovers	1-2	4248	Dinsdale
26	26	STOCKPORT COUNTY	1-2	6643	Maidment
27	2 Feb	Halifax Town	2-4	3927	Pringle, Savage
28	9	DONCASTER ROVERS	2-1	5168	Dinsdale, Pegg
29	16	BRADFORD CITY	3-4	4523	Pringle, Dinsdale(2)
30	23	Accrington Stanley	1-0	3377	Dinsdale
31	2 Mar	Barrow	3-2	8256	Dinsdale, Pegg(2)
32	9	CHESTERFIELD	1-0	5371	Kitching
33	16	Wrexham	1-2	6888	Kitching
34	23	NEW BRIGHTON	4-0	4033	Kitching(2), Pegg, Fisher
35	29	CARLISLE UNITED	3-0	8734	Kitching(2), Maidment
36	30	Rochdale	2-0	4848	Kitching, Jenkins
37	1 Apr	ASHINGTON	3-1	5068	Maidment, Kitching(2)
38	6	SOUTHPORT	4-1	4170	Kitching(2), Pegg(2)
39	13	Darlington	1-2	2454	Kitching
40	20	NELSON	5-1	4036	Kitching(2), Maidment, Fisher, Pegg
41	27	South Shields	0-1	2542	
42	4 May	Southport	1-2	2244	Sykes

F.A. CUP

1R	24 Nov	Lancaster Town	3-1	4325	Dinsdale(2), Pringle
2R	8 Dec	Carlisle United	1-0	13700	Roberts
3R	12 Jan	LEICESTER CITY	0-1	16849	

LINCOLNSHIRE CUP

SF	13 Mar	BOSTON	3-1	1265	Fisher, Savage(2)
F	11 May	GRIMSBY TOWN	0-1	7374	

Final League Table

```
                Pl.  Home              Away           F.  A.  Pts
                     W  D  L  F  A    W  D  L  F  A
 1 Bradford City 42  17  2 2 82 18   10  7  4 46 25  128 43  63
 2 Stockport County 42 19 2 0 77 23   9  4  8 34 35  111 58  62
 3 Wrexham      42  17  2 2 59 25    8  9  4 32 44   91 69  52
 4 Wigan Borough 42 16  4 1 55 16    5  5 11 27 33   82 49  51
 5 Doncaster Rovers 42 14 3 4 39 20  6  7  8 37 46   76 66  50
 6 Lincoln City 42  15  3 3 58 18    6  3 12 33 49   91 67  48
 7 Tranmere Rovers 42 15 3 3 55 21   7  0 14 24 56   79 77  47
 8 Carlisle United 42 15 3 3 61 27   4  5 12 25 50   86 77  46
 9 Crewe Alexandra 42 11 6 4 47 23   7  2 12 33 45   80 68  44
10 South Shields 42 13 5 3 57 24    5  3 13 26 50   83 74  44
11 Chesterfield 42  13  2 6 46 28    5  3 13 25 49   71 77  41
12 Southport    42  13  5 3 52 27    3 15 23 58    75 85  40
13 Halifax Town 42  11  7 3 42 24    2  6 13 21 38   63 62  39
14 New Brighton 42  11  3 7 40 28    6 11 24 43    64 71  39
15 Nelson       42  14  1 6 48 28    3  4 14 29 62   77 90  39
16 Rotherham United 42 12 5 4 44 23  3  4 14 16 54   60 77  39
17 Rochdale     42  12  4 5 55 34    1  6 14 24 62   79 96  36
18 Accrington Stanley 42 11 5 5 42 22  2 3 16 26 60  68 82  34
19 Darlington   42  12  6 3 47 26    1  1 19 17 62   64 88  33
20 Barrow       42   7  6 8 42 37    3  2 12 22 56   64 93  28
21 Hartlepools United 42 9 4 8 35 38  1 2 18 24 74  59 112  26
22 Ashington    42   6  5 10 31 52   2  2 17 14 63   45 115 23
```

SEASON 1929-30
DIVISION THREE (NORTH)

Players: Kendall J.W., Worthy A., York A.E., Savage R.E., Hunter C., Hale A., Jenkins E.T., Maidment T., Kitching H., Robinson W.A., Ellis W.T., Pringle H., Mitchell T, Sykes E.A.A., Roberts H., Thursby R.S., McConville P., Young A., Lax W., Foulkes C.E., Fisher J., Burnikell W.F., Meeson A.W., Pegg F.E.

No.	Date	Opposition	Res.	Att.	Goalscorers
1	31 Aug	ROCHDALE	0-0	6415	
2	2 Sep	Rotherham United	0-1	6605	
3	7	South Shields	1-3	5071	Maidment
4	9	ROTHERHAM UNITED	1-1	5739	Savage
5	14	ACCRINGTON STANLEY	3-3	6040	Ellis, Pringle, Roberts
6	16	PORT VALE	3-2	5842	Robinson(3)
7	21	Darlington	1-1	5498	Robinson
8	28	HARTLEPOOLS UNITED	2-2	5792	Maidment, Robinson
9	5 Oct	Doncaster Rovers	0-0	4467	
10	12	CHESTERFIELD	2-1	5612	Robinson, Thursby
11	19	YORK CITY	3-0	5310	Maidment, Ellis, Thursby
12	26	Crewe Alexandra	1-1	4688	Thursby
13	2 Nov	SOUTHPORT	1-1	5190	Ellis
14	9	Nelson	0-0	3692	
15	16	CARLISLE UNITED	4-1	5298	Roberts, Maidment, Thursby, Pringle
16	23	Wigan Borough	1-4	2932	Roberts
17	7 Dec	Barrow	1-2	3052	Pringle
18	21	New Brighton	4-1	2582	Hunter, Maidment, Jenkins(2)
19	25	Halifax Town	1-1	4618	Ellis
20	26	HALIFAX TOWN	0-1	10304	
21	1 Jan	Stockport County	1-1	9972	Pringle
22	4	SOUTH SHIELDS	2-2	5675	Roberts, Maidment
23	18	Accrington Stanley	3-0	4513	Ellis, Thursby, Pringle
24	25	DARLINGTON	2-2	6801	Ellis, Maidment
25	1 Feb	Hartlepools United	0-4	1716	
26	8	DONCASTER ROVERS	3-1	5914	Jenkins, Robinson, Lax
27	15	Chesterfield	1-2	3932	Fisher
28	19	WREXHAM	3-0	2631	Maidment, Roberts, Ellis
29	22	York City	0-1	5298	
30	1 Mar	CREWE ALEXANDRA	2-2	4629	Jenkins, Kitching
31	8	Southport	2-3	3154	Roberts(2)
32	15	NELSON	4-1	2057	Jenkins(3), Kitching
33	22	Carlisle United	4-2	4191	Roberts(4)
34	29	WIGAN BOROUGH	2-0	3941	Ellis, Pringle
35	5 Apr	Wrexham	1-3	3023	Roberts
36	8	Rochdale	4-3	1046	Ellis(2), Roberts(2)
37	12	BARROW	3-0	3597	Ellis, Maidment, Roberts
38	18	Tranmere Rovers	1-0	8095	Maidment
39	19	Port Vale	2-5	7649	Roberts, Jenkins
40	21	TRANMERE ROVERS	8-0	4842	Maidment(3), Roberts(4), Kitching
41	23	STOCKPORT COUNTY	1-0	5385	Maidment
42	26	NEW BRIGHTON	5-3	3431	Kitching, Jenkins(3), Roberts

Apps. 31 41 26 41 14 29 25 38 11 17 31 26 3 25 23 17 17 17 11 2 5 1 11
Goals 1 1 11 14 4 7 11 6 21 5 1 1

F.A. CUP

| 1R | 30 Nov | WIGAN BOROUGH | 3-1 | 8079 | Maidment(2), Thursby |
| 2R | 14 Dec | Queens Park Rangers | 1-2 | 13097 | Maidment |

LINCOLNSHIRE CUP

SF	13 Mar	Boston	3-3	2090	Maidment(2), Jenkins
SFr	31	BOSTON	2-0	1686	Worthy, Jenkins
F	10 May	Grimsby Town	1-7	7369	Maidment

Final League Table

		Pl.	Home W D L F A	Away W D L F A	F.	A.	Pts
1	Port Vale	42	17 2 2 64 18	13 5 3 39 19	103	37	67
2	Stockport County	42	15 3 3 67 20	8 4 9 39 24	106	44	63
3	Darlington	42	14 2 5 71 29	8 4 9 37 44	108	73	50
4	Chesterfield	42	18 1 2 53 15	4 5 12 23 41	76	56	50
5	**Lincoln City**	42	**12 8 1 54 23**	**5 6 10 29 38**	**83**	**61**	**48**
6	York City	42	11 7 3 43 20	4 9 8 34 44	77	64	46
7	South Shields	42	11 6 4 49 32	7 4 10 28 42	77	74	46
8	Hartlepools United	42	13 4 4 50 24	4 7 10 31 50	81	74	45
9	Southport	42	11 5 5 49 31	4 8 9 32 43	81	74	43
10	Rochdale	42	14 3 4 57 30	4 4 13 32 61	89	91	43
11	Crewe Alexandra	42	12 5 4 55 28	5 3 13 27 43	82	71	42
12	Tranmere Rovers	42	12 4 5 57 35	4 5 12 26 51	83	86	41
13	New Brighton	42	13 4 4 48 22	3 4 14 21 57	69	79	40
14	Doncaster Rovers	42	13 5 3 39 22	2 4 15 23 47	62	69	39
15	Carlisle United	42	13 4 4 63 34	3 3 15 27 67	90	101	39
16	Accrington Stanley	42	11 4 6 55 30	3 5 13 29 51	84	81	37
17	Wrexham	42	10 5 6 42 28	3 3 15 25 60	67	88	34
18	Wigan Borough	42	12 4 5 44 26	1 3 17 16 62	60	88	33
19	Nelson	42	9 4 8 31 25	4 3 14 20 55	51	80	33
20	Rotherham United	42	9 4 8 46 40	2 4 15 21 73	67	113	30
21	Halifax Town	42	7 7 7 27 26	3 1 17 17 53	44	79	28
22	Barrow	42	9 4 8 31 28	2 1 18 10 70	41	98	27

SEASON 1930-31
DIVISION THREE (NORTH)

No.	Date	Opposition	Res.	Att.	Goalscorers
1	30 Aug	New Brighton	1-2	4963	Dinsdale
2	1 Sep	WIGAN BOROUGH	2-0	6398	Dinsdale, Young
3	6	STOCKPORT COUNTY	6-1	7418	Cartwright(2), Lax(2), Dinsdale, Kitching
4	9	Nelson	2-1	3955	Pegg, T.Maidment
5	13	Gateshead	1-0	7505	Dinsdale
6	15	NELSON	2-0	6741	T.Maidment, Cartwright
7	20	DONCASTER ROVERS	1-0	6722	Lax
8	27	Hull City	3-1	12638	T.Maidment, Lax, Cartwright
9	4 Oct	BARROW	5-0	7329	T.Maidment(3), Worthy, Lax
10	11	HARTLEPOOLS UNITED	1-0	7516	Dinsdale
11	18	Southport	2-1	3479	Kitching, Lax
12	25	CHESTERFIELD	1-1	10840	Worthy
13	1 Nov	Rochdale	2-4	4307	Lax, Kitching
14	8	CREWE ALEXANDRA	3-1	7561	Lax, Cartwright, Savage
15	15	Wrexham	2-2	9616	T.Maidment, Kitching
16	22	TRANMERE ROVERS	1-3	9381	Kitching
17	6 Dec	YORK CITY	4-1	5679	T.Maidment(2), Dinsdale, Worthy
18	15	Rotherham United	2-2	2668	Dinsdale, Peg
19	20	ACCRINGTON STANLEY	5-2	5731	Cartwright(2), T.Maidment, Lax, Dinsdale
20	26	DARLINGTON	1-0	6002	Dinsdale
21	27	NEW BRIGHTON	4-0	8418	Kitching(2), Lax, Dinsdale
22	1 Jan	Darlington	1-0	5908	Pegg
23	3	Stockport County	2-4	14804	Cartwright, Dinsdale
24	15	Carlisle United	6-3	4621	Dinsdale(3), Pringle, T.Maidment(2)
25	17	GATESHEAD	0-0	7091	
26	24	Doncaster Rovers	1-0	5137	Cartwright
27	31	HULL CITY	3-0	9737	Lax, Cartwright, Kitching
28	7 Feb	Barrow	2-3	7678	Cartwright, Dinsdale
29	14	Hartlepools United	3-0	3706	Dinsdale, Pegg, T.Maidment
30	21	SOUTHPORT	3-3	8950	Kitching, Pegg, Dinsdale
31	7 Mar	ROCHDALE	5-0	6040	Pegg(3), Cartwright, Dinsdale
32	14	Crewe Alexandra	0-2	4459	
33	21	WREXHAM	3-2	7334	Whalley, Young, Lax
34	28	Tranmere Rovers	3-3	15402	Halliday(2), Lax
35	3 Apr	HALIFAX TOWN	4-1	10728	March(2), Lax, Halliday
36	4	CARLISLE UNITED	5-1	9011	Lax(2), Halliday, Worthy, March
37	6	Halifax Town	2-3	4616	Halliday, Whalley
38	11	York City	1-1	6004	Young
39	18	ROTHERHAM UNITED	1-3	7857	March
40	22	Chesterfield	2-3	20092	Dinsdale, Lax
41	25	Accrington Stanley	3-5	3844	Whalley(2), Dinsdale
42	2 May	Wigan Borough	1-0	2878	March

F.A. CUP

| 1R | 29 Nov | BARROW | 8-3 | 3800 | T.Maidment, Cartwright, * |
| 2R | 13 Dec | Scarborough | 4-6 | 6318 | Cartwright, Lax, Dinsdale(2) |

* Additional scorers: Dinsdale(3), Lax(2), Kitching

LINCOLNSHIRE CUP

| SF | 13 Apr | Scunthorpe United | 4-2 | | Dinsdale(2), Whalley, Worthy |
| F | 9 May | GRIMSBY TOWN | 2-2* | 3616 | OG, Thursby |

* replay played in 1931/32 season

Final League Table

		Pl.	Home W D L F A	Away W D L F A	F.	A.	Pts
1	Chesterfield	42	19 1 1 66 22	7 5 9 36 35	102	57	58
2	*Lincoln City*	42	16 3 2 60 19	9 4 8 42 40	102	59	57
3	Wrexham	42	16 4 1 61 25	5 8 8 33 37	94	62	54
4	Tranmere Rovers	42	16 3 2 73 26	8 3 10 38 48	111	74	54
5	Southport	42	15 3 3 52 19	7 6 8 36 37	88	56	53
6	Hull City	42	12 7 2 64 20	8 3 10 35 35	99	55	50
7	Stockport County	42	15 5 1 54 19	5 4 12 23 42	77	61	49
8	Carlisle United	42	13 4 4 68 32	7 1 13 30 49	98	81	45
9	Gateshead	42	14 4 3 46 22	2 9 10 25 51	71	73	45
10	Wigan Borough	42	14 4 3 48 25	5 1 15 28 61	76	86	43
11	Darlington	42	9 6 6 44 30	7 4 10 27 29	71	59	42
12	York City	42	15 3 3 59 30	3 3 15 26 52	85	82	42
13	Accrington Stanley	42	14 2 5 51 31	1 7 13 33 77	84	108	39
14	Rotherham United	42	9 6 6 50 34	4 6 11 31 49	81	83	38
15	Doncaster Rovers	42	9 8 4 40 18	4 3 14 25 47	65	65	37
16	Barrow	42	13 4 4 45 23	2 3 16 23 66	68	89	37
17	Halifax Town	42	11 6 4 30 16	2 3 16 25 73	55	89	35
18	Crewe Alexandra	42	13 2 6 52 35	1 4 16 14 58	66	93	34
19	New Brighton	42	12 4 5 36 25	1 3 17 13 51	49	76	33
20	Hartlepools United	42	10 2 9 47 37	2 4 15 20 49	67	86	30
21	Rochdale	42	9 1 11 42 50	3 5 13 20 57	62	107	30
22	Nelson	42	6 7 8 28 40	0 0 21 15 73	43	113	19

1930-31
Back : Wynter (trainer), Wright (treasurer), Boatman, Dinsdale, Davies, Jim Maidment, Meeson, Cowling, Savage, Begg, Hilton, Higham, Ludkin (assistant trainer), Knott (assistant secretary).
Centre : Parkes (secretary/manager), Cottam (director), Ward, Tom Maidment, Cartwright, Kitching, Young, Worthy, Sykes, Lax, Anderson, McConville, Taylor (director), Simpson (chairman).
Front : Thursby, Burnikell, Whalley, Pringle, Buckley, Pegg.

1931-32
Back : Wynter (trainer), Knott (assistant secretary), Cottam (director), Applewhite (director), Worthy, McPhail, Smith, Jubb (director), Parkes (secretary/ manager), Moore (director), Ludkin (assistant trainer).
Centre : Wright (treasurer), Taylor (dir.), Burnikell, Buckley, Young, Charles Pringle, Simpson (dir.), Irving (dir.).
Front : Cartwright, Keetley, Riley, Hall, Harry Pringle, Whyte.

SEASON 1931-32
DIVISION THREE (NORTH)

Players (column headers): McPhail D., Anderson R., McConville P., Pringle C.R., Young A., Buckley W., Cartwright P., Keetley F., Hall B.A.C., Pringle H., Whyte G., Lincoln A., Riley H., Worthy A., Halliday J.H., Burnikell W.F., Thursby R.S., Murray J., Edwards W.J., Smith J., Beel G.W., March H.J., Shepherd L.

No.	Date	Opposition	Res.	Att.	Goalscorers
1	29 Aug	DARLINGTON	2-0	8060	Hall, Whyte
2	31	HARTLEPOOLS UNITED	6-0	6539	Whyte, Hall, Keetley(2), Lincoln(2)
3	5 Sep	Halifax Town	0-3	4109	
4	12	WALSALL	3-0	7567	Buckley, Cartwright, Riley
5	19	Gateshead	3-2	14633	Hall, Riley, Halliday
6	26	NEW BRIGHTON	3-0	7335	Riley, Halliday, Hall
7	3 Oct	Barrow	2-0	9697	Riley, Thursby
8	10	HULL CITY	1-0	9492	Hall
9	17	STOCKPORT COUNTY	1-2	7747	Hall
10	24	Rotherham United	1-0	4714	Keetley
11	31	TRANMERE ROVERS	4-2	7623	Riley(2), Hall(2)
12	7 Nov	York City	1-1	4626	Keetley
13	14	SOUTHPORT	7-0	8030	Keetley(2), Riley, Hall(4)
14	21	Doncaster Rovers	3-0	5856	Hall(2), Riley
15	5 Dec	Crewe Alexandra	1-8	5356	Keetley
16	19	Wrexham	3-1	6198	Cartwright, Hall(2)
17	25	Chester	1-2	10184	Hall
18	26	CHESTER	4-0	12856	Cartwright, Hall(3)
19	1 Jan	Accrington Stanley	2-2	6571	Hall(2)
20	8	Darlington	6-0	6761	Keetley(2), Hall(3), Cartwright
21	9	ROCHDALE	3-0	6737	Cartwright(2), Hall
22	16	HALIFAX TOWN	9-1	7086	Riley(2), Hall, Keetley(6)
23	23	Walsall	3-0	5421	Keetley, Hall, Riley
24	30	GATESHEAD	1-0	14178	Hall
25	6 Feb	New Brighton	1-2	2768	Hall
26	13	BARROW	3-1	7617	Riley(2), Beel
27	20	Hull City	1-4	13608	Beel
28	24	CARLISLE UNITED	3-1	5384	Whyte, Hall, Keetley
29	27	Stockport County	1-0	9753	Beel
30	5 Mar	ROTHERHAM UNITED	3-1	7997	Beel, Keetley, Hall
31	12	Tranmere Rovers	0-1	7638	
32	19	YORK CITY	1-1	7327	Hall
33	25	ACCRINGTON STANLEY	5-1	11796	Whyte, Hall, Riley, Beel(2)
34	26	Southport	1-1	6398	Hall
35	2 Apr	DONCASTER ROVERS	1-2	7551	Hall
36	9	Rochdale	5-3	1938	Whyte(2), Riley, Cartwright, H.Pringle
37	16	CREWE ALEXANDRA	5-1	8359	Hall(3), Riley(2)
38	23	Carlisle United	3-0	3412	Hall, Cartwright, Whyte
39	30	WREXHAM	0-0	14938	
40	7 May	Hartlepools United	3-4	3723	Hall(2), C.Pringle

Apps: 40, 4, 17, 35, 38, 26, 34, 27, 40, 3, 33, 36, 3, 19, 2, 1, 1, 23, 9
Goals: 1, 1, 8, 18, 42, 1, 7, 2, 17, 2, 1, 6

F.A. CUP

1R	28 Nov	Manchester Central	3-0	4827	Riley(2), Hall
2R	12 Dec	LUTON TOWN	2-2	12613	Hall(2)
2Rr	16	Luton Town	1-4	9264	Hall

LINCOLNSHIRE CUP

SF	6 Apr	GRANTHAM TOWN	5-1		Hall(2), Burnikell, H.Pringle(2)
F	14 May	GRIMSBY TOWN	1-1*	7929	Hall

* replay played in 1932-33 season

LINCOLNSHIRE CUP (1930-31 competition)

Fr	22 Sep	Grimsby Town	1-0		Hall

Final League Table

		Pl.	Home W D L F A	Away W D L F A	F. A.	Pts
1	Lincoln City	40	16 2 2 65 13	10 3 7 41 34	106 47	57
2	Gateshead	40	15 3 2 59 20	10 4 6 35 28	94 48	57
3	Chester	40	16 2 2 54 22	5 6 9 24 38	78 60	50
4	Tranmere Rovers	40	15 4 1 76 23	4 7 9 31 35	107 58	49
5	Barrow	40	16 1 3 59 23	8 0 12 27 36	86 59	49
6	Crewe Alexandra	40	15 3 2 64 24	6 3 11 31 42	95 66	48
7	Southport	40	14 5 1 44 15	4 5 11 14 38	58 53	46
8	Hull City	40	14 1 5 52 21	6 4 10 30 32	82 53	45
9	York City	40	14 3 3 49 24	4 4 12 27 57	76 81	43
10	Wrexham	40	14 2 4 42 25	4 5 11 22 44	64 69	43
11	Darlington	40	12 1 7 41 27	5 3 12 25 42	66 69	38
12	Stockport County	40	12 3 5 31 15	1 8 11 24 38	55 53	37
13	Hartlepools United	40	10 4 6 47 37	6 1 13 31 63	78 100	37
14	Accrington Stanley	40	14 4 2 56 20	1 2 17 19 60	75 80	36
15	Doncaster Rovers	40	12 3 5 38 27	4 1 15 21 53	59 80	36
16	Walsall	40	12 3 5 42 30	4 0 16 15 55	57 85	35
17	Halifax Town	40	11 6 3 36 18	2 2 16 25 69	61 87	34
18	Carlisle United	40	9 7 4 40 23	2 4 14 24 56	64 79	33
19	Rotherham United	40	10 3 7 41 23	4 1 15 22 49	63 72	32
20	New Brighton	40	8 5 7 25 23	0 3 17 13 53	38 76	24
21	Rochdale	40	4 2 14 33 63	0 1 19 15 72	48 135	11

Wigan Borough resigned, record deleted.

SEASON 1932-33
DIVISION TWO

No.	Date	Opposition	Res.	Att.	Goalscorers
1	27 Aug	Notts County	1-1	20987	Keetley
2	29	SWANSEA TOWN	2-0	12613	Keetley, Riley
3	3 Sep	PORT VALE	0-1	11276	
4	5	Swansea Town	1-3	4403	Keetley
5	10	Millwall	0-2	14392	
6	17	SOUTHAMPTON	1-0	11158	Cooper
7	24	Bury	2-2	9391	Hall(2)
8	1 Oct	GRIMSBY TOWN	6-3	14102	Keetley(2), Hall(2), Wilkinson(2)
9	8	WEST HAM UNITED	6-0	9887	Cooper(3), Wilkinson, Hall(2)
10	15	Fulham	2-3	25500	Hall, Keetley
11	22	Oldham Athletic	2-5	6548	Riley(2)
12	29	PRESTON NORTH END	2-1	9207	Horne, Wilkinson
13	5 Nov	Burnley	0-0	9046	
14	12	TOTTENHAM HOTSPUR	2-2	11654	Hall(2)
15	19	Charlton Athletic	2-4	6953	Hall(2)
16	26	NOTTINGHAM FOREST	1-1	10069	Cartwright
17	3 Dec	Plymouth Argyle	3-0	18347	Hall(2), Riley
18	10	STOKE CITY	2-3	10787	Keetley, Hall
19	17	Manchester United	1-4	18021	Riley
20	24	BRADFORD PARK AVENUE	2-2	9239	Atkinson, Hall
21	26	CHESTERFIELD	5-3	9314	Riley, Young, Atkinson(2), Wilkinson
22	27	Chesterfield	0-3	12792	
23	31	NOTTS COUNTY	1-1	9260	Reed
24	7 Jan	Port Vale	2-3	7263	Reed, Horne
25	21	MILLWALL	3-0	5933	Wilkinson, Keetley(2)
26	28	Southampton	0-4	7225	
27	4 Feb	BURY	2-1	7565	Horne(2)
28	11	Grimsby Town	3-3	11088	Young, Hall, Atkinson
29	4 Mar	OLDHAM ATHLETIC	1-3	7524	Atkinson
30	11	Preston North End	0-5	11244	
31	18	BURNLEY	1-4	8617	Reed
32	25	Tottenham Hotspur	2-3	33930	Hall, Horne
33	27	West Ham United	0-0	9836	
34	1 Apr	CHARLTON ATHLETIC	1-1	7745	Cooper
35	5	FULHAM	3-0	8023	Whyte, Wilkinson, Hall
36	8	Nottingham Forest	2-2	9600	Hall(2)
37	14	BRADFORD CITY	0-0	13435	
38	15	PLYMOUTH ARGYLE	2-0	9012	Riley, Hall
39	18	Bradford City	1-1	9735	Riley
40	22	Stoke City	2-5	15791	Hall, Horne
41	29	MANCHESTER UNITED	3-2	8507	Reed, Hall, Wilkinson
42	6 May	Bradford Park Avenue	0-6	5709	

F.A. CUP

3R	14 Jan	BLACKBURN ROVERS	1-5	13276	Horne

LINCOLNSHIRE CUP

SF	8 Mar	GAINSBOROUGH TRINITY	7-0		Reed(4), Riley, Cartwright, Atkinson
F	25 Apr	Grimsby Town	1-3		Hall

LINCOLNSHIRE CUP (1931-32 competition)

Fr	13 Sep	Grimsby Town	4-3		Hall(2), C.Pringle, Horne

Final League Table

```
                    Pl.   Home           Away          F.  A.  Pts
                         W  D  L  F  A  W  D  L  F  A
 1 Stoke City       42  13  3  5 40 15 12  3  6 38 24  78 39  56
 2 Tottenham Hotspur 42  14  7  0 58 19  6  8  7 38 32  96 51  55
 3 Fulham           42  12  5  4 46 31  8  5  8 32 34  78 65  50
 4 Bury             42  13  7  1 55 23  7  2 12 29 36  84 59  49
 5 Nottingham Forest 42   9  8  4 37 28  8  7  6 30 31  67 59  49
 6 Manchester United 42  11  5  5 40 24  4  8  9 31 44  71 68  43
 7 Millwall         42  11  7  3 40 20  5  4 12 19 37  59 57  43
 8 Bradford Park Ave. 42 13  4  4 51 27  4  4 13 26 44  77 71  42
 9 Preston North End 42 12  2  7 53 36  4  8  9 21 34  74 70  42
10 Swansea Town     42  17  0  4 36 12  2  4 15 14 42  50 54  42
11 Bradford City    42  10  6  5 43 24  4  7 10 22 37  65 61  41
12 Southampton      42  15  3  3 48 22  3  2 16 18 44  66 66  41
13 Grimsby Town     42   8 10  3 49 34  6  3 12 30 50  79 84  41
14 Plymouth Argyle  42  13  4  4 45 22  3  5 13 18 45  63 67  41
15 Notts County     42  10  4  7 41 31  5  6 10 26 47  67 78  40
16 Oldham Athletic  42  10  4  7 38 31  5  4 12 29 49  67 80  38
17 Port Vale        42  12  3  6 49 27  2  7 12 17 52  66 79  38
18 Lincoln City     42  11  6  4 46 28  1  7 13 26 59  72 87  37
19 Burnley          42   8  9  4 35 20  3  5 13 32 59  67 79  36
20 West Ham United  42  12  6  3 56 31  1  3 17 19 62  75 93  35
21 Chesterfield     42  10  5  6 36 25  2  5 14 25 59  61 84  34
22 Charlton Athletic 42   9  3  9 35 35  3  4 14 25 56  60 91  31
```

SEASON 1933-34
DIVISION TWO

No.	Date	Opposition	Res.	Att.	Goalscorers
1	26 Aug	MILLWALL	0-1	9642	
2	2 Sep	Manchester United	1-1	16987	Keetley
3	4	NOTTS COUNTY	0-1	8647	
4	9	Bury	2-0	8591	Reed, Keetley
5	13	Notts County	0-2	13709	
6	16	HULL CITY	2-1	8820	Keetley, Reed
7	23	Fulham	0-1	13646	
8	30	SOUTHAMPTON	1-1	8761	Keetley
9	7 Oct	Blackpool	0-2	18579	
10	14	BRADFORD CITY	0-1	6792	
11	21	PLYMOUTH ARGYLE	1-1	6024	Jenkins
12	28	West Ham United	1-4	19380	Keetley
13	4 Nov	Nottingham Forest	0-0	6203	
14	11	Grimsby Town	0-3	11791	
15	18	BRADFORD PARK AVENUE	2-1	5951	Rowe(2)
16	25	Preston North End	1-2	10335	Rowe
17	2 Dec	OLDHAM ATHLETIC	1-1	6875	Horne
18	9	Burnley	1-3	7993	Rowe
19	16	BRENTFORD	0-2	6080	
20	23	Bolton Wanderers	2-1	9174	Campbell, Horne
21	25	PORT VALE	1-0	11584	OG
22	26	Port Vale	0-1	13910	
23	30	Millwall	1-4	12225	Reed
24	6 Jan	MANCHESTER UNITED	5-1	6075	Reed(2), Whyte, Campbell, Wilkinson
25	20	Bury	1-2	6652	Reed
26	3 Feb	FULHAM	5-0	5357	Whyte(2), Campbell, Horne, Reed
27	8	Hull City	0-2	6481	
28	10	Southampton	1-3	8044	Campbell
29	17	BLACKPOOL	2-2	5968	Whyte, Wilkinson
30	24	Bradford City	0-3	8339	
31	3 Mar	Plymouth Argyle	0-3	10913	
32	10	WEST HAM UNITED	0-2	5213	
33	17	Nottingham Forest	2-6	8101	Wilkinson, Dodgin
34	24	GRIMSBY TOWN	3-3	8723	Urwin, Smith, OG
35	30	SWANSEA TOWN	1-0	9353	Horne
36	31	Bradford Park Avenue	1-2	10855	Smith
37	2 Apr	Swansea Town	0-1	9500	
38	7	PRESTON NORTH END	0-1	5185	
39	14	Oldham Athletic	0-3	4461	
40	21	BURNLEY	4-0	3483	Wilkinson, Rowe, Campbell(2)
41	28	Brentford	0-5	12184	
42	5 May	BOLTON WANDERERS	2-2	6412	Marklew, Iverson

2 own goals

F.A. CUP

3R	13 Jan	Leicester City	0-3	25987	

LINCOLNSHIRE CUP

SF	14 Mar	GAINSBOROUGH TRINITY	7-0	643	Urwin, Smith, Wilkinson(3), Campbell(2)
F	26 Apr	Grimsby Town	2-2		Whyte, Horne
Fr	3 May	GRIMSBY TOWN	2-1 *	3296	Marklew, Wilkinson

* After extra time

Final League Table

```
                Pl.    Home            Away           F.  A.  Pts
                    W  D  L  F  A   W  D  L  F  A
 1 Grimsby Town    42 15  3  3 62 28 12  2  7 41 31 103 59  59
 2 Preston North End 42 15  3  3 47 20  8  3 10 24 32  71 52  52
 3 Bolton Wanderers 42 14  2  5 45 22  7  7  7 34 33  79 55  51
 4 Brentford       42 15  2  4 52 24  7  5  9 33 36  85 60  51
 5 Bradford Park Ave. 42 16  2  3 63 27  7  1 13 23 40  86 67  49
 6 Bradford City   42 14  4  3 46 25  6  2 13 27 42  73 67  46
 7 West Ham United 42 13  3  5 51 28  4  8  9 27 42  78 70  45
 8 Port Vale       42 14  4  3 39 14  5  3 13 21 41  60 55  45
 9 Oldham Athletic 42 12  5  4 48 28  5  5 11 24 32  72 60  44
10 Plymouth Argyle 42 12  7  2 43 20  3  6 12 26 50  69 70  43
11 Blackpool       42 10  8  3 39 27  5  5 11 23 37  62 64  43
12 Bury            42 12  4  5 43 31  5  5 11 27 42  70 73  43
13 Burnley         42 14  2  5 40 29  4  4 13 20 43  60 72  42
14 Southampton     42 15  2  4 40 21  0  6 15 14 37  54 58  38
15 Hull City       42 11  6  4 33 20  2  8 11 19 48  52 68  38
16 Fulham          42 13  3  5 29 17  2  4 15 19 50  48 67  37
17 Nottingham Forest 42 11  4  6 50 27  2  5 14 23 47  73 74  35
18 Notts County    42  9  7  5 32 22  3  4 14 21 40  53 62  35
19 Swansea Town    42 10  9  2 36 19  0  6 15 15 41  51 60  35
20 Manchester United 42  9  3  9 29 33  5  3 13 30 52  59 85  34
21 Millwall        42  8  8  5 21 17  3  3 15 18 51  39 68  33
22 Lincoln City    42  7  7  7 31 23  2  1 18 13 52  44 75  26
```

SEASON 1934-35
DIVISION THREE (NORTH)

No.	Date	Opposition	Res.	Att.	Goalscorers
1	25 Aug	ROCHDALE	3-0	6765	Iverson, Reed, Campbell
2	29	Mansfield Town	4-3	8669	Reed(3), OG
3	1 Sep	York City	2-1	5977	Horne, Campbell
4	3	MANSFIELD TOWN	4-0	8376	Wilinson, Reed(2), Whyte
5	8	Tranmere Rovers	1-2	9383	Robinson
6	15	WREXHAM	1-3	7490	Horne
7	22	Halifax Town	1-2	8382	Robinson
8	29	ROTHERHAM UNITED	4-0	5249	Marklew(2), Wilkinson(2)
9	6 Oct	Walsall	0-0	5642	
10	13	CHESTERFIELD	2-0	6436	Wilkinson, Campbell
11	20	DARLINGTON	2-4	6562	Iverson, Robinson
12	27	Accrington Stanley	0-3	2609	
13	3 Nov	GATESHEAD	5-0	4244	Reed(3), Iverson(2)
14	10	Stockport County	2-1	9950	Reed, Campbell
15	17	CREWE ALEXANDRA	1-1	4399	Reed
16	1 Dec	DONCASTER ROVERS	0-2	4871	
17	15	CHESTER	0-0	4394	
18	22	New Brighton	2-0	2852	Iverson, Reed
19	26	CARLISLE UNITED	4-2	8592	Wilkinson(2), Reed, Campbell
20	29	Rochdale	0-2	4531	
21	1 Jan	Carlisle United	1-2	3773	Iverson
22	5	YORK CITY	3-1	3900	Horne, Campbell(2)
23	12	Hartlepools United	5-1	2694	Iverson(3), Campbell, Wilkinson
24	19	TRANMERE ROVERS	2-2	6481	Walker, Iverson
25	26	Wrexham	2-2	3729	Iverson, Walker
26	2 Feb	HALIFAX TOWN	2-3	5021	Iverson, McAleer
27	9	Rotherham United	0-5	6371	
28	16	WALSALL	5-1	2902	Horne(2), Campbell(2), OG
29	23	Chesterfield	1-3	5418	Horne
30	2 Mar	Darlington	1-4	4429	Campbell
31	9	ACCRINGTON STANLEY	1-0	2448	Robinson
32	16	Gateshead	2-0	2687	Horne, Dickinson
33	23	STOCKPORT COUNTY	3-0	3109	Robinson(2), Dickinson
34	30	Crewe Alexandra	0-1	3347	
35	2 Apr	Southport	3-3	773	Dickinson, Robinson(2)
36	6	HARTLEPOOLS UNITED	2-1	2847	Campbell(2)
37	13	Doncaster Rovers	3-1	13494	McAleer, Whyte, Robinson
38	19	BARROW	6-0	7325	Robinson(2), McAleer(3), Campbell
39	20	SOUTHPORT	4-1	5233	Whyte, Robinson, Campbell(2)
40	22	Barrow	1-1	4170	Robinson
41	27	Chester	1-0	3733	Robinson
42	4 May	NEW BRIGHTON	1-0	3128	Campbell

2 own goals

F.A. CUP

1R	24 Nov	Shildon	2-2	6675	Wilkinson(2)
1Rr	28	SHILDON	4-0	3867	Burke, Reed(3)
2R	8 Dec	Swindon Town	3-4	14931	Reed, Campbell, Iverson

DIVISION THREE (NORTH) CUP

1R	28 Jan	Walsall	1-1	992	Iverson
1Rr	6 Feb	WALSALL	2-3 *	1596	Burke, Iverson

* After extra time

LINCOLNSHIRE CUP

F	24 Sep	GRIMSBY TOWN	5-0	2334	Reed, Iverson, Wilkinson(2), Campbell

Final League Table

		Pl.	Home W	D	L	F	A	Away W	D	L	F	A	F.	A.	Pts
1	Doncaster Rovers	42	16	0	5	53	21	10	5	6	34	23	87	44	57
2	Halifax Town	42	17	2	2	50	24	8	3	10	26	43	76	67	55
3	Chester	42	14	3	4	62	27	6	10	5	29	31	91	58	54
4	*Lincoln City*	42	14	3	4	55	21	8	4	9	32	37	87	58	51
5	Darlington	42	15	5	1	50	15	6	4	11	30	44	80	59	51
6	Tranmere Rovers	42	15	4	2	53	20	5	7	9	21	35	74	55	51
7	Stockport County	42	15	2	4	57	22	7	1	13	33	50	90	72	47
8	Mansfield Town	42	16	3	2	55	25	3	6	12	20	37	75	62	47
9	Rotherham United	42	14	3	4	56	21	5	3	13	30	52	86	73	45
10	Chesterfield	42	13	4	4	46	21	4	6	11	25	31	71	52	44
11	Wrexham	42	12	5	4	47	25	4	6	11	29	44	76	69	43
12	Hartlepools United	42	12	4	5	52	34	5	3	13	28	44	80	78	41
13	Crewe Alexandra	42	12	6	3	41	25	2	5	14	25	61	66	86	39
14	Walsall	42	11	7	3	51	18	2	3	16	30	54	81	72	36
15	York City	42	12	5	4	50	20	3	1	17	26	62	76	82	36
16	New Brighton	42	12	3	6	32	25	5	2	14	27	51	59	76	36
17	Barrow	42	11	5	5	37	31	2	4	15	21	56	58	87	35
18	Accrington Stanley	42	11	5	5	44	36	1	5	15	19	53	63	89	34
19	Gateshead	42	12	4	5	36	28	1	4	16	22	68	58	96	34
20	Rochdale	42	9	5	7	39	35	2	6	13	14	36	53	71	33
21	Southport	42	6	6	9	27	36	4	6	11	28	49	55	85	32
22	Carlisle United	42	7	6	8	34	36	1	1	19	17	66	51	102	23

1934-35
Back : Home, Gray, Reddish, McPhail, Smith, Barber, Whyte.
Front : Buckley, Campbell, Iverson, Reed, Thomas Robinson, Wilkinson.

1935-36
Back   Home, Sellars, Ernie Robinson, McPhail, Smith, Wright (trainer), Meacock.
Front   Walker, Burke, Campbell, Green, Whyte, Moulson.

SEASON 1935-36
DIVISION THREE (NORTH)

No.	Date	Opposition	Res.	Att.	Goalscorers
1	31 Aug	ACCRINGTON STANLEY	6-0	7190	Burke(2), Whyte, Campbell, Green
2	2 Sep	Crewe Alexandra	1-2	5195	Campbell
3	7	Southport	3-0	3971	Bulger, Campbell, Green
4	9	CREWE ALEXANDRA	6-2	6714	Campbell(3), Horne(2), Green
5	14	CHESTER	1-1	8051	Bulger
6	16	STOCKPORT COUNTY	3-0	7020	Horne(3)
7	21	Oldham Athletic	3-2	7794	Horne, Campbell(2)
8	28	Rochdale	0-0	7052	
9	5 Oct	YORK CITY	3-2	5885	Whyte, Campbell, Bulger
10	12	Barrow	0-0	6255	
11	19	WREXHAM	3-1	5662	Bulger, Whyte, Campbell
12	26	Rotherham United	1-1	9360	Bulger
13	2 Nov	MANSFIELD TOWN	1-2	6623	Campbell
14	9	Hartlepools United	1-1	3560	Campbell
15	16	CARLISLE UNITED	2-0	5415	Green, Whyte
16	23	Walsall	1-4	8081	Whyte
17	7 Dec	Gateshead	0-4	2825	
18	21	Halifax Town	1-2	5002	Towler
19	26	NEW BRIGHTON	2-0	5185	Sellars, Towler
20	28	Accrington Stanley	2-2	3673	Towler, Horne
21	1 Jan	New Brighton	5-0	4319	Hill(2), Horne, Sellars, Campbell
22	4	SOUTHPORT	4-0	4809	Hill, Smith, Campbell, Towler
23	25	OLDHAM ATHLETIC	2-1	5039	Towler(2)
24	1 Feb	ROCHDALE	5-1	4835	Hill, Campbell(2), Towler, Horne
25	8	York City	1-2	3485	Towler
26	15	BARROW	2-0	3834	Towler, Campbell
27	22	Wrexham	1-1	2309	Campbell
28	7 Mar	Mansfield Town	2-2	5007	Horne, Hill
29	14	ROTHERHAM UNITED	4-0	4087	Campbell(2), Horne, Whyte
30	18	HARTLEPOOLS UNITED	1-0	2598	Campbell
31	21	Carlisle United	1-4	5642	Horne
32	28	WALSALL	4-1	3966	Towler(3), Bulger
33	4 Apr	Tranmere Rovers	1-1	9389	OG
34	10	CHESTERFIELD	0-1	14586	
35	11	GATESHEAD	5-0	3713	Bulger(2), Horne, Green, Campbell
36	13	Chesterfield	1-0	15282	Campbell
37	18	Darlington	0-1	3006	
38	20	DARLINGTON	2-1	2542	Towler, Ranson
39	22	Chester	2-4	4726	Campbell, Green
40	25	HALIFAX TOWN	3-1	2189	Bulger, Dransfield, Campbell
41	27	TRANMERE ROVERS	5-0	3568	Campbell(2), Towler, Bulger, Horne
42	2 May	Stockport County	0-4	4509	

1 own goal

F.A. CUP

| 1R | 30 Nov | Walsall | 0-2 | 11707 | |

DIVISION THREE (NORTH) CUP

1R	30 Oct	ROTHERHAM UNITED	2-1	1745	Sellars, Campbell
3R	11 Mar	Chesterfield	3-0	1258	Littledyke, Hill, Horne
SF	23 Apr	CHESTER	2-3	1680	Campbell, Green

Bye in 2R

LINCOLNSHIRE CUP

| F | 24 Sep | Grimsby Town | 0-4 | | |

Final League Table

	Pl.	Home W	D	L	F	A	Away W	D	L	F	A	F.	A.	Pts
1 Chesterfield	42	15	3	3	60	14	9	9	3	32	25	92	39	60
2 Chester	42	14	5	2	69	18	8	6	7	31	27	100	45	55
3 Tranmere Rovers	42	17	2	2	75	28	5	9	7	18	30	93	58	55
4 *Lincoln City*	42	18	1	2	64	14	4	8	9	27	37	91	51	53
5 Stockport County	42	15	2	4	45	18	5	6	10	20	31	65	49	48
6 Crewe Alexandra	42	14	4	3	55	31	5	5	11	25	45	80	76	47
7 Oldham Athletic	42	13	5	3	60	25	5	4	12	26	48	86	73	45
8 Hartlepools United	42	13	6	2	41	18	2	6	13	16	43	57	61	42
9 Accrington Stanley	42	12	5	4	43	24	5	3	13	20	48	63	72	42
10 Walsall	42	15	4	2	58	13	1	7	13	21	46	79	59	41
11 Rotherham United	42	14	3	4	52	13	2	6	13	17	53	69	66	41
12 Darlington	42	16	3	2	60	26	1	3	17	14	53	74	79	40
13 Carlisle United	42	13	5	3	44	19	1	7	13	12	43	56	62	40
14 Gateshead	42	11	10	0	37	18	2	4	15	19	58	56	76	40
15 Barrow	42	9	9	3	33	16	4	3	14	25	49	58	65	38
16 York City	42	10	8	3	41	28	3	4	14	21	67	62	95	38
17 Halifax Town	42	12	3	6	34	22	3	4	14	23	39	57	61	37
18 Wrexham	42	12	6	3	39	18	3	4	14	27	57	66	75	37
19 Mansfield Town	42	13	6	3	55	25	1	4	16	25	66	80	91	37
20 Rochdale	42	8	10	3	35	26	2	3	16	23	62	58	88	33
21 Southport	42	9	8	4	31	26	2	1	18	17	64	48	90	31
22 New Brighton	42	8	5	8	29	33	1	1	19	14	69	43	102	24

SEASON 1936-37
DIVISION THREE (NORTH)

No.	Date	Opposition	Res.	Att.	Goalscorers
1	29 Aug	Accrington Stanley	2-1	5300	Callender(2)
2	31	OLDHAM ATHLETIC	2-0	8797	Raw, Whyte
3	5 Sep	SOUTHPORT	4-1	7306	Campbell(3), Whyte
4	7	Oldham Athletic	0-1	3813	
5	12	NEW BRIGHTON	1-0	5647	Deacon
6	14	STOCKPORT COUNTY	0-2	7011	
7	19	Hull City	1-1	10462	Campbell
8	26	GATESHEAD	4-0	5329	Campbell(2), Deacon, Horne
9	3 Oct	Darlington	2-2	5375	Callender, Burdett
10	10	WREXHAM	6-2	5082	Towler, Campbell, Horne(2), *
11	17	Tranmere Rovers	2-2	9019	Deacon(2)
12	24	HALIFAX TOWN	4-1	6062	Campbell(3), Callender
13	31	Mansfield Town	2-2	13228	Towler, Callender
14	7 Nov	CREWE ALEXANDRA	2-4	5756	Callender, Horne
15	14	Chester	3-7	8343	Raw, Campbell, OG
16	21	ROCHDALE	5-3	4595	Campbell(5)
17	5 Dec	YORK CITY	3-1	4758	Horne, Campbell, Deacon
18	19	HARTLEPOOLS UNITED	3-0	4032	OG, Campbell, Callender
19	25	ROTHERHAM UNITED	3-0	9425	Raw, Campbell, Spencer
20	26	ACCRINGTON STANLEY	3-3	9305	Callender, Deacon, Whyte
21	28	Rotherham United	1-3	3308	Campbell
22	2 Jan	Southport	1-2	4837	Raw
23	9	New Brighton	2-1	3635	Campbell, Callender
24	16	Barrow	4-0	3176	Campbell, White(2), Towler
25	23	HULL CITY	5-0	5098	White(2),Campbell,Towler,Callender
26	6 Feb	DARLINGTON	4-3	6463	Campbell(3), White
27	13	Wrexham	3-0	5387	Campbell, Callender, Towler
28	20	TRANMERE ROVERS	1-0	6515	Campbell
29	27	Halifax Town	3-2	4303	Campbell, Towler(2)
30	6 Mar	MANSFIELD TOWN	2-0	7877	Campbell, Towler
31	13	Crewe Alexandra	1-2	4119	Callender
32	20	CHESTER	3-0	11498	Towler(2), Campbell
33	26	Port Vale	1-1	8185	Deacon
34	27	Rochdale	3-2	6630	Campbell, Callender, Whyte
35	29	PORT VALE	1-0	13715	OG
36	3 Apr	BARROW	6-0	7658	Burdett,Deacon(2),Whyte,Towler(2)
37	7	Gateshead	5-0	1224	Campbell(3), Callender, Burdett
38	10	York City	0-0	5086	
39	15	Carlisle United	1-3	8710	Deacon
40	17	CARLISLE UNITED	3-0	7582	Whyte, White, Callender
41	24	Hartlepools United	1-3	5552	Raw
42	1 May	Stockport County	0-2	26135	

* Additional scorers: Deacon, Callender

F.A. CUP

1R	28 Nov	NEW BRIGHTON	1-1	6899	Towler
1Rr	2 Dec	New Brighton	3-2*	5079	Towler, Campbell, Horne
2R	12	OLDHAM ATHLETIC	2-3	7403	Towler(2)

* After extra time

DIVISION THREE (NORTH) CUP

1R	7 Oct	HARTLEPOOLS UNITED	0-2	1115	

LINCOLNSHIRE CUP

F	23 Sep	GRIMSBY TOWN	1-6	2523	Horne

Final League Table

		Pl.	Home W D L F A	Away W D L F A	F. A.	Pts
1	Stockport County	42	17 3 1 59 18	6 11 4 25 21	84 39	60
2	*Lincoln City*	42	18 1 2 65 20	7 6 8 38 37	103 57	57
3	Chester	42	15 5 1 68 21	7 4 10 19 36	87 57	53
4	Oldham Athletic	42	13 7 1 49 25	7 4 10 28 34	77 59	51
5	Hull City	42	13 6 2 39 20	4 6 11 29 47	68 69	46
6	Hartlepools United	42	16 1 4 53 21	3 6 12 22 48	75 69	45
7	Halifax Town	42	12 4 5 40 20	6 5 10 28 43	68 63	45
8	Wrexham	42	13 2 6 41 21	4 9 8 30 36	71 57	44
9	Mansfield Town	42	13 1 7 64 35	5 7 9 27 41	91 76	44
10	Carlisle United	42	13 6 2 42 19	5 2 14 23 49	65 68	44
11	Port Vale	42	12 6 3 39 23	5 4 12 19 41	58 64	44
12	York City	42	13 3 5 54 27	3 8 10 25 43	79 70	43
13	Accrington Stanley	42	14 2 5 51 26	2 7 12 25 43	76 69	41
14	Southport	42	10 8 3 39 28	2 5 14 34 59	73 87	37
15	New Brighton	42	10 8 3 36 16	3 3 15 19 54	55 70	37
16	Barrow	42	11 5 5 42 25	2 5 14 28 61	70 86	36
17	Rotherham United	42	11 7 3 52 28	0 1 18 26 63	78 91	35
18	Rochdale	42	12 3 6 44 27	1 6 14 25 59	69 86	35
19	Tranmere Rovers	42	10 8 3 52 30	2 1 18 19 58	71 88	33
20	Crewe Alexandra	42	6 8 7 31 34	4 4 13 24 52	55 83	32
21	Gateshead	42	9 8 4 40 31	2 2 17 23 67	63 98	32
22	Darlington	42	6 8 7 42 46	2 6 13 24 50	66 96	30

Back : Knott (assistant secretary), Meacock, Hartshorne, Moulson, McPhail, Hill, Johnny Campbell, Whyte, John Callender, Corbett, Young (asst.trainer).
Centre : Wright (trainer), Dransfield, Burdett, McClelland (sec./manager), Taylor, Dowall, Deacon.
Front : Robinson, W.Campbell, Raw, Horne.

SEASON 1937-38
DIVISION THREE (NORTH)

No.	Date	Opposition	Res.	Att.	Goalscorers
1	28 Aug	HARTLEPOOLS UNITED	2-1	8779	Campbell, Whyte
2	1 Sep	Wrexham	0-1	9205	
3	4	Carlisle United	1-0	7766	Clare
4	6	WREXHAM	7-1	7631	Campbell(4), Deacon, Clare, White
5	11	Hull City	1-1	10615	Campbell
6	13	BARROW	5-0	6833	Deacon, White(2), Clare, Callender
7	18	NEW BRIGHTON	4-1	8935	Bean, Campbell(2), Callender
8	25	Gateshead	1-1	20792	Campbell
9	2 Oct	OLDHAM ATHLETIC	0-1	9438	
10	9	Darlington	4-1	7152	Callender, Campbell(2), Deacon
11	16	ACCRINGTON STANLEY	2-0	8198	Clare, Callender
12	23	Chester	1-1	6507	Campbell
13	30	ROTHERHAM UNITED	5-0	8054	Callender, Deacon, Towler(2), Whyte
14	6 Nov	Rochdale	1-0	9074	Callender
15	13	DONCASTER ROVERS	2-2	12500	Deacon, Whyte
16	20	Southport	1-1	5748	Towler
17	4 Dec	York City	1-3	3418	Clare
18	27	PORT VALE	1-0	13354	Callender
19	28	Port Vale	0-1	5740	
20	1 Jan	Hartlepools United	0-2	5126	
21	15	CARLISLE UNITED	0-1	5845	
22	22	HULL CITY	2-1	9107	Whyte, Towler
23	26	BRADFORD CITY	4-0	3479	Callender, Whyte, Burdett, White
24	29	New Brighton	1-0	2898	Burdett
25	5 Feb	GATESHEAD	3-2	10944	Towler(2), Burdett
26	12	Oldham Athletic	2-2	12018	Callender, Burdett
27	19	DARLINGTON	0-0	7796	
28	26	Accrington Stanley	3-0	3985	White, Burdett(2)
29	5 Mar	CHESTER	1-1	10157	Burdett
30	12	Rotherham United	0-4	10443	
31	19	ROCHDALE	2-0	6836	Deacon(2)
32	26	Doncaster Rovers	0-3	13787	
33	2 Apr	SOUTHPORT	1-3	5946	Burdett
34	9	Bradford City	0-2	5762	
35	15	Crewe Alexandra	0-2	7783	
36	16	YORK CITY	2-0	7088	Clare, Raw
37	18	CREWE ALEXANDRA	3-2	6308	Marlow, Young, Raw
38	23	Tranmere Rovers	0-2	12881	
39	25	Halifax Town	0-2	1772	
40	30	HALIFAX TOWN	2-0	3108	Callender, OG
41	3 May	TRANMERE ROVERS	0-1	5657	
42	7	Barrow	1-4	1946	Clare

1 own goal

F.A. CUP

1R	27 Nov	Rochdale	1-1	10920	Deacon
1Rr	1 Dec	ROCHDALE	2-0	6474	Whyte, Campbell
2R	15	Mansfield Town	1-2	8062	Campbell

DIVISION THREE (NORTH) CUP

1R	28 Oct	Doncaster Rovers	2-7	2544	White, Kerr

LINCOLNSHIRE CUP

F	21 Sep	Grimsby Town	1-4		Burdett

Final League Table

	Pl.	Home W D L F A	Away W D L F A	F. A. Pts
1 Tranmere Rovers	42	15 4 2 57 21	8 6 7 24 20	81 41 56
2 Doncaster Rovers	42	15 4 2 48 16	6 8 7 26 33	74 49 54
3 Hull City	42	11 8 2 51 19	9 5 7 29 24	80 43 53
4 Oldham Athletic	42	16 4 1 48 18	3 9 9 19 28	67 46 51
5 Gateshead	42	15 5 1 53 20	5 6 10 31 39	84 59 51
6 Rotherham United	42	13 6 2 45 21	7 4 10 23 35	68 56 50
7 Lincoln City	42	14 3 4 48 17	5 5 11 18 33	66 50 46
8 Crewe Alexandra	42	14 3 4 47 17	4 6 11 24 36	71 53 45
9 Chester	42	13 4 4 54 31	3 8 10 23 41	77 72 44
10 Wrexham	42	14 4 3 37 15	2 7 12 21 48	58 63 43
11 York City	42	11 4 6 40 25	5 6 10 30 43	70 68 42
12 Carlisle United	42	11 5 5 35 19	4 4 13 22 48	57 67 39
13 New Brighton	42	12 5 4 43 18	3 3 15 17 43	60 61 38
14 Bradford City	42	12 6 3 46 21	2 4 15 20 48	66 69 38
15 Port Vale	42	11 8 2 45 27	1 6 14 20 46	65 73 38
16 Southport	42	8 8 5 30 26	4 6 11 23 56	53 82 38
17 Rochdale	42	7 10 4 38 27	6 1 14 29 51	67 78 37
18 Halifax Town	42	9 7 5 24 19	3 5 13 20 47	44 66 36
19 Darlington	42	10 4 7 37 31	1 6 14 17 48	54 79 32
20 Hartlepools United	42	10 8 3 36 20	0 4 17 17 60	53 80 32
21 Barrow	42	9 6 6 28 20	2 4 15 13 51	41 71 32
22 Accrington Stanley	42	9 2 10 31 31	2 5 14 14 43	45 75 29

1937-38
Back : Raw, Robinson, Meacock, Ainsworth, McPhail, Bland, Nevin, Whyte, Corbett, Wyllie, Hartshorne.
Centre : Wright (trainer), Edward Young, John Callender, Burdett, Deacon, McClelland (secretary/manager), Clare, Marlow, White, Campbell, Alf Young (assistant trainer). Front : Forman, Tom Callender, Nightingale, Wilson.

1938-39
Back : Hartshorne, Mellors (assistant trainer), Corbett, Gibb, Whyte, Culley,------,McPhail, Tom Callender, Hinton, ------, Shilton, Wilson, Griffin, Holmes,Young (trainer), Nevin, Knott (assistant secretary).
Centre : Kirkland, Mowatt, Clotworthy, Hancock, McClelland (secretary-manager), Campbell, Deacon, Clare, Bean.
Front : Rudkin, Robinson, Round, Cottam, Burdett, Marlow.

SEASON 1938-39
DIVISION THREE (NORTH)

No.	Date	Opposition	Res.	Att.	Goalscorers
1	27 Aug	Barrow	2-2	9835	Campbell, Deacon
2	29	BARNSLEY	2-4	8501	Clare, Deacon
3	3 Sep	CHESTER	0-3	4844	
4	7	New Brighton	2-3	6009	Mowatt, Deacon
5	10	Bradford City	0-3	7044	
6	12	NEW BRIGHTON	0-0	4159	
7	17	HULL CITY	0-3	5983	
8	24	Crewe Alexandra	0-6	5344	
9	1 Oct	Stockport County	3-3	10261	Leach, Holmes, OG
10	8	ACCRINGTON STANLEY	3-0	4422	Marlow(3)
11	15	CARLISLE UNITED	2-1	5085	Clare(2)
12	22	Darlington	1-3	4130	Marlow
13	29	HARTLEPOOLS UNITED	2-2	4682	Wilson, Campbell
14	5 Nov	Gateshead	0-4	4623	
15	12	WREXHAM	8-3	5314	Clare(3), Wilson(3), Whyte, Ponting
16	19	York City	3-1	5333	Ponting(2), Clare
17	3 Dec	Rotherham United	3-1	5607	Ponting(2), Clare
18	17	Southport	1-4	5374	Clare
19	24	BARROW	1-1	4207	Wilson
20	26	Halifax Town	0-2	7793	
21	27	HALIFAX TOWN	0-0	8391	
22	31	Chester	0-0	6079	
23	11 Jan	ROCHDALE	2-2	1847	Hancock, Ponting
24	14	BRADFORD CITY	4-0	4516	Ponting(2), Wilson, Hancock
25	21	Hull City	2-4	4962	Rudkin, Wilson
26	28	CREWE ALEXANDRA	3-2	5197	Ponting(2), Deacon
27	4 Feb	Stockport County	3-2	6202	Ponting, Whyte, Campbell
28	11	Accrington Stanley	4-3	2825	Clare, Campbell, Ponting(2)
29	18	Carlisle United	3-4	3869	Clare, Campbell, Wilson
30	25	DARLINGTON	3-0	4975	Ponting, Hancock(2)
31	4 Mar	Hartlepools United	1-2	2393	Clare
32	11	GATESHEAD	1-0	5796	Clare
33	18	Wrexham	0-1	2627	
34	25	YORK CITY	3-3	4178	Clare(2), Leach
35	1 Apr	Rochdale	0-4	4314	
36	7	OLDHAM ATHLETIC	1-0	7844	Ponting
37	8	ROTHERHAM UNITED	0-1	5192	
38	10	Oldham Athletic	0-1	5797	
39	15	Doncaster Rovers	1-4	6585	Clare
40	22	SOUTHPORT	0-1	2493	
41	29	Barnsley	0-4	5234	
42	6 May	DONCASTER ROVERS	2-5	3082	Campbell, Burdett

1 own goal

F.A. CUP

1R	26 Nov	BARROW	4-1	8201	Wilson, Hancock, Deacon, Ponting
2R	10 Dec	BROMLEY	8-1	9751	Clare(2), Ponting(3), Wilson *
3R	7 Jan	Portsmouth	0-4	27432	

* Additional scorers: Deacon, Whyte

FOOTBALL LEAGUE JUBILEE FUND

	20 Aug	GRIMSBY TOWN	2-1	4732	Campbell(2)

LINCOLNSHIRE CUP - no competition held

Final League Table

		Pl.	Home W D L F A	Away W D L F A	F. A. Pts
1	Barnsley	42	18 2 1 60 12	12 5 4 34 22	94 34 67
2	Doncaster Rovers	42	12 5 4 47 21	9 9 3 40 26	87 47 56
3	Bradford City	42	16 2 3 59 21	6 6 9 30 35	89 56 52
4	Southport	42	14 5 2 47 16	6 5 10 28 38	75 54 50
5	Oldham Athletic	42	16 1 4 51 21	6 4 11 25 38	76 59 49
6	Chester	42	12 5 4 54 31	8 4 9 34 39	88 70 49
7	Hull City	42	13 5 3 57 25	5 5 11 26 49	83 74 46
8	Crewe Alexandra	42	12 5 4 54 23	7 1 13 28 47	82 70 44
9	Stockport County	42	13 6 2 57 24	4 3 14 34 53	91 77 43
10	Gateshead	42	12 1 8 45 24	3 8 10 29 43	74 67 42
11	Rotherham United	42	12 4 5 45 21	5 4 12 19 43	64 64 42
12	Halifax Town	42	9 10 2 33 22	4 6 11 19 32	52 54 42
13	Barrow	42	11 5 5 46 22	5 4 12 20 43	66 65 41
14	Wrexham	42	15 2 4 46 28	2 5 14 20 51	66 79 41
15	Rochdale	42	10 5 6 58 29	5 4 12 34 53	92 82 39
16	New Brighton	42	11 2 8 46 32	4 7 10 22 41	68 73 39
17	*Lincoln City*	*42*	*9 6 6 40 33*	*3 3 15 26 59*	*66 92 33*
18	Darlington	42	12 2 7 43 30	1 5 15 19 62	62 92 33
19	Carlisle United	42	10 5 6 44 33	3 2 16 22 78	66 111 33
20	York City	42	8 5 8 37 34	4 3 14 27 58	64 92 32
21	Hartlepools United	42	10 4 7 36 33	2 3 16 19 61	55 94 31
22	Accrington Stanley	42	6 5 10 30 39	1 1 19 19 64	49 103 20

SEASON 1939-40

FOOTBALL LEAGUE JUBILEE FUND

No.	Date	Opposition	Res.	Att.	Goalscorers										
	19 Aug	Grimsby Town	2-3	2000	Clare, Ponting	Gormlie	Hartshorne	T.Callender	Rix	Askew	Bean	Hoyland	Clayton	Ponting	Deacon	Clare

DIVISION THREE (NORTH)

1	26 Aug	Hull City	2-2	6000	Clayton, Clare	"	"	"	"	"	"	"	"	"	"	"
2	28	DARLINGTON	0-2	5344		"	"	"	"	"	"	Holmes	"	"	"	"
3	2 Sep	GATESHEAD	4-3	2856	Ponting(3), Clare	"	Bean	"	"	"	Hardy	Hoyland	"	"	"	"

REGIONAL LEAGUE - EAST MIDLANDS

1	21 Oct	Chesterfield	0-8		Connor	Seagrave	Hartshorne	Bean	Jessop	Rix	J.Callender	Bell	"	Riley	Clare
2	28	BARNSLEY	1-3	Campbell	Mellors	"	Hodgson	Musson	"	Hardy	J.Callender	Campbell	Bett	"	"
3	11 Nov	Grimsby Town	3-7	Bett(2), Campbell	Hetherington	Bean	Seagrave	Eggleston	"	"	J.Callender	Campbell	Ponting	"	S.Cooper
4	18	SHEFFIELD UNITED	1-2	Dunderdale	G.Moulson	G.Hall	Bean	Jessop	C.Moulson	"	Hoyland	Bett	Dunderdale	S.Cooper	Clare
5	25	Nottingham Forest	1-0	Dunderdale	"	"	"	"	"	"	"	"	"	"	"
6	2 Dec	MANSFIELD TOWN	3-2	Dunderdale(2), Bett	"	"	"	"	"	Hann	"	"	"	"	"
7	6 Jan	ROTHERHAM UNITED	0-1		"	"	"	"	"	Campbell	"	"	"	Hardy	"
8	24 Feb	Barnsley	7-1	Clare(2), Dunderdale(4), Hoyland	"	"	"	"	"	Hardy	"	"	"	S.Cooper	"
9	2 Mar	Doncaster Rovers	1-3	Clare	"	"	Hardy	"	"	Campbell	"	"	"	"	"
10	9	GRIMSBY TOWN	4-1	Dunderdale(3), Clare	"	"	Bean	"	"	Hardy	"	"	"	"	"
11	16	Sheffield United	0-1		"	"	"	"	"	"	"	"	"	"	"
12	22	SHEFFIELD WEDNESDAY	4-2	Bett(2), Dunderdale, Clare	"	"	"	"	"	"	"	"	"	"	"
13	23	NOTTINGHAM FOREST	1-0	Cooper	"	"	"	Campbell	Jessop	"	"	"	"	"	"
14	25	CHESTERFIELD	1-4	Dunderdale	"	"	"	"	"	"	"	"	"	"	"
15	30	Mansfield Town	5-4	Dunderdale(2),Campbell(2),Cooper	"	"	"	Jessop	Bailey	"	Campbell	"	"	"	"
16	20 Apr	DONCASTER ROVERS	3-2	Dunderdale, Cooper, Clare	"	"	"	"	C.Moulson	"	Hoyland	"	"	"	"
17	4 May	NOTTS COUNTY	3-4	Dunderdale(2), Bett	"	"	"	"	"	"	Campbell	"	"	"	"
18	9	Sheffield Wednesday	3-2	Dunderdale(2), Bett	"	"	"	"	"	"	"	"	"	"	"
19	11	Rotherham United	1-3	McCall	"	"	"	"	"	"	"	McCall	"	Bett	S.Cooper
20	1 Jun	Notts County	0-3		"	"	"	"	"	"	"	Bett	"	S.Cooper	Clare

P20 W9 D0 L11 F42 A53 Pts18 Pos.7th (of 11 teams)

WAR CUP

| 1R | 13 Apr | Hull City | 0-1 | | " | " | " | " | Bailey | " | " | J.Parr | " | Deacon | " |

Back : Young (asst.trainer), Knott (asst.sec.), Tom Callender, Clare, Ponting, Gray, Gormlie, Singleton, Connor, Clayton, Thompson, Askew, Hartshorne, Mellors (trainer).
Centre : Staley (director), Applewhite (director), Broome, Evans, Newey, Wright (chairman), Deacon, Hardy, Holmes, Fasham (director), Giles (director).
Front : Grant, Hoyland, Jeavons, Rix.

SEASON 1940-41
NORTH REGIONAL LEAGUE

No.	Date	Opposition	Res.	Att.	Goalscorers	G.Moulson	G.Hall	Bean	Jessop	C.Moulson	Hardy	H.Barton	Bett	Dunderdale	Campbell	Clare
1	31 Aug	GRIMSBY TOWN	2-2		Barton, Clare	G.Moulson	G.Hall	Bean	Jessop	C.Moulson	Hardy	A.Hall	"	"	Bell	"
2	7 Sep	Grimsby Town	1-2		Bell	"	"	"	"	"	"	A.Hall	"	"	Bell	"
3	14	SHEFFIELD UNITED	9-2		Clare,Bett(3),Dunderdale(2),Towler(3)	"	"	"	"	"	"	"	"	"	Towler	"
4	21	Chesterfield	0-2			"	"	"	"	"	"	H.Barton	"	"	"	"
5	28	ROTHERHAM UNITED	2-2		A.Hall, G.Hall	"	"	"	"	"	"	"	"	A.Hall	"	"
6	5 Oct	York City	2-1		A.Hall, Bett	"	Johnston	"	"	"	"	Brelsford	"	"	"	"
7	12	YORK CITY	4-2		A.Hall(3), Towler	"	"	"	"	"	"	"	"	"	"	"
8	26	Sheffield United	3-3		A.Hall, Jones, Towler	"	G.Hall	"	"	"	"	Edrich	L.Jones	"	"	"
9	2 Nov	HULL CITY	1-1		Clare	"	"	"	Johnston	"	"	Brelsford	A.Hall	Broadhurst	"	"
10	9	CHESTERFIELD	2-0		A.Hall, Dunderdale	"	"	"	"	"	"	Marlow	"	Dunderdale	"	"
11	16	BARNSLEY	2-3		Bett, Clare	"	"	"	"	"	"	Bett	L.Jones	"	"	"
12	23	Rotherham United	3-0		Towler, Clare, A.Hall	"	"	"	"	"	"	Marlow	A.Hall	"	"	"
13	30	Hull City	2-1		Towler, Dunderdale	"	"	"	"	"	"	"	"	"	"	"
14	25 Dec	Doncaster Rovers	0-0			"	"	Forman	"	"	"	"	"	"	"	"
15	25	DONCASTER ROVERS	3-1		Towler(3)	"	"	"	Johnston	"	"	"	"	"	"	"
16	28	Barnsley	0-6			"	"	A.Turner	"	"	"	"	"	"	"	"
17	11 Jan	Nottingham Forest	2-4		OG, Towler	"	"	Bean	Forman	"	"	"	"	"	"	"
18	18	NOTTINGHAM FOREST	2-1		Dunderdale, Hardy	"	"	"	Johnston	"	"	"	"	"	"	"
19	1 Feb	MANSFIELD TOWN	4-2		Towler(2), A.Hall, Dunderdale	"	"	"	"	"	"	Dean	"	"	"	"
20	8	Leicester City	1-4		Dunderdale	"	"	"	"	"	"	"	"	"	"	"
21	1 Mar	Bradford Park Avenue	0-4			"	"	"	"	Wheat	E.Smith	Lascelles	"	"	"	"
22	8	SHEFFIELD WEDNESDAY	4-1		Dunderdale, Wightman, Towler(2)	"	"	"	"	C.Moulson	Wightman	E.Smith	Dickie	"	"	"
23	29	MANSFIELD TOWN	3-1		Towler(3)	"	"	"	"	"	Hardy	Bett	Dean	E.Smith	"	"
24	5 Apr	Mansfield Town	1-1		Towler	"	Bell	"	E.Smith	"	"	Marlow	A.Hall	Dunderdale	"	"
25	12	LEICESTER CITY	5-4		Meek, Clare, Towler(3)	"	G.Hall	"	Johnston	"	"	Marsh	Meek	Hullett	"	"
26	14	Leicester City	1-1		Towler	"	"	"	"	"	"	Marlow	Fox	A.Hall	"	"
27	19	BRADFORD PARK AVENUE	6-2		Doherty(4), Clare, Meek	"	"	"	"	"	"	Meek	Doherty	"	"	"

P27 W13 D7 L7 F65 A53 Goal Ave.1.226 Pos.9th (out of 36 teams) Nb. League positions were decided on goal average. Match 14 - kick off time 10.45am; match 15 - kick off time 3.00pm
Matches 17-20 and 25 also counted for the Midlands Cup (M17-1RIL; M18-1R2L; M19-2R*; M20-SF1L; M25-SF2L) * 3 first round losers with best goal average went into 2R.

FOOTBALL LEAGUE WAR CUP NORTH

						G.Moulson	G.Hall	Bean	Johnston	C.Moulson	Hardy	Forman	A.Hall	Dunderdale	Towler	Clare
1R1L	15 Feb	Hull City	1-4		Towler	G.Moulson	G.Hall	Bean	Johnston	C.Moulson	Hardy	Lascelles	"	"	"	"
1R2L	22	HULL CITY	3-2		Clare, Dunderdale, Hardy	"	"	"	"	"	"	Lascelles	"	"	"	"

SEASON 1941-42
FOOTBALL LEAGUE NORTH (FIRST CHAMPIONSHIP)

No.	Date	Opposition	Res.	Att.	Goalscorers	G.Moulson	Bean	Ross	Johnston	C.Moulson	Hardy	Farrell	A.Hall	Knott	Towler	Clare
1	30 Aug	Chesterfield	2-1		Knott, Towler	G.Moulson	Bean	Ross	Johnston	C.Moulson	Hardy	Farrell	A.Hall	Knott	Towler	Clare
2	6 Sep	CHESTERFIELD	5-1		Johnston, Towler(3), Knott	"	"	Hardy	"	"	Dickie	J.Parr	Meek	"	"	"
3	13	BARNSLEY	3-2		Doherty, Towler, C.Moulson	"	H.Turner	Bean	"	"	Hardy	Marlow	Doherty	"	"	"
4	20	Barnsley	2-1		Knott(2)	"	Bean	Ross	"	"	"	"	Watson	A.Hall	"	"
5	27	Sheffield Wednesday	1-1		Towler	"	"	"	"	"	"	"	A.Hall	"	"	"
6	4 Oct	SHEFFIELD WEDNESDAY	6-0		Knott(4), Hullett, Towler	"	"	"	"	"	"	Hullett	Meek	Knott	"	"
7	11	ROTHERHAM UNITED	3-0		Clare, Towler, Meek	"	"	"	"	"	"	Meek	Dickie	A.Hall	"	"
8	18	Rotherham United	3-2		Meek, Towler, Marlow	"	"	"	Wightman	"	"	Marlow	Meek	Knott	"	"
9	25	Grimsby Town	3-1		Towler(2), Marlow	"	"	"	Marsh	"	"	"	"	"	"	"
10	1 Nov	GRIMSBY TOWN	1-1		Clare	"	"	"	Wightman	"	"	"	"	Dickie	"	"
11	8	YORK CITY	3-3		Meek, Doherty(2)	"	"	"	"	"	"	"	"	Knott	Doherty	"
12	15	York City	2-4		Clare(2)	"	"	"	Johnston	"	"	Farrell	Anderson	"	Day	"
13	22	DONCASTER ROVERS	3-1		Cheetham(2), Towler	"	"	"	"	"	"	Barber	Knott	Cheetham	Towler	"
14	29	Doncaster Rovers	3-1		Cheetham(2), Meek	"	"	"	"	"	"	Knott	Meek	"	"	"
15	6 Dec	Sheffield United	0-9			"	"	"	"	"	"	"	"	"	"	"
16	13	SHEFFIELD UNITED	3-0		Towler, Cheetham(2)	"	Nicholson	Bean	Dickie	"	"	"	"	"	"	"
17	20	Mansfield Town	5-0		Knott(3), Towler, Cheetham	"	"	"	Johnston	"	"	"	"	"	"	"
18	25	MANSFIELD TOWN	6-0		Knott(4), Marlow, Meek	"	"	"	"	"	"	Marlow	"	Knott	"	"

P18 W13 D3 L2 F54 A28 Pts.29 Pos.2nd (out of 38 teams)

FOOTBALL LEAGUE NORTH (SECOND CHAMPIONSHIP)

						G.Moulson	Nicholson	Bean	Dickie	Johnston	Hardy	Knott	Meek	Cheetham	Towler	Clare
1	27 Dec	DONCASTER ROVERS	9-3		Knott(5),Meek,Towler,Cheetham(2)	G.Moulson	Nicholson	Bean	Dickie	Johnston	Hardy	Knott	Meek	Cheetham	Towler	Clare
2	3 Jan	Leeds United	1-5		Towler	"	"	"	"	Johnston	C.Moulson	"	"	"	"	"
3	10	MANSFIELD TOWN	7-2		Cheetham(2),Meek(2),Clare(2),Towler	"	"	"	"	"	"	Meek	Dickie	"	"	"
4	24	GRIMSBY TOWN	1-2		Cheetham	"	"	"	"	"	"	Marlow	"	"	"	"
5	14 Feb	NOTTINGHAM FOREST	0-3			"	"	"	"	"	Dickie	Knott	Meek	"	"	Marlow
6	21	Rotherham United	1-0		Towler	"	"	"	"	"	Hardy	"	Bett	"	"	"
7	28	ROTHERHAM UNITED	4-2		Towler(3), Knott	"	"	"	"	"	"	"	"	"	"	Meek
8	21 Mar	Doncaster Rovers	2-0		Hullett, Clare	"	"	"	"	"	"	Marlow	"	Hullett	"	Clare
9	28	Grimsby Town	2-4		Knott(2)	"	"	"	"	"	"	Knott	Meek	Cheetham	Marlow	"
10	4 Apr	NOTTINGHAM FOREST	6-5		Clare,Towler(2),Hullett(2),Marlow	"	"	"	"	"	"	Marlow	Bett	Hullett	Towler	"
11	6	Nottingham Forest	2-4		Towler, Jones	"	"	"	"	"	"	"	"	Towler	L.Jones	"
12	11	Mansfield Town	8-1		Hullett(7), Towler	"	"	"	Marsh	"	"	Knott	"	Hullett	Towler	"
13	18	MANSFIELD TOWN	2-2		Towler, Bett	"	"	"	"	"	"	"	"	"	"	"

P13 W7 D1 L5 F45 A31 Pts.15 (did not qualify for final table as played less than 18 matches) Matches 1-9 also counted for League War Cup Qualifying Competition: P9 W5 D0 L4 F27 A21 Pts.(adjusted to 10 matches)
11.11 Pos. 19th (out of 51 teams) Top 32 qualified for knock out stages. Matches 10 & 11 were also the two legs of the League War Cup Round 1.

SEASON 1942-43
FOOTBALL LEAGUE NORTH (FIRST CHAMPIONSHIP)

No.	Date	Opposition	Res.	Att.	Goalscorers											
1	29 Aug	NOTTINGHAM FOREST	3-3		Wardle, Clare, Towler	G.Moulson	C.Moulson	Bean	Johnston	Nicholson	Hardy	Wardle	Bett	Marsh	Towler	Clare
2	5 Sep	Nottingham Forest	1-0		Stillyards	"	Nicholson	"	"	C.Moulson	"	"	Osborne	Stillyards	"	"
3	12	Grimsby Town	2-5		OG, Wardle	"	"	"	"	"	"	"	Makinson	"	"	"
4	19	GRIMSBY TOWN	2-2		Wardle, Knott	"	Hardy	"	"	"	Dickie	"	Bett	Knott	"	"
5	26	Doncaster Rovers	2-0		Wardle, Bett	"	A.Thompson	"	Marsh	"	Hardy	"	"	Cheetham	"	"
6	3 Oct	DONCASTER ROVERS	3-0		Towler(3)	"	"	"	"	"	"	"	"	"	"	"
7	10	MANSFIELD TOWN	7-1		Towler(3), Cheetham(4)	"	Wightman	"	"	"	"	"	"	"	"	"
8	17	Mansfield Town	4-3		Brown, Cheetham, Towler, Bett	"	Winslow	"	"	"	"	W.Brown	"	"	"	"
9	24	Notts County	6-3		Cheetham(2),Towler(2),Bett,Clare	"	Hardy	"	"	"	Dickie	Wardle	"	"	"	"
10	31	NOTTS COUNTY	8-1		Wardle(3),Cheetham(2),Towler,Bett(2)	"	"	"	"	"	"	"	"	"	"	"
11	7 Nov	Grimsby Town	2-2		Towler, C.Moulson	"	"	"	"	"	"	"	"	"	"	"
12	14	GRIMSBY TOWN	2-2		Towler, Bett	"	"	"	"	"	"	"	"	"	"	"
13	21	ROTHERHAM UNITED	1-1		Towler	"	"	"	Makinson	"	Johnston	"	"	Stillyards	"	"
14	28	Rotherham United	0-3			"	"	Wightman	Johnston	"	Dickie	"	"	W.Cooper	"	"
15	5 Dec	Nottingham Forest	1-4		Clare	"	Wightman	Bean	Marsh	"	Hardy	W.Brown	Dickie	Towler	Lewis	"
16	12	NOTTINGHAM FOREST	4-1		Cheetham, Wardle(2), Towler	Platts	Hardy	"	"	Wightman	Dickie	Wardle	Bett	Cheetham	Towler	"
17	19	Notts County	2-4		Wardle(2)	"	"	"	Johnston	"	"	"	"	Rogers	"	"
18	25	NOTTS COUNTY	8-1		Knott(2), Towler(2), Wightman, *	G.Moulson	"	"	Wightman	C.Moulson	"	Stillyards	"	Knott	"	"

* Additional scorers - Bett(2), Stillyards   P18 W9 D5 L4 F58 A36 Pts.23 Pos.11th (out of 48 teams)

FOOTBALL LEAGUE WAR CUP-NORTH (QUALIFYING COMPETITION)

1	26 Dec	Sheffield Wednesday	3-4		Towler, Bett, Dickie	G.Moulson	Hardy	Bean	Wightman	C.Moulson	Dickie	Wardle	Bett	Knott	Towler	Clare
2	2 Jan	SHEFFIELD WEDNESDAY	0-3			"	"	"	Marsh	"	Wightman	"	"	Dunderdale	"	"
3	9	NOTTS COUNTY	0-2			"	"	"	Johnston	"	"	"	"	"	"	"
4	16	Notts County	2-1		Bett, Clare	"	Wightman	"	"	"	Hardy	Bett	Yorston	Tyson	"	"
5	23	Mansfield Town	3-2		Clare(2), Towler	"	"	"	"	"	"	"	"	"	"	"
6	30	MANSFIELD TOWN	8-1		Yorston(2),Bett,Towler,Hardy,OG,Clare(2)	"	A.Thompson	"	"	"	"	"	"	Clare	"	Lewis
7	6 Feb	GRIMSBY TOWN	1-1		Lewis	Platts	"	"	"	"	"	"	Dickie	"	"	"
8	13	Grimsby Town	0-1			"	"	"	"	"	"	"	"	Marsh	"	Clare
9	20	NOTTINGHAM FOREST	4-0		Dryden, Towler(2), Clare	Bly	"	Marsh	Johnston	"	"	"	Dryden	"	"
10	27	Nottingham Forest	2-3		Dickie, Towler	Theaker	"	"	"	"	Dryden	"	Dorsett	"	"

P10 W4 D1 L5 F23 A18 Pts.9 Pos.36th (out of 54 teams), top 32 qualified for knock out stages.

SEASON 1943-44
FOOTBALL LEAGUE NORTH (FIRST CHAMPIONSHIP)

No.	Date	Opposition	Res.	Att.	Goalscorers											
1	28 Aug	NOTTS COUNTY	4-5		Bett, Warburton, Knott(2)	J.Smith	Hardy	Bean	Johnston	C.Moulson	Marsh	Warburton	Bett	Knott	L.Parker	Clare
2	4 Sep	Notts County	0-0			Platts	A.Thompson	"	Hardy	Johnston	Towler	D.Thompson	"	"	Lewis	"
3	11	NOTTINGHAM FOREST	3-0		Lewis, D.Thompson, Stillyards	"	Topping	"	"	"	"	"	Lyon	Stillyards	"	"
4	18	Nottingham Forest	1-8		O'Donnell	"	"	Readett	Marsh	"	Hardy	"	Bett	O'Donnell	Towler	"
5	25	DONCASTER ROVERS	2-1		Bett, O'Donnell	"	A.Thompson	Bean	"	"	"	"	"	Knott	"	O'Donnell
6	2 Oct	Doncaster Rovers	1-3		D.Thompson	"	Topping	"	"	"	"	"	"	O'Donnell	"	Clare
7	9	GRIMSBY TOWN	2-2		Lewis, O'Donnell	J.Smith	"	"	"	"	"	"	"	"	Lewis	"
8	16	Grimsby Town	2-3		Lewis(2)	Oakley	"	"	"	"	"	"	"	Stillyards	"	"
9	23	Mansfield Town	0-1			J.Smith	A.Thompson	"	"	"	"	Mason	"	Knott	"	"
10	30	MANSFIELD TOWN	7-2		Clare, Lello(4), Lewis, D.Thompson	"	Topping	"	"	"	"	D.Thompson	"	Lello	"	"
11	6 Nov	GRIMSBY TOWN	4-0		Bett, Lello, Lewis, Clare	"	"	"	"	"	"	"	"	McDermott	"	"
12	13	Grimsby Town	2-3		Lewis, Clare	"	Hardy	"	"	"	McDermott	Knott	"	"	"	"
13	20	Rotherham United	2-1		Parker, Clare	Bradley	"	"	"	"	Keen	Burton	Curry	Clare	H.Parker	B.Cartwright
14	27	ROTHERHAM UNITED	5-1		Bett(2), Bray, Lello(2)	J.Smith	A.Thompson	"	Hardy	"	"	Stillyards	Bett	Lello	Clare	Bray
15	4 Dec	NOTTINGHAM FOREST	2-2		Lello, Clare	"	Hardy	"	Marsh	"	"	Bray	"	"	Lewis	Clare
16	11	Nottingham Forest	1-1		Clare	Bradley	Corkhill	"	"	"	Hardy	Buttery	"	Clare	"	Bray
17	18	NOTTS COUNTY	8-5		Lello(7), Lewis	Dawson	"	A.Thompson	"	Hardy	Haines	Smith	"	Lello	"	Clare
18	25	Notts County	5-2		Bett(3), Haines, Grummett	J.Smith	"	Bean	Thomas	Johnston	Hardy	Bray	"	Haines	Grummett	"

P18 W8 D4 L6 F51 A40 Pts.20 Pos.15th (out of 50 teams)

FOOTBALL LEAGUE NORTH (SECOND CHAMPIONSHIP)

1	26 Dec	Mansfield Town	1-2		Bett	Bradley	Shimwell	Bean	Haines	Johnston	Hardy	Rudkin	Bett	Lello	Lewis	Clare
2	1 Jan	MANSFIELD TOWN	3-2		Marsh, Lello, Clare	"	Hardy	"	Marsh	"	S.Green	Haines	"	"	Grummett	"
3	8	DONCASTER ROVERS	4-5		Lello(2), Bray, Haines	"	"	A.Thompson	"	"	Hardy	Lowrey	Haines	"	Clare	Bray
4	22	GRIMSBY TOWN	1-3		Lello	J.Smith	Hollis	"	"	"	"	"	Bett	"	Lewis	Clare
5	29	Grimsby Town	0-3			Parkin	"	"	"	"	"	Bray	"	"	"	"
6	5 Feb	Sheffield United	2-6		Lello, Bett	N.Jones	"	"	"	"	Douglas	"	Keggan	"	Grummett	"
7	12	SHEFFIELD UNITED	0-0			J.Smith	Bean	G.Williams	"	"	"	"	"	"	Bellis	"
8	19	ROTHERHAM UNITED	2-4		Lello, Lowry	Adkins	A.Thompson	Bean	"	Hollis	"	Lowrey	"	"	"	Bray
9	26	Rotherham United	1-6		Bellis	"	Hardy	"	"	Douglas	Johnston	"	"	Haines	"	Clare
10	4 Mar	Doncaster Rovers	1-6		Clare	Oakley	Hepworth	"	Johnston	"	Hardy	"	Marsh	Clare	Grummett	Marlow
11	11	DONCASTER ROVERS	2-7		Bett, Hatfield	Adkins	Hardy	Darley	Clawson	Johnston	Haines	Taylor	Bett	Hatfield	Bellis	Clare
12	18	Mansfield Town	0-4			Mellors	"	R.Barton	Douglas	"	"	Bray	"	"	Marlow	"
13	25	MANSFIELD TOWN	3-0		Bray(2), E.Rutherford	J.Smith	"	Bean	Marsh	"	Douglas	E.Rutherford	Taylor	"	J.Parr	Bray
14	1 Apr	SHEFFIELD WEDNESDAY	2-1		Lee, Lowrie	G.Moulson	"	"	"	Johnston	Millington	Marsh	"	J.Parr	Lowrie	Bett	Lee
15	8	Sheffield Wednesday	0-2			"	"	"	"	A.Hall	"	Johnston	"	"	"	Lewis	"
16	10	GRIMSBY TOWN	1-1		E.Rutherford	J.Rutherford	"	"	Marsh	Johnston	H.Green	J.Parr	Clare	Grummett	Bray
17	15	BRADFORD CITY	0-1			G.Moulson	"	"	"	"	L.Jones	"	"	"	Bett	"
18	22	Bradford City	2-3		Ranshaw, Marsh	Binns	"	"	"	"	Page	McGinn	Bett	Robledo	Grummett	Ranshaw

P18 W3 D2 L12 F25 A56 Pts.8 Pos.53rd (out of 56 teams)
Matches 1-9 also counted for League Cup North Qualifying Competition: P9 W1 D1 L7 F14 A31 Pts.3 Pos.53rd (out of 56 teams). Top 32 qualified for knock out stages
Matches 14-15 also counted as the two legs of Combined Counties Cup, Round 1.

SEASON 1944-45
FOOTBALL LEAGUE NORTH (FIRST CHAMPIONSHIP)

No.	Date	Opposition	Res.	Att.	Goalscorers										
1	26 Aug	NOTTS COUNTY	4-2		Boyes, Beaumont, E.Rutherford(2)	Ravenscroft	Hardy	Bean	Johnston	Douglas	Marsh	E.Rutherford	Boyes	Haines	Beaumont	Pawlaw
2	2 Sep	Notts County	5-4		Boyes, Rowley(3), Pawlaw	"	"	"	"	G.Johnson	B.Cartwright	"	Rowley	"	Boyes	"
3	9	Chesterfield	1-3		Haines	"	"	"	"	Douglas	Marsh	"	Boyes	"	W.Williams	"
4	16	CHESTERFIELD	0-1			"	"	"	"	"	"	"	"	Stillyards	Beaumont	"
5	23	MANSFIELD TOWN	3-1		Haines(2), Clare	"	"	"	"	"	B.Cartwright	F.Cooper	Marsh	Haines	Clare	"
6	30	Mansfield Town	0-1			"	"	"	"	"	"	"	"	"	Drysdale	Clare
7	7 Oct	Rotherham United	0-1			Mills	"	"	"	"	"	E.Rutherford	"	"	Clare	Pawlaw
8	14	ROTHERHAM UNITED	2-6		Pawlaw, Haines	Ravenscroft	"	"	Marsh	"	Johnston	"	Gillan	"	"	"
9	21	Grimsby Town	0-4			"	"	"	B.Cartwright	"	"	"	Beaumont	Sleight	Davidson	Liddell
10	28	GRIMSBY TOWN	5-2		Collindridge(2),Douglas,Clare,Acton	Groves	"	"	Douglas	Johnston	Haines	Worthington	Hutchinson	Collindridge	Acton	Clare
11	4 Nov	SHEFFIELD WEDNESDAY	0-3			"	"	"	"	"	"	"	"	Beaumont	Laing	"
12	11	Sheffield Wednesday	1-2		Haines	"	"	"	Marsh	Douglas	B.Cartwright	E.Rutherford	Bett	Haines	Grummett	Worthington
13	18	Nottingham Forest	2-2		Hutchinson(2)	"	"	G.Hall	"	"	Haines	"	Hutchinson	Lello	Davidson	Gordon
14	25	NOTTINGHAM FOREST	2-2		Clare, Hutchinson	"	"	Bean	"	G.Hall	B.Cartwright	"	"	Haines	"	Clare
15	2 Dec	BARNSLEY	2-5		Hutchinson, Gordon	"	G.Hall	Hardy	"	Douglas	Johnston	Gordon	"	"	Dulson	"
16	9	Barnsley	3-5		Haines(3)	"	Hardy	Bean	"	"	Flack	"	"	"	Grummett	"
17	16	Doncaster Rovers	2-9		Haines, Hutchinson	"	"	"	"	Johnston	"	"	"	"	Davidson	Grummett
18	23	DONCASTER ROVERS	0-3			"	"	"	Johnston	Metcalfe	B.Cartwright	E.Rutherford	"	Lello	"	Pawlaw

P18 W4 D2 L12 F32 A56 Pts.10 Pos.51st (out of 54 teams)

FOOTBALL LEAGUE NORTH (SECOND CHAMPIONSHIP)

No.	Date	Opposition	Res.		Goalscorers										
1	25 Dec	Grimsby Town	2-2		Hutchinson, Haines	Groves	Hardy	Bean	Rossington	Johnston	B.Cartwright	Beaumont	Hutchinson	Stillyards	Haines	Clare
2	30	GRIMSBY TOWN	0-2			"	"	"	"	"	"	Stillyards	Marsh	Finan	"	"
3	6 Jan	Doncaster Rovers	1-6		Haines	"	"	"	"	"	Marsh	Worthington	Hutchinson	Haines	Grummett	"
4	13	DONCASTER ROVERS	1-3		Haines	"	G.Hall	"	Marsh	"	Hardy	Rossington	"	"	"	Marlow
5	27	Sheffield United	2-10		Hutchinson(2)	Manning	"	"	Rossington	"	"	Collins	Jessop	Hutchinson	"	"
6	3 Feb	Rotherham United	2-3		Haines, Hutchinson	Groves	Watford	"	Marsh	"	"	Harper	"	Haines	"	"
7	10	ROTHERHAM UNITED	2-2		Marlow, Haines	Ravenscroft	"	"	"	"	"	Russell	"	"	Rossington	"
8	17	SHEFFIELD WEDNESDAY	5-3		Bett, Marlow(2), Haines(2)	"	"	"	"	"	"	Rossington	"	"	Bett	"
9	24	Sheffield Wednesday	3-1		Marsh, Hutchinson, Grummett	"	"	"	"	"	"	"	"	"	Grummett	"
10	3 Mar	NOTTS COUNTY	3-2		Hutchinson(2), Haines	"	"	"	"	"	"	"	"	"	Marlow	Clare
11	10	SHEFFIELD UNITED	3-1		Haines, Marsh, Marlow	"	"	"	"	"	"	"	"	"	Collins	Marlow
12	24	Hull City	4-1		Rossington, Marlow(3)	"	Walker	"	"	"	"	"	"	"	Russell	"
13	31	Grimsby Town	2-4		Gordon, Haines	"	Watford	"	"	T.Callender	"	"	"	"	Gordon	"
14	2 Apr	GRIMSBY TOWN	3-3		Haines, Marsh, McCormick	"	"	"	"	Johnston	"	"	"	"	McCormick	"
15	7	HULL CITY	4-2		Marlow(2), Haines, Rossington	"	"	"	"	B.Cartwright	"	"	"	"	Grummett	"
16	14	Grimsby Town	3-4		Cheetham(2), Marlow	"	"	"	"	"	"	"	Haines	Cheetham	"	"
17	21	GRIMSBY TOWN	2-2		Grainger, Hutchinson	"	"	"	Haines	"	"	Grainger	Hutchinson	"	"	"

P17 W6 D4 L7 F42 A51 Pts.16 Pos.46th (out of 60 teams)

Matches 1-9 and 11 also counted for League Cup North Qualifying Competition: P10 W3 D2 L5 F21 A33 Pts.8 Pos.43rd (out of 63 teams). Top 32 qualified for knock out stages.

Matches 16 & 17 also counted as the two legs of the Lincolnshire Hospital Cup Final.

SEASON 1945-46

DIVISION THREE NORTH: EAST

No.	Date	Opposition	Res.	Att.	Goalscorers										
1	25 Aug	ROTHERHAM UNITED	1-1	4628	OG	Parkin	Walker	Bean	Marsh	Archer	Hardy	Grainger	Davies	Tench	Grummett	Marlow
2	1 Sep	Rotherham United	0-3	6353		Parkin	Wilkinson	Marsh	Marsh	Archer	Hardy	Grainger	Davies	Tench	Grummett	Marlow
3	8	Bradford City	1-5	5060	Howarth	Ravenscroft	Walker	Parkinson	Johnson	Archer	Hardy	Grummett	Davies	Howarth	Cheetham	Marlow
4	15	BRADFORD CITY	2-3	4306	Marlow, Bean	Ravenscroft	Walker	Bean	Marsh	Archer	Hardy	Davies	Smedley	Howarth	Grummett	Marlow
5	22	CARLISLE UNITED	5-0	4754	Cheetham(3), Smedley, Marlow	Parkin	Walker	Bean	Marsh	Franklin	Hardy	Davies	Smedley	Cheetham	Grummett	Marlow
6	29	Carlisle United	3-4	5414	Smedley, Cheetham, Marlow	Parkin	Walker	Bean	Marsh	Archer	Hardy	Davies	Smedley	Cheetham	T. Callender	Marlow
7	6 Oct	Gateshead	1-6	5263	Cheetham	Parkin	Walker	Bean	Marsh	Archer	Hardy	Davies	Smedley	Cheetham	Grummett	Marlow
8	13	GATESHEAD	1-4	5768	Cheetham	Parkin	G.Cartwright	Bean	Marsh	Walker	Hardy	Davies	Lello	Cheetham	Grummett	Hepple
9	20	York City	0-3	4884		Parkin	G.Cartwright	Walker	Marsh	Bean	Hardy	Davies	Smedley	Cheetham	Grummett	Marlow
10	27	YORK CITY	2-2	5365	Cheetham, Davies	Parkin	G.Cartwright	Walker	Wroe	Bean	Hardy	Davies	Grummett	Cheetham	Smedley	Marlow
11	3 Nov	Halifax Town	2-6	2785	Cheetham, Smedley	Parkin	G.Cartwright	Walker	Wroe	Bean	Hardy	Davies	Grummett	Cheetham	Smedley	Marlow
12	10	HALIFAX TOWN	1-2	6426	Davies	Parkin	G.Cartwright	Bean	Keen	Wilson	Hardy	Davies	Hellings	Cheetham	Smedley	Marlow
13	1 Dec	Darlington	1-6	5421	Haines	Parkin	G.Cartwright	Bean	Wroe	Hartshorne	Keen	Wilkinson	Haines	Stillyards	Hepple	Marlow
14	22	HARTLEPOOLS UNITED	4-2	3567	Wilkinson, Marlow, Cheetham(2)	Parkin	G.Cartwright	Bean	Wroe	Emery	Hardy	Wilkinson	Davies	Cheetham	Grummett	Marlow
15	25	Doncaster Rovers	1-3	6302	Marlow	Parkin	G.Cartwright	Bean	Wroe	Emery	Hardy	Wilkinson	Davies	Cheetham	Grummett	Marlow
16	26	DONCASTER ROVERS	4-0	7977	Cheetham(2), Davies(2)	Parkin	Wilkinson	Bean	Wroe	Emery	Hardy	Davies	Stillyards	Cheetham	Grummett	Marlow
17	29	DARLINGTON	1-3	6195	Cheetham	Ravenscroft	Wilkinson	Bean	Wroe	Emery	Hardy	Davies	Stillyards	Cheetham	Grummett	Marlow
18	1 Jan	Hartlepools United	4-1	4689	Grummett(3), OG	Lumsden	G.Cartwright	Bean	Wroe	Franklin	Ruecroft	Wilkinson	Davies	Cheetham	Grummett	Marlow

P18 W4 D2 L12 F34 A54 Pts.10 Pos.9th (out of 10 teams)

DIVISION THREE NORTH (EAST) CUP QUALIFYING COMPETITION

No.	Date	Opposition	Res.	Att.	Goalscorers										
1	12 Jan	DONCASTER ROVERS	2-3	6619	Marlow, Cheetham	Parkin	G.Cartwright	Bean	Wroe	Franklin	Haines	Wilkinson	Davies	Cheetham	Grummett	Marlow
2	19	Doncaster Rovers	0-3	3987		Lumsden	G.Cartwright	Bean	Wroe	Emery	Hardy	Davies	Haines	Cheetham	Grummett	Marlow
3	26	Halifax Town	3-1	2285	Cheetham(2), Marlow	Woodbridge	G.Cartwright	Bean	Wroe	Emery	Hardy	Davies	Cheetham	Hellings	Grummett	Marlow
4	2 Feb	HALIFAX TOWN	2-3	5705	Hellings, Marlow	Woodbridge	G.Cartwright	Bean	Wroe	Emery	Hardy	Davies	Cheetham	Hellings	Grummett	Marlow
5	9	ROTHERHAM UNITED	1-5	5536	Marlow	Woodbridge	G.Cartwright	Bean	Hann	Emery	Hardy	Hoyland	Powell	Hellings	Grummett	Marlow
6	16	Rotherham United	1-6	8374	Cheetham	Lumsden	Thompson	Bean	Wroe	G.Cartwright	Hardy	Hoyland	Smedley	Cheetham	Grummett	Marlow
7	23	Darlington	2-7	4377	Grummett, Marlow	Lumsden	G.Cartwright	Bean	Wroe	Johnson	Settle	Grant	Haines	Cheetham	Grummett	Marlow
8	2 Mar	DARLINGTON	6-2	4209	Grummett,Thompson,Grant(2), *	Skelton	Thompson	Bean	Settle	Johnson	Hardy	Davies	Stillyards	Grant	Grummett	Ranshaw
9	9	York City	2-6	4827	Stillyards, Grummett	Skelton	Thompson	Bean	Settle	Johnson	Hardy	Davies	Stillyards	Grant	Grummett	Ranshaw
10	13	YORK CITY	2-2	1643	Grant, Grummett	Raynor	Thompson	Bean	Settle	Johnson	Hardy	Davies	Stillyards	Grant	Grummett	Ranshaw

P10 W2 D1 L7 F21 A38 Pts.15 Pos.10th (out of 10 teams) Top 8 clubs qualified for knock out stages.
* Additional scorers: Stillyards, Ranshaw

DIVISION THREE NORTH - SECOND CHAMPIONSHIP

No.	Date	Opposition	Res.	Att.	Goalscorers										
1	23 Mar	HALIFAX TOWN	1-1	3783	Cheetham	Gadsby	Thompson	Bean	Settle	Johnson	Stillyards	Collins	Grant	Cheetham	Grummett	Ranshaw
2	30	Halifax Town	3-2	4000	Cheetham(2), Marlow	Gadsby	Thompson	Bean	Settle	Johnson	Stillyards	Grant	C.Smith	Cheetham	Grummett	Marlow
3	6 Apr	Rochdale	3-2	4987	Cheetham, Grant, C.Smith	Gadsby	Thompson	Bean	Settle	Johnson	Stillyards	Grant	C.Smith	Cheetham	Grummett	Marlow
4	13	ROCHDALE	1-2	4942	Grant	Gadsby	Thompson	Bean	Settle	Johnson	Stillyards	Grant	C.Smith	Cheetham	Grummett	Marlow
5	20	TRANMERE ROVERS	3-0	6263	Hutchinson, Ranshaw, Cheetham	Gadsby	Thompson	Bean	Settle	Johnson	Stillyards	Grant	C.Smith	Cheetham	Hutchinson	Ranshaw
6	22	Tranmere Rovers	0-3	7000		Gadsby	Thompson	Bean	Settle	Johnson	Stillyards	Rossington	Hutchinson	Cheetham	Grummett	Ranshaw
7	27	Accrington Stanley	1-2	1772	Grummett	Gadsby	Thompson	Bean	Settle	Johnson	Stillyards	Grant	Hutchinson	Cheetham	Grummett	Ranshaw
8	4 May	ACCRINGTON STANLEY	5-1	4441	Cheetham,Grummett,Davies, *	Daniels	Thompson	Bean	Settle	Johnson	Stillyards	Davies	Hutchinson	Cheetham	Grummett	Marlow

P8 W4 D1 L3 F12 A13 Pts.9 Pos.8th (out of 20 teams)
* Additional scorers: Wilkinson, Marlow

F.A. CUP

1R1	17 Nov	Yorkshire Amateurs	0-1	1718		Parkin	G.Cartwright	Bean	Wroe	Emery	Hardy	Wilkinson	Davies	Cheetham	Grummett	Smedley
1R2	24	YORKSHIRE AMATEURS	5-1	6287	Cheetham(2), Marlow, Wroe, OG	Parkin	G.Cartwright	Bean	Wroe	Emery	Hardy	Wilkinson	Stillyards	Cheetham	Grummett	Marlow
2R1	8 Dec	Rotherham United	1-2	8145	Marlow	Parkin	G.Cartwright	Bean	Wroe	Emery	Hardy	Wilkinson	Stillyards	Cheetham	Grummett	Marlow
2R2	15	ROTHERHAM UNITED	1-2	8004	Marlow	Parkin	G.Cartwright	Bean	Wroe	Emery	Hardy	Wilkinson	Stillyards	Cheetham	Grummett	Marlow

LINCOLNSHIRE CUP

F1	1 May	Grimsby Town	1-1		Marlow	Daniels	Thompson	Bean	Settle	Johnson	Stillyards	Davies	Hutchinson	Cheetham	Grummett	Marlow
F2	11	GRIMSBY TOWN	4-1	6123	Cheetham,Marlow,Grummett,Davies	Daniels	Thompson	Bean	Settle	Emery	Stillyards	Davies	Hutchinson	Cheetham	Grummett	Marlow

SEASON 1946-47
DIVISION THREE (NORTH)

No.	Date	Opposition	Res.	Att.	Goalscorers
1	31 Aug	Hull City	0-0	25586	
2	4 Sep	DARLINGTON	2-0	7375	Parr, Grummett
3	7	GATESHEAD	4-0	9099	Cheetham, Parr, Marlow, Grummett
4	11	York City	4-2	6930	Parr(2), Davies, Grummett
5	14	Hartlepools United	0-2	8027	
6	21	CREWE ALEXANDRA	1-3	8060	Cheetham
7	28	Oldham Athletic	1-3	14478	Davies
8	5 Oct	Southport	3-1	4321	Marlow, Cheetham, Davies
9	12	ROTHERHAM UNITED	4-0	9653	Stillyards, Cheetham(2), Davies
10	19	BRADFORD CITY	0-1	9726	
11	26	Barrow	3-1	8785	Cheetham, Davies, Thompson
12	2 Nov	ACCRINGTON STANLEY	1-1	8235	Parr
13	9	Carlisle United	0-1	11821	
14	16	HALIFAX TOWN	3-1	7944	Marlow(2), Smedley
15	23	New Brighton	2-4	4017	Marlow, Hutchinson
16	7 Dec	DONCASTER ROVERS	3-5	10917	Marlow, Hutchinson, Cheetham
17	21	Stockport County	2-3	6824	Hutchinson, Dagg
18	25	Tranmere Rovers	2-5	6938	Cheetham, Smedley
19	26	TRANMERE ROVERS	2-1	11633	Cheetham, Marlow
20	28	HULL CITY	0-3	10996	
21	1 Jan	Darlington	3-4	8652	Cheetham(2), Hutchinson
22	4	Gateshead	0-3	5263	
23	18	HARTLEPOOLS UNITED	5-2	7414	Cheetham(2), Davies(2), Parr
24	22	ROCHDALE	2-3	3249	Hutchinson, Cheetham
25	25	Crewe Alexandra	5-0	4421	Hutchinson(2), Cheetham(2), Marlow
26	1 Feb	OLDHAM ATHLETIC	1-3	5579	Hutchinson
27	18 Mar	CARLISLE UNITED	3-1	6267	Cheetham, Parr(2)
28	29	NEW BRIGHTON	5-1	5058	Cheetham(2), Hutchinsn, Marlow, Davies
29	4 Apr	Chester	0-3	6921	
30	5	Rochdale	0-2	6634	
31	7	CHESTER	2-2	8785	Davies, Hutchinson
32	12	Doncaster Rovers	1-1	19571	OG
33	19	Wrexham	1-4	7544	Hutchinson
34	26	STOCKPORT COUNTY	4-0	5550	Hutchinson(2), Cheetham(2)
35	3 May	YORK CITY	2-2	6443	OG, Hutchinson
36	10	Rotherham United	0-3	11667	
37	17	SOUTHPORT	4-2	5158	Smedley, Marlow, Parr, Cheetham
38	24	WREXHAM	3-1	6173	OG, Parr, Dooley
39	26	BARROW	1-0	6596	Dooley
40	31	Accrington Stanley	4-8	2504	Cheetham(3), Hutchinson
41	7 Jun	Halifax Town	3-2	2513	Cheetham, Smedley, Grummett
42	14	Bradford City	0-3	5705	

3 own goals

F.A. CUP

1R	30 Nov	Stockton	4-2	8057	Cheetham, Hutchinson, Davies, Marlow
2R	14 Dec	WREXHAM	1-1	8173	Marlow
2Rr	18	Wrexham	3-3 *	9740	Hutchinson, Cheetham(2)
2R2r	23	Wrexham #	2-1	2683	Marlow, Cheetham
3R	11 Jan	NOTTINGHAM FOREST	0-1	17092	

* After extra time
# Played at Maine Road, Manchester

LINCOLNSHIRE CUP

| F | 21 May | GRIMSBY TOWN | 1-2 | 4597 | Dooley |

Final League Table

```
                    Pl.   Home              Away            F.   A.  Pts
                          W  D  L  F  A     W  D  L  F  A
 1  Doncaster Rovers  42  15  5  1 67 16   18  1  2 56 24  123  40  72
 2  Rotherham United  42  20  1  0 81 19    9  5  7 33 34  114  53  64
 3  Chester           42  17  2  2 53 13    8  4  9 42 38   95  51  56
 4  Stockport County  42  17  0  4 50 19    7  2 12 28 34   78  53  50
 5  Bradford City     42  12  5  4 40 20    8  5  8 22 27   62  47  50
 6  Rochdale          42   9  5  7 39 25   10  5  6 41 39   80  64  48
 7  Wrexham           42  13  5  3 43 21    4  7 10 22 30   65  51  46
 8  Crewe Alexandra   42  12  4  5 39 26    5 11 31 48   70  74  43
 9  Barrow            42  10  2  9 28 24    7  5  9 26 38   54  62  41
10  Tranmere Rovers   42  11  5  5 43 33    6  2 13 23 44   66  77  41
11  Hull City         42   9  5  7 25 19    7  3 11 24 34   49  53  40
12  Lincoln City      42  12  3  6 52 32    5  2 14 34 55   86  87  39
13  Hartlepools Utd   42  10  5  6 36 26    5  4 12 28 47   64  73  39
14  Gateshead         42  10  8  3 39 33    6  3 12 23 39   62  72  38
15  York City         42   6  4 11 35 42    8  5  8 32 39   67  81  37
16  Carlisle United   42  10  5  6 45 38    4  4 13 25 55   70  93  37
17  Darlington        42  12  4  5 48 26    3  2 16 20 54   68  80  36
18  New Brighton      42  11  3  7 37 30    3  5 13 20 47   57  77  36
19  Oldham Athletic   42   6  5 10 29 31    6  3 12 26 49   55  80  32
20  Accrington Stanley 42  8  3 10 37 38    6  1 14 19 54   56  92  32
21  Southport         42   6  5 10 35 41    1  6 14 18 44   53  85  25
22  Halifax Town      42   6  3 12 28 36    2  3 16 15 56   43  92  22
```

SEASON 1947-48
DIVISION THREE (NORTH)

No.	Date	Opposition	Res.	Att.	Goalscorers
1	23 Aug	HULL CITY	2-3	11116	Hutchinson, Marlow
2	26	Southport	1-1	7547	Cheetham
3	30	Stockport County	1-1	13199	Marlow
4	3 Sep	SOUTHPORT	3-1	9091	Hutchinson(2), Cheetham
5	6	BRADFORD CITY	3-0	11397	Walshaw(2), Marlow
6	10	NEW BRIGHTON	1-2	10092	Cheetham
7	13	Barrow	1-0	9238	OG
8	20	WREXHAM	2-1	11443	Hutchinson(2)
9	27	Halifax Town	1-0	7162	Hutchinson
10	4 Oct	ROCHDALE	3-0	12246	Hutchinson(2), McCormick
11	11	DARLINGTON	3-1	12077	Walshaw(2), Hutchinson
12	18	Tranmere Rovers	4-1	11985	Marlow, Hutchinson, McCormick, Walshaw
13	25	OLDHAM ATHLETIC	0-2	13783	
14	1 Nov	York City	1-0	9816	Hutchinson
15	8	MANSFIELD TOWN	0-0	15127	
16	15	Chester	1-1	7849	Walshaw
17	22	CREWE ALEXANDRA	0-0	11815	
18	6 Dec	Rotherham United	3-1	13320	Hutchinson, Storey, Bean
19	20	Hull City	1-0	20923	Storey
20	25	ACCRINGTON STANLEY	2-3	14352	Hutchinson(2)
21	27	Accrington Stanley	1-2	9293	Bean
22	1 Jan	New Brighton	1-0	3321	Marlow
23	3	STOCKPORT COUNTY	3-0	12777	Hutchinson(2), Marlow
24	10	Carlisle United	5-2	14068	Marlow(3), Hutchinson(2)
25	17	Bradford City	4-2	12859	Marlow, Parr, Lester, McCormick
26	24	Hartlepools United	2-1	8090	Hutchinson, McCormick
27	31	BARROW	2-1	15289	Hutchinson, Bean
28	7 Feb	Wrexham	0-3	12612	
29	14	HALIFAX TOWN	3-1	12552	Windle, Grummett, Lester
30	28	Darlington	3-1	7631	Hutchinson, Lester, Owen
31	6 Mar	TRANMERE ROVERS	2-0	12653	Hutchinson, McCormick
32	12	Oldham Athletic	0-0	14574	
33	20	YORK CITY	0-0	11703	
34	26	GATESHEAD	3-0	17657	Windle(3)
35	27	Mansfield Town	2-0	18863	Hutchinson, Parr
36	29	Gateshead	2-3	9673	Lester, Hutchinson
37	3 Apr	CHESTER	4-2	13066	Windle, Hutchinson(2), Bean
38	6	Rochdale	1-1	8467	Stillyards
39	10	Crewe Alexandra	0-3	7463	
40	17	CARLISLE UNITED	3-0	15337	Hutchinson(3)
41	24	Rotherham United	2-0	20177	Windle, McCormick
42	1 May	HARTLEPOOLS UNITED	5-0	20024	Hutchinson(3), Lester(2)

1 own goal

F.A. CUP

| 1R | 29 Nov | WORKINGTON | 0-2 | 9218 | |

LINCOLNSHIRE CUP

| F | 8 May | Grimsby Town | 2-0 | 8000 | Windle, Hutchinson |

Final League Table

		Pl.	W	Home D	L	F	A	W	Away D	L	F	A	F.	A.	Pts
1	Lincoln City	42	14	3	4	47	18	12	5	4	34	22	81	40	60
2	Rotherham United	42	15	4	2	56	18	10	5	6	39	31	95	49	59
3	Wrexham	42	14	3	4	49	23	7	5	9	25	31	74	54	50
4	Gateshead	42	11	5	5	48	28	8	6	7	27	29	75	57	49
5	Hull City	42	12	5	4	38	21	6	6	9	21	27	59	48	47
6	Accrington Stanley	42	13	1	7	36	24	7	5	9	26	35	62	59	46
7	Barrow	42	9	4	8	24	19	7	9	5	25	21	49	40	45
8	Mansfield Town	42	11	4	6	37	24	6	7	8	20	27	57	51	45
9	Carlisle United	42	10	4	7	50	35	8	3	10	38	42	88	77	43
10	Crewe Alexandra	42	12	4	5	41	24	6	3	12	20	39	61	63	43
11	Oldham Athletic	42	6	10	5	25	25	8	3	10	38	39	63	64	41
12	Rochdale	42	12	4	5	32	23	3	7	11	16	49	48	72	41
13	York City	42	8	7	6	38	25	5	7	9	27	35	65	60	40
14	Bradford City	42	10	4	7	38	27	5	6	10	27	39	65	66	40
15	Southport	42	10	4	7	34	27	4	7	10	26	36	60	63	39
16	Darlington	42	7	8	6	30	31	6	5	10	24	39	54	70	39
17	Stockport County	42	9	6	6	42	28	4	6	11	21	39	63	67	38
18	Tranmere Rovers	42	10	1	10	30	28	6	3	12	24	44	54	72	36
19	Hartlepools United	42	10	6	5	34	23	4	2	15	17	50	51	73	36
20	Chester	42	11	6	4	44	25	2	3	16	20	42	64	67	35
21	Halifax Town	42	4	10	7	25	27	3	3	15	18	49	43	76	27
22	New Brighton	42	5	6	10	20	28	3	3	15	18	53	38	81	25

1947-48
Back : Grummett, Stillyards, Moulson, Johnson, Owen, Bean.
Front : McCormick, Hutchinson, Lester, Parr, Windle.

1949-50
Back : Dinsdale, Wright, Grummett, Finch, Windsor.
Centre : Doherty, Stafford, Stillyards, Green, Emery, Dick Young, Owen, Ramsay, Bickerstaffe.
Front : Bett, Parr, Waby, Dodds, Payne, Eastham, Windle, Jarvis.

SEASON 1948-49
DIVISION TWO

No.	Date	Opposition	Res.	Att.	Goalscorers
1	21 Aug	West Ham United	2-2	31079	Parr, Windle
2	25	BURY	1-1	17627	Bean
3	28	TOTTENHAM HOTSPUR	0-0	19540	
4	1 Sep	Bury	1-3	14417	Windle
5	4	Brentford	1-2	22414	Lester
6	8	West Bromwich Albion	0-5	13009	
7	11	LEICESTER CITY	2-0	17103	Bean, Hutchinson
8	15	WEST BROMWICH ALBION	0-3	14902	
9	18	Leeds United	1-3	33963	Bett
10	25	COVENTRY CITY	1-0	14863	Bett
11	2 Oct	Sheffield Wednesday	2-2	42558	Grummett, Hutchinson
12	9	Grimsby Town	2-2	22189	Dodds(2)
13	16	NOTTINGHAM FOREST	1-3	19980	Dodds
14	23	Fulham	1-2	24760	Hutchinson
15	30	PLYMOUTH ARGYLE	1-2	15091	Dodds
16	6 Nov	Blackburn Rovers	1-7	25603	Marlow
17	13	CARDIFF CITY	0-0	14438	
18	20	Queens Park Rangers	0-2	19465	
19	27	LUTON TOWN	4-4	10817	Docherty(2), Hutchinson, Dodds
20	4 Dec	BRADFORD PARK AVENUE	3-6	14171	Hutchinson(3)
21	11	SOUTHAMPTON	1-2	14340	Dodds
22	18	WEST HAM UNITED	4-3	15609	Bean, Dodds(3)
23	25	CHESTERFIELD	2-2	18418	Hutchinson, Windle
24	27	Chesterfield	1-3	20473	Lester
25	1 Jan	Tottenham Hotspur	2-1	33218	Dodds(2)
26	15	BRENTFORD	3-1	13125	OG, Dodds(2)
27	22	Leicester City	3-5	35324	Bean(2), OG
28	5 Feb	LEEDS UNITED	0-0	18060	
29	12	Southampton	0-4	22782	
30	19	Coventry City	0-2	23452	
31	26	SHEFFIELD WEDNESDAY	3-1	20660	Grummett, Windsor, Dodds
32	5 Mar	GRIMSBY TOWN	2-3	23146	Dodds, Eastham
33	12	Nottingham Forest	1-1	28065	Lester
34	19	FULHAM	0-3	13199	
35	26	Plymouth Argyle	0-0	18532	
36	2 Apr	BLACKBURN ROVERS	3-0	11749	Smedley(2), Lester
37	9	Cardiff City	1-3	32585	Smedley
38	15	BARNSLEY	0-1	15551	
39	16	QUEENS PARK RANGERS	0-0	11306	
40	18	Barnsley	0-2	17346	
41	23	Luton Town	0-6	12643	
42	4 May	Bradford Park Avenue	3-0	6054	Dodds(2), Wright

2 own goals.

F.A. CUP

3R	8 Jan	WEST BROMWICH ALBION	0-1	19602	

LINCOLNSHIRE CUP

F	8 May	GRIMSBY TOWN	2-1*	5000	Windsor, Lester

* After extra time

Final League Table

		Pl.	Home W D L F A	Away W D L F A	F.	A.	Pts
1	Fulham	42	16 4 1 52 14	8 5 8 25 23	77	37	57
2	West Bromwich Alb.	42	16 3 2 47 16	8 5 8 22 23	69	39	56
3	Southampton	42	16 4 1 48 10	7 5 9 21 26	69	36	55
4	Cardiff City	42	14 4 3 45 21	5 9 7 17 26	62	47	51
5	Tottenham Hotspur	42	14 4 3 50 18	3 12 6 22 26	72	44	50
6	Chesterfield	42	9 7 5 24 18	6 10 5 27 27	51	45	47
7	West Ham United	42	13 5 3 38 23	5 5 11 18 35	56	58	46
8	Sheffield Wed.	42	12 6 3 36 17	3 7 11 27 39	63	56	43
9	Barnsley	42	10 7 4 40 18	4 5 12 22 43	62	61	40
10	Luton Town	42	11 6 4 32 16	3 6 12 23 41	55	57	40
11	Grimsby Town	42	10 5 6 44 28	5 5 11 28 48	72	76	40
12	Bury	42	12 5 4 41 23	5 1 15 26 53	67	76	40
13	Queen's Park Rgs.	42	11 4 6 31 26	3 7 11 13 36	44	62	39
14	Blackburn Rovers	42	12 5 4 41 23	3 3 15 12 40	53	63	38
15	Leeds United	42	11 6 4 36 21	1 7 13 19 42	55	63	37
16	Coventry City	42	12 3 6 35 20	3 4 14 20 44	55	64	37
17	Bradford Park Ave.	42	8 8 5 37 26	5 3 13 28 52	65	78	37
18	Brentford	42	7 10 4 28 21	4 4 13 14 32	42	53	36
19	Leicester City	42	6 6 10 5 41 38	4 6 11 21 41	62	79	36
20	Plymouth Argyle	42	11 4 6 33 25	1 8 12 16 39	49	64	36
21	Nottingham Forest	42	9 6 6 22 14	5 1 15 28 40	50	54	35
22	**Lincoln City**	42	6 7 8 31 35	2 5 14 22 56	53	91	28

SEASON 1949-50
DIVISION THREE (NORTH)

No.	Date	Opposition	Res.	Att.	Goalscorers
1	20 Aug	OLDHAM ATHLETIC	1-2	14917	Dodds
2	24	YORK CITY	1-0	11881	Dodds
3	27	Wrexham	0-4	13216	
4	29	York City	2-1	9007	Finch, Docherty
5	3 Sep	ACCRINGTON STANLEY	1-0	13817	Dodds
6	6	Barrow	0-0	7241	
7	10	Mansfield Town	1-2	16813	Troops
8	17	CARLISLE UNITED	2-1	11166	Grummett, Young
9	24	Rotherham United	3-1	11096	Finch, Dodds(2)
10	1 Oct	GATESHEAD	2-0	13405	Grummett(2)
11	8	Hartlepools United	1-2	10871	Troops
12	15	DARLINGTON	2-0	14303	Robinson, Dodds
13	22	New Brighton	0-1	5626	
14	29	HALIFAX TOWN	1-0	12498	Robinson
15	5 Nov	Rochdale	0-2	8867	
16	12	BRADFORD CITY	2-2	11328	Finch, Burnett
17	19	Chester	1-3	5312	Robinson
18	3 Dec	Stockport County	1-1	7939	Grummett
19	17	Oldham Athletic	2-0	11464	Dodds(2)
20	24	WREXHAM	2-0	11206	Robinson(2)
21	26	Crewe Alexandra	2-3	11648	Troops(2)
22	27	CREWE ALEXANDRA	2-0	15198	Dodds(2)
23	31	Accrington Stanley	0-2	5691	
24	14 Jan	MANSFIELD TOWN	1-0	15018	Dodds
25	21	Carlisle United	2-0	12892	Finch, Windle
26	28	SOUTHPORT	1-1	10180	Owen
27	4 Feb	ROTHERHAM UNITED	0-0	13329	
28	11	DONCASTER ROVERS	1-0	20306	Troops
29	18	Gateshead	1-2	10751	Dodds
30	25	CHESTER	2-0	8634	OG, Whittle
31	4 Mar	Southport	1-1	6047	Dodds
32	11	NEW BRIGHTON	1-2	10160	Troops
33	18	Halifax Town	1-0	5461	Dodds
34	25	ROCHDALE	2-0	11009	Dodds, Whittle
35	1 Apr	Bradford City	1-0	9192	Windle
36	7	TRANMERE ROVERS	0-0	14370	
37	8	HARTLEPOOLS UNITED	6-0	9116	Windle(2), Dodds(2), Green, Troops
38	10	Tranmere Rovers	2-2	8022	Green, Windle
39	15	Darlington	0-2	5076	
40	22	STOCKPORT COUNTY	1-1	10087	Dodds
41	29	Doncaster Rovers	4-1	11712	Windle(2), Dodds(2)
42	6	BARROW	4-0	8855	Dodds, Whittle(2), Boden

1 own goal

F.A. CUP

1R	26 Nov	Carlisle United	0-1	17240	

LINCOLNSHIRE CUP

F	13 May	Grimsby Town	1-2	8821	Whittle

Final League Table

		Pl.	Home				Away			F.	A.	Pts
			W	D	L	F	A	W	D	L	F	A	
1	Doncaster Rovers	42	9	9	3	30	15	10	8	3	36	23	66	38	55
2	Gateshead	42	13	5	3	51	23	10	2	9	36	31	87	54	53
3	Rochdale	42	15	3	3	42	13	6	6	9	26	28	68	41	51
4	Lincoln City	42	14	5	2	35	9	7	4	10	25	30	60	39	51
5	Tranmere Rovers	42	15	3	3	35	21	4	8	9	16	27	51	48	49
6	Rotherham United	42	10	6	5	46	28	9	4	8	34	31	80	59	48
7	Crewe Alexandra	42	10	6	5	38	27	7	8	6	30	28	68	55	48
8	Mansfield Town	42	12	4	5	37	20	6	8	7	29	34	66	54	48
9	Carlisle United	42	12	6	3	39	20	4	9	8	29	31	68	51	47
10	Stockport County	42	14	2	5	33	21	5	5	11	22	31	55	52	45
11	Oldham Athletic	42	10	4	7	32	31	6	7	8	26	32	58	63	43
12	Chester	42	12	3	6	47	33	5	3	13	23	46	70	79	40
13	Accrington Stanley	42	12	5	4	41	21	4	2	15	16	41	57	62	39
14	New Brighton	42	10	5	6	27	25	4	5	12	18	38	45	63	38
15	Barrow	42	9	6	6	27	20	5	3	13	20	33	47	53	37
16	Southport	42	7	10	4	29	26	5	3	13	22	45	51	71	37
17	Darlington	42	9	8	4	35	27	2	5	14	21	42	56	69	35
18	Hartlepools United	42	10	3	8	37	35	4	2	15	15	44	52	79	33
19	Bradford City	42	11	1	9	38	32	1	7	13	23	44	61	76	32
20	Wrexham	42	8	7	6	24	17	2	5	14	15	37	39	54	32
21	Halifax Town	42	9	5	7	35	31	3	3	15	23	54	58	85	32
22	York City	42	6	7	8	29	33	6	0	15	23	37	52	70	31

SEASON 1950-51
DIVISION THREE (NORTH)

No.	Date	Opposition	Res.	Att.	Goalscorers
1	19 Aug	CHESTER	2-1	10793	Whittle, Boden
2	22	SCUNTHORPE UNITED	2-1	16857	Garvie, Owen
3	26	Shrewsbury Town	2-1	11019	Windle, Finch
4	30	Scunthorpe United	1-1	14840	Windle
5	2 Sep	Mansfield Town	1-1	13111	Whittle
6	6	Bradford City	0-0	9082	
7	9	DARLINGTON	3-0	11514	Garvie, Whittle, McCready
8	13	BRADFORD CITY	1-4	12313	Green
9	16	Stockport County	0-2	11582	
10	23	HALIFAX TOWN	3-1	11358	Graver, Wright, Whittle
11	30	Hartlepools United	2-2	6729	Graver, Green
12	7 Oct	SOUTHPORT	1-2	10957	Windle
13	14	Accrington Stanley	1-3	5785	Graver
14	21	BRADFORD PARK AVENUE	1-3	10929	Owen
15	28	Tranmere Rovers	1-0	11220	Garvie
16	4 Nov	WREXHAM	2-1	8650	Finch, Garvie
17	11	Oldham Athletic	0-0	21742	
18	18	CARLISLE UNITED	1-1	9480	Garvie
19	2 Dec	BARROW	3-0	7852	Finch, Garvie, Green
20	22	SHREWSBURY TOWN	5-0	6634	Graver(2), Finch, Garvie, Windle
21	25	ROCHDALE	4-2	9873	Finch(3), Garvie
22	30	MANSFIELD TOWN	3-0	7904	Garvie(2), Windle
23	6 Jan	New Brighton	1-0	2256	Graver
24	13	Darlington	1-1	6108	Finch
25	20	STOCKPORT COUNTY	6-0	10521	Whittle(4), Graver, Green
26	27	NEW BRIGHTON	3-0	11332	Garvie(2), Whittle
27	3 Feb	Halifax Town	1-4	8760	Whittle
28	10	Crewe Alexandra	4-0	7467	Garvie, Finch, Green, Troops
29	17	HARTLEPOOLS UNITED	1-0	10336	Graver
30	24	Southport	2-0	4710	Garvie(2)
31	3 Mar	ACCRINGTON STANLEY	9-1	10745	Garvie(3),Finch(2),Graver(3),Windle
32	10	Bradford Park Avenue	1-2	10203	Graver
33	17	TRANMERE ROVERS	2-1	10596	Whittle, Garvie
34	23	GATESHEAD	2-1	11245	Graver, Troops
35	24	Wrexham	3-2	10705	Garvie, Whittle, Graver
36	26	Gateshead	2-1	5672	Troops, Garvie
37	31	OLDHAM ATHLETIC	2-0	10383	Graver(2)
38	7 Apr	Carlisle United	0-2	8859	
39	11	Chester	1-2	4730	Emery
40	14	YORK CITY	2-1	8363	Graver, Green
41	16	York City	2-2	6623	Green, Whittle
42	17	Rochdale	0-3	3533	
43	21	Barrow	1-3	6983	Young
44	28	ROTHERHAM UNITED	0-2	14714	
45	30	Rotherham United	0-3	15396	
46	5 May	CREWE ALEXANDRA	4-1	6781	Whittle, Finch, Graver(2)

F.A. CUP

| 1R | 25 Nov | SOUTHPORT | 1-1 | 9964 | Graver |
| 1Rr | 28 | Southport | 2-3 | 5798 | Troops, Windle |

LINCOLNSHIRE CUP

| F | 19 May | GRIMSBY TOWN | 3-0 | 7250 | Finch, Graver, Young |

Final League Table

	Pl.	W	D	L	F	A	W	D	L	F	A	F.	A.	Pts
1 Rotherham United	46	16	3	4	55	16	15	6	2	48	25	103	41	71
2 Mansfield Town	46	17	6	0	54	19	9	6	8	24	29	78	48	64
3 Carlisle United	46	18	4	1	44	17	7	8	8	35	33	79	50	62
4 Tranmere Rovers	46	15	5	3	51	26	9	6	8	32	36	83	62	59
5 *Lincoln City*	*46*	*18*	*1*	*4*	*62*	*23*	*7*	*9*	*7*	*27*	*35*	*89*	*58*	*58*
6 Bradford Park Ave.	46	15	3	5	46	23	8	5	10	44	49	90	72	54
7 Bradford City	46	13	4	6	55	30	8	6	9	35	33	90	63	52
8 Gateshead	46	17	1	5	60	21	4	7	12	24	41	84	62	50
9 Crewe Alexandra	46	14	5	7	38	26	8	5	10	23	34	61	60	48
10 Stockport County	46	15	3	5	45	26	5	5	13	18	37	63	63	48
11 Rochdale	46	11	6	6	38	18	6	5	12	31	44	69	62	45
12 Scunthorpe United	46	10	12	1	32	9	3	6	14	26	48	58	57	44
13 Chester	46	11	6	6	42	30	6	3	14	20	34	62	64	43
14 Wrexham	46	12	6	5	37	28	6	0	14	18	43	55	71	42
15 Oldham Athletic	46	10	5	8	47	36	6	3	14	26	37	73	73	40
16 Hartlepools United	46	14	5	4	55	26	2	2	19	9	40	64	66	39
17 York City	46	7	12	4	37	24	5	3	15	29	53	66	77	39
18 Darlington	46	10	8	5	35	29	3	5	15	24	48	59	77	39
19 Barrow	46	12	3	8	38	27	4	3	16	13	49	51	76	38
20 Shrewsbury Town	46	11	3	9	28	30	4	4	15	15	44	43	74	37
21 Southport	46	9	4	10	29	25	4	6	13	27	47	56	72	36
22 Halifax Town	46	11	6	6	36	24	0	6	17	14	45	50	69	34
23 Accrington Stanley	46	10	4	9	28	29	1	6	16	14	72	42	101	32
24 New Brighton	46	7	6	10	22	32	4	2	17	18	58	40	90	30

1950-51
Back : Anderson (manager), Gray, Dick Young, Bickerstaffe, Emery,
Wright, Troops, Alf Young (trainer), Mann (secretary).
Front : Finch, Whittle, Grummett, Garvie, Windle, McCready, Owen.

1951-52
Back : Anderson (manager), Mann (secretary), Green, Wright, Jones, Emery, Graham, Owen, Young (trainer).
Front : Troops, Garvie, Gibson, Graver, Whittle, Finch.

SEASON 1951-52
DIVISION THREE (NORTH)

No.	Date	Opposition	Res.	Att.	Goalscorers
1	18 Aug	YORK CITY	3-1	12016	Whittle, Graver, Troops
2	22	Grimsby Town	3-2	21479	Graver, Green, Garvie
3	25	Bradford City	1-1	14545	Garvie
4	29	GRIMSBY TOWN	0-2	19522	
5	1 Sep	HARTLEPOOLS UNITED	4-3	11888	Graver(2), Varney, Garvie
6	6	Scunthorpe United	3-1	12967	Graver, Varney(2)
7	8	Oldham Athletic	1-4	20948	Graver
8	12	SCUNTHORPE UNITED	4-1	14220	Whittle, Graver, Garvie, Troops
9	15	DARLINGTON	7-2	10515	Graver(3),Whittle,Troops(2),Garvie
10	22	Gateshead	1-3	13287	Whittle
11	29	CREWE ALEXANDRA	11-1	11269	Graver(6),Troops,Johnson,Green *
12	6 Oct	Chesterfield	2-2	13288	Garvie(2)
13	13	BRADFORD PARK AVENUE	2-0	12013	Whittle, Finch
14	20	Halifax Town	3-1	6328	Garvie, Finch, Whittle
15	27	MANSFIELD TOWN	1-2	16364	Finch
16	3 Nov	Rochdale	1-0	2457	Graver
17	10	ACCRINGTON STANLEY	2-2	11822	Graver, Garvie
18	17	Carlisle United	4-1	11099	Whittle, Troops, Garvie, Finch
19	1 Dec	Workington	3-0	5784	Finch, Graver(2)
20	8	BARROW	3-0	10636	Whittle, Finch, Graver
21	22	BRADFORD CITY	2-1	11204	Garvie, Graver
22	25	Wrexham	2-4	11087	Whittle, Troops
23	26	WREXHAM	3-2	15247	Graver(2), Whittle
24	29	Hartlepools United	1-1	11420	Graver
25	1 Jan	Tranmere Rovers	2-2	8510	Graver, Finch
26	5	OLDHAM ATHLETIC	4-0	15056	Garvie, Graver(3)
27	19	Darlington	1-1	5019	Finch
28	23	CHESTER	4-1	7682	Finch, Green, Graver(2)
29	26	GATESHEAD	1-1	12907	Gibson
30	2 Feb	Chester	1-1	5537	Graver
31	9	Crewe Alexandra	2-0	8547	Garvie, Gibson
32	16	CHESTERFIELD	5-1	15058	Gibson, Troops, Whittle(2), Green
33	23	TRANMERE ROVERS	3-0	15311	Clark, Gibson, Whittle
34	1 Mar	Bradford Park Avenue	1-1	17468	Finch
35	8	HALIFAX TOWN	4-1	15439	Whittle, Troops, Graver, Garvie
36	15	Mansfield Town	0-1	19043	
37	22	ROCHDALE	2-0	13646	Gibson(2)
38	29	Accrington Stanley	3-1	3358	Finch, Graver(2)
39	31	York City	0-1	6736	
40	5 Apr	CARLISLE UNITED	2-2	12093	Troops, Graver
41	11	Southport	3-0	8001	Troops(2), Garvie
42	12	Stockport County	1-1	18736	Finch
43	14	SOUTHPORT	4-0	17960	Finch, Troops, Garvie, Whittle
44	19	WORKINGTON	7-0	14277	Whittle(3),Gibson,Troops(2),Garvie
45	23	STOCKPORT COUNTY	2-1	21501	Garvie(2)
46	26	Barrow	2-1	4344	Finch, Gibson

* Additional scorers: Whittle, Grummett.

F.A. CUP

1R	24 Nov	Crewe Alexandra	4-2	9400	Garvie, Graver, Whittle, Young
2R	15 Dec	GRIMSBY TOWN	3-1	21757	Graver(2), Garvie
3R	12 Jan	Portsmouth	0-4	41093	

LINCOLNSHIRE CUP

F	10 May	Scunthorpe United	0-1	8098	

Final League Table

		Pl.	Home W D L F A	Away W D L F A	F. A. Pts
1	Lincoln City	46	19 2 2 80 23	11 7 5 41 29	121 52 69
2	Grimsby Town	46	19 2 2 59 14	10 6 7 37 31	96 45 66
3	Stockport County	46	12 9 2 47 17	11 4 8 27 23	74 40 59
4	Oldham Athletic	46	19 2 2 65 22	5 7 11 25 39	90 61 57
5	Gateshead	46	14 7 2 41 17	7 4 12 25 32	66 49 53
6	Mansfield Town	46	17 3 3 50 23	5 5 13 23 37	73 60 52
7	Carlisle United	46	13 6 4 51 28	6 6 11 23 36	74 64 50
8	Bradford Park Ave.	46	13 6 4 31 24	9 6 8 31 33	62 57 51
9	Hartlepools United	46	17 3 3 47 19	4 5 14 24 46	71 65 50
10	York City	46	16 4 3 53 19	2 9 12 20 33	73 52 49
11	Tranmere Rovers	46	17 2 4 59 29	4 4 15 17 42	76 71 48
12	Barrow	46	13 5 5 33 19	4 7 12 24 42	57 61 46
13	Chesterfield	46	15 5 1 47 16	2 4 17 18 50	65 66 45
14	Scunthorpe United	46	10 11 2 39 23	4 5 14 26 51	65 74 44
15	Bradford City	46	12 5 6 40 32	4 5 14 21 36	61 68 42
16	Crewe Alexandra	46	12 6 5 42 28	5 2 16 21 54	63 82 42
17	Southport	46	12 6 5 36 22	3 5 15 17 49	53 71 41
18	Wrexham	46	14 5 4 41 22	1 4 18 22 51	63 73 39
19	Chester	46	13 6 4 46 30	2 5 16 26 55	72 85 39
20	Halifax Town	46	11 4 8 31 23	3 3 17 30 74	61 97 35
21	Rochdale	46	10 5 8 32 34	1 8 14 15 45	47 79 35
22	Accrington Stanley	46	6 8 9 30 34	4 4 15 31 58	61 92 32
23	Darlington	46	10 5 8 39 34	1 4 18 25 69	64 103 31
24	Workington	46	8 4 11 33 34	3 3 17 17 57	50 91 29

SEASON 1952-53
DIVISION TWO

No.	Date	Opposition	Res.	Att.	Goalscorers
1	23 Aug	Brentford	0-1	27787	
2	27	BLACKBURN ROVERS	4-1	21042	Graver(2), Whittle, Troops
3	30	DONCASTER ROVERS	2-0	20775	Graver, Troops
4	1 Sep	Blackburn Rovers	2-0	25118	Gibson, Garvie
5	6	Swansea Town	1-1	21570	Whittle
6	10	NOTTINGHAM FOREST	2-3	21726	Graver, Whittle
7	13	HUDDERSFIELD TOWN	2-2	22029	Graver(2)
8	17	Nottingham Forest	1-1	24159	Graver
9	20	Sheffield United	1-6	33429	Graver
10	27	BARNSLEY	1-1	15293	Garvie
11	4 Oct	Fulham	2-4	24801	Whittle, Gibson
12	11	ROTHERHAM UNITED	1-3	19626	Whittle
13	18	Plymouth Argyle	0-0	23427	
14	25	LEEDS UNITED	1-1	15491	Graver
15	1 Nov	Luton Town	0-4	17538	
16	8	BIRMINGHAM CITY	1-1	16293	Johnson
17	15	Bury	2-2	11332	OG, Graver
18	22	SOUTHAMPTON	2-2	13126	Graver, Johnson
19	29	Notts County	1-1	18802	Varney
20	6 Dec	LEICESTER CITY	3-2	17221	Birch(2), Green
21	13	West Ham United	1-5	14436	Graver
22	20	BRENTFORD	0-0	11953	
23	26	EVERTON	1-1	19524	Birch
24	3 Jan	Doncaster Rovers	0-2	14206	
25	17	SWANSEA TOWN	3-1	14002	Birch, Garvie, Troops
26	24	Huddersfield Town	0-5	26512	
27	7 Feb	SHEFFIELD UNITED	3-2	17049	Graver, Garvie, Whittle
28	14	Barnsley	1-1	7867	Whittle
29	21	FULHAM	2-2	15042	Graver, Kerr
30	28	Rotherham United	2-3	16751	Finch, Graver
31	7 Mar	PLYMOUTH ARGYLE	0-0	14508	
32	14	Leeds United	1-2	18293	Garvie
33	21	LUTON TOWN	1-2	15510	Whittle
34	28	Birmingham City	2-2	13429	Munro, Whittle
35	3 Apr	HULL CITY	2-1	18445	Garvie, Whittle
36	4	BURY	4-0	14586	Garvie(2), Graver(2)
37	6	Hull City	1-1	26802	Garvie
38	11	Southampton	0-1	14922	
39	18	NOTTS COUNTY	3-0	14747	Garvie, Munro, Whittle
40	22	Everton	3-0	24217	Birch(2), Whittle
41	25	Leicester City	2-3	20923	Birch, Whittle
42	1 May	WEST HAM UNITED	3-1	14285	Graver, Whittle, Birch

1 own goal

F.A. CUP

3R	10 Jan	SOUTHAMPTON	1-1	14466	Birch
3Rr	14	Southampton	1-2	16750	Finch

LINCOLNSHIRE CUP

SF	15 Apr	GRIMSBY TOWN	0-3	3516	

Final League Table

		Pl.	Home					Away					F.	A.	Pts
			W	D	L	F	A	W	D	L	F	A			
1	Sheffield United	42	15	3	3	60	27	10	7	4	37	28	97	55	60
2	Huddersfield Town	42	14	4	3	51	14	10	6	5	33	19	84	33	58
3	Luton Town	42	15	1	5	53	17	7	7	7	31	32	84	49	52
4	Plymouth Argyle	42	12	5	4	37	24	8	4	9	28	36	65	60	49
5	Leicester City	42	13	6	2	55	29	5	6	10	34	45	89	74	48
6	Birmingham City	42	11	3	7	44	38	8	7	6	27	28	71	66	48
7	Nottingham Forest	42	11	5	5	46	32	7	3	11	31	35	77	67	44
8	Fulham	42	14	1	6	52	28	3	9	9	29	43	81	71	44
9	Blackburn Rovers	42	12	6	3	40	20	6	4	11	28	45	68	65	44
10	Leeds United	42	12	3	6	42	24	2	11	9	29	39	71	63	43
11	Swansea Town	42	10	9	2	45	26	5	3	13	33	55	78	81	42
12	Rotherham United	42	9	7	5	41	30	7	2	12	34	44	75	74	41
13	Doncaster Rovers	42	9	9	3	26	17	3	7	11	32	47	58	64	40
14	West Ham United	42	9	5	7	38	28	4	8	9	20	32	58	60	39
15	*Lincoln City*	*42*	*9*	*9*	*3*	*41*	*26*	*2*	*8*	*11*	*23*	*45*	*64*	*71*	*39*
16	Everton	42	9	8	4	38	23	3	6	12	33	52	71	75	38
17	Brentford	42	8	8	5	38	29	5	3	13	21	47	59	76	37
18	Hull City	42	11	6	4	36	19	3	2	16	21	50	57	69	36
19	Notts County	42	11	5	5	41	31	3	3	15	19	57	60	88	36
20	Bury	42	10	6	5	33	30	3	3	15	20	51	53	81	35
21	Southampton	42	5	7	9	45	44	5	6	10	23	41	68	85	33
22	Barnsley	42	4	4	13	31	46	1	4	16	16	62	47	108	18

1952-53
Back : Anderson (manager), Dick Young (coach), Gibson, Wright, Jones,
Graham, Lowery, Emery, Owen, Alf Young (trainer).
Front : Troops, Garvie, Graver, Whittle, Finch.

1954-55
Back : Giles (director), Linighan, Troops, Smith, Green, Warrington, Downie, Dykes, Wright, Bell (asst. trainer),
Alf Young (trainer), Dick Young (player/coach), Anderson (manager), Allen (director).
Centre : Neal, Munro, Gibson, Graver, Garvie, Birch, Emery, Graham.
Front : Middleton, Clews, Burlison, Hails, Owen, Finch.

SEASON 1953-54
DIVISION TWO

Players (columns): Lowery J., Green H., Graham J.D., Wright J.D., Emery A.J., Owen R.G., Munro J.F., Birch B., Graver A.M., Whittle E., Finch A.R., McDowall D., Troops H., Shaw B., Jones J.A., Hails W., Garvie J., Dykes D.W., Gibson R.H., Killin H.R., Young R.H., Clews M.D., Kerr J., Warrington A., Taylor C.H.

No.	Date	Opposition	Res	Att.	Goalscorers
1	19 Aug	West Ham United	0-5	17045	
2	22	Doncaster Rovers	1-1	16531	Graver
3	26	BURY	0-0	14564	
4	29	BLACKBURN ROVERS	8-0	12246	Whittle, Graver(4), Finch, Munro(2)
5	3 Sep	Bury	1-1	10701	Finch
6	5	Derby County	0-2	21810	
7	9	OLDHAM ATHLETIC	3-1	13821	McDowall, Whittle, Graver
8	12	BRENTFORD	2-1	16592	Graver, Whittle
9	14	Oldham Athletic	0-1	17624	
10	19	Bristol Rovers	1-0	24658	McDowall
11	26	LEEDS UNITED	2-0	17979	McDowall, Graver
12	3 Oct	NOTTS COUNTY	3-0	16448	Graver(2), Finch
13	10	Birmingham City	0-1	21948	
14	17	NOTTINGHAM FOREST	2-2	21936	Whittle, Graver
15	24	Luton Town	0-1	15578	
16	31	PLYMOUTH ARGYLE	2-0	13270	Graver(2)
17	7 Nov	Swansea Town	2-4	10074	Whittle, Graver
18	14	ROTHERHAM UNITED	4-3	15460	Whittle(3), Graver
19	21	Leicester City	2-9	30343	Whittle, Graver
20	28	STOKE CITY	1-1	14740	Whittle
21	5 Dec	Fulham	1-4	18726	Graver
22	12	WEST HAM UNITED	1-2	12886	Whittle
23	19	DONCASTER ROVERS	0-2	12904	
24	26	Hull City	0-3	26476	
25	28	HULL CITY	3-0	16910	Graver, Shaw, Gibson
26	2 Jan	Blackburn Rovers	0-6	16276	
27	16	DERBY COUNTY	2-2	13116	Graver, Birch
28	23	Brentford	1-0	11431	Munro
29	6 Feb	BRISTOL ROVERS	1-2	11986	Finch
30	13	Leeds United	2-5	15325	Graver, McDowall
31	20	Notts County	1-1	21109	Munro
32	27	BIRMINGHAM CITY	0-1	13924	
33	6 Mar	Nottingham Forest	2-4	20986	Garvie, Graver
34	13	LUTON TOWN	1-1	11195	Garvie
35	20	Plymouth Argyle	2-1	14036	Finch, Munro
36	27	LEICESTER CITY	3-1	16990	Graver, Garvie, Munro
37	3 Apr	Stoke City	1-4	11371	Garvie
38	10	SWANSEA TOWN	3-1	12583	Finch, Graver, OG
39	16	Everton	1-3	61231	Garvie
40	17	Rotherham United	1-4	12313	Garvie
41	19	EVERTON	1-1	17593	Garvie
42	24	FULHAM	4-2	11810	Garvie(3), Graver

Apps: 34, 35, 29, 37, 41, 42, 40, 17, 40, 25, 39, 17, 8, 8, 7, 3, 13, 10, 4, 7, 1, 3, 1, 1
Goals: 6, 1, 24, 11, 6, 4, 1, 10, 1
1 own goal

F.A. CUP

Round	Date	Opposition	Res	Att.	Goalscorers
3R	9 Jan	WALSALL	1-1	13890	Graver
3Rr	14	Walsall	1-1 *	16536	Finch
3R2r	18	Walsall #	2-1	12365	OG, Whittle
4R	30	PRESTON NORTH END	0-2	23027	

* After extra time
# Played at City Ground, Nottingham

LINCOLNSHIRE CUP

Round	Date	Opposition	Res	Att.	Goalscorers
SF	8 Apr	Scunthorpe United	1-2	4779	McDowall

Final League Table

	Pl.	Home W	D	L	F	A	Away W	D	L	F	A	F.	A.	Pts
1 Leicester City	42	15	4	2	63	23	8	6	7	34	37	97	60	56
2 Everton	42	13	6	2	55	27	7	10	4	37	31	92	58	56
3 Blackburn Rovers	42	15	4	2	54	16	8	5	8	32	34	86	50	55
4 Nottingham Forest	42	15	5	1	61	19	5	7	9	25	32	86	59	52
5 Rotherham United	42	13	4	4	51	26	8	3	10	29	41	80	67	49
6 Luton Town	42	11	7	3	36	23	7	5	9	28	36	64	59	48
7 Birmingham City	42	12	6	3	49	18	6	5	10	29	40	78	58	47
8 Fulham	42	12	3	6	62	39	5	7	9	36	46	98	85	44
9 Bristol Rovers	42	10	7	4	32	19	4	9	8	32	39	64	58	44
10 Leeds United	42	12	5	4	56	30	3	8	10	33	51	89	81	43
11 Stoke City	42	8	8	5	43	28	4	9	8	28	32	71	60	41
12 Doncaster Rovers	42	9	5	7	32	28	7	4	10	27	35	59	63	41
13 West Ham United	42	11	6	4	44	20	4	3	14	23	49	67	69	39
14 Notts County	42	8	6	7	26	29	5	7	9	28	45	54	74	39
15 Hull City	42	14	1	6	47	22	2	5	14	17	44	64	66	38
16 *Lincoln City*	42	11	6	4	46	23	3	3	15	19	60	65	83	37
17 Bury	42	9	7	5	39	32	2	7	12	15	40	54	72	36
18 Derby County	42	9	5	7	38	35	3	6	12	26	47	64	82	35
19 Plymouth Argyle	42	6	12	3	38	31	3	4	14	27	51	65	82	34
20 Swansea Town	42	11	5	5	34	25	2	3	16	24	57	58	82	34
21 Brentford	42	9	5	7	25	26	1	6	14	15	52	40	78	31
22 Oldham Athletic	42	6	7	8	26	31	2	2	17	14	58	40	89	25

SEASON 1954-55
DIVISION TWO

No.	Date	Opposition	Res.	Att.	Goalscorers	Downie M.	Green H.	Graham D.	Wright J.D.	Emery A.J.	Owen R.G.	Munro J.F.	Garvie J.	Graver A.M.	Birch B.	Finch A.R.	Dykes D.W.	Troops H.	Clews M.D.	Middleton F.T.	Neal R.M.	Gibson R.H.	Hails W.	Shaw B.	Littler J.E.	Withers A.	Birkbeck J.	Linighan B.
1	21 Aug	BURY	3-2	15394	Graver, Finch, Birch	1	2	3	4	5	6	7	8	9	10	11												
2	25	HULL CITY	0-1	13827		1		3	4	5	6	7	8	9	10	11	2											
3	28	Leeds United	3-2	22326	Finch, Dykes, Garvie	1			4	5	6		8	9	10	7	2	3	11									
4	30	Hull City	0-4	21818		1			4	5	6		8	9	10	7	2	3	11									
5	4 Sep	NOTTINGHAM FOREST	2-1	14167	Birch, Graver	1			4	5	6	7	8	9	10	11	2	3										
6	8	LUTON TOWN	1-2	13450	Owen	1			4	5	6	7	8	9	10	11	2	3										
7	11	Ipswich Town	2-1	17831	Gibson, Middleton	1				5		7	8		10	11	2	3		4	6	9						
8	15	Luton Town	1-2	11972	Gibson	1				5		7	8		10	11	2	3		4	6	9						
9	18	BIRMINGHAM CITY	1-1	14581	Finch	1				5		7	8		10	11	2	3		4	6	9						
10	25	Middlesbrough	1-2	23706	Graver	1				5		7	8	9		11	2	3		4	6	10						
11	2 Oct	STOKE CITY	1-4	13724	Graver	1				5		7		9		10	2	3	11	4	6		8					
12	9	Port Vale	3-1	19724	Neal(2), Birch	1	2		4	5		7	8	9	10	11		3			6							
13	16	DONCASTER ROVERS	5-1	13737	Neal, Finch, Munro, Birch, Graver	1	2		4	5		7	8	9	10	11		3			6							
14	23	Notts County	1-2	19474	Neal	1	2		4	5		7		9	10	11		3		8	6							
15	30	LIVERPOOL	3-3	13952	Graver, Garvie(2)	1	2			5		7	8	9	10	11		3		4	6							
16	6 Nov	Bristol Rovers	2-2	22119	Finch, Garvie	1		2		5		7	8	9	10	11		3		4	6							
17	13	PLYMOUTH ARGYLE	3-2	11865	Graver, Garvie, Birch	1		2		5		7	8	9	10	11		3		4	6							
18	20	Fulham	2-3	21024	Birch, Munro	1				5		7	8	9	10	11	2	3			6		4					
19	27	SWANSEA TOWN	2-2	11698	Graver, Munro	1			4	5		7	8	9	10	11	2	3			6							
20	4 Dec	Derby County	0-3	10883		1				5	4	7	8	9	10	11	2	3			6							
21	11	WEST HAM UNITED	2-1	11100	Dykes, Graver	1				5		7	8	9	10	11	2	3		4	6							
22	18	Bury	1-3	11761	Munro	1				5		7	8		10	11	2	3		4	6			9				
23	25	Rotherham United	0-3	14990		1	3			5		7	8		10	11	2			4	6			9				
24	27	ROTHERHAM UNITED	2-3	18897	Garvie(2)	1	2			5		7	8			11	10	3		4	6			9				
25	1 Jan	LEEDS UNITED	2-0	12231	Littler, Dykes	1	2			5		7	8			11	10	3		4	6			9				
26	15	Nottingham Forest	1-1	6707	Birch	1	2			5		7	8		10	11		3		4	6							
27	5 Feb	Birmingham City	3-3	20313	Gibson, Garvie, Finch	1	2			5		7	8		10	11		3		4	6	9						
28	12	MIDDLESBROUGH	3-3	8368	Finch, Neal, Munro	1	2			5		7	8		10	11		3		4	6	9						
29	19	Stoke City	2-4	12365	Gibson(2)	1	2			5		7	8		10	11		3		4	6	9						
30	5 Mar	Doncaster Rovers	1-1	11772	Gibson	1	2			5		7	8			11		3		4	6	9			10			
31	16	NOTTS COUNTY	1-2	8082	Finch	1	2			5		7	8			11		3		4	6	9			10			
32	19	Liverpool	4-2	31805	Garvie, Middleton, Gibson(2)	1	2			5		7	8			10		3		4	6	9			11			
33	26	BRISTOL ROVERS	0-2	6509		1	2			5		7	8			10		3		4	6	9			11			
34	2 Apr	Plymouth Argyle	0-1	9912		1	2			5		7	8			10		3		4	6	9			11			
35	8	Blackburn Rovers	0-1	29700		1	2			5		7	8			10		3		4	6	9			11			
36	9	FULHAM	2-2	12417	Garvie, OG	1	2			5			8		10	11		3		4	6	9	7					
37	11	BLACKBURN ROVERS	2-1	14745	Littler, Garvie	1	2			5			8		10	11		3		4	6		7		9			
38	16	Swansea Town	1-3	17558	Finch	1	2			5			8		10	11		3		4	6		7		9			
39	23	DERBY COUNTY	3-0	9419	Munro, Finch, Garvie	1	2			5		7	8			11		3		4	6	9	10					
40	27	IPSWICH TOWN	1-1	8201	Gibson	1	2			5		7	8			11		3		4	6	9	10					
41	30	West Ham United	1-0	10201	Garvie	1	2			5		7	8			11		3	11	4	6						9	
42	4 May	PORT VALE	0-1	7044		1	2			5		7	8			11		3		4	6	9					10	
		Apps.				42	5	24	10	42	7	37	40	18	28	42	18	39	4	31	36	18	6	1	6	6	2	
		Goals										1	6	13	9	7	10	3		2		5	9		2			

1 own goal

F.A. CUP

3R	8 Jan	LIVERPOOL	1-1	15302	Munro	1	2			5		7	8			11	10	3		4	6			9				
3Rr	12	Liverpool	0-1 *	32179		1	2			5		7	8		10	11		3		4	6	9						

* After extra time

LINCOLNSHIRE CUP

SF	19 Oct	Grimsby Town	2-0	3981	Gibson, Finch	1	2		4	5		7	8			11		3			6	9	10					
F	14 May	SCUNTHORPE UNITED	3-5 *		Garvie(2), Munro	1	2			7	8			11		3		4	6	9		10					5	

* After extra time

Final League Table

```
                    Pl.   Home              Away              F.   A.  Pts
                          W  D  L  F  A   W  D  L  F  A
 1  Birmingham City  42  14  4  3 56 22   8  6  7 36 25  92  47  54
 2  Luton Town       42  18  2  1 55 18   5  6 10 33 35  88  53  54
 3  Rotherham United 42  17  1  3 59 22   8  3 10 35 42  94  64  54
 4  Leeds United     42  14  4  3 43 19   9  3  9 27 34  70  53  53
 5  Stoke City       42  12  5  4 38 17   9  5  7 31 29  69  46  52
 6  Blackburn Rovers 42  14  4  3 73 31   8  2 11 41 48 114  79  50
 7  Notts County     42  14  3  4 46 27   7  3 11 28 44  74  71  48
 8  West Ham United  42  12  4  5 46 28   6  6  9 28 42  74  70  46
 9  Bristol Rovers   42  15  4  2 52 23   4  3 14 23 47  75  70  45
10  Swansea Town     42  15  3  3 58 28   2  6 13 28 55  86  83  43
11  Liverpool        42  11  7  3 55 37   5  3 13 37 59  92  96  42
12  Middlesbrough    42  13  1  7 48 31   5  5 11 25 51  73  82  42
13  Bury             42  10  5  6 44 35   5  6 10 33 37  77  72  41
14  Fulham           42  10  5  6 46 29   4  6 11 30 50  76  79  39
15  Nottingham Forest 42  8  4  9 29 29   8  3 10 29 33  58  62  39
16  Lincoln City     42  8  6  7 39 35   5  4 12 29 44  68  79  36
17  Port Vale        42  10  6  5 31 21   2  5 14 17 50  48  71  35
18  Doncaster Rovers 42  10  5  6 35 34   4  2 15 23 61  58  95  35
19  Hull City        42   7  5  9 30 35   5  5 11 14 34  44  69  34
20  Plymouth Argyle  42  10  4  7 29 26   2  3 16 28 56  57  82  31
21  Ipswich Town     42  10  3  8 37 28   1  3 17 20 64  57  92  28
22  Derby County     42   6  6  9 39 34   1  3 17 14 48  53  82  23
```

SEASON 1955-56
DIVISION TWO

No.	Date	Opposition	Res.	Att.	Goalscorers
1	20 Aug	Blackburn Rovers	2-0	22397	Graver, Munro
2	24	HULL CITY	2-0	13291	Graver, Garvie
3	27	BURY	4-2	12573	Finch(2), OG, Garvie
4	29	Hull City	1-2	14810	Middleton
5	3 Sep	LEICESTER CITY	7-1	16547	Finch(2),Northcott(2),Munro(2),Graver
6	7	SHEFFIELD WEDNESDAY	2-2	21025	Graver, Troops
7	10	Liverpool	1-2	39816	Garvie
8	17	PLYMOUTH ARGYLE	1-0	13460	Northcott
9	24	Stoke City	0-3	20534	
10	1 Oct	BRISTOL ROVERS	2-0	15202	Garvie, Neal
11	8	Barnsley	0-1	14819	
12	15	MIDDLESBROUGH	1-2	12532	Troops
13	22	Leeds United	0-1	17378	
14	29	WEST HAM UNITED	1-1	11078	Middleton
15	5 Nov	Port Vale	1-1	16561	Bannan
16	12	ROTHERHAM UNITED	1-1	12160	Bannan
17	19	Swansea Town	2-0	20990	Northcott, Middleton
18	26	NOTTS COUNTY	2-0	12815	Munro, Northcott
19	3 Dec	Bristol City	1-5	26329	OG
20	10	FULHAM	6-1	11635	Finch(2),Northcott(2),Bannan,Middleton
21	17	BLACKBURN ROVERS	3-0	11465	Finch, Bannan, Northcott
22	24	Bury	3-3	9392	OG, Middleton(2)
23	26	DONCASTER ROVERS	1-1	18083	Garvie
24	27	Doncaster Rovers	0-2	18323	
25	31	Leicester City	0-4	34418	
26	21 Jan	Plymouth Argyle	4-1	13632	Neal, Bannan(2), Gibson
27	11 Feb	Bristol Rovers	0-3	17469	
28	18	SWANSEA TOWN	3-1	7842	Gibson(2), Northcott
29	3 Mar	LEEDS UNITED	1-1	13713	Neal
30	10	Fulham	0-3	19196	
31	17	PORT VALE	1-0	10635	Gibson
32	24	Rotherham United	2-2	9681	Northcott, Finch
33	31	BARNSLEY	4-0	11787	Northcott(3), Gibson
34	2 Apr	NOTTINGHAM FOREST	1-3	18190	Munro
35	3	Nottingham Forest	2-2	22238	Northcott(2)
36	7	Notts County	2-2	14234	Gibson, Northcott
37	14	BRISTOL CITY	2-0	10318	Withers, Gibson
38	18	Middlesbrough	2-4	8298	Northcott, Neal
39	21	West Ham United	4-2	13347	Northcott(2), Withers, Bannan
40	25	STOKE CITY	2-1	12005	Hawkings(2)
41	28	Sheffield Wednesday	3-5	31084	Northcott, Withers, Munro
42	2 May	LIVERPOOL	2-0	11069	Gibson, Withers

3 own goals

F.A. CUP

| 3R | 7 Jan | SOUTHEND UNITED | 2-3 | 11229 | Bannan, Troops |

LINCOLNSHIRE CUP

| SF | 18 Oct | Grimsby Town | 2-1 | 4858 | Garvie, Graver |
| F | 12 May | Scunthorpe United | 1-1 * | 4242 | Withers |

* After extra time, the trophy was shared

Final League Table

		Pl.	Home W D L F A	Away W D L F A	F. A. Pts
1	Sheffield Wed.	42	13 5 3 60 28	8 8 5 41 34	101 62 55
2	Leeds United	42	17 3 1 51 18	6 3 12 29 42	80 60 52
3	Liverpool	42	14 3 4 52 25	7 3 11 33 38	85 63 48
4	Blackburn Rovers	42	13 4 4 55 29	8 2 11 29 36	84 65 48
5	Leicester City	42	15 3 3 63 23	6 3 12 31 55	94 78 48
6	Bristol Rovers	42	13 5 3 53 33	8 3 10 31 37	84 70 48
7	Nottingham Forest	42	9 5 7 30 26	10 4 7 38 37	68 63 47
8	*Lincoln City*	*42*	*14 5 2 49 17*	*4 5 12 30 48*	*79 65 46*
9	Fulham	42	15 2 4 59 27	5 4 12 30 52	89 79 46
10	Swansea Town	42	14 4 3 49 23	6 2 13 34 58	83 81 46
11	Bristol City	42	14 4 3 49 20	5 3 13 31 44	80 64 45
12	Port Vale	42	12 4 5 38 21	4 9 8 22 37	60 58 45
13	Stoke City	42	13 2 6 47 27	7 2 12 24 35	71 62 44
14	Middlesbrough	42	11 4 6 46 31	5 4 12 30 47	76 78 40
15	Bury	42	9 5 7 44 39	7 3 11 42 51	86 90 40
16	West Ham United	42	12 4 5 52 27	2 7 12 22 42	74 69 39
17	Doncaster Rovers	42	11 5 5 45 30	1 6 14 24 66	69 96 35
18	Barnsley	42	10 5 6 33 35	1 7 13 14 49	47 84 34
19	Rotherham United	42	7 5 9 29 34	5 4 12 27 41	56 75 33
20	Notts County	42	8 5 8 39 37	3 4 14 16 45	55 82 31
21	Plymouth Argyle	42	7 6 8 33 25	3 2 16 21 62	54 87 28
22	Hull City	42	6 4 11 32 45	4 2 15 21 52	53 97 26

1955-56
Back : Dick Young (coach), Middleton, Dykes, Downie,
Emery, Neal, Troops, Anderson (manager), Alf Young (trainer).
Front : Graham, Munro, Garvie, Graver, Finch, Holder, Withers, Northcott.

1956-57
Back : Anderson (manager), Bob Jackson, Walton, Middleton, Gibson, Dykes,
Neal, Capper, Northcott, Holder, Young (trainer).
Front : Emery, Troops, Smillie, Withers, Munro, Finch, Buick, Graham.

SEASON 1956-57
DIVISION TWO

No.	Date	Opposition	Res.	Att.	Goalscorers
1	18 Aug	BRISTOL CITY	1-1	12727	Bannan
2	22	PORT VALE	4-0	11863	Gibson, Withers(2), Bannan
3	25	Blackburn Rovers	4-3	23863	Bannan, Withers(2), Northcott
4	27	Port Vale	1-1	13595	Bannan
5	1 Sep	WEST HAM UNITED	0-2	13131	
6	5	Barnsley	2-5	9377	Munro, Northcott
7	8	Nottingham Forest	1-1	26780	Hawkings
8	15	FULHAM	1-0	11476	Munro
9	22	Swansea Town	2-1	12941	Gibson, Middleton
10	29	GRIMSBY TOWN	1-0	18973	Munro
11	6 Oct	Doncaster Rovers	1-3	16197	Gibson
12	13	STOKE CITY	0-1	13066	
13	20	Huddersfield Town	1-0	16999	OG
14	27	LEICESTER CITY	2-3	19450	Hawkings, Withers
15	3 Nov	Bristol Rovers	1-0	22320	Northcott
16	10	NOTTS COUNTY	1-0	11615	Gibson
17	17	Liverpool	0-4	29762	
18	24	LEYTON ORIENT	0-2	10386	
19	1 Dec	Middlesbrough	0-3	24598	
20	8	BURY	2-0	9260	Bannan, Munro
21	15	Bristol City	1-5	12772	Northcott
22	22	BLACKBURN ROVERS	1-2	7396	Watson
23	25	Sheffield United	0-2	19954	
24	26	SHEFFIELD UNITED	4-1	8079	Northcott(2), Watson, Hawkings
25	29	West Ham United	1-2	16790	Bannan
26	12 Jan	NOTTINGHAM FOREST	0-2	13214	
27	19	Fulham	1-0	17052	Hawkings
28	2 Feb	SWANSEA TOWN	0-2	10629	
29	9	Grimsby Town	0-2	18749	
30	16	DONCASTER ROVERS	4-1	9204	Bannan(2), OG, Withers
31	23	Stoke City	0-8	10813	
32	2 Mar	HUDDERSFIELD TOWN	1-2	9917	Neal
33	9	Leicester City	3-4	33195	Smillie, Northcott, Bannan
34	16	BRISTOL ROVERS	1-0	8907	Smillie
35	23	Notts County	0-3	17375	
36	30	LIVERPOOL	3-3	8451	Bannan(2), Northcott
37	6 Apr	Leyton Orient	1-2	13523	Neal
38	13	MIDDLESBROUGH	1-1	8601	Northcott
39	19	ROTHERHAM UNITED	3-3	11150	Bannan, Smillie, Finch
40	20	Bury	0-1	9460	
41	22	Rotherham United	0-3	7646	
42	27	BARNSLEY	4-1	7282	Linnecor(2), Northcott, Smillie

2 own goals

F.A. CUP

Rd	Date	Opposition	Res.	Att.	Goalscorers
3R	5 Jan	Peterborough United	2-2	23000	Watson, Troops
3Rr	9	PETERBOROUGH UNITED	4-5 *	18122	Bannan(2), Neal, Northcott

* After extra time

LINCOLNSHIRE CUP

Rd	Date	Opposition	Res.	Att.	
SF	1 Oct	Scunthorpe United	0-1		

Final League Table

	Pl.	Home W	D	L	F	A	Away W	D	L	F	A	F.	A.	Pts
1 Leicester City	42	14	5	2	68	36	11	6	4	41	31	109	67	61
2 Nottingham Forest	42	13	4	4	50	29	9	6	6	44	26	94	55	54
3 Liverpool	42	16	1	4	53	26	5	10	6	29	28	82	54	53
4 Blackburn Rovers	42	12	6	3	49	32	9	4	8	34	43	83	75	52
5 Stoke City	42	16	2	3	64	18	4	6	11	19	40	83	58	48
6 Middlesbrough	42	12	5	4	51	29	7	5	9	33	31	84	60	48
7 Sheffield United	42	11	6	4	45	28	8	2	11	42	48	87	76	46
8 West Ham United	42	12	4	5	31	24	7	4	10	28	39	59	63	46
9 Bristol Rovers	42	12	5	4	47	19	6	4	11	34	48	81	67	45
10 Swansea Town	42	12	3	6	53	34	7	4	10	37	56	90	90	45
11 Fulham	42	11	1	7	53	32	6	3	12	31	44	84	76	42
12 Huddersfield Town	42	10	3	8	33	27	8	3	10	35	47	68	74	42
13 Bristol City	42	13	2	6	49	32	3	7	11	25	47	74	79	41
14 Doncaster Rovers	42	12	5	4	51	21	3	5	13	26	56	77	77	40
15 Leyton Orient	42	7	8	6	34	38	8	2	11	32	46	66	84	40
16 Grimsby Town	42	12	4	5	41	26	5	1	15	20	36	61	62	39
17 Rotherham United	42	9	7	5	37	26	4	4	13	37	49	74	75	37
18 Lincoln City	**42**	**9**	**4**	**8**	**34**	**27**	**5**	**2**	**14**	**20**	**53**	**54**	**80**	**34**
19 Barnsley	42	8	7	6	39	35	4	3	14	20	54	59	89	34
20 Notts County	42	7	6	8	34	32	2	6	13	24	54	58	86	30
21 Bury	42	5	3	13	37	47	3	6	12	23	49	60	96	25
22 Port Vale	42	7	4	10	31	42	1	2	18	26	59	57	101	22

SEASON 1957-58
DIVISION TWO

No.	Date	Opposition	Res.	Att.	Goalscorers
1	24 Aug	West Ham United	2-2	18907	Grainger, Smillie
2	29	Swansea Town	1-5	22462	Grainger
3	31	SHEFFIELD UNITED	2-2	12579	Linnecor, Grainger
4	4 Sep	SWANSEA TOWN	4-0	10516	Linnecor, Withers(3)
5	7	Blackburn Rovers	1-0	20984	Northcott
6	11	DERBY COUNTY	1-1	12152	OG
7	14	IPSWICH TOWN	2-1	12579	OG, Smillie
8	18	Derby County	2-3	18058	Withers, Buick
9	21	Notts County	0-1	18059	
10	28	GRIMSBY TOWN	1-4	17342	Withers
11	5 Oct	BRISTOL ROVERS	0-1	9247	
12	12	Stoke City	1-1	20791	Northcott
13	26	Cardiff City	2-3	14515	Northcott, Linnecor
14	2 Nov	LIVERPOOL	0-1	10083	
15	9	Middlesbrough	1-3	20705	Northcott
16	16	LEYTON ORIENT	2-0	6244	Grainger(2)
17	23	Charlton Athletic	1-4	16022	Chapman
18	30	DONCASTER ROVERS	1-1	10017	Grainger
19	7 Dec	Rotherham United	2-1	8393	Grainger, Troops
20	14	HUDDERSFIELD TOWN	1-0	8473	Grainger
21	21	West Ham United	1-6	8384	Grainger
22	25	FULHAM	0-1	8029	
23	26	Fulham	1-4	18978	Grainger
24	28	Sheffield United	0-4	23424	
25	11 Jan	BLACKBURN ROVERS	1-1	9023	Hannah
26	18	Ipswich Town	1-1	16384	Troops
27	1 Feb	NOTTS COUNTY	2-2	8573	Chapman(2)
28	8	Grimsby Town	0-4	13594	
29	19	Bristol Rovers	0-3	13021	
30	22	CHARLTON ATHLETIC	2-3	8613	Neale, Hannah
31	1 Mar	Bristol City	0-4	20041	
32	15	Liverpool	0-1	31403	
33	22	MIDDLESBROUGH	2-3	8901	Harbertson, Brook
34	29	Leyton Orient	0-1	9637	
35	5 Apr	STOKE CITY	1-3	8169	Harbertson
36	7	BARNSLEY	1-3	7004	
37	8	Barnsley	3-1	11501	Hannah, Harbertson, Chapman
38	12	Doncaster Rovers	3-1	9459	Hannah, Chapman, Harbertson
39	19	ROTHERHAM UNITED	2-0	9139	Harbertson, Smillie
40	23	BRISTOL CITY	4-0	10011	Chapman, Smillie, Harbertson(2)
41	26	Huddersfield Town	1-0	8464	Harbertson
42	30	CARDIFF CITY	3-1	18001	Chapman(2), Harbertson

2 own goals

F.A. CUP

3R	4 Jan	WOLVERHAMPTON WAND	0-1	21741	

LINCOLNSHIRE CUP

SF	7 Nov	Scunthorpe United	2-2 *	5220	Finch, Watson
SFr	19 Mar	SCUNTHORPE UNITED	1-2	769	Smillie

* After extra time

Final League Table

	Pl.	W	D	L	F	A	W	D	L	F	A	F.	A.	Pts
1 West Ham United	42	12	8	1	56	25	11	3	7	45	29	101	54	57
2 Blackburn Rovers	42	13	7	1	50	18	9	5	7	43	39	93	57	56
3 Charlton Athletic	42	15	3	3	65	33	9	4	8	42	36	107	69	55
4 Liverpool	42	17	3	1	50	13	5	7	9	29	41	79	54	54
5 Fulham	42	13	5	3	53	24	7	7	7	44	35	97	59	52
6 Sheffield United	42	12	5	4	38	22	9	5	7	37	28	75	50	52
7 Middlesbrough	42	13	3	5	52	29	6	4	11	31	45	83	74	45
8 Ipswich Town	42	13	4	4	45	29	3	8	10	23	40	68	69	44
9 Huddersfield Town	42	9	8	4	28	24	5	8	8	35	42	63	66	44
10 Bristol Rovers	42	12	5	4	52	31	5	3	13	33	49	85	80	42
11 Stoke City	42	9	4	8	49	36	9	2	10	26	37	75	73	42
12 Leyton Orient	42	14	2	5	53	27	4	3	14	24	52	77	79	41
13 Grimsby Town	42	13	4	4	54	30	4	2	15	32	53	86	83	40
14 Barnsley	42	10	6	5	40	25	4	6	11	30	49	70	74	40
15 Cardiff City	42	10	6	5	44	31	4	4	13	19	46	63	77	37
16 Derby County	42	11	3	7	37	36	3	5	13	23	45	60	81	36
17 Bristol City	42	9	5	7	35	31	4	4	13	28	57	63	88	35
18 Rotherham United	42	8	8	3	10	38	44	6	2	13	27	57	65	101	33
19 Swansea Town	42	8	3	10	48	45	3	6	12	24	54	72	99	31
20 Lincoln City	**42**	**6**	**6**	**9**	**33**	**35**	**5**	**3**	**13**	**22**	**47**	**55**	**82**	**31**
21 Notts County	42	9	3	9	24	31	3	3	15	20	49	44	80	30
22 Doncaster Rovers	42	7	5	9	34	40	1	6	14	22	48	56	88	27

1957-58
Back : McGlen (trainer), Bob Jackson, Lord, Dykes, Grainger, Troops, Munro, Buick,
Thompson, Downie, Walton, Green, Giles (director), Hunter (director), Mawer (director).
Front : Finch, Middleton, Northcott, Smillie, Withers, Emery, Capper, Brown, Whitehead, Watson, Linnecor

1958-59
Back: Linnecor, Dykes, Emery, Thompson, Middleton, Bob Jackson.
Front : Buick, Coxon, Hannah, Harbertson, Chapman, Withers, Smith.

SEASON 1958-59
DIVISION TWO

No.	Date	Opposition	Res.	Att.	Goalscorers
1	23 Aug	SUNDERLAND	3-1	17386	Harbertson, Chapman(2)
2	26	Grimsby Town	2-4	22408	Harbertson, Chapman
3	30	Stoke City	0-1	20561	
4	3 Sep	GRIMSBY TOWN	4-4	19631	Linnecor, Grainger(2), Dykes
5	6	SWANSEA TOWN	1-2	12001	Withers
6	10	FULHAM	2-4	13092	Chapman, Withers
7	13	Ipswich Town	1-4	14498	Chapman
8	17	Fulham	2-4	20591	Harbertson, Chapman
9	20	BRISTOL ROVERS	4-1	9233	Chapman, Withers, OG, McClelland
10	27	Derby County	0-1	18290	
11	4 Oct	LEYTON ORIENT	2-0	9777	OG, Chapman
12	11	Liverpool	2-3	31344	Smillie, Linnecor
13	18	MIDDLESBROUGH	1-1	10803	Harbertson
14	25	Charlton Athletic	2-3	18053	Smillie, Graver
15	1 Nov	BRIGHTON & HOVE ALBION	4-2	11252	McClelland, Chapman, Graver, Coxon
16	8	Cardiff City	0-3	15689	
17	15	HUDDERSFIELD TOWN	1-1	9361	Chapman
18	22	Barnsley	2-2	10277	Chapman, Graver
19	29	ROTHERHAM UNITED	1-0	7766	Graver
20	6 Dec	Sheffield United	1-6	14426	Graver
21	13	BRISTOL CITY	0-2	7041	
22	20	Sunderland	0-2	20178	
23	26	Sheffield Wednesday	0-7	34486	
24	27	SHEFFIELD WEDNESDAY	0-1	15629	
25	3 Jan	STOKE CITY	3-1	8813	Harbertson, Graver, McClelland
26	17	Swansea Town	1-3	7809	Smillie
27	31	IPSWICH TOWN	3-1	9784	McClelland, Graver, Chapman
28	7 Feb	Bristol Rovers	0-3	15208	
29	14	DERBY COUNTY	1-4	11476	Grainger
30	21	Leyton Orient	0-0	10106	
31	28	CARDIFF CITY	4-2	8736	Graver, McClelland, Wright, Middletn
32	7 Mar	Middlesbrough	2-1	14396	Wright, McClelland
33	14	CHARLTON ATHLETIC	3-3	9647	McClelland, Green, Grainger
34	21	Brighton & Hove Albion	1-2	19916	Chapman
35	27	SCUNTHORPE UNITED	3-3	14679	Graver(3)
36	28	LIVERPOOL	2-1	11017	Chapman, Graver
37	30	Scunthorpe United	1-3	13742	Harbertson
38	4 Apr	Huddersfield Town	1-2	12646	McClelland
39	11	BARNSLEY	2-1	9394	Chapman, Graver
40	18	Rotherham United	0-1	11930	
41	21	Bristol City	0-1	10369	
42	25	SHEFFIELD UNITED	1-2	11506	McClelland

2 own goals

F.A. CUP

3R	10 Jan	Leicester City	1-1	25623	McClelland
3Rr	14	LEICESTER CITY	0-2	8212	

LINCOLNSHIRE CUP

SP	29 Sep	BOSTON UNITED	5-2	2034	Withrs(2),Chapmn,Cxon,Commons
F	8 Dec	Scunthorpe United	1-2	4467	Grainger

Final League Table

		Pl.	Home W D L F A	Away W D L F A	F. A.	Pts
1	Sheffield Wed.	42	18 2 1 68 13	10 4 7 38 35	106 48	62
2	Fulham	42	18 1 2 65 26	9 5 7 31 35	96 61	60
3	Sheffield United	42	16 2 3 54 15	7 5 9 28 33	82 48	53
4	Liverpool	42	15 3 3 57 25	9 2 10 30 37	87 62	53
5	Stoke City	42	16 2 3 48 19	5 5 11 24 39	72 58	49
6	Bristol Rovers	42	13 5 3 46 23	5 7 9 34 41	80 64	48
7	Derby County	42	15 1 5 46 29	5 7 9 28 42	74 71	48
8	Charlton Athletic	42	13 5 3 53 33	5 4 12 39 57	92 90	43
9	Cardiff City	42	12 2 7 37 26	6 5 10 28 39	65 65	43
10	Bristol City	42	11 3 7 43 27	6 4 11 31 43	74 70	41
11	Swansea Town	42	12 5 4 52 30	4 4 13 27 51	79 81	41
12	Brighton & Hove A.	42	10 9 2 46 29	5 2 14 28 61	74 90	41
13	Middlesbrough	42	9 9 7 51 26	6 3 12 36 45	87 71	40
14	Huddersfield Town	42	12 3 6 39 20	4 5 12 23 35	62 55	40
15	Sunderland	42	13 4 4 42 23	3 4 14 22 52	64 75	40
16	Ipswich Town	42	12 4 5 37 27	5 2 14 25 50	62 77	40
17	Leyton Orient	42	9 4 8 43 30	5 4 12 28 48	71 78	36
18	Scunthorpe United	42	7 6 8 32 37	5 3 13 23 47	55 84	33
19	*Lincoln City*	42	10 5 6 45 37	1 2 18 18 56	63 83	29
20	Rotherham United	42	9 5 7 32 28	1 4 16 10 54	42 82	29
21	Grimsby Town	42	7 7 7 41 36	2 3 16 21 54	62 90	28
22	Barnsley	42	8 4 9 34 34	2 3 16 21 57	55 91	27

SEASON 1959-60
DIVISION TWO

No.	Date	Opposition	Res.	Att.	Goalscorers
1	22 Aug	Swansea Town	1-2	19398	Graver
2	26	PORTSMOUTH	0-2	12604	
3	29	BRISTOL ROVERS	0-1	9284	
4	2 Sep	Portsmouth	2-1	18827	Smillie, OG
5	5	Ipswich Town	0-3	13042	
6	9	STOKE CITY	3-0	8867	Linnecor(2), McClelland
7	12	HUDDERSFIELD TOWN	0-2	10410	
8	16	Stoke City	1-6	13543	Chapman
9	19	Leyton Orient	0-4	11764	
10	26	CARDIFF CITY	2-3	8401	McClelland, Chapman
11	3 Oct	ASTON VILLA	0-0	13812	
12	10	Hull City	5-0	17170	Linnecr,Middletn,McClellnd,Hrbertsn(2)
13	17	SHEFFIELD UNITED	2-0	12108	Graver, Harbertson
14	24	Middlesbrough	2-3	24007	Graver(2)
15	31	DERBY COUNTY	6-2	12309	Harbertson(2),McClelland(3),Smillie
16	7 Nov	Plymouth Argyle	2-0	17405	Allen, McClelland
17	14	LIVERPOOL	4-2	10799	Graver(2), McClelland, Linnecor
18	21	Charlton Athletic	2-2	13340	Linnecor(2)
19	28	BRISTOL CITY	3-1	10667	Linnecor, McClelland(2)
20	5 Dec	Scunthorpe United	0-5	13945	
21	12	ROTHERHAM UNITED	0-1	13950	
22	19	SWANSEA TOWN	2-0	6122	Graver(2)
23	26	Sunderland	4-2	23848	Smillie, Chapman, Linnecor(2)
24	28	SUNDERLAND	0-0	16483	
25	2 Jan	Bristol Rovers	3-3	14130	Linnecor, McClelland, Graver
26	16	IPSWICH TOWN	0-1	8542	
27	23	Huddersfield Town	0-3	14995	
28	6 Feb	LEYTON ORIENT	2-2	9020	McClelland, Harbertson
29	13	Cardiff City	2-6	16231	Commons, McClelland
30	27	HULL CITY	3-0	10043	McClelland,Hawkeswrth,Hrbertson
31	1 Mar	Aston Villa	1-1	33962	McClelland
32	5	Sheffield United	2-3	22872	Hawksworth(2)
33	12	MIDDLESBROUGH	5-2	9780	McClelland,Linnecor,Hawksworth(2),Chapmn
34	19	Bristol City	0-1	16221	
35	26	PLYMOUTH ARGYLE	0-1	6478	
36	2 Apr	Liverpool	3-1	24081	Linnecor(3)
37	9	CHARLTON ATHLETIC	5-3	9906	Graver(3),Hawksworth,McClelland
38	15	BRIGHTON & HOVE ALBION	2-1	13129	Hawksworth(2)
39	16	Rotherham United	0-1	9887	
40	18	Brighton & Hove Albion	3-3	15682	Chapman, Hawksworth(2)
41	23	SCUNTHORPE UNITED	2-1	12691	Chapman(2)
42	30	Derby County	1-3	10440	McClelland

F.A. CUP

3R	9 Jan	BURNLEY	1-1	21693	Harbertson
3Rr	12	Burnley	0-2	35456	

LINCOLNSHIRE CUP

SF	28 Sep	SCUNTHORPE UNITED	3-0	1702	Linnecor, Commons, McClelland
F	24 Nov	Boston United	1-2	5477	McClelland

Final League Table

		Pl.	Home W	D	L	F	A	Away W	D	L	F	A	F.	A.	Pts
1	Aston Villa	42	17	3	1	62	19	8	6	7	27	24	89	43	59
2	Cardiff City	42	15	2	4	55	36	8	10	3	35	26	90	62	58
3	Liverpool	42	15	3	3	59	28	5	7	9	31	38	90	66	50
4	Sheffield United	42	12	5	4	43	22	7	7	7	25	29	68	51	50
5	Middlesbrough	42	14	5	2	56	21	5	5	11	34	43	90	64	48
6	Huddersfield Town	42	13	5	5	44	20	6	6	9	29	32	73	52	47
7	Charlton Athletic	42	12	7	2	55	28	5	6	10	35	59	90	87	47
8	Rotherham United	42	9	9	3	31	23	8	4	9	30	37	61	60	47
9	Bristol Rovers	42	12	6	3	42	28	6	5	10	30	50	72	78	47
10	Leyton Orient	42	12	4	5	47	25	3	10	8	29	36	76	61	44
11	Ipswich Town	42	12	5	4	48	24	7	1	13	30	44	78	68	44
12	Swansea Town	42	12	6	3	54	32	3	4	14	28	52	82	84	40
13	*Lincoln City*	*42*	*11*	*3*	*7*	*41*	*25*	*5*	*4*	*12*	*34*	*53*	*75*	*78*	*39*
14	Brighton & Hove A.	42	7	8	6	35	32	6	4	11	32	44	67	76	38
15	Scunthorpe United	42	9	7	5	38	26	4	3	14	19	45	57	71	36
16	Sunderland	42	8	5	8	35	29	4	6	11	17	36	52	65	36
17	Stoke City	42	8	3	10	40	38	6	4	11	26	45	66	83	35
18	Derby County	42	9	4	8	31	28	5	3	13	30	49	61	77	35
19	Plymouth Argyle	42	10	6	5	42	36	3	3	15	19	53	61	89	35
20	Portsmouth	42	6	9	6	36	36	4	6	11	23	41	59	77	32
21	Hull City	42	7	6	8	27	30	3	4	14	21	46	48	76	30
22	Bristol City	42	8	3	10	27	31	3	2	16	33	66	60	97	27

1959-60
Back : McGlen (trainer), Greenhalgh (assistant trainer), Jackson, Harbertson,
Smith, Heath, Thompson, McEvoy, Buick, Chapman, Anderson (manager).
Front : Middleton, Wright, McClelland, Graver, Commons, Vickers, Dunwell, Linnecor, Allen.

1960-61
Back : McGlen (trainer), Bob Jackson, Chapman, Haines, Heath, Middleton, Buick, Graver, Anderson (manager).
Front : Greenhalgh (assistant trainer), Allen, McClelland, Dunwell, Wright, Harvey, Commons, Linnecor.

SEASON 1960-61
DIVISION TWO

No.	Date	Opposition	Res.	Att.	Goalscorers
1	20 Aug	Portsmouth	0-3	18959	
2	24	ROTHERHAM UNITED	0-1	10859	
3	27	HUDDERSFIELD TOWN	0-0	8639	
4	29	Rotherham United	0-2	9606	
5	3 Sep	Sunderland	2-2	26512	Graver, Chapman
6	6	Swansea Town	2-1	7680	Chapman(2)
7	10	PLYMOUTH ARGYLE	3-1	9351	Graver, Linnecor, Hawksworth
8	14	SWANSEA TOWN	2-0	7513	Chapman, McClelland
9	17	Norwich City	1-5	24956	Hawksworth
10	24	CHARLTON ATHLETIC	2-2	8160	Chapman(2)
11	1 Oct	Sheffield United	1-2	14365	Linnecor
12	8	LIVERPOOL	1-2	7699	Hawksworth
13	15	Bristol Rovers	1-3	15334	Hawksworth
14	22	DERBY COUNTY	3-4	9325	Linnecor(2), Middleton
15	29	Leyton Orient	2-1	5793	Chapman, Graver
16	5 Nov	SCUNTHORPE UNITED	0-2	10262	
17	12	Ipswich Town	1-3	10197	Graver
18	19	BRIGHTON & HOVE ALBION	2-1	4397	Graver, OG
19	26	Middlesbrough	1-1	13053	Chapman
20	3 Dec	LEEDS UNITED	2-3	5678	Chapman, Graver
21	10	Southampton	3-2	15159	Chapman(2), Graver
22	17	PORTSMOUTH	2-3	6143	Linnecor, Wright
23	26	Luton Town	0-3	15283	
24	27	LUTON TOWN	1-1	10345	Green
25	31	Huddersfield Town	1-4	11564	McClelland
26	14 Jan	SUNDERLAND	1-2	9012	Linnecor
27	21	Plymouth Argyle	1-1	12671	Linnecor
28	4 Feb	NORWICH CITY	1-4	8276	Graver
29	11	Charlton Athletic	0-3	9735	
30	22	SHEFFIELD UNITED	0-5	5263	
31	25	Liverpool	0-2	24759	
32	4 Mar	BRISTOL ROVERS	1-2	5723	Middleton
33	11	Derby County	1-3	10530	Dunwell
34	18	SOUTHAMPTON	0-3	5182	
35	25	Scunthorpe United	1-3	6981	Chapman
36	31	STOKE CITY	1-1	6751	McClelland
37	1 Apr	MIDDLESBROUGH	5-2	5115	Smith, Bannister, Chapman(3)
38	3	Stoke City	0-0	6383	
39	8	Brighton & Hove Albion	0-1	14952	
40	15	IPSWICH TOWN	1-4	7820	OG
41	22	Leeds United	0-7	8432	
42	29	LEYTON ORIENT	2-0	3996	Middleton, Buick

2 own goals

F.A. CUP

3R	7 Jan	WEST BROMWICH ALBION	3-1	14957	Graver, Linnecor, McClelland
4R	28	Sheffield United	1-3	21651	Graver

LEAGUE CUP

1R	12 Oct	BRADFORD PARK AVENUE	2-2	1737	Chapman, Linnecor
1Rr	19	Bradford Park Avenue	0-1	3415	

LINCOLNSHIRE CUP

SF	7 Nov	Grimsby Town	3-8	2648	Graver, Linnecor(2)

Final League Table

		Pl.	Home W D L F A	Away W D L F A	F. A.	Pts
1	Ipswich Town	42	15 3 3 55 24	11 4 6 45 31	100 55	59
2	Sheffield United	42	16 2 3 49 22	10 4 7 32 29	81 51	58
3	Liverpool	42	14 5 2 49 21	7 5 9 38 37	87 58	52
4	Norwich City	42	15 3 3 46 20	5 6 10 24 33	70 53	49
5	Middlesbrough	42	13 6 2 44 20	5 6 10 39 54	83 74	48
6	Sunderland	42	12 5 4 47 24	5 8 8 28 36	75 60	47
7	Swansea Town	42	14 3 4 49 26	4 7 10 28 47	77 73	47
8	Southampton	42	12 4 5 57 35	6 4 11 27 46	84 81	44
9	Scunthorpe United	42	9 8 4 39 25	5 7 9 30 39	69 64	43
10	Charlton Athletic	42	12 3 6 60 42	4 8 9 37 49	97 91	43
11	Plymouth Argyle	42	13 4 4 52 32	4 4 13 29 50	81 82	42
12	Derby County	42	9 6 6 46 36	6 4 11 34 45	80 80	40
13	Luton Town	42	13 5 3 48 27	2 4 15 23 52	71 79	39
14	Leeds United	42	7 7 7 41 38	7 3 11 34 45	75 83	38
15	Rotherham United	42	9 7 5 37 24	3 6 12 28 40	65 64	37
16	Brighton & Hove A.	42	9 6 6 33 26	5 3 13 28 49	61 75	37
17	Bristol Rovers	42	13 4 4 52 35	2 3 16 21 57	73 92	37
18	Stoke City	42	9 6 6 39 26	3 6 12 12 33	51 59	36
19	Leyton Orient	42	10 5 6 31 29	4 3 14 24 49	55 78	36
20	Huddersfield Town	42	7 5 9 33 33	6 4 11 29 38	62 71	35
21	Portsmouth	42	10 6 5 38 27	1 5 15 26 64	64 91	33
22	**Lincoln City**	42	5 4 12 30 43	3 4 14 18 52	48 95	24

SEASON 1961-62
DIVISION THREE

No.	Date	Opposition	Res.	Att.	Goalscorers
1	19 Aug	BOURNEMOUTH	0-2	7597	
2	23	Bradford Park Avenue	0-2	10854	
3	26	Watford	3-3	12790	Calland(2), McClelland
4	30	BRADFORD PARK AVENUE	3-2	5948	Calland, Holmes, Buick
5	2 Sep	HULL CITY	0-3	6495	
6	6	Portsmouth	0-0	13275	
7	9	Northampton Town	2-2	11850	Harbertson, Barrett
8	16	BRISTOL CITY	1-1	4090	McClelland
9	20	Crystal Palace	3-1	19601	Tracey, Barrett, Punter
10	23	Torquay United	1-3	4693	Punter
11	27	CRYSTAL PALACE	3-2	3793	Bannister, Punter, Barrett
12	30	Swindon Town	0-4	9593	
13	7 Oct	Grimsby Town	1-4	9061	Harbertson
14	9	Queens Park Rangers	3-1	10151	Bannister(2), Linnecor
15	14	COVENTRY CITY	1-2	5009	OG
16	21	Peterborough United	4-5	13502	Linnecor(2), Punter(2)
17	28	PORT VALE	1-1	4708	Holmes
18	11 Nov	SOUTHEND UNITED	2-0	3881	Punter, Bannister
19	18	Notts County	0-1	9215	
20	2 Dec	Brentford	0-1	7976	
21	9	READING	2-3	4178	Moore, Holmes
22	16	Bournemouth	0-0	8635	
23	23	WATFORD	0-0	4436	
24	26	Barnsley	1-0	5572	Punter
25	13 Jan	Hull City	0-1	4634	
26	20	NORTHAMPTON TOWN	0-0	5720	
27	31	BARNSLEY	2-2	5317	Middleton, Broadbent
28	3 Feb	Bristol City	0-2	12190	
29	7	SHREWSBURY TOWN	1-2	5508	Tracey
30	10	Torquay United	4-3	4789	Scanlon, Broadbent(2), Harbertson
31	16	SWINDON TOWN	2-2	5622	Linnecor, Scanlon
32	23	GRIMSBY TOWN	1-1	13989	Bannister
33	2 Mar	Coventry City	2-2	9147	Linnecor(2)
34	10	PETERBOROUGH UNITED	1-2	11052	Punter
35	17	Port Vale	0-4	6239	
36	23	NEWPORT COUNTY	3-2	5539	Green(3)
37	26	Newport County	0-4	3062	
38	31	Southend United	0-0	5323	
39	6 Apr	NOTTS COUNTY	2-2	6111	Green, Scanlon
40	14	Shrewsbury Town	0-0	4227	
41	21	BRENTFORD	3-3	5482	Green(2), Linnecor
42	23	HALIFAX TOWN	0-1	5355	
43	24	Halifax Town	3-0	4160	Barrett, OG, Tracey
44	27	Reading	0-4	5357	
45	30	QUEENS PARK RANGERS	0-5	6815	
46	2 May	PORTSMOUTH	2-2	3617	Tracey(2)

2 own goals

F.A. CUP

| 1R | 4 Nov | Crewe Alexandra | 0-2 | 7267 | |

LEAGUE CUP

| 1R | 13 Sep | ACCRINGTON STANLEY | 1-0 | 2681 | Tracey |
| 2R | 4 Oct | Norwich City | 2-3 | 16011 | Harbertson(2) |

LINCOLNSHIRE CUP

| SF | 18 Oct | GAINSBOROUGH TRINITY | 5-1 | 243 | Buick(3), Holmes, Harbertson |
| F | 19 Mar | Scunthorpe United | 2-0 | 2513 | Punter, Green |

Final League Table

		Pl.	Home W D L F A	Away W D L F A	F. A. Pts
1	Portsmouth	46	15 6 2 48 23	12 5 6 39 24	87 47 65
2	Grimsby Town	46	18 3 2 49 18	10 3 10 31 38	80 56 62
3	Bournemouth	46	14 8 1 42 18	7 9 7 27 27	69 45 59
4	Queen's Park Rgs.	46	15 3 5 65 31	9 8 6 46 42	111 73 59
5	Peterborough Utd.	46	16 4 3 69 38	10 6 7 47 44	107 82 58
6	Bristol City	46	15 3 5 56 27	8 5 10 38 45	94 72 54
7	Reading	46	14 5 4 46 24	8 4 11 31 42	77 66 53
8	Northampton Town	46	12 6 5 52 24	8 5 10 33 33	85 57 51
9	Swindon Town	46	11 8 4 48 26	6 7 10 30 45	78 71 49
10	Hull City	46	15 2 6 43 20	5 6 12 24 34	67 54 48
11	Bradford Park Ave.	46	13 5 5 47 27	7 2 14 33 51	80 78 47
12	Port Vale	46	12 4 7 41 23	5 7 11 24 35	65 58 45
13	Notts County	46	14 5 4 44 23	3 4 16 23 51	67 74 43
14	Coventry City	46	11 6 6 38 26	5 5 13 26 45	64 71 43
15	Crystal Palace	46	8 8 7 50 41	6 6 11 33 39	83 80 42
16	Southend United	46	10 7 6 41 23	3 9 11 26 43	57 69 42
17	Watford	46	10 9 4 37 26	4 4 15 26 48	63 74 41
18	Halifax Town	46	9 5 9 34 35	6 5 12 28 49	62 84 40
19	Shrewsbury Town	46	8 7 8 46 37	5 5 13 27 47	73 84 38
20	Barnsley	46	9 8 6 45 41	6 4 13 26 54	71 95 38
21	Torquay United	46	9 4 10 48 44	6 2 15 28 56	76 100 36
22	*Lincoln City*	46	4 10 9 31 43	5 7 11 26 44	57 87 35
23	Brentford	46	11 3 9 34 29	2 5 16 19 64	53 93 34
24	Newport County	46	6 5 12 29 38	1 3 19 17 64	46 102 22

1961-62
Back: McGlen(trainer), Chapman, Haines, Wardle, Heath, Smith, Barnard, Tracey, Middleton, Anderson(manager).
Front : Greenhalgh (assistant trainer), Bob Jackson, Parker, McClelland, Linnecor, Buick.

1962-63
Back : Anderson (manager), Franks, Warner, Broadbent, Carling, Haines, Kelly,
Bob Jackson, Barnard, McGlen (trainer).
Front : Jones, Campbell, Jeff Smith, Linnecor, Scanlon.

SEASON 1962-63
DIVISION FOUR

No.	Date	Opposition	Res.	Att.	Goalscorers
1	18 Aug	TRANMERE ROVERS	4-2	5549	Holmes, Campbell, Linnecor(2)
2	22	Oxford United	1-2	10368	Scanlon
3	25	Torquay United	0-0	6539	
4	29	OXFORD UNITED	1-0	7576	Campbell
5	1 Sep	Chesterfield	2-2	6514	Kelly, Campbell
6	3	Newport County	1-2	6864	Kelly
7	8	OLDHAM ATHLETIC	1-2	5915	Bannister
8	12	NEWPORT COUNTY	6-3	5211	Punter(2), OG, Linnecor(2), Bannister
9	15	Barrow	1-2	4476	Punter
10	22	HARTLEPOOLS UNITED	4-1	5014	Campbell(2), Punter, Broadbent
11	26	BRADFORD CITY	3-2	6411	Punter(2), OG
12	29	Darlington	0-0	5025	
13	3 Oct	Exeter City	1-1	4490	Punter
14	6	WORKINGTON	3-2	6251	Scanlon, Punter(2)
15	10	EXETER CITY	4-1	6338	Linnecor(2), Scanlon(2)
16	13	Mansfield Town	0-2	12801	
17	19	DONCASTER ROVERS	1-2	10265	Punter
18	27	Stockport County	2-1	3228	Scanlon, Campbell
19	10 Nov	Crewe Alexandra	1-1	5546	Bannister
20	17	CHESTER	1-3	5125	Campbell
21	1 Dec	BRENTFORD	1-3	5620	Bannister
22	15	Tranmere Rovers	0-3	4680	
23	21	TORQUAY UNITED	3-0	4041	Bannister(3)
24	26	ALDERSHOT	2-4	4071	Campbell(2)
25	19 Jan	Oldham Athletic	1-4	10561	Punter
26	23 Feb	Workington	1-1	2963	Scanlon
27	9 Mar	Doncaster Rovers	0-3	4041	
28	13	Bradford City	2-2	2869	Scanlon, Franks
29	16	STOCKPORT COUNTY	0-0	3289	
30	23	Gillingham	0-3	6135	
31	27	MANSFIELD TOWN	2-6	5990	Scanlon, Linnecor
32	29	YORK CITY	2-4	2227	Linnecor, Punter
33	3 Apr	Aldershot	2-1	4653	Rooney, Holmes
34	6	Chester	2-3	4125	Rooney, Holmes
35	12	Southport	0-0	3397	
36	13	CREWE ALEXANDRA	1-2	3322	Linnecor
37	15	SOUTHPORT	0-2	2987	
38	20	Brentford	2-3	11384	Holmes(2)
39	22	York City	1-3	5082	Campbell
40	27	ROCHDALE	3-0	2281	Campbell, Franks, Punter
41	1 May	DARLINGTON	2-1	2579	Middleton, Campbell
42	4	Hartlepools United	0-3	2683	
43	7	Rochdale	0-1	2101	
44	11	CHESTERFIELD	1-3	2383	Franks
45	15	GILLINGHAM	2-1	1993	Gedney, Franks
46	18	BARROW	1-2	2051	Franks

2 own goals

F.A. CUP

1R	3 Nov	DARLINGTON	1-1	7675	Scanlon
1Rr	7	Darlington	2-1	8152	Campbell(2)
2R	24 Nov	HALIFAX TOWN	1-0	7009	Campbell
3R	6 Mar	COVENTRY CITY	1-5	7440	Punter

LEAGUE CUP

1R	5 Sep	York City	2-2	6744	Punter, Bannister
1Rr	19	YORK CITY	2-0	4790	Punter, Bannister
2R	24	Bury	2-2	4706	Broadbent, Punter
2Rr	8 Oct	BURY	2-3	7981	Franks, Linnecor

LINCOLNSHIRE CUP competition cancelled due to bad weather.

Final League Table

		Pl.	Home						Away					F.	A.	Pts
			W	D	L	F	A	W	D	L	F	A				
1	Brentford	46	18	2	3	59	31	9	6	8	39	33	98	64	62
2	Oldham Athletic	46	18	4	1	65	23	6	7	10	30	37	95	60	59
3	Crewe Alexandra	46	15	4	4	50	21	9	7	7	36	37	86	58	59
4	Mansfield Town	46	16	4	3	61	20	8	5	10	47	49	108	69	57
5	Gillingham	46	17	3	3	49	23	5	10	8	22	26	71	49	57
6	Torquay United	46	14	8	1	45	20	6	8	9	30	36	75	56	56
7	Rochdale	46	16	6	1	48	21	4	5	14	19	38	67	59	51
8	Tranmere Rovers	46	15	3	5	57	25	5	7	11	24	42	81	67	50
9	Barrow	46	14	7	2	52	26	5	5	13	30	54	82	80	50
10	Workington	46	13	4	6	42	20	4	9	10	34	48	76	68	47
11	Aldershot	46	9	9	5	42	32	6	8	9	31	37	73	69	47
12	Darlington	46	13	3	7	44	33	6	3	14	28	54	72	87	44
13	Southport	46	11	9	3	47	35	4	5	14	25	71	72	106	44
14	York City	46	12	6	5	42	25	4	5	14	25	37	67	62	43
15	Chesterfield	46	7	10	6	43	29	6	6	11	27	35	70	64	42
16	Doncaster Rovers	46	9	10	4	36	26	5	4	14	28	51	64	77	42
17	Exeter City	46	9	6	8	27	32	7	4	12	30	45	57	77	42
18	Oxford United	46	10	10	3	44	27	3	5	15	26	44	70	71	41
19	Stockport County	46	9	7	7	34	29	6	3	14	22	41	56	70	40
20	Newport County	46	11	6	6	44	29	3	5	15	32	61	76	90	39
21	Chester	46	11	5	7	31	23	4	4	15	20	43	51	66	39
22	*Lincoln City*	46	11	1	11	48	46	2	8	13	20	43	68	89	35
23	Bradford City	46	8	5	10	37	40	5	1	17	27	53	64	93	32
24	Hartlepools United	46	5	7	11	33	39	2	4	17	23	65	56	104	25

SEASON 1963-64
DIVISION FOUR

No.	Date	Opposition	Res.	Att.	Goalscorers
1	24 Aug	SOUTHPORT	2-0	5089	Morton(2)
2	26	Stockport County	0-4	7075	
3	31	Exeter City	0-0	5452	
4	7 Sep	HARTLEPOOLS UNITED	4-2	6110	Bannister, Campbell(2), Morton
5	11	STOCKPORT COUNTY	2-0	7822	Bannister
6	14	Darlington	1-1	3194	Campbell
7	18	Gillingham	0-1	6949	
8	21	TRANMERE ROVERS	0-1	7329	
9	28	Halifax Town	2-0	4470	Campbell, Holmes
10	2 Oct	GILLINGHAM	0-3	8968	
11	5	TORQUAY UNITED	3-2	5256	Neal(2), Morton
12	9	Aldershot	0-2	6609	
13	12	Chesterfield	3-1	7540	OG, Moore, Wilkinson
14	16	ALDERSHOT	3-3	7477	Wilkinson, Rooney, Moore
15	19	DONCASTER ROVERS	3-1	6932	Wilkinson, Holmes, Morton
16	22	Carlisle United	0-5	10257	
17	26	Brighton & Hove Albion	1-5	10053	Houghton
18	30	CARLISLE UNITED	0-2	7013	
19	2 Nov	CHESTER	3-2	5523	Houghton, Morton, Bannister
20	9	York City	0-0	4346	
21	23	Rochdale	2-2	2407	Houghton, Heward
22	30	OXFORD UNITED	3-2	5135	Milner, Houghton(2)
23	14 Dec	Southport	0-1	2176	
24	21	EXETER CITY	1-1	3841	Neal
25	26	BRADFORD PARK AVENUE	3-0	6606	Morton(3)
26	28	Bradford Park Avenue	1-0	6939	Morton
27	11 Jan	Hartlepools United	2-1	4330	Linnecor, Morton
28	18	DARLINGTON	3-1	6394	Linnecor, Houghton, Neal
29	25	Workington	1-1	3235	Morton
30	31	Tranmere Rovers	0-3	7126	
31	8 Feb	HALIFAX TOWN	4-0	5936	Morton, Houghton(3)
32	15	Torquay United	2-2	4922	Houghton, Linnecor
33	22	CHESTERFIELD	5-2	5926	Linnecor(3), Houghton(2)
34	29	Doncaster Rovers	0-0	9474	
35	7 Mar	BRIGHTON & HOVE ALBION	0-2	5591	
36	13	Chester	1-3	5077	Houghton
37	20	YORK CITY	3-2	5222	Linnecor, Houghton, Moore
38	28	Newport County	2-4	2050	Heward, Linnecor
39	30	BRADFORD CITY	1-2	4997	Fell
40	31	Bradford City	0-4	8049	
41	4 Apr	ROCHDALE	2-0	3643	Bracewell, Morton
42	11	Oxford United	0-2	5876	
43	18	WORKINGTON	0-2	3802	
44	22	NEWPORT COUNTY	2-1	2803	Morton, Milner
45	25	Barrow	0-2	1752	
46	29	BARROW	3-0	2546	Morton(3)

F.A. CUP

1R	16 Nov	Hartlepools United	1-0	5698	Holmes
2R	7 Dec	SOUTHPORT	2-0	6719	Morton, Wilkinson
3R	4 Jan	SHEFFIELD UNITED	0-4	18374	

LEAGUE CUP

1R	4 Sep	HARTLEPOOLS UNITED	3-2	4748	Morton, Rooney, Campbell
2R	25	York City	1-1	5594	Campbell
2Rr	14 Oct	YORK CITY	2-0	5055	Morton, Moore
3R	4 Nov	Millwall	1-1	6761	Neal
3Rr	12	MILLWALL	1-2	4940	Wilkinson

LINCOLNSHIRE CUP

F	30 Apr	SCUNTHORPE UNITED	1-1 *	936	Fell

* after extra time, trophy shared.

Final League Table

		Pl.	Home W D L F A	Away W D L F A	F. A. Pts
1	Gillingham	46	16 7 0 37 10	7 7 9 22 20	59 30 60
2	Carlisle United	46	17 3 3 70 20	8 7 8 43 38	113 58 60
3	Workington	46	15 6 2 46 19	9 5 9 30 33	76 52 59
4	Exeter City	46	12 9 2 39 14	8 9 6 23 23	62 37 58
5	Bradford City	46	15 3 5 45 24	10 3 10 31 38	76 62 56
6	Torquay United	46	15 6 2 60 20	5 14 20 34	80 54 51
7	Tranmere Rovers	46	16 6 1 60 20	4 5 14 20 34	80 54 51
7	Tranmere Rovers	46	12 4 7 46 30	8 7 8 39 43	85 73 51
8	Brighton & Hove A.	46	13 3 7 45 22	6 9 8 26 30	71 52 50
9	Aldershot	46	15 3 5 58 28	4 7 12 25 50	83 78 48
10	Halifax Town	46	14 4 5 47 28	3 10 10 30 49	77 77 48
11	Lincoln City	46	15 2 6 49 31	4 7 12 18 44	67 75 47
12	Chester	46	17 3 3 47 18	2 5 16 18 42	65 60 46
13	Bradford Park Ave.	46	13 5 5 50 34	5 4 14 25 47	75 81 45
14	Doncaster Rovers	46	11 8 4 46 23	4 4 15 24 52	70 75 42
15	Newport County	46	12 8 3 45 24	5 4 14 24 49	64 73 42
16	Chesterfield	46	11 6 6 29 27	4 7 12 21 44	57 71 42
17	Stockport County	46	12 7 4 32 19	3 5 15 18 49	50 68 42
18	Oxford United	46	10 7 6 37 27	4 6 13 22 36	59 63 41
19	Darlington	46	10 7 6 40 30	3 4 16 26 56	66 93 40
20	Rochdale	46	9 8 6 36 24	3 7 13 20 35	56 59 39
21	Southport	46	10 5 5 42 29	3 7 13 17 21	59 63 35
22	York City	46	9 3 11 29 26	5 4 14 23 40	52 66 35
23	Hartlepools United	46	9 8 6 30 36	1 6 16 17 26	54 93 33
24	Barrow	46	4 10 9 30 36	2 8 13 21 57	51 93 30

1963-64
Back : Eyre, Green, Graves, Carling, Morton, Bannister, Heward, Bob Jackson.
Front : Jeff Smith, Spears, Holmes, Linnecor, Campbell, Rooney, Alf Jones.

1964-65
Back : Milner, Jeff Smith, Holmes, Houghton, Graves, Jones, Larkin, Chapman, Moulson (coach).
Front : Fell, Brooks, Barton, Hawksby, Morton.

SEASON 1964-65
DIVISION FOUR

No.	Date	Opposition	Res.	Att.	Goalscorers
1	22 Aug	HARTLEPOOLS UNITED	4-2	5222	OG, Houghton, Fell, Fencott
2	24	Barrow	2-2	5403	Fencott, Thompson
3	29	Rochdale	0-2	4306	
4	5 Sep	MILLWALL	2-2	4738	Milner, Fell
5	9	OXFORD UNITED	0-2	5571	
6	12	Bradford City	1-0	2898	Fell
7	16	Oxford United	0-2	10772	
8	19	CHESTER	2-2	3897	Houghton, Fell
9	23	BARROW	1-0	5305	Holmes
10	26	Torquay United	2-0	4658	Fell, Fencott
11	30	HALIFAX TOWN	2-3	6578	Jackson, Hawksby
12	3 Oct	STOCKPORT COUNTY	6-0	5180	Houghton, Morton(2), Holmes, Jones, Fencott
13	6	Halifax Town	1-2	2608	Moore
14	10	CHESTERFIELD	0-2	5469	
15	14	BRIGHTON & HOVE ALBION	0-1	5681	
16	17	Doncaster Rovers	2-1	9235	Grummett(2)
17	20	Brighton & Hove Albion	0-4	16887	
18	24	ALDERSHOT	3-1	3504	Hawksby, Holmes(2)
19	26	Newport County	0-7	4173	
20	31	Bradford Park Avenue	1-3	7984	Houghton
21	7 Nov	SOUTHPORT	3-0	4007	Fencott, Jones, Houghton
22	20	TRANMERE ROVERS	1-2	5553	Fencott
23	28	Darlington	1-3	3494	Milner
24	12 Dec	Hartlepools United	0-3	3102	
25	18	ROCHDALE	1-1	3177	Milner
26	26	NOTTS COUNTY	1-0	4969	OG
27	28	Notts County	1-2	4472	Larkin
28	2 Jan	Millwall	1-2	7146	Fell
29	16	BRADFORD CITY	0-2	2863	
30	23	Chester	1-5	7432	Jones
31	30	Wrexham	3-5	4303	Hawksby, Fencott, Chapman
32	6 Feb	TORQUAY UNITED	0-1	3311	
33	13	Stockport County	1-3	3400	Chapman
34	17	CREWE ALEXANDRA	1-2	3229	Milner
35	20	Chesterfield	0-1	4405	
36	27	DONCASTER ROVERS	0-2	5193	
37	12 Mar	BRADFORD PARK AVENUE	2-2	3772	Chapman, Houghton
38	20	Southport	4-4	1320	Houghton(2), OG, Chapman
39	26	WREXHAM	0-2	4255	
40	30	Aldershot	2-3	3463	Larkin, Fencott
41	2 Apr	Tranmere Rovers	0-4	12143	
42	10	DARLINGTON	2-0	2569	Chapman, Fell
43	16	YORK CITY	0-1	6478	
44	17	Crewe Alexandra	0-5	3575	
45	19	York City	0-3	10800	
46	24	NEWPORT COUNTY	4-3	2408	Barton, Hawksby, Fell(2)

3 own goals

F.A. CUP

1R	14 Nov	Tranmere Rovers	0-0	11524	
1Rr	18	TRANMERE ROVERS	1-0	5526	Hawksby
2R	5 Dec	Hull City	1-1	10177	Houghton
2Rr	9	HULL CITY	3-1	8383	Houghton, Fencott, Milner
3R	9 Jan	Rotherham United	1-5	12456	Houghton

LEAGUE CUP

| 1R | 2 Sep | Barnsley | 1-2 | 4262 | OG |

LINCOLNSHIRE CUP - No Competition.

Final League Table

		Pl.	Home W	D	L	F	A	Away W	D	L	F	A	F.	A.	Pts
1	Brighton & Hove A.	46	18	5	0	68	20	8	6	9	34	37	102	57	63
2	Millwall	46	13	10	0	45	15	10	6	7	33	30	78	45	62
3	York City	46	20	1	2	63	21	8	5	10	28	35	91	56	62
4	Oxford United	46	18	4	1	54	13	5	11	7	33	31	87	44	61
5	Tranmere Rovers	46	20	2	1	72	20	7	4	12	27	36	99	56	60
6	Rochdale	46	15	4	4	46	22	7	10	6	28	31	74	53	58
7	Bradford Park Ave.	46	14	8	1	52	22	6	9	8	34	40	86	62	57
8	Chester	46	19	1	3	75	26	6	5	12	44	55	119	81	56
9	Doncaster Rovers	46	13	6	4	46	25	7	5	11	38	47	84	72	51
10	Crewe Alexandra	46	11	8	4	55	34	7	5	11	35	47	90	81	49
11	Torquay United	46	11	5	7	41	33	10	2	11	29	37	70	70	49
12	Chesterfield	46	13	5	5	36	22	7	3	13	22	48	58	70	48
13	Notts County	46	12	7	4	43	23	3	7	13	18	50	61	73	44
14	Wrexham	46	12	5	6	59	37	5	4	14	25	55	84	92	43
15	Hartlepools United	46	11	10	2	44	28	4	3	16	17	57	61	85	43
16	Newport County	46	14	5	4	54	26	3	3	17	31	55	85	81	42
17	Darlington	46	14	2	7	52	30	4	4	15	32	57	84	87	42
18	Aldershot	46	14	3	6	46	25	1	4	18	18	59	64	84	37
19	Bradford City	46	9	2	12	37	36	3	6	14	33	52	70	88	32
20	Southport	46	5	9	9	35	45	3	7	13	23	44	58	89	32
21	Barrow	46	9	4	10	30	38	3	2	18	29	67	59	105	30
22	*Lincoln City*	46	8	4	11	35	33	3	2	18	23	66	58	99	28
23	Halifax Town	46	9	4	10	37	37	2	2	19	17	66	54	103	28
24	Stockport County	46	8	4	11	30	34	2	3	18	14	53	44	87	27

Final League Tables 1965/66 to 1972/73

1965/66 Division 4

		Pl.	Home					Away					F.	A.	Pts
			W	D	L	F	A	W	D	L	F	A			
1	Doncaster Rovers	46	15	6	2	49	21	9	5	9	36	33	85	54	59
2	Darlington	46	16	3	4	41	17	9	6	8	31	36	72	53	59
3	Torquay United	46	17	2	4	43	20	7	8	8	29	29	72	49	58
4	Colchester United	46	13	7	3	45	21	10	3	10	25	26	70	47	56
5	Tranmere Rovers	46	15	1	7	56	32	9	7	7	37	34	93	66	56
6	Luton Town	46	19	2	2	65	27	5	6	12	25	43	90	70	56
7	Chester	46	15	5	3	52	27	5	7	11	27	43	79	70	52
8	Notts County	46	9	8	6	32	25	10	4	9	29	28	61	53	50
9	Newport County	46	14	6	3	46	24	4	6	13	29	51	75	75	48
10	Southport	46	15	6	2	47	20	3	6	14	21	49	68	69	48
11	Bradford Park Ave.	46	14	2	7	59	31	7	3	13	43	61	102	92	47
12	Barrow	46	12	8	3	48	31	4	7	12	24	45	72	76	47
13	Stockport County	46	12	4	7	42	29	6	2	15	29	41	71	70	42
14	Crewe Alexandra	46	12	4	7	42	23	4	5	14	19	40	61	63	41
15	Halifax Town	46	11	6	6	46	31	4	5	14	21	44	67	75	41
16	Barnsley	46	11	6	6	43	24	4	4	15	31	54	74	78	40
17	Aldershot	46	12	6	5	47	27	3	4	16	28	57	75	84	40
18	Hartlepools United	46	13	4	6	44	22	3	4	16	19	53	63	75	40
19	Port Vale	46	12	7	4	38	18	3	2	18	10	41	48	59	39
20	Chesterfield	46	8	9	6	37	35	5	4	14	25	43	62	78	39
21	Rochdale	46	12	1	10	46	27	4	4	15	25	60	71	87	37
22	*Lincoln City*	*46*	*9*	*7*	*7*	*37*	*29*	*4*	*4*	*15*	*20*	*53*	*57*	*82*	*37*
23	Bradford City	46	10	5	8	37	34	2	8	13	26	60	63	94	37
24	Wrexham	46	10	4	9	43	43	3	5	15	29	61	72	104	35

1966/67 Division 4

		Pl.	Home					Away					F.	A.	Pts
			W	D	L	F	A	W	D	L	F	A			
1	Stockport County	46	16	5	2	41	18	10	7	6	28	24	69	42	64
2	Southport	46	19	2	2	47	15	4	11	8	22	27	69	42	59
3	Barrow	46	12	8	3	35	18	12	3	8	41	36	76	54	59
4	Tranmere Rovers	46	14	6	3	42	20	8	8	7	24	23	66	43	58
5	Crewe Alexandra	46	14	5	4	42	26	7	7	9	28	29	70	55	54
6	Southend United	46	15	5	3	44	12	7	4	12	26	37	70	49	53
7	Wrexham	46	11	12	0	46	20	5	8	10	30	42	76	62	52
8	Hartlepools United	46	15	3	5	44	29	7	4	12	22	35	66	64	51
9	Brentford	46	13	7	3	36	19	5	6	12	22	37	58	56	49
10	Aldershot	46	14	4	5	48	19	4	8	11	24	38	72	57	48
11	Bradford City	46	13	4	6	48	31	6	6	11	26	31	74	62	48
12	Halifax Town	46	10	11	2	37	27	5	3	15	22	41	59	68	44
13	Port Vale	46	9	7	7	33	27	5	8	10	22	31	55	58	43
14	Exeter City	46	11	6	6	30	24	3	9	11	20	36	50	60	43
15	Chesterfield	46	13	6	4	33	16	4	2	17	27	47	60	63	42
16	Barnsley	46	8	7	8	30	28	5	8	10	30	36	60	64	41
17	Luton Town	46	15	5	3	47	23	1	4	18	12	50	59	73	41
18	Newport County	46	9	9	5	35	23	3	7	13	21	40	56	63	40
19	Chester	46	8	5	10	24	32	7	5	11	30	46	54	78	40
20	Notts County	46	10	7	6	31	25	3	4	16	22	47	53	72	37
21	Rochdale	46	10	4	9	30	27	3	7	13	23	48	53	75	37
22	York City	46	11	5	7	45	31	1	6	16	20	48	65	79	35
23	Bradford Park Ave.	46	7	6	10	30	34	4	7	12	22	45	52	79	35
24	*Lincoln City*	*46*	*7*	*8*	*8*	*39*	*39*	*2*	*5*	*16*	*19*	*43*	*58*	*82*	*31*

1967/68 Division 4

		Pl.	Home					Away					F.	A.	Pts
			W	D	L	F	A	W	D	L	F	A			
1	Luton Town	46	19	3	1	55	16	8	9	6	32	28	87	44	66
2	Barnsley	46	17	6	0	43	14	7	7	9	25	32	68	46	61
3	Hartlepools United	46	15	7	1	34	12	10	3	10	26	34	60	46	60
4	Crewe Alexandra	46	13	10	0	44	18	7	8	8	30	31	74	49	58
5	Bradford City	46	14	5	4	41	22	9	6	8	31	29	72	51	57
6	Southend United	46	12	8	3	45	21	8	6	9	32	37	77	58	54
7	Chesterfield	46	15	4	4	47	20	6	7	10	24	30	71	50	53
8	Wrexham	46	17	3	3	47	12	3	10	10	25	41	72	53	53
9	Aldershot	46	10	11	2	36	19	8	6	9	34	36	70	55	53
10	Doncaster Rovers	46	12	8	3	36	16	6	7	10	30	40	66	56	51
11	Halifax Town	46	10	6	7	34	24	5	10	8	18	25	52	49	46
12	Newport County	46	11	7	5	32	22	5	6	12	26	41	58	63	45
13	*Lincoln City*	*46*	*11*	*3*	*9*	*41*	*31*	*6*	*6*	*11*	*30*	*37*	*71*	*68*	*43*
14	Brentford	46	13	4	6	41	24	5	3	15	20	40	61	64	43
15	Swansea Town	46	11	8	4	38	25	5	2	16	25	52	63	77	42
16	Darlington	46	6	11	6	31	27	6	6	11	16	26	47	53	41
17	Notts County	46	10	7	6	27	27	5	4	14	26	52	53	79	41
18	Port Vale	46	10	5	8	41	31	2	10	11	20	41	61	72	39
19	Rochdale	46	9	8	6	35	32	3	6	14	16	40	51	72	38
20	Exeter City	46	9	7	7	30	30	2	9	12	15	35	45	65	38
21	York City	46	9	6	8	44	30	2	8	13	21	38	65	68	36
22	Chester	46	6	6	11	35	38	3	8	12	22	40	57	78	32
23	Workington	46	8	8	7	35	29	2	3	18	19	58	54	87	31
24	Bradford Park Ave.	46	3	7	13	18	35	1	8	14	12	47	30	82	23

1968/69 Division 4

		Pl.	Home					Away					F.	A.	Pts
			W	D	L	F	A	W	D	L	F	A			
1	Doncaster Rovers	46	13	8	2	42	16	8	9	6	23	22	65	38	59
2	Halifax Town	46	15	5	3	36	18	5	12	6	17	19	53	37	57
3	Rochdale	46	14	7	2	47	11	4	13	6	21	24	68	35	56
4	Bradford City	46	11	10	2	36	18	7	10	6	29	28	65	46	56
5	Darlington	46	11	6	6	40	26	6	12	5	22	19	62	45	52
6	Colchester United	46	12	8	3	31	17	8	4	11	26	36	57	53	52
7	Southend United	46	15	3	5	51	21	4	10	9	27	40	78	61	51
8	*Lincoln City*	*46*	*13*	*6*	*4*	*38*	*19*	*4*	*11*	*8*	*16*	*33*	*54*	*52*	*51*
9	Wrexham	46	13	7	3	41	22	5	7	11	20	30	61	52	50
10	Swansea Town	46	11	8	4	35	20	8	3	12	23	34	58	54	49
11	Brentford	46	12	7	4	40	24	6	5	12	24	41	64	65	48
12	Workington	46	8	11	4	24	17	7	6	10	16	26	40	43	47
13	Port Vale	46	12	8	3	33	15	4	6	13	13	31	46	46	46
14	Chester	46	12	4	7	43	24	4	9	10	33	42	76	66	45
15	Aldershot	46	13	3	7	42	23	6	4	13	24	43	66	66	45
16	Scunthorpe United	46	10	5	8	28	22	8	3	12	33	38	61	60	44
17	Exeter City	46	11	8	4	45	24	5	3	15	21	41	66	65	43
18	Peterborough Utd.	46	8	9	6	32	23	5	7	11	28	34	60	57	42
19	Notts County	46	10	8	5	33	22	2	10	11	15	35	48	57	42
20	Chesterfield	46	7	7	9	24	22	6	8	9	19	28	43	50	41
21	York City	46	12	8	3	36	25	2	3	18	17	50	53	75	39
22	Newport County	46	9	9	5	31	26	2	5	16	18	48	49	74	36
23	Grimsby Town	46	5	7	11	25	31	4	8	11	22	38	47	69	33
24	Bradford Park Ave.	46	5	8	10	19	34	0	2	21	13	72	32	106	20

1969/70 Division 4

		Pl.	Home					Away					F.	A.	Pts
			W	D	L	F	A	W	D	L	F	A			
1	Chesterfield	46	19	1	3	55	12	8	9	6	22	20	77	32	64
2	Wrexham	46	17	6	0	56	16	9	3	11	28	33	84	49	61
3	Swansea Town	46	14	8	1	43	14	7	10	6	23	31	66	45	60
4	Port Vale	46	13	9	1	39	10	7	10	6	22	23	61	33	59
5	Brentford	46	14	8	1	36	11	6	8	9	22	28	58	39	56
6	Aldershot	46	16	5	2	52	22	4	8	11	26	43	78	65	53
7	Notts County	46	14	4	5	44	21	8	4	11	29	41	73	62	52
8	*Lincoln City*	*46*	*11*	*8*	*4*	*38*	*20*	*6*	*8*	*9*	*28*	*32*	*66*	*52*	*50*
9	Peterborough Utd.	46	13	8	2	51	21	4	6	13	26	48	77	69	48
10	Colchester United	46	14	5	4	38	22	3	9	11	26	41	64	63	48
11	Chester	46	14	3	6	39	23	7	3	13	19	43	58	66	48
12	Scunthorpe United	46	11	6	6	34	23	7	4	12	33	42	67	65	46
13	York City	46	14	7	2	38	16	2	7	14	17	46	55	62	46
14	Northampton Town	46	11	7	5	41	19	5	5	13	23	36	64	55	44
15	Crewe Alexandra	46	12	6	5	37	18	4	6	13	14	33	51	51	44
16	Grimsby Town	46	9	9	5	33	24	5	6	12	21	34	54	58	43
17	Southend United	46	12	8	3	40	28	3	2	18	19	57	59	85	40
18	Exeter City	46	13	5	5	48	20	1	6	16	9	39	57	59	39
19	Oldham Athletic	46	11	4	8	45	28	2	9	12	15	37	60	65	39
20	Workington	46	9	9	5	31	21	3	5	15	15	43	46	64	38
21	Newport County	46	12	3	8	39	24	1	8	14	14	50	53	74	37
22	Darlington	46	8	7	8	31	27	5	3	15	22	46	53	73	36
23	Hartlepool	46	7	7	9	31	30	3	3	17	11	52	42	82	30
24	Bradford Park Ave.	46	6	5	12	23	32	0	6	17	18	64	41	96	23

1970/71 Division 4

		Pl.	Home					Away					F.	A.	Pts
			W	D	L	F	A	W	D	L	F	A			
1	Notts County	46	19	4	0	59	12	11	5	7	30	24	89	36	69
2	Bournemouth	46	16	5	2	51	15	8	7	8	30	31	81	46	60
3	Oldham Athletic	46	14	6	3	57	29	10	5	8	31	34	88	63	59
4	York City	46	16	6	1	45	14	7	4	12	33	40	78	54	56
5	Chester	46	17	2	4	42	18	7	5	11	27	37	69	55	55
6	Colchester United	46	14	6	3	44	19	7	6	10	26	35	70	54	54
7	Northampton Town	46	15	4	4	39	24	4	9	10	24	35	63	59	51
8	Southport	46	15	2	6	42	24	6	4	13	21	33	63	57	48
9	Exeter City	46	12	7	4	40	23	5	7	11	27	45	67	68	48
10	Workington	46	13	7	3	28	13	5	5	13	20	36	48	49	48
11	Stockport County	46	12	8	3	28	17	4	6	13	21	48	49	65	46
12	Darlington	46	15	3	5	42	22	2	8	13	16	35	58	57	45
13	Aldershot	46	8	10	5	32	23	6	7	10	34	48	66	71	45
14	Brentford	46	13	3	7	45	27	5	5	13	21	35	66	62	44
15	Crewe Alexandra	46	13	1	9	49	35	5	7	11	26	41	75	76	44
16	Peterborough Utd.	46	14	3	6	46	23	4	4	15	24	48	70	71	43
17	Scunthorpe United	46	9	7	7	36	23	6	6	11	20	38	56	61	43
18	Southend United	46	8	11	4	32	24	6	4	13	21	42	53	66	43
19	Grimsby Town	46	13	4	6	37	26	5	3	15	20	45	57	71	43
20	Cambridge United	46	9	9	5	31	27	6	4	13	20	39	51	66	43
21	*Lincoln City*	*46*	*11*	*4*	*8*	*45*	*33*	*2*	*9*	*12*	*25*	*38*	*70*	*71*	*39*
22	Newport County	46	8	3	12	32	36	2	5	16	23	49	55	85	28
23	Hartlepool	46	6	10	7	28	27	2	2	19	6	47	34	74	28
24	Barrow	46	5	5	13	25	38	2	3	18	26	52	51	90	22

1971/72 Division 4

		Pl.	Home					Away					F.	A.	Pts
			W	D	L	F	A	W	D	L	F	A			
1	Grimsby Town	46	18	3	2	61	26	10	4	9	27	30	88	56	63
2	Southend United	46	18	2	3	56	26	6	10	7	25	29	81	55	60
3	Brentford	46	16	2	5	52	21	8	9	6	24	23	76	44	59
4	Scunthorpe United	46	13	8	2	34	15	9	5	9	22	22	56	37	57
5	*Lincoln City*	*46*	*17*	*5*	*1*	*46*	*15*	*4*	*9*	*10*	*31*	*44*	*77*	*59*	*56*
6	Workington	46	12	9	2	34	7	4	10	9	16	27	50	34	51
7	Southport	46	15	5	3	48	21	3	9	11	18	25	66	46	50
8	Peterborough Utd.	46	14	6	3	51	24	3	10	10	31	40	82	64	50
9	Bury	46	16	4	3	55	22	3	8	12	18	37	73	59	50
10	Cambridge United	46	11	8	4	38	22	6	6	11	24	38	62	60	48
11	Colchester United	46	13	6	4	38	23	6	4	13	32	46	70	69	48
12	Doncaster Rovers	46	11	8	4	35	24	5	6	12	21	39	56	63	46
13	Gillingham	46	11	5	7	33	24	5	8	10	28	43	61	67	45
14	Newport County	46	13	5	5	34	20	5	3	15	26	52	60	72	44
15	Exeter City	46	11	5	7	40	30	5	6	12	21	38	61	68	43
16	Reading	46	14	3	6	37	26	3	5	15	19	50	56	76	42
17	Aldershot	46	5	13	5	27	20	4	9	10	21	34	48	54	40
18	Hartlepool	46	14	2	7	39	25	3	4	16	19	44	58	69	40
19	Darlington	46	9	9	5	37	24	5	2	16	27	58	64	82	39
20	Chester	46	10	11	2	34	16	0	7	16	13	40	47	56	38
21	Northampton Town	46	8	9	6	43	27	4	4	15	23	52	66	79	37
22	Barrow	46	8	8	7	23	26	5	3	15	17	45	40	71	37
23	Stockport County	46	7	10	6	33	32	2	4	17	22	55	55	87	32
24	Crewe Alexandra	46	9	4	10	27	25	1	5	17	16	44	43	69	29

1972/73 Division 4

		Pl.	Home					Away					F.	A.	Pts
			W	D	L	F	A	W	D	L	F	A			
1	Southport	46	17	4	2	40	19	9	6	8	31	29	71	48	62
2	Hereford United	46	18	4	1	39	12	5	8	10	17	26	56	38	58
3	Cambridge United	46	15	6	2	40	23	5	11	7	27	34	67	57	57
4	Aldershot	46	14	6	3	33	14	8	6	9	27	24	60	38	56
5	Newport County	46	14	6	3	37	18	8	6	9	27	26	64	44	56
6	Mansfield Town	46	15	7	1	52	17	5	7	11	26	34	78	51	54
7	Reading	46	14	7	2	33	7	3	11	9	18	31	51	38	52
8	Exeter City	46	13	8	2	40	18	5	6	12	17	33	57	51	50
9	Gillingham	46	15	4	4	44	20	4	7	12	19	38	63	58	49
10	*Lincoln City*	*46*	*12*	*7*	*4*	*38*	*27*	*4*	*9*	*10*	*26*	*30*	*64*	*57*	*48*
11	Stockport County	46	14	7	2	38	18	4	5	14	15	35	53	53	48
12	Bury	46	11	7	5	37	19	3	11	9	21	32	58	51	46
13	Workington	46	15	7	1	44	20	2	5	16	15	41	59	61	46
14	Barnsley	46	9	8	6	32	24	5	8	10	26	36	58	60	44
15	Chester	46	11	6	6	40	19	3	9	11	21	33	61	52	43
16	Bradford City	46	12	6	5	42	25	4	5	14	19	40	61	65	43
17	Doncaster Rovers	46	10	8	5	28	19	5	4	14	21	39	49	58	42
18	Torquay United	46	8	10	5	23	17	4	7	12	21	30	44	47	41
19	Peterborough Utd.	46	10	8	5	42	29	4	5	14	29	47	71	76	41
20	Hartlepool	46	8	10	5	17	15	4	7	12	17	34	34	49	41
21	Crewe Alexandra	46	7	8	8	18	23	2	10	11	20	38	38	61	36
22	Colchester United	46	8	8	7	36	28	2	3	18	12	48	48	76	31
23	Northampton Town	46	7	6	10	24	30	3	5	15	16	43	40	73	31
24	Darlington	46	5	9	9	28	41	2	6	15	14	44	42	85	29

SEASON 1965-66
DIVISION FOUR

No.	Date	Opposition	Res.	Att.	Goalscorers
1	21 Aug	Doncaster Rovers	0-4	11566	
2	23	Darlington	2-0	6333	Hutchinson, Larkin
3	28	NOTTS COUNTY	1-2	6613	Farrall
4	4 Sep	Chester	2-4	6742	Hutchinson(2)
5	11	HALIFAX TOWN	3-3	4454	Hutchinson, Chapman(2)
6	15	DARLINGTON	4-1	5107	Farrall, Hutchinson(2), Chapman
7	18	Port Vale	0-3	4605	
8	24	CREWE ALEXANDRA	1-1	5084	Hutchinson
9	2 Oct	Bradford City	0-2	2684	
10	6	TRANMERE ROVERS	1-0	4269	Hutchinson
11	9	Wrexham	1-0	4313	Hutchinson
12	15	BRADFORD PARK AVENUE	1-1	6426	Hutchinson
13	23	Aldershot	0-2	4093	
14	30	NEWPORT COUNTY	1-1	3759	Chapman
15	6 Nov	Torquay United	1-4	5576	Chapman
16	20	Rochdale	1-0	2574	Holmes
17	22	Tranmere Rovers	2-3	6936	Hutchinson(2)
18	27	LUTON TOWN	2-2	2941	Chapman(2)
19	11 Dec	HARTLEPOOLS UNITED	3-1	3332	Hutchinson, Holmes
20	18	Bradford Park Avenue	2-4	4576	Hutchinson(2)
21	1 Jan	WREXHAM	0-2	4035	
22	8	Chesterfield	0-1	3174	
23	15	ALDERSHOT	2-1	1955	Hutchinson(2)
24	28	DONCASTER ROVERS	0-3	7499	
25	5 Feb	Notts County	1-2	5122	Hutchinson
26	12	COLCHESTER UNITED	0-2	2421	
27	19	CHESTER	2-2	3111	Allison, Bonson
28	21	Stockport County	1-2	8403	Bonson
29	26	Halifax Town	2-2	2984	Smith, Allison
30	5 Mar	Colchester United	0-3	5055	
31	9	CHESTERFIELD	0-2	3371	
32	12	PORT VALE	0-1	2238	
33	15	STOCKPORT COUNTY	1-2	2638	Allison
34	18	Crewe Alexandra	0-7	3740	
35	22	BARNSLEY	4-1	2368	Allison(2), Bonson(2)
36	25	BRADFORD CITY	1-0	3368	Allison
37	2 Apr	TORQUAY UNITED	1-1	2472	Grummett
38	8	SOUTHPORT	4-0	4389	Bonson(3), Fencott
39	11	Southport	1-5	3844	Godbold
40	16	ROCHDALE	2-0	2884	Fencott(2)
41	23	Luton Town	0-0	9621	
42	26	Barnsley	1-0	2287	Bonson
43	30	BARROW	4-0	3703	Godbold, Fencott, Bonson(2)
44	2 May	Newport County	0-0	2176	
45	7	Hartlepools United	1-3	4904	Bonson
46	12	Barrow	2-2	2858	Bonson, Allison

F.A. CUP

| 1R | 12 Nov | BARNSLEY | 1-3 | 6378 | Ellis |

LEAGUE CUP

| 1R | 1 Sep | YORK CITY | 2-2 | 3725 | Hutchinson, Chapman |
| 1Rr | 7 | York City | 2-4 | 7987 | Chapman, Hutchinson |

LINCOLNSHIRE CUP

| SF | 29 Mar | GRIMSBY TOWN | 1-1 * | 1359 | Barton |
| F | 24 May | Scunthorpe United | 2-2 | 1183 | Godbold, Bonson |

* Semi-final won the toss of a coin.
Trophy shared.

1965-66
Back : Jones, Milner, Brooks, Farmer, Wakeham, Farrell, Larkin, Hudson.
Centre : Fencott, Holmes, Hutchinson, Chapman (player/coach), Hawksby, Fell, Barton.
Front : Hawbrook, Whittle.

1966-67
Back : Loxley (trainer/coach), Jones, Milner, Brooks, Treharne, Dixon-Cave,
Grummett, Bonson, Chapman (player/coach), McGlen (trainer).
Front : Heard, Holmes, Fencott, Allison, Hubbard, Whittle, Hawbrook, Scott, Anderson.

SEASON 1966-67
DIVISION FOUR

No.	Date	Opposition	Res.	Att.	Goalscorers
1	20 Aug	NEWPORT COUNTY	2-2	4182	Holmes, Chapman
2	27	Chesterfield	1-3	5998	Chapman
3	2 Sep	STOCKPORT COUNTY	0-1	5582	
4	7	BRENTFORD	3-1	4505	Chapman(2), Anderson
5	10	Rochdale	0-1	2905	
6	17	SOUTHPORT	0-4	4340	
7	24	Notts County	1-2	5167	Chapman
8	27	Brentford	2-2	6231	Godbold, Anderson
9	1 Oct	CHESTER	2-3	2818	Chapman, Bonson
10	7	HALIFAX TOWN	3-3	3956	Chapman(2), Fencott
11	15	Hartlepools United	0-5	3987	
12	22	EXETER CITY	1-1	3030	Chapman
13	26	Aldershot	0-1	5035	
14	29	Bradford City	1-2	4813	Allison
15	5 Nov	TRANMERE ROVERS	2-0	3159	Bonson, Anderson
16	12	Southend United	0-3	6761	
17	16	CREWE ALEXANDRA	1-1	2671	Allison
18	19	Wrexham	1-1	3423	Allison
19	3 Dec	LUTON TOWN	8-1	2893	Holmes,Cobb(3),Bonson(2),Chapman(2)
20	10	Barnsley	1-2	9394	Allison
21	27	Port Vale	0-1	5268	
22	31	CHESTERFIELD	2-1	4614	Chapman, Cobb
23	14 Jan	ROCHDALE	0-2	3983	
24	21	Southport	1-2	3497	Holmes
25	4 Feb	NOTTS COUNTY	2-1	5122	Cobb, Chapman
26	11	Chester	1-0	4251	Chapman
27	18	Barrow	1-2	5740	Scott
28	25	Halifax Town	0-0	4531	
29	4 Mar	HARTLEPOOLS UNITED	3-0	4667	Anderson(2), Ford
30	11	BARROW	2-1	5056	OG, Chapman
31	13	Newport County	0-0	2246	
32	18	Exeter City	0-1	3142	
33	24	YORK CITY	2-2	7389	Ford, Anderson
34	25	ALDERSHOT	0-4	5087	
35	27	York City	1-3	3923	Allison
36	31	Tranmere Rovers	0-1	6851	
37	5 Apr	Crewe Alexandra	0-3	4187	
38	8	SOUTHEND UNITED	2-2	3116	Ford, Cobb
39	11	Bradford Park Avenue	1-2	3713	Hubbard
40	15	Wrexham	0-0	5108	
41	22	BRADFORD CITY	1-4	3138	Chapman
42	26	BRADFORD PARK AVENUE	2-2	2155	Chapman(2)
43	29	Luton Town	1-2	5382	Chapman
44	3 May	Port Vale	2-2	3085	Allison, Chapman
45	6	BARNSLEY	0-1	2860	
46	26	Stockport County	5-4	9662	Ford,Holmes,Thom,Lewis,Grummett

1 own goal

F.A. CUP

| 1R | 26 Nov | SCUNTHORPE UNITED | 3-4 | 6223 | Chapman, Bonson, Grummett |

LEAGUE CUP

1R	24 Aug	HULL CITY	1-0	6238	Bonson
2R	14 Sep	HUDDERSFIELD TOWN	2-1	6442	Anderson, Bonson
3R	5 Oct	Leicester City	0-5	14491	

LINCOLNSHIRE CUP

| F | 14 Feb | SCUNTHORPE UNITED | 3-0 | 1557 | Holmes, Smith, Allison |

SEASON 1967-68
DIVISION FOUR

No.	Date	Opposition	Res.	Att.	Goalscorers
1	19 Aug	ALDERSHOT	1-1	6466	Grummett
2	26	Workington	4-2	2245	Holmes(2), Ford, Harford
3	2 Sep	Rochdale	2-1	2467	Ford(2)
4	6	DARLINGTON	1-2	7718	Ford
5	9	HALIFAX TOWN	1-0	6200	Holmes
6	16	Bradford City	1-2	4065	Ford
7	23	CREWE ALEXANDRA	2-4	6437	Holmes, Gregson
8	25	Darlington	1-1	4427	Ford
9	30	Notts County	0-0	6238	
10	4 Oct	CHESTERFIELD	2-2	7207	Cobb, Harford
11	7	NEWPORT COUNTY	2-1	6576	Ford, Holmes
12	13	Hartlepools United	1-1	5031	Ford
13	21	SWANSEA TOWN	3-0	7661	Grummett, Holmes(2)
14	23	Chesterfield	0-2	11807	
15	28	Barnsley	1-2	9290	Gregson
16	4 Nov	WREXHAM	0-2	7382	
17	11	Southend United	1-2	8943	Holmes
18	18	LUTON TOWN	2-3	6052	Pilgrim, Corner
19	25	Doncaster Rovers	0-0	5627	
20	2 Dec	BRADFORD PARK AVENUE	5-1	5015	Ford(3), Grummett, Peden
21	16	Aldershot	2-3	4263	Grummett, Cobb
22	23	WORKINGTON	3-0	5634	Thom, Grummett, Holmes
23	26	CHESTER	3-0	8740	Holmes, Grummett, Ford
24	30	Chester	0-6	2876	
25	6 Jan	ROCHDALE	3-2	5480	Holmes, Grummett(2)
26	13	Halifax Town	0-1	5028	
27	20	BRADFORD CITY	2-0	6719	Grummett, Gregson
28	27	York City	1-3	6398	Thom
29	3 Feb	Crewe Alexandra	1-2	5678	Peden
30	10	NOTTS COUNTY	1-3	6554	Cobb
31	16	Port Vale	1-1	4187	Holmes
32	24	Luton Town	2-4	11159	Grummett, Thom
33	2 Mar	HARTLEPOOLS UNITED	1-2	4363	OG
34	9	York City	0-1	4716	
35	16	Swansea Town	2-2	3775	Grummett, Peden
36	23	BARNSLEY	0-1	7772	
37	30	Wrexham	1-3	3395	Holmes
38	6 Apr	SOUTHEND UNITED	4-2	4898	Kearns, Corner(2), Holmes
39	12	Exeter City	1-0	3853	Cobb
40	13	Newport County	1-0	2541	Harford
41	14	EXETER CITY	1-1	8129	Corner
42	20	DONCASTER ROVERS	2-0	7793	OG, Peden
43	23	Brentford	3-1	4903	Kearns, Brooks, Corner
44	27	Bradford Park Avenue	5-1	2259	Kearns(2), Corner(3)
45	4 May	BRENTFORD	1-0	8071	Kearns
46	11	PORT VALE	0-1	6649	

Apps. 46 38 46 5 46 46 31 44 30 39 38 5 9 3 8 18 3 15 0 1 13 10 12
Subs. 5 1 1 2 1 2 1 1
Goals 4 3 11 3 14 12 4 3 1 8 1 5
2 own goals

F.A. CUP

1R	9 Dec	Southport	1-3	5105	Cobb

LEAGUE CUP

1R	23 Aug	Mansfield Town	3-2	5944	Cobb, Holmes(2)
2R	13 Sep	NEWCASTLE UNITED	2-1	15454	Grummett, Peden
3R	11 Oct	TORQUAY UNITED	4-2	13532	Lewis(2), Holmes, Peden
4R	1 Nov	Derby County	1-1	25079	Thom
4Rr	15	DERBY COUNTY	0-3	23196	

LINCOLNSHIRE CUP

SF	14 Feb	SCUNTHORPE UNITED	4-0	1988	Peden, Grummett(2), Lewis
F	26 Mar	GRIMSBY TOWN	2-3	2682	Grummett, OG

1967-68
Back : Gray (manager), Samuel, Brown, Lancaster, Adlard, Harford,
Tennant, Brooks, Grummett, Peden, Loxley (trainer).
Centre: Cobb, Gregson, Holmes, Ford, Thom, Lewis, Hubbard, York, Wells. Front : Hawley, Emmingham.

1968-69
Back : Loxley (trainer), Hubbard, Corner, Grummett, Peden, Kennedy, Jim Smith,
Graham Taylor, Kearns, Harford, Brooks, Gray (manager).
Front : Holmes, Parker, Dave Smith, Hughes, Thom, Lewis, Fletcher.

SEASON 1968-69
DIVISION FOUR

No.	Date	Opposition	Res.	Att.	Goalscorers
1	10 Aug	NOTTS COUNTY	5-0	8177	Peden, Taylor, OG, Lewis(2)
2	17	Halifax Town	1-0	4536	Harford
3	24	NEWPORT COUNTY	1-0	8038	Hughes
4	28	SOUTHEND UNITED	2-1	10203	Kearns, Corner
5	31	Darlington	0-5	5078	
6	7 Sep	SWANSEA TOWN	0-1	7521	
7	14	Wrexham	1-0	6235	Holmes
8	16	Bradford Park Avenue	1-1	3433	Peden
9	21	GRIMSBY TOWN	3-0	9140	Kearns, Lewis, D.Smith
10	28	Workington	1-1	2506	OG
11	5 Oct	Port Vale	1-1	6152	Hubbard
12	7	Southend United	0-3	10097	
13	12	YORK CITY	3-0	7247	D.Smith, Kearns, Lewis
14	16	CHESTERFIELD	2-2	7635	Hughes, Corner
15	19	Bradford City	0-2	6142	
16	26	COLCHESTER UNITED	0-3	6633	
17	2 Nov	Doncaster Rovers	2-0	5497	Kearns, D.Smith
18	6	Exeter City	0-3	4332	
19	9	BRENTFORD	1-0	6121	Peden
20	23	CHESTER	2-0	6033	Corner, D.Smith
21	30	Scunthorpe United	0-0	5855	
22	14 Dec	York City	1-1	2577	Hughes
23	21	BRADFORD CITY	2-0	6990	D.Smith, Svarc
24	26	PORT VALE	0-1	12208	
25	11 Jan	DONCASTER ROVERS	1-1	9794	Kearns
26	13	Peterborough United	0-0	6527	
27	18	Brentford	2-2	6572	Corner, Harford
28	25	EXETER CITY	3-2	9105	D.Smith, Peden, OG
29	1 Feb	Rochdale	0-0	8621	
30	15	SCUNTHORPE UNITED	1-2	8186	Hubbard
31	1 Mar	Notts County	0-0	5870	
32	5	PETERBOROUGH UNITED	1-1	7677	D.Smith
33	8	HALIFAX TOWN	0-0	6974	
34	10	Rochdale	1-2	5803	Lewis
35	15	Newport County	1-2	1688	Grummett
36	17	Chesterfield	1-1	3164	Fletcher
37	22	DARLINGTON	2-1	6059	Lewis, Fletcher
38	24	Colchester United	1-1	6787	Harford
39	29	Swansea Town	0-5	3377	
40	4 Apr	Aldershot	1-0	8264	Fletcher
41	5	WORKINGTON	4-1	7143	Fletcher(3), D.Smith
42	7	BRADFORD PARK AVENUE	3-2	8092	Fletcher(2), Peden
43	12	Grimsby Town	1-1	5113	Kearns
44	16	ALDERSHOT	2-1	7057	D.Smith, Fletcher
45	19	WREXHAM	0-0	7321	
46	23	Chester	0-2	2468	

3 own goals

F.A. CUP

1R	16 Nov	Macclesfield Town	3-1	6809	Kearns, Thom, D.Smith
2R	7 Dec	Chester	1-1	6065	Corner
2Rr	11	CHESTER	2-1	9703	Kearns, D.Smith
3R	4 Jan	Birmingham City	1-2	31429	J.Smith

LEAGUE CUP

| 1R | 14 Aug | MANSFIELD TOWN | 2-1 | 8840 | Corner, Peden |
| 2R | 3 Sep | Scunthorpe United | 1-2 | 11098 | Taylor |

LINCOLNSHIRE CUP

1R	23 Oct	Grimsby Town	0-0	762	
1Rr	29	GRIMSBY TOWN	1-1 *	1910	Peden
1R2r	31 Mar	GRIMSBY TOWN	3-2	937	Harrison, D.Smith(2)
SF	28 Apr	Gainsborough Trinity	5-3 *		Grummett(2), J.Smith, Harford, Jeffrey
F	3 May	SCUNTHORPE UNITED	4-1 *	1090	Jeffrey(2), D.Smith, J.Smith

* after extra time

SEASON 1969-70
DIVISION FOUR

No.	Date	Opposition	Res.	Att.	Goalscorers
1	9 Aug	COLCHESTER UNITED	3-3	7061	Fletchre(2), Harford
2	16	York City	0-2	3408	
3	23	SOUTHEND UNITED	3-3	6556	Fletcher, Jeffrey, W.Taylor
4	27	PORT VALE	0-0	6865	
5	30	Northampton Town	1-1	6026	Fletcher
6	6 Sep	OLDHAM ATHLETIC	0-1	6420	
7	13	Peterborough United	1-2	5859	Hubbard
8	17	Notts County	0-2	6479	
9	20	CHESTER	2-0	4482	Hubbard, Harford
10	27	Grimsby Town	2-0	6718	Fletcher, Jeffrey
11	29	Brentford	1-2	8210	Jeffrey
12	4 Oct	EXETER CITY	1-0	5791	Fletcher
13	8	YORK CITY	4-0	7515	Fletcher, W.Taylor(2), Lewis
14	11	Aldershot	1-1	5926	Meath
15	18	SCUNTHORPE UNITED	1-2	8172	Fletcher
16	25	Swansea Town	2-2	7568	Fletcher(2)
17	1 Nov	WORKINGTON	1-1	6236	W.Taylor
18	8	Newport County	1-3	2346	Hughes
19	22	Darlington	3-0	2713	Helliwell, Fletcher(2)
20	26	Crewe Alexandra	1-3	2297	Smith
21	13 Dec	PETERBOROUGH UNITED	3-0	5407	Smith, Lewis, Fletcher
22	26	Southend United	2-2	7755	Meath, Smith
23	27	NORTHAMPTON TOWN	0-0	7866	
24	3 Jan	BRENTFORD	1-0	4991	Smith
25	10	Chester	2-1	5768	Meath, Fletcher
26	17	GRIMSBY TOWN	2-0	9296	Meath(2)
27	24	Chesterfield	0-4	10426	
28	31	Exeter City	2-1	5336	Smith, Svarc
29	7 Feb	ALDERSHOT	1-1	6511	Harford
30	10	Oldham Athletic	1-1	2391	Hubbard
31	21	SWANSEA TOWN	0-0	6183	
32	28	Scunthorpe United	1-2	7130	Gaston
33	2 Mar	Wrexham	0-0	7677	
34	14	Hartlepool	3-0	2555	Hughes, OG, W.Taylor
35	18	CHESTERFIELD	0-2	7519	
36	21	WREXHAM	0-0	4456	
37	23	Bradford Park Avenue	5-2	4350	OG,Peden,Fletcher,Hghes,Grmmett
38	27	NEWPORT COUNTY	3-0	6394	Smith, Hubbard, Holmes
39	28	Bradford Park Avenue	3-0	2427	Hughes, Smith(2)
40	30	Workington	1-1	2950	Hughes
41	4 Apr	Port Vale	0-0	7414	
42	8	CREWE ALEXANDRA	2-1	4850	Hubbard, Fletcher
43	15	NOTTS COUNTY	2-4	5518	Grummett(2)
44	18	HARTLEPOOL	3-0	3772	Svarc(2), Peden
45	22	Colchester United	0-2	2611	
46	25	DARLINGTON	1-0	3407	Svarc

2 own goals

F.A. CUP

1R	15 Nov	SOUTHPORT	2-0	5846	Smith, Fletcher
2R	6 Dec	Bradford City	0-3	9614	

LEAGUE CUP

1R	13 Aug	Watford	1-2	10086	Hubbard

LINCOLNSHIRE CUP

1R	22 Sep	Grantham Town	5-1	1656	Jeffrey,D.Smith,Grummett(2),Harford
SF	19 Jan	Gainsborough Trinity	3-3	2905	Meath, Svarc, Smith
SFr	10 Apr	GAINSBOROUGH TRINITY	3-0	2172	Fletcher, Hubbard, Grummett
F	4 May	Boston United	3-2	3004	Svarc(2), OG

1969-70
Back : Peden, Grummett, Kennedy, Brooks, Harford, Hubbard.
Front : Dave Smith, Holmes, Thom, Hughes, Graham Taylor.

1970-71
Back : Billy Taylor, Grummett, Mawer, Meath, McInally, Harford, Freeman, Trevis, Peden.
Centre : Loxley (manager/coach), Fletcher, Dave Smith, Hubbard, Graham Taylor. Front : Alexander, Svarc, Scott.

SEASON 1970-71
DIVISION FOUR

No.	Date	Opposition	Res.	Att.	Goalscorers
1	15 Aug	Cambridge United	1-1	6843	Trevis
2	22	BRENTFORD	2-0	6813	Freeman(2)
3	29	York City	0-2	4401	
4	2 Sep	Chester	0-1	4709	
5	5	WORKINGTON	3-1	5071	Hubbard, Smith, Freeman
6	12	Barrow	4-1	2707	Trevis, Hubbard, Smith, W.Taylor
7	19	SOUTHEND UNITED	1-2	7011	Trevis
8	23	GRIMSBY TOWN	3-0	8844	Freeman(2), Hubbard
9	26	Aldershot	2-0	5559	Smith, Hubbard
10	3 Oct	EXETER CITY	4-1	6548	Hubbard, Trevis(3)
11	9	Stockport County	3-4	5251	Hubbard(2), Trevis
12	17	CAMBRIDGE UNITED	0-1	7132	
13	20	Southport	0-1	2449	
14	24	PETERBOROUGH UNITED	2-1	6419	Fletcher, Trevis
15	31	Bournemouth	0-3	6477	
16	7 Nov	SCUNTHORPE UNITED	4-1	7469	OG, Freeman, Fletcher, Hubbard
17	11	Notts County	0-0	10276	
18	14	Oldham Athletic	2-4	9688	Hubbard, Peden
19	18	NORTHAMPTON TOWN	1-3	3889	Trevis
20	28	DARLINGTON	2-1	4339	Trevis, Svarc
21	5 Dec	Hartlepool	0-0	1965	
22	19	Brentford	1-2	5966	Svarc
23	26	COLCHESTER UNITED	1-2	5919	Svarc
24	9 Jan	Northampton Town	1-2	5957	Svarc
25	16	SOUTHPORT	3-0	4292	Freeman, Svarc, Hughes
26	23	CREWE ALEXANDRA	2-2	4261	Svarc(2)
27	30	Darlington	2-3	2753	Fletcher, Hubbard
28	6 Feb	HARTLEPOOL	2-0	3993	Hubbard, Trevis
29	13	Crewe Alexandra	1-3	2838	Svarc
30	20	NOTTS COUNTY	0-1	10849	
31	27	BOURNEMOUTH	1-2	4988	Hubbard
32	6 Mar	Peterborough United	1-1	4292	Smith
33	9	Grimsby Town	1-1	4394	Hubbard
34	13	OLDHAM ATHLETIC	2-1	5297	Fletcher, Trevis
35	17	NEWPORT COUNTY	1-1	4407	Hubbard
36	20	Scunthorpe United	1-2	5919	Harford
37	27	Workington	1-2	1760	Smith
38	3 Apr	YORK CITY	4-5	4208	Smith, Ward, Hubbard, W.Taylor
39	9	BARROW	0-3	4518	
40	10	Colchester United	1-1	6430	Hubbard
41	12	Exeter City	0-0	4614	
42	17	STOCKPORT COUNTY	1-1	3761	Hubbard
43	20	Newport County	2-2	3397	Smith, Hubbard
44	28	CHESTER	2-0	3086	Freeman, Svarc
45	1 May	ALDERSHOT	4-4	3568	Trevis, Freeman(2), Svarc
46	3	Southend United	1-1	4710	Svarc

F.A. CUP

1R	21 Nov	BARROW	2-1	5143	Svarc, Smith
2R	12 Dec	BRADFORD CITY	2-2	7081	Trevis, Svarc
2Rr	16	Bradford City	2-2 *	6991	Fletcher, Svarc
2R2r	21	Bradford City #	4-1	3296	Freeman(2), Svarc, W.Taylor
3R	2 Jan	Torquay United	3-4	8147	Freeman(2), Hubbard

* after extra time
# played at Belle Vue Ground, Doncaster

LEAGUE CUP

1R	19 Aug	GRIMSBY TOWN	2-1	7615	Freeman, Trevis
2R	9 Sep	SUNDERLAND	2-1	10789	Trevis, Freeman
3R	7 Oct	Crystal Palace	0-4	16988	

LINCOLNSHIRE CUP

SF	1 Mar	Grimsby Town	1-3	1223	Hubbard

SEASON 1971-72
DIVISION FOUR

No.	Date	Opposition	Res.	Att.	Goalscorers
1	14 Aug	COLCHESTER UNITED	2-0	6607	Hubbard, Smith
2	21	Scunthorpe United	1-2	5155	Trevis
3	28	NEWPORT COUNTY	3-1	5275	Gilliver(2), Hubbard
4	1 Sep	Crewe Alexandra	1-3	2581	Trevis
5	3	Stockport County	2-4	2399	D.Kennedy, Gilliver
6	11	READING	0-0	5621	
7	18	Workington	0-0	2291	
8	25	CAMBRIDGE UNITED	3-1	5679	Hubbard(2), Gilliver
9	29	GRIMSBY TOWN	3-0	15015	McMahon, Hubbard, Freeman
10	2 Oct	Barrow	2-2	2308	Hubbard(2)
11	9	EXETER CITY	4-1	6085	Hubbard, Freeman(3)
12	15	Colchester United	2-5	5834	Freeman(2)
13	19	Doncaster Rovers	0-2	5272	
14	23	PETERBOROUGH UNITED	3-2	6784	Smith, Freeman, Gilliver
15	30	Bury	1-0	3158	Hubbard
16	6 Nov	NORTHAMPTON TOWN	2-0	6529	Hubbard, Gilliver
17	12	Southport	1-1	4868	Freeman
18	27	Darlington	3-3	2520	Hubbard, Freeman(2)
19	4 Dec	ALDERSHOT	2-2	5366	Hubbard(2)
20	11	Newport County	0-2	2987	
21	18	STOCKPORT COUNTY	2-1	5248	Hubbard(2)
22	27	Southend United	1-2	15628	Trevis
23	1 Jan	WORKINGTON	1-0	5539	Freeman
24	15	BRENTFORD	4-1	7552	McNeil, Spencer, Ward(2)
25	22	Grimsby Town	2-2	15856	McNeil, Freeman
26	29	DONCASTER ROVERS	2-0	7568	Worsdale, McNeil
27	5 Feb	HARTLEPOOL	2-1	7261	McNeil, Spencer
28	12	Peterborough United	4-4	6611	Spencer(2), Smith, Worsdale
29	19	BURY	2-0	7332	Spencer, McMahon
30	26	Northampton Town	3-2	4970	Worsdale(2), McNeil
31	4 Mar	SOUTHPORT	2-1	8001	McNeil, Worsdale
32	9	GILLINGHAM	1-1	8621	Ward
33	11	Exeter City	2-1	2970	Freeman, Gilliver
34	13	Brentford	0-2	12065	
35	18	SCUNTHORPE UNITED	1-0	16498	Gilliver
36	21	Chester	1-2	2372	McNeil
37	25	Reading	1-0	4663	Trevis
38	1 Apr	SOUTHEND UNITED	0-0	12199	
39	3	Cambridge United	0-0	6588	
40	8	Hartlepool	1-2	5975	McNeil
41	12	BARROW	3-2	9432	Ward, McNeil(2)
42	15	DARLINGTON	0-1	9555	
43	19	Gillingham	3-3	3538	McNeil, Ward, Spencer
44	22	Aldershot	0-0	3087	
45	26	CREWE ALEXANDRA	0-0	4064	
46	29	CHESTER	4-0	3033	McNeil(2), Spencer(2)

F.A. CUP

| 1R | 20 Nov | BURY | 1-2 | 6063 | Gilliver |

LEAGUE CUP

1R	18 Aug	Scunthorpe United	1-0	5915	Gilliver
2R	8 Sep	Blackburn Rovers	0-0	6457	
2Rr	15	BLACKBURN ROVERS	4-1	7838	Hubbard(3), OG
3R	5 Oct	Queens Park Rangers	2-4	12723	Freeman, Hubbard

LINCOLNSHIRE CUP

| 1R | 2 Nov | BOSTON UNITED | 3-0 | 1724 | McMahon, Hubbard(2) |
| SF | 3 May | Scunthorpe United | 1-3 | 1786 | Gilliver |

1971-72
Back : Loxley (trainer), Gilliver, David Kennedy, Meath, Freeman, McInally, Branston, Trevis, McMahon, Lawton, Herd (manager).
Centre : Bloor, Worsdale, Dave Smith, Hubbard, Ward, Taylor, Svarc, Scott. Front : Osgar, Brankin, Drinkell.

1972-73
Back : McGeough, Peden, Spencer, McNeil, Symm, Bloor.
Centre : Herd (manager), Freeman, Meath, Branston, John Kennedy, McInally, David Kennedy, Trevis, Bradley, Loxley (trainer). Front : Ward, Taylor, Worsdale, McMahon, Dave Smith, Walls.

SEASON 1972-73
DIVISION FOUR

No.	Date	Opposition	Res.	Att.	Goalscorers
1	12 Aug	HARTLEPOOL	1-2	5789	McNeil
2	19	Darlington	1-1	2090	McNeil
3	26	ALDERSHOT	0-2	4447	
4	30	Workington	3-0	1987	Bradley(2), McNeil
5	2 Sep	Crewe Alexandra	1-1	2283	Bradley
6	9	HEREFORD UNITED	4-1	4971	Bradley(2), McNeil(2)
7	16	Bury	4-0	2927	Bradley, Freeman(3)
8	20	Reading	1-1	4679	Bradley
9	23	DONCASTER ROVERS	2-1	6455	McNeil, Freeman
10	27	TORQUAY UNITED	3-1	6630	McNeil, Freeman, Bradley
11	30	Peterborough United	2-2	4757	McNeil(2)
12	7 Oct	COLCHESTER UNITED	3-2	6268	McNeil(2), Bradley
13	11	NORTHAMPTON TOWN	1-1	6198	Freeman
14	14	Chester	1-2	3813	Freeman
15	21	GILLINGHAM	1-0	5215	Bradley
16	28	Stockport County	1-2	3623	McNeil
17	4 Nov	Torquay United	0-2	1938	
18	6	Exeter City	0-2	4319	
19	11	READING	0-0	4004	
20	25	MANSFIELD TOWN	1-1	6657	McNeil
21	2 Dec	Bradford City	1-3	3382	Bradley
22	16	Newport County	2-2	2847	Peden, Bradley
23	23	BARNSLEY	1-2	4029	OG
24	26	Doncaster Rovers	1-1	3325	Worsdale
25	6 Jan	Aldershot	0-0	3127	
26	13	EXETER CITY	2-2	3729	Peden, McNeil
27	20	CREWE ALEXANDRA	1-1	2429	Ward
28	27	Hereford United	1-2	8579	OG
29	3 Feb	Northampton Town	0-0	2381	
30	10	BURY	2-2	3347	Trevis, McNeil
31	17	Hartlepool	0-1	2892	
32	24	NEWPORT COUNTY	0-2	3023	
33	28	DARLINGTON	1-0	2479	Branston
34	3 Mar	Colchester United	2-0	2649	McNeil(2)
35	7	Cambridge United	1-2	3736	Peden
36	10	CHESTER	1-0	3593	Harding
37	17	Gillingham	1-1	3479	Ward
38	21	SOUTHPORT	3-1	4107	Ward(2), McNeil
39	24	STOCKPORT COUNTY	5-3	3562	Ward(3), Harding(2)
40	31	Mansfield Town	2-0	5277	Ward, Heath
41	7 Apr	BRADFORD CITY	2-1	4369	Symm(2)
42	14	Southport	0-1	4284	
43	20	PETERBOROUGH UNITED	1-0	5231	Symm
44	21	CAMBRIDGE UNITED	2-1	4801	McNeil(2)
45	24	Barnsley	1-4	2807	McNeil
46	28	WORKINGTON	1-1	3280	Worsdale

2 own goals

F.A. CUP

1R	18 Nov	BLACKBURN ROVERS	2-2	5128	Freeman, Bradley
1Rr	27	Blackburn Rovers	1-4	9006	Smith

LEAGUE CUP

1R	16 Aug	Mansfield Town	1-3	4642	Freeman

LINCOLNSHIRE CUP

1R	6 Sep	SCUNTHORPE UNITED	3-0	1416	McNeil(2), Bradley
SF	11 Dec	Boston United	0-2	1200	

WATNEY CUP

1R	29 Jul	BURNLEY	0-1	7425	

Final League Tables 1973/74 to 1980/81

1973/74 Division 4

		Pl.	Home					Away					F.	A.	Pts
			W	D	L	F	A	W	D	L	F	A			
1	Peterborough Utd.	46	19	4	0	49	10	8	7	8	26	28	75	38	65
2	Gillingham	46	16	5	2	51	16	9	7	7	39	33	90	49	62
3	Colchester United	46	16	5	2	46	14	8	7	8	27	22	73	36	60
4	Bury	46	18	3	2	51	14	6	8	9	30	35	81	49	59
5	Northampton Town	46	14	7	2	39	14	6	6	11	24	34	63	48	53
6	Reading	46	11	9	3	37	13	5	10	8	21	24	58	37	51
7	Chester	46	13	6	4	31	19	4	9	10	23	36	54	55	49
8	Bradford City	46	14	7	2	45	20	3	7	13	13	32	58	52	48
9	Newport County	46	13	6	4	39	23	3	8	12	17	42	56	65	45
10	Exeter City	45	12	5	6	37	20	6	3	13	21	35	58	55	44
11	Hartlepool	46	11	4	8	29	16	5	8	10	19	31	48	47	44
12	*Lincoln City*	*46*	*10*	*8*	*5*	*40*	*30*	*6*	*4*	*13*	*23*	*37*	*63*	*67*	*44*
13	Barnsley	46	15	5	3	42	16	2	5	16	16	48	58	64	44
14	Swansea City	46	11	6	6	28	15	5	5	13	17	31	45	46	43
15	Rotherham United	46	10	9	4	33	22	5	4	14	23	36	56	58	43
16	Torquay United	46	11	7	5	37	23	2	10	11	15	34	52	57	43
17	Mansfield Town	46	13	8	2	47	24	0	9	14	15	45	62	69	43
18	Scunthorpe United	45	12	7	3	33	17	2	5	16	14	47	47	64	42
19	Brentford	46	9	7	7	31	20	3	9	11	17	30	48	50	40
20	Darlington	46	9	8	6	29	24	4	5	14	11	38	40	62	39
21	Crewe Alexandra	46	11	5	7	28	30	3	5	15	15	41	43	71	38
22	Doncaster Rovers	46	10	7	6	32	22	2	4	17	15	58	47	80	35
23	Workington	46	10	8	5	33	26	1	5	17	10	48	43	74	35
24	Stockport County	46	4	12	7	22	25	3	8	12	22	44	44	69	34

1974/75 Division 4

		Pl.	Home					Away					F.	A.	Pts
			W	D	L	F	A	W	D	L	F	A			
1	Mansfield Town	46	17	6	0	55	15	11	6	6	35	25	90	40	68
2	Shrewsbury Town	46	16	3	4	46	18	10	7	6	34	25	80	43	62
3	Rotherham United	46	13	7	3	40	19	9	8	6	31	22	71	41	59
4	Chester	46	17	5	1	48	9	6	6	11	16	29	64	38	57
5	*Lincoln City*	*46*	*14*	*8*	*1*	*47*	*14*	*7*	*7*	*9*	*32*	*34*	*79*	*48*	*57*
6	Cambridge United	46	15	5	3	43	16	5	9	9	19	28	62	44	54
7	Reading	46	13	6	4	38	20	8	4	11	25	27	63	47	52
8	Brentford	46	15	6	2	38	14	3	7	13	15	31	53	45	49
9	Exeter City	46	14	3	6	33	24	5	8	10	27	39	60	63	49
10	Bradford City	46	10	5	8	32	21	7	8	8	24	30	56	51	47
11	Southport	46	13	7	3	36	19	2	10	11	20	37	56	56	47
12	Newport County	46	13	5	5	43	30	6	4	13	25	45	68	75	47
13	Hartlepool	46	13	6	4	40	24	3	5	15	12	38	52	62	43
14	Torquay United	46	10	7	6	30	25	4	7	12	16	36	46	61	42
15	Barnsley	46	10	7	6	34	24	5	4	14	28	41	62	65	41
16	Northampton Town	46	12	6	5	43	22	3	5	15	24	51	67	73	41
17	Doncaster Rovers	46	10	9	4	41	29	4	3	16	24	50	65	79	40
18	Crewe Alexandra	46	9	9	5	22	16	2	9	12	12	31	34	47	40
19	Rochdale	46	9	9	5	35	22	4	4	15	24	53	59	75	39
20	Stockport County	46	10	8	5	26	27	2	6	15	17	43	43	70	38
21	Darlington	46	11	4	8	38	27	2	6	15	16	40	54	67	36
22	Swansea City	46	9	4	10	25	31	6	2	15	21	42	46	73	36
23	Workington	46	7	5	11	23	29	3	6	14	13	37	36	66	31
24	Scunthorpe United	46	7	8	8	27	29	0	7	16	14	49	41	78	29

1975/76 Division 4

		Pl.	Home					Away					F.	A.	Pts
			W	D	L	F	A	W	D	L	F	A			
1	*Lincoln City*	*46*	*21*	*2*	*0*	*71*	*15*	*11*	*8*	*4*	*40*	*24*	*111*	*39*	*74*
2	Northampton Town	46	18	5	0	62	20	11	5	7	25	20	87	40	68
3	Reading	46	19	3	1	42	9	5	9	9	28	42	70	51	60
4	Tranmere Rovers	46	18	3	2	61	16	6	7	10	28	39	89	55	58
5	Huddersfield Town	46	11	6	6	28	17	10	8	5	28	24	56	41	56
6	Bournemouth	46	15	5	3	39	16	5	7	11	18	32	57	48	52
7	Exeter City	46	13	7	3	37	17	5	7	11	19	30	56	47	50
8	Watford	46	16	4	3	38	18	6	2	15	24	44	62	62	50
9	Torquay United	46	12	6	5	31	24	6	8	9	24	39	55	63	50
10	Doncaster Rovers	46	10	6	7	42	31	9	5	9	33	38	75	69	49
11	Swansea City	46	14	8	1	51	21	2	7	14	15	36	66	57	47
12	Barnsley	46	12	8	3	34	16	2	8	13	18	32	52	48	44
13	Cambridge United	46	7	10	6	36	28	7	5	11	22	34	58	62	43
14	Hartlepool	46	10	6	7	37	29	6	4	13	25	49	62	78	42
15	Rochdale	46	7	11	5	27	23	5	7	11	13	31	40	54	42
16	Crewe Alexandra	46	10	7	6	36	21	3	8	12	22	36	58	57	41
17	Bradford City	46	9	7	7	35	26	3	10	10	28	39	63	65	41
18	Brentford	46	12	7	4	37	18	2	6	15	19	42	56	60	41
19	Scunthorpe United	46	11	3	9	31	24	3	7	13	19	35	50	59	38
20	Darlington	46	11	7	5	30	14	3	3	17	18	43	48	57	38
21	Stockport County	46	8	7	8	23	23	5	5	13	20	53	43	76	38
22	Newport County	46	8	7	8	35	33	5	2	16	22	57	57	90	35
23	Southport	46	6	6	11	27	31	2	4	17	14	46	41	77	26
24	Workington	46	5	4	14	19	43	2	3	18	11	44	30	87	21

1976/77 Division 3

		Pl.	Home					Away					F.	A.	Pts
			W	D	L	F	A	W	D	L	F	A			
1	Mansfield Town	46	17	6	0	52	13	11	2	10	26	29	78	42	64
2	Brighton & Hove A.	46	19	3	1	63	14	6	8	9	20	26	83	40	61
3	Crystal Palace	46	17	5	1	46	15	6	8	9	22	25	68	40	59
4	Rotherham United	46	11	9	3	30	15	11	6	6	39	29	69	44	59
5	Wrexham	46	15	6	2	47	22	9	4	10	33	32	80	54	58
6	Preston North End	46	15	4	4	48	21	6	8	9	16	22	64	43	54
7	Bury	46	15	2	6	41	21	8	6	9	23	38	64	59	54
8	Sheffield Wed.	46	15	4	4	39	18	7	5	11	26	37	65	55	53
9	*Lincoln City*	*46*	*12*	*9*	*2*	*50*	*30*	*7*	*5*	*11*	*27*	*40*	*77*	*70*	*52*
10	Shrewsbury Town	46	13	7	3	40	21	5	4	14	25	38	65	59	47
11	Swindon Town	46	12	6	5	48	33	3	9	11	20	42	68	75	45
12	Gillingham	46	11	8	4	31	21	5	4	14	24	43	55	64	44
13	Chester	46	14	3	6	28	20	4	5	14	20	38	48	58	44
14	Tranmere Rovers	46	10	7	6	31	23	3	10	10	20	30	51	53	43
15	Walsall	46	8	7	8	39	32	5	8	10	18	33	57	65	41
16	Peterborough Utd.	46	11	4	8	33	28	2	11	10	22	37	55	65	41
17	Oxford United	46	9	8	6	34	29	3	7	13	21	36	55	65	39
18	Chesterfield	46	10	6	7	30	20	4	4	15	26	44	56	64	38
19	Port Vale	46	9	7	7	29	28	2	9	12	18	43	47	71	38
20	Portsmouth	46	8	9	6	28	26	3	5	15	25	44	53	70	36
21	Reading	46	10	5	8	29	24	3	4	16	20	49	49	73	35
22	Northampton Town	46	9	4	10	33	29	4	4	15	27	46	60	75	34
23	Grimsby Town	46	10	6	7	29	22	2	3	18	16	47	45	69	33
24	York City	46	7	8	8	25	34	3	4	16	25	55	50	89	32

1977/78 Division 3

		Pl.	Home					Away					F.	A.	Pts
			W	D	L	F	A	W	D	L	F	A			
1	Wrexham	46	14	8	1	48	19	9	7	7	30	26	78	45	61
2	Cambridge United	46	19	3	1	49	11	4	9	10	23	40	72	51	58
3	Preston North End	46	16	5	2	48	19	4	11	8	15	19	63	38	56
4	Peterborough Utd.	46	15	7	1	32	11	5	9	9	15	22	47	33	56
5	Chester	46	14	8	1	41	24	2	14	7	18	32	59	56	54
6	Walsall	46	12	8	3	35	17	6	9	8	26	33	61	50	53
7	Gillingham	46	11	10	2	36	21	4	10	9	31	39	67	60	50
8	Colchester United	46	10	11	2	36	16	5	7	11	19	28	55	44	48
9	Chesterfield	46	14	6	3	40	16	3	8	12	18	33	58	49	48
10	Swindon Town	46	12	7	4	40	22	4	9	10	27	38	67	60	48
11	Shrewsbury Town	46	11	7	5	42	23	5	8	10	21	34	63	57	47
12	Tranmere Rovers	46	13	7	3	39	19	3	8	12	18	33	57	52	47
13	Carlisle United	46	10	9	4	32	26	4	10	9	27	33	59	59	47
14	Sheffield Wed.	46	13	7	3	28	14	2	9	12	22	38	50	52	46
15	Bury	46	7	13	3	34	22	6	6	11	28	34	62	56	45
16	*Lincoln City*	*46*	*10*	*8*	*5*	*35*	*26*	*5*	*7*	*11*	*18*	*35*	*53*	*61*	*45*
17	Exeter City	46	11	8	4	30	18	4	6	13	19	41	49	59	44
18	Oxford United	46	11	10	2	38	21	2	4	17	26	46	64	67	40
19	Plymouth Argyle	46	7	8	8	33	28	4	9	10	28	40	61	68	39
20	Rotherham United	46	11	5	7	26	19	2	8	13	25	49	51	68	39
21	Port Vale	46	7	11	5	28	23	1	9	13	18	44	46	67	36
22	Bradford City	46	11	6	6	40	29	1	4	18	16	57	56	86	34
23	Hereford United	46	9	9	5	28	22	0	5	18	6	38	34	60	32
24	Portsmouth	46	4	11	8	31	38	3	6	14	10	37	41	75	31

1978/79 Division 3

		Pl.	Home					Away					F.	A.	Pts
			W	D	L	F	A	W	D	L	F	A			
1	Shrewsbury Town	46	14	9	0	36	11	7	10	6	25	30	61	41	61
2	Watford	46	15	5	3	47	22	9	7	7	36	30	83	52	60
3	Swansea City	46	16	6	1	57	32	8	6	9	26	29	83	61	60
4	Gillingham	46	15	7	1	39	15	6	10	7	26	27	65	42	59
5	Swindon Town	46	17	2	4	44	14	8	5	10	30	38	74	52	57
6	Carlisle United	46	11	10	2	31	13	4	12	7	22	29	53	42	52
7	Colchester United	46	13	9	1	35	19	4	8	11	25	36	60	55	51
8	Hull City	46	12	9	2	36	14	7	2	14	30	47	66	61	49
9	Exeter City	46	14	6	3	38	18	3	9	11	23	38	61	56	49
10	Brentford	46	14	4	5	35	19	5	5	13	18	30	53	49	47
11	Oxford United	46	10	8	5	27	20	4	10	9	17	30	44	50	46
12	Blackpool	46	12	5	6	38	19	6	4	13	23	40	61	59	45
13	Southend United	46	11	6	6	30	17	4	9	10	21	32	51	49	45
14	Sheffield Wed.	46	9	8	6	30	22	4	11	8	23	31	53	53	45
15	Plymouth Argyle	46	11	9	3	40	27	4	5	14	27	41	67	68	44
16	Chester	46	11	9	3	42	21	3	7	13	15	40	57	61	44
17	Rotherham United	46	13	3	7	30	23	4	7	12	19	32	49	55	44
18	Mansfield Town	46	7	11	5	30	24	5	8	10	21	28	51	52	43
19	Bury	46	6	11	6	35	32	5	9	9	24	33	59	65	42
20	Chesterfield	46	10	5	8	35	34	3	9	11	16	31	51	65	40
21	Peterborough Utd.	46	8	7	8	26	24	3	7	13	18	39	44	63	36
22	Walsall	46	7	6	10	34	32	3	6	14	22	39	56	71	32
23	Tranmere Rovers	46	4	12	7	26	31	2	4	17	19	47	45	78	28
24	*Lincoln City*	*46*	*5*	*7*	*11*	*26*	*38*	*2*	*4*	*17*	*15*	*50*	*41*	*88*	*25*

1979/80 Division 4

		Pl.	Home					Away					F.	A.	Pts
			W	D	L	F	A	W	D	L	F	A			
1	Huddersfield Town	46	16	5	2	61	18	11	7	5	40	30	101	48	66
2	Walsall	46	12	9	2	43	23	11	9	3	32	24	75	47	64
3	Newport County	46	16	5	2	47	22	11	2	10	36	28	83	50	61
4	Portsmouth	46	15	5	3	62	23	9	7	7	29	26	91	49	60
5	Bradford City	46	14	6	3	44	14	10	6	7	33	36	77	50	60
6	Wigan Athletic	46	13	5	5	42	26	8	8	7	34	35	76	61	55
7	*Lincoln City*	*46*	*14*	*8*	*1*	*43*	*12*	*4*	*9*	*10*	*21*	*30*	*64*	*42*	*53*
8	Peterborough Utd.	46	14	3	6	39	22	7	7	9	19	25	58	47	52
9	Torquay United	46	13	7	3	47	25	2	10	11	23	44	70	69	47
10	Aldershot	46	10	7	6	35	23	6	6	11	27	30	62	53	45
11	Bournemouth	46	8	9	6	32	25	5	9	9	20	26	52	51	44
12	Doncaster Rovers	46	11	6	6	37	27	4	8	11	25	36	62	63	44
13	Northampton Town	46	14	5	4	33	16	2	7	14	18	50	51	66	44
14	Scunthorpe United	46	11	9	3	37	23	3	6	14	21	52	58	75	43
15	Tranmere Rovers	46	10	4	9	32	24	4	9	10	18	32	50	56	41
16	Stockport County	46	9	7	7	30	31	5	5	13	18	41	48	72	40
17	York City	46	9	6	8	35	34	5	5	13	30	48	65	82	39
18	Halifax Town	46	11	9	3	29	20	2	4	17	17	52	46	72	39
19	Hartlepool United	46	10	7	6	36	28	4	3	16	23	36	59	64	38
20	Port Vale	46	8	6	9	34	24	4	6	13	22	46	56	70	36
21	Hereford United	46	8	7	8	22	21	3	7	13	16	31	38	52	36
22	Darlington	46	7	11	5	33	26	2	6	15	17	48	50	74	35
23	Crewe Alexandra	46	10	6	7	25	27	1	7	15	10	41	35	68	35
24	Rochdale	46	6	7	10	20	28	1	6	16	13	51	33	79	27

1980/81 Division 4

		Pl.	Home					Away					F.	A.	Pts
			W	D	L	F	A	W	D	L	F	A			
1	Southend United	46	19	4	0	47	6	11	3	9	32	25	79	31	67
2	*Lincoln City*	*46*	*15*	*7*	*1*	*44*	*11*	*10*	*8*	*5*	*22*	*14*	*66*	*25*	*65*
3	Doncaster Rovers	46	15	4	4	36	20	7	8	8	23	29	59	49	56
4	Wimbledon	46	15	4	4	42	17	8	5	10	22	29	64	46	55
5	Peterborough Utd.	46	11	8	4	37	21	6	10	7	31	33	68	54	52
6	Aldershot	46	12	9	2	28	11	6	5	12	15	30	43	41	50
7	Mansfield Town	46	13	5	5	36	15	7	4	12	22	29	58	44	49
8	Darlington	46	13	6	4	43	23	6	5	12	22	36	65	59	49
9	Hartlepool United	46	14	3	6	42	22	6	6	11	22	39	64	61	49
10	Northampton Town	46	11	7	5	42	26	7	6	10	23	41	65	67	49
11	Wigan Athletic	46	13	4	6	29	16	5	7	11	22	39	51	55	47
12	Bury	46	10	8	5	38	21	7	3	13	32	41	70	62	45
13	Bournemouth	46	9	8	6	30	21	7	5	11	17	27	47	48	45
14	Bradford City	46	9	9	5	30	24	5	7	11	23	36	53	60	44
15	Rochdale	46	11	6	6	33	25	3	9	11	27	45	60	70	43
16	Scunthorpe United	46	8	12	3	40	31	3	8	12	20	38	60	69	42
17	Torquay United	46	13	2	8	38	26	5	3	15	17	37	55	63	41
18	Crewe Alexandra	46	10	7	6	28	20	3	7	13	20	41	48	61	40
19	Port Vale	46	10	8	5	40	23	2	7	14	17	47	57	70	39
20	Stockport County	46	10	5	8	29	25	6	2	15	15	32	44	57	39
21	Tranmere Rovers	46	12	5	6	41	24	1	5	17	18	49	59	73	36
22	Hereford United	46	8	8	7	29	20	3	5	15	9	42	38	62	35
23	Halifax Town	46	9	3	11	28	32	2	9	12	16	39	44	71	34
24	York City	46	10	2	11	31	23	2	7	14	16	43	47	66	33

SEASON 1973-74
DIVISION FOUR

No.	Date	Opposition	Res.	Att.	Goalscorers
1	25 Aug	SCUNTHORPE UNITED	1-0	6327	McNeil
2	1 Sep	Torquay United	1-2	2654	Smith
3	8	STOCKPORT COUNTY	1-1	4132	Cooper
4	12	PETERBOROUGH UNITED	1-1	5863	McNeil
5	15	Workington	1-1	1194	Harding
6	18	Barnsley	1-0	2778	Ward
7	22	BRADFORD CITY	0-1	4456	
8	26	Chester	3-2	2924	Smith, Symm, Branfoot
9	3 Oct	BARNSLEY	1-1	3841	Smith
10	6	BRENTFORD	3-2	4056	Ward(2), McNeil
11	13	Reading	0-0	7282	
12	20	DARLINGTON	2-1	3946	Harding, Ward
13	22	Peterborough United	0-1	9125	
14	27	Hartlepool	2-0	1898	Ward, Branfoot
15	3 Nov	NEWPORT COUNTY	3-0	4389	Spencer, Ward, Smith
16	10	Swansea City	0-3	1855	
17	13	Bury	1-2	3683	McNeil
18	17	EXETER CITY	2-1	4100	McNeil, Harding
19	1 Dec	CREWE ALEXANDRA	4-2	2443	Smith, Ward(2), Harding
20	8	Northampton Town	0-1	3464	
21	22	CHESTER	2-2	3142	McNeil(2)
22	26	Mansfield Town	3-4	4529	McNeil(3)
23	29	Stockport County	2-2	2246	McNeil, Graham
24	1 Jan	TORQUAY UNITED	3-0	5139	Worsdale, Harding(2)
25	5	Colchester United	1-4	4398	McNeil
26	12	WORKINGTON	2-0	3254	McNeil, Ward
27	19	Scunthorpe United	1-1	5624	McNeil
28	27	ROTHERHAM UNITED	2-1	6157	McNeil, Ward
29	3 Feb	GILLINGHAM	2-3	7150	Spencer, Ward
30	10	Bradford City	0-4	6510	
31	17	READING	0-2	4866	
32	23	Brentford	1-2	4171	McNeil
33	3 Mar	MANSFIELD TOWN	1-1	2615	Ward
34	9	HARTLEPOOL	0-1	1800	
35	17	Darlington	3-0	3132	McNeil, Ward, Cooper
36	23	SWANSEA CITY	2-2	2353	Ward(2)
37	27	COLCHESTER UNITED	0-1	2638	
38	30	Newport County	1-0	1908	Ward
39	2 Apr	Rotherham United	0-2	2685	
40	6	BURY	4-3	2328	McNeil, Booth(3)
41	13	Exeter City	1-0	3627	Graham
42	15	DONCASTER ROVERS	3-3	2863	Ellis, McNeil, Ward
43	16	Doncaster Rovers	0-2	2385	
44	20	NORTHAMPTON TOWN	1-1	2530	OG
45	24	Gillingham	0-2	9094	
46	27	Crewe Alexandra	1-2	1372	Worsdale

1 own goal

F.A. CUP

1R	24 Nov	Doncaster Rovers	0-1	3628	

LEAGUE CUP

1R	28 Aug	Rotherham United	1-2	3455	Symm

LINCOLNSHIRE CUP (Competition not completed)

SF	30 Apr	BOSTON UNITED	4-1	623	Ward(2), Ellis, Graham

1973-74
Back : Graham, Cooper, McNeil, Kennedy, Fleming, Leigh, Peden.
Front : Booth, Worsdale, Branfoot, Dave Smith, Ward.

1974-75
Back : Kerr (trainer), Cooper, Leigh, Branfoot, Gordon, Anthony, Krzywicki, Ellis, Loxley (physio).
Centre : Ward, McGeough, Dave Smith, Symm, Graham, Heath, Harding.   Front : Slater, Sellars, Wiggett.

SEASON 1974-75
DIVISION FOUR

No.	Date	Opposition	Res.	Att.	Goalscorers	Grotier P.D.	Branfoot I.G.	Leigh D.	Byron G.F.	Ellis S.	Cooper T.	Krzywicki R.L.	Ward J.P.	Graham P.	Booth D.	Harding A.	Smith D.	McGeough J.	Symm C.	Cliff E.	Hill K.G.	Coker A.O.	Freeman R.P.	Neale P.A.	O'Connor P.K.	Wiggett D.J.	Gordon J.S.	Anthony C.
1	17 Aug	CHESTER	2-1	2903	Branfoot, Harding	1	2	3	4*	5	6	7	8	9	10	11	12											
2	24	Crewe Alexandra	0-1	2522		1	2	3		5	6	7	8	9	4	11*	10	12										
3	31	EXETER CITY	5-0	2751	Ward, Graham(2), Smith, OG	1	2	3	12	5	6	7	8	9	4		11	10*										
4	7 Sep	Rotherham United	2-2	3681	Ward, Smith	1	2	3		5	6	7	8		4	8	11	10										
5	14	NORTHAMPTON TOWN	2-2	3113	Booth, Ward	1	2	3		5	6	7	8	9	4	11*	12	10										
6	18	SOUTHPORT	1-1	2953	Krzywicki	1	2	3		5	6	7	8	9	4		11	10										
7	21	Cambridge United	0-5	2825		1	2	3		5	6	7	8	9	4		11	10*	12									
8	24	Swansea City	2-1	1801	Graham	1	2	3		5	6	7*	8	9	4	11		10	12									
9	28	ROCHDALE	3-0	2461	Graham(2), Krzywicki	1	2	3		5	6	7	8	9	4		11	10										
10	5 Oct	BRADFORD CITY	2-1	2970	Ward(2)	1	6			5		7	8	9	2	11	10		4	3								
11	12	Brentford	1-1	4973	Harding	1	6		12	5		7*	8	9	2	11	10		4	3								
12	15	Doncaster Rovers	2-2	2034	Symm, Graham	1	2			5	6	12	8	9	4	11*	10		7	3								
13	19	WORKINGTON	3-0	3049	Ellis(2), Symm	1	2	3		5	6	7	8	9	10	12	11*		4									
14	26	Darlington	4-1	2810	Graham, Krzywicki, Branfoot, Smith	1	2	3		5	6	7	8	9	4		11	10										
15	2 Nov	Shrewsbury Town	4-0	4349	Krzywicki, Graham, Smith, Ward	1	2	3		5	6	7*	8	9	4	11	10		12									
16	8	TORQUAY UNITED	3-1	6126	Graham, Krzywicki, Harding	1	2	3		5	6	7	8	9	4	11	10											
17	13	DONCASTER ROVERS	4-0	5300	Ellis, Booth, Harding, Branfoot	1	2	3		5	6	7	8	9	4	11*	10		12									
18	16	Barnsley	2-0	4567	Ellis, Krzywicki	1	2	3		5	6	7		9	8	11	10		4									
19	6 Dec	READING	1-1	7005	Symm	1	2	3	4		6			9	8	11	10		7		5							
20	20	STOCKPORT COUNTY	2-0	5636	Ellis(2)	1	2	3		5	6	12		9	4	11	10		7*				8					
21	26	Northampton Town	0-1	7275		1	2	3		5	6	12		9	4	11	10		7*				8					
22	28	SCUNTHORPE UNITED	1-0	7883	Ellis	1	2	3	4	5	6	7		9*	10		11		12				8					
23	11 Jan	Reading	0-1	4388		1	2	3		5	6				4	11	10		7*				8	9	12			
24	17	HARTLEPOOL	2-0	5459	Coker, Harding	1	2	3		5	6	7			4*	11	10						8	9	12			
25	20	Stockport County	0-0	2040		1	2	3		5	6	7*			4	11	10						8	9	12			
26	1 Feb	Torquay United	3-1	2579	O'Connor, Freeman, Ellis	1	2			5	6	12		9	4	11	10						8	3	7*			
27	8	SHREWSBURY TOWN	3-0	8579	Branfoot, Smith, Freeman	1	2	3		5	6			12	9*	4	11	10					8		7			
28	12	Hartlepool	0-2	2632		1	2	3		5	6		8		4	11	10							9*	12	7		
29	22	BARNSLEY	3-0	6464	Freeman, Ward, Smith	1	2	3		5	6	12	8		4	11	10							9		7*		
30	25	MANSFIELD TOWN	0-0	13108		1	2	3		5	6	7		9	4	11	10							8				
31	1 Mar	Exeter City	2-1	2978	Ellis, Ward	1	2	3		5	6	7	12	9	4	11*	10							8				
32	3	Newport County	1-1	2064	Ward	1	2	3		5	6	12	8	9	4		11		7					10*				
33	8	SWANSEA CITY	1-3	6200	Ward	1	2	3		5	6	7	8	9	10		11		4									
34	15	Rochdale	1-1	1517	Ellis	1	2	3		5			8	9	4	11	10		7							6		
35	19	Chester	1-4	6975	Graham	1	2	3		5	6	11	8	9	4	12	10		7*									
36	22	ROTHERHAM UNITED	2-0	8031	Harding, Ward	1	2	3		5	6	7	8	9	4	11	10											
37	31	CAMBRIDGE UNITED	0-0	8292		1	2	3		5	6	7	8	9	4	11	10											
38	1 Apr	Scunthorpe United	1-1	6044	Harding	1	2	3		5	6	7	8	9	4	11	10											
39	5	DARLINGTON	1-1	5158	Graham	1	2	3*		5	6	7	8	9	4	11	10		12									
40	9	NEWPORT COUNTY	5-2	5613	Krzywicki, Harding(2), Ellis, Cooper	1		12	5	6	7*	8	9	2	11	10	4							3				
41	12	Bradford City	2-1	3207	Cooper, Graham	1	3			5	6		8	9	4	11	10		7					2				
42	14	Mansfield Town	1-3	14392	Ward	1	3			5	6	7	8	9	2	11	10		4									
43	19	BRENTFORD	1-1	6956	Ward	1	3			5	6	7*	8	9	4	11	10							12	2			
44	23	CREWE ALEXANDRA	0-0	7274		1	2			5	6	7	8		4	11	10							9	3			
45	26	Workington	2-0	1531	Ellis, Branfoot	1	2			5	6	7	8	9	4	11	10								3			
46	28	Southport	2-3	2310	Krzywicki, Ellis	1	2	3*		5	6	7	8	9	4	11	10							12				
					Apps.	46	42	39	3	45	43	34	34	39	46	38	43	6	16	3	1	1	6	11	6	4	1	
					Subs.				3			6	2			2	2	1	6					2	4			
					Goals		5			13	2	8	13	12	2	9	6		3				1	3		1		

1 own goal

F.A. CUP

1R	23 Nov	Port Vale	2-2	4840	OG, Krzywicki	1	2	3	12	5	6	7		9	8	11	10		4*									
1Rr	27	PORT VALE	2-0	6284	Graham, Harding	1	2	3	4	5	6	7		9	8	11	10											
2R	14 Dec	Hartlepool	0-0	2838		1	2	3	4		6			9	8	11	10		7		5							
2Rr	17	HARTLEPOOL	1-0	4985	Cooper	1	2	3	4	5	6			9	8	11	10		7									
3R	4 Jan	Swindon Town	0-2	11791		1	2	3		5	6	9*			4	11	10		7				8		12			

LEAGUE CUP

1R	20 Aug	Rotherham United	1-1	2725	Ellis	1	2	3		5	6	7	8*	9	4	11	10	12										
1Rr	28	ROTHERHAM UNITED	1-1 *	3254	Smith	1	2	3		5	6	7	8	9	4		11	10										
1R2r	3 Sep	Rotherham United	1-2	3664	Ellis	1	2	3		5	6	7	8	9*	4	12	11	10										

* after extra time

LINCOLNSHIRE CUP

SF	17 Feb	Boston United	3-0	1300	Ward, Krzywicki, Harding		6	3	10		5	9	8			11			4						7		1	2
F	29 Apr	GRIMSBY TOWN	2-0	2311	Ward, Freeman	1	2	3		5	6	7	8	9	4*	11	10							12				

SEASON 1975-76
DIVISION FOUR

No.	Date	Opposition	Res.	Att.	Goalscorers	Grotier P.D.	Branfoot I.G.	Leigh D.	Fleming J.J.	Cooper T.	Wiggett D.J.	Krzywicki R.L.	Freeman R.P.	Graham P.	Smith D.	Harding A.	Ward J.P.	Ellis S.	Neale P.A.	Booth D.	Sellars P.	Bowery B.N.	Woodcock A.S.	Gordon J.S.
1	16 Aug	Newport County	1-3	2830	Freeman	1	2	3	4*	5	6	7	8	9	10	11	12							
2	22	TORQUAY UNITED	4-2	4128	Ward, Fleming, Branfoot, Freeman	1	2	3	4	6		7	12	9*	10	11	8	5						
3	30	Hartlepool	2-2	1908	Smith, Fleming	1	6	3	7				12	9*	10	11	8	5	2	4				
4	6 Sep	READING	3-1	4327	Ellis, Harding, Graham	1	2	3	7*	6			9	12	10	11	8	5		4				
5	13	Huddersfield Town	1-0	5209	Fleming	1	2	3	7	6			9		10	11	8	5		4				
6	20	EXETER CITY	4-1	5088	Freeman, Ward(2), Cooper	1	2	3	7	6			9	12	10	11*	8	5		4				
7	24	Southport	2-1	871	Ward, Freeman	1	2	3	7	6			9	12	10	11*	8	5		4				
8	27	Darlington	0-0	2580		1	2	3	7	6			9*	12	10	11	8	5		4				
9	4 Oct	SWANSEA CITY	4-0	5323	Freeman, Smith, Ward(2)	1	2	3	7	6			9	12	10*	11	8	5		4				
10	11	BRENTFORD	3-1	6312	Ward(2), Ellis	1	2	3	7	6		12	10*	9	11		8	5		4				
11	18	Northampton Town	0-1	6566		1	2	3	4	6		7	9	12	11		8*	5		10				
12	21	Cambridge United	4-2	3330	Graham, Freeman(2), Ward	1	2	3	7	6				10	9	11	8	5		4				
13	25	AFC BOURNEMOUTH	1-0	7431	Ellis	1	2	3	7	6		12	10	9*	11		8	5		4				
14	1 Nov	Crewe Alexandra	3-2	2707	Graham(3)	1	2		7	6				9	10	11	8	5	3	4				
15	4	TRANMERE ROVERS	2-2	11026	Graham, Ward	1	2		7*	6			12	9	10	11	8	5	3	4				
16	8	ROCHDALE	2-0	7063	Krzywicki, Graham	1	2	3	10	6		7	12	9		11	8*	5		4				
17	15	Workington	3-0	1237	Freeman, Graham, Fleming	1	2	3	7	6			8	9	10	11		5		4				
18	28	SCUNTHORPE UNITED	3-0	8494	Freeman(2), Graham	1	2	3		6		7	8	9	10	11	12	5*		4				
19	6 Dec	Watford	3-1	4178	Harding, Graham(2)	1	5	3*	7	6			8	9	10	11	12		2	4				
20	20	BRADFORD CITY	4-2	6780	Harding(2), Ward, Ellis	1	2		7	6			8*	9	10	11	12	5	3	4				
21	26	Doncaster Rovers	4-2	14353	Freeman(2), Ward(2)	1	2	3	7	6			9		10	11	8	5		4				
22	27	BARNSLEY	2-1	12074	Ellis, Cooper	1	2	3	7	6		11	9		10		8	5		4				
23	10 Jan	HARTLEPOOL	3-0	7581	Smith, Ellis, Ward	1	2	3	7	6		11	9		10		8	5		4				
24	17	Exeter City	0-0	3858		1	2	3	7	6		11	9		10		8	5		4				
25	31	CAMBRIDGE UNITED	3-0	7440	Ward, Freeman, Fleming	1	2	3	7	6		11	9		10		8	5		4				
26	6 Feb	Tranmere Rovers	0-2	4869		1	2	3	7	6		11	9		10		8	5		4				
27	14	Rochdale	0-0	2439		1	2	3		6		7	9		10	11	8	5		4				
28	21	WORKINGTON	4-1	7069	Neale, OG, Ward, Freeman	1	2	3		6*		7	9		10	11	8	5	4		12			
29	25	SOUTHPORT	6-0	8080	Ellis,Neale(2),Bowery,Woodcock,Ward	1	2	3	12	6					10		8	5	7	4*		9	11	
30	6 Mar	CREWE ALEXANDRA	2-0	7211	Ward, Smith	1	2	3		6					10	11	8	5	7*	4		9		
31	9	Swansea City	2-2	3908	Branfoot, Ward	1	2	3		6		9			10	11	8	5	7*	4		12		
32	13	Brentford	0-1	5386		1	2*	3		6					10	11	8	5	7	4		12	9	
33	17	NORTHAMPTON TOWN	3-1	13880	Fleming, Krzywicki, Smith	1	2		7	6		9*			10	11	8	5	3	4			12	
34	20	Scunthorpe United	2-0	10322	Ellis, Ward	1	2		7	6		9*			10	11	8	5	3	4			12	
35	23	HUDDERSFIELD TOWN	0-0	11290		1	2		7	6		9*	12		10	11	8	5	3	4				
36	26	WATFORD	5-1	8798	Freeman(2),Fleming,Branfoot,Smith	1	2		7	6			12	9	10	11	8*	5	3	4				
37	31	Bradford City	5-1	4019	Harding, Ellis, Freeman(2), Neale	1	2		7	6			12	9*	10	11	8	5	3	4				
38	3 Apr	NEWPORT COUNTY	4-1	8178	Ward(2), Harding, Fleming	1	2		7	6				9	10	11	8	5	3	4				
39	7	DARLINGTON	2-1	10655	Booth, Smith	1	2		7	6				9	10	11	8	5	3	4				
40	10	Reading	1-1	15900	Ward	1	2		7	6				9	10	11	8	5	3	4				
41	12	Stockport County	3-0	3703	Krzywicki, Harding, Smith	1	2		7	6				9	10	11	8	5	3	4				
42	16	STOCKPORT COUNTY	2-0	10906	Freeman, Ellis	1	2		7	6		12	9	4	10	11	8	5	3*					
43	17	DONCASTER ROVERS	5-0	14096	Branfoot,Freeman(2), Harding,Ellis	1	2		7	6				9	10	11	8	5	3	4				
44	19	Barnsley	1-0	8697	Freeman	1	2		7	6			12	9	10	11	8*	5	3	4				
45	24	Torquay United	2-2	4364	Ellis, Freeman	1	2		7	6	3		12	9	10	11	8	5		4*				
46	26	AFC Bournemouth	1-1	4284	Ward	1	2		7*	6	3	12	9		10	11	8	5		4				
					Apps.	46	46	29	39	45	3	21	30	13	45	36	41	44	22	42	0	2	2	
					Subs.				1			1	7	5		6			4			1	2	2
					Goals		4		8	2		3	23	11	8	8	24	12	4	1		1	1	

1 own goal

F.A. CUP

1R	22 Nov	Boston United	1-0	6500	Freeman	1	2	3	7	6			8	9	10	11*	12	5		4				
2R	13 Dec	Mansfield Town	2-1	8466	Branfoot, Freeman		2		7	6			10	9	11		8	5	3	4				1
3R	3 Jan	Aldershot	2-1	6825	Ward, Ellis	1	2	3	7	6		11	9		10		8	5		4				
4R	24	West Bromwich Albion	2-3	26388	Ellis, Fleming	1	2	3	7	6		11	9		10*		8	5	12	4				

LEAGUE CUP

1R1L	20 Aug	CHESTERFIELD	4-2	4168	Ward(4)	1	5	3	4	6		7		9	10	11	8		2					
1R2L	25	Chesterfield	2-3	4286	Graham, Ellis	1	6	3	7				8	9	10	11		5	2	4				
2R	10 Sep	STOKE CITY	2-1	13472	Harding, Booth	1	2	3	7	6				9		10	11	8	5		4			
3R	8 Oct	Leicester City	1-2	17063	Smith	1	2	3	7	6				9	10	11	8	5		4				

LINCOLNSHIRE CUP

SF	2 Aug	Grimsby Town	2-3	1800	Fleming, Krzywicki	1	2	3	4	5	6	7		9	10	11	8							

1975-76
Back : Krzywicki, Gordon, Loxley (physio), Grotier, Wiggett.
Centre : Taylor (manager), Cooper, Ellis, Branfoot, Guest, Leigh, Ward,
Freeman, Kerr (assistant manager). Front : Dave Smith, Graham, Booth, Fleming, Sellars, Harding.

1976-77
Back : Graham, Branfoot, Ellis, Tony Loxley, Cooper.
Second Row: Taylor (manager), Guest, Freeman, Grotier, Gordon, Ward, Krzywicki, Kerr (trainer/coach).
Third Row : Fleming, Leigh, Wiggett, Dave Smith, Booth, Gallagher. Front : Potts, Sellars, Cox.

SEASON 1976-77
DIVISION THREE

No.	Date	Opposition	Res.	Att.	Goalscorers	Grotier P.D.	Branfoot I.G.	Leigh D.	Booth D.	Bolton I.R.	Cooper T.	Hubbard P.J.	Ward J.P.	Freeman R.P.	Smith D.	Harding A.	Graham P.	Neale P.A.	Ellis S.	Fleming J.J.	Guest B.J.	Cockerill G.	Crombie D.M.	Gordon J.S.	Cox M.L.	Gallagher J.C.	Krzywicki R.L.
1	21 Aug	SHREWSBURY TOWN	1-1	6372	Cooper	1	2	3	4	5	6	7*	8	9	10	11	12										
2	28	Northampton Town	0-1	6350		1			4		6	7	8*	9	10	11		3	5	12							
3	4 Sep	PORT VALE	2-0	6059	Ellis(2)	1	2		4		6		8	9	10	11		3	5	7							
4	11	Portsmouth	1-1	7865	Ward	1	2		4		6		8	9	10	11		3	5	7							
5	14	Walsall	3-1	5356	OG, Ward, Freeman	1	2		4		6		8	9	10	11		3	5	7							
6	18	SWINDON TOWN	0-0	7679		1	2		4		6	12	8	9	10	11		3	5	7*							
7	25	Chesterfield	4-1	4426	Booth, Freeman, Ward(2)	1	2		4		6	12	8	9	10	11*		3	5	7							
8	2 Oct	SHEFFIELD WEDNESDAY	1-1	14706	Freeman	1	2		4*		6	12	8	9	10	11		3	5	7							
9	9	Wrexham	0-3	7753		1	2		4		6	7	8	9	10*	11	12	3	5								
10	16	Gillingham	1-0	6053	Ward	1	2		4		6	7	8	9	10			3	5	11							
11	23	READING	3-1	6502	Cooper, Ward(2)	1	2		4		6	7	8	9	10	12		3	5	11*							
12	26	Oxford United	2-1	5199	Ward, Freeman	1	2		4		6	12	8	9	10	11		3	5	7*							
13	29	ROTHERHAM UNITED	2-2	9318	Freeman, Hubbard	1	2		4		6	7	8	9	10	11		3	5								
14	3 Nov	BURY	2-3	6869	Hubbard, Smith	1	2		4		6	7	8	9	10	11		3	5								
15	6	Mansfield Town	1-3	8232	Smith	1	2		4		6	7	8	9	10	11		3	5								
16	13	TRANMERE ROVERS	2-2	6407	Freeman(2)	1	2		4		6	7		8	10	11	9	3	5								
17	27	Preston North End	0-3	7964		1	2		4*		6	7	8		10		12	3	5	11						.	
18	27 Dec	GRIMSBY TOWN	2-0	11645	Graham, Ward	1			4		6	7	8		10	11	9	3	5		2						
19	18 Jan	WALSALL	4-1	5223	Harding, Hubbard(2), Smith	1			4		6	7	8	9*	10	11		3	5	12	2						
20	22	Shrewsbury Town	1-2	5074	Ellis	1		12	4		6	7	8*		10	11	9	3	5		2						
21	29	Brighton & Hove Albion	0-4	18632		1	2	12	4		6	7	8		10	11	9*	3	5								
22	5 Feb	NORTHAMPTON TOWN	5-4	5869	Hubbard(2), Ellis, Graham(2)	1	6		4			7	8*		10	11	9	3	5		2	12					
23	15	MANSFIELD TOWN	3-2	9588	Guest, Cooper, Graham	1			4		6	7	8		10	11	9	3	5		2						
24	22	York City	2-2	2953	Ward, OG	1	2		4		6	7	8	12	10	11	9*	3	5								
25	26	Swindon Town	2-2	8862	Harding, Freeman	1	2		4		6	7	8	9	10	11		3	5								
26	2 Mar	CRYSTAL PALACE	3-2	8288	Ward, Graham, Smith	1	2		4		6	7	8	9*	10	11	12	3	5								
27	5	CHESTERFIELD	3-2	7193	Graham(2), Ellis	1	2		4		6		8		10	11	9	3	5	7							
28	8	Rotherham United	0-1	10045		1	2		4		6		8	9	10	11		3	5	7	12						
29	12	Sheffield Wednesday	1-1	15047	Hubbard	1	2		4		6	8			10	11	9	3	5	7							
30	15	PORTSMOUTH	2-1	4648	Booth, Hubbard	1	2		4		6	8			10	11	9	3	5	7							
31	18	WREXHAM	1-1	7753	Hubbard	1	2		4		6*	7	8		10	11	9	3	5	12							
32	21	Port Vale	0-1	3987		1	6		4*			7	8	12	10	11	9	3	5		2						
33	26	GILLINGHAM	4-0	5126	Graham, Leigh, Ward(2)	1	2	3	4			7	8			11	9		10	5			6				
34	29	CHESTER	3-3	5567	Graham(2), Ward	1		3	4			7	8		10	11	9	2	5				6				
35	2 Apr	Reading	2-1	4417	Leigh, OG	1		3	4			7	8		10*	11	9	2	5	12			6				
36	8	Grimsby Town	2-1	8725	Ellis(2)	1		3	4			7	8		10	11	9*	2	5	12			6				
37	9	YORK CITY	2-0	6920	Graham, Smith	1	2	3				4*	8	12	10	11	9		5	7			6				
38	11	Bury	0-3	5676		1		3	4			12	8		10	11	9*	2	5	7			6				
39	16	OXFORD UNITED	0-1	4963		1		3	4			12	8		10*	11	9	2	5	7			6				
40	20	BRIGHTON & HOVE ALBION	2-2	7512	Harding, Ward	1	2	3	4			7	8		10	11	9	6	5								
41	23	Tranmere Rovers	2-2	2290	Hubbard, Neale	1		3	4	5		7	9			11		10		12	2	8*	6				
42	26	Peterborough United	2-1	4974	Graham, Harding	1		3	4	5		7	8			11	9	10			2		6				
43	30	PRESTON NORTH END	2-0	5357	Graham, Ward			3	4	5		7	8			11	9	10			2		6	1			
44	3 May	Chester	0-1	1964				3	4	5		7	8*		11	12	9				2	10	6	1			
45	7	Crystal Palace	1-4	18370	Harding	1		3	4	5*		7	8		10	11	9				2		6		12		
46	11	PETERBOROUGH UNITED	1-1	5081	Harding		5	3	4			12	8			11	9*			7	2		6				10
					Apps.	44	32	15	45	1	35	34	43	21	41	42	25	41	39	18	12	2	13	2	0	1	
					Subs.			2				7		3			2		4			6			2		1
					Goals			2	2		3	10	16	8	5	6	13	1	7		1						

3 own goals

F.A. CUP

1R	20 Nov	MORECAMBE	1-0	6111	Freeman	1	2		4		6	7*	12	8	10			9	3	5	11						
2R	11 Dec	NUNEATON BOROUGH	6-0	7058	Harding,Ellis(3),Ward,Graham(2)	1			4		6	7	8		10	11	9	3	5		2						
3R	8 Jan	Burnley	2-2	11583	Ward, Harding	1			4		6	7	8		10	11		3	5								
3Rr	12	BURNLEY	0-1	11414		1			4		6	7	8*	9	10	11		3	5	12	2						

LEAGUE CUP

1R1L	14 Aug	Doncaster Rovers	1-1	5594	Graham		2	3		5	6		8	10	11	9			4			1				7
1R2L	18	DONCASTER ROVERS	1-1	7089	Graham	1	2	3	12	5	6	7*		8	10	11	9		4								
1R2Lr	24	Doncaster Rovers	2-2 *	3726	Ellis, Hubbard	1	2	3	4*		6	7	8	9	10	11			5								12

* Played at City Ground, Nottingham, after extra time. Lost 2-3 on penalties.

LINCOLNSHIRE CUP

G	31 Jul	Grimsby Town	2-1	2083	Branfoot, Grotier	1	5	3	4		6		8		10	11	9*			7	2						12
G	3 Aug	Scunthorpe United	2-1	2038	Ward, Grotier	1	5		4*		6		8	9	10	11				7	2						12
F	22 Sep	Boston United	1-3	2200	Ward	1	2	3	4		6		8		10	11	9		5								7

SEASON 1977-78
DIVISION THREE

No.	Date	Opposition	Res.	Att.	Goalscorers
1	20 Aug	Bury	0-1	4160	
2	24	WALSALL	2-2	3723	Ward(2)
3	26	SHREWSBURY TOWN	1-3	4714	Ward
4	3 Sep	Port Vale	1-2	3520	Harding
5	10	PETERBOROUGH UNITED	0-1	4898	
6	14	Oxford United	0-1	4416	
7	17	Portsmouth	2-0	11370	Graham, OG
8	23	CHESTERFIELD	1-0	6290	Graham
9	28	HEREFORD UNITED	0-0	4973	
10	1 Oct	Wrexham	0-1	5939	
11	4	Carlisle United	3-2	4041	Fleming(2), Harding
12	8	SWINDON TOWN	3-1	4852	Graham, Hubbard, Booth
13	15	EXETER CITY	1-2	4804	Graham
14	22	Sheffield Wednesday	0-2	13303	
15	29	Rotherham United	0-0	5088	
16	5 Nov	CHESTER	2-1	4270	Jones, Graham
17	12	Cambridge United	0-5	4834	
18	19	PRESTON NORTH END	2-2	3924	Harding, Graham
19	3 Dec	Bradford City	2-2	3203	Cockerill, D.Smith
20	10	GILLINGHAM	0-2	3902	
21	26	Colchester United	1-1	5840	Graham
22	27	TRANMERE ROVERS	1-1	6463	Leigh
23	31	Chester	2-2	3525	Harford, Neale
24	2 Jan	PLYMOUTH ARGYLE	2-2	6262	OG, Neale
25	14	BURY	0-0	4274	
26	21	Shrewsbury Town	1-1	3385	Graham
27	28	PORT VALE	3-0	3205	Cooper, Harford(2)
28	4 Feb	Peterborough United	1-0	5662	Harding
29	7	Walsall	1-3	5082	Jones
30	11	PORTSMOUTH	1-0	4100	Jones
31	24	WREXHAM	0-1	6060	
32	1 Mar	Chesterfield	0-0	4556	
33	4	Swindon Town	0-1	7149	
34	8	OXFORD UNITED	1-0	3888	Hubbard
35	11	Exeter City	0-3	4280	
36	13	Plymouth Argyle	2-1	5208	Wigginton, Harding
37	18	SHEFFIELD WEDNESDAY	3-1	8811	Harford, Wigginton, Jones
38	24	ROTHERHAM UNITED	3-3	5795	Harford(2), Hoult
39	25	Tranmere Rovers	1-3	2587	Cooper
40	27	COLCHESTER UNITED	0-0	4709	
41	5 Apr	Hereford United	1-1	3974	Wigginton
42	8	CAMBRIDGE UNITED	4-1	4783	Harford(2), Hobson, Graham
43	15	Preston North End	0-4	11208	
44	22	BRADFORD CITY	3-2	4121	Wigginton, Neale, Fleming
45	26	CARLISLE UNITED	2-1	3384	Harford, Hobson
46	29	Gillingham	0-0	5481	

2 own goals

F.A. CUP

Round	Date	Opposition	Res.	Att.	Goalscorers
1R	26 Nov	Preston North End	2-3	6965	Harding, Wigginton

LEAGUE CUP

Round	Date	Opposition	Res.	Att.	Goalscorers
1R1L	13 Aug	Mansfield Town	1-0	6735	Ward
1R2L	17	MANSFIELD TOWN	0-0	5761	
2R	30	Bolton Wanderers	0-1	11467	

LINCOLNSHIRE CUP

Round	Date	Opposition	Res.	Att.	Goalscorers
G	30 Jul	Grimsby Town	2-2	1059	Graham(2)
G	2 Aug	Scunthorpe United	1-1	1231	Grotier

1977-78
Back : Cooper, Hubbard, Chris Smith, Mick Smith, Cordon, Grotier, Gallagher, Stephen Ward, Branfoot.(coach).
Centre: Bert Loxley (physio), Burrows, Cockerill, Graham, Tony Loxley, Crombie, John Ward, Harford, Worth(coach).
Front : Laybourne, Cox, Guest, Dave Smith, Kerr (manager), Booth, Leigh, Fleming, Harding.

1978-79
Back : Eden, Wright, Laybourne, Cockerill, Harding, Hubbard.
Centre : Bert Loxley (physio), Cooper, Harford, Wigginton, Fox, Grotier, Ward, Guest, Branfoot (coach).
Front : Sunley, Hobson, Leigh, Jones, Bell (manager), Fleming, Tony Loxley, Hughes, Mick Smith.

SEASON 1978-79
DIVISION THREE

No.	Date	Opposition	Res.	Att.	Goalscorers
1	19 Aug	TRANMERE ROVERS	2-1	2835	Hobson, Sunley
2	22	Swansea City	0-3	17085	
3	26	Plymouth Argyle	1-2	7806	Harding
4	2 Sep	SHEFFIELD WEDNESDAY	1-2	7007	Cooper
5	9	Rotherham United	0-2	4427	
6	13	Watford	0-5	5924	
7	16	CARLISLE UNITED	1-1	2577	Cockerill
8	23	Shrewsbury Town	0-2	2902	
9	25	Brentford	1-2	6107	Cockerill
10	29	WALSALL	1-1	3071	Ward
11	7 Oct	Blackpool	0-2	7080	
12	13	COLCHESTER UNITED	0-0	3541	
13	17	Gillingham	2-4	5783	Wigginton, Leigh
14	21	SWINDON TOWN	0-2	2932	
15	27	Southend United	0-2	7601	
16	4 Nov	MANSFIELD TOWN	0-1	3644	
17	11	Sheffield Wednesday	0-0	12740	
18	18	PLYMOUTH ARGYLE	3-3	3444	Fleming(2), Hobson
19	9 Dec	OXFORD UNITED	2-2	2996	Tynan, Wigginton
20	23	CHESTERFIELD	0-1	2991	
21	26	Peterborough United	1-0	4592	Watson
22	30	Exeter City	2-3	3810	Hobson, Cockerill
23	6 Jan	Watford	0-2	12142	
24	20	Carlisle United	0-2	3892	
25	23	Colchester United	0-2	2861	
26	3 Mar	Swindon Town	0-6	6856	
27	7	Chester	1-5	2745	Sunley
28	10	SOUTHEND UNITED	1-1	2558	Fleming
29	13	Walsall	1-4	2794	Harford
30	21	BRENTFORD	1-0	2060	Ward
31	24	SWANSEA CITY	2-1	3568	Harford, Fleming
32	26	Tranmere Rovers	0-0	1222	
33	31	Hull City	0-0	4103	
34	4 Apr	ROTHERHAM UNITED	3-0	3347	Sunley, Cockerill, Ward
35	7	CHESTER	0-0	3489	
36	14	PETERBOROUGH UNITED	0-1	4610	
37	16	Bury	2-2	3455	Laybourne, Fleming
38	17	Chesterfield	3-1	3364	Neale, Cockerill(2)
39	21	EXETER CITY	0-1	2673	
40	25	GILLINGHAM	2-4	1864	Sunley, Fleming
41	28	Oxford United	1-2	3497	Harford
42	2 May	SHREWSBURY TOWN	1-2	1685	Harford
43	5	HULL CITY	4-2	2532	Watson, Hobson(2), Harford
44	7	BLACKPOOL	1-2	1949	Harford
45	9	BURY	1-4	1571	Harford
46	11	Mansfield Town	0-2	4386	

F.A. CUP

1R	25 Nov	Blackpool	1-2	4375	Ward

LEAGUE CUP

1R1L	12 Aug	Bradford City	0-2	4980	
1R2L	16	BRADFORD CITY	1-1	3806	Hughes

LINCOLNSHIRE CUP

G	29 Jul	SCUNTHORPE UNITED	2-1	1229	Sunley, Harford
G	5 Aug	Grimsby Town	1-0	1518	Hubbard
F	4 Oct	Boston United	0-2	2500	

SEASON 1979-80
DIVISION FOUR

No.	Date	Opposition	Res.	Att.	Goalscorers
1	18 Aug	PETERBOROUGH UNITED	0-1	4801	
2	22	Crewe Alexandra	2-0	2238	Harford, Cunningham
3	25	York City	2-0	2716	Carr, Hobson
4	1 Sep	HUDDERSFIELD TOWN	2-0	4381	Harford(2)
5	8	Bradford City	1-1	5298	Cockerill
6	15	DONCASTER ROVERS	1-1	4834	Hobson
7	18	Walsall	0-3	5193	
8	22	TRANMERE ROVERS	3-0	3357	Cunningham, Guest, Hobson
9	29	Newport County	1-1	4042	Harford
10	3 Oct	WALSALL	2-2	4275	Carr, Hobson
11	6	Port Vale	2-1	3127	Harford, Hobson
12	10	CREWE ALEXANDRA	3-0	3411	Sunley, Cockerill, Harford
13	13	SCUNTHORPE UNITED	4-0	5011	Cockerill, OG, Sunley, Harford
14	20	Wigan Athletic	1-2	5454	OG
15	23	Aldershot	0-2	3945	
16	27	STOCKPORT COUNTY	1-0	3786	Harford
17	3 Nov	Peterborough United	1-3	4681	Saunders
18	10	AFC BOURNEMOUTH	1-1	3548	Cunningham
19	17	Portsmouth	0-4	14620	
20	30	HARTLEPOOL UNITED	3-3	3526	Bell, Harford, Hobson
21	8 Dec	Halifax Town	0-1	1991	
22	29	YORK CITY	1-1	3577	Bell
23	12 Jan	Huddersfield Town	2-3	8108	Harford, Cunningham
24	26	TORQUAY UNITED	2-0	3489	Cunningham, Hobson
25	30	BRADFORD CITY	1-0	3875	OG
26	2 Feb	Doncaster Rovers	1-1	3627	Harford
27	6	HEREFORD UNITED	2-0	2978	Keeley, Cunningham
28	9	Tranmere Rovers	0-1	2021	
29	13	NORTHAMPTON TOWN	0-0	3652	
30	16	NEWPORT COUNTY	2-1	3422	Bell, Ramsay
31	23	Scunthorpe United	0-1	3838	
32	29	WIGAN ATHLETIC	4-0	3820	Harford(3), Bell
33	4 Mar	Darlington	1-1	1935	Keeley
34	8	Stockport County	1-2	2536	Cunningham
35	11	Rochdale	1-1	1108	Keeley
36	15	PORT VALE	3-0	2969	Cunningham(2), Bell
37	19	ALDERSHOT	1-1	2440	Peake
38	22	AFC Bournemouth	0-0	2674	
39	29	PORTSMOUTH	1-0	4839	Turner
40	2 Apr	Hereford United	0-0	2773	
41	5	ROCHDALE	0-0	3635	
42	7	Northampton Town	0-0	3371	
43	12	DARLINGTON	2-1	2994	Cunningham, Ramsay
44	19	Hartlepool United	0-0	1706	
45	25	HALIFAX TOWN	4-0	2772	Shipley(2), Cunningham, Harford
46	3 May	Torquay United	5-2	2010	Cunningham, Hobson(3), Harford

3 own goals

F.A. CUP

1R	24 Nov	Sheffield Wednesday	0-3	11226	

LEAGUE CUP

1R1L	11 Aug	BARNSLEY	2-1	6733	Peake, Cunningham
1R2L	14	Barnsley	1-2 *	11914	Cunningham

* after extra time, lost 3-4 on penalties

LINCOLNSHIRE CUP

G	22 Jul	Scunthorpe United	1-2	937	Cunningham
G	6 Aug	GRIMSBY TOWN	0-0	1662	

1979-80
Back : Tony Loxley, Cockerill, Mick Smith, Saunders, Harford.
Centre : Grotier, Lawrence (coach), Fleming, Sunley, Ward, Hughes, Watson, Sheridan (coach), Fox.
Front : Lyons, Carr, Hobson, Laybourne, Bert Loxley (physio), Cunningham,
Murphy (manager), Peake, Wright, Guest, Burrows.

1980-81
Back : Bell, Ward, Creane, Cunningham, Saunders, Steve Thompson, Hibberd, Travis.
Second Row : Lawrence (coach), Naylor, Harford, Keeley, Boulton, Biggins, Peake, Fox, Loxley (physio).
Third Row : Burrows, Trevor Thompson, Turner, Ramsay, Sheridan (coach), Murphy (manager),
Hobson, Shipley, Hughes, Carr.   Front : McLauchlan, Gilbert,

SEASON 1980-81
DIVISION FOUR

No.	Date	Opposition	Res.	Att.	Goalscorers
1	16 Aug	PETERBOROUGH UNITED	1-1	5189	Harford
2	20	Torquay United	2-1	3683	Harford(2)
3	23	WIGAN ATHLETIC	2-0	3921	Hobson, Cunningham
4	30	Crewe Alexandra	3-0	2121	Hobson(2), OG
5	6 Sep	HALIFAX TOWN	3-0	3802	Hobson(2), S.Thompson
6	13	Stockport County	0-0	3289	
7	17	ALDERSHOT	0-1	4446	
8	20	Wimbledon	1-0	2380	Hobson
9	27	SCUNTHORPE UNITED	2-2	4336	Harford, Hughes
10	30	Aldershot	0-0	4970	
11	4 Oct	Doncaster Rovers	1-0	9693	Hobson
12	8	ROCHDALE	3-0	3641	Neale, Hobson, Peake
13	11	YORK CITY	1-1	4144	Hobson
14	18	Hartlepool United	0-2	2712	
15	22	Bradford City	2-1	2832	Harford, Neale
16	25	NORTHAMPTON TOWN	8-0	4060	Hobson(4), Harford(2), Shipley(2)
17	29	TRANMERE ROVERS	2-0	4657	Neale, J.T.Thompson
18	1 Nov	Hereford United	2-0	2755	Neale(2)
19	4	Rochdale	0-1	2257	
20	8	SOUTHEND UNITED	2-1	7237	Neale, Hobson
21	12	TORQUAY UNITED	5-0	5086	Harford(3), Neale, Shipley
22	15	Peterborough United	0-1	5817	
23	6 Dec	BURY	2-1	3564	Turner, Neale
24	20	AFC BOURNEMOUTH	2-0	3458	Hobson, Shipley
25	26	Port Vale	1-0	4239	Turner
26	27	MANSFIELD TOWN	1-1	8535	Carr
27	10 Jan	BRADFORD CITY	1-1	4731	Turner
28	24	CREWE ALEXANDRA	2-1	4917	Neale, S.Thompson
29	31	Wigan Athletic	2-0	5190	Cunningham, Turner
30	7 Feb	STOCKPORT COUNTY	1-0	4434	Cunningham
31	14	Halifax Town	3-1	4444	Hobson(2), Shipley
32	21	Scunthorpe United	2-2	5032	Hobson(2)
33	28	WIMBLEDON	0-0	4019	
34	3 Mar	Tranmere Rovers	0-0	1535	
35	7	DONCASTER ROVERS	1-1	8832	Cunningham
36	10	Darlington	0-0	2076	
37	14	York City	0-1	2222	
38	21	HARTLEPOOL UNITED	2-0	3969	Biggins, Shipley
39	28	Northampton Town	1-1	2424	Hobson
40	4 Apr	HEREFORD UNITED	1-0	3799	Hobson
41	11	Southend United	0-0	12391	
42	18	Mansfield Town	0-2	4771	
43	20	PORT VALE	1-0	3784	Cunningham
44	25	AFC Bournemouth	1-0	3542	Shipley
45	2 May	DARLINGTON	1-0	3888	Cunningham
46	4	Bury	1-1	2968	Shipley

1 own goal

F.A. CUP

Rd	Date	Opposition	Res.	Att.	Goalscorers
1R	22 Nov	GATESHEAD	1-0	4543	Turner
2R	13 Dec	Bury	0-2	3375	

LEAGUE CUP

Rd	Date	Opposition	Res.	Att.	Goalscorers
1R1L	9 Aug	HULL CITY	5-0	3538	Harford(3), Bell, Shipley
1R2L	12	Hull City	2-0	2933	Harford(2)
2R1L	27	SWINDON TOWN	1-1	4940	Shipley
2R2L	2 Sep	Swindon Town	0-2	4907	

LINCOLNSHIRE CUP

Rd	Date	Opposition	Res.	Att.	Goalscorers
G	29 Jul	GRIMSBY TOWN	1-0	1365	Cunningham
G	2 Aug	SCUNTHORPE UNITED	2-1	1156	Harford, Cunningham
F	14 Oct	GRANTHAM TOWN	3-0	734	Peake, Hobson, Shipley

Final League Tables 1981/82 to 1988/89

1981/82 Division 3

		Pl.	Home					Away					F.	A.	Pts
			W	D	L	F	A	W	D	L	F	A			
1	Burnley	46	13	7	3	37	20	8	10	5	29	25	66	45	80
2	Carlisle United	46	17	4	2	44	21	6	7	10	21	29	65	50	80
3	Fulham	46	12	9	2	44	22	9	6	8	33	29	77	51	78
4	*Lincoln City*	*46*	*13*	*7*	*3*	*40*	*16*	*8*	*7*	*8*	*26*	*24*	*66*	*40*	*77*
5	Oxford United	46	10	8	5	28	18	9	6	8	35	31	63	49	71
6	Gillingham	46	14	5	4	44	26	6	6	11	20	30	64	56	71
7	Southend United	46	11	7	5	35	23	7	8	8	28	28	63	51	69
8	Brentford	46	8	6	9	28	22	11	5	7	28	25	56	47	68
9	Millwall	46	12	4	7	36	28	6	9	8	26	34	62	62	67
10	Plymouth Argyle	46	12	5	6	37	24	6	6	11	27	32	64	56	65
11	Chesterfield	46	12	4	7	33	27	6	6	11	24	31	57	58	64
12	Reading	46	11	6	6	43	35	6	5	12	24	40	67	75	62
13	Portsmouth	46	11	10	2	33	14	3	9	11	23	37	56	51	61
14	Preston North End	46	10	7	6	25	22	6	6	11	25	34	50	56	61
15	Bristol Rovers	46	12	4	7	35	28	6	5	12	23	37	58	65	61
16	Newport County	46	9	10	4	28	21	5	6	12	26	33	54	54	58
17	Huddersfield Town	46	10	5	8	38	25	5	7	11	26	34	64	59	57
18	Exeter City	46	14	4	5	46	33	2	5	16	25	51	71	84	57
19	Doncaster Rovers	46	9	9	5	31	24	4	8	11	24	44	55	68	56
20	Walsall	46	10	7	6	32	23	3	7	13	19	32	51	55	53
21	Wimbledon	46	10	6	7	33	27	4	5	14	28	48	61	75	53
22	Swindon Town	46	9	5	9	37	36	4	8	11	18	35	55	71	52
23	Bristol City	46	7	6	10	24	29	4	7	12	16	36	40	65	46
24	Chester	46	2	10	11	16	30	5	1	17	20	48	36	78	32

1982/83 Division 3

		Pl.	Home					Away					F.	A.	Pts
			W	D	L	F	A	W	D	L	F	A			
1	Portsmouth	46	16	4	3	43	19	11	6	6	31	22	74	41	91
2	Cardiff City	46	17	5	1	45	14	8	6	9	31	36	76	50	86
3	Huddersfield Town	46	15	8	0	56	18	8	5	10	28	31	84	49	82
4	Newport County	46	13	7	3	40	20	10	2	11	36	34	76	54	78
5	Oxford United	46	12	9	2	41	23	10	3	10	30	30	71	53	78
6	*Lincoln City*	*46*	*17*	*1*	*5*	*55*	*22*	*6*	*6*	*11*	*22*	*29*	*77*	*51*	*76*
7	Bristol Rovers	46	16	4	3	55	21	6	5	12	29	37	84	58	75
8	Plymouth Argyle	46	15	2	6	37	23	4	6	13	24	43	61	66	65
9	Brentford	46	14	4	5	50	28	4	6	13	38	49	88	77	64
10	Walsall	46	14	5	4	38	19	3	8	12	26	44	64	63	64
11	Sheffield United	46	16	3	4	44	20	3	4	16	18	44	62	64	64
12	Bradford City	46	11	7	5	41	27	5	6	12	27	42	68	69	61
13	Gillingham	46	12	4	7	37	29	4	9	10	21	30	58	59	61
14	Bournemouth	46	11	7	5	35	20	5	6	12	24	48	59	68	61
15	Southend United	46	10	8	5	41	28	5	6	12	25	37	66	65	59
16	Preston North End	46	11	10	2	35	17	4	3	16	25	52	60	69	58
17	Millwall	46	12	7	4	41	24	2	6	15	23	53	64	77	55
18	Wigan Athletic	46	10	4	9	35	33	5	5	13	25	39	60	72	54
19	Exeter City	46	12	4	7	49	43	2	8	13	32	61	81	104	54
20	Orient	46	10	6	7	44	38	5	3	15	20	50	64	88	54
21	Reading	46	10	8	5	37	28	2	9	12	27	51	64	79	53
22	Wrexham	46	11	6	6	40	26	1	9	13	16	50	56	76	51
23	Doncaster Rovers	46	6	8	9	38	44	3	3	17	19	53	57	97	38
24	Chesterfield	46	6	6	11	28	28	2	7	14	15	40	43	68	37

1983/84 Division 3

		Pl.	Home					Away					F.	A.	Pts
			W	D	L	F	A	W	D	L	F	A			
1	Oxford United	46	17	5	1	58	22	11	6	6	33	28	91	50	95
2	Wimbledon	46	15	5	3	58	35	11	4	8	39	41	97	76	87
3	Sheffield United	46	14	7	2	56	18	10	4	9	30	35	86	53	83
4	Hull City	46	16	5	2	42	11	7	9	7	29	27	71	38	83
5	Bristol Rovers	46	16	5	2	47	21	6	8	9	21	33	68	54	79
6	Walsall	46	14	4	5	44	22	8	5	10	24	39	68	61	75
7	Bradford City	46	11	9	3	46	30	9	2	12	27	35	73	65	71
8	Gillingham	46	13	4	6	50	29	7	6	10	24	40	74	69	70
9	Millwall	46	16	4	3	42	18	2	9	12	29	47	71	65	67
10	Bolton Wanderers	46	13	4	6	36	17	5	6	12	20	43	56	60	64
11	Orient	46	13	5	5	40	27	5	4	14	31	54	71	81	63
12	Burnley	46	12	5	6	52	25	4	9	10	24	36	76	61	62
13	Newport County	46	11	9	3	35	27	5	5	13	23	48	58	75	62
14	*Lincoln City*	*46*	*11*	*4*	*8*	*42*	*29*	*6*	*6*	*11*	*17*	*33*	*59*	*62*	*61*
15	Wigan Athletic	46	11	5	7	26	18	5	8	10	20	38	46	56	61
16	Preston North End	46	12	5	6	42	27	3	6	14	24	39	66	66	56
17	Bournemouth	46	11	5	7	38	27	5	2	16	25	46	63	73	55
18	Rotherham United	46	10	5	8	29	17	5	4	14	28	47	57	64	54
19	Plymouth Argyle	46	11	8	4	38	17	2	4	17	18	45	56	62	51
20	Brentford	46	8	9	6	41	30	3	7	13	28	49	69	79	49
21	Scunthorpe United	46	9	9	5	40	31	0	10	13	14	42	54	73	46
22	Southend United	46	8	9	6	34	24	2	5	16	21	52	55	76	44
23	Port Vale	46	10	4	9	33	29	1	6	16	18	54	51	83	43
24	Exeter City	46	4	8	11	27	39	2	7	14	23	45	50	84	33

1984/85 Division 3

		Pl.	Home					Away					F.	A.	Pts
			W	D	L	F	A	W	D	L	F	A			
1	Bradford City	46	15	6	2	44	23	13	4	6	33	22	77	45	94
2	Millwall	46	18	5	0	44	12	8	7	8	29	30	73	42	90
3	Hull City	46	16	4	3	46	20	9	8	6	32	29	78	49	87
4	Gillingham	46	15	5	3	54	29	10	3	10	26	33	80	62	83
5	Bristol City	46	17	2	4	46	19	7	7	9	28	28	74	47	81
6	Bristol Rovers	46	15	6	2	37	13	6	6	11	29	35	66	48	75
7	Derby County	46	14	7	2	40	20	5	6	12	25	34	65	54	70
8	York City	46	13	5	5	42	22	7	4	12	28	35	70	57	69
9	Reading	46	8	7	8	31	29	11	5	7	37	33	68	62	69
10	Bournemouth	46	16	3	4	42	16	3	8	12	15	30	57	46	68
11	Walsall	46	9	7	7	33	22	9	6	8	25	30	58	52	67
12	Rotherham United	46	11	6	6	36	24	7	5	11	19	31	55	55	65
13	Brentford	46	13	5	5	42	27	3	9	11	20	37	62	64	62
14	Doncaster Rovers	46	11	5	7	42	33	6	3	14	30	41	72	74	59
15	Plymouth Argyle	46	11	7	5	33	23	4	7	12	29	42	62	65	59
16	Wigan Athletic	46	12	6	5	36	22	3	8	12	24	42	60	64	59
17	Bolton Wanderers	46	12	5	6	38	22	4	1	18	31	53	69	75	54
18	Newport County	46	9	6	8	30	30	4	7	12	25	37	55	67	52
19	*Lincoln City*	*46*	*8*	*11*	*4*	*32*	*20*	*3*	*7*	*13*	*18*	*31*	*50*	*51*	*51*
20	Swansea City	46	7	5	11	31	39	5	6	12	22	41	53	80	47
21	Burnley	46	6	8	9	30	24	5	5	13	30	49	60	73	46
22	Orient	46	7	7	9	30	36	4	6	13	21	40	51	76	46
23	Preston North End	46	9	5	9	33	41	4	2	17	18	59	51	100	46
24	Cambridge United	46	2	3	18	17	48	2	6	15	20	47	37	95	21

1985/86 Division 3

		Pl.	Home					Away					F.	A.	Pts
			W	D	L	F	A	W	D	L	F	A			
1	Reading	46	16	3	4	39	22	13	4	6	28	29	67	51	94
2	Plymouth Argyle	46	17	3	3	56	20	9	6	8	32	33	88	53	87
3	Derby County	46	13	7	3	45	20	10	8	5	35	21	80	41	84
4	Wigan Athletic	46	17	4	2	54	17	6	10	7	28	31	82	48	83
5	Gillingham	46	14	5	4	48	17	8	8	7	33	37	81	54	79
6	Walsall	46	15	7	1	59	23	7	2	14	31	41	90	64	75
7	York City	46	16	4	3	49	17	4	7	12	28	41	77	58	71
8	Notts County	46	12	6	5	42	26	7	8	8	29	34	71	60	71
9	Bristol City	46	14	5	4	43	19	4	9	10	26	41	69	60	68
10	Brentford	46	8	8	7	29	29	10	4	9	29	32	58	61	66
11	Doncaster Rovers	46	7	10	6	20	21	9	6	8	25	31	45	52	64
12	Blackpool	46	11	6	6	38	19	6	6	11	28	36	66	55	63
13	Darlington	46	10	7	6	39	33	5	6	12	22	45	61	78	58
14	Rotherham United	46	13	5	5	44	18	2	7	14	17	41	61	59	57
15	Bournemouth	46	9	6	8	41	31	6	3	14	24	41	65	72	54
16	Bristol Rovers	46	9	8	6	27	21	5	4	14	24	54	51	75	54
17	Chesterfield	46	10	6	7	41	30	3	8	12	20	34	61	64	53
18	Bolton Wanderers	46	10	4	9	35	30	5	4	14	19	38	54	68	53
19	Newport County	46	7	8	8	35	33	4	10	9	17	32	52	65	51
20	Bury	46	11	7	5	46	26	1	6	16	17	41	63	67	49
21	*Lincoln City*	*46*	*7*	*9*	*7*	*33*	*34*	*3*	*7*	*13*	*22*	*43*	*55*	*77*	*46*
22	Cardiff City	46	7	5	11	22	29	5	4	14	31	54	53	83	45
23	Wolverhampton W.	46	6	6	11	29	47	5	4	14	28	51	57	98	43
24	Swansea City	46	9	6	8	27	27	2	4	17	16	60	43	87	43

1986/87 Division 4

		Pl.	Home					Away					F.	A.	Pts
			W	D	L	F	A	W	D	L	F	A			
1	Northampton Town	46	20	2	1	56	20	10	7	6	47	33	103	53	99
2	Preston North End	46	16	4	3	36	18	10	8	5	36	29	72	47	90
3	Southend United	46	14	4	5	43	27	11	1	11	25	28	68	55	80
4	Wolverhampton W.	46	12	3	8	36	24	12	4	7	33	26	69	50	79
5	Colchester United	46	15	3	5	41	20	6	4	13	23	36	64	56	70
6	Aldershot	46	13	5	5	40	22	7	5	11	24	35	64	57	70
7	Orient	46	15	2	6	40	25	5	7	11	24	36	64	61	69
8	Scunthorpe United	46	15	3	5	52	27	3	9	11	21	30	73	57	66
9	Wrexham	46	8	13	2	38	24	7	7	9	32	27	70	51	65
10	Peterborough Utd.	46	10	7	6	29	21	7	7	9	28	29	57	50	65
11	Cambridge United	46	12	6	5	37	23	5	5	13	23	39	60	62	62
12	Swansea City	46	13	3	7	31	21	4	8	11	25	40	56	61	62
13	Cardiff City	46	6	12	5	24	18	9	4	10	24	32	48	50	61
14	Exeter City	46	11	10	2	37	17	0	13	10	16	32	53	49	56
15	Halifax Town	46	10	5	8	32	32	5	5	13	27	42	59	74	55
16	Hereford United	46	10	6	7	33	23	4	5	14	27	38	60	61	53
17	Crewe Alexandra	46	8	9	6	38	35	5	5	13	32	37	70	72	53
18	Hartlepool United	46	6	11	6	24	30	5	7	11	20	35	44	65	51
19	Stockport County	46	9	6	8	25	27	4	6	13	15	42	40	69	51
20	Tranmere Rovers	46	6	10	7	32	37	5	7	11	22	35	54	72	50
21	Rochdale	46	8	8	7	31	30	3	9	11	23	43	54	73	50
22	Burnley	46	9	7	7	31	35	3	6	14	22	39	53	74	49
23	Torquay United	46	8	8	7	28	29	2	10	11	28	43	56	72	48
24	*Lincoln City*	*46*	*8*	*7*	*8*	*30*	*27*	*4*	*5*	*14*	*15*	*38*	*45*	*65*	*48*

1987/88 GM Vauxhall Conference

		Pl.	Home					Away					F.	A.	Pts
			W	D	L	F	A	W	D	L	F	A			
1	*Lincoln City*	*42*	*16*	*4*	*1*	*53*	*13*	*8*	*6*	*7*	*33*	*35*	*86*	*48*	*82*
2	Barnet	42	15	4	2	57	23	8	7	6	36	22	93	43	80
3	KetteringTown	42	13	5	3	37	20	9	4	8	31	28	68	48	75
4	Runcorn	42	14	4	3	42	20	7	7	7	26	27	74	68	47
5	Telford United	42	11	5	5	33	23	9	5	7	32	27	65	50	70
6	Stafford Rangers	42	12	4	5	43	25	8	5	8	36	33	79	58	69
7	Kidderminster Harr.	42	11	8	2	42	28	7	7	7	33	38	75	66	69
8	Sutton United	42	9	8	4	41	25	7	10	4	36	29	77	54	66
9	Maidstone United	42	8	5	8	38	33	10	4	7	41	31	79	64	63
10	Weymouth	42	13	7	1	33	13	5	2	14	20	30	53	43	63
11	MacclesfieldTown	42	10	5	6	36	27	8	4	9	28	35	64	62	63
12	Enfield	42	8	5	8	35	34	7	5	9	33	44	68	78	55
13	Cheltenham Town	42	6	11	4	36	32	5	9	7	28	35	64	67	53
14	Altrincham	42	11	5	5	41	21	3	5	13	18	38	59	59	52
15	Fisher Athletic	42	8	7	6	28	23	5	6	10	30	38	52	58	61
16	Boston United	42	9	5	7	33	25	5	2	14	27	50	60	75	49
17	Northwich Victoria	42	8	6	7	30	25	2	11	8	16	32	46	57	47
18	Wycombe Wanderers	42	8	5	8	32	43	3	8	10	18	33	50	73	46
19	Welling United	42	8	4	9	33	32	3	5	13	17	40	50	72	42
20	Bath City	42	7	5	9	27	32	2	5	14	21	44	48	76	37
21	Wealdstone	42	3	11	7	20	33	2	6	13	19	43	39	76	32
22	Dagenham	42	4	3	14	20	46	1	3	17	17	58	37	104	21

1988/89 Division 4

		Pl.	Home					Away					F.	A.	Pts
			W	D	L	F	A	W	D	L	F	A			
1	Rotherham United	46	13	6	4	44	18	9	10	4	32	17	76	35	82
2	Tranmere Rovers	46	15	6	2	34	13	6	11	6	28	30	62	43	80
3	Crewe Alexandra	46	13	7	3	42	24	8	8	7	25	24	67	48	78
4	Scunthorpe United	46	11	9	3	40	22	10	5	8	37	35	77	57	77
5	Scarborough	46	12	7	4	33	23	9	7	7	34	29	67	52	77
6	Leyton Orient	46	16	2	5	61	19	5	10	8	25	31	86	50	75
7	Wrexham	46	12	7	4	44	28	7	7	9	33	35	77	63	71
8	Cambridge United	46	13	7	3	45	25	5	7	11	26	37	71	62	68
9	Grimsby Town	46	11	9	3	33	18	6	6	11	32	41	65	59	66
10	*Lincoln City*	*46*	*12*	*6*	*5*	*39*	*26*	*6*	*4*	*13*	*25*	*34*	*64*	*60*	*64*
11	York City	46	10	8	5	43	27	7	5	11	19	36	62	63	64
12	Carlisle United	46	9	6	8	26	25	6	9	8	27	27	53	52	60
13	Exeter City	46	14	4	5	46	23	4	2	17	19	45	65	68	60
14	Torquay United	46	15	2	6	32	23	2	6	15	13	37	45	60	59
15	Hereford United	46	11	8	4	40	27	3	8	12	26	45	66	72	58
16	Burnley	46	12	6	5	35	20	2	7	14	17	41	52	61	55
17	Peterborough Utd.	46	10	3	10	29	32	4	9	10	23	42	52	74	54
18	Rochdale	46	10	10	3	32	26	3	4	16	24	56	56	82	53
19	Hartlepool United	46	10	6	7	33	33	4	4	15	17	45	50	78	52
20	Stockport County	46	8	10	5	31	20	2	11	10	23	32	54	52	51
21	Halifax Town	46	10	7	6	42	27	3	4	16	27	48	69	75	50
22	Colchester United	46	8	7	8	35	30	4	7	12	25	48	60	78	50
23	Doncaster Rovers	46	9	6	8	32	32	4	4	15	17	46	49	78	49
24	Darlington	46	3	12	8	28	38	5	6	12	25	38	53	76	42

SEASON 1981-82
DIVISION THREE

No.	Date	Opposition	Res.	Att.	Goalscorers
1	29 Aug	Portsmouth	1-1	10867	Cammack
2	5 Sep	FULHAM	1-1	4062	Shipley
3	12	Plymouth Argyle	2-0	3323	Gilbert, Cockerill
4	19	CARLISLE UNITED	0-0	3754	
5	23	MILLWALL	0-1	4056	
6	26	Bristol Rovers	2-0	6112	Cunningham, Cammack
7	29	Walsall	1-2	3653	Cunningham
8	3 Oct	NEWPORT COUNTY	2-2	3484	Cammack, Hobson
9	10	WIMBLEDON	5-1	3330	Cockerill(2), Cunningham, *
10	17	Brentford	1-3	4187	Cunningham
11	20	Doncaster Rovers	1-4	8261	Bell
12	24	BRISTOL CITY	1-2	3819	Bell
13	31	Oxford United	1-1	4163	Bell
14	4 Nov	PRESTON NORTH END	1-2	3723	Shipley
15	7	Southend United	2-0	5318	Cockerill, Shipley
16	14	CHESTERFIELD	2-1	5978	Cunningham, Shipley
17	28	SWINDON TOWN	2-0	3171	OG, Cunningham
18	5 Dec	Reading	2-3	3219	Cammack, Shipley
19	16 Jan	GILLINGHAM	2-0	2796	S.Thompson, Bell
20	23	PORTSMOUTH	1-1	3337	Bell
21	30	Carlisle United	0-1	3890	
22	3 Feb	CHESTER	3-0	2218	Peake, Cammack, Shipley
23	6	PLYMOUTH ARGYLE	2-0	3010	S.Thompson, Cockerill
24	9	Millwall	1-1	3198	Shipley
25	13	Newport County	0-0	3735	
26	20	WALSALL	1-1	3291	Shipley
27	27	Wimbledon	1-1	2094	Cockerill
28	2 Mar	Huddersfield Town	2-0	5874	Cunningham, Peake
29	6	BRENTFORD	1-0	2880	Hobson
30	10	DONCASTER ROVERS	5-0	5227	OG, Hobson(3), Hibberd
31	13	Bristol City	1-0	6570	Cunningham
32	16	Preston North End	1-1	4885	Cunningham
33	20	OXFORD UNITED	2-1	4514	Peake, Cockerill
34	24	Exeter City	2-1	3081	Hibberd(2)
35	27	SOUTHEND UNITED	1-1	5495	OG
36	31	BURNLEY	1-1	6188	Cockerill
37	3 Apr	Chesterfield	2-0	7443	Cunningham, Hobson
38	10	Burnley	0-1	10911	
39	12	HUDDERSFIELD TOWN	2-0	8243	Cunningham, Neale
40	17	READING	2-1	5028	Shipley, Peake
41	24	Swindon Town	0-1	4222	
42	1 May	BRISTOL ROVERS	1-0	4070	Cockerill
43	4	Gillingham	0-1	3245	
44	8	Chester	2-1	1371	Cockerill, Shipley
45	15	EXETER CITY	2-0	5489	Shipley, Cockerill
46	18	Fulham	1-1	20461	Carr

* extra scorers – Cammack, Hobson

F.A. CUP

1R	21 Nov	PORT VALE	2-2	3950	S.Thompson, Cammack
1Rr	30	Port Vale	0-0 *	4769	
1R2r	2 Dec	Port Vale	0-2	5373	

* after extra time

LEAGUE CUP

1R1L	2 Sep	HULL CITY	3-0	3498	Shipley, Hobson, Cunningham
1R2L	15	Hull City	1-1	2702	Carr
2R1L	7 Oct	NOTTS COUNTY	1-1	4943	Peake
2R2L	27	Notts County	3-2	6292	Cunningham, Cockerill, Shipley
3R	10 Nov	Watford	2-2	12198	W.Turner, Shipley
3Rr	27	WATFORD	2-3	8763	Cunningham(2)

FOOTBALL LEAGUE GROUP CUP

G	15 Aug	NOTTS COUNTY	1-1	2959	Hobson
G	19	NORWICH CITY	0-1	1990	
G	22	Peterborough United	1-3	2684	Shipley

LINCOLNSHIRE CUP

G	12 Aug	GRIMSBY TOWN	1-0	2000	Hobson
G	18	Scunthorpe United	2-2	1139	Cunningham, Shipley
F	27 Jan	Boston United	1-1 *	1119	S.Thompson

* after extra time; won 3-1 on penalties

1981-82
Back : Lawrence (coach), Phil Turner, Creane, Steve Thompson, Naylor,
Cunningham, Felgate, Keeley, Carr, Bell, Loxley (physio).
Second Row : Gilbert, Ramsay, Cammack, Hobson, Hibberd, Peake, Cockerill, Trevor Thompson, Shipley.
Third Row : Mitchell (commercial manager), Blades (director), Dove (director), Houlston (chairman), Murphy
(manager), Sheridan (coach), Green (director), Davey (director), Sills (director), Sorby (secretary).
Front : McLauchlan, Strodder, Bellhouse, Brown.

1982-83
Back: Hobson, Hibberd, Neale, Simmonite, Strodder, Thompson, Felgate, Peake, Cockerill, Carr, Bell, Beavon, Burke.
Front : Shipley, Hough (secretary), Reames (director), Pickering (assistant manager),
Houlston (chairman), Murphy (manager), Overton (director), Pryor (director), Turner.

SEASON 1982-83
DIVISION THREE

No.	Date	Opposition	Res.	Att.	Goalscorers
1	28 Aug	WIGAN ATHLETIC	2-1	3348	Shipley(2)
2	4 Sep	Southend United	0-2	3178	
3	7	Wrexham	1-0	2971	Cunningham
4	11	READING	4-0	2790	Cunningham(2), S.Thompson, Bell
5	18	Bristol Rovers	2-1	4182	Shipley, Turner
6	25	ORIENT	2-0	3116	Bell(2)
7	29	SHEFFIELD UNITED	3-0	8550	Hobson(2), Peake
8	2 Oct	Newport County	0-1	3749	
9	9	DONCASTER ROVERS	5-1	4785	Shipley(2), Hobson, OG, Cockerill
10	16	Plymouth Argyle	2-0	2921	Bell, Hobson
11	20	EXETER CITY	4-1	3699	Bell(3), Hobson
12	23	Brentford	0-2	8017	
13	30	BRADFORD CITY	1-0	5296	Burke
14	2 Nov	Portsmouth	1-4	12429	Bell
15	6	Chesterfield	3-1	4265	Hobson(2), Bell
16	13	CARDIFF CITY	2-1	6585	Bell, OG
17	4 Dec	MILLWALL	3-1	4245	Bell, Neale, Cockerill
18	18	AFC BOURNEMOUTH	9-0	4138	Hobson(3), OG, Cockerill(2), Bell(3)
19	27	Walsall	1-1	5284	Cockerill
20	28	HUDDERSFIELD TOWN	1-2	11832	Cockerill
21	1 Jan	Gillingham	2-0	5535	Bell, Shipley
22	3	PRESTON NORTH END	3-0	5889	Shipley, Bell, Turner
23	15	Wigan Athletic	1-2	4731	Burke
24	22	BRISTOL ROVERS	2-1	5342	Bell, Hobson
25	29	Reading	1-1	2683	S.Thompson
26	5 Feb	Orient	1-1	2583	Neale
27	16	PORTSMOUTH	0-3	6311	
28	19	Doncaster Rovers	2-2	4667	Hobson, Bell
29	23	SOUTHEND UNITED	0-1	4000	
30	26	PLYMOUTH ARGYLE	1-2	3915	Bell
31	2 Mar	Exeter City	1-3	2505	Bell
32	5	BRENTFORD	2-1	3698	Cockerill, Bell
33	12	Bradford City	1-1	5026	Burke
34	16	Oxford United	0-1	5321	
35	19	CHESTERFIELD	2-0	4454	Shipley(2)
36	23	NEWPORT COUNTY	1-4	4742	Bell
37	26	Cardiff City	0-1	8021	
38	2 Apr	Huddersfield Town	1-1	13028	Hobson
39	4	WALSALL	2-1	4671	Moss, Bell
40	9	Millwall	1-2	3775	Bell
41	16	WREXHAM	2-0	3515	Turner, Moss
42	23	AFC Bournemouth	0-1	5010	
43	30	OXFORD UNITED	1-1	2812	OG
44	2 Mar	Preston North End	0-1	6503	
45	7	Sheffield United	1-0	11842	Cockerill
46	14	GILLINGHAM	3-1	2441	Shipley, Burke(2)

4 own goals

F.A. CUP

1R	29 Nov	Hartlepool United	0-3	2204	

MILK CUP

1R1L	31 Aug	York City	1-2	1972	Hobson
1R2L	15 Sep	York City	3-1	2716	Cunningham(2), Hobson
2R1L	6 Oct	LEICESTER CITY	2-0	6755	Bell, Shipley
2R2L	29	Leicester City	1-0	10000	Bell
3R	10 Nov	WEST HAM UNITED	1-1	13899	Bell
3Rr	29	West Ham United	1-2 *	13686	OG

* after extra time

FOOTBALL LEAGUE TROPHY

G	14 Aug	Scunthorpe United	1-1	1022	Cunningham
G	18	GRIMSBY TOWN	2-1	1430	Cockerill, S.Thompson
G	21	SHEFFIELD UNITED	3-1	2820	Cockerill(2), Cunningham
QF	8 Dec	NORWICH CITY	3-1	3853	Bell(3)
SF	8 Feb	Chester	3-1 *	1058	Cockerill, Peake, Turner
F	20 Apr	MILLWALL	2-3	3142	Burke(2)

* after extra time

LINCOLNSHIRE CUP

G	9 Aug	Grimsby Town	4-0	1161	Peake, Shipley, Turner(2)
G	11	SCUNTHORPE UNITED	1-3	699	Turner

SEASON 1983-84
DIVISION THREE

No.	Date	Opposition	Res.	Att.	Goalscorers
1	27 Aug	Oxford United	0-3	4393	
2	3 Sep	SHEFFIELD UNITED	0-2	6686	
3	7	Orient	2-0	2899	Jack(2)
4	10	Brentford	0-3	4777	
5	17	PLYMOUTH ARGYLE	3-1	3103	Hobson(2), Jack
6	24	Hull City	0-2	7523	
7	28	Exeter City	3-0	2775	Jack(2), Shipley
8	1 Oct	AFC BOURNEMOUTH	3-0	3528	Cockerill(2), Jack
9	8	Wigan Athletic	0-2	3864	
10	15	MILLWALL	2-2	3190	Turner, Thompson
11	18	Newport County	0-1	3450	
12	22	BURNLEY	3-1	3793	Shipley, Turner, Fashanu
13	29	Preston North End	2-1	4440	Thomas(2)
14	2 Nov	BOLTON WANDERERS	0-0	3988	
15	5	Gillingham	0-2	4428	
16	12	SCUNTHORPE UNITED	2-1	4657	OG, Jack
17	26	BRISTOL ROVERS	4-0	3709	Fashanu(3), Jack
18	3 Dec	Wimbledon	1-3	2434	Shipley
19	17	Port Vale	1-0	2861	Cockerill
20	26	WALSALL	2-1	4886	Hobson, Thomas
21	27	Southend United	0-2	3010	
22	31	BRADFORD CITY	2-3	3984	Strodder, Shipley
23	2 Jan	Rotherham United	1-1	4595	OG
24	14	OXFORD UNITED	2-2	3344	Saxby, Thomas
25	21	Plymouth Argyle	2-2	3804	Thomas, Cockerill
26	1 Feb	BRENTFORD	2-0	2266	Cockerill, Jack
27	4	AFC Bournemouth	0-3	3597	
28	7	Sheffield United	0-0	9765	
29	11	HULL CITY	1-3	5370	Turner
30	14	Bolton Wanderers	2-0	5450	Hobson, Thomas
31	18	PRESTON NORTH END	2-1	2780	Thomas, Fashanu
32	25	Burnley	0-4	6652	
33	3 Mar	NEWPORT COUNTY	2-3	1780	Walker, Thomas
34	7	GILLINGHAM	4-0	1575	Hobson, Neale, Walker, Cockerill
35	10	Scunthorpe United	0-0	3889	
36	17	WIGAN ATHLETIC	0-1	2030	
37	31	EXETER CITY	1-1	1498	Burke
38	7 Apr	Orient	1-1	2174	Thomas
39	14	WIMBLEDON	1-2	1986	Redfearn
40	21	Walsall	1-0	3660	Fashanu
41	23	SOUTHEND UNITED	1-2	1834	Thomas
42	28	Bristol Rovers	1-3	3254	Burke
43	1 May	Millwall	2-0	2825	Thomas, Hobson
44	5	ROTHERHAM UNITED	0-1	2140	
45	7	Bradford City	0-0	3167	
46	12	PORT VALE	3-2	1372	Thomas(3)

F.A. CUP

1R	19 Nov	Port Vale	2-1	3647	Jack, Shipley
2R	10 Dec	SHEFFIELD UNITED	0-0	7554	
2Rr	19	Sheffield United	0-1	12547	

MILK CUP

1R1L	30 Aug	Hull City	0-0	6396	
1R2L	14 Sep	HULL CITY	3-1 *	4630	Shipley, Thomas, Houghton
2R1L	5 Oct	Tottenham Hotspur	1-3	20241	Shipley
2R2L	26	TOTTENHAM HOTSPUR	2-1	12239	Thomas, Jack

* after extra time

ASSOCIATE MEMBERS CUP

1R	22 Feb	DONCASTER ROVERS	0-2	1941	

LINCOLNSHIRE CUP

1R	30 Jan	Grimsby Town	0-5	579	

1983-84
Back : Hobson, Jack, Strodder, Thompson, Felgate, Houghton, Cockerill, Simmonite, Burke.
Centre : Pickering (assistant manager), Shipley, Overton (director), Houlston (chairman), Murphy (manager), Pryor (director), Reames (director), Hough (secretary), Turner, Loxley (physio).   Front : Moyses, Jones, Hall.

1984-85
Back : McCarrick, Thomas, Neale, Thompson, Houghton, Naylor,
Fashanu, Felgate, Walker, Strodder, Simmonite, Jack, Turner.
Centre : Hobson, Hough (secretary), Overton (director), Houlston (chairman),
Pickering (assistant manager), Murphy (manager), Loxley (physio), Pryor (director),
Reames (director), Rodman (marketing manager), Shipley.   Front : Hall, Gamble.

SEASON 1984-85
DIVISION THREE

No.	Date	Opposition	Res.	Att.	Goalscorers
1	25 Aug	HULL CITY	0-0	4139	
2	1 Sep	Rotherham United	0-0	4161	
3	8	PLYMOUTH ARGYLE	2-2	2171	Hobson, Turner
4	14	Doncaster Rovers	2-3	4962	Shipley, Hobson
5	18	Wigan Athletic	0-1	2518	
6	22	BRISTOL ROVERS	1-2	2173	Redfearn
7	29	Derby County	0-2	12244	
8	6 Oct	PRESTON NORTH END	4-0	1906	Fashanu, Jack, McGinley, Shipley
9	13	Burnley	2-1	4315	Shipley, Fashanu
10	20	AFC BOURNEMOUTH	0-0	2340	
11	23	Millwall	0-2	5625	
12	27	READING	5-1	2422	Fashanu, Jack, Turner, Walker, Shipley
13	3 Nov	Bolton Wanderers	0-1	4019	
14	7	NEWPORT COUNTY	2-2	2331	Fashanu, Jack
15	10	Brentford	2-2	4115	Jack(2)
16	24	YORK CITY	2-1	2864	Jack, Hobson
17	28	CAMBRIDGE UNITED	1-1	1869	McGinley
18	1 Dec	Bristol City	1-2	7270	Strodder
19	15	GILLINGHAM	2-0	1920	OG, McGinley
20	22	BRADFORD CITY	1-2	3554	Thomas
21	26	Orient	0-1	2315	
22	29	Walsall	0-0	4613	
23	1 Jan	SWANSEA CITY	1-0	2529	Strodder
24	2 Feb	DERBY COUNTY	0-0	5911	
25	16	WIGAN ATHLETIC	1-0	2286	Hobson
26	23	BOLTON WANDERERS	2-0	2448	White, Redfearn
27	2 Mar	Reading	1-1	3938	OG
28	6	MILLWALL	0-1	2881	
29	9	AFC Bournemouth	1-3	2955	Thomas
30	13	ROTHERHAM UNITED	3-3	2157	McGinley, Hobson, Redfearn
31	16	BURNLEY	3-1	2137	Walker, Thomas(2)
32	19	Hull City	0-1	7029	
33	23	Preston North End	1-0	2927	Turner
34	30	Newport County	1-2	1307	Hobson
35	2 Apr	Bristol Rovers	0-0	4159	
36	6	ORIENT	0-0	2160	
37	9	Swansea City	2-2	4506	OG, Redfearn
38	13	BRENTFORD	1-1	1980	Shipley
39	16	Plymouth Argyle	0-2	4278	
40	20	York City	1-2	3309	Jack
41	24	DONCASTER ROVERS	0-2	1824	
42	27	BRISTOL CITY	1-1	1908	Thompson
43	30	Cambridge United	2-0	1235	Shipley(2)
44	4 May	Gillingham	2-3	3219	OG, Hobson
45	6	WALSALL	0-0	1473	
46	11	Bradford City	0-0 *	11076	

* Match abandoned after 42 minutes, score allowed to stand.

4 own goals

F.A. CUP

1R	17 Nov	TELFORD UNITED	1-1	3329	Redfearn
1Rr	30	Telford United	1-2	3343	Walker

MILK CUP

1R1L	29 Aug	HULL CITY	0-2	3465	
1R2L	4 Sep	Hull City	1-4	4642	OG

FREIGHT ROVER TROPHY

1R1L	23 Jan	Hartlepool United	1-2	1202	OG
1R2L	6 Feb	HARTLEPOOL UNITED	4-0	1316	White(2), Walker, Hobson
2R	26 Mar	Darlington	3-1	1648	Walker, McGinley, Hobson
NQF	22 Apr	York City	3-2	4010	Jack, Hobson, Thompson
NSF	8 May	WIGAN ATHLETIC	1-3	1782	Hobson

LINCOLNSHIRE CUP

G	4 Aug	BOSTON UNITED	1-0	369	Thomas
G	7	Grantham Town	2-2		Simmonite, Thomas
F	9 Oct	Gainsborough Trinity	1-0	758	Fashanu

SEASON 1985-86
DIVISION THREE

No.	Date	Opposition	Res.	Att.	Goalscorers
1	12 Aug	GILLINGHAM	1-0	2099	Redfearn
2	24	Rotherham United	0-1	3356	
3	26	WALSALL	3-2	2282	McGinley(2), Toman
4	31	Bury	0-4	2877	
5	8 Sep	DONCASTER ROVERS	3-3	3205	Redfearn, McGinley, Ward
6	14	Bristol Rovers	0-0	3067	
7	17	Bolton Wanderers	1-1	3928	Ward
8	21	BRENTFORD	3-0	1856	Turner(2), Toman
9	28	Wolverhampton Wanderers	1-1	3501	Toman
10	2 Oct	AFC BOURNEMOUTH	3-2	1862	Ward, McGinley, Redfearn
11	5	NEWPORT COUNTY	1-1	1989	McGinley
12	11	Swansea City	1-3	3600	Redfearn
13	19	READING	0-1	4007	
14	22	Plymouth Argyle	1-2	6552	Ward
15	27	Notts County	2-3	6120	Latchford, Toman
16	2 Nov	BLACKPOOL	0-3	2371	
17	6	BRISTOL CITY	1-1	1379	Redfearn
18	9	Derby County	0-7	10560	
19	24	YORK CITY	3-4	2455	McGinley, Redfearn, Turner
20	30	Wigan Athletic	2-3	2714	Latchford, Mair
21	14 Dec	CARDIFF CITY	0-4	2127	
22	22	ROTHERHAM UNITED	0-0	3007	
23	26	Chesterfield	2-2	2631	White, Ward
24	28	Walsall	1-2	4493	Daniel
25	1 Jan	DARLINGTON	1-1	2304	McGinley
26	11	BURY	2-0	2226	McInnes(2)
27	18	Gillingham	0-2	3797	
28	1 Feb	Doncaster Rovers	1-1	2723	Daniel
29	25	Blackpool	0-2	1995	
30	4 Mar	AFC Bournemouth	2-2	1873	West, Gamble
31	8	Newport County	2-1	1540	Mair, Kilmore
32	12	Reading	2-0	5012	Redfearn, Gamble
33	16	SWANSEA CITY	4-1	2846	Turner, Gamble(2), Mair
34	22	NOTTS COUNTY	0-2	3468	
35	25	BOLTON WANDERERS	1-1	2329	Kilmore
36	29	Darlington	0-1	3102	
37	31	CHESTERFIELD	2-1	2461	Kilmore, White
38	5 Apr	Bristol City	1-1	5375	White
39	12	DERBY COUNTY	0-1	6237	
40	16	PLYMOUTH ARGYLE	0-1	2197	
41	19	York City	1-2	3874	Strodder
42	22	Brentford	1-0	3011	Ward
43	26	WIGAN ATHLETIC	0-0	3074	
44	30	BRISTOL ROVERS	2-2	2233	Ward, Redfearn
45	3 May	Cardiff City	1-2	1904	Kilmore
46	5	WOLVERHAMPTON WANDS.	2-3	2174	Gamble, Ward

F.A. CUP

1R	16 Nov	BLACKPOOL	0-1	2596	

MILK CUP

1R1L	20 Aug	York City	1-2	3630	Burke
1R2L	4 Sep	YORK CITY	1-2	2257	S.Richards

FREIGHT ROVER TROPHY

1R	18 Jan	SCUNTHORPE UNITED	1-3	1235	Daniel
1R	11 Feb	Halifax Town	1-1	150	McInnes

LINCOLNSHIRE CUP

G	5 Aug	SCUNTHORPE UNITED	2-0	395	Redfearn, McGinley
G	9	Gainsborough Trinity	2-1	400	Latchford, White
F	30 Oct	Boston United	0-4	1398	

1985-86
Back : McInnes, Redfearn, Steve Richards, Toman, Cooper, Mitchell.
Centre : Turner, Gamble, Strodder, White, Swinburne, West, McGinley, Hodson, Nicholson.
Front : Parkin, Kerr (manager), Mair, Kilmore, Daniel, Gary Richards, Franklin, Loxley (physio), Buck.

1986-87
Back : McInnes, Turner, Gamble, West, Swinburne, Butler, Strodder, McGinley, Kilmore, Mitchell.
Centre : Cook, Cooper, Redfearn, Loxley (physio), Daniel, Hodson, Franklin.
Front : Ranshaw, Buck, Hare, Parkin, Nicholson.

SEASON 1986-87
DIVISION FOUR

No.	Date	Opposition	Res.	Att.	Goalscorers
1	23 Aug	COLCHESTER UNITED	3-1	2303	McInnes, Lund, Cooper
2	30	Wrexham	1-1	2395	McInnes
3	6 Sep	PRESTON NORTH END	1-1	2305	Lund
4	13	Aldershot	0-4	1443	
5	16	Cardiff City	1-1	2406	Simmons
6	20	SOUTHEND UNITED	1-3	1950	Simmons
7	27	Cambridge United	1-1	2542	Lund
8	30	ORIENT	2-0	1443	Simmons, Kilmore
9	5 Oct	HARTLEPOOL UNITED	1-4	2101	Simmons
10	11	Exeter City	0-2	2499	
11	18	ROCHDALE	1-1	1357	OG
12	21	Torquay United	1-0	1112	Gamble
13	25	Peterborough United	1-0	2384	Strodder
14	1 Nov	TRANMERE ROVERS	3-1	1461	Gamble, Strodder, Buckley
15	4	CREWE ALEXANDRA	2-1	1762	Gamble, Lund
16	8	Hereford United	0-0	2305	
17	22	Burnley	1-3	2177	Lund
18	29	WOLVERHAMPTON WANDS.	3-0	2277	Lund, Mitchell, Simmons
19	13 Dec	SWANSEA CITY	4-0	1988	Lund(3), Buckley
20	21	Northampton Town	1-3	7063	Lund
21	26	STOCKPORT COUNTY	0-0	2773	
22	27	Scunthorpe United	1-2	4299	Lund
23	3 Jan	BURNLEY	2-1	2343	Lund, Cooper
24	10	Colchester United	0-2	1768	
25	24	Preston North End	0-3	7821	
26	7 Feb	CARDIFF CITY	0-1	1954	
27	14	Southend United	0-1	2539	
28	22	CAMBRIDGE UNITED	0-3	1958	
29	24	Halifax Town	2-1	1088	McGinley(2)
30	28	Orient	1-2	2900	Mitchell
31	3 Mar	Tranmere Rovers	0-2	1445	
32	8	PETERBOROUGH UNITED	1-2	3316	Lund
33	14	Rochdale	1-1	1490	Kilmore
34	17	TORQUAY UNITED	1-1	1186	West
35	21	EXETER CITY	1-1	1558	Gamble
36	29	Hartlepool United	1-2	1483	McGinley
37	31	ALDERSHOT	0-2	1498	
38	4 Apr	HEREFORD UNITED	0-0	1198	
39	11	Crewe Alexandra	2-1	1350	McGinley, West
40	14	WREXHAM	0-1	1540	
41	18	HALIFAX TOWN	0-0	1673	
42	20	Stockport County	0-1	2529	
43	26	NORTHAMPTON TOWN	3-1	4012	Gilligan, Gamble, OG
44	2 May	Wolverhampton Wanderers	0-3	7285	
45	4	SCUNTHORPE UNITED	1-2	2567	McGinley
46	9	Swansea City	0-2	2544	

F.A. CUP

| 1R | 15 Nov | Wigan Athletic | 1-3 | 3547 | Lund |

LITTLEWOODS CHALLENGE CUP

1R1L	26	Wolverhampton Wanderers	2-1	3256	Kilmore, Mitchell
1R2L	2 Sep	WOLVERHAMPTON WANDS.	0-1 *	2396	
2R1L	23	Charlton Athletic	1-3	2319	Lund
2R2L	8 Oct	CHARLTON ATHLETIC	0-1	2070	

* after extra time; 2-2 on aggregate, won on away goals

FREIGHT ROVER TROPHY

Prel	25 Nov	SCUNTHORPE UNITED	1-0	1003	Lund
Prel	6 Dec	Hartlepool United	0-0	938	
1R	21 Jan	Chester City	1-1 *	1194	Simmons

* after extra time; lost 4-5 on penalties

LINCOLNSHIRE CUP

| 1R | 6 Aug | BOSTON UNITED * | 0-3 | 1107 | |

* played at York Street, Boston

SEASON 1987-88
GM VAUXHALL CONFERENCE

No.	Date	Opposition	Res.	Att.	Goalscorers
1	22 Aug	Barnet	2-4	2598	Cumming, Waitt
2	26	Weymouth	0-3	3583	
3	29	DAGENHAM	3-0	1995	Mossman(2), Hunter
4	31	RUNCORN	1-0	2330	Waitt
5	5 Sep	Stafford Rangers	4-1	2111	Waitt(3), Clarke
6	8	Altrincham	0-0	2398	
7	19	ENFIELD	4-0	2503	Cumming, McGinley, Smith(2)
8	22	Runcorn	1-4	970	Smith
9	26	Telford United	1-0	2025	Smith
10	30	KETTERING TOWN	0-1	3156	
11	3 Oct	BATH CITY	3-0	2494	Waitt(2), Brown
12	10	Maidstone United	2-1	1101	Waitt, Smith
13	17	Wealdstone	0-0	1107	
14	28	BARNET	2-1	4624	Matthewson, McGinley
15	31	CHELTENHAM TOWN	5-1	2341	Evans(2), McGinley, Cumming, Sertori
16	7 Nov	Wycombe Wanderers	2-1	2105	Cumming, Brown
17	21	WEYMOUTH	0-0	3890	
18	25	MACCLESFIELD TOWN	3-0	2544	Brown, McGinley(2)
19	28	Sutton United	1-4	1013	Cumming
20	12 Dec	NORTHWICH VICTORIA	3-2	2301	Brown(2), McGinley
21	26	Boston United	2-1	5822	OG, Brown
22	28	KIDDERMINSTER HARRIERS	5-3	4121	Cumming, Evans, Nicholson, Smith, Clarke
23	2 Jan	Northwich Victoria	3-2	1207	Brown, Evans, McGinley
24	9	FISHER ATHLETIC	3-0	3751	Evans, Smith, Clarke
25	16	Welling United	4-1	1339	McGinley(2), Matthewson, Brown
26	17 Feb	SUTTON UNITED	1-1	3201	Matthewson
27	20	TELFORD UNITED	0-0	3500	
28	27	Dagenham	3-0	832	Brown(2), Clarke
29	2 Mar	WELLING UNITED	2-1	3218	Evans, Sertori
30	12	Kidderminster Harriers	3-3	2635	Brown, Smith, Evans
31	19	Enfield	0-0	1390	
32	26	ALTRINCHAM	5-0	2720	McGinley(2), Clarke, Moore, Brown
33	1 Apr	Fisher Athletic	1-1	1705	Cumming
34	4	BOSTON UNITED	5-1	7542	Matthewson, OG, McGinley, Sertori(2)
35	9	Cheltenham Town	3-3	1715	McGinley, Matthewson, Sertori
36	12	Maccesfield Town	0-2	2050	
37	16	WEALDSTONE	3-0	4159	McGinley, Brown(2)
38	19	Bath City	1-2	1336	Matthewson
39	23	Kettering Town	0-2	4135	
40	27	MAIDSTONE UNITED	1-1	4892	McGinley
41	30	STAFFORD RANGERS	2-1	4402	Brown, Evans
42	2 May	WYCOMBE WANDERERS	2-0	9432	Sertori, Brown

2 own goals

F.A. CUP

4QF	24 Oct	Brigg Town *	4-1	2023	McGinley(2), Waitt, Cumming
1R	14 Nov	CREWE ALEXANDRA	2-1	3892	McGinley, Cumming
2R	5 Dec	Mansfield Town	3-4	5671	Smith, Brown, Clarke

* played at Sincil Bank

F.A. TROPHY

1R	19 Oct	South Liverpool	1-1	307	Cumming
1Rr	23	SOUTH LIVERPOOL	2-2 *	1847	Brown, Smith
1R2r	4 Jan	SOUTH LIVERPOOL	3-1	1848	Smith, Mossman(2)
2R	27	CAMBRIDGE CITY	2-1	2566	OG, Brown
3R	13 Feb	MAIDSTONE UNITED	2-1	2372	Smith, Matthewson
4R	5 Mar	Enfield	0-1	2239	

* after extra time

GMAC CUP

1R	7 Oct	MATLOCK TOWN	2-1	1296	Brown, McGinley
2R	4 Nov	BEDWORTH UNITED	4-1	1139	OG, McGinley, Sertori, Nicholson
3R	8 Dec	Telford United	1-2 *	1015	Smith

* after extra time

LINCOLNSHIRE CUP

1R	4 Aug	Grimsby Town	3-1	1000	Waitt, Cumming, Gamble
SF	11	Gainsborough Trinity	2-2 *	450	McGinley(2)

* after extra time, lost 6-7 on penalties

1987-88
Back : Buckley, Simmons, Mossman, Sertori, Hunter, Batch, Waitt, McGinley, Matthewson, Moore, Evans.
Front: Clarke, Franklin, Nicholson, Murphy (manager), Cumming, Bate (asst./manager), Brown, Paul Smith, Gamble.

1988-89
Back : Brown, Bressington, James, McGinley, Angell, Wallington, Batch, Scott, Sertori, Cook, Evans, Casey.
Front : Nicholson, Clarke, Matthewson, Cumming, Murphy (manager), Paul Smith, Davis, Buckley, Gamble.

SEASON 1988-89
DIVISION FOUR

No.	Date	Opposition	Res.	Att.	Goalscorers
1	27 Aug	HARTLEPOOL UNITED	0-1	3361	
2	3 Sep	Wrexham	0-3	2312	
3	10	CREWE ALEXANDRA	2-2	2651	Evans, Smith
4	17	Peterborough United	1-1	4256	Smith
5	20	Cambridge United	3-2	2776	Hobson, Sertori(2)
6	24	HEREFORD UNITED	2-0	2915	Gamble, Hobson
7	1 Oct	Colchester United	3-1	1529	Hobson(2), OG
8	5	SCUNTHORPE UNITED	1-0	5443	Gamble
9	8	Torquay United	0-1	2105	
10	15	SCARBOROUGH	2-2	4535	Clarke, Gamble
11	22	DARLINGTON	3-2	3705	Gamble, Nicholson, Sertori
12	24	Tranmere Rovers	0-1	3498	
13	29	CARLISLE UNITED	0-2	3727	
14	5 Nov	Rotherham United	0-2	4506	
15	8	Burnley	4-1	8742	Hobson(3), Sertori
16	12	EXETER CITY	2-0	3461	Hobson(2)
17	26	HALIFAX TOWN	2-1	3379	Cumming, Matthewson
18	3 Dec	Leyton Orient	1-3	3093	Cumming
19	17	Stockport County	0-1	2355	
20	26	GRIMSBY TOWN	2-2	8038	Smith, Hobson
21	28	DONCASTER ROVERS	3-1	5213	Smith(2), Matthewson
22	2 Jan	York City	1-2	3589	Smith
23	7	ROCHDALE	2-2	1515	Smith, Cumming
24	14	WREXHAM	4-3	3860	Schofield, Hobson(2), Cumming
25	21	Hartlepool United	2-3	2860	Brown, McGinley
26	28	PETERBOROUGH UNITED	1-1	4150	Brown
27	4 Feb	CAMBRIDGE UNITED	3-0	3239	Dunkley(2), Hobson
28	11	Hereford United	2-3	2113	Dunkley, Hobson
29	18	TORQUAY UNITED	1-0	3423	Bressington
30	25	Scarborough	1-1	3293	Clarke
31	1 Mar	TRANMERE ROVERS	2-1	3560	Clarke, OG
32	4	Darlington	1-2	2169	Dunkley
33	11	ROTHERHAM UNITED	0-1	5186	
34	15	Carlisle United	1-2	2691	Hobson
35	18	Crewe Alexandra	0-2	3106	
36	25	YORK CITY	2-1	3710	Smith(2)
37	27	Grimsby Town	0-1	8618	
38	1 Apr	STOCKPORT COUNTY	0-0	3400	
39	5	ROCHDALE	4-1	2033	Clarke, Smith, Schofield, Evans
40	8	Doncaster Rovers	1-0	2124	Cumming
41	15	COLCHESTER UNITED	1-1	3519	McGinley
42	22	Scunthorpe United	0-0	5729	
43	29	Halifax Town	1-0	1261	Brown
44	1 May	BURNLEY	2-3	3594	Davis, Gamble
45	6	LEYTON ORIENT	0-1	3579	
46	13	Exeter City	1-0	2249	Davis

F.A. CUP

1R	19 Nov	Altrincham	2-3	2169	Davis, Sertori

LITTLEWOODS CHALLENGE CUP

1R1L	30 Aug	Crewe Alexandra	1-1	1860	Brown
1R2L	7 Sep	CREWE ALEXANDRA	2-1	2616	OG, Gamble
2R1L	28	SOUTHAMPTON	1-1	5404	Clarke
2R2L	11 Oct	Southampton	1-3	6401	Clarke

SHERPA VAN TROPHY

Prel	22 Nov	Southend United	1-2	1176	Cumming
Prel	30	COLCHESTER UNITED	1-2	1448	Gamble

LINCOLNSHIRE CUP

1R	3 Aug	GAINSBOROUGH TRINITY	0-2	518	

2 own goals

Final League Tables 1989/90 to 1996/97

1989/90 Division 4

		Pl.	Home					Away					F.	A.	Pts
			W	D	L	F	A	W	D	L	F	A			
1	Exeter City	46	20	3	0	50	14	8	2	13	33	34	83	48	89
2	Grimsby Town	46	14	4	5	41	20	8	9	6	29	27	70	47	79
3	Southend United	46	15	3	5	35	14	7	6	10	26	34	61	48	75
4	Stockport County	46	13	6	4	45	27	8	5	10	23	35	68	62	74
5	Maidstone United	46	14	4	5	49	21	8	3	12	28	40	77	61	73
6	Cambridge United	46	14	3	6	45	30	7	7	9	31	36	76	66	73
7	Chesterfield	46	12	9	2	41	19	7	5	11	22	31	63	50	71
8	Carlisle United	46	15	4	4	38	20	6	4	13	23	40	61	60	71
9	Peterborough Utd.	46	10	8	5	35	23	7	9	7	24	23	59	46	68
10	*Lincoln City*	*46*	*11*	*6*	*6*	*30*	*27*	*7*	*8*	*8*	*18*	*21*	*48*	*48*	*68*
11	Scunthorpe United	46	9	9	5	42	25	8	6	9	27	29	69	54	66
12	Rochdale	46	11	4	8	28	23	9	2	12	24	32	52	55	66
13	York City	46	10	5	8	29	24	6	11	6	26	29	55	53	64
14	Gillingham	46	9	8	6	28	21	8	3	12	18	27	46	48	62
15	Torquay United	46	12	2	9	33	29	3	10	10	20	37	53	66	57
16	Burnley	46	6	10	7	19	18	8	4	11	26	37	45	55	56
17	Hereford United	46	7	4	12	31	32	8	6	9	25	30	56	62	55
18	Scarborough	46	10	5	8	35	28	5	5	13	25	45	60	73	55
19	Hartlepool United	46	12	4	7	45	33	3	6	14	21	55	66	88	55
20	Doncaster Rovers	46	7	7	9	29	29	7	2	14	24	31	53	60	51
21	Wrexham	46	8	8	7	28	28	5	4	14	23	39	51	67	51
22	Aldershot	46	8	7	8	28	26	4	7	12	21	43	49	69	50
23	Halifax Town	46	5	9	9	31	29	7	4	12	26	36	57	65	49
24	Colchester United	46	9	3	11	26	25	2	7	14	22	50	48	75	43

1990/91 Division 4

		Pl.	Home					Away					F.	A.	Pts
			W	D	L	F	A	W	D	L	F	A			
1	Darlington	46	13	8	2	36	14	9	9	5	32	24	68	38	83
2	Stockport County	46	16	6	1	54	19	7	7	9	30	28	84	47	82
3	Hartlepool United	46	15	5	3	35	15	9	5	9	32	33	67	48	82
4	Peterborough Utd.	46	13	9	1	38	15	8	8	7	29	30	67	45	80
5	Blackpool	46	17	3	3	55	17	6	7	10	23	30	78	47	79
6	Burnley	46	17	5	1	46	16	6	5	12	24	35	70	51	79
7	Torquay United	46	14	7	2	37	13	4	11	8	27	34	64	47	72
8	Scunthorpe United	46	17	4	2	51	20	3	7	13	20	42	71	62	71
9	Scarborough	46	13	5	5	36	21	6	7	10	23	35	59	56	69
10	Northampton Town	46	14	5	4	34	21	4	8	11	23	37	57	58	67
11	Doncaster Rovers	46	12	5	6	36	22	5	9	9	20	24	56	46	65
12	Rochdale	46	10	9	4	29	22	5	8	10	21	31	50	53	62
13	Cardiff City	46	10	6	7	26	23	5	9	9	17	31	43	54	60
14	*Lincoln City*	*46*	*10*	*7*	*6*	*32*	*27*	*4*	*10*	*9*	*18*	*34*	*50*	*61*	*59*
15	Gillingham	46	9	9	5	35	27	3	9	11	22	33	57	60	54
16	Walsall	46	7	12	4	25	17	5	5	13	23	34	48	51	53
17	Hereford United	46	9	10	4	32	19	4	4	15	21	39	53	58	53
18	Chesterfield	46	8	12	3	33	26	5	2	16	14	36	47	62	53
19	Maidstone United	46	9	5	9	42	34	4	7	12	24	37	66	71	51
20	Carlisle United	46	12	3	8	30	30	1	6	16	17	59	47	89	48
21	York City	46	8	6	9	21	23	3	7	13	24	34	45	57	46
22	Halifax Town	46	9	6	8	34	29	3	4	16	25	50	59	79	46
23	Aldershot	46	8	7	8	38	43	2	4	17	23	58	61	101	41
24	Wrexham	46	8	7	8	33	34	2	3	18	15	40	48	74	40

1991/92 Division 4

		Pl.	Home					Away					F.	A.	Pts
			W	D	L	F	A	W	D	L	F	A			
1	Burnley	42	14	4	3	42	16	11	4	6	37	27	79	43	83
2	Rotherham United	42	12	6	3	38	16	10	5	6	32	21	70	37	77
3	Mansfield Town	42	13	4	4	43	26	10	4	7	32	27	75	53	77
4	Blackpool	42	17	3	1	48	13	5	7	9	23	32	71	45	76
5	Scunthorpe United	42	14	5	2	39	18	7	4	10	25	41	64	59	72
6	Crewe Alexandra	42	12	6	3	33	20	8	4	9	33	31	66	51	70
7	Barnet	42	16	1	4	48	23	5	5	11	33	38	81	61	69
8	Rochdale	42	12	6	3	34	22	6	7	8	23	31	57	53	67
9	Cardiff City	42	13	3	5	42	26	4	12	5	24	27	66	53	66
10	*Lincoln City*	*42*	*9*	*5*	*7*	*21*	*24*	*8*	*6*	*7*	*29*	*20*	*50*	*44*	*62*
11	Gillingham	42	12	5	4	41	19	3	7	11	22	34	63	53	57
12	Scarborough	42	12	5	4	39	28	3	7	11	25	40	64	68	57
13	Chesterfield	42	6	7	8	26	28	8	4	9	23	33	49	61	53
14	Wrexham	42	11	4	6	31	26	3	5	13	21	47	52	73	51
15	Walsall	42	5	10	6	28	26	7	3	11	20	32	48	58	49
16	Northampton Town	42	5	9	7	25	23	6	4	11	21	34	46	57	46
17	Hereford United	42	9	4	8	31	24	3	4	14	13	33	44	57	44
18	Maidstone United	42	6	9	6	24	22	2	9	10	21	34	45	56	42
19	York City	42	6	9	6	26	23	2	7	12	16	35	42	58	40
20	Halifax Town	42	7	5	9	23	35	3	3	15	11	40	34	75	38
21	Doncaster Rovers	42	6	2	13	21	35	3	6	12	19	30	40	65	35
22	Carlisle United	42	5	9	7	24	27	2	4	15	17	40	41	67	34

1992/93 Division 3 (Divisions re-numbered)

		Pl.	Home					Away					F.	A.	Pts
			W	D	L	F	A	W	D	L	F	A			
1	Cardiff City	42	13	7	1	42	20	12	1	8	35	27	77	47	83
2	Wrexham	42	14	3	4	48	26	9	8	4	27	26	75	52	80
3	Barnet	42	16	4	1	45	19	7	6	8	21	29	66	48	79
4	York City	42	13	6	2	41	15	8	6	7	31	30	72	45	75
5	Walsall	42	11	6	4	42	31	11	1	9	34	30	76	61	73
6	Crewe Alexandra	42	13	3	5	47	23	8	4	9	28	33	75	56	70
7	Bury	42	10	7	4	36	19	8	2	11	27	36	63	55	63
8	*Lincoln City*	*42*	*10*	*6*	*5*	*31*	*20*	*8*	*3*	*10*	*26*	*33*	*57*	*53*	*63*
9	Shrewsbury Town	42	11	3	7	36	30	6	8	7	21	22	57	52	62
10	Colchester United	42	13	3	5	38	26	5	2	14	29	50	67	76	59
11	Rochdale	42	10	3	8	38	29	6	7	8	32	41	70	70	58
12	Chesterfield	42	11	3	7	32	28	4	8	9	27	35	59	63	56
13	Scarborough	42	7	7	7	32	30	8	2	11	34	41	66	71	54
14	Scunthorpe United	42	8	7	6	38	25	6	5	10	19	29	57	54	54
15	Darlington	42	5	6	10	23	31	7	8	6	25	22	48	53	50
16	Doncaster Rovers	42	6	5	10	22	28	5	9	7	20	29	42	57	47
17	Hereford United	42	7	9	5	31	27	3	6	12	16	33	47	60	45
18	Carlisle United	42	7	5	9	29	27	4	6	11	22	38	51	65	44
19	Torquay United	42	6	4	11	18	26	6	3	12	27	41	45	67	43
20	Northampton Town	42	6	5	10	19	28	5	3	13	29	46	48	74	41
21	Gillingham	42	9	4	8	32	28	0	9	12	16	36	48	64	40
22	Halifax Town	42	3	5	13	20	35	6	4	11	25	33	45	68	36

1993/94 Division 3

		Pl.	Home					Away					F.	A.	Pts
			W	D	L	F	A	W	D	L	F	A			
1	Shrewsbury Town	42	10	8	3	28	17	12	5	4	35	22	63	39	79
2	Chester City	42	13	5	3	35	18	8	6	7	34	28	69	46	74
3	Crewe Alexandra	42	12	4	5	45	30	9	6	6	35	31	80	61	73
4	Wycombe Wanderers	42	11	6	4	34	21	8	7	6	33	32	67	53	70
5	Preston North End	42	13	5	3	46	23	5	8	8	33	37	79	60	67
6	Torquay United	42	8	10	3	30	24	9	6	6	34	32	64	56	67
7	Carlisle United	42	10	4	7	35	23	8	6	7	22	19	57	42	64
8	Chesterfield	42	8	8	5	32	22	8	6	7	23	26	55	48	62
9	Rochdale	42	10	5	6	38	22	6	7	8	25	29	63	51	60
10	Walsall	42	7	5	9	28	26	10	4	7	20	27	48	53	60
11	Scunthorpe United	42	9	7	5	40	26	6	7	8	24	30	64	56	59
12	Mansfield Town	42	9	3	9	28	30	6	7	8	25	32	53	62	55
13	Bury	42	9	6	6	33	22	5	5	11	22	34	55	56	53
14	Scarborough	42	8	4	9	29	28	7	4	10	26	33	55	61	53
15	Doncaster Rovers	42	8	6	7	24	26	6	4	11	20	31	44	57	52
16	Gillingham	42	8	8	5	27	23	4	7	10	17	28	44	51	51
17	Colchester United	42	8	4	9	31	33	5	6	10	25	38	56	71	49
18	*Lincoln City*	*42*	*7*	*4*	*10*	*26*	*29*	*5*	*7*	*9*	*26*	*34*	*52*	*63*	*47*
19	Wigan Athletic	42	6	7	8	33	33	5	5	11	18	37	51	70	45
20	Hereford United	42	6	4	11	34	33	6	2	13	26	46	60	79	42
21	Darlington	42	7	5	9	24	28	3	6	12	18	36	42	64	41
22	Northampton Town	42	6	7	8	25	23	3	4	14	19	43	44	66	38

1994/95 Division 3

		Pl.	Home					Away					F.	A.	Pts
			W	D	L	F	A	W	D	L	F	A			
1	Carlisle United	42	14	5	2	34	14	13	5	3	33	17	67	31	91
2	Walsall	42	15	3	3	42	18	9	8	4	33	22	75	40	83
3	Chesterfield	42	11	7	3	26	10	12	5	4	36	27	62	37	81
4	Bury	42	13	7	1	39	13	10	4	7	34	23	73	36	80
5	Preston North End	42	13	3	5	37	17	6	7	8	21	24	58	41	67
6	Mansfield Town	42	10	5	6	45	27	8	6	7	39	32	84	59	65
7	Scunthorpe United	42	12	2	7	40	30	6	6	9	28	33	68	63	62
8	Fulham	42	11	5	5	39	22	5	9	7	21	32	60	54	62
9	Doncaster Rovers	42	9	5	7	28	20	8	5	8	30	23	58	43	61
10	Colchester United	42	8	5	8	29	30	8	5	8	27	34	56	64	58
11	Barnet	42	8	7	6	37	27	7	4	10	19	36	56	63	56
12	*Lincoln City*	*42*	*10*	*7*	*4*	*34*	*22*	*5*	*4*	*12*	*20*	*33*	*54*	*55*	*56*
13	Torquay United	42	10	8	3	35	25	4	5	12	19	32	54	57	55
14	Wigan Athletic	42	7	6	8	28	30	7	4	10	25	30	53	60	52
15	Rochdale	42	8	6	7	25	23	4	8	9	19	44	44	67	50
16	Hereford United	42	9	6	6	22	19	3	7	11	23	43	45	62	49
17	Northampton Town	42	8	5	8	25	29	2	9	10	20	38	45	67	44
18	Hartlepool United	42	9	5	7	33	32	2	5	14	10	37	43	69	43
19	Gillingham	42	8	7	6	31	25	2	4	15	15	39	46	64	41
20	Darlington	42	7	5	9	25	24	4	3	14	18	33	43	57	41
21	Scarborough	42	4	7	10	26	31	4	3	14	23	39	49	70	34
22	Exeter City	42	5	5	11	25	36	3	5	13	11	34	36	70	34

1995/96 Division 3

		Pl.	Home					Away					F.	A.	Pts
			W	D	L	F	A	W	D	L	F	A			
1	Preston North End	46	11	8	4	44	22	12	9	2	34	16	78	38	86
2	Gillingham	46	16	6	1	33	6	6	11	6	16	14	49	20	83
3	Bury	46	11	6	6	33	21	11	7	5	33	27	66	48	79
4	Plymouth Argyle	46	14	5	4	41	20	8	7	8	27	29	68	49	78
5	Darlington	46	10	6	7	30	21	10	12	1	30	21	60	42	78
6	Hereford United	46	13	5	5	40	22	7	9	7	25	25	65	47	74
7	Colchester United	46	13	7	3	37	22	5	11	7	24	29	61	51	72
8	Chester City	46	11	9	3	45	22	7	7	9	27	31	72	53	70
9	Barnet	46	13	6	4	40	19	5	10	8	25	26	65	45	70
10	Wigan Athletic	46	15	3	5	36	21	5	7	11	26	35	62	56	70
11	Northampton Town	46	9	10	4	32	22	9	3	11	19	22	51	44	67
12	Scunthorpe United	46	8	8	7	36	30	7	7	9	31	31	67	61	60
13	Doncaster Rovers	46	11	6	6	25	19	5	5	13	24	41	49	60	59
14	Exeter City	46	9	9	5	25	22	4	9	10	21	31	46	53	57
15	Rochdale	46	7	8	8	32	33	7	5	11	25	28	57	61	55
16	Cambridge United	46	8	8	7	34	30	6	4	13	27	41	61	71	54
17	Fulham	46	10	9	4	39	26	2	8	13	18	37	57	63	53
18	*Lincoln City*	*46*	*8*	*7*	*8*	*32*	*26*	*5*	*7*	*11*	*25*	*47*	*57*	*73*	*53*
19	Mansfield Town	46	6	10	7	25	29	5	10	8	29	35	54	64	53
20	Hartlepool United	46	8	9	6	30	24	4	4	15	17	43	47	67	49
21	Leyton Orient	46	11	4	8	29	22	1	7	15	15	41	44	63	47
22	Cardiff City	46	8	6	9	24	22	3	6	14	17	42	41	64	45
23	Scarborough	46	5	11	7	22	28	3	5	15	17	41	39	69	40
24	Torquay United	46	4	9	10	17	36	1	5	17	13	48	30	84	29

1996/97 Division 3

		Pl.	Home					Away					F.	A.	Pts
			W	D	L	F	A	W	D	L	F	A			
1	Wigan Athletic	46	17	3	3	53	21	9	6	8	31	30	84	51	87
2	Fulham	46	13	5	5	41	20	12	7	4	31	18	72	38	87
3	Carlisle United	46	16	3	4	41	21	8	9	6	26	23	67	44	84
4	Northampton Town	46	14	4	5	43	17	6	8	9	24	27	67	44	72
5	Swansea City	46	13	5	5	37	20	8	3	12	25	38	62	58	71
6	Chester City	46	11	8	4	30	16	7	8	8	25	27	55	43	70
7	Cardiff City	46	11	4	8	30	23	9	5	9	26	31	56	54	69
8	Colchester United	46	11	9	3	36	23	6	8	9	26	28	62	51	68
9	*Lincoln City*	*46*	*10*	*8*	*5*	*35*	*25*	*8*	*4*	*11*	*35*	*44*	*70*	*69*	*66*
10	Cambridge United	46	11	5	7	30	27	7	6	10	23	32	53	59	65
11	Mansfield Town	46	9	8	6	21	17	7	8	8	26	28	47	45	64
12	Scarborough	46	9	9	5	36	31	7	6	10	29	37	65	68	63
13	Scunthorpe United	46	11	3	9	36	33	7	6	10	23	29	59	62	63
14	Rochdale	46	10	6	7	34	24	4	10	9	24	34	58	58	58
15	Barnet	46	9	9	5	32	23	5	7	11	14	28	46	51	58
16	Leyton Orient	46	11	6	6	28	20	4	6	13	22	38	50	58	57
17	Hull City	46	9	8	6	29	26	4	10	9	15	24	44	50	57
18	Darlington	46	11	5	7	37	28	3	5	15	27	50	64	78	52
19	Doncaster Rovers	46	9	7	7	29	23	5	3	15	23	43	52	66	52
20	Hartlepool United	46	8	6	9	33	32	6	3	14	20	34	53	66	51
21	Torquay United	46	9	4	10	24	24	4	7	12	22	38	46	62	50
22	Exeter City	46	6	9	8	25	30	6	3	14	23	43	48	73	48
23	Brighton & Hove A.	46	12	6	5	41	27	1	4	18	12	43	53	70	47
24	Hereford United	46	6	8	9	26	25	5	6	12	24	40	50	65	47

SEASON 1989-90
DIVISION FOUR

No.	Date	Opposition	Res.	Att.	Goalscorers
1	19 Aug	SCUNTHORPE UNITED	1-0	4504	Carmichael
2	26	Aldershot	1-0	1786	Carmichael
3	2 Sep	DONCASTER ROVERS	2-1	3906	Bressington, Groves
4	9	Torquay United	3-0	2081	G.Brown, Sertori(2)
5	16	YORK CITY	0-0	4149	
6	23	Wrexham	2-0	2002	Sertori(2)
7	27	PETERBOROUGH UNITED	1-0	6106	Clarke
8	30	Southend United	0-2	4833	
9	7 Oct	Chesterfield	0-0	4723	
10	14	HALIFAX TOWN	2-1	4071	Sertori, Waitt
11	18	Maidstone United	0-2	2199	
12	21	GRIMSBY TOWN	1-1	6251	P.Smith
13	28	Hereford United	2-2	2392	Carmichael, P.Smith
14	1 Nov	STOCKPORT COUNTY	0-0	5003	
15	4	Exeter City	0-3	3674	
16	11	Gillingham	1-3	3612	Bressington
17	25	BURNLEY	1-0	4079	Schofield
18	2 Dec	Colchester United	1-0	2517	Nicholson
19	16	Rochdale	0-1	1216	
20	26	CAMBRIDGE UNITED	4-3	4111	OG, Hobson, Carmichael, P.Smith
21	30	CARLISLE UNITED	1-3	4793	Hobson
22	1 Jan	Scarborough	0-2	2441	
23	6	Hartlepool United	1-1	2499	Hobson
24	13	ALDERSHOT	0-1	3188	
25	20	Scunthorpe United	1-1	3830	Puttnam
26	3 Feb	WREXHAM	1-0	3030	Lormor
27	10	York City	0-0	2687	
28	13	Doncaster Rovers	1-0	3079	Hobson
29	17	COLCHESTER UNITED	2-1	3284	Lormor, P.Smith
30	24	Burnley	0-0	5897	
31	3 Mar	HARTLEPOOL UNITED	4-1	3503	Cornforth, Lormor(2), Clarke
32	7	SOUTHEND UNITED	2-0	4860	OG, Schofield
33	13	Peterborough United	0-1	6204	
34	17	CHESTERFIELD	1-1	5251	Lormor
35	20	Halifax Town	1-0	1423	P.Smith
36	25	MAIDSTONE UNITED	1-2	4302	G.Brown
37	31	Grimsby Town	0-1	11427	
38	4 Apr	TORQUAY UNITED	2-2	2573	Hobson, Scott
39	7	HEREFORD UNITED	1-0	2501	Lormor
40	9	Stockport County	1-1	3394	Hobson
41	14	SCARBOROUGH	0-0	3310	
42	17	Cambridge United	1-2	4121	Lormor
43	21	ROCHDALE	1-2	2470	Lormor
44	24	Carlisle United	2-1	5064	Hobson, Carmichael
45	28	Gillingham	1-1	2654	Scott
46	5 May	EXETER CITY	1-5	4772	Hobson

2 own goals

F.A. CUP

1R	18 Nov	BILLINGHAM SYNTHONIA	1-0	2903	Nicholson
2R	9 Dec	Rochdale	0-3	2369	

LITTLEWOODS CHALLENGE CUP

1R1L	22 Aug	Wolverhampton Wanderers	0-1	11071	
1R2L	30	WOLVERHAMPTON WANDS.	0-2	6733	

LEYLAND DAF CUP

Prel	7 Nov	Halifax Town	0-3	824	
Prel	29	CHESTERFIELD	3-0	1178	Sertori(2), Carmichael
1R	9 Jan	Bolton Wanderers	1-2	4420	Hobson

LINCOLNSHIRE CUP

1R	9 Aug	SCUNTHORPE UNITED	2-1	856	Carmichael, Sertori
SF	15	Spalding United	0-5	535	

Additional players: Bowling I. 1R/1; West D. 1R/7#; Briggs S. 1R/12; Hurford L. 1R/14 & SF/14

1989-90
Back : Schofield, Cook, Sertori, Holmes, Wallington, Waitt, Bowling, James, Thompson, Davis, Bressington.
Front : Brown, Andersen, Casey, Murphy (manager), Pickering (asst. manager), Paul Smith, Nicholson, Clarke.

1990-91
Back : Edwards (chief scout), Nicholson, Lormor, Brown, Bowling, Dunphy,
Wallington, Davis, Scott, Carmichael, Brook (physio), Clarke (manager).
Front : Casey, Schofield, Stoutt, Puttnam, Barron (director), Overton (director),
Reames (chairman), Staples (director), Davey (director), Dixon, Neil Smith, Paul Smith, Bressington.

SEASON 1990-91
DIVISION FOUR

No.	Date	Opposition	Res.	Att.	Goalscorers
1	25 Aug	Burnley	2-2	6106	Brown, P.Smith
2	1 Sep	HALIFAX TOWN	1-0	2947	Schofield
3	15	CARDIFF CITY	0-0	3152	
4	19	CHESTERFIELD	1-1	2855	Puttnam
5	22	Scunthorpe United	1-2	2844	Warren
6	29	Maidstone United	1-4	2190	Casey
7	3 Oct	HEREFORD UNITED	1-1	2205	P.Smith
8	6	ALDERSHOT	2-2	2755	P.Smith(2)
9	13	Peterborough United	0-2	4766	
10	20	Doncaster Rovers	0-1	2968	
11	24	ROCHDALE	1-2	1974	Nicholson
12	27	NORTHAMPTON TOWN	3-1	3352	Nicholson, P.Smith, Casey
13	3 Nov	Carlisle United	0-0	3095	
14	10	Stockport County	0-4	2644	
15	24	DARLINGTON	0-3	2182	
16	1 Dec	SCARBOROUGH	2-0	2204	Schofield, P.Smith
17	15	Hartlepool United	0-2	2055	
18	22	GILLINGHAM	1-1	2685	Puttnam
19	29	Blackpool	0-5	2519	
20	1 Jan	WREXHAM	0-0	2527	
21	5	WALSALL	2-1	2500	Casey, Dobson
22	12	Halifax Town	1-1	1447	Davis
23	19	BURNLEY	1-0	4167	Carmichael
24	26	Cardiff City	1-0	2513	Alexander
25	2 Feb	Chesterfield	1-1	3588	Casey
26	19	Walsall	0-0	3582	
27	23	STOCKPORT COUNTY	0-3	3257	
28	26	York City	0-1	1808	
29	2 Mar	Scarborough	0-3	1432	
30	5	Torquay United	1-0	2330	Puttnam
31	9	HARTLEPOOL UNITED	3-1	2575	Lormor(2), Puttnam
32	13	Hereford United	1-0	2195	Lormor
33	16	MAIDSTONE UNITED	2-1	2583	Alexander, Lormor
34	20	PETERBOROUGH UNITED	0-2	5524	
35	23	Aldershot	3-0	1653	Nicholson, Lee, Alexander
36	26	YORK CITY	2-1	2564	Davis, Lee
37	30	TORQUAY UNITED	3-2	3315	Schofield, Puttnam, Stoutt
38	1 Apr	Gillingham	2-2	3765	Lormor, Puttnam
39	6	BLACKPOOL	0-1	4003	
40	9	Darlington	1-1	4241	Lormor
41	13	Wrexham	2-2	1269	Lormor(2)
42	17	SCUNTHORPE UNITED	1-2	3212	Nicholson
43	20	Doncaster Rovers	0-0	3363	
44	27	Rochdale	0-0	1481	
45	30	Northampton Town	1-1	2544	Lee
46	11 May	CARLISLE UNITED	6-2	2323	Lormor(4), Carmichael, D.West

F.A. CUP

| 1R | 17 Nov | CREWE ALEXANDRA | 1-4 | 3596 | Lormor |

Additional player: Thompson S.P. 5*

RUMBELOWS LEAGUE CUP

| 1R1L | 28 Aug | Halifax Town | 0-2 | 1239 | |
| 1R2L | 5 Sep | HALIFAX TOWN | 1-0 | 2376 | Davis |

Additional player: Dixon A. 1R1L/12

LEYLAND DAF CUP

| Prel | 27 Nov | Birmingham City | 0-2 | 2922 | |
| Prel | 12 Dec | WALSALL | 1-1 | 868 | Davis |

LINCOLNSHIRE CUP

1R	1 Aug	SPALDING UNITED	7-2	694	Puttnam, Lormor, P.Smith(4), Dunphy
SF	4	Scunthorpe United	2-2*	610	P.Smith, Puttnam
F	13 May	GRIMSBY TOWN	3-2	953	Lormor(2), D.West

* after extra time, won 5-4 on penalties

Additional player: Dunphy S. 1R & SF/5

SEASON 1991-92
DIVISION FOUR

Players (columns): Dickins M.J., Smith P.M., Clarke D.A., West D., Carmichael M., Brown G.A., Finney K., Ward P.T., Lee J.B., Dobson P., Puttnam D.P., Alexander K., West G., Nicholson S.M., Hoult R., Schofield J.D., Bowling I., Costello P., Smith N., Lormor A., Dye D.C., Bressington G., Kabia J.T., Dixon B.M., Dunphy S., Chapman D.P.

No.	Date	Opposition	Res.	Att.	Goalscorers
1	17 Aug	Cardiff City	2-1	5137	Carmichael, Dobson
2	24	ROTHERHAM UNITED	0-2	4134	
3	31	Rochdale	0-1	2086	
4	4 Sep	BARNET	0-6	3067	
5	14	Carlisle United	2-0	2149	Lee(2)
6	17	Maidstone United	2-0	1113	P.Smith, Puttnam
7	21	CHESTERFIELD	1-2	2896	Dobson
8	28	Hereford United	0-3	2801	
9	5 Oct	HALIFAX TOWN	0-0	2092	
10	13	Blackpool	0-3	5086	
11	19	York City	1-1	1893	P.Smith
12	26	BURNLEY	0-3	3235	
13	5 Nov	Walsall	0-0	2555	
14	9	Northampton Town	0-1	2575	
15	23	SCUNTHORPE UNITED	4-2	3078	Finney, Lormor(3)
16	30	Doncaster Rovers	5-1	1999	Lormor, Puttnam, Finney, Lee, Carmichael
17	17 Dec	SCARBOROUGH	0-2	1752	
18	21	Rotherham United	1-1	3293	G.West
19	26	CARDIFF CITY	0-0	3162	
20	28	ROCHDALE	0-3	2916	
21	1 Jan	Barnet	0-1	3739	
22	4	GILLINGHAM	1-0	2169	Dobson
23	11	Crewe Alexandra	0-1	3060	
24	18	WREXHAM	0-0	2213	
25	8 Feb	Burnley	0-1	9748	
26	12	DONCASTER ROVERS	2-0	2011	Lee, Dobson
27	15	Scarborough	1-1	1614	P.Smith
28	22	CREWE ALEXANDRA	2-2	2261	Lormor, Lee
29	29	Gillingham	3-1	3160	Puttnam, Kabia(2)
30	3 Mar	Wrexham	1-1	2716	Puttnam
31	7	MANSFIELD TOWN	2-0	4387	Nicholson, Lormor
32	11	WALSALL	1-0	2021	Puttnam
33	18	YORK CITY	0-0	1875	
34	21	NORTHAMPTON TOWN	1-2	2486	Brown
35	24	Mansfield Town	0-0	3604	
36	28	Scunthorpe United	2-0	2697	Schofield, D.West
37	1 Apr	CARLISLE UNITED	1-0	2118	D.West
38	11	MAIDSTONE UNITED	1-0	2241	Carmichael
39	18	Chesterfield	5-1	2748	Lormor, Dunphy, Puttnam, *
40	20	HEREFORD UNITED	3-0	2358	D.West, Carmichael, Lee
41	25	Halifax Town	4-1	1296	Lormor(2), OG, Alexander
42	2 May	BLACKPOOL	2-0	7884	Carmichael(2)

* Additional scorers – Carmichael, Kabia

Apps: 20, 39, 27, 19, 36, 37, 21, 28, 33, 4, 37, 5, 14, 28, 2, 39, 20, 3, 0, 33, 0, 2, 10, 0, 5, 0
Subs: —, 1, 13, 4, —, —, 2, 1, 2, 7, 2, 10, 4, 1, —, —, —, 1, 2, 2, 1, 5, 3, —, 1
Goals: 3, —, 3, 7, 1, 2, —, 6, 4, 6, 1, 1, —, 1, —, —, 9, —, 3, —, 1

1 own goal

F.A. CUP

| 1R | 16 Nov | Stockport County | 1-3 | 3864 | Lee |

RUMBELOWS LEAGUE CUP

| 1R1L | 20 Aug | Chester City | 0-1 | 1018 | |
| 1R2L | 28 | CHESTER CITY | 4-3 * | 2170 | Schofield(2), Dobson, Ward |

* after extra time, lost on away goals

AUTOGLASS TROPHY

| Prel | 19 Nov | Shrewsbury Town | 0-1 | 615 | |
| Prel | 4 Dec | WEST BROMWICH ALBION | 1-2 | 1861 | G.West |

LINCOLNSHIRE CUP

| 1R | 29 Jul | GAINSBOROUGH TRINITY | 3-2 * | 312 | Lee, Finney, N.Smith |
| SF | 3 Aug | GRIMSBY TOWN | 1-2 | 956 | OG |

* after extra time

1991-92
Back : Dobson, Neil Smith, Ward, Brown, Puttnam, Nicholson, West.
Second Row : Chapman, Bowling, Finney, Lormor, Dunphy, Alexander, Lee, Carmichael, Dickins, Hill.
Third Row : Paul Smith, Bressington, Colin Clarke (assistant manager),
Thompson (manager), McDiarmid (physio), Schofield, David Clarke.
Front : Barker, Diamond, Donnelly, Whittle, Hackett, Carbon, Dixon, Charles, Parkinson, Hunt.

1992-93
Back : Dobson, Ward, Kabia, Schofield, Puttnam, Dean West, Clarke.
Second Row : Bressington, Dunphy, Gary West, Morgan, Bowling, Lee, Carmichael, Finney, Brown, Lormor.
Third Row : Chapman, Whittle, Carbon, Donnelly, Alexander (youth coach),
Thompson (manager), McDiarmid (physio), Spencer, Parkinson.
Front : Dixon, Wright, Rawlinson, Irlam, Oseni, Huckerby, Charles, Williams, Gilliat.

SEASON 1992-93
DIVISION THREE (Divisions renumbered)

No.	Date	Opposition	Res.	Att.	Goalscorers
1	15 Aug	Colchester United	1-2	4131	West
2	22	YORK CITY	0-1	3032	
3	29	Carlisle United	0-2	4023	
4	1 Sep	Hereford United	2-0	1403	Lee, Clarke
5	5	SCUNTHORPE UNITED	1-0	3764	Lee
6	12	HALIFAX TOWN	2-1	2689	Carmichael, Lee
7	18	Doncaster Rovers	0-0	2936	
8	26	SHREWSBURY TOWN	0-1	2746	
9	3 Oct	Northampton Town	2-0	1922	Clarke, Kabia
10	10	WALSALL	0-2	3095	
11	17	Bury	2-1	2208	Costello, Lee
12	24	BARNET	4-1	2955	Costello, Bressington, OG, Lee
13	31	Darlington	3-1	2051	Costello(2), Lee
14	3 Nov	Scarborough	1-0	2084	Dunphy
15	7	WREXHAM	0-0	3699	
16	21	Crewe Alexandra	2-1	3208	Carmichael, Smith
17	28	GILLINGHAM	1-1	3175	Baraclough
18	19 Dec	Rochdale	1-5	1793	Matthews
19	28	CARDIFF CITY	3-2	4359	Puttnam, Matthews, West
20	16 Jan	Shrewsbury Town	2-3	2506	Bressington, Matthews
21	23	DONCASTER ROVERS	2-1	3269	Costello(2)
22	26	CARLISLE UNITED	2-1	2947	Lee, Smith
23	30	York City	0-2	3948	
24	6 Feb	COLCHESTER UNITED	1-1	3380	Bressington
25	13	Scunthorpe United	1-1	3748	Bressington
26	16	Halifax Town	1-2	1260	West
27	20	HEREFORD UNITED	2-0	2875	Matthews(2)
28	27	Walsall	2-1	3345	Baraclough, Lee
29	2 Mar	Chesterfield	1-2	2842	Matthews
30	6	NORTHAMPTON TOWN	2-0	3328	Baraclough, Matthews
31	9	TORQUAY UNITED	2-2	2781	Matthews, Baraclough
32	13	Wrexham	0-2	5246	
33	20	SCARBOROUGH	3-0	3725	Baraclough, Lee, Matthews
34	23	Gillingham	1-3	2906	Matthews
35	27	CREWE ALEXANDRA	1-1	4235	Carmichael
36	10 Apr	CHESTERFIELD	1-1	4271	Lee
37	12	Cardiff City	1-3	11257	Matthews
38	17	ROCHDALE	1-2	2922	Lee
39	20	Torquay United	2-1	3688	Carmichael, Smith
40	24	BURY	1-2	3651	Puttnam
41	1 May	Barnet	1-1	4422	Lee
42	8	DARLINGTON	2-0	3107	Costello, Brown

1 own goal

F.A. CUP

1R	14 Nov	STAFFORD RANGERS	0-0	3380	
1Rr	25	Stafford Rangers	1-2	2309	Costello

COCA COLA CUP

1R1L	18 Aug	Doncaster Rovers	3-0	2507	Finney, Bressington, Carmichael
1R2L	25	DONCASTER ROVERS	1-1	1996	Dunphy
2R1L	22 Sep	Crystal Palace	1-3	6947	Bressington
2R2L	6 Oct	CRYSTAL PALACE	1-1	6255	Puttnam

AUTOGLASS TROPHY

1R	1 Dec	ROTHERHAM UNITED	0-1	1066	
1R	14	Scunthorpe United	2-2	1263	Costello, Carmichael

LINCOLNSHIRE CUP

1R	4 Aug	GRANTHAM TOWN	3-0	352	Kabia, Ward, West
SF	21 Apr	Boston United	0-3	356	

SEASON 1993-94
DIVISION THREE

No.	Date	Opposition	Res.	Att.	Goalscorers
1	14 Aug	Colchester United	0-1	3198	
2	21	DARLINGTON	1-1	2699	Baraclough
3	28	Hereford United	2-1	1900	Baraclough, D.Johnson
4	31	CHESTER CITY	0-3	4038	
5	4 Sep	PRESTON NORTH END	0-2	3793	
6	11	Mansfield Town	0-1	2678	
7	18	BURY	2-2	2469	D.Johnson, Jones
8	25	NORTHAMPTON TOWN	4-3	2705	West, D.Johnson, Jones, Puttnam
9	2 Oct	Crewe Alexandra	2-2	3361	Clarke, Brown
10	9	DONCASTER ROVERS	2-1	3901	West(2)
11	16	Wycombe Wanderers	3-2	5623	West, Baraclough, Matthews
12	23	CHESTERFIELD	1-2	3591	D.Johnson
13	30	Rochdale	1-0	2551	Loughlan
14	2 Nov	Carlisle United	3-3	5098	West, Lormor, M.Smith
15	6	TORQUAY UNITED	1-0	3244	Hill
16	20	Walsall	2-5	4580	Hill, Brown
17	27	GILLINGHAM	3-1	2979	Baraclough, Matthews, Schofield
18	11 Dec	Darlington	2-3	1936	D.Johnson, Matthews
19	27	SCUNTHORPE UNITED	2-0	6030	D.Johnson, West
20	1 Jan	SCARBOROUGH	0-1	3812	
21	15	WYCOMBE WANDERERS	1-3	3735	Williams
22	22	Doncaster Rovers	0-1	2374	
23	29	ROCHDALE	1-1	2703	Schofield
24	1 Feb	Chester City	1-1	2648	Mardenborough
25	5	Chesterfield	2-2	3104	Brown, Loughlan
26	12	WIGAN ATHLETIC	0-1	2534	
27	19	HEREFORD UNITED	3-1	2277	Campbell, Matthews(2)
28	26	Preston North End	0-2	5941	
29	1 Mar	Shrewsbury Town	2-1	4706	Hill, Huckerby
30	5	MANSFIELD TOWN	1-2	3384	Baraclough
31	12	Bury	0-1	2214	
32	15	COLCHESTER UNITED	2-0	1631	Mardenborough, Matthews
33	19	Northampton Town	0-0	3868	
34	26	CREWE ALEXANDRA	1-2	3007	Daws
35	29	Wigan Athletic	1-0	1349	OG
36	2 Apr	Scunthorpe United	0-2	3571	
37	4	SHREWSBURY TOWN	0-1	2823	
38	9	Scarborough	2-2	1314	Matthews, OG
39	16	CARLISLE UNITED	0-0	2738	
40	23	Torquay United	2-3	3270	D.Johnson(2)
41	30	WALSALL	1-2	2665	Daws
42	7 May	Gillingham	1-1	2840	Daws

Extra players – D.J.Flitcroft - 8/21, 11/21*; J.Burridge - 19,20,22,23/GK

2 own goals

N.B. SQUAD NUMBERS USED (GK = Goalkeeper)

F.A. CUP

1R	13 Nov	Witton Albion	2-0	1450	West, Lormor
2R	4 Dec	BOLTON WANDERERS	1-3	6250	D.Johnson

COCO COLA CUP

1R1L	17 Aug	Port Vale	2-2	5175	Lormor(2)
1R2L	24	PORT VALE	0-0	3642*	
2R1L	21 Sep	EVERTON	3-4	9153	D.Johnson, Matthews, Brown
2R2L	6 Oct	Everton	2-4	8375	D.Johnson, Baraclough

* after extra time, won on away goals

Additional player: Flitcroft D.J. 2R1L/S*

AUTOGLASS TROPHY

1R	28 Sep	MANSFIELD TOWN	1-0	1449	D.Johnson
1R	10 Nov	Chesterfield	2-1	1475	Hill, Loughlan
2R	30	DARLINGTON	3-2	1434	Loughlan, Williams, Matthews
NQF	11 Jan	CHESTER CITY	1-0	1733	Brown
NSF	8 Feb	Carlisle United	1-2	6246	D.Johnson

Additional player: Dickins M.J. 2R/GK

LINCOLNSHIRE CUP

1R	31 Jul	GRANTHAM TOWN	2-3	519	Mardenborough, Costello

Additional player: Chapman D.P. 1R/19#

1993-94
Back : Ward, Carbon, Dunphy, Pollitt, Lee, Kabia, Lormor.
Centre : Stoutt (youth coach), Clarke, Costello, Parkinson, Brown, Baraclough,
Matthews, Paul Smith, McDiarmid (physio).
Front : Dixon, Chapman, Mardenborough, Alexander (manager), Puttnam, Hill, Schofield.

1994-95
Back : Riley (physio) Alan Johnson, Brown, Daley, Dixon, Williams, Onwere, Carbon,
David Johnson, Matthews, Paul Smith, Greenall, Lord (assistant manager).
Centre : Platnauer, Hebberd, Hill, Foley, Huckerby, Leaning, Bannister, West,
Puttnam, Daws, Mark Smith (youth team coach).
Front : Thomas (director), Hicks (director), Davey (vice chairman), Ellis (manager),
Reames (chairman), Sills (director), Woolsey (director), Hough (secretary).

SEASON 1994-95
DIVISION THREE

No.	Date	Opposition	Res.	Att.	Goalscorers
1	13 Aug	EXETER CITY	2-0	3439	Daws, D.Johnson
2	20	Walsall	1-2	3813	West
3	27	TORQUAY UNITED	1-2	3164	Daley
4	30	Rochdale	0-1	1974	
5	3 Sep	Preston North End	0-4	8837	
6	10	MANSFIELD TOWN	3-2	2575	Daley, West, Puttnam
7	13	WIGAN ATHLETIC	1-0	2030	Schfield
8	17	Exeter City	0-1	2180	
9	24	Hartlepool United	3-0	1419	West, Greenall, Puttnam
10	1 Oct	NORTHAMPTON TOWN	2-2	3248	Brown, Puttnam
11	8	CARLISLE UNITED	1-1	3097	Bannister
12	15	Bury	0-2	3139	
13	22	SCARBOROUGH	2-0	2396	Bannister, Daley
14	29	Hereford United	3-0	2485	Matthews, Daley, Puttnam
15	5 Nov	BARNET	1-2	2741	Matthews
16	19	Fulham	1-1	3955	Bannister
17	26	GILLINGHAM	1-1	2919	West
18	10 Dec	WALSALL	1-1	2717	Brown
19	17	Torquay United	1-2	2004	Daws
20	26	Scunthorpe United	0-2	4785	
21	27	DARLINGOTN	3-1	2964	D.Johnson, Carbon(2)
22	31	Chesterfield	0-1	3325	
23	14 Jan	DONCASTER ROVERS	1-0	2771	Daws
24	28	HEREFORD UNITED	2-0	2545	Hill, Carbon
25	4 Feb	Gillingham	0-0	4196	
26	7	Scarborough	1-1	1217	Daws
27	18	DONCASTER ROVERS	0-3	2291	
28	21	COLCHESTER UNITED	2-0	1969	Bannister, D.Johnson
29	25	Northampton Town	1-3	4821	Greenall
30	4 Mar	HARTLEPOOL UNITED	3-0	6477	Bannister, Carbon, Daws
31	11	Mansfield Town	2-6	3396	Daws, Brown
32	18	ROCHDALE	2-2	2939	West, D.Johnson
33	25	PRESTON NORTH END	1-1	5487	West
34	1 Apr	Wigan Athletic	1-0	1696	Hill
35	4	Barnet	1-2	1616	Carbon
36	8	CHESTERFIELD	0-1	5141	
37	11	FULHAM	2-0	2932	Carbon, Hill
38	15	Darlington	0-0	1664	
39	17	SCUNTHORPE UNITED	3-3	3330	Carbon, Greenall, Williams
40	22	Colchester United	2-1	2654	Bannister, Huckerby
41	29	BURY	0-3	3928	
42	6 May	Carlisle United	3-1	12412	Bannister, Huckerby, Daws

F.A. CUP

1R	12 Nov	Hull City	1-0	5758	Bannister
2R	3 Dec	HUDDERSFIELD TOWN	1-0	4143	D.Johnson
3R	8 Jan	Crystal Palace	1-5	6541	Greenall

COCO COLA CUP

1R1L	16 Aug	CHESTER CITY	2-0	2531	Carbon, Schofield
1R2L	23	Chester City	3-2	1568	Schofield, West, D.Johnson
2R1L	20 Sep	CRYSTAL PALACE	1-0	4310	D.Johnson
2R2L	4 Oct	Crystal Palace	0-3 *	6870	

* after extra time

AUTO WINDSCREEN SHIELD

1R	17 Oct	Doncaster Rovers	0-1	1480	
1R	8 Nov	HULL CITY	1-0	1626	West
2R	30	Huddersfield Town	2-3 *	5738	Daley, A.Johnson

* after extra time, lost on sudden death

LINCOLNSHIRE CUP

1R	30 Jul	Gainsborough Trinity	1-0	550	D.Johnson
SF	6 Aug	Grimsby Town	0-2	853	

SEASON 1995-96
DIVISION THREE

No.	Date	Opposition	Res.	Att.	Goalscorers
1	12 Aug	Preston North End	2-1	7813	Puttnam, West
2	19	GILLINGHAM	0-3	2822	
3	26	Colchester United	0-3	2939	
4	28	SCUNTHORPE UNITED	2-2	2674	Daws, Onwere
5	2 Sep	Barnet	1-3	1813	Huckerby
6	9	ROCHDALE	1-2	2408	Onwere
7	12	BURY	2-2	1851	Onwere, Daws
8	16	Chester City	1-5	3049	Daws
9	23	CAMBRIDGE UNITED	1-3	2614	D.Johnson
10	30	Plymouth Argyle	0-3	6643	
11	7 Oct	DARLINGTON	0-2	2564	
12	14	Scarborough	0-0	1848	
13	21	CARDIFF CITY	0-1	2453	
14	28	Exeter City	1-1	3252	Barnett
15	1 Nov	Mansfield Town	2-1	2398	Onwere, Holmes
16	4	HARTLEPOOL UNITED	1-1	2939	Huckerby
17	18	Torquay United	2-0	2553	Ainsworth(2)
18	25	NORTHAMPTON TOWN	1-0	3287	S.Brown
19	9 Dec	Cambridge United	1-2	2472	Westley
20	16	PLYMOUTH ARGYLE	0-0	2801	
21	23	Wigan Athletic	1-1	2334	S.Brown
22	26	FULHAM	4-0	3693	S.Brown, Ainsworth(2), Whitney
23	13 Jan	Gillingham	0-2	8047	
24	16	LEYTON ORIENT	1-0	1841	Carbon
25	20	Preston North End	0-0	5185	
26	3 Feb	COLCHESTER UNITED	0-0	2531	
27	5	Doncaster Rovers	1-1	2083	Minett
28	13	HEREFORD UNITED	2-1	1884	Minett, Whitney
29	17	Bury	1-7	3096	Carbon
30	24	CHESTER CITY	0-0	2533	
31	27	Rochdale	3-3	1253	Carbon, Ainsworth, OG
32	2 Mar	Fulham	2-1	4245	Ainsworth(2)
33	5	Scunthorpe United	3-2	2411	Ainsworth(2), Daley
34	9	WIGAN ATHLETIC	2-4	3282	Alcide, Ainsworth
35	16	Leyton Orient	0-2	3129	
36	19	BARNET	1-2	1872	Bos
37	23	DONCASTER ROVERS	4-0	3240	Alcide(2), Minett(2)
38	27	Hereford United	0-1	1631	
39	30	Darlington	2-3	2146	Bos, Ainsworth
40	2 Apr	SCARBOROUGH	3-1	2010	Bos(2), Ainsworth
41	6	EXETER CITY	0-1	2723	
42	8	Cardiff City	1-1	2657	Alcide
43	13	MANSFIELD TOWN	2-1	2992	OG, Bos
44	20	Hartlepool United	0-3	3012	
45	27	Northampton Town	1-1	5166	Minett
46	4 May	TORQUAY UNITED	5-0	5814	Alcide(2), Storey, Barnett, Holmes

Additional players: Platnauer N.R. 1/14; Williams S.R. 2/12, 5/9#, 8/14; Dyer A.C. 3/9#; Davis D.J. 6,9,10/6; Bound M.T. 7,8/6, 9/5*, 11/14; Appleton M.A. 8,9/8, 10/11, 11/2; Hulme K. 10/7*, 11/11, 12/4, 13/4*, 14/12; Westley S.L.M. 11-19/5 (9 apps, 1 goal); Storey B.B. 43/14, 46/12 (0 + 2 apps, 1 goal)

F.A. CUP

1R	11 Nov	Stockport County	0-5	3952	

Additional players: Westley S.L.M. 5; Hulme K. 10*

COCA COLA CUP

| 1R1L | 15 Aug | Notts County | 0-2 | 3494 | |
| 1R2L | 22 | NOTTS COUNTY | 0-2 | 2636 | |

Additional players: Williams S.R. 1R1L/14; Dyer A.C. 1R2L/11

AUTO WINDSCREEN SHIELD

1R	26 Sep	ROCHDALE	4-3	1238	Huckerby(2), D.Johnson(2)
1R	7 Nov	Darlington	1-0	984	G.Brown
2R	28	PRESTON NORTH END	2-1	1729	Onwere, S.Brown
NQF	9 Jan	Rotherham United	1-3	1825	Ainsworth

Additional players: Bound M.T. 1st 1R/6; Davis D.J. 1st 1R/7; Appleton M.A. 1st 1R/8; Hulme K. 2nd 1R/8, 2R/12; Westley S.L.M. 2R/5

LINCOLNSHIRE CUP

| G | 29 Jul | Boston United | 0-0 | 823 | |
| G | 1 Aug | Grantham Town | 2-1 | 365 | Carbon, D.Johnson |

Additional players: Williams S.R. 1st G/12

1995-96
Back : Platnauer, Daley, Williams, Grant Brown, Dixon, Carbon, Leaning,
David Johnson, Alan Johnson, Wanless, Allon, Lord (assistant manager).
Front : Onwere, Huckerby, West, Puttnam, Ellis (manager), Minett, Daws, Mudd, Greenall.

1996-97
Back : Holmes, Storey, Whitney, Richardson, Vaughan, Davies, Fraser, Austin.
Centre : Cain (kit manager), Bonnell (scout), Alcide, Lawrence, Robertson, Bos, Hone, Grant Brown,
Challinor, Cleary (physio), Whyte (youth development officer).
Front : Sterling, Fleming, Ainsworth, Steve Brown, Beck (manager),
Westley (reserve coach), Minett, Dennis, Barnett, Gibson.

SEASON 1996-97
DIVISION THREE

No.	Date	Opposition	Res.	Att.	Goalscorers
1	17 Aug	Torquay United	1-2	2645	Ainsworth
2	24	LEYTON ORIENT	1-1	3067	Ainsworth
3	27	CAMBRIDGE UNITED	1-1	2407	Dennis
4	30	Swansea City	2-1	3111	Ainsworth(2)
5	7 Sep	Chester City	1-4	1802	Holmes
6	10	HULL CITY	0-1	3069	
7	14	BARNET	1-0	2484	Martin
8	21	Wigan Athletic	0-1	3394	
9	28	CARDIFF CITY	2-0	2925	Alcide, Taylor
10	1 Oct	Brighton & Hove Albion	3-1	4411	Ainsworth, Alcide, G.Brown
11	5	EXETER CITY	2-3	3115	Ainsworth, Dennis
12	12	Scunthorpe United	0-2	3274	
13	15	Rochdale	0-2	1411	
14	19	SCARBOROUGH	1-1	2611	Taylor
15	26	COLCHESTER UNITED	3-2	2768	Ainsworth, Martin, OG
16	29	Doncaster Rovers	3-1	1913	Alcide(2), Ainsworth
17	2 Nov	Fulham	2-1	6945	Ainsworth, Whitney
18	9	DARLINGTON	2-0	3259	Whitney(2)
19	19	Hereford United	1-1	1363	Ainsworth
20	23	MANSFIELD TOWN	0-0	3548	
21	30	Colchester United	1-7	2738	Martin
22	3 Dec	CARLISLE UNITED	1-1	2033	Alcide
23	14	NORTHAMPTON TOWN	1-1	2702	Ainsworth
24	21	Hartlepool United	1-2	1344	Bos
25	26	Hull City	1-2	4892	Stant
26	11 Jan	Cardiff City	3-1	2033	Stant, OG, Ainsworth
27	18	BRIGHTON & HOVE ALBION	2-1	3056	Stant, Ainsworth
28	25	DONCASTER ROVERS	3-1	3262	Stant(2), Martin
29	28	CHESTER CITY	0-0	2330	
30	1 Feb	Darlington	2-5	2265	Ainsworth(2)
31	4	WIGAN ATHLETIC	1-3	2241	Cort
32	8	FULHAM	2-0	3948	Ainsworth, Stant
33	15	Mansfield Town	2-2	3037	Ainsworth, Stant
34	22	HEREFORD UNITED	3-3	2957	Holmes, Stant, Alcide
35	25	Barnet	0-1	1194	
36	1 Mar	Carlisle United	0-1	4958	
37	8	HARTLEPOOL UNITED	2-1	2915	Ainsworth(2)
38	15	Northampton Town	1-1	5266	Holmes
39	22	Leyton Orient	3-2	4121	Ainsworth, S.Brown, Stant
40	29	TORQUAY UNITED	1-2	3455	Alcide
41	31	Cambridge United	3-1	3656	Robertson, OG, Stant
42	5 Apr	SWANSEA CITY	4-0	3348	Alcide, Ainsworth, Stant(2)
43	12	Exeter City	3-3	2818	S.Brown, Stant, Holmes
44	19	SCUNTHORPE UNITED	2-0	4755	Ainsworth, Stant
45	26	Scarborough	2-0	3607	Stant(2)
46	3 May	ROCHDALE	0-2	6495	

3 own goals

F.A. CUP

| 1R | 16 Nov | Burnley | 1-2 | 6484 | Bos |

COCA COLA CUP

1R1L	20 Aug	Hartlepool United	2-2	2073	Bos, Alcide
1R2L	3 Sep	HARTLEPOOL UNITED	3-2	2389	Martin, Holmes, Alcide
2R1L	17	MANCHESTER CITY	4-1	7599	Fleming, Holmes, Bos, Whitney
2R2L	24	Manchester City	1-0	14242	Bos
3R	23 Oct	Southampton	2-2	14516	Hone, Ainsworth
3Rr	12 Nov	SOUTHAMPTON	1-3	10523	Ainsworth

AUTO WINDSCREEN SHIELD

| 2R | 14 Jan | Blackpool | 0-4 | 1578 | |

1R - Bye

LINCOLNSHIRE CUP

| 1R | 1 Aug | Lincoln United | 0-1 | 463 | |

Additional players: Storey B.B. 11", Anderson R. 15

FRIENDLY AND MINOR CUP GAMES, ETC :
INTRODUCTION

The qualifications for inclusion in this list are that the game was a public match, that it was recognised as a first team game and that the City team which appeared was either of full strength or near to full strength. It includes games played up to the end of the 1996/97 season. Closed door and private practice games are excluded on the basis of not being public fixtures - this includes a number of pre-season friendlies played on RAF bases in the 1970s and 1980s and the match with the Qatar national side in September 1975. Games excluded on the grounds that a first team did not appear include most of the fixtures with March Town in the 1950s, ties in the Sleaford Invitation Cup and the two fixtures with the British Police (April 1988 and March 1989).The 1926/27 tie against Gainsborough Trinity in the Cranwell RAF Memorial Shield and the 1996/97 Syd North Trophy match against Horncastle Town are not included for similar reasons. Occasions when the first team appeared by agreement in a competition for which the reserves were entered have also been discounted; there are a number of Midland League fixtures prior to 1915, which for this reason have been excluded.

Games **have** been listed in cases where there is some doubt as to whether the game should be included. Games marked * denote result not traced.

1884/85
Oct	4	Sleaford	H 9-1
	11	Nottingham Forest XI	H 2-4
Nov	8	Sheffield Brincliffe	H 5-0
	15	Derby Midland	A 1-6
	29	Lockwood Brothers	H 0-4
Dec	20	Newark	H 8-1
	29	Sheffield	H 6-2
Jan	6	Cambridge Univ. Wands.	H 1-2
	10	Notts Wanderers	H 1-1
	24	Sheffield Collegiate	H 2-1
	31	Long Eaton Rangers	A 0-2
Feb	7	Notts County XI	H 1-0
	14	Mellors Ltd (Nottm.)	H 2-0
	28	Derby Midland	H 1-3
Mar	14	Long Eaton Rangers	H 1-5
	21	Sheffield	A 1-1
Apr	4	Mellors Ltd (Nottm.)	H 3-0
	6	Wirksworth	H 0-1
	18	Notts Amateurs	H 4-0
	25	Grimsby Town	A 0-0

1885/86
Sep	5	Lincoln Butchers	H13-0
	26	Grimsby Town	A 2-2
Oct	3	Mexborough	H 4-0
	10	Derby St Lukes	H 3-1
	17	Newark	H 7-0
	24	Nottingham Forest XI	H 7-0
Nov	7	Nottingham Forest XI	A 0-0
	16	Blackburn Rovers	H 0-1
	21	Derby St Lukes	H 1-1
	28	Derby St Lukes	A 0-2
Dec	5	Notts County XI	H 4-0
	10	Grantham Town	A 2-2
	26	Sheffield	H 3-0
	28	Louth	H 5-0
Jan	2	Notts Rangers	H 1-1
	16	Derby Midland	H 2-3
	23	Attercliffe	H 5-0
Feb	4	Grantham Town	H 7-0
	6	Notts Rangers	A 0-2
	13	Mexborough	A 0-2
	20	Burton-on-Trent Strollers	H 6-0
	25	Notts County XI	A 1-2
	27	Brigg Town	A 3-0
Mar	20	Basford Rovers	H 5-0
	27	Accrington XI	H 3-4
	30	Preston North End	H 0-4
Apr	3	Brigg Town	H 6-0
	10	Notts Rangers	H 1-2
	17	Lockwood Brothers	H 2-0
	23	Lincoln Ramblers	H12-1
(Benefit for Charity Organization Society)			
	24	London Nondescripts	H 7-1
	26	Derby Midland	H 3-0
	29	T.H.White's XI	H 2-1
May	19	T.H.White's XI	H 6-0

1886/87
Aug		Mellors Ltd (Nottm.)	H 4-0
	11	Jardines (Nottm.)	H 3-0
	16	Basford Rovers	H 4-0
	23	Sneinton Rovers	H 6-0
Sep	4	Wednesbury Old Athletic	H 3-0

(1886/87 contd.)
	11	Aston Villa	A 1-4
	18	Birmingham Excelsior	H 5-0
	25	Mellors Ltd (Nottm.)	H13-0
Oct	2	Derby Junction	H 4-3
	9	Jardines (Nottm.)	H 1-0
	16	Oswaldtwistle Rovers	H 2-1
	23	Heeley	H 5-0
	30	Liverpool Oakfield Rovers	H 7-1
Nov	13	Cambridge University	H 6-0
Dec	18	Brigg Town	H 1-0
	25	Long Eaton Rangers	H 0-2
	27	Sheffield	H 4-0
Feb	5	Derby Midland	H 1-2
	12	Walsall Swifts	H 2-1
	21	Preston North End	H 0-2
	26	Mexborough	H 4-0
Mar	19	Sheffield Wednesday	H 1-0
	26	Lincoln Ramblers	H 4-0
Apr	8	London Strollers	H 4-0
	9	Mitchell St Georges	H 1-2
	11	Jardines (Nottm.)	H 4-2
	13	Corinthians	H 0-5
	16	Accrington & District	H 3-1
	30	Derby Midland	H 5-1
May	7	Boston Town	A 4-2
	14	Gainsborough Trinity	H 0-1
(Benefit for Lincoln County Hospital)			
	21	Horncastle	H 6-2
(Benefit for Horncastle player)			

1887/88
Aug	17	Basford Rovers	H 3-0
Sep	3	Derby Junction	H 4-1
	10	Mexborough	H 7-1
	17	Boston Town	H 7-0
	24	Grimsby Town	H 3-1
Oct	1	Notts Rangers	H 1-1
	8	Gainsborough Trinity	A 1-2
	17	Lockwood Brothers	A 1-1
	29	West Bromwich Albion	A 1-4
Nov	12	Nottingham Forest	H 1-1
	19	Oswaldtwistle Rovers	H 4-1
	28	Sheffield Wednesday	A 1-5
Dec	10	West Bromwich Albion	H 1-6
	17	Loughborough	H 5-1
	24	Derby Midland	H 3-0
	26	Sheffield	H 7-0
	27	Burton Swifts	H 6-0
	28	Rotherham Town	A 8-2
	31	Staveley	H 4-1
Jan	2	Clyde	H 2-4
	7	Heeley	H 2-0
	14	Notts Jardines	H 2-0
	28	Bolton Wanderers	H 4-3
Feb	4	Nottingham Forest	A 0-2
	11	Burslem Port Vale	H 2-3
	18	Long Eaton Rangers	A 2-2
Mar	3	Rotherham Town	H 4-1
	10	Lockwood Brothers	H 5-0
	17	Middlesbrough	H 1-0
	24	Sheffield Wednesday	H 1-2
	30	Rawtenstall	H 5-1
	31	Doncaster Rovers	H 1-2
Apr	2	North Wales Wanderers	H 2-1

(1887/88 contd.)
	3	London Strollers	H 4-2
	7	Gainsborough Trinity	H 3-1
	14	Lindum	H 1-1
	21	Long Eaton Rangers	H 3-1
	28	Gainsborough Trinity	H 2-1
May	5	Boston Town	A 2-2
	12	Derby St Lukes	H 1-2
(Benefit for Joe Duckworth)			

1888/89
Sep	1	Notts Mellors	H 0-2
	22	Basford Rovers	H13-1
	29	Canadian Touring XI	H 1-3
Oct	15	Notts County	H 3-1
	27	Notts Olympic	H 5-1
Nov	3	Mitchell St Georges	H 4-1
	6	Rotherham Town	A 2-2
	10	Sheffield Wednesday	H 1-6
	17	Middlesbrough	A 0-2
	24	Sunderland	H 1-1
Dec	8	Notts Rangers	H 3-3
	15	Sheffield	H 5-1
	24	Sheffield Wednesday	A 0-5
	26	Lincoln Rangers	H 8-4
	29	Halliwell	H 2-4
Jan	12	Derby St Lukes	H 4-0
	19	Rotherham Town	H 4-0
Feb	2	Lincolnshire Regiment	H10-1
	9	Derby County	H 0-1
	16	Heeley	H 6-1
	27	Notts County	H 4-1
(Played under floodlights)			
Mar	21	Gainsborough Trinity	A 1-0
(Played under floodlights)			
	30	Bolton Wanderers	H 2-3
Apr	13	Boston Town	H 3-2
	20	Warwick County	H 2-1
May	4	Boston Town	A 4-1
	11	Doncaster Rovers	H 5-0
(Benefit for former players)			

1889/90
Sep	21	Sheffield United	H 0-1
Oct	5	Sunderland Albion	A 1-6
	12	Halliwell	H 2-4
	14	Sheffield United	A 1-3
Nov	2	Notts Jardines	H 2-1
	23	Derby Junction	H 8-0
Dec	14	Grimsby Town	H 0-0
	21	Rotherham Swifts	H 8-0
	25	Sheffield United	H 5-1
	26	London Casuals	H 6-1
Jan	11	Grimsby Town	A 1-3
Feb	8	Middlesbrough Ironopolis	A 0-1
	15	Manchester	H10-1
Mar	15	Derby St Lukes	H 5-0
	19	Gainsborough Trinity	H 3-0
(Played under floodlights)			
	25	Grantham Rovers	A 1-0
Apr	4	Notts County	H 2-2
	12	Wolverhampton Wands.	A 3-4
May	3	Grimsby Town	H 2-4
	10	Derby County	H 2-4
	17	Notts Jardines	H 5-1
	24	Grimsby Town	H 1-1

1921/22
Mar	27	Grimsby Town	H	3-3
		(Lincoln Hospital Cup)		
Apr	4	Grimsby Town	A	1-5
		(Lincoln Hospital Cup - replay)		

1922/23
May	4	Nottingham Forest	H	1-2
		(Lincoln Hospital Cup)		

1923/24
Apr	28	Arthur Atkin's XI	H	3-3
		(Benefit for Arthur Atkin)		
	30	Notts County	H	3-0
		(Lincoln Hospital Cup)		

1924/25
Nov	26	Gainsborough Trinity	H	3-1
		(Cranwell RAF Memorial Shield - Rl)		
Jan	10	Blackburn Rovers Res.	H	2-1
Apr	6	Grantham	H	3-I
		(Cranwell RAF Memorial Shield - SF)		
	20	Notts County	H	0-0
		(Lincoln Hospital Cup)		
	27	Grimsby Town	H	3-0
		(Cranwell RAF Memorial Shield - F)		

1925/26
Oct	14	Arsenal	H	3-0
		(Benefit for Alf Jewett)		
	28	York City	A	1-2
Dec	29	Gainsborough Trinity	A	2-3
		(Cranwell RAF Memorial Shield - Rl)		
May	3	Chesterfield	H	0-4
		(Lincoln Hospital Cup)		

1926/27
Apr	25	Chesterfield	H	6-0
		(Lincoln Hospital Cup)		
May	2	Chesterfield	A	1-7
		(Chesterfield Hospital Cup)		

1927/28
Sep	19	Grimsby Town	H	4-1
		(Benefit for Harry Pringle)		

1930/31
Jan	10	Sheffield Wed. Res.	A	6-8

1935/36
Dec	14	Millwall	H	2-2
Jan	8	Dutch National 'B' XI	A	2-4
		(In Rotterdam)		

1936/37
Apr	28	Grimsby Town	H	2-2
(Benefit for Dan McPhail and George Whyte)				

1937/38
Jan	19	Dutch National XI	A	0-5
		(in Rotterdam)		
May	4	Bernard Towler's XI	H	4-4
		(Benefit for Bernard Towler)		

1938/39
May	3	Derby County	H	0-2
		(Benefit for John Campbell)		

1939/40
Sep	30	Nottingham Forest	H	0-6
Oct	14	Scunthorpe United	A	2-5
Nov	4	Rotherham United	H	6-3
Dec	16	York City	A	3-3
	25	Mansfield Town	A	2-2
	26	Mansfield Town	H	4-1
	30	Peterborough United	A	1-4
Jan	13	York City	H	4-3

1940/41
Oct	19	Nottingham Forest	H	2-3
Dec	7	Infantry Training Corps	H	6-5
Mar	15	RAF XI	H	3-4

1941/42
Jan	17	RAF XI	A	5-2
(In aid of RAF Benevolent Fund,				
played at Skegness Grammar School)				
Mar	14	RAF XI	H	1-2

1942/43
Aug	22	RAF XI	H	2-1

1943/44
Aug	21	RAF Station 'S'	H	5-2

1944/45
Aug	19	RAF Skegness	H	6-2

1946/47
Sep	25	Nottingham Forest	H	0-3
		(Benefit for Billy Bean)		
Jun	11	Bill Whittaker's XI	A	1-0
		(Ruskington Cup)		

1947/48
Dec	13	Port Vale	A	1-2
Apr	28	Chesterfield	H	1-0
		(Benefit for Geoff Marlow)		

1948/49
May	7	Mansfield Town	H	2-1
	30	KR	A	2-0
		(Tour of Iceland)		
Jun	1	Valur Reykjavik	A	2-0
	2	Fram/Vikingur XI	A	1-0
	3	Combined Reykjavik XI	A	1-4

1949/50
Sep	21	Mac's All Star XI	H	3-2
		(Benefit for Joe McClelland)		
Dec	10	Brighton and Hove Alb.	H	3-1
Jan	7	Leyton Orient	H	4-1

1950/51
Sep	20	Jimmy Grummett's XI	H	4-2
		(Benefit for Jimmy Grummett)		
	27	George Stillyards' XI	H	1-1
		(Benefit for George Stillyards)		
Dec	9	Southend United	H	4-4
May	9	Transport (Eire)	H	6-1
		(Festival of Britain)		
	12	Sligo Rovers (Eire)	H	3-0
		(Festival of Britain)		

1951/52
May	1	Grimsby Town	A	2-1

1952/53
Sep	29	Selected XI	H	4-2
(Benefit for Tony Emery and Bobby Owen)				
Jan	31	Portsmouth	A	2-2
Mar	11	Brentford	H	2-2
(In aid of Mayor's Flood Relief Fund)				
May	16	Jersey Saturday League XI	A	1-0
	19	Jersey/Guernsey XI	A	6-1

1953/54
Mar	23	Grimsby Town	A	1-1

1954/55
Oct	26	Carlisle United	A	2-4
Nov	3	Aldershot	A	4-3
Jan	29	Leicester City	H	3-4
Mar	12	Manchester United	H	2-3

1955/56
Oct	4	Carlisle United	A	1-2
	24	North Shields	A	3-2
Jan	23	Exeter City	A	1-3
	28	Bury	H	2-2
Apr	23	Spartak FK (Yugoslavia)	H	2-1

1956/57
Nov	6	Brentford	A	0-2
Jan	26	Doncaster Rovers	H	2-2
May	1	Newcastle United	H	2-2
		(Benefit for Doug Graham)		

1957/58
Oct	28	Plymouth Argyle	A	1-3
Feb	15	Hull City	H	2-5

1958/59
Oct	20	Walsall	A	1-3
Jan	24	Barnsley	H	2-1
Apr	28	March Town United	A	5-3

1959/60
Oct	31	Headington United	A	4-2
Jan	30	Grimsby Town	H	1-2
May	15	Limerick	A	4-1
		(Tour of Eire)		
	17	Shelbourne	A	3-1
	19	Waterford	A	7-6

1962/63
Aug	10	Grimsby Town	H	0-2

1963/64
Aug	14	Grimsby Town	H	4-3
May	1	Lincoln City Old Star XI	H	5-5
		(Players Benefit Fund)		

1964/65
Aug	12	Grimsby Town	H	2-6
	14	Grimsby Town	A	1-5
Apr	30	Lincoln City Old Star XI	H	8-8
		(Benefit)		

1965/66
Aug	7	Gainsborough Trinity	A	1-0
	10	Burton Albion	A	2-2
	13	Mansfield Town	H	0-5
Jan	22	Scunthorpe United	H	1-5
May	9	Jimmy Hill's Internat. XI	H	8-4
		(Benefit for Roger Holmes)		

1966/67
Aug	12	Boston FC	H	3-0
	15	Boston United	H	1-1
Oct	10	Ex-Wolverhampton W. XI	H	*
		(Benefit)		
May	9	Heart of Midlothian	H	3-0
	17	Boston United	A	4-3
		(Mather Cup)		

1967/68
Aug	5	Scunthorpe United	H	1-1
	9	Peterborough United	H	3-3
	16	Nottingham Forest XI	H	2-1
May	17	Norwich City	H	3-3

1968/69
Jul	23	Barnsley	H	2-0
Aug	2	Queen of the South	H	3-2
Feb	24	Bohemians (Prague,Czech.)	H	1-1
	26	Sheffield United	H	3-2

1969/70
Jul	26	Stockport County	H	1-1
	28	Kettering Town	A	2-3
	30	Middlesbrough	H	0-2
Aug	1	Glentoran	A	2-1
	2	Ards	A	2-2
	5	Kettering Town	H	3-2
Apr	28	All Star XI	H	5-4
		(Benefit for John Harrison)		
	30	Gainsborough Trinity	A	7-4
		(Benefit for Russell Green)		

1970/71
Aug	1	Northampton Town	H	2-1
	4	Walsall	A	2-3
	8	Chesterfield	H	3-0
Mar	31	Lunds BK (Sweden)	H	2-0
Apr	14	Lincoln City Old Stars	H	9-5
		(Benefit for Roger Holmes)		

1971/72
Jul	31	Stoke City XI	H	2-1
Aug	4	Port Vale	H	2-1
	7	Wigan Athletic	H	0-0
	9	Kettering Town	A	2-2
Mar	15	All Star XI	H	7-9
		(Benefit for Nobby Lawton)		

1972/73
Aug	2	Notts County	H	1-0
	5	Manchester United XI	H	4-0
Dec	5	Crystal Palace	H	3-1
		(Benefit for Trevor Meath)		

1973/74
Aug	11	Chesterfield	A	1-3
	16	Bishop Auckland	H	10-1
	20	Nottingham Forest	H	2-0
Dec	5	Chelsea	H	2-4
		(Benefit for John Kennedy and		
		George Peden; attendance 6,591)		

1890/91
Sep	6	Sheffield Wednesday	A 3-3
	10	Notts Jardines	H 6-0
	13	Sheffield Wednesday	H 2-1
Oct	11	Grimsby Town	H 2-1
	28	Grimsby Town	A 0-1
		(Benefit for Jimmy Lundie)	
Nov	8	Grimsby Town	A 3-5
Dec	20	Long Eaton Rangers	H 4-2
	26	London Casuals	H 3-3
	27	South Bank	H 6-1
Jan	31	Darlington	H 0-2
Mar	5	Grantham Rovers	A 1-0
		(Grantham Charity Cup - R3)	
	12	Norfolk County	A 4-2
	27	Notts County	H 0-1
	30	Middlesbrough Ironopolis	A 0-2
Apr	4	Derby County	H 2-1
	18	Sheffield United	H 0-1
	24	Gainsborough Trinity	H 3-0
	29	Doncaster Rovers	H 9-3
	30	Doncaster Rovers	A 0-2

1891/92
Sep	2	Notts County	H 0-4
	5	Grimsby Town	A 3-3
	9	Grimsby Town	H 1-0
		(Benefit for Herbert Simpson)	
	12	Sheffield Wednesday	A 4-7
	16	Canadian Touring XI	H 1-2
	23	Gainsborough Trinity	A 0-2
Oct	17	Rotherham Town	H 6-1
Nov	12	Grantham Rovers	A 1-4
	14	Burslem Port Vale	H 2-0
Dec	5	Woolwich Arsenal	A 1-3
	26	Casuals	H 4-4
Jan	2	Long Eaton Rangers	H 5-2
	23	Gainsborough Trinity	A 2-2
Feb	24	Barton Town	H *
		(Lincs. & District Charity Cup - Rl)	
	27	Gainsborough Trinity	H 1-2
Mar	2	Everton	H 0-3
	19	Sheffield United	A 2-2
	28	Doncaster Rovers	A 2-1
	31	Newark	A 1-3
		(Lincs. & District Charity Cup - SF)	
Apr	6	Gainsborough Trinity	H 2-2
	18	Newcastle West End	A 1-3
	19	Rotherham Town	A 1-6
	23	Sheffield United	H 2-2
	30	Grimsby Town	H 0-1

1892/93
Sep	3	Nottingham Forest	A 1-3
	10	Gainsborough Trinity	A 2-1
	14	Nottingham Forest	H 2-3
	17	Rotherham Town	H 3-1
	29	Grimsby Town	A 2-2
(At Mablethorpe to celebrate the opening of Louth to Sutton-on-Sea railway line - match abandoned)
Oct	20	Grimsby Town	A 3-5
		(Benefit for David Riddoch)	
Nov	5	Woolwich Arsenal	A 0-4
	26	Grimsby Town	H 3-6
Dec	27	London Casuals	H 1-1
Jan	21	Ist Royal Scots	H 3-2
Mar	11	Grantham Rovers	H 1-2
	18	Newark	H 3-1
		(Lincoln Charity Cup - SF)	
	25	Grimsby Town	A 2-4
Apr	4	Rotherham Town	A 0-4
	20	Gainsborough Trinity	H 3-0
		(Lincoln Charity Cup - F)	
	22	Burton Wanderers	H 4-0
	26	Grimsby Town	H 2-3
		(Benefit for Arthur Marriott)	
	29	Gainsborough Trinity	H 3-0

1893/94
Sep	6	Grantham Rovers	H 3-0
	20	Casuals (Lincoln)	H 7-1
	30	Burton Wanderers	H 2-0
Oct	4	Gainsborough Trinity	H 1-3

(1893/94 contd.)
Nov	18	Darlington	H 1-0
	25	Ist Royal Scots	H 2-2
Dec	16	Millwall Athletic	A 0-4
Jan	6	Gainsborough Trinity	A 4-8
	27	Mansfield Greenhalgh's	H 4-1
	31	Sheffield United	H 1-0
		(played under floodlights)	
Mar	3	Lincoln League XI	H 8-0
	8	Grimsby Town	A 0-2
	13	Grantham Rovers	A 4-0
	28	Gainsborough Trinity	A 0-0
Apr	4	Grimsby Town	H 4-2
	14	Doncaster Rovers	A 2-1
	18	Burnley	H 1-2
		(Benefit for Quentin Neill & George Shaw)	
	21	Long Eaton Rangers	H 0-1
		(Lincoln Charity Cup - SF)	
	28	Gainsborough Trinity	H 4-0

1894/95
Sep	5	Gainsborough Trinity	A 4-0
	12	Sheffield Wednesday	H 5-3
	19	Gainsborough Trinity	H 4-0
	31	Sheffield Wednesday	A 0-5
Nov	9	Northwich Victoria	H 2-2
	24	Scottish Borderers Reg't.	H 7-0
Dec	15	Grimsby Town	H 0-2
Feb	2	Grimsby Town	A 0-0
	9	Gainsborough Trinity	A 0-2
Apr	15	3rd Battn.Grenadier Guards	A 3-1
	27	Rotherham Town	H 3-3
	30	Gainsborough Trinity	H 2-0
		(Lincs. Charity Cup - F)	

1895/96
Sep	2	Gainsborough Trinity	H 0-0
	11	Gainsborough Trinity	A 3-4
Dec	7	Grimsby Town	A 2-1
	14	Gainsborough Trinity	A 1-3
	25	Newark	H 3-1
Jan	1	Middlesbrough	A 3-8
	18	Grimsby Town	H 2-1
Mar	21	Glossop North End	A 3-2
(Abandoned after 80 mins due to crowd trouble)
	30	Royal Ordnance	A 0-1
Apr	6	Ilkeston Town	A 1-2
	23	Grantham Rovers	A 2-4
		(Benefit for Harry Woods)	
	25	London Caledonians	A 3-2

1896/97
Sep	1	New Brompton	A 0-6
	2	Sheffield United	H 0-1
	7	Southampton St Marys	A 1-0
	9	Derby County	H 4-1
	16	Gainsborough Trinity	H 1-1
	22	Stockport County	A 0-3
Oct	10	Gainsborough Trinity	A 1-5
	17	Ealing	A 4-1
	26	Walsall	H 0-3
		(Kettering Charity Cup - Rl)	
	31	Southampton St Marys	H 1-1
Nov	28	Luton Town	A 0-2
Jan	1	Middlesbrough	A 2-4
	30	Lindum	H 4-0
Feb	27	Manchester City Reserves	H 1-4
Mar	11	Notts County	A 1-3
		(Lord Burford Charity Cup - SF)	
	17	Lindum	H 5-1
	24	Nottingham Forest	H 2-2

1897/98
Sep	6	Small Heath	A 0-4
	13	Notts County	H 0-2
	29	Lindum	H 8-1
Oct	25	Burslem Port Vale	A 1-5
Dec	11	Darlington	H 1-2
	28	London Casuals	H 3-2
Mar	24	Grimsby Town	A 2-3
		(Benefit for Tommy McCairns)	
	26	Burslem Port Vale	H 0-4
Apr	2	Lincoln Amateur XI	H 3-0

(1897/98 contd.)
		Tottenham Hotspur	A 1-2
Apr	20	Grimsby Town	H 2-2
		(Benefit for John Irving)	
	23	Newark	H 8-0
	30	Manchester City Reserves	H 1-0

1898/99
Sep	29	Grimsby Town	A 1-2
Dec	10	Gainsborough Trinity	H 0-0
Jan	28	London Caledonians	A 1-1
Apr	29	Attercliffe	H 3-1

1899/1900
Sep	13	Grimsby Town	H 2-0
	19	Grimsby Town	A 1-2
Nov	15	Lindum	H 6-1
		(In aid of Transvaal War Fund)	
Dec	9	London Casuals	A 2-3
Jan	27	Gainsborough Trinity	H 1-0
Mar	27	Notts County	H 3-1
Apr	4	Glossop	H 0-1

1900/01
Oct	1	Grimsby Town	H 6-1
Mar	20	Gainsborough Trinity	A 2-4
		(Benefit for George Hall)	
Apr	6	Derby County	H 3-0
	15	Sunderland	H 0-0
		(Benefit for Will Gibson)	
	20	Leicester Fosse	H 2-1

1901/02
Sep	2	Gainsborough Trinity	H 3-1
Apr	28	Grimsby Town	A 1-2
		(Benefit for George Mountain)	
	30	Grimsby Town	H 0-3
		(Benefit for Charlie Bannister)	

1902/03
Nov	1	Sheffield United	A 1-1
	15	Doncaster Rovers	H 4-0

1903/04
Feb	7	Barnsley	H 0-2
Mar	26	Watford	A 0-2
Apr	20	Grimsby Town	H 1-1
		(Benefit for William McMillan)	

1904/05
Oct	20	Hull City	A 0-1
Mar	11	Leeds City	A 3-1

1906/07
Sep	26	Notts County	H 3-3
		(Benefit for George Fraser)	
Apr	15	Leeds City	A 1-2

1907/08
Feb	26	Horncastle United	A 3-0

1908/09
Oct	28	Hull City	H 0-1
Nov	11	Notts County	H 1-1
	25	Gainsborough Trinity	H 3-1
Feb	13	Gainsborough Trinity	H 3-1
Mar	31	Horncastle United	A 9-1
Apr	19	Midland League XI	H 0-1

1915/16
Dec	26	Hull City	H 1-1

1916/17
Apr	14	Rustons Aircraftmen	H 3-0

1917/18
Dec	5	North Staffordshire Reg't.	H 4-4
May	4	Newland Athletic	H 6-0
		(Lincs. Senior Charity Cup - SF)	
	11	Grimsby Town	H 1-0
		(Lincs. Senior Charity Cup - F)	

1920/21
Apr	9	Midland League XI	H 2-0
May	2	Millwall Athletic	H 1-2
		(Lincoln Hospital Cup)	

1974/75
Aug	3	Oxford United	H 1-1
	6	Chelmsford City	A 0-1
	8	Charlton Athletic	H 1-4
	10	Watford	H 0-1
May	5	Grantham Town	A 3-1

(Benefit for Dennis Benskin, Bob Norris, and Jimmy Bloomer)

1975/76
Aug	6	Spalding United	A 2-0

(Spalding RAFA Cup)
	9	Skegness Town	A 2-0
Mar	1	Ipswich Town	H 1-0

(Benefit for Terry Heath)
Apr	28	Coventry City	H 2-2
May	6	Rotherham United	A 0-1

(Norman Noble Memorial Match)
	17	Boston United	A 2-2

(Won 7-5 on pens; Mather Cup and benefit for Fred Taylor)
	24	Sheffield United	A 2-2

(Lost 7-8 on pens; Gibraltar Rock Tournament, played in Gibraltar)
	26	Blackburn Rovers	A 3-3

(Lost 10-11 on pens; Gibraltar Rock Tournament, played in Gibraltar)

1976/77
Aug	4	Sheffield Wednesday	A 0-1

(Shipp Cup)
	7	Peterborough United	A 1-2

(Shipp Cup)
	9	Cambridge United	A 1-1

(Shipp Cup)
May	16	Sheffield United	H 2-2

(Benefit for Percy Freeman)

1977/78
Aug	6	Corby Town	A 0-0
Dec	5	Worksop Town	A 3-0

(Benefit for Adrian Wall)
	16	Scunthorpe United	A 3-1

1978/79
May	15	Watford	H 0-2

(Benefit for Dave Smith)

1979/80
Jul	23	17th/21st Lancers	A 8-0
	24	Dorchester Town	A 2-1

(Played at Bovington Camp)
Oct	29	Tulsa Roughnecks (USA)	H 8-2
Nov	12	Ledbury Town	A 4-1

(Opening of floodlights)
Dec	14	Chesterfield	H 0-0

(Abandoned 52 mins, rain)
Apr	16	Nottingham Forest	H 2-1

(Benefit for Bert Loxley)
	21	Hinckley Athletic	A 3-1

(Hinckley centenary match)

1980/81
Jul	26	Raith Rovers	H 1-1
Aug	4	Boston FC	A 2-1
Jan	26	Jersey FA XI	A 2-1
May	4	Luton Town	H 0-1
	7	Boston United	A 0-1

(Mather Cup)

1981/82
Jan	4	Boston FC	H 4-0
	12	Luton Town	H 0-0

(Abandoned 51 mins, fog)
Apr	19	Gravesend	A 3-1

(Benefit for Kenny Burrett)
	27	Gainsborough Trinity	A 1-0

(Benefit for Wilson Rose)
Jun	10	VFL 1907 Neustadt (W.Germ.)	A 2-1

(Neustadt 75th anniversary match)

1982/83
Aug	7	Skegness Town	A 2-1
Dec	22	Gainsborough Trinity	A 7-0

(Abandoned 70 mins)
Jan	11	Worksop Town	A 3-0

1983/84
Aug	6	Bourne Town	A 3-0
	9	Crewe Alexandra	A 0-0
	13	Coventry City	H 2-1
	16	Sheffield Wednesday	H 2-2
	20	Mansfield Town	H 3-0
Jan	11	Spalding United	A 2-0
May	13	Sheffield United	H 3-3

(In aid of British Olympic Fund)

1984/85
Aug	1	Harworth Colliery	A 0-0
	11	Notts County	H 4-0
	15	Harrogate Rail	A 3-0
	18	Chesterfield	A 0-1
Sep	19	Watford	H 1-1

(Benefit for Phil Neale)
Jan	28	Nuneaton Borough	A 1-3

1985/86
Jul	30	Spalding United	A 3-0
	31	Sunderland	H 1-3
Aug	3	Middlesbrough	H 1-2
	7	Peterborough United	H 0-3
Oct	15	Gainsborough Trinity	A 0-3
Mar	19	Lincoln Sunday League	H 4-1

(Lincoln Sunday League Benevolent Fund)
May	7	Welbourn	A 9-0

(In aid of St Chad's Church Fund)

1986/87
Jul	24	RAF Cranwell	A 5-0
	28	Collingham	A 8-0
	30	Ruston Athletic	A 4-0
Aug	1	Ingham	A 5-0
	4	Lincoln United	A 4-2
	8	Boston FC	H 2-0
	10	Red Arrows	H 19-0
	11	Nettleham	A 1-1
	12	Croft United	A 0-5
	14	Mablethorpe	A 6-0
	18	Harworth Colliery	A 1-1
	19	Market Rasen Town	A 0-1
	20	Sleaford Town	A 3-0
Jan	29	Matlock Town	H 5-1
Feb	3	Louth United	A 2-0

1987/88
Jul	28	Boston FC	A 3-0
Aug	8	Chesterfield	H 3-3
	15	Frickley Athletic	A 0-2
May	8	Nottingham Forest	H 2-2

(Official opening of St Andrews Stand)
	12	Scarborough	H 1-3

1988/89
Jul	26	SEME/REME XI	A 4-3
	29	Alton Town	A 2-0
Aug	6	Seattle Storm (USA)	H 2-2
	10	Shepshed Charterhouse	A 2-2
	12	Hayes	A 2-0
	15	Leicester City	H 1-4
	20	Charlton Athletic	H 0-4
Oct	19	Enfield	H 3-1

(GMVC Championship Shield)
Mar	21	Orgryte (Sweden)	H 2-2
Apr	23	Bradford City	A 1-3

(In aid of Hillsborough Disaster Fund)

1989/90
Jul	27	Boston FC	A 1-0
	29	Fisher Athletic	A 2-2
Aug	1	REME	A 5-1
	3	Alton Town	A 4-0

(1989/90 contd.)
Aug	5	Bradford City	A 1-4

(Yorkshire and Humberside Cup)
	8	Barnsley	A 2-0

(Yorkshire and Humberside Cup)
	12	Huddersfield Town	H 0-3

(Yorkshire and Humberside Cup)
Dec	22	Gainsborough Trinity	A 5-0
Feb	19	Moscow Torpedo (USSR)	H 2-1

1990/91
Aug	8	Leicester United	A 7-0
	11	Whitby Town	A 4-1

(Yorkshire and Humberside Cup)
	15	Hull City	H 1-1

(Yorkshire and Humberside Cup)
	18	Leeds United	H 0-4

(Yorkshire and Humberside Cup)
Apr	23	Sheffield United	H 2-0

(Benefit for Alan Roberts)
May	7	Nettleham	A 4-2

(Opening of new stand)

1991/92
Jul	23	Burton Albion	A 3-0
	27	Kings Lynn	A 1-0
	31	Ipswich Town	H 1-1
Aug	6	Luton Town	H 2-2
	10	Otelul Galati (Romania)	H 1-2
Apr	4	Oakham United	H 3-2

1992/93
Jul	22	Kempston Rovers	A 4-0
	25	Worksop Town	A 1-0

(Opening of Sandy Lane ground)
	28	Notts County	H 0-1
Aug	1	Middlesbrough	H 5-1
	8	Dagenham & Redbridge	A 0-2

1993/94
Jul	17	Kempston Rovers	A 1-0
	21	Gainsborough Trinity	A 2-4
	24	Frickley Athletic	A 1-3
	27	Barnet	H 3-1
Aug	2	Sleaford Town	A 7-0

(Sleaford Invitation Cup)
	4	Nottingham Forest	H 1-5

1994/95
Jul	26	Wisbech Town	A 4-1
	27	Stamford Town	A 4-0
	28	Spalding United	A 2-0
Aug	1	Kettering Town	A 2-2
	4	Ilkeston Town	A 3-3
	9	Worksop Town	A 3-1

1995/96
Jul	21	Horncastle Town	A 3-2

(Syd North Trophy)
	24	Bradford City	A 0-1

(Played at W. Riding FA ground, Woodlesford; Yorkshire Electricity Cup)
	26	Huddersfield Town	H 1-3

(Yorkshire Electricity Cup)
Aug	3	Lincoln United	A 3-3

(Won 5-3 on pens; Lincoln Challenge Cup)
	5	Nottingham Forest	H 1-3

(Attendance 7,499)
Jan	6	Rushden & Diamonds	A 2-1

1996/97
Jul	27	Norwich City	H 1-1
	30	Kettering Town	A 1-1
	31	Aston Villa	H 0-1
Aug	3	Derby County	H 1-0
	9	Newcastle U.	H 0-2

(Attendance 10,069)
	12	Boston United	H 0-3

BIBLIOGRAPHY

Lincoln City F.C. Directors' Meeting Minutes :
1929 to 1959, 1970 to 1975, 1977 to 1981.
The Football League Appearance Registers.
The Football League Attendance Books.
Lincoln City F.C. Official Programme.
Benny Dix (G.H. Grosse) Cock o'the North (W.H.Smith, 1932).
Sawyer,J.J. 'Down the years with Lincoln City' (G.W.Betton, 1954).
O'Neill,Geoff and Holliday,John Lincoln City F.C. Centenary Souvenir 1883-1983 (Lincoln City F.C. and Lincolnshire Standard, 1983).
Lincoln City F.C. Co. Ltd. Photo Album (Le Butt, 1948).
Lincoln City F.C. Souvenir handbook 1951-52 (Cook's Publicity, 1952).
Lincoln City F.C. Official yearbook 1975-76 (Lincoln City F.C., 1975).
Lincoln City F.C. Promotion book (Lincoln City F.C., 1976).
Sullivan, Neville Lincoln City F.C. Official Souvenir Booklet (Integral Publishing, 1988).
Sullivan,Neville Lincoln City F.C. yearbook 1990 (Lincoln City F.C., 1990).
Lincoln City bygones (Lincolnshire Echo, 1991).
'100 years at Sincil Bank' (Lincolnshire Echo, 1996).
'Critique' (Ed.) The Lincolnshire Football Guide 1924/25, 1925/26, 1926/27. (Lincolnshire Chronicle 1924 to 1926).
The Imps Supporters Club official magazine Nos 1 to 3. (Supporters Magazines Ltd. 1967)).

AUTOBIOGRAPHIES

Eyre,Fred. ' Kicked into touch' (Senior Publications, 1981).
Neale,Phil. 'A double life' (Ringpress, 1990).
Smith, Jim and Dawson, Mark. 'Bald Eagle' (Mainstream, 1990).

NEWSPAPERS :

Athletic News.
Football Echo.
Lincoln Daily News.
The Lincoln Gazette and Lincolnshire Times.
The Lincoln Leader and County Advertiser.
The Lincolnshire Chronicle.
Lincolnshire Echo.

BACKGROUND INFORMATION :

Batchelor, Denzil. ' Soccer : a history of association football' (Batsford,1954).
Mason, Tony. 'Association Football and English Society 1863-1915' (Harvester Press,1980).
Wagg, Stephen. 'The football world : a contemporary social history' (Harvester Press,1984).
Walvin,James. ' The people's game.The social history of British football' (Allen Lane,1975).
Inglis,Simon. 'League football and the men who made it. The official centenary history of the Football League' 1888-1988 (Willow,1988).
Green,Geoffrey. ' The history of the Football Association' (Naldrett,1953).
Rollin,Jack. 'Soccer at War 1939-45' (Collins Willow,1985).
Rippon,Anton. ' Soccer : the road to crisis' (Moorland Publishing,1983).
[Chapter 13 includes an interview with Gilbert Blades on the events of 1982-83]
Inglis,Simon. ' Soccer in the dock.A history of British football scandals 1900 to 1965' (Collins Willow,1985). [Chapter 5 covers the match fixing of 1919-20].

1997-98
Back: Holmes, Robertson, Richardson, Vaughan, Hone, Alcide.
Centre: Bimson, Miller, Gowshall, Whitney, Stones, Austin, Chandler, Thorpe, Oakes (physio).
Front: Barnett, Fleming, Ainsworth, Beck (manager), Westley (asst. manager), Steve Brown, Martin, Stant.

ADVANCED SUBSCRIBERS

Andy Graver
Tony Emery
Graham Taylor
Mr.& Mrs.T.Nannestad, North Hykeham
Eleanor Nannestad, Lincoln
Niyousha Haki, Birmingham
Proushat Haki, Birmingham
Houram Haki, Tehran, Iran
Dr. Abbas Haki, Rasht, Iran
Mrs. Talatt Haki, Rasht, Iran
Mr. & Mrs. Lung, Isleworth
Chris Parkin, BBC Radio Lincolnshire
Lincolnshire County Library Services
Mr. F.T.Middleton, Hartlepool
Maurice Hodson, North Hykeham
Martin Burton
Dave Tyler, Worcester Imp
John Groom, Canterbury, Kent
Steve Broughton, Gosport, Hants.
Owen Coupland, Lichfield
Andrew Ditcher
Tim Wray, Yeovilton, Somerset
Chris Travers, Sleaford
Geoffrey R. Smith, Peterborough
Philip Smowton, Windsor, Berks.
Terry & Caroline Cole, March, Cambs.
Robert Knox, Peterborough (Navenby)
Robin Smith, Peterborough, Cambs.
Chris, Hayley Burton, Skegness
Malcolm Carrott, Wellesbourne, Warwick
Paul Carrott, Wellesbourne, Warwick
Neil Carrott, Wellesbourne, Warwick
Paul Blewitt, Lincoln
Steve Hircoe, Netherfield, Nottingham
Peter Wells, Stamford, Lincs.
John Wells, Peterborough
Mike Dean, Maidenhead, Berkshire
Brian & Martin Strawson
Simon Shaw, Nettleham, Lincoln
Charles Shaw, Nettleham, Lincoln
Mr.Michael Denis Barker, Lincoln
Gary Edward Parkin, Cambridge
Andrew Cottingham, Fulbeck
Alan & Hugh Johnson, Leasingham
Sean Sackfield, Lincoln
Dave Small, North Hykeham
J.S. Taylor, Screveton, Notts.
Matthew Bibby, Billinghay
Ron Osgerby, Nettleham, Lincoln

Cyril Gavin, Lincoln
Matthew Gavin, Scunthorpe
Les Abbott And Family
Sarah Scarlett, Lincoln
Ben Scott
Roger Malyon, Ewell, Surrey
John Burman, Kings Lynn
Jeremy Chappell, Dallas, Texas
Robert Chappell, Newbury, Berks.
Andy Poole, Darlington
John Holland, East Yorkshire
Ray Muldoon, Enfield, Middlesex
Simon Edwards, Newcastle
Simon Dobbs, Birmingham
Steve Kester, Hitchin, Herts.
Kevin Cole, Godmanchester, Cambs.
John Cartwright, London SE2
A. Rankin, California, U.S.A.
Mick Grant, Aylesbury, Bucks.
John W. Picker, Bedford
Geoffrey Piper, Thornton Hough
Christopher Barnes
Philip Jarvis, Loddington, Leics.
Rob Jarvis, West Bridgeford, Notts.
Ric Jarvis, Billinghay, Lincs.
Clive Woodhead, Formby, Merseyside
John Bates, Market Deeping
Colin Ford, Chelmsford, Essex
Alan Wilkins, Leicester
Hugh Howitt, Chelmsford, Essex
Ian Higgins, Pulborough, Sussex
Jeremy Brinkworth, Madrid, Spain
Stephen Alexander, Lincoln
Paul Jackson, Lincoln
David Fox, Sleaford
Anthony Smith, Welwyn Garden
Gordon Malcolm Graham, Lincoln
Andrew Kelly, Lincoln
Michael Napper, Clevedon, Somerset
Andrew Pearce, Waddington
Mr. Ernest Roper
Richard Blanchard, Lincoln
Terry Seaton, West End, Lincoln
Clarence Vickers, Gillingham, Kent
Peter Vickers, Gillingham, Kent
Roger Bates, Carlton Scroop
Matthew Codd, Heighington, Lincoln
Alan Everett, Lincoln
Phil Skayman, Bracebridge, Lincoln

Phil Marshall, Leeds.
Robert Cook, Sleaford
James Olsen, Nettleham
Roger Huxley, Lincoln
John Jackson, Lincoln
Tony Otter, Lincoln
Keith Hookham, Hinckley Branch
David A. Briggs, Cleethorpes
Harvey Lyngaas, Cockermouth, Cumbria
Phil Brown, Bottesford, Notts.
Bryan Stainton, Lincoln
Martin John Osborne, Lincoln
Neil Denton, Birch, Colchester
Roger Denton, Bracebridge Heath
D. Speed, Lincoln
Norman, Michael & Andrew Foster
Steve Madden, Raunds Imp
Jane Kilmister, Lincoln
Ian Bath, Lincoln
David Knight, Sherringham, Norfolk
Joan Butler nee Pattison, Nottingham
Nicholas James Birkett, Southwell
Dave Ellis, Fairlight, East Sussex
Glenn Woolley, Baston, Lincs.
E. Grantham
Billy Cobb, Sherwood, Nottingham
Neil Price, Bristol
Mr. Michael Anthony Harrod
Philip Thompson, Lincoln
Melanie Theaker, Lincoln
Kev Barwise, Lincoln
Ken Mumby, Coleford, Gloucestershire
Nick Hunter, Lincoln
Nicholas of Oxberry, Lincoln
R. Holland, Englands No. 1
David Cattle, Lincoln
Paul Wilcockson, Lincoln
Kevin Britt, Lincoln (11)
David Rollinson, Trentham, Staffs.
Neil Cuckson, Radcliffe, Manchester
Ian Cuckson, Melbourne, Australia
Glyn Botfield, Lincoln
John Swaby, Lincoln
Leigh Bentley, Lincoln
Leah Bailey, Billinghay, Lincoln
Patrick Heppenstall, Lincoln
Alvin & Tracey Nixon, Lincoln
Christopher Inman, Laughterton
Chris Child, Welton

ADVANCED SUBSCRIBERS (CONTINUED)

Anthony Lee, Sudbrooke	John Byrne, Barrhead	Martin Simons, Belgium
Joseph Dobson, Langworth, Lincoln	Alan Davies	A.N. Other
Matthew Dobson, Langworth, Lincoln	Richard Wells	Christer Svensson
Peter Chapman, Newport, Shropshire	B.H. Standish	David and Matthew Fleckney
Raymond Shaw	George Mason, Liverpool	S. Metcalfe, Rochdale
David Keats, Thornton Heath	Geoffrey Wright	John Rawnsley, Pudsey
G.D. Painter	Roger Sharp	Gordon R. Davies
W. Grier	Dave McPherson, Colchester	Terry Frost
G.T. Allman	Dave Parine	Agnes and Ivar Hansson
Mark Tyler, Rayleigh, Essex	Fred Lee, Plymouth Argyle	P.J. Newport
Derek Hyde	David J. Godfrey	John Stephen Holbrook
John Treleven	Arthur Atkins	David Robbins
David Earnshaw, Belper	Keith Coburn	Trond Isaksen, Norway
Derrick Sawyer, Doug Wright Lincoln's greatest	Donald Noble, Dunkeld, Pethshire	Richard Shore
Graham Spackman	Dave Windross, York City	Willy Østby, Norway
Martin Cripps	W.D. Phillips	David Beck
Denis Manders	Philip Pike, Caernarfon	Lawrence Dickinson
Mr. Philip H. Whitehead	Gary Parle, Lincoln	Alan Hindley
Peter Cogle, Aberdeen	Andrew & Janet Waterman	Peter Baxter
J. Ringrose	David Jowett	R. Stocken
David Downs and Marion	Gordon Small	Roger Wash
Steve Emms	Chris Brewer	Robert Michael Smith
Peter Pickup, Gainsborough Fan.	Sarah and Andrew Kirkham	John Motson
P. Graham, Lincoln	Ray Bickel	B.J. Tabner
Jonny Stokkeland, Kvinesdal, Norway	Peter Kirby, Maidstone	Michael Campbell
Bob Lilliman	Lucy and Peter Barratt	Colin Cameron
Gordon Macey, Q.P.R. Historian	Phil Hollow	C.M. Walker
Gary	G.S. Briggs	J.W. Stratton, West London
Chris Marsh, Chesterfield	Paul Johnson - Birmingham City	Arran Matthews, Tylers Green
Moira and Fred Furness	Svein Borge Pettersen, Sandefjord	Nicholas Matthews, Tylers Green

---

YORE PUBLICATIONS

We specialise in books normally of an historic nature, especially fully detailed and well illustrated Football League club histories (over twenty to date). Also those with a diverse appeal, such as the *'Rejected F.C.'* series (compendium histories of the former Football League and Scottish League clubs, each in three volumes), *'The Code War'* (The history of football in respect of its splitting into the three 'codes'), *'Theatre of Dreams - The History of Old Trafford', 'The Little Red Book of Chinese Football'* (A history of football in the area, plus the Author's football travels in China and Hong Kong), plus non-League football, notably the *'Gone But Not Forgotten'* series (each booklet issued every six months, covering the histories of former grounds and clubs). We were the publisher of the Lincoln City 'Who's Who book (now out of print).

We publish a free newsletter three times per year. For your first copy please send a S.A.E. to:

YORE PUBLICATIONS, 12 The Furrows, Harefield, Middlesex, UB9 6AT